THE DEATH PENALTY IN AMERICA

HUGO ADAM BEDAU was born in Portland, Oregon. He is presently Associate Professor of Philosophy at Tufts University. He received a B.A. degree from the University of Redlands, an A.M. degree from Boston University, and his M.A. and Ph.D. degrees from Harvard. During the academic year 1957–58 he was a Danforth Teacher Fellow, and while doing research for *The Death Penalty in America,* he held a Carnegie Fellowship in Law and Philosophy at the Harvard Law School. Before joining the faculty at Tufts, he taught philosophy at Dartmouth College, Princeton University, Rutgers University, Swarthmore College, and Reed College. He is the author of articles and book reviews that have appeared in many periodicals.

The Death Penalty in America

AN ANTHOLOGY

EDITED BY

HUGO ADAM BEDAU

REVISED EDITION

Anchor Books
Doubleday & Company, Inc.
Garden City, New York

The Anchor Books edition
is the first publication of
The Death Penalty in America

Revised Anchor Books edition: 1967

Library of Congress Catalog Card Number 68–12040
Copyright © 1964, 1967 by Hugo Adam Bedau
Printed in the United States of America

PREFACE

Despite the wealth of discussion that the death penalty has inspired in this country during the past several years, no volume has been published in which all the issues are presented against the background of the latest available research. Unfortunately, much of the information necessary for a thorough study of capital punishment in the United States has never been published or else it is inaccessible except to the scholar with a major research library at his disposal. In preparing this volume, I have been able to examine most of the published and unpublished legal, criminological, penological, and psychological literature touching the subject. The book has been designed to allow the partisans and the authorities on both sides of disputed questions to speak for themselves. The result, I hope, has been to bring under one cover a selection of the best recent writing on capital punishment and, through the footnotes, Index, and Bibliography, a guide to its farthest reaches.

Several principles of selection and organization have been in my mind while writing and editing the book. First of all, a deliberate effort has been made to avoid any extensive discussion of the controversial cases of Caryl Chessman, Julius and Ethel Rosenberg, and Sacco and Vanzetti. I have not, for example, even mentioned them in my essay in Chapter Eight on errors of justice, though one of the reasons these cases have become notorious throughout the world is that in each instance massive injustice was committed. The intrinsic importance of these cases has, understandably enough, permitted them to obtrude upon almost every discussion of capital punishment in America. The powerful emotions aroused and the far-reaching political and social consequences of each case have usually carried the controversy far beyond the question of capital punishment itself. Rarely has this helped to put the larger question in a clearer light. Little if any harm will come from ignoring these cases in this book. There is plenty of authoritative literature available on each, and some of it has been listed in the Bibliography.

Analysis and evaluation of the practice of capital punishment in other countries has also been rigorously excluded, except at the beginning of the General Introduction, where for several reasons the history of the death penalty in England has had to be sketched. During the past decade, Great Britain, Canada, Ceylon, Australia, and New Zealand, to mention only Commonwealth countries, have given unusually careful study to all aspects of this issue. The results of these inquiries, embodied in several official reports, are required reading for anyone with a serious interest in capital punishment. But to give an adequate account of the experience of these nations with the death penalty would have enlarged beyond reason the scope and bulk of this volume. Fortunately, one may now consult the survey by James Avery Joyce, *Capital Punishment: A World View* (Toronto: Thos. Nelson, 1961; New York: Grove Press, 1962), which conveniently summarizes the salient points on the history and status of the death penalty elsewhere in the world. An even more comprehensive analysis is available from the United Nations, prepared by the distinguished French jurist, Marc Ancel: *Capital Punishment* (1962).

Because of the rarity of executions in the United States for any crime except murder, and also because of the dearth of research on capital crimes such as treason, rape, and kidnapping, I have concentrated the discussion throughout the book upon the crime of murder. Wherever it was appropriate and possible, however, data on other capital crimes has also been included.

The only essay in the book not from my own hand which appears now for the first time is Herbert L. Cobin's account of "Abolition and Restoration of the Death Penalty in Delaware." The thirty-three selections which have been reprinted here are, with a few minor exceptions, exactly as they were in the original. The few omissions, revisions, or additions have been indicated at the appropriate places. Only with Sara R. Ehrmann's article, "The Human Side of Capital Punishment," did it seem necessary to avoid substantial repetitions of material elsewhere in the book. Accordingly, about fifteen per cent of her article was deleted. One result of reprinting so many essays without a running editorial commentary has been occasional overlap and even contradiction among them. The perceptive reader should have no difficulty in making up his own mind which writer's position on disputed questions is probably nearer to the truth.

The six essays I have written for this volume are a result of the inherent difficulties in carrying out the conception of a book such as this. A desire for the earliest possible publication prevented commissioning articles on several subjects. Yet in a few cases, these topics were so fundamental that they could not be omitted. Where nothing about such questions was available or where the existing literature was either too out-of-date or too inaccurate, I felt I owed the reader a brief essay even if I had to write it myself. No one is more conscious than I am of the inadequacies of the results; they will not endanger my standing as an amateur social scientist.

Although my own opposition to the death penalty will be evident throughout, I have tried to keep my convictions from distorting my account of the views of those who disagree with me, especially in those cases where their writings have been reprinted here. If the reader, to his annoyance, finds that I have succeeded badly in maintaining the necessary editorial neutrality, I can only assure him that the idea of this book was not conceived in dispassionate scholarly curiosity, and that there are any number of passages in the articles reprinted, including some by my fellow abolitionists, with which I heartily disagree though I managed to curb my desire to single them out for comment. The one deliberate exception to this policy is in my concluding essay to Chapter Four, where I undertake to reply to the specific arguments offered by Professors Jacques

Barzun and Sidney Hook in their essays reprinted in Chapter Three.

There remains only the pleasant task of thanking all those whose cooperation made this book possible. The authors and publishers who permitted their work to be republished here deserve and have my thanks. My appreciation and apologies go to those who granted me permission to reprint selections which, on account of limitations of space, I regretfully could not include.

To my many friends in New Jersey with whom I came to maturity on the issue of capital punishment, I feel a special warmth and indebtedness. Chief among these is Edmund Goerke, Jr., with whom for several years I had an almost daily association during which the need for a book such as this slowly became apparent to both of us. I am glad that the publication of this volume has given me a chance to credit him and several others as they deserve (see below, Chapter Seven).

Considerable help in writing my earlier publications on capital punishment, which provided the basis of this book, has been received from many criminologists and penologists. If I single out for special mention James A. McCafferty, it is only because he has again and again put his own work aside to give me the benefit of his researches in this area. I have also been fortunate to have the encouragement of several leaders in the abolition movement in the United States. Sara R. Ehrmann and Herbert L. Cobin in particular have made an indispensable contribution to this book.

It would not have been possible to complete this book in the short period of time devoted to the actual research, editing and writing were it not for the incomparable facilities of the Harvard University Libraries which were available to me during the academic year 1961–1962, when I undertook a program of study at Harvard Law School as a Carnegie Fellow in Law and Philosophy. Though the preparation of this book was no part of the purpose of my fellowship, the project benefited considerably from that year of study.

My mentor in criminal law at Harvard, Norval Morris,

and my colleague at Reed College, Marvin Levich, have generously read portions of earlier drafts. Professor Morris guided me away from several historical and legal errors in the General Introduction and in the Introduction to Chapter Eight. Professor Levich had no difficulty in showing me several ways to improve my concluding essay in Chapter Four. He and Professor Morris, of course, are in no way to be blamed for any mistakes and shortcomings which remain.

Kay Dunn, of the publisher's editorial staff, has been both understanding and exacting in advising me on every aspect of the manuscript. Several of my essays in the volume are vastly improved, thanks to her detailed suggestions.

Last to be acknowledged but first in every respect is the debt I owe to my wife, Jan. It was her moral consciousness that awakened my own concern over capital punishment. Her ideas and suggestions are the source of much that is best in the book; she alone advised me from beginning to end and especially on the sections I have written. To her (and to my daughter, Lauren) I credit the early completion of several editorial chores. From her companionship I have derived whatever pleasure I have had in preparing this book.

Hugo Adam Bedau

April 1963

PREFACE TO REVISED EDITION

Several revisions appear in this printing of the book, though by no means enough to call the result a new edition. Constraints of space have prevented me from making many changes I would have liked. The only revisions affecting the table of contents occur in Chapter Five; there, I have replaced two older nationwide public opinion polls with two quite recent ones. New items published since

1962 have been added to the Bibliography, but at the expense of dropping some of the original entries. Several of these newer essays are of great value, and nothing would have pleased me more than to reprint them here. To do so would have posed insuperable editorial problems, however. In the material I have written, three essays proved especially in need of updating: Chapter One, and "Offenses Punishable by Death" and "Volume and Rate of Capital Crimes," both in Chapter Two. Elsewhere, I have contented myself with removing such plain errors and infelicities as I could find, along with bringing up to date any number of minor points in the text and references. The one section most deserving of expansion, but left unchanged because of lack of space, was my catalogue of judicial miscarriages, "Murder, Errors of Justice, and Capital Punishment," in Chapter Eight. Subsequent research has added more than a score of cases to my list, most of them quite recent and several involving last-minute rescues from the executioner. Several of these cases are discussed in the book by Edward Radin, *The Innocents* (1964).

I am also happy to express my appreciation to several correspondents whose help has eased my task in revising the first edition. I am also grateful to the many reviewers who wrote so generously and approvingly of this book when it first appeared. Encouraged by that reception, I have decided to collect several of my own scattered writings on capital punishment published over the past decade; they are to appear in book form under the title, *The Right to Life*.

H. A. B.

June 1967

CONTENTS

Chapter One

GENERAL INTRODUCTION

American criminal law was not created out of nothing by the original colonists and the Founding Fathers. Rather, it took its shape directly from English criminal law of the sixteenth, seventeenth and eighteenth centuries. In order to appreciate the structure that this tradition imparted to the American law of capital punishment, it is necessary to review, if only briefly, the experience in England with the death penalty during our nation's formative years. Accordingly, in the following paragraphs, we shall examine the main features of the capital laws of England as a foundation for a study of the pattern of capital laws in colonial America. With this background of English and early American law in mind, we will then be in a position to appreciate the major American innovations in capital punishment developed during the past century and a half (privacy of executions, redefinition of the crime of murder, new methods of execution, and optional death penalties), innovations that give distinctive shape to this mode of punishment as it now exists in our country.

Capital Punishment in England and America: "The Bloody Code"

By the end of the fifteenth century, English law recognized eight major capital crimes: treason (including attempts and conspiracies), petty treason (killing of a husband by his wife), murder (killing a person with "malice"), larceny, robbery, burglary, rape and arson.[1] Under the Tudors and Stuarts, many more crimes entered this category. By 1688 there were nearly fifty. During the reign of George II, nearly three dozen more were added, and under George III the total was increased by sixty. The highpoint was reached shortly after 1800. One estimate put the

[1] Theodore Plucknett, *A Concise History of the Common Law* (5th ed., 1956), pp. 424–454.

number of capital crimes at 223 as late as 1819. It is impossible to detail here the incredible variety of offenses involved. Crimes of every description against the state, against the person, against property, against the public peace were made punishable by death. Even with fairly lax enforcement after 1800, between 2,000 and 3,000 persons were sentenced to death each year from 1805 to 1810.[2]

Conviction of a capital offense, whether or not sentence was executed, resulted in attainder: forfeiture of all lands and property, and denial of all right of inheritance ("corruption of blood"). Although appeal of the death sentence itself to a higher tribunal was all but impossible, the descendants of an executed criminal occasionally succeeded in appealing the attainder.

The usual mode of execution was hanging, though there were several crimes for which this was deemed insufficient. The bodies of pirates were hung in chains from specially built gibbet irons along the wharves of London. Throughout England, the rotting corpses of executed criminals dotted the countryside, a grim warning to other malefactors. Executions were always conducted in public and often became the scene of drunken revels. Thackeray's vivid description is famous; he wrote in part:

> I must confess . . . that the sight has left on my mind an extraordinary feeling of terror and shame. It seems to me that I have been abetting an act of frightful wickedness and violence, performed by a set of men against one of their fellows; and I pray God that it may soon be out of the power of any man in England to witness such a hideous and degrading sight. Forty thousand persons (say the Sheriffs), of all ranks and degrees—mechanics, gentlemen, pickpockets, members of both Houses of Parliament, street-walkers, newspaper-writers, gather together before Newgate at a very early hour: the most part of them give up their

[2] Leon Radzinowicz, *A History of English Criminal Law* (1948), I, pp. 3–5, 153.

natural quiet night's rest, in order to partake of this
hideous debauchery, which is more exciting than sleep,
or than wine, or the last new ballet, or any other
amusement they can have . . .[3]

Traitors, whether guilty of petty or high treason, were
subject to especially aggravated forms of execution. Burning to death was the fate of many a woman convicted of
killing her husband. As late as 1786, a crowd of thousands
watched as one Phoebe Harris was burned at the stake. But
the worst punishment was reserved for criminals guilty of
high treason. When Sir Walter Raleigh touched the heads-
man's sword, he is supposed to have quipped, " 'Tis a
sharp medicine." Beheading was the least of it. The standard practice, according to the great authority on English
law, Sir William Blackstone, consisted of drawing, hanging, disemboweling, and then beheading, followed by quartering.[4] In 1812, this death sentence was pronounced in
England on seven men convicted of high treason:

That you and each of you, be taken to the place
from whence you came, and from thence be drawn
on a hurdle to the place of execution, where you shall
be hanged by the neck, not till you are dead; that you
be severally taken down, while yet alive, and your
bowels be taken out and burnt before your faces—
that your heads be then cut off, and your bodies cut
into four quarters, to be at the King's disposal. And
God have mercy on your souls.[5]

This "bloody code," as Arthur Koestler has called it,
with its scores of capital offenses and almost daily public
executions, was considerably mitigated by benefit of clergy
and the Royal prerogative of mercy. Benefit of clergy arose
from the struggle between church and state in England,
and it originally provided that priests, monks and other

[3] William Thackeray, "Going to see a Man Hanged," *Fraser's
Magazine* (August 1840), p. 156.
[4] William Blackstone, *Commentaries on the Law of England*
(1769), IV, p. 92.
[5] Quoted in G. Ryley Scott, *The History of Capital Punishment* (1950), p. 179.

clerics were to be remanded from secular to ecclesiastical jurisdiction for trial on indictment of felony. In later centuries, this privilege was applied in ordinary criminal courts to more and more persons and for an ever larger number of felonies. Eventually, all persons accused of capital crimes were spared a death sentence if the crime was a first felony offense and if it was clergyable, provided only the criminal could recite the "Neck verse" (the opening lines of Psalm LI), this being construed by the court as proof of his literate (and thus clerical) status. Benefit of clergy became in effect the fictional device whereby first offenders were given a lesser punishment.[6]

A far different practice having a comparable effect was the trial court's frequent recommendation to the Crown that mercy be granted. Such recommendations were natural enough, since the judge had no alternative upon the conviction of an accused but to sentence him to death; all felonies carried a mandatory death penalty. Because the court's plea for mercy was usually granted (even during the years when Parliament was increasing the number of capital crimes!), hundreds of persons convicted and sentenced to death were not executed. Instead, they were transported to the colonies. During the last decade of the eighteenth century, in London and Middlesex alone, more than two-thirds of all death sentences were reversed through the Royal prerogative of mercy. Although death sentences issued annually throughout England sometimes ran in the thousands, by the 1800's executions apparently never exceeded seventy.[7]

Near the end of his *Commentaries,* Blackstone paused to reflect on the system of criminal justice whose workings he had so thoroughly described (and which has been only

---

[6] Thus, the phrase, "without benefit of clergy," which came to be attached to capital statutes during the nineteenth century in England and in America, meant not that a condemned man must go to his grave without the consolations of a spiritual advisor during his last moments, but that his conviction for a capital crime was not subject to a reduction in sentence on the ground that it was a first offense.

[7] Radzinowicz, *op. cit.,* pp. 151, 153.

summarily outlined above). He said, speaking particularly of the methods of execution,

> Disgusting as this catalogue may seem, it will afford pleasure to an English reader and do honor to the English law, to compare it with that shocking apparatus of death and torment to be met with in the criminal codes of almost every other nation in Europe.[8]

It would never have occurred to Blackstone to measure England's criminal law by that prescribed in her colonies across the Atlantic. But were he to have made the comparison, he would have found it somewhat less than flattering to the mother country.

The American colonies had no uniform criminal law. The range of variation during the seventeenth and eighteenth centuries, so far as capital punishment is concerned, was considerable. It may be gauged from the differences in the penal codes of Massachusetts, Pennsylvania, and North Carolina. The earliest recorded set of capital statutes on these shores are those of the Massachusetts Bay Colony, dating from 1636. This early codification, titled "The Capitall Lawes of New-England," lists in order the following crimes: idolatry, witchcraft, blasphemy, murder ("manslaughter, committed upon premeditate malice, hatred, or cruelty, not in a man's necessary and just defense, nor by mere casualtie, against his will"), assault in sudden anger, sodomy, buggery, adultery, statutory rape, rape (punishment of death optional), man-stealing, perjury in a capital trial, and rebellion (including attempts and conspiracies).[9] Each of these crimes was accompanied in the statute with an Old Testament text as its authority. How rigorously these laws were enforced is not known, nor is it known why the rest of the nearly three dozen capital laws in the Mosaic Code were not also adopted in the Bay Colony.

---

[8] Blackstone, *op. cit.,* p. 377.

[9] George Haskins, " 'The Capitall Lawes of New-England'," *Harvard Law School Bulletin* (February 1956), pp. 10–11. A brief survey of the development of capital laws in Massachusetts after 1636 is available in Massachusetts, *Report on the Death Penalty* (1958), pp. 98–103.

In later decades, this theocratic criminal code gave way in all but a few respects to purely secular needs. Before 1700, arson and treason, as well as the third offense of theft of goods valued at over forty shillings, were made capital, despite the absence of any biblical justification. By 1785, the Commonwealth of Massachusetts recognized nine capital crimes, and they bore only slight resemblance to the thirteen "Capitall Lawes" of the Bay Colony: treason, piracy, murder, sodomy, buggery, rape, robbery, arson and burglary.[10]

Far milder than the Massachusetts laws were those adopted in South Jersey and Pennsylvania by the original Quaker colonists. The Royal charter for South Jersey in 1646 did not prescribe the death penalty for any crime, and there was no execution in this colony until 1691.[11] In Pennsylvania, William Penn's Great Act of 1682 specifically confined the death penalty to the crimes of treason and murder. These ambitious efforts to reduce the number of capital crimes were defeated early in the eighteenth century when the colonies were required to adopt, at the direction of the Crown, a far harsher penal code. By the time of the War of Independence, many of the colonies had roughly comparable capital statutes. Murder, treason, piracy, arson, rape, robbery, burglary, sodomy, and, from time to time, counterfeiting, horse-theft, and slave rebellion—all were usually punishable by death. Benefit of clergy was never widely permitted,[12] and hanging was the usual method of inflicting the death penalty.

Some states, however, preserved a severer code. As late as 1837, North Carolina required death for all the follow-

[10] "Capital Punishment in the United States," *Law Reporter* (March 1846), p. 487.

[11] This case is of unusual interest, for it involved the attempt to detect the murderer by means of "the right of bier," the superstition that if a murderer is brought near his victim's corpse, it will bleed ("blood will out") and thus identify him. See Joseph Sickler (ed.), *Rex et Regina v. Lutherland* (1948).

[12] For a full study of this subject, as well as for much else of value on the history of capital punishment in England and America, see George Dalzell, *Benefit of Clergy in America* (1955).

ing crimes: murder, rape, statutory rape, arson, castration, burglary, highway robbery, stealing bank notes, slave-stealing, "the crime against nature" (buggery, sodomy, bestiality), duelling if death ensues, burning a public building, assault with intent to kill, breaking out of jail if under a capital indictment, concealing a slave with intent to free him, taking a free Negro or mulatto out of the state with intent to sell him into slavery; the second offense of forgery, mayhem, inciting slaves to insurrection, or of circulating seditious literature among slaves; being an accessory to murder, robbery, burglary, arson, or mayhem. Highway robbery and bigamy, both capitally punishable, were also clergyable.[13] This harsh code persisted so long in North Carolina partly because the state had no penitentiary and thus had no suitable alternative to the death penalty.

The Movement for Reform

In England, the first of hundreds of capital statutes to be repealed early in the last century was a law enacted in 1565 which made picking pockets a capital offense; it was abolished in 1810 "without opposition or comment."[14] Penal reform in America dates from about the same period,[15] and was inspired by the same continental thinkers who stimulated reform in England. In May 1787, Dr. Benjamin Rush (1745–1813) gave a lecture in Benjamin Franklin's house in Philadelphia to a group of friends, recommending the construction of a "House of Reform," a penitentiary, so that criminals could be taken off the streets and detained until purged of their antisocial habits. A little

[13] *Revised Statutes of North Carolina* (1837), chapter 34. Virginia laws of a slightly earlier date punished Negro slaves with death for any of seventy crimes, though for whites only five crimes were capital. See Charles Spear, *Essays on the Punishment of Death* (1844), pp. 227–231.

[14] Radzinowicz, *op. cit.,* pp. 498–500.

[15] On the subject in general, see Louis Filler, "Movements to Abolish the Death Penalty in the United States," *The Annals* (November 1952), and David Davis, "The Movement to Abolish Capital Punishment in America, 1787–1861," *American Historical Review* (October 1957). The next few paragraphs are based almost entirely on these articles.

over a year later, Rush followed this lecture with an essay, entitled "Inquiry into the Justice and Policy of Punishing Murder by Death." He argued its impolicy and injustice. This essay, published a few years later, became the first of several memorable pamphlets originating in this country to urge the cause of abolition, and Dr. Rush is usually credited with being the father of the movement to abolish capital punishment in the United States.

Rush's argument was based on the analysis originating with the Italian jurist, Cesare Beccaria, whose book, *On Crimes and Punishments,* had been published a generation earlier and had stirred all European intellectuals. The main points of Rush's argument were simple enough: scriptural support for the death penalty was spurious; the threat of hanging does not deter but increases crime; when a government puts one of its citizens to death, it exceeds the powers entrusted to it. In the years immediately following the publication of Rush's essay, several other prominent citizens in Philadelphia, notably Franklin and the Attorney General, William Bradford, gave their support to reform of the capital laws. In 1794, they achieved the repeal of the death penalty for all crimes in Pennsylvania except for the crime of "first degree" murder.

These reforms in Pennsylvania had few immediate influences in other states. Whereas in England, Samuel Romilly began to make a Parliamentary career for himself in the service of penal reform, in the United States no major public figures emerged as leaders in this movement until several decades later. The most distinguished American lawyer in this group was Edward Livingston (1764–1836). Under commission from the Louisiana legislature, and inspired by the radical approach to crime and punishment being preached with such persuasiveness in France and England, Livingston prepared a revolutionary penal code for Louisiana. At the center of his proposals, he insisted, was "the total abolition of capital punishment."[16] The legislature was not convinced, and it rejected most of his recommendations, including this one. Livingston did not

---

[16] *The Complete Works of Edward Livingston* (1873), II, p. 224.

live long enough to learn that during the next half-century, the leading piece of anti-capital punishment propaganda in the United States was a thirty-page excerpt from his model Louisiana code.[17]

Not until the 1830's did the literary efforts of Rush and Livingston begin to bear fruit. By this time, the legislatures in several states (notably Maine, Massachusetts, Ohio, New Jersey, New York and Pennsylvania) were besieged each year with petitions on behalf of abolition from their constituents. Special legislative committees were formed to receive these messages, hold hearings, and submit recommendations. Anti-gallows societies came into being in every state along the eastern seaboard, and in 1845 an American Society for the Abolition of Capital Punishment was organized.[18] With the forces arrayed against slavery and saloons, the anti-gallows societies were among the most prominent groups struggling for social reform in America.

The highwater mark was reached in the later 1840's, when Horace Greeley, the editor and founder of the *New York Tribune,* became one of the nation's leading critics of the death penalty. In New York, Massachusetts and Pennsylvania, abolition bills were constantly before the legislature. Then, in 1846, the Territory of Michigan voted to abolish hanging and to replace it with life imprisonment for all crimes save treason. This law took effect on March 1, 1847, and Michigan became the first English-speaking jurisdiction in the world to abolish the death penalty, for all practical purposes.[19] In 1852, Rhode Island abolished the gallows for all crimes, including treason; the next year Wisconsin did likewise. In several other states, capital punishment for many lesser crimes was replaced by life im-

---

[17] *Ibid.,* pp. 192–224. It was taken from Livingston's "Introductory Report to the System of Penal Law Prepared for the State of Louisiana," completed in 1824 but not published until 1833.

[18] Albert Post, "Early Efforts to Abolish Capital Punishment in Pennsylvania," *Pennsylvania Magazine of History and Biography* (January 1944), p. 49.

[19] See Louis Burbey, "History of Execution in What is Now the State of Michigan," *Michigan History Magazine* (Autumn 1938).

prisonment, and other reforms affecting the administration of the death penalty were adopted. By the middle of the last century in most of the northern and eastern states, only treason and murder universally remained as capitally punishable crimes. Few states outside the South had more than one or two additional capital offenses. The anti-gallows movement rapidly lost its momentum, however, as the moral and political energies of the nation became increasingly absorbed in the struggle over slavery.

After the Civil War and the Reconstruction Era, both Iowa and Maine abolished the death penalty, only to restore it promptly. In 1887, Maine again abolished it, thereby becoming the first American jurisdiction which has twice voted to end the death penalty. During this period, the federal government, after extensive debate in Congress, did reduce its dozens of capital crimes to three: murder, treason and rape (and for none was death mandatory). Colorado abolished the death penalty for a few years, but reinstated it in the face of what at the time seemed the threat of mob rule. In that state, public dissatisfaction with mere imprisonment twice resulted in lynchings during the abolition years.

Between the peak of the Progressive Era and the years when women got the vote and whiskey got the gate, no less than eight states—Kansas, Minnesota, Washington, Oregon, North and South Dakota, Tennessee, and Arizona—abolished the death penalty for murder and for most other crimes. In only a few states did the reform last, however. By 1921, Tennessee, Arizona, Washington, Oregon and Missouri had reinstated it. During the Prohibition Era, when law enforcement often verged on total collapse, the abolitionists were nearly routed in several states. Had it not been for the persuasive voices of Clarence Darrow, the great "attorney for the damned," and of Lewis E. Lawes, the renowned warden of Sing Sing Prison, and the organization in 1927 of the American League to Abolish Capital Punishment, the lawless era of the twenties might have seen the death penalty reintroduced in every state in the Union.

Throughout this period in England, the abolition movement remained somewhat more popular. Primarily through the dedicated efforts of Roy Calvert, a Select Committee of the House of Commons studied the issue and published a scholarly report in 1931. Although they recommended an experimental period of five years without the death penalty,[20] no action was taken by the government. Immediately after the end of World War II, while the Labor Party controlled the government, several Labor M.P.s struggled to have their Party vote out the death penalty, as abolition was one of the social reforms that labor and socialist parties in many countries had promised for decades. Even so, the government was not receptive. In 1949 it created a Royal Commission on Capital Punishment and suspended all executions. But the Commission was expressly forbidden to consider whether the death penalty should be abolished. Nevertheless, it was these investigations, stretching over four years, which set off the current wave of agitation against the death penalty in the Commonwealth countries and in the United States.

It was quite clear that the Royal Commissioners favored complete abolition as the best solution to the complex legal and penal problems they were forced to face, even though their explicit recommendations (eventually embodied in an unrecognizable form in the Homicide Act of 1957) were required to fall short of this radical position. No sooner was their report published than the Canadian Parliament established its own inquiry into capital punishment, and several United States experts gave testimony at these hearings. Concurrently, debates at the United Nations often touched on the compatibility of the state's right to kill and the individual's right to live.[21] Many of the delegates, especially the Scandinavian, Benelux, and Latin American representatives, were from nations that had long abandoned recourse to the executioner in peace time. Thus it

[20] Great Britain, *Select Committee Report on Capital Punishment* (1931), p. c, §475. In general, see Elizabeth Tuttle, *The Crusade Against Capital Punishment in Great Britain* (1961).

[21] See James Avery Joyce, "Capital Punishment at UN," *Contemporary Review* (March 1962), and "The United Nations and the Issue of Capital Punishment," *U. N. Monthly Chronicle* (1966).

TABLE 1
ABOLITION OF DEATH PENALTIES IN THE UNITED STATES

Jurisdiction	Date of Abolition	Date of Restoration	Date of Reabolition
Michigan	1846[a]	—	—
Rhode Island	1852[b]	—	—
Wisconsin	1853	—	—
Iowa	1872	1878	1965
Maine	1876[c]	1883	1887
Colorado	1897	1901	—
Kansas	1907[d]	1935	—
Minnesota	1911	—	—
Washington	1913	1919	—
Oregon	1914	1920	1964
North Dakota	1915[e]	—	—
South Dakota	1915	1917	—
Tennessee	1915[f]	1917	—
Arizona	1916	1918	—
Missouri	1917	1919	—
Puerto Rico	1917	1919	1929
Alaska	1957	—	—
Hawaii	1957	—	—
Virgin Islands	1957	—	—
Delaware	1958	1961	—
West Virginia	1965	—	—
Vermont	1965[g]	—	—
New York	1965[h]	—	—

[a] Death penalty retained for treason until 1963.

[b] Death penalty restored in 1882 for any life term convict who commits murder.

[c] In 1837 a law was passed to provide that no condemned person could be executed until one year after his sentencing and then only upon a warrant from the Governor.

[d] In 1872 a law was passed similar to the 1837 Maine statute (see note c above).

[e] Death penalty retained for murder by a prisoner serving a life term for murder.

[f] Death penalty retained for rape.

[g] Death penalty retained for murder of a police officer on duty or guard or by a prisoner guilty of a prior murder, kidnapping for ransom, and killing or destruction of vital property by a group during wartime.

[h] Death penalty retained for murder of a police officer on duty, or of anyone by a prisoner under life sentence.

was that several American organizations, notably the Society of Friends and the American League to Abolish Capital Punishment, were encouraged to restimulate public interest against the death penalty in the United States as well.

By the later 1950's, abolition groups were once again active and moderately well organized in nearly two dozen death penalty states in this country. Public hearings on abolition bills were again echoing in legislative chambers, reminiscent of the 1840's and 1910's. Except for Delaware, where the death penalty was abolished in 1958, abolitionists were able to obtain no more than a few legislative committee reports in their favor. Suddenly, in November 1964, all capital penalties in Oregon were voted out by a large majority, and the log jam was broken. Within six months, New York and three other states followed suit.

The checkered pattern of experiment with abolition in the United States from 1846 to date is summarized in Table 1.

Major Trends in Capital Punishment

The focus of the abolition movement in America has always been on reform of the punishment for murder, as most death sentences and executions have been for this crime. Not many observers have noticed that in recent years capital punishment for certain other crimes has been quietly removed from the statute books, even though the death penalty for murder has remained unaltered. For instance, in 1961, Nevada dropped trainwrecking from its list of capital crimes, and Illinois repealed the death penalty for dynamiting. On the whole, however, many more capital statutes have been added during this century than have been removed, and considerable publicity has surrounded these additions. The best known example is the crime of kidnapping, which, in one form or another (usually kidnapping for ransom, or kidnapping where the victim is not released unharmed), was elevated to capital status in over two dozen states during the 1930's, after the death of the kidnapped Lindbergh baby in 1932. Revenge and deterrence seem to be about equally powerful motives in the minds of most of those who favored making this crime a capital offense.

There have been other occasions when particularly shocking crimes have provoked this response. After President William McKinley was assassinated in 1901, Connecticut and New Jersey made murder or attempted murder of a high public official a capital crime. Airplane bombings in 1958–59, air piracy in 1960–61, led Congress to make such crimes punishable by death under Federal law. Most capital statutes added during the past generation cannot be traced to any such spectacular causes; e.g., providing narcotics to a minor (1946, Federal law), espionage violations of the Atomic Energy Act (1946, Federal law), assault by a life term prisoner (1939, Pennsylvania; 1941, California), armed robbery (1955, Tennessee; 1957, Georgia), third offense of a capital crime after having received mercy at the prior convictions (1955, South Carolina). Very few death sentences have issued from these novel laws, and even fewer executions. Yet their number and variety is undeniable evidence that the death penalty is still believed in many quarters to be an effective deterrent and an appropriate punishment for several different kinds of crime.

The ostensible failure of the abolition movement in this country, after a century and a half of effort, may be in part attributable to the weakness of the arguments and the fickleness of the sentiments on which they are based. It may also be because only a few Americans in each generation bother to inform themselves on the facts surrounding the actual use of the death penalty and on the merits of the abolitionist's position. Furthermore, support for the death penalty may rest on attitudes that are nearly universal, unconscious and impervious to rational persuasion. But it is far more likely that the very reforms in the administration of capital punishment, the hard-won results of the struggle for abolition during the last century, have paradoxically become the major obstacles to further statutory repeal. They have mitigated the rigidity and brutality of this form of punishment to a point where the average citizen no longer regards it as an affront to his moral sensibilities. As a consequence, he has no strong motive to press for further reduction, much less complete abolition, of the death penalty. The reforms referred to here are several, but four of them are particularly important: the disappearance of violent and repulsive modes of carrying out the sentence; the protection of the general public from exposure to executions; the limitation of the death penalty to the highest degree of murder; and the extension of authority to the trial jury in capital cases to grant imprisonment rather than death as the punishment.[22] As all these reforms originated in the United States, and as each is an integral part of our present system of capital punishment in every jurisdiction, they deserve the closest attention.

Methods of Execution. The variety of ways in which men have put one another to death under the law is appalling. History records such exotic practices (fortunately, largely unknown in the Anglo-American tradition) as flaying and impaling, boiling in oil, crucifixion, pulling asunder, breaking on the wheel, burying alive, and sawing in half. But not so many generations ago, in both England and America, criminals were occasionally pressed to death, drawn and quartered, and burned at the stake. Had any of these punishments survived the eighteenth century, there is little doubt that public reaction would have forced an end to capital punishment long ago.

Originally, the purpose of *peine forte et dure* (pressing to death) was to force an accused person to plead to an indictment. Such tactics became necessary because anyone

[22] Reform has also moved with a comparable effect in three other directions (not discussed below): toward a statutory minimum age of sixteen, below which a capital indictment may not issue (this is usually accomplished by restricting jurisdiction over juveniles to special courts); toward a statutory requirement of an automatic writ of error to issue upon a death sentence, with an accompanying stay of execution, ordering a review of the case by a higher court; and toward a two-stage trial, in which the jury first determines the question of guilt and then, if it decides on a conviction and after hearing further testimony relevant to the sentence, whether the punishment shall be death or a term of imprisonment. Some states, e.g., California, have all three provisions.

who refused to plead to a felony indictment (that is, refused to plead either guilty or innocent) could avoid forfeiture even if he was later found guilty. The effect of pressing on an uncooperative accused was, and was intended to be, fatal. As early as 1426, pressing was used in England, though it never seems to have enjoyed wide popularity with the courts. Its sole recorded use in this country seems to have been during the notorious Salem witchcraft trials, in 1692, when one Giles Cory was pressed to death for refusal to plead to the charge of witchcraft.[23]

Burning at the stake is intimately connected with the punishment of witchcraft and heresy, having been endorsed for these crimes by several medieval Christian theologians. In civilized countries, such as England, if we may believe Blackstone, it was the practice to strangle the condemned person before the flames reached him. There are records showing that in New York and New Jersey, and probably elsewhere in the American colonies, rebellious Negro slaves were burned at the stake during the early and middle eighteenth century. Except for these occasional excesses, however, burning at the stake seems to have played no part among standard methods of execution actually practiced on these shores.

It is somewhat curious that any of these barbarous and inhumane methods of execution survived as long as they did, for the English Bill of Rights of 1689 proscribed "cruel and unusual punishments." This phrase worked its way through several of the early American state constitutions into the federal Bill of Rights (in the Eighth Amendment) of 1789. Supreme Court opinions interpreting this clause have been few, but they agree in declaring that the intent of the Framers of the Constitution was to rule out, once and for all, the aggravations attendant on execution, e.g., drawing and quartering, pressing, or burning.[24] These

[23] Some details of the case (which figures in Arthur Miller's play, *The Crucible*) are available in Dalzell, *op. cit.*, pp. 182–185.

[24] See Wilkerson v. Utah, 99 U. S. 130 (1878) at p. 135, and subsequent decisions. In this opinion, the Court held that there was nothing "cruel and unusual" in Utah's practice of allowing

practices had all but totally disappeared by 1789 and they had never taken firm root here, anyway; but their express exclusion by Jefferson, Madison and the other authors of the Bill of Rights was a service to the interests of a free and humane people. Except when executing spies, traitors and deserters, who could be shot under martial law, the sole acceptable mode of execution in the United States for a century after the adoption of the Eighth Amendment was hanging.

In the 1880's, as one story has it, in order to fight the growing success of the Westinghouse Company, which was pressing for nationwide electrification with alternating current, the advocates of direct current staged public demonstrations to show how dangerous their competitor's product really was: if it could kill animals—and awed spectators saw that, indeed, it could—it could kill human beings as well. Within a few years, this somber warning was turned completely around, and in 1888, the New York legislature approved the dismantling of its gallows and the construction of an "electric chair," on the theory that in all respects, scientific and humane, executing a condemned man by electrocution was superior to executing him by hanging.[25] On August 6, 1890, after his lawyer had unsuccessfully argued the unconstitutionality of this "unusual" method of execution, one William Kemmler became the first criminal to be put to death by electricity. Although the execution was little short of torture for Kemmler (the apparatus was makeshift and the executioner clumsy), the fad had started. Authorities on electricity, such as Thomas Edison and Niccola Tesla, continued to debate whether electrocution was so horrible that it never should have been invented. The late Robert G. Elliot, electrocutioner of 387 men and women, assured the public in his memoirs that the condemned man loses consciousness immediately with the first jolt of current.[26] The matter remains controver-

a condemned man to choose either the firing squad or the hangman for his executioner.

[25] See the *Report* of the New York Legislative Commission on Capital Punishment (1888), pp. 52–92.

[26] Robert Elliot, *Agent of Death* (1940).

sial to this day. Despite the record of bungled executions,[27] the unavoidable absence of first-hand testimony, and the invariable odor of burning flesh that accompanies every electrocution, most official observers favor the electric chair. However ironical it may be, it is a fact that electrocution was originally adopted and is still employed in two dozen states on the grounds of its superiority to hanging as a civilized method of killing criminals.

Not satisfied with shooting, hanging or electrocution, the Nevada legislature passed a bill in 1921 to provide that a condemned person should be executed in his cell, while asleep and without any warning, with a dose of lethal gas. Governor Emmet Boyle, an avowed opponent of capital punishment, signed the bill, confident that it would be declared unconstitutional on the grounds of "cruel and unusual punishment." Nothing much was done one way or the other until one Gee Jon was found guilty of murder and sentenced to death. When the Nevada Supreme Court upheld the constitutionality of lethal gas, a chamber was hurriedly constructed after practical obstacles were discovered in the original plan for holding the execution in the prisoner's cell. On February 8, 1924, Jon became the first person to be legally executed with a lethal dose of cyanide gas. A Nevada newspaper editorial hailed the event: "It brings us one step further from the savage state where we seek vengeance and retaliatory pain infliction."[28]

It is doubtful whether any serious scientific inquiry has ever substantiated the claims advanced on behalf of either electrocution or gassing. According to a 1953 Gallup Poll, the American public strongly favored electrocution over lethal gas, while hanging and shooting had very few supporters (twelve per cent registered no opinion, or recommended "drugs" or "any of them, but let the prisoner choose"). Also during 1953, though few Americans knew

[27] Several were cited by the defense in the remarkable case of Louisiana *ex rel.* Francis v. Resweber, 329 U. S. 459 (1947); some are mentioned in Barrett Prettyman, Jr., *Death and the Supreme Court* (1961), pp. 105 ff.

[28] A.P. dispatch from Carson City, Nevada; see e.g. *Newark News* of April 8, 1960.

it, the British Royal Commission on Capital Punishment stated:

> . . . we cannot recommend that either electrocution or the gas chamber should replace hanging as the method of judicial execution in this country. In the attributes we have called "humanity" [rapidity with which unconsciousness is induced] and "certainty" [simplicity of the apparatus] the advantage lies, on balance, with hanging; and though in one aspect of what we have called "decency" [decorum with which executions can be conducted, and absence of mutilation to the body of the condemned man] the other methods are preferable, we cannot regard this as enough to turn the scale.[29]

When representatives of the British Medical Association were cautiously sounded out on the question whether they would be willing to endorse and administer death sentences by lethal injections, they made it quite clear to the Royal Commissioners that they wanted nothing to do with it, no matter how humane, certain and decent it might be.

In this country, voices are occasionally still heard, protesting the risks, indignities and mutilations incident on hangings, shootings, electrocutions and gassings. "Contemporary methods of execution," it has been said, "are unnecessarily cruel"; they are "archaic, inefficient, degrading for everyone involved."[30] Novelties, such as allowing the condemned man to choose the method of his execution, or even to administer it to himself, or to become the subject of medical experiments until he dies of a fatal one, have lately been suggested.[31] But these objections and suggestions seem to go almost entirely unheeded. Retentionists

[29] Great Britain, Royal Commission on Capital Punishment, *Report* (1953), p. 256.

[30] Respectively, Clarence Farrer, in *American Journal of Psychiatry* (1958), p. 567, and Rufus King, "Some Reflections on Do-It-Yourself Capital Punishment," *American Bar Association Journal* (July 1961), p. 669.

[31] King, *op. cit.*, and Jack Kevorkian, "Capital Punishment or Capital Gain?" *Journal of Criminal Law, Criminology and Police Science* (May–June 1959).

—those who favor keeping, adopting or extending the death penalty—usually have no curiosity about the regrettable details of actual executions, and abolitionists, being totally out of sympathy with the whole business, have no interest in finding a more humane way to do what they disapprove of on principle.

Private Executions. The strongest argument in favor of public executions and of cruel methods of inflicting the death penalty was that such procedures greatly increased the deterrent effect. Hence, the desirability of having children and the criminal fringe of society witness these spectacles. Also, the notion of executions hidden from public view suggested to many the unsavory aspects of secret Star Chamber proceedings. Thackeray's reaction (quoted in part above), however, seems to have been the judgment of most sensitive witnesses: "I feel myself ashamed and degraded at the brutal curiosity which took me to that brutal sight." It was probable, too, that the deterrent effect of attending an execution was considerably overrated. A classic tale has it that when pick-pocketing was a capital crime in England, pick-pockets plied their trade at the foot of the gallows while the other spectators watched a pick-pocket being hanged! The story is probably apocryphal[32] (as is another oft-told tale, that in England during Henry VIII's reign, over 72,000 persons were hanged[33]), but it illustrates the point. Somewhat more reliable may be the observation of the chaplain at Bristol Prison, England, who reported that all but three of the 167 men sentenced to death whom he had interviewed had, at one time or another, witnessed a hanging.[34] Nor could terror and hatred of the criminal increase if he took his punishment like a man. As the

[32] See Radzinowicz, *op. cit.,* p. 498. The story may have started from a chance remark in the testimony given before the first Royal Commission on Capital Punishment; see its *Report* (1886), p. 302 (#2294).

[33] Thorsten Sellin, "Two Myths in the History of Capital Punishment," *Journal of Criminal Law, Criminology and Police Science* (July–August 1959); and Radzinowicz, *op. cit.,* p. 139.

[34] Spear, *op. cit.,* p. 53.

New York Legislative Commission on Capital Punishment observed,

> . . . the very boldness with which he [the condemned man] marched from the cell to the scaffold is extolled as an act of heroism and as evidence of courage and valor. "He was game to the last" has been many a ruffian's eulogy.[35]

But public executions continued well into the last century. Dr. Benjamin Rush, in his address of 1787 delivered in Franklin's house, attacked "The Effects of Public Punishments Upon Criminals and Upon Society." In response to his arguments and the support they aroused, the Walnut Street Jail was built in Philadelphia three years later. From this primitive beginning sprang the whole penitentiary system, and a realistic alternative to hangings at last was available. But nothing was done about public executions until New York, in 1830, imposed some control on the county sheriffs, requiring them (but only at their discretion!) to hold executions away from public view. Not until 1835 did New York increase the stringency of this law so as to prohibit public executions. Within the next few years, several other states followed suit, and this reform—at most, merely a sop to abolitionists—was underway.

The reform was by no means universal or thoroughgoing, however. Pennsylvania and New Jersey, for instance, stipulated only that executions should take place within the walls or buildings of the county jail. Since in most cases the gallows was erected out of doors in the jail yard, it was a simple enough matter for any interested spectator to watch the entire proceeding from a vantage point well outside the walls. Not until nearly the end of the last century were such abuses prohibited. Even so, flagrantly public executions continued in some states until quite recently. The last such event in the United States is said to have been the hanging of a Negro in Owensboro, Kentucky in August 1936. A news service photograph taken moments after the "drop" shows some 20,000 people packed around the gallows, with the dead man dangling at the end of his

[35] New York, *op. cit.*, p. 93.

rope. Several spectators are atop a nearby utility pole, and others are leaning out of windows a block away. The platform is jammed with official witnesses.[36] Two years later, Kentucky passed a statute prohibiting all but official witnesses from attending future executions.

Even today, however, most states allow considerable discretion to the warden in charge of an execution as to how many persons shall qualify as official guests and witnesses. Wardens and executioners have often told how the announcement of an execution (required by law) brings a flood of requests for permission to attend. Such requests, they say, are never granted. But if the condemned man is enough of a celebrity, the mass news media will send their representatives, and these, plus the officials directly and indirectly involved, often swell the total to several dozen, as in the execution of Julius and Ethel Rosenberg at Sing Sing in 1953 and of Caryl Chessman at San Quentin in 1960.

The relative privacy of executions nowadays (even photographs of the condemned man dying are almost invariably strictly prohibited) means that the average American literally does not know what is being done when the government, in his name and presumably on his behalf, executes a criminal. Lately, it has been suggested, though with what seriousness it is hard to gauge, that executions should be televised for public viewing.[37] More than one abolitionist has wistfully recalled the days when all executions were holiday occasions, confident that if this were to happen today, the whole practice of killing criminals would be rapidly outlawed. The adage, "out of sight, out of mind," goes some distance toward explaining why even the op-

[36] The photo is reproduced in Negley Teeters, "Public Executions in Pennsylvania, 1682 to 1834," *Journal of the Lancaster County Historical Society* (Spring 1960), p. 117.

[37] Vigorous opposition to this idea was expressed by convicts in *The San Quentin News* (March 5, 1959), p. 2. Their former warden, however, seems to support it, though only in order to educate and shock the public and thereby to secure greater support for abolition; see Clinton Duffy, *88 Men and 2 Women* (1962), p. 21.

ponents of the death penalty today are not as evangelical as were the reformers in the last century.

Actually, the relative loss of ardor and persistency among today's abolitionists probably has its main explanation elsewhere. Capital punishment today is not thought to be the dreadful evil it once was, partly because the number of persons executed has been drastically reduced. Whereas there is now about one execution a week in the nation, with a population of 180 million people, in 1900, with a population half that size, executions were held on an average three times as often. Reliable statistics on the annual number of executions prior to 1930 are unavailable, but there is no doubt that the number has steadily decreased during the last generation. Although executions seem to be fewer and fewer, the number of death sentences shows a slower decline. Hence, an increasing number of men each year are awaiting execution under sentence of death. This circumstance tends to veil the fact that for a century and a half, the ratio of death sentences to convictions for capital crimes has itself been steadily decreasing. When we add to this the widespread belief that only the worst murderers and other felons are even sentenced to death, thanks to the American innovations of degrees of murder and jury discretion in sentencing, it is not difficult to understand why the abolition movement has achieved so few successes during the past decade.

Degrees of Murder. Since time immemorial, death has been regarded as the supremely suitable manner of punishing murderers. The Bible, somewhat cryptically, tells us, "Whoso sheddeth man's blood, by man shall his blood be shed" (Genesis IX:6). But what is the crime of murder, as distinct from the fact of homicide? Blackstone, speaking for the English tradition, declared:

. . . all homicide is malicious, and . . . amounts to murder unless where *justified* by the command or permission of the law; *excused* on account of accident or self-preservation; or *alleviated* into manslaughter, by being either the involuntary consequence of some act not statutorily lawful, or (if voluntary) occasioned by some sudden and sufficiently violent provocation.[38]

The effect of this definition, which became a standard interpretation of the law of murder in this country, was to make into "murder," and thus punishable by death, all homicide not involuntary, provoked, justified or excused.

With the intention of giving the trial jury an opportunity to exclude from the punishment of death all murderers whose crime was not of the gravest nature, William Bradford, the Attorney General in Pennsylvania and a friend of Dr. Rush's, proposed the following now classic division of murder into "degrees":

> . . . all murder, which shall be perpetrated by means of poison, or by lying in wait, or by any other kinds of wilful, deliberate and premeditated killing, or which shall be committed in the perpetration or attempt to perpetrate any arson, rape, robbery, or burglary, shall be deemed murder of the first degree; and all other kinds of murder shall be deemed murder in the second degree; and the jury, before whom any person indicted for murder shall be tried, shall, if they find such person guilty thereof, ascertain in their verdict, whether it be murder of the first or second degree . . .[39]

To this was added the stipulation, "That no crime whatsoever hereafter committed (except murder of the first degree) shall be punished with death in the State of Pennsylvania." The legislature adopted this statute in 1794. With certain minor modifications, the distinction of degrees of murder, with the death penalty limited to first degree murder, was quickly adopted in Virginia (1796), somewhat later in Ohio (1815), and during the next generation in most other states, until today all but a few states use it.

[38] Blackstone, *op. cit.*, p. 201.
[39] Quoted in Edwin Keedy, "History of the Pennsylvania Statute Creating Degrees of Murder," *University of Pennsylvania Law Review* (May 1949), pp. 772–773.

The distinction of murder into degrees has often been disputed as an improvement over the common law notion of murder. It is arguable whether the common law concept of "malice" is really clarified by the equally shadowy notions of wilfulness, deliberateness and premeditation.[40] But it was an effective compromise of the policy that murderers shall be punished with death, since it left for the jury to decide in each case whether the accused, though he may be guilty, had committed his crime with sufficient conscious calculation to deserve the maximum punishment. One of the main objections to the doctrine of degrees of murder is that it can often have just the opposite of the intended effect. For example, a mean, impulsive and violently brutal person who kills suddenly and without a weapon nor in the course of another felony (and thus kills in absence of wilfulness, deliberation or premeditation) may be as great (or even greater) a menace to society than is another person who carefully plans the death of some one victim, e.g., a doctor who decides to put a hopelessly incurable patient out of his misery. Indeed, in the latter case, a jury might wish to mete out light, or even no, punishment. But it could do so only by flouting the letter of the law, since the doctor's crime is clearly first degree murder.

After weighing the merits of the doctrine of degrees of murder for more than a century, the English have concluded that it is a clumsy tool for demarking the class of murderers meriting execution. The Report of the Royal Commission trenchantly observes:

There are strong reasons for believing that it must inevitably be found impracticable to define a class of murders in which alone the infliction of the death penalty is appropriate. The crux of the matter is that any legal definition must be expressed in terms of objective characteristics of the offense, whereas the choice of the appropriate penalty must be based on a much wider range of considerations, which cannot

[40] The classic criticism of the doctrine is by Benjamin Cardozo, in his essay, "What Medicine Can Do for Law" (1928), reprinted in his *Selected Writings* (1947), pp. 382–384.

be defined but are essentially a matter for the exercise of discretion.[41]

Besides the difficulties surrounding the distinction of degrees of murder, another equally disastrous tendency originated in the same 1794 Pennsylvania statute and has spread throughout American criminal law. Under the common law of England, all homicides not excusable or justifiable were murder and punishable by death. In the sixteenth century, manslaughter was made non-capital on the ground that such homicide lacked the required *mens rea,* or criminal intent, to deserve such severe punishment. But according to the Pennsylvania statute, first degree murder includes not only wilful, deliberate and premeditated homicide; it includes also all "homicides in or in the attempt to perpetrate arson, rape, robbery or burglary." This notion that killings in the course of a felony (other than the felony of murder itself) are on a par with wilful, deliberate and premeditated killing seems a complete throwback to the primitive theory that a person is to be punished not for what he intends to do (e.g., rob a store) but for what results from his action (e.g., the death, however unintended, of the store keeper). The most remarkable feature of the concept of felony murder is the way it has grown in several states so as to encompass homicides done in the course of *any* felony (where "felony" is defined as any crime punishable by death or by more than a year in prison), and to allow a felon to be punished as a first degree murderer for a homicide committed by a co-felon or even by a *police officer!*[42] Considerable experience with this doctrine has shown not only that it has thoroughly defeated any hope its originators may have had to mitigate the se-

[41] Royal Commission, *op. cit.,* p. 173. How little effect the Commission's advice had may be seen from the fact that the Homicide Act passed by Parliament in 1957 attempted to draw this distinction in the very way the Commission declared to be impossible. See, on this and other points, Sidney Prevezer, "The English Homicide Act," *Columbia Law Review* (May 1957).

[42] See especially Norval Morris, "The Felon's Responsibility for the Lethal Acts of Others," *University of Pennsylvania Law Review* (November 1956), and Note, "Felony Murder As a First Degree Offense," *Yale Law Review* (January 1957).

verity and inequity of capital punishment—rather, its effect has been exactly the opposite—but also that it makes for bad law, so much so that the American Law Institute has recently advocated abandoning the entire doctrine.[43]

Jury Discretion. The early reformers may have dimly sensed what was to come, and while they deserve the credit for inventing the distinction of degrees of murder, they also deserve the blame for expanding the concept of felony murder. They and their successors must have seen the need for a better solution to the problem of making the punishment fit the crime and of limiting the severity of punishment, whenever possible, to something less than death.

The solution seems obvious enough now, though only quite recently has it been universally adopted: make the punishment fit both the crime and the criminal by abolishing all mandatory death penalties, and instead authorize the jury in capital trials to sentence a guilty person either to death or to life imprisonment. The democracy of the idea was one source of its appeal. To give discretion to the jury meant that the Governor's arbitrary power to extend clemency would be considerably curbed, if not by law at least by force of public opinion, and thus this vestige of the old Royal privilege would be curtailed in favor of popular expression of the community's will.[44]

But by far the most pronounced argument in favor of ending mandatory death penalties, echoed on every side, was the extreme difficulty of obtaining convictions in cases where a conviction is tantamount to a death sentence. Because this difficulty was one of the strongest complaints against capital punishment, retentionists may have recognized that they could cut the ground from under the abolitionists by adopting the simple expedient of discretionary death sentences. Abolitionists may well have looked with some dismay on this development, as they could hardly

[43] See American Law Institute, *Model Penal Code Tentative Draft No. 9* (1959), pp. 33–39, 115–120, especially pp. 65–70; and the *Proceedings* of the Institute's Thirty-sixth Annual Meeting (1959), pp. 123–133.

[44] On this subject, see Christen Jensen, *The Pardoning Power in the American States* (1922).

fail to appreciate how much more difficult this reform would make achievement of their ultimate aim, while at the same time they could not deny that it was a step in the right direction.

A history of the principle of jury discretion in capital trials has yet to be written,[45] and the suggestions in the above paragraphs are largely speculations. We do not in fact know whether the idea of jury discretion was invented by abolitionists, retentionists, or some third party seeking a middle way. Nor do we know where or when the idea originated (it should be noticed that it apparently was a feature of the Massachusetts "Capitall Lawes" of 1636 for the crime of rape), nor when it was first applied to the punishment for murder. We do know that in Maryland, where the jury had the power to fix degrees of murder, the death penalty became optional in 1809 for treason, rape and arson, but not for homicide;[46] that Louisiana in 1846 may have been the first state to make all its capital crimes optionally punishable by life imprisonment;[47] and that jury discretion was introduced specifically for the punishment of murder in California in 1873, in Illinois the next year, and in Georgia the following year. According to one report, some thirty-two states had given either the judge or the jury discretion as to the punishment in capital cases by the year 1926.[48] Between 1949 and 1958, five more states (Massachusetts, Connecticut, North Carolina, New Mexico and Vermont) introduced this procedure.[49]

At present, twenty-two jurisdictions—just half the total—

[45] The leading article is by Robert Knowlton, "Problems of Jury Discretion in Capital Cases," *University of Pennsylvania Law Review* (June 1953). For current American Law in this area, see American Law Institute, *op. cit.,* pp. 121–126.

[46] *Dorsey's Maryland Laws* (1809), pp. 573 ff.; cf. "Capital Punishment in the United States," *Law Reporter* (March 1846), p. 484.

[47] Act of June 1, 1846, cited in *State v. Lewis* (1848), 3 *Louisiana Annotated Reports* 398.

[48] Raymond Bye, "Recent History and Present Status of Capital Punishment in the United States," *Journal of Criminal Law, Criminology and Police Science* (August 1926), p. 239.

[49] Sara Ehrmann, "Capital Punishment Today—Why?" in Herbert Bloch (ed.), *Crime in America* (1961), pp. 81, 91.

have made all their capital crimes optionally punishable by death or by imprisonment. It is interesting to note that many of those states which were the first to accept the doctrine of degrees of murder were among the last to add the doctrine of jury discretion for this crime. Ohio did not accept it until 1898, New Jersey until 1916, Pennsylvania until 1925. When the District of Columbia abolished the mandatory death sentence for murder in March 1962,[50] New York remained the last stronghold of this practice in the United States. After considerable pressure, including pleas from the District Attorney of New York County, the Legislature abolished this restriction in April 1963, and Governor Nelson Rockefeller signed it into law, to take effect the following July.

It often used to be maintained by abolitionists that if the death penalty were abolished, convictions would increase.[51] There seems to be little or no evidence that this is so.[52] Had the practice of jury discretion, however, not been introduced in most death penalty states over fifty years ago, there might have been considerable evidence to support this claim. There is some slight evidence in this direction, in favor of the view that the change from a mandatory to an optional death sentence for murder has resulted in significantly more convictions of first degree murder. In Philadelphia, for instance, in the last year of mandatory death penalties (1924), there were 118 indictments for first degree murder, but only six convictions were sustained by the courts after appeals. Some twenty years later (1947), out of 102 such indictments, twenty-six con-

[50] For an instructive public debate over the mandatory death penalty, see the *Congressional Record,* March 14, 1962, pp. 3771–3801.

[51] See, e.g., Maynard Shipley, "Does Capital Punishment Prevent Convictions?" *American Law Review* (May–June 1909), and the remark of the Governor of Minnesota, that in the three years after abolition (1911–1913), convictions for murder increased "approximately fifty per cent," cited in Lamar Beman (ed.), *Selected Articles on Capital Punishment* (1925), p. 355.

[52] Raymond Bye, *Capital Punishment in the United States* (1919), pp. 50–55.

victions were obtained and in twelve of these the jury had granted mercy, i.e., life imprisonment.[53] On the other hand, far more cases went to trial in 1947 than in 1924. Under the mandatory law, twenty-one first degree murder indictments were not opposed by the accused, giving full sentencing discretion to the judge; whereas in 1947, under the law that gave sentencing discretion to the jury, only seven defendants were willing to leave their fate in the hands of the judge. Presumably, they thought they would have a better chance of mercy from the jury. But no nationwide statistics are available against which we can place these data; they may or they may not be representative.

Whereas Americans seem to have their doubts about complete abolition of the death penalty for the crime of murder (since only twenty-one states have ever abolished it, and half of these later reintroduced it), the optional death penalty has been thoroughly accepted. There seems to be but one case of backsliding. Vermont adopted jury discretion in 1911, and a veritable crime wave of twenty murders occurred the next year. Although it subsided noticeably after one Elroy Kent was sentenced to death (with the jury exercising its discretion in favor of the death penalty), the legislature voted overwhelmingly to return to the mandatory death penalty for murder in 1913.[54] More than forty years were to pass before Vermont reabolished this mandatory law. Today there is no jurisdiction in the United States in which the jury is denied sentencing discretion for the crime of murder.

Conclusion

It would be premature at this juncture to attempt to estimate either the merits or the probability of complete abolition of the death penalty in this country. Supporters of abolition in the past have been noticeably sanguine in their predictions. Thirty-five years ago, Raymond Bye, one of the sociologists to pioneer in the study of this subject, remarked, "There is reason to believe that in the course of

[53] Thomas White, "Punishment for Murder in the First Degree," *The Shingle* (March 1948), p. 62.
[54] Reported in Beman (ed.), *op. cit.*, p. 8.

the present century the use of the death penalty will finally pass away."[55] A decade ago, another observer said that "the over-all, international trend is toward the progressive abolition of capital punishment."[56] It is difficult to believe these predictions, if that is what they are. As these lines are being written, the Soviet Union has announced executions under *ex post facto* laws for currency speculation,[57] the French government is in an uproar over the failure of a special tribunal to issue a death sentence to renegade Army generals, the Union of South Africa has decided to impose the death penalty on its colored population for a host of crimes, South Korea has executed six soldiers for embezzlement of military funds, and Israel has announced that the notorious Adolf Eichmann has been hanged. The political executions in Cuba, Algeria, and the Congo are too infamous to need comment.

Yet it is true that in the United States, as the next chapter will show, nearly half the states now use the death penalty so sparingly that it plays almost no part in their program of law enforcement and criminal treatment. Of all the persons today in state and federal prisons, only about one in a thousand is under sentence of death.[58] The obvious inference is that the death penalty in our country is an anachronism, a vestigial survivor of an earlier era when the possibilities of an incarcerative and rehabilitative penology were hardly imagined. Although killing persons in the name of the law for racial, political, and military crimes remains one of the familiar social phenomena elsewhere in the modern world, yet the infrequency with which ordinary peacetime criminal offenses against persons and property are punished with death outside the United States[59] focuses

[55] Bye, *op. cit.* note 48 *supra*, p. 245.

[56] Frank Hartung, "Trends in the Use of Capital Punishment," *The Annals* (November 1952), p. 19.

[57] See particularly "The Death Penalty and the USSR," *Bulletin of the International Commission of Jurists* (November 1961), pp. 55–62.

[58] James McCafferty, "Major Trends in the Use of Capital Punishment," *Federal Probation* (September 1961), p. 21.

[59] Until recently no reliable survey of the status of capital punishment in foreign countries existed; cf. Sara Ehrmann, *op.*

attention on the persistence of this ancient practice in our own land. It is for the rest of this book to describe in detail the surroundings and the consequences of this practice, and to weigh the results as they bear on the justification of capital punishment in the present and for the future.

Chapter Two

THE LAWS, THE CRIMES, AND THE EXECUTIONS

INTRODUCTION

Anyone who hopes to understand the place of capital punishment in contemporary American society must have a grasp of the latest information on at least four aspects of the subject. First, one needs to know what crimes, in each American jurisdiction, are at present punishable by death. Next, one needs to know how many of each of these crimes actually occur. Third, one must understand the scope of liability for a death sentence, especially as it affects juveniles. Lastly, one should have some idea of the ultimate fate of a typical group of persons originally sentenced to death, and a record (by jurisdiction, year, and crime) of those who have been executed. All this information is in this chapter.

Probably few Americans have any idea just how many crimes still carry a death penalty—anywhere from thirty-three to sixty-seven, depending on how they are classified and counted. They range from the familiar ones such as murder, kidnapping, rape, and treason, to such crimes as desecrating a grave (Georgia), attempting to set fire to a

---

cit., p. 92, James Avery Joyce, *Capital Punishment* (1961), p. 261, and *Bulletin of the International Commission of Jurists* (November 1961), p. 63. Now, however, the reader should consult Marc Ancel, *The Death Penalty in European Countries* (1962), published by the Council of Europe, and his comprehensive worldwide report released under auspices of the United Nations, *Capital Punishment* (1962).

prison (Arkansas), and sexual intercourse with a girl under eighteen, so-called "statutory rape" (Nevada and Texas). It is all the more important, therefore, to know that all the nearly four thousand legal executions in this country since 1930 were for one or another of only seven of these crimes.

The volume of capital crimes, coupled with the execution statistics, shows that by far the most important capital crime is murder. It is desirable, therefore, to increase one's knowledge of the facts of this crime, especially, since part of the factual dispute between abolitionists and retentionists turns on the nature, incidence, and disposition of murderers. For this purpose one cannot do better than to study Professor Marvin Wolfgang's outstanding monograph, *Patterns in Criminal Homicide* (1958). A brief digest of his findings in his own words is reprinted below. (It would be desirable, of course, to supplement this analysis of criminal homicide with a comparable analysis of other capital crimes; in particular, rape, armed robbery and kidnapping. But no such research seems to have been published.) One of the noteworthy aspects of Wolfgang's investigation for our purposes is that he nowhere invokes the use or disuse of the death penalty to explain any of the characteristics of homicide. Some armchair criminologists may regard this as a major defect in the hypotheses that guide his analysis; professionals would have been surprised if he had been able to make reliable inferences on the basis of a correlation of the two phenomena.

Most capital statutes play no role in contemporary penology at all. It is significant that though only nine states at present have legally abolished the death penalty, it is so infrequently used in another dozen states that they have, for all practical purposes, abolished it, too. Finally, it may come as something of a paradox to learn that in the last few years, when the number of persons executed has been dropping steadily, the number under sentence of death and awaiting execution has never been greater. What this means is that the courts are increasingly being used by more and more prisoners to delay and, in some cases, avert the execution of the death sentence.

It has not been possible to provide some of the information many readers will want. A survey of American legal procedures involved in appealing a capital conviction and in obtaining executive clemency would have been instructive, because the laws vary significantly from state to state and because both appeal and clemency are an integral aspect of our present system of capital punishment. But no legal scholar has yet published a study of this subject, and it was not possible to prepare even a preliminary sketch of these procedures specially for this volume. (What literature there is on these subjects has been cited in the introduction to Chapter Eight.) Others may wish to have certain statistical information, e.g., on how many death sentences are appealed annually, on what grounds, in which states, and with what results. Some information on the disposition of capital offenders will be found in this chapter in Mr. McCafferty's article, in Chapter Eight, and at the end of this introduction. But the information provided barely scratches the surface of the judicial criminal statistics needed, but so far unavailable, in this area. This chapter also does not provide any scientific analysis of the current methods of execution, their physical effects on the condemned men, and their psychological effects on witnesses at executions and on other prisoners. This subject deserves more investigation than it has so far received. Reports from eye-witnesses at executions are not lacking,[1] but none seemed appropriate for reprinting here.

However, rough statistics on two matters not available in the selections below (nor anywhere else) can be supplied here: the total number of persons legally executed during this century in the United States; and the ratio of executions to murders, i.e., the likelihood of a murderer being executed. Unfortunately, even in these two instances

[1] On electrocutions, see Charles Potter, "I Saw a Man Electrocuted," *Reader's Digest* (February 1938), and the books by Robert Elliot and Lewis Lawes on executions in Sing Sing Prison. On lethal gas, see Sylvan Shane, "Window on a Gas Chamber," *The Nation* (February 24, 1962), and the books by Byron Eshelman and Clinton Duffy on executions in San Quentin Prison.

an estimate must suffice, because there is no reliable nationwide count of executions prior to 1930.

The latest *National Prisoner Statistics* "Executions" bulletin, of June 1967, reports a total of 3,857 legal executions between 1930 and 1966. Between 1901 and 1917, data collected by the *Chicago Tribune* indicates that there was a total of 1,858 executions.[2] We have no total for the year 1900, though the *Tribune* data show that for the five year period from 1896 through 1900 there were 610 executions. If we take the annual average for the years 1896–1900 and assign it arbitrarily as the total for 1900, we get an estimated 122 executions. For the years from 1925 through 1929, Professors Barnes and Teeters reported (without indicating their source) a total of 564 executions.[3] Their figures need to be corrected upward, according to data since published by Professor Sellin,[4] bringing the total for this period to at least 591. This leaves only the years 1918 through 1924 unaccounted for. If we arbitrarily assign as the total for these seven years seven times the average of the annual averages for the years 1901–1917 and 1925–1929 (as corrected), i.e., 114, we have an estimated seven-year total of 798 executions. The totals may be tabulated as follows:

TABLE 1

TOTAL LEGAL EXECUTIONS IN THE UNITED STATES SINCE 1900

Years	Number of Executions
1900	122 (estimated)
1901–1917	1,858
1918–1924	798 (estimated)
1925–1929	591
1930–1966	3,857
Grand Total	7,226

[2] Raymond Bye, *Capital Punishment in the United States* (1919), pp. 56–58.

[3] Harry Elmer Barnes and Negley Teeters, *New Horizons in Criminology* (1943), p. 425.

[4] Thorsten Sellin, "A Note on Capital Executions in the United States," *British Journal of Delinquency* (July 1950), p. 7.

This total of 7,226 legal executions in the United States from 1900 through 1966 is probably an underestimate.

It is somewhat more difficult to estimate the ratio of executions to murders. For reasons set forth at length later in this chapter, the number of murders, as distinct from the number of homicides—that is, as distinct from manslaughters (both negligent and non-negligent) and justifiable and excusable homicides—is almost impossible to determine. Earlier in the century, Raymond Bye estimated that there was about one execution for every seventy or seventy-five homicides (1:70–75).[5] Lewis Lawes estimated an even lower ratio, 1:85.[6] According to the data reported below for the second quarter of this century, a somewhat higher ratio is indicated. Slightly over a quarter of a million (260,000) total homicides between 1930 and 1960 have been reported. Given some 3,724 executions during this period, the ratio is 1:69. As we enter the second half of this century, with 717 executions and some 77,000 homicides in the most recent decade (1950–1959), the ratio is a very low 1:107. If we use the figures for "murders and non-negligent manslaughters," as reported in the *Uniform Crime Reports*, the ratio is still 1:103. However, Professor Wolfgang has estimated that only fifteen per cent of all criminal homicides are capital crimes (see below, p. 467). Using this percentage, the ratio of executions to murders for the past decade soars to 1:10, and for the past three decades (1930–1959) it is about 1:16. What these ratios show is that during the past decade, ninety-nine times out of a hundred, killing someone did not result in the killer's execution; and that even when someone committed first degree murder, nine times out of ten he did not pay the supreme penalty.

In this light, it is instructive to consider the statistics on the actual disposition of those under sentence of death. The public does not ordinarily realize how many different ways execution of death sentence can be avoided. Mr. McCafferty's analysis shows what happened to all those

5 Bye, *op. cit.*, p. 58.
6 Lewis Lawes, *Man's Judgment of Death* (1924), p. 34.

under sentence of death during 1960. As a supplement to his data, the following two tables, one on death sentences in New York from 1889 to 1927, and the other on death sentences in New Jersey from 1907 to 1960, may be of some value. A more informative analysis would require a study of decennial variations in the use made of the different ways to dispose of a death sentence. For instance, of the thirty-four commutations of death sentences in New

TABLE 2

DISPOSITION OF DEATH SENTENCES IN NEW YORK, 1889–1927[a]

Total death sentences	437(6)[b]		
Died under sentence of death		273(2)	
Executed			266(2)
Suicide			3
Natural death			2
Drowned while escaping			2
Conviction reversed on appeal		56(2)	
Acquitted			31(1)
Reconvicted			25(1)
Manslaughter				4
Second degree murder				14(1)
First degree murder				7
Commuted to life imprisonment					1
Awaiting execution					1
Executed					5
Commuted to life imprisonment		74(2)	
Pardoned			3
Discharged			7
In prison, in hospital for the criminally insane, or died in prison			64
Awaiting execution		13	
Transferred to hospital for criminally insane		11	

[a] Source: Lewis Lawes, *Life and Death In Sing Sing* (1928), p. 146.
[b] Figures in parentheses indicate the number of women included in the totals.

Jersey, thirty-one occurred before 1945, and this suggests that in that state executive clemency has practically disappeared as a device for nullifying a death sentence. Undoubtedly, many such variations would show up in a careful study of the subject for all the states in the Union. Meanwhile, the data in these two tables show that a considerable number of death sentences are never carried out.[7]

TABLE 3

DISPOSITION OF DEATH SENTENCES IN
NEW JERSEY, 1907–1960[a]

Total death sentences	232(3)[b]		
Died under sentence of death		160	
Executed			157
Suicide			1
Natural death			1
Killed in escape attempt			1
Conviction reversed on appeal		38	
Acquitted			5
Reconvicted			30
Less than death sentence			21
Death sentence executed			6
Transferred to hospital for the criminally insane			1
Suicide			2
Commuted to life imprisonment		34(3)	
Discharged			23(3)
Died in prison			6
Still in prison or in hospital for the criminally insane			5
Awaiting execution		7	
Transferred to hospital for the criminally insane		1	
Died under suspended sentence		1	

a Source: Inmate admission and classification records, New Jersey State Prison, Trenton, N. J.

b Figures in parentheses indicate the number of women included in the totals.

7 For an analysis of disposition of death sentences in other states, see California, *Assembly Report on the Death Penalty* (1957), p. 14; Ohio, *Report on Capital Punishment* (1961), p. 51; and Maryland, *Report* (1962), pp. 10–11.

OFFENSES PUNISHABLE BY DEATH

When one attempts to specify as of any given date the offenses punishable by death in the United States, irrespective of whether anyone commits these crimes or is executed for them, one must cope with the fact that there are several dozen jurisdictions competent to impose death penalties—the fifty states, the District of Columbia, Puerto Rico, the Virgin Islands, and the federal government under both civil law (extending to territorial, maritime and interstate matters) and military law. No two of these fifty-five jurisdictions employ capital punishment in exactly the same way, except for Alaska, Hawaii, Iowa, Maine, Michigan, Minnesota, Oregon, P. R., V. I., West Virginia, and Wisconsin, all of which have totally abolished it. Since all such provisions are subject to rapid statutory change, it is improbable that anyone knows, from year to year, the precise procedural and substantive law of capital crimes in all American jurisdictions.[1]

Classifying and counting the capital crimes, once they have been identified in the statute books, presents some problems. In many states, a particular offense will be defined as murder (or as murder in the first degree), though it is not punished by death; in other states, the same or a very similar offense will carry the death penalty but will not be regarded as murder. The policy adopted here has been to classify each crime separately listed (or having

[1] Developments in capital laws have frequently been reported in the *Journal of Criminal Law, Criminology and Police Science*. See Raymond Bye, "Recent History and Present Status of Capital Punishment in the United States" (August 1926), pp. 240–244; Lee Emerson Deets, "Changes in Capital Punishment Policy Since 1939" (March–April 1948), pp. 590–591; Richard Reifsnyder, "Capital Crimes in the States" (March–April 1955), pp. 690–693; Leonard Savitz, "Capital Crimes as Defined in American Statutory Law" (September–October 1955), pp. 355–363. See also James McCafferty, *Capital Punishment in the United States* (1954) and *The Congressional Record* (March 1, 1962), pp. 3019–3023. The present survey is in considerable debt to the last three sources, and especially to Professor Savitz's article.

no necessary connection with another offense) as a separate crime and to count it as such. Thus, in the case of capitally punishable homicides, unless a crime is specifically stated to be murder (or, in a few cases, punishable as murder), it is regarded as a separate crime. Similarly, attempted rape is distinguished from rape and from assault with intent to rape; carnal knowledge, or "statutory rape," is distinguished from all other forms of rape; several different kinds of kidnapping, robbery, and burglary are likewise distinguished for purposes of classification and counting. No attempt has been made, however, to do full justice to all the statutory subtleties nor to the interpretations of the statutes by the courts.

Murder, or, in the states that recognize degrees of murder, first degree murder, carries a death penalty in every United States jurisdiction except Vermont, New York, North Dakota, Rhode Island and the eleven abolition areas.[2] The crime of murder is variously defined by statute and judicial interpretation, and only the broader distinctions will be noticed here.[3] Aside from the traditional definition of murder as killing "with malice aforethought," or as "wilful, deliberate, premeditated" killing, an enormous variety of unpremeditated and even unintentional killing is encompassed in the crime of murder.

First of all, so-called "felony murder" considerably enlarges the kinds of homicides regarded as first degree murder. Seven states define murder as any killing in the commission of "any felony"—Alabama, Kansas, New Mexico, New York, North Carolina, Oklahoma, South Carolina, South Dakota. One state defines murder as all killing in the commission of any crime punishable by life imprisonment or death—Massachusetts. All the remaining states define as murder all killing done in the commission of arson, burglary, rape and robbery. Homicide can also become first degree murder if it occurs in the course of any of several other felonies, as follows: mayhem—Arizona,

---

[2] In the following remarks on murder, the definitions of murder in these abolition jurisdictions are not taken into account.
[3] For details, see American Law Institute, *Model Penal Code Tentative Draft No. 9* (1959), Appendix C.

California, Colorado, District of Columbia, Idaho, Iowa, Maryland, Missouri, Montana; kidnapping—District of Columbia, Florida, Idaho, Illinois, Louisiana, New Jersey, New Hampshire, Pennsylvania; sodomy—Federal (civil and military), Florida, Maryland, New Jersey, North Dakota; larceny—Arkansas, Tennessee, Washington.

Secondly, certain other homicides are stipulated by statute to be first degree murder: killing someone in a duel—Alabama, Arkansas, Florida, Illinois, Indiana, Iowa, Massachusetts, Mississippi, Nebraska, Nevada, Oklahoma, Texas, Utah, Virginia, West Virginia, Wyoming; causing death by train wrecking (including, in some cases, aircraft and motor vehicle destruction)—Colorado, Connecticut, District of Columbia, Florida, Georgia, Idaho, Illinois, Indiana, Kentucky, Maryland, Montana, Nebraska, New York, Ohio, Oregon, Pennsylvania, Virginia, Washington, West Virginia, Wyoming; causing death of a woman by abortion—Arkansas, Colorado, Illinois, Kentucky, Mississippi, Texas, West Virginia; lynching—Georgia, Pennsylvania, Virginia, West Virginia; perjury resulting in the death of an innocent person—Illinois, Nebraska, Nevada, Vermont; killing a police officer on duty—Ohio, Oregon, Tennessee (if he is making an arrest in connection with gambling); a prisoner killing any person while attempting to escape prison—Maryland, Nevada; bombing which causes death—Connecticut, Iowa; killing someone by shooting at a train—Virginia, West Virginia; accidentally killing someone while attempting to commit suicide—South Carolina; inciting someone to commit suicide—South Carolina; causing death by stabbing someone—South Carolina; a convict killing a guard—Ohio; causing death by knowingly selling wood alcohol or other poisonous liquid as a beverage—Illinois; police officer causing death by exceeding the bounds of moderation—Arkansas; captain of a boat causing death by deliberately ramming his craft into another—Arkansas; killing during the advocacy of criminal syndicalism—Kentucky; causing death in a fight by the sudden use of a hitherto concealed deadly weapon, the victim having no such weapon—Alabama; killing a kidnapped person—Connecticut; a prisoner killing a hostage—Oregon; foeticide

—Alabama; killing by a prisoner under life sentence—Nevada; causing death during the commission of, or while inciting the commission of criminal anarchy—Colorado; causing death by an act of sabotage—Alabama; causing death by any deliberate injury or alarm—Arkansas; death during a lewd act with a minor—California; causing death by armed housebreaking—District of Columbia; killing certain federal officials or employees—Federal civil.

In addition to all these crimes classified by statute within the crime of murder and punishable by death, many states have made some sixteen kinds of homicide capitally punishable, without including them under the statutory offense of murder: lynching—Alabama, Indiana, Kentucky, South Carolina, Texas; perjury (including subornation) that results in the execution of an innocent person—Arizona, California, Colorado, Idaho, Montana, Nevada; innocence of the person executed not required—Texas; murder by a life term prisoner—Alabama, Rhode Island; causing death by train wrecking—California, Connecticut, Federal civil, Montana, North Carolina; causing death by mishandling a poisonous reptile—Georgia; foeticide—Georgia; murder by a prisoner guilty of a prior murder—New York, North Dakota, Vermont; causing death in a bank robbery—Federal civil; killing by a group of persons during wartime—Vermont; killing the President, Vice President, a Governor or Vice Governor—Ohio; causing death by violent entry on a mining site—Colorado; causing death during criminal anarchy—Colorado; killing a police officer or guard—New York, Vermont; murder and insurrection or rebellion against certain nations—Federal civil; assassination of the President or Vice President—Federal civil; causing death by explosives transported interstate with intent to commit a crime—Federal civil; causing death by malicious destruction of an aircraft or motor vehicle engaged in foreign or interstate commerce, or of the terminal facilities thereof—Federal civil.

Besides all these capitally punishable homicides, there are more than a score of other capital crimes, thirteen of which—treason, kidnapping, rape, carnal knowledge (or "statutory rape"), robbery, bombing, assault by a life prisoner, train wrecking, burglary, arson, perjury, machine gunning, and espionage—are punishable by death in two or more jurisdictions.

Treason[4]—Alabama, Arizona, Arkansas, California, Connecticut, Federal civil, Georgia, Illinois, Indiana, Kansas, Louisiana, Mississippi, Missouri, Montana, Nevada, New Jersey, North Dakota, Oregon, Texas, Vermont, Virginia, Washington.

Kidnapping—Maryland, Mississippi; kidnapping for ransom—Florida, Georgia, Illinois, Indiana, Kansas, Kentucky, Missouri, Montana, Nebraska, New Jersey, Ohio, Oklahoma, Tennessee, Texas, Utah, Vermont, Virginia,[5] Washington; kidnapping for ransom where the victim is not released unharmed—Alabama,[6] Arizona, Arkansas,[7] California, Colorado, Federal civil,[8] Nevada, New Mexico, South Dakota, Wyoming; kidnapping where the victim is not released alive before the trial—South Carolina; kidnapping where the victim suffers bodily harm, or threat thereof—Kansas, Louisiana.

Rape—Alabama, Arkansas,[9] District of Columbia, Federal civil, Florida, Georgia, Kentucky, Louisiana, Maryland,[10] Mississippi, Missouri, Nevada,[11] North Carolina, Oklahoma, South Carolina,[11] Tennessee, Texas, Virginia.[12]

Carnal Knowledge[13]—Alabama (12),[9] District of Co-

---

[4] Except in the case of the federal government, these capital laws proscribing treason are directed at traitors to the *state* governments.

[5] Includes kidnapping of a female for purposes of prostitution or concubinage.

[6] Includes the separate crime of attempted kidnapping.

[7] Includes kidnapping to maim, rob or torture, or to prevent arrest or detection after commission of a felony.

[8] Includes kidnapping the President if his death ensues.

[9] Includes the separate crime of giving a female a stupor-inducing drug with the intent to rape.

[10] Includes the separate crime of carnal knowledge of an imbecile or a lunatic.

[11] Includes the separate crime of aggravated assault to commit rape.

[12] Includes the separate crime of attempted rape.

[13] Number in parentheses indicates the victim's age below which the offense, even if without force and with consent, is deemed capitally punishable. Liability in several cases depends

lumbia (16), Florida (10), Georgia (14), Kentucky (12), Maryland (14), Mississippi (12),[9] Missouri (16), Nevada (18), North Carolina (12), Oklahoma (16),[9,10] South Carolina (16), Tennessee (12),[9] Texas (18), Virginia (14).

Robbery—Alabama, Missouri; armed robbery—Georgia, Kentucky, Mississippi, Missouri, Oklahoma, South Carolina, Tennessee, Texas; armed bank robbery or aggravated robbery—Virginia; train robbery—Alabama, Arizona (includes any train wrecking or railroad bridge burning if done with intent to commit train robbery).

Bombing (includes bomb throwing and dynamiting)—Alabama, Florida, Georgia, Mississippi, Missouri, Nevada, Texas.

Assault with a deadly weapon by a life term prisoner—Arizona, California, Colorado (if escaping), Utah.

Train wrecking—California (if harm results), Wyoming.

Burglary—Alabama, North Carolina, Virginia; armed burglary—Kentucky.

Arson—Georgia, North Carolina, Virginia; if maiming results—Alabama; of a prison by a convict—Arkansas.

Perjury in a capital case—Georgia (only if conviction results), Kansas, Missouri.

Espionage (gathering information for a foreign country during wartime, or giving information to an enemy during wartime)—Federal civil, South Carolina.

Machine gunning—Florida, Virginia.

Seven jurisdictions have singled out particular forms of *assault* for punishment by death: assault with intent to rob—Kentucky; assault with intent to kill by a life term prisoner—Pennsylvania; assault with a deadly weapon while in disguise—Tennessee; assault (or conspiracy) to kill a prison guard or official by a life term prisoner—Alabama; assault on any chief of state or his successor—New Jersey; assault with intent to rape—Maryland; aggravated assault—Nevada.

Lastly, there are fifteen other offenses having nothing in common except that they are acts thought by some leg-

on the age of the male and prior chastity of the female; for details see below, under the jurisdiction in question.

islature to deserve the death penalty: insurrection (including attempts)—Georgia; forcing a woman to marry—Arkansas; second conviction for selling narcotics to a minor—Colorado; intentionally interfering with the war effort—Florida; committing any felony on a train after boarding with such intent—Wyoming; desecration of a grave (unless convicted solely on circumstantial evidence)—Georgia; castration—Georgia; attempt to kill the President or a foreign ambassador—Connecticut; instigation of a minor by a relative or spouse to commit a capital crime—Texas; destruction of vital property by a group during wartime—Vermont; abducting anyone during a bank robbery—Federal civil; third conviction of any offense, or offenses, optionally punishable by death—South Carolina; piracy of interstate or foreign commercial aircraft—Federal civil; supplying heroin to a minor—Federal civil; certain espionage violations of the Atomic Energy Act—Federal civil.

In addition to this list of capital crimes under the civil jurisdictions in the United States, there are nearly a dozen additional capital crimes under the Uniform Code of Military Justice for the armed forces. Many apply only during wartime: desertion, spying, misconduct in the face of the enemy, compelling a subordinate to surrender, aiding the enemy, assault or wilful disobedience of a superior, misbehavior while on duty as a sentinel. Several others, however, obtain also in peacetime: murder, rape, forcing a safeguard, improperly using a counter-sign, mutiny or sedition (including attempts and, if the act is attempted, solicitation), and failure to suppress mutiny or sedition.

This completes the list of capital crimes under civil and military law in force in the United States (as of January 1967). In most cases, a death sentence is *optional* upon conviction of one of the foregoing crimes (usually, it is for the jury to determine the sentence; in a few states, it is for the judge to decide[14]). Many offenses, however,

14 For details, see Robert Knowlton, "Problems of Jury Discretion in Capital Cases," *University of Pennsylvania Law Review* (June 1953). E.g., in Georgia, the judge may set aside any death sentence if the conviction was obtained solely on circumstantial evidence.

TABLE 1
CAPITAL CRIMES IN THE UNITED STATES
BY TYPE OF OFFENSE, JURISDICTIONS, AND EXECUTIONS

Type of Offense	Number of Capital Jurisdictions[a]	Number of Mandatory Jurisdictions	Number of Executing Jurisdictions[b]
Capitally punishable homicide	44	9	44
Murder	40	0	[d]
Other homicide[c]	20	8	[d]
Kidnapping[e]	34	1	6
Treason	21	11	0
Rape[f]	19	0	18
Carnal knowledge[g]	15	0	[d]
Robbery[h]	10	0	7
Perjury in a capital case[i]	10	6	0
Bombing[j]	7	0	0
Assault by life term prisoner[k]	5	3	1
Burglary[l]	4	0	2
Arson	4	0	0
Train wrecking	2	0	0
Train robbery	2	0	0
Espionage[m]	2	0	1
Other[n]	17	5	0
Total[o]	44	22	45

a Fifty-five jurisdictions: Fifty states, District of Columbia, Puerto Rico, Virgin Islands, Federal civil and military.
b Source: *National Prisoner Statistics,* "Executions 1961." Alaska and Hawaii excluded. Executions in years prior to 1930 excluded.
c Includes sixteen special capital homicide statutes.
d Information not available; see note b.
e Included kidnapping, kidnapping for ransom, kidnapping with

carry a *mandatory* death penalty, as follows: treason[15]—
Arizona, California, Connecticut, Kansas, Louisiana, Mississippi, Montana, Nevada, New Jersey, Vermont, Virginia, Washington; perjury in a capital case where an execution results—Texas; perjury where an innocent person is executed—Arizona, California, Colorado, Idaho,
Montana; train wrecking, if death results—California, Montana, North Carolina; murder in the commission of rape
(including attempts)—Massachusetts; killing the President,
Vice President, Governor or Vice Governor—Ohio; murder in wartime by a group of persons—Vermont; murder by a life term prisoner—Alabama, Rhode Island; assault with a deadly weapon by a life term prisoner—
Arizona, California (if the victim is a non-inmate and
dies), Colorado (if escaping); assault on a prison guard
or official by a prisoner—Alabama; kidnapping for ransom
where the victim is harmed—Arkansas; attempt to kill the
President or a foreign ambassador—Connecticut; destruction of vital property by a group in wartime—Vermont;
arson of a prison by a convict—Arkansas; spying in wartime—Federal military.

It may be useful to have the foregoing information arranged in tabular form to display for each kind of offense
the number of jurisdictions which treat it as a capital crime,
how many have kept it mandatory, and how many have

bodily harm, kidnapping for ransom and with bodily harm, taking
a hostage.

f Includes rape, attempted rape, assault with intent to rape, drugging with intent to rape.

g Includes carnal knowledge of a minor and of a mentally deficient
or mentally ill person.

h Includes robbery, aggravated robbery, armed robbery, bank
robbery.

i Includes perjury and subornation leading to the death of a guilty
person or to the death of an innocent person.

j Includes bombing, dynamiting, and bomb throwing.

k Includes assault and assault with a deadly weapon.

l Includes burglary and armed burglary.

m Includes gathering or giving information to an enemy or foreign
power during wartime.

n Includes twenty-one special capital statutes.

o Because of duplications, the totals are less than the sum of the
numbers in each column.

15 Some states prohibit even executive clemency for traitors.

actually punished it with death since 1930. (Table 1) As the annotations show, the total number of different capital crimes is either sixty-seven, fifty-three, forty-seven, or thirty-three, depending on whether or not all the forms of capitally punishable homicide are included under the single crime of murder or are counted separately, and whether or not each of the several forms of kidnapping, rape, robbery, bombing, assault and espionage are counted as separate crimes.

Finally, we may arrange the information for each of the fifty-five jurisdictions, showing the crimes which each punishes by death and whether the offense is optional or mandatory (if the latter, it is italicized).

Alabama—Murder, kidnapping for ransom where the victim is not released unharmed, attempted kidnapping, rape, carnal knowledge of a female under twelve or a female who has been drugged for the purpose, treason, robbery, train robbery, burglary, lynching, dynamiting, *assault* (or conspiracy) *to kill a prison guard or official by a life term prisoner, murder by a life term prisoner*, death or maiming during arson.

Alaska—None.

Arizona—Murder, kidnapping for ransom where the victim is not released unharmed, *perjury in a capital case resulting in the death of an innocent person, armed assault by a life term prisoner*, train robbery, *treason*.

Arkansas—Murder, *kidnapping for ramsom where the victim is not released unharmed*, kidnapping to maim, rob or torture, or to prevent arrest or detection after commission of a felony, drugging a female with intent to rape, forcing a woman to marry, treason, *arson of a prison by a convict*.

California—Murder, kidnapping for ransom if victim is harmed, *treason, perjury in a capital case resulting in the death of an innocent person, armed assault by a life term prisoner* (*if the victim is a non-inmate and dies*), train wrecking (*if harm results*).

Colorado—Murder, kidnapping for ransom where the victim suffers bodily harm, causing death during criminal anarchy, causing death by violent entry upon a mining site, second conviction of selling narcotics to a minor, *perjury in a capital case leading to the death of an innocent person, armed assault by an escaping life term prisoner.*

Connecticut—Murder, *treason, attempt on the life of the President or foreign ambassador,* causing death by arson, causing death by train wrecking.

Delaware—Murder.

District of Columbia—Murder, rape, carnal knowledge (16).[16]

Florida—Murder, rape, carnal knowledge (10), kidnapping for ransom, bombing, machine gunning, intentional interference with the war effort.

Georgia—Murder, kidnapping for ransom, rape, carnal knowledge (14), treason, armed robbery, dynamiting, arson, castration, desecration of a grave, insurrection (including attempts), perjury in a capital case resulting in conviction, causing death by mishandling a poisonous reptile, foeticide.

Hawaii—None.

Idaho—Murder, kidnapping, *perjury in a capital case resulting in the execution of an innocent person.*

Illinois—Murder, kidnapping for ransom, treason.

Indiana—Murder, kidnapping for ransom, treason, lynching.

Iowa—None.

Kansas—Murder, kidnapping for ransom or with bodily harm to the victim, *treason,* perjury in a capital case.

Kentucky—Murder, kidnapping for ransom, rape, carnal knowledge (12), armed robbery, armed burglary, assault to rob, lynching.

Louisiana—Murder, kidnapping with bodily harm to the victim, rape ("aggravated rape"), *treason.*

Maine—None.

Maryland—Murder, kidnapping, rape, assault to commit rape, carnal knowledge (14; or any age if victim is mentally deficient or insane).

Massachusetts—Murder (*in the commission of rape*).

Michigan—None.

Minnesota—None.

[16] See note 13 above.

Mississippi—Murder, kidnapping, rape, armed robbery, bombing, carnal knowledge, including attempts (12; any age if drugged with intent to rape), *treason.*

Missouri—Murder, kidnapping for ransom, rape, carnal knowledge (16), treason, robbery, bombing, perjury in a capital case.

Montana—Murder (*if caused by train wrecking*), kidnapping for ransom, *treason, perjury in a capital case resulting in the execution of an innocent person.*

Nebraska—Murder, kidnapping for ransom with bodily harm to the victim.

Nevada—Murder, kidnapping for ransom with bodily harm to the victim, aggravated rape, aggravated carnal knowledge (18, unless the male is under 16), aggravated assault, *treason*, dynamiting, perjury in a capital case resulting in the death of an innocent person.

New Hampshire—Murder.

New Jersey—Murder, kidnapping for ransom, *treason*, assault on a chief of state or his successor.

New Mexico—Murder, kidnapping for ransom with bodily harm to the victim.

New York—Murder of a peace officer on duty or by a prisoner under life sentence.

North Carolina—Murder (*if caused by train wrecking*), rape, carnal knowledge (12), burglary, arson.

North Dakota—Treason, murder by a convict under life sentence for murder.

Ohio—Murder, kidnapping for ransom, *killing a federal or state chief of state.*

Oklahoma—Murder, kidnapping for ransom, rape, carnal knowledge (16; 18 if the victim is previously chaste; or of a mentally deficient or insane person unless male is under 18 or, if over 14, with proof of physical capacity), armed robbery.

Oregon—None.

Pennsylvania—Murder, assault with intent to kill by a life term prisoner.

Puerto Rico—None.

Rhode Island—Murder by a life term prisoner.

South Carolina—Murder, kidnapping where victim is not

released alive before the trial, rape, assault with intent to rape, carnal knowledge (16; unless male is under 18 and female over 14 and previously unchaste), lynching, gathering or delivering information or aid to the enemy during wartime, causing death in a duel, third conviction for crime(s) optionally punishable by death.

South Dakota—Murder, kidnapping for ransom where the victim is bodily harmed.

Tennessee—Murder, kidnapping for ransom, rape, carnal knowledge (12; or any age if drugged with intent to rape), armed robbery, armed assault while disguised.

Texas—Murder, kidnapping for ransom, rape, carnal knowledge (18; unless victim is over 15 and previously unchaste), treason, *perjury in a capital case resulting in an execution,* lynching, armed robbery, bombing, instigation of a minor by a relative or spouse to commit a capital crime.

Utah—Murder, kidnapping for ransom, armed assault by a life term prisoner.

Vermont—Murder of a guard or policeman acting in line of duty or by a person guilty of a previous murder, kidnapping for ransom, *treason, killing or destruction of vital property by a group in wartime.*

Virginia—Murder, *treason,* kidnapping for ransom, rape, kidnapping of a female to coerce her into prostitution or concubinage, carnal knowledge (14), attempted rape, aggravated robbery, armed bank robbery, burglary, arson, using a machine gun while committing (or attempting to commit) any crime.

Virgin Islands—None.

Washington—Murder, kidnapping for ransom, *treason.*

West Virginia—None.

Wisconsin—None.

Wyoming—Murder, kidnapping for ransom where the victim is not released unharmed, committing any felony on a train after boarding with such intent, train wrecking.

Federal civil—Murder, kidnapping for ransom where the victim is not released unharmed, rape, treason, taking a hostage or causing death during a bank robbery, gathering information for a foreign power or giving information to an enemy during wartime, aircraft piracy, supplying heroin to a minor, causing death by malicious destruction of aircraft or motor vehicles or the terminal facilities thereof, causing death by explosives transported interstate with intent to commit a crime, causing death by train wrecking, espionage violations of the Atomic Energy Act, death resulting from illegally mailing certain articles, murder and insurrection or rebellion against certain countries, assassination of President or Vice President.

Federal military—Murder, rape, mutiny or sedition (including attempts and, if the act is attempted, solicitation), failure to suppress mutiny or sedition, forcing a safeguard, improper use of a countersign; in wartime only: *Spying*, misconduct in the presence of the enemy, desertion, aiding the enemy, assault or wilful disobedience of a superior, misbehavior while on duty or as a sentinel, compelling a subordinate to surrender.

JUVENILES AND CAPITAL PUNISHMENT

Even though a state prescribes the death penalty for a given crime, not everyone who commits such an offense and who is arrested is actually subjected to a possible death sentence. A guilty person may escape trial for his crime by a plea of *non vult* (no defense), or the court may determine that he is unfit to be tried by reason of his insanity. If the former, the judge in most cases will sentence him to prison. If the latter, most jurisdictions require that he be committed to a hospital for the criminally insane. It is even possible that the prosecutor will decide not to press charges against the guilty party, though this is rare in a capital crime. But by far the commonest reason for exempting a person from trial on a capital indictment, even when he is guilty, is his age.

The Standard Juvenile Court Law of 1959, a piece of model criminal legislation prepared by the National Council on Crime and Delinquency, would prohibit execution of "any child under sixteen" and give jurisdiction to the regular adult criminal courts at their discretion to indict on a capital or a felony charge any person sixteen to eighteen.[1] The following article "Right to Execute Children Scored," from *The New York Times** shows how widely the actual laws governing juveniles in this country deviate from even these modest standards.

In Georgia's Reidsville Prison a fifteen-year-old Negro boy, Preston Cobb Jr., is under sentence of death for killing a seventy-year-old white farmer.

There have been protests and appeals from all over the world, moving the case from the obscurity of a rural county in Georgia to the arena of public controversy. The issue is not over the boy's guilt. It is over his age, and the state's legal right to execute a child.

Criticism has focused on laws and legal ruling that permitted the state to try the youth as an adult. At the center of the issue, there is this question: At what point is a youngster too young to be executed? In Georgia, by law, the death penalty can be given to a child as young as ten. But Georgia is not alone in this category.

An Associated Press survey of legal possibilities in criminal proceedings involving children shows: In sixteen states it is legally possible to execute children as young as seven. In three states death could be given children of eight. In three, including Georgia, youngsters of ten are subject to the death penalty. In the nineteen other states having the death penalty, the minimum age ranges from twelve to eighteen. All fifty states possess the power and authority to try children as adults—and give them the same punishment as adults—in cases of capital crimes.

Dr. Ralph S. Banay, associate director of the Research on Social Deviation, New York, said:

> The apparent philosophy behind statutes concerning juvenile offenders is that a child has not reached a

[1] Sol Rubin, "Developments in Correctional Law," *N. P. P. A. Journal* (1960), pp. 82 ff., and "Developments in Correctional Law," *Crime and Delinquency* (1961), pp. 69 f. A tabular analysis of capital laws as they affect juveniles (as of 1955) is available in Leonard Savitz, "Capital Crimes as Defined in American Statutory Law," *Journal of Criminal Law, Criminology and Police Science* (September–October 1955), p. 356.

* Reprinted, with permission, from *The New York Times*, Sunday, January 7, 1962, p. 81.

degree of intellectual and emotional development that would qualify him as fully responsible for his acts. The laws, however, embody an obvious contradiction: for when the offense is too obnoxious or repugnant, complete responsibility is placed upon the child and he must face the full weight of the law.

In substance, this is the situation in the United States today: Despite the protection given children through the juvenile court systems—in which they cannot be tried as criminals—all states can prosecute and punish children as if they were adults. The trial of children in adult criminal courts is not the scheme of vengeful prosecutors but ideally and theoretically another way to give the child the greater protection of constitutional rights. The irony is that this legal machinery to protect children can cut both ways.

The machinery is not rusty. Sometimes it delivers death; most times prison sentences that in some cases amount to living death. At least seventy teen-agers have been executed in the last half-century. The youngest was a Negro boy of fourteen, George Stinney Jr., who was electrocuted for murder June 16, 1944, in South Carolina. Few females of any age have been put to death, but one was a Negro girl of seventeen. Virginia Christian was executed for murder in Virginia's electric chair August 16, 1912.

Prisons throughout the nation today house teen-agers— or adults who were children when their crimes were committed. Edward Bell was thirteen when he was sentenced in 1960 to a life term for rape, and James Frank King was twelve when he was sentenced in 1958 to life for murder, in Florida—a state that has executed four sixteen-year-olds. Young Bell and King were white. King's sentence has since been commuted to an indefinite term. Lee Arthur Vester, a fourteen-year-old Negro, recently began serving a fifty-year term for murder and, in 1960, Edward Vargas entered prison for a minimum forty years for murder, in Illinois. Today, in Indiana, a nine-year-old boy— Ronnie Wing—is in custody of juvenile authorities while possible procedures are being studied. Immediately after the slaying of a thirteen-year-old girl, he was held on a preliminary charge of first degree murder. In Illinois, a thirteen-year-old—Steven Schloneger—has been charged with murder in the death of a seven-year-old neighbor girl.

The right to inflict death on youngsters drew sharp condemnation at a recent University of Chicago conference on "Justice for the Child." More than seventy of the nation's leading juvenile court jurists, attorneys, probation officers, educators, welfare and social workers at a seminar expressed outrage "that any state retains the power to execute a minor." "Justice for the child means exactly that, and there can be no justice in executing a child, any child, anywhere," they said.

The juvenile court is not a court in the usual sense. Basically, it is a place where a hearing is conducted to decide what action can be taken in a case involving a juvenile. The court's fundamental aim was stated in the laws by which Illinois created the first juvenile courts in the nation in 1899. It is "that the care of, custody and discipline of a child [found to be delinquent, dependent or neglected] shall approximate as nearly as may be that which should be given by its parents."

There is no uniformity to the age limits that would bring a person under jurisdiction of the juvenile court, or bar him. Ages are keyed to varying definitions of "child" and "juvenile" and "minor." The broad standard came from common law. Under the common law yardstick, children of seven were deemed absolutely innocent—that is, lacking the mental competence required for criminal liability. Children between seven and fourteen were presumed to lack such capacity. But this could be overcome by showing that the child was sufficiently intelligent to understand what he had done. At fourteen, a child was presumed to have adult intelligence and stand liable for his actions.

The common law groupings, which largely set age standards for criminal capacity, do not coincide with statutes setting juvenile court jurisdictions. The result is that while a state may consider a fifteen-year-old as a child, it may at the same time be able to hold a ten-year-old responsible for certain crimes. Because of the difference in laws and their interpretations, there is a hodge-podge of legal possibilities that apparently contradict each state's laws concerning juvenile court jurisdiction.

In New York, a fifteen-year-old charged with a serious crime can be transferred to jurisdiction of the criminal court. In Iowa, the juvenile court has no jurisdiction in any case in which the punishment for an adult could be life in prison or the death penalty. Indiana's juvenile courts can waive any capital case—without regard to age—to criminal jurisdiction. Georgia's juvenile court jurisdiction applies to all those sixteen and under regardless of the offense. But the state Supreme Court has ruled that in capital cases the jurisdiction belongs to the Superior Court. This permitted the trial of Preston Cobb Jr. and could determine what course will be taken in two other murders, one committed by a sixteen-year-old Negro boy and the other by a fifteen-year-old white boy.

Sparked by the Cobb case, there is a growing movement in Georgia to raise to eighteen the age limit of persons liable to capital punishment. Governor S. Ernest Vandiver —who has no clemency powers—has expressed belief the state pardon and parole board would commute young Cobb's death sentence if such a law was enacted.

VOLUME AND RATE OF CAPITAL CRIMES

In a word, there is no exact information anywhere as to the volume of capital crimes in the United States. Difficult as it is to specify the capital laws for the nation as a whole, it is impossible with the present sort of criminal statistics to specify the exact amount of capital crimes for even one jurisdiction in even one year for even one crime! Ten years ago, George B. Vold complained, "There are no general statistics available as to the number of offenses committed per year for which death is the required penalty."[1] Nothing has changed in the interim. We are not, of course, totally ignorant of the extent of crime in America, nor are the available criminal statistics wholly useless for

[1] George B. Vold, "Extent and Trend of Capital Crimes in the United States," *The Annals* (November 1952), p. 1.

our purposes. Even a brief examination of the facts reveals that the vast majority of crimes in America are non-capital and that the vast majority of crimes punishable by death either never occur or are never actually punished by death.

According to the *National Prisoner Statistics,* there are only seven capital crimes for which the death sentence has been carried out since 1930: murder, rape, armed robbery, kidnapping, espionage, burglary and assault by a life term prisoner. Thus, when one speaks about the volume of capital crimes in the United States, one refers for all practical purposes to the volume of these seven crimes. The most reliable, up-to-date, and readily accessible criminal statistics in the country—indeed, the only nation-wide ones —are those published annually since 1930 by the Federal Bureau of Investigation in the *Uniform Crime Reports.* Although this source makes no attempt to classify crimes by the mode of punishment, it does record the volume of certain major crimes against the person, and murder, rape, armed robbery and burglary are among these crimes. Kidnapping, however, is not reported in this source, and except for disconnected bits of information which have appeared from time to time in hearings before Congress and in the *Reports* of the United States Attorney General, we have no reliable information on the extent of this capital crime at all.

(A brief digression on the subject is perhaps in point here. The Director of the Federal Bureau of Investigation, J. Edgar Hoover, has reported that between 1932 and 1959, a total of 844 persons have been convicted of kidnapping in state and federal courts, that only two kidnappings have gone unsolved, and that there have been five executions under the federal law for kidnapping (in 1936, 1938, two in 1953, and 1956).[2] But how many kidnappings there were from, say, 1920 to 1933, or what the annual number of kidnappings was in each American jurisdiction between 1920 and 1960—these are questions we cannot answer. Information available in the annual *Re-*

[2] Cited by Herbert Wechsler, in *New York Law Forum* (August 1961), pp. 252–253. No government source is given.

ports of the Attorney General show that, according to Mr. Hoover, the number of convictions under the federal kidnapping law for the seven years 1955 through 1961 averaged twenty-eight, whereas for the nine years 1933 through 1941 the average was forty-four.[3] Testimony before Congress back in 1932 and prior to the enactment of the federal "Lindbergh law" indicated that in 501 cities during 1931 alone, there were some 279 kidnappings.[4] However, in 1941, Mr. Hoover reported that in all the years since 1932 the F. B. I. had investigated only 156 cases of kidnapping and threatened kidnapping, resulting in 317 convictions.[5] These two sets of facts are an indication of the volume of kidnapping during the 1930s and of the trend in this crime during the past three decades. In general, the data at present available, of which the above is a fair sample, are so crude that it is almost impossible to draw any reliable inferences concerning the possible effects of capital punishment on the crime of kidnapping.)

Murder, rape, robbery and burglary receive special definitions in *Uniform Crime Reports,* and these must be understood in order to interpret the crime totals entered in this source. (Although aggravated assault is almost nowhere a capital crime, I have included it below and elsewhere in this essay because many attempted murders fall into this category.) Here are the definitions:[6]

1. Criminal homicide.—(a) Murder and non-negligent manslaughter: all willful felonious homicides as

[3] Frequently, there are discrepancies in the Attorney General's *Reports* between the number of convictions under the federal kidnapping law as reported under Mr. Hoover's name and as reported under the Attorney General's name; e.g., the *Report* for 1934 has the former alleging seventy-nine convictions (p. 132) and the latter alleging sixty-nine convictions (p. 68). Wherever possible, I have relied in the text above on Mr. Hoover's figures.

[4] Cited in Horace L. Bomar, Jr., "The Lindbergh Law," *Law and Contemporary Problems* (1934), p. 435, referring to the Hearing on H. R. 5657 before the House Committee on the Judiciary, seventy-first Congress, Second Session (1932), p. 5.

[5] *Report of the Attorney General* (1939), p. 154.

[6] *Uniform Crime Reports, 1965,* p. 47.

distinguished from deaths caused by negligence. Excludes attempts to kill, assaults to kill, suicides, accidental deaths, or justifiable homicides. Justifiable homicides are limited to: (1) the killing of a person by a peace officer in line of duty; (2) the killing of a person in the act of committing a felony by a private citizen. (b) Manslaughter by negligence: any death which the police investigation establishes was primarily attributable to gross negligence of some individual other than the victim.

2. *Forcible rape.*—Rape by force, assault to rape and attempted rape. Excludes statutory offenses (no force used—victim under age of consent).

3. *Robbery.*—Stealing or taking anything of value from the person by force or violence or by putting in fear, such as strong-arm robbery, stickups, armed robbery, assault to rob, and attempt to rob.

4. *Aggravated assault.*—Assault with intent to kill or for the purpose of inflicting severe bodily injury by shooting, cutting, stabbing, maiming, poisoning, scalding, or by the use of acids, explosives, or other means. Excludes simple assaults, assault and battery, fighting, etc.

5. *Burglary—breaking or entering.*—Burglary, housebreaking, safecracking, or any unlawful entry to commit a felony or a theft, even though no force was used to gain entrance and attempts. Burglary followed by larceny is not counted again as larceny.

These definitions undoubtedly help to bring uniformity into the classification of crimes as they are reported from thousands of police departments all over the nation. But the crimes totalled under these headings are not an accurate count of the capital crimes in the nation. Some may argue that each of these crimes *ought* to be punishable by death, and the point is debatable. But the truth is that very few of these crimes are legally punishable in this way. There are several reasons why this is so.

First and most important, the national totals of crimes such as murder, rape and robbery vastly overstate the number of capitally punishable murders, rapes and robberies, because by no means do all of these crimes occur in jurisdictions where they are punishable by death. As an example, consider forcible rape. In 1960, seventeen states, Washington, D. C., and the federal government punished rape with death (not including homicide in the course of rape, which is usually felony murder and widely punishable by death). Accordingly, whereas *Uniform Crime Reports* show that a total of 15,560 forcible rapes occurred during 1960, the maximum that should be counted as capital crimes cannot exceed the 4,735 which occurred in these nineteen jurisdictions.[7] Yet even this number is far in excess of the actual number of capital rapes. Rape nowhere carries a mandatory death penalty, and therefore considerable discretion enters into the decision by the county prosecutor whether or not to seek a death sentence for any particular rapist. *National Prisoner Statistics* show that nine-tenths of all executions for rape since 1930 have been of non-white males; thus there is small likelihood that many white rapists in 1960 were prosecuted with an intent to secure a death sentence. Similarly, it seems reasonable to assume that in no more than a few cases where the victim is non-white is the rapist (whether white or not) likely to be sentenced to death. But these considerations, if they are sound, require us to eliminate about three-fourths of the 4,735 rapes as non-capital crimes, and leaves us with about 1,250, which is an estimate of the number of forcible rapes perpetrated by non-white males against white females, and thus likely to be treated as capital crimes. And this number is but one-twelfth of the original total given in *Uniform Crime Reports* for the year. Furthermore, since the F. B. I. definition of "forcible rape" in-

---

[7] Alabama (272), Arkansas (156), Florida (418), Georgia (299), Kentucky (167), Louisiana (311), Maryland (226), Mississippi (112), Missouri (474), Nevada (36), North Carolina (334), Oklahoma (229), South Carolina (224), Tennessee (187), Texas (891), Virginia (288), West Virginia (81). *Uniform Crime Reports* enters no totals for the federal jurisdiction.

cludes not only the completed crime of rape by force, but also "assault to rape and attempted rape," whereas only a few jurisdictions count such crimes as capitally punishable, the total must probably be reduced still further. Similar reductions for similar reasons would have to be made from the national totals reported in *Uniform Crime Reports* for every category of crime to arrive at the subtotals that represent the capital crimes. This is especially true in the case of burglary and armed robbery, for less than a dozen jurisdictions still punish these crimes with death.

Comparable difficulties occur in attempting to determine the actual total of capitally punishable homicides. Since some states have no death penalty for murder, the national totals of "murder and non-negligent manslaughter" will exceed the number of homicides punishable by death. What is even more important, the F. B. I. does not distinguish between total murders (or first degree murders), which alone carry the death penalty, and all lesser forms of non-negligent criminal homicide, in particular second degree murder and voluntary manslaughter, crimes usually punished by imprisonment. Instead, all voluntary or non-negligent criminal homicides are lumped together in *Uniform Crime Reports* under the title, "murder and non-negligent manslaughter." (This must be kept in mind when the term, "murder," is used in the tables below.) What one wants to know, of course, is what fraction of the totals entered in this fashion are murders; and what fraction of this fraction are capitally punishable homicides, i.e., murders where a normal adult (not a child, juvenile, or lunatic) is the criminal and where a capital indictment might issue (excluding, therefore, those cases where the murderer commits suicide). It is impossible to supply this information at present. Probably the annual nationwide total of capitally punishable homicides is no greater than the total number of possible indictments for (first degree) murder that might be issued in any given year, though it is probably considerably more than the total number of convictions eventually obtained on these indictments. But we have no accurate idea of what this total number of murder indictments might be.

Even judicial criminal statistics, which show how the courts actually dispose of the cases which come before them, would not reveal to us the number of crimes that could have been treated as capitally punishable; such statistics would reveal only how many were treated in this way. (Therefore, the absence of any nationwide judicial criminal statistics is not disastrous for our purposes. The Bureau of the Census attempted, between 1931 and 1946, to collect and publish such data in the annual series, *Judicial Criminal Statistics*. But the reports as published never gave more than fragmentary data on the nation as a whole.) Raw criminal statistics, which is all that *Uniform Crime Reports* contains, can never be taken as an accurate basis for estimating either the total possible (first degree) murder indictments or the total actual convictions where a death sentence might have resulted.

One can conclude only that the number of capitally punishable homicides in the United States is far less than the total of murders and non-negligent manslaughters reported for any one year by the F. B. I. Professor Marvin Wolfgang, in his article reprinted in a later chapter, estimates that only fifteen per cent of all "criminal homicides" are "capital crimes."[8] Bensing and Schroeder, in their study of criminal homicide in Greater Cleveland for the years 1947–1953, indicated that exactly twenty-five per cent (116 of 454) of all homicides during this period issued in first degree murder indictments.[9] Whether even 1,000 of the 9,140 "murders and non-negligent manslaughters" reported for 1960 in *Uniform Crime Reports* should qualify as capitally punishable homicides, as that term has been defined in this essay, is doubtful.

Notice, too, that *Uniform Crime Reports* offers no breakdown of murders into those which are wilful, premeditated,

[8] In his *Patterns in Criminal Homicide* (1958), pp. 300–302, Wolfgang reports that twenty per cent of those convicted of criminal homicide were found guilty of first degree murder; but his figures also show (pp. 24 f.) that of the total number of homicidal crimes, only thirteen per cent resulted in a conviction of first degree murder.

[9] Robert C. Bensing and Oliver Schroeder, Jr., *Homicide in an Urban Community* (1960), pp. 5, 22.

and deliberate, as distinct from those which are committed in the course of rape, burglary, robbery and other felonies, so-called "felony murders." Nor does this source classify robberies into armed and unarmed robberies. Hence, it is impossible, using the *Reports,* to tell whether the presence of capital punishment correlates directly with a lower volume of felony murders and armed robberies, as many believe it should. Here, as with kidnapping, we simply lack the relevant data. These are but some of the many questions that depend for their answers on accurate knowledge of the volume of certain crimes, but that are unanswerable at present in the absence of better nationwide criminal statistics.[10]

Two more features of the crime totals as found in *Uniform Crime Reports* deserve notice. The crimes recorded in the *Reports* are not all the crimes "known to the police," but only those known to police departments that classify and report them to Washington. At its latest and best, the *Reports* cover approximately 8,000 law enforcement agencies reporting ninety-two per cent of the total United States population.[11] But as recently as 1957, the combined total of urban and rural police departments submitting re-

[10] The American Law Institute reports (*Model Penal Code, Tentative Draft No. 9* [1959], p. 38) that in Philadelphia between 1948 and 1952, a total of 1,133 rapes, 6,432 robberies, and 27,669 burglaries led to a total of forty-three homicides or "felony murders" (four, thirty-eight, and one, respectively, for these three felonies), and that six of these resulted in death sentences. Professor Wolfgang reports that during the same period in Philadelphia there were a total of 588 criminal homicides (*Patterns in Criminal Homicide* [1958], p. 15). If these data are representative of the nation as a whole, less than .2 per cent of all felonies become felony murders, while about seven per cent of all criminal homicides are felony murders. If we use the data Professor Wolfgang offers in his book (p. 240), this last figure drops to five per cent. However, the total of 1,133 rapes which resulted in thirty-eight murders reported by the American Law Institute is about half the percentage of felony murders for this crime reported in a previous study; see Edwin H. Sutherland, "The Sexual Psychopath Laws," *Journal of Criminal Law, Criminology and Police Science* (January–February 1950), p. 545.

[11] *Uniform Crime Reports, 1965,* p. 43.

ports represented only about eighty-three per cent of the population.[12] Furthermore, the crimes recorded are only the crimes *known* to the police. How many murders, for instance, have gone undetected and thus unreported? How many rapes have never been reported to the police by the victims or their families? The number may be small, but it is not zero. The result is that an estimate of the actual national volume of a particular crime requires a double extrapolation from the reported figures: one, to cover all those crimes committed in reporting districts which are not included in reports because they were not detected; and another, to cover all the crimes committed in districts not covered by reports at all. Thus, *Uniform Crime Reports* can be used only for a rough estimate of the annual volume of capital crimes in the nation.

With all these qualifications before us, let us now look at the volume of murder, rape, robbery, aggravated assault and burglary for the most recent years as we find it in this source. It appears from these data that the total *volume* of "murder and non-negligent manslaughter" increased very slightly between 1960 and 1965, and that the *rates* for this crime took a similar upward turn. It is also apparent from these tables that this crime increased less rapidly than any other major crime. What inferences we should draw from these increases I shall discuss later.

The figures given in Tables 1 and 2 do not indicate the degree of variation in the volume of these crimes from region to region, state to state. Tables 3 and 4 show how striking these variations are for the crime of "murder and non-negligent manslaughter." The variations indicated by these two tables only scratch the surface. Professor Wolfgang's study of criminal homicide in Philadelphia shows that males (rather than females) between the ages of twenty and twenty-four (whether Negro or white) are far more homicide-prone than any other age-sex grouping (see below, p. 78). Bensing and Schroeder, in their study, pinpointed the locus of murder in Cleveland to particular districts and even to particular streets. They remarked, "It

[12] *Uniform Crime Reports, 1957,* p. 119.

Table 1
Volume of Selected Crimes, 1960–1965

Crime	1960	1961	1962	1963	1964	1965
			Year			
Murder	9,140[a]	8,600	8,400	8,500	9,250	9,850
Forcible rape	15,560	16,010	16,310	16,400	20,550	22,470
Aggravated assault	130,230	133,020	139,600	147,800	184,900	206,700
Robbery	88,970	91,660	95,260	100,160	111,750	118,920
Burglary	821,100	852,500	892,800	975,900	1,110,500	1,173,200

SOURCE: *Uniform Crime Reports, 1960–1965.*

[a] This total was reported in *Uniform Crime Reports, 1961*, p. 2, as 8,970; the total in the table is taken from *ibid*, 1960, p. 2.

TABLE 2
RATE OF SELECTED CRIMES, 1960–1965
(Per 100,000 Population)

Crime	Year					
	1960	1961	1962	1963	1964	1965
Murder	5.1[a]	4.7	4.5	4.5	4.8	5.1
Forcible rape	8.7	8.8	8.8	8.7	10.7	11.6
Aggravated assault	72.6	72.7	75.1	78.4	96.6	106.8
Robbery	49.6	50.1	51.3	53.1	58.4	61.4
Burglary	264.8	466.0	480.4	517.6	580.4	605.3

SOURCE: *Uniform Crime Reports, 1960–1965.*

[a] This rate was subsequently reported in *Uniform Crime Reports, 1961*, p. 3, as 5.3, and in *ibid., 1962*, p. 3, as 4.9; the rate in the table is taken from *ibid., 1960*, p. 2.

can safely be generalized . . . that the areas with the very highest homicide rates are the areas with the lowest socio-economic status, the most undesirable neighborhood conditions, the greatest financial dependency, the most acute problems of space and crowded housing conditions, the least stability of population, the greatest social maladjustment and family and individual adjustment problems, and the poorest health."[13] All these factors, of course, fail to register on anything but the most detailed geographical and demographical analysis of crime.

As the discussion later in this volume will show, the statistical investigations of the deterrent efficacy of capital punishment are usually based on reference to general homicide statistics. These statistics are collected by state and federal bureaus of vital statistics from death certificates, and include non-criminal as well as criminal homicides. Unlike both police and judicial criminal statistics, vital statistics make no attempt to appraise the legal status of the killing; nothing is indicated in homicide classifications except the cause of death, i.e., gun shot, stab wound, etc. The

[13] Bensing and Schroeder, *op. cit.*, p. 184.

TABLE 3
MURDER RATES BY REGIONS, 1964–1965
(Per 100,000 Population)

Region	Year	Murder Rate
New England		
(Conn., Mass., Me.,	1964	1.7
N.H., R.I., Vt.)	1965	2.1
Middle Atlantic	1964	3.9
(N.J., N.Y., Pa.)	1965	4.0
East North Central		
(Ill., Ind., Mich.,	1964	3.7
Ohio, Wis.)	1965	4.0
West North Central		
(Iowa, Kan., Minn.,	1964	2.5
Mo., Neb., N.D., S.D.)	1965	3.1
South Atlantic		
(Del., Fla., Ga., Md.,	1964	8.2
N.C., S.C., Va., W.Va.)	1965	8.4
East South Central		
(Ala., Ky., Miss.,	1964	7.4
Tenn.)	1965	8.4
West South Central		
(Ark., La., Okla.,	1964	7.3
Texas)	1965	7.0
Mountain		
(Ariz., Colo., Idaho,		
Mont., Nev., N.M.,	1964	4.3
Utah, Wyo.)	1965	3.9
Pacific		
(Alaska, Calif., Hawaii,	1964	3.7
Ore., Wash.)	1965	4.3

SOURCE: *Uniform Crime Reports, 1965,* pp. 52–55.

sole advantage such statistics have over the F. B. I.'s police criminal statistics on the volume of "murder and non-negligent manslaughter" is that they are the only statistics available for study if one wants to compare trends in killings during years prior to the past decade or so. Yet the deterrent efficacy of capital punishment for homicide is manifest, presumably, only for those homicides which are

TABLE 4
MURDER RATES BY STATES, 1965
(Per 100,000 Population)

State	Rate	State	Rate
Alabama	11.4	Montana	1.7
Alaska	6.3	Nebraska	2.4
Arizona	5.0	Nevada	8.4
Arkansas	5.9	New Hampshire	2.7
California	4.7	New Jersey	3.2
Colorado	3.5	New Mexico	6.1
Connecticut	1.3	New York	4.6
Delaware	5.1	North Carolina	7.9
Florida	8.9	North Dakota	0.9
Georgia	11.3	Ohio	3.6
Hawaii	3.2	Oklahoma	4.4
Idaho	2.0	Oregon	3.4
Illinois	5.2	Pennsylvania	3.5
Indiana	3.5	Rhode Island	2.1
Iowa	1.3	South Carolina	9.6
Kansas	2.7	South Dakota	1.6
Kentucky	5.3	Tennessee	8.0
Louisiana	8.1	Texas	7.5
Maine	2.1	Utah	1.5
Maryland	6.7	Vermont	0.5
Massachusetts	2.4	Virginia	6.6
Michigan	4.4	Washington	2.2
Minnesota	1.4	West Virginia	4.0
Mississippi	8.9	Wisconsin	1.5
Missouri	6.7	Wyoming	2.9

SOURCE: *Uniform Crime Reports, 1965*, pp. 52–55.

or might be capitally punishable. Such homicides will by no means be equivalent in number to all homicides, as totalled for purposes of vital statistics. So the question has often been raised whether it is not misleading to use statistics on general homicide for this purpose when this classification of deaths is so inclusive.

One of the first criminologists to discuss the statistical relationship between general homicides and capitally punishable homicides was the late Professor Edwin H. Sutherland. In 1925, he pointed out that although (a) the *number* of homicides far exceeded the number of first degree murders (and, by inference, the number of capitally punishable homicides), (b) the *ratio* of the two was sufficiently constant to use the former as a guide to the latter.[14] We have already discussed (a) at length above, and there is no doubt that it is true. But what about (b)? It is extremely difficult to determine what evidence it is based on. Sutherland himself offered none, but advanced it as a plausible assumption. In the intervening generation, no criminologist has done any better.

One would expect that the number of deaths caused by homicide would exceed the number of murders and even the number of all criminal homicides. Sutherland, for instance, estimated that nearly one-third of all homicides were non-criminal, i.e., justifiable or excusable.[15] The vital statistics and *Uniform Crime Reports* totals recorded in Table 5 for the period 1930 to 1965 bear out this general assumption, though they suggest that he over-estimated the proportion of non-criminal homicides. Criminal homicide during the past generation seems to approach nearly ninety per cent of the total, not sixty-seven per cent. The only significant exception to this rule occurs after 1957, when annual total homicides suddenly total less than annual murders and non-negligent manslaughters.[16]

[14] Edwin H. Sutherland, "Murder and the Death Penalty," *Journal of Criminal Law, Criminology and Police Science* (February 1925), p. 523.

[15] Sutherland, *op. cit.*, p. 522.

[16] Inquiries bringing this curious fact to the attention of the Federal Bureau of Investigation and to the National Center for Vital Statistics were answered without clarifying the situation. All that is clear is that beginning with *Uniform Crime Reports, 1959,* the F. B. I. initiated a new program for gathering and analyzing police criminal statistics, and that its national totals for all crimes show a corresponding increase in subsequent years. But how it suddenly happened, as these data suggest, that coroners, medical examiners and private physicians (who fill out death certificates) undercounted or underreported the total homicides for 1960, or that the Office of Vital Statistics underestimated the total national homicides by fifteen per cent, or that the police overcounted the criminal homicides by a thousand, remains a complete mystery. Perhaps

TABLE 5
POPULATION, HOMICIDE, AND MURDER, 1930–1960

Year	Total Resident Population (in thousands)[a]	Homicides[a]	Murders[b]	Homicide Rate (Per 100,000 Population)[a]	Murder Rate (Per 100,000 Population)[c]
1930	123,077	10,617	—	8.9	—
1931	124,044	11,160	—	9.3	—
1932	124,840	11,035	—	9.2	7.0
1933	125,579	12,124	—	9.6	7.1
1934	126,374	12,055	—	9.5	6.7
1935	127,250	10,587	—	8.3	6.0
1936	128,053	10,232	7,894	8.0	6.2
1937	128,825	9,811	7,859	7.6	6.1
1938	129,825	8,799	7,438	6.8	5.7
1939	130,954	8,394	7,514	6.4	5.7
1940	131,954	8,208	7,540	6.3	5.7
1941	133,121	—	7,562	6.0	5.7
1942	133,920	7,743	7,569	5.8	5.7
1943	134,245	6,690	6,517	5.0	4.8
1944	132,885	6,553	6,552	4.9	4.9
1945	132,481	7,412	6,847	5.6	5.2
1946	140,054	8,794	8,442	6.3	6.0
1947	143,446	8,555	7,760	6.0	5.4
1948	146,093	8,536	7,620	5.8	5.2

Year	Population				
1949	148,665	8,033	6,990	5.4	4.7
1950	151,234	7,942	7,020	5.3	4.6
1951	153,384	7,495	6,820	4.9	4.4
1952	155,761	8,054	7,210	5.2	4.6
1953	158,313	7,880	7,120	5.0	4.5
1954	161,191	7,735	6,850	4.8	4.2
1955	164,302	7,418	6,850	4.5	4.2
1956	167,261	7,629	6,970	4.6	4.2
1957	170,295	7,641	8,060	4.5	4.7
1958	173,239	7,100d	8,222	4.5	4.7
1959	176,511	8,159	8,585	4.6	4.9
1960	179,992	8,464	9,140	4.7	5.1
1961	183,057	8,578	8,600	4.7	4.7
1962	185,890	9,013	8,400	4.7	4.5
1963	188,658	9,225	8,500	4.9	4.5
1964	191,372	9,814	9,250	5.1	4.8
1965	193,795	10,712	9,850	5.5	5.1

a SOURCE: *Statistical Abstract of the United States*, annually. Includes Alaska since 1959 and Hawaii since 1960. No homicide total published in this source for the year 1941. Recalculation of the population totals, based on newer census data, have resulted in slight increases for all the more recent years; cf., e.g., the *Abstracts* for 1962 and for 1965 on population estimates subsequent to 1940. Data for 1965 are taken from *Monthly Vital Statistics Report*, vol. 16, No. 1, Supplement (April 14, 1967), p. 6.

b SOURCE: *Uniform Crime Reports*, annually. No totals were published for the years 1930–1935.

c Rates for the years 1932–1936 are taken from *Uniform Crime Reports*; for all other years prior to 1960 they are calculated directly, and they do not always agree with the rates published for these years in the *Reports*.

d Reported as an "estimate."

We may notice, first, that the last two columns of Table 5 show that the pattern of annual homicide and murder rates between 1930 and 1960 parallel each other fairly well, especially between 1942 and 1956. We may infer from this that the fluctuations in the annual volume of total homicide is fairly closely paralleled by the pattern of the annual volume of criminal homicide. But this parallel does not directly confirm the view of Sutherland and other criminologists, including Professor Thorsten Sellin (see below, p. 277), that the homicide death rate is adequate for an estimate of the first degree murder rate, and thus that one can estimate the trend in the latter from a knowledge of the former. None of the data in Table 5 reports the volume of murder nor, *a fortiori*, of capitally punishable homicide. If we had national figures for a few years, at least, on the volume of capitally punishable homicides, or of first degree murder, or of the percentage of murders in the F. B. I.'s category of "murders and non-negligent manslaughters," then we could test the assumption that annual total homicides parallel annual capital homicides. As it is now, we can only take it on the authority of experienced criminologists that the former is an adequate symptom of the latter. Since so much in the debate over the deterrent efficacy of the death penalty seems to turn on the validity of this assumption, it is regrettable that so little evidence can be offered to support it.

One question raised earlier, as to the significance of the apparent rise of murder, both in volume and in rate, as recorded in Tables 1 and 2, is answerable on the basis of Table 5. Whether we use criminal or vital statistics to measure death by homicide, it is obvious that the recent upturn in this figure remains consistent with the generally *downward* trend in killings since 1930, a trend that per-

---

criminologists and vital statisticians will closely watch these totals in future years and eventually advance some explanation of the discrepancy that occurred during 1957–1960. In the text, it is assumed that some such explanation will be forthcoming and that the hitherto prevailing view, that total homicides (as measured by vital statistics) can never be less than criminal homicides (as measured by police statistics), will be vindicated.

sisted despite several slight and short-lived increases in recent decades. Since the slight increase recorded for the years 1957–1960 has not persisted during 1961–1962, it probably represents no trend and is of no theoretical significance.

One should not infer, however, that this generally downward pattern in the volume of death by homicide since 1930 is a result of any increased respect for the lives of others. As some criminologists have pointed out (see below, p. 80) many crimes no longer end up in the homicide column simply because the victims are given more prompt and more skillful medical attention than they would have received even a quarter century ago.

The task of identifying the relationship between the volume of total homicides and the sub-class of capitally punishable homicides is no less acute when we shift from the national to the state level. Moreover, it is at the state, not the national, level that knowledge of the annual volume of capitally punishable homicide is especially useful; statistical tests of the deterrent efficacy of the death penalty in America usually concentrate on the differences in volume of homicide between abolition and non-abolition states. Until 1957, *Uniform Crime Reports* did not measure the total volume of criminal homicide for each state, but only for the nation as a whole and for selected urban and rural areas. Because the areas measured differed from year to year, it is impossible to use this source as a measure of criminal homicide at the state level except after 1957.

Granting the inadequacies of the data presented in this essay as a basis for answering the original question, viz., the volume of capital crimes in this country, year by year, crime by crime, state by state, nevertheless some general impressions do emerge. First, the annual totals of serious crimes as reported in the most reliable available source, *Uniform Crime Reports,* are far in excess of the totals which are capitally punishable. Second, capitally punishable homicide is probably a fairly constant fraction of the total volume of homicide, irrespective of how homicide itself is measured (by judicial, police or vital statistics). Third, the long range trend in the rates of homicide and of "murder and non-negligent manslaughter," and by inference, of capitally punishable homicide, for the nation as a whole is a slow but steady decrease. Serious inquiry into the finer details of the volume of capital crime in this nation may yield more significant generalizations than these. But until extensive further research is undertaken, we shall have to content ourselves with rather crude conclusions such as those offered here.[17]

A SOCIOLOGICAL ANALYSIS OF CRIMINAL HOMICIDE*

BY MARVIN E. WOLFGANG**

Murder and other types of criminal homicide are deviations of the most serious and visible kind in our society. Public concern, the amount of time the police spend in detection and investigation, the ratio of the number of police to the number of these crimes, and the quantity of stories in literature and the drama that use murder as a central theme all attest to the interest we have in homicide. However, the television or literary mystery usually is concerned with the relatively rare premeditated type of killing. Most homicides have typical forms and are crimes of passion that arise from a world of violence.

The typical criminal slayer is a young man in his twenties who kills another man only slightly older. Both are of the same race; if Negro, the slaying is commonly with a knife, if white, it is a beating with fists and feet on a public street.

---

[17] For further discussion of the general problem of the volume of crime and the quality of criminal statistics in America, see: Donald Cressey, "The State of Criminal Statistics," *National Probation and Parole Journal* (July 1957), pp. 230–241; Ronald Beattie, "Criminal Statistics in the United States—1960," *Journal of Criminal Law, Criminology and Police Science* (May–June 1960), pp. 49–65; Thorsten Sellin, "Crime and Delinquency in the United States: An Over-All View," *The Annals* (January 1962), pp. 11–23.

* Reprinted from *Federal Probation*, vol. 25 (March 1961), pp. 48–55.

** Associate Professor of Sociology, University of Pennsylvania, and President, Pennsylvania Prison Society.

Men kill and are killed between four and five times more frequently than women, but when a woman kills she most likely has a man as her victim and does it with a butcher knife in the kitchen. A woman killing a woman is extremely rare, for she is most commonly slain by her husband or other close friend by a beating in the bedroom.

These are some of the findings of a study more fully described in my book, *Patterns in Criminal Homicide*. Since publication of this book, a variety of requests for a summary discussion have come to my desk, partly, I imagine, because of the recent renewed interest in the sociopsychological aspects of criminal homicide reflected in Guttmacher's *The Mind of the Murderer*, Palmer's *A Study of Murder*, and in Bohannan's *African Homicide and Suicide*. What follows, therefore, is an abbreviated analysis of my own sociological study with suggestive theoretical points of departure for additional research. For detailed information of the research methods and interpretive analysis of criminal homicide, the reader is referred to the present author's book.

The popular press and even some of our national, state, and municipal police officials sometimes confuse murder with other types of criminal homicide. As every capable policeman should know, homicide is the killing of another person and is divided into criminal and noncriminal homicide. The former category comprises murder (commonly in the first and second degree) as well as voluntary (nonnegligent) and involuntary (negligent) manslaughter. Noncriminal homicide is excusable, or a killing in self-defense, and justifiable homicide, or homicide performed as a legal duty by a peace officer or executioner. Confusion of these terms, mixing criminal with noncriminal cases, and mislabeling murder for other types of criminal homicides, has occurred in both professional and popular studies.

In order to produce some clarity among these terms and to provide a sociological and statistical analysis of criminal homicide, research was conducted in Philadelphia, using all criminal homicides recorded by the Philadelphia Homicide Squad from January 1, 1948 through December 31, 1952. Excusable and justifiable homicides were excluded from the study and concentration was only on criminal cases listed by the police. I spent many long hours over several years collecting the data and participating in arrest and interrogation of offenders, and I have the highest respect for the police officers with whom I came into contact during that period. The homicide detectives consistently showed due respect for the constitutional rights of persons they arrested as well as an attitude of understanding rather than that of vengeance and retribution. These are, of course, qualities desirable in all police officers, for their function is to protect as well as to apprehend, to make suspects available for prosecution, but not to judge guilty.

It is almost axiomatic in criminal statistics that for purposes of determining the amount and type of crime committed in a community, police statistics yield the most valid data. Too many cases are lost through court trials to use court statistics, and to use prison data means a still further reduction of cases that are highly selected to result in incarceration instead of probation or some other form of disposition. For this reason, police statistics were used to obtain the most valid picture of criminal homicides over this five year period.

Another important aspect of the research design was to distinguish between victims and offenders in terms of their major social characteristics. Usually this distinction is not maintained in studies of homicide, especially in those that rely only on mortality statistics published by the Office of Vital Statistics from death certifications. The Philadelphia study and review of the literature on criminal homicide reveal that much confusion of terminology pervades the field; that data about victims often are confused with data about offenders; rates per population unit are sometimes confused with reports about proportionate distributions or percentages of criminal slayings. We have emphasized constantly the invalidity of inferring characteristics about victims from criminal statistics, some of which supply data only for offenders; or of inferring characteristics about offenders from mortality statistics, which supply data only for victims.

Most previous research has examined *either* the victim *or* the offender. In the present work, analysis has been made of *both* victims and offenders, separately, as distinct units, but also as mutual participants in the homicide. A broad social approach is interested both in the active, "to kill," and in the passive, "to be killed." It is one type of analysis to consider victims as a social group and offenders as another social group; it is quite a different and more refined type of analysis to consider specific victim-offender relationships, and to find race, sex, age, and other patterns among them.

During the period from 1948 through 1952 there were 588 cases of criminal homicide in Philadelphia; i.e., there were 588 victims. Because several people were sometimes involved in killing one person, there were 621 offenders arrested by the police and taken into custody. In terms of a mean annual rate per 100,000 population in the city, the victim rate was 5.7 and the offender rate 6.0. This is neither high nor low. Compared with eighteen other cities across the country, each of which had a population of a quarter of a million or more in 1950, Philadelphia ranks ninth, with the range between Miami having a victim rate of 15.1 and Milwaukee having a low of 2.3. New York's rate was only 3.7, Los Angeles 4.0, and Chicago 7.8. The rate for Pennsylvania as a whole for 1950 was only 3.5, but the most fair comparison is between cities of comparable size.[1]

The years 1948–52 were advantageous years for research purposes because the census fell exactly in the middle of this period so that the population statistics for 1950 could be used for computing a rate for any of the single five years or for all of them together. Moreover, it should be noted that the data collected from police files and used to analyze suggested associations and questions are expressed in numerical and percentage frequency distributions, in rates per 100,000 population in some cases, and in

---

[1] It is obvious to any student in the field that there are many criminal offenses committed that are never reported or recorded by the public authorities. This generalization is applicable to criminal homicide as it is to other offenses. But a theoretical analysis of the social visibility of crime, or the varying degrees of high and low reportability of specific offenses, leads us to suggest that there is a relatively low ratio between offenses committed and those known to the police in cases of criminal homicide.

ratios. In order to safeguard against loose generalizations, several tests of statistical significance were employed.[2]

Research has shown that although criminal homicide is largely an unplanned act, there are nonetheless in the act regular uniformities and patterns. We have found, as previous research has noted, that there is a statistically significant association between criminal homicide and the race and sex of both victim and offender. Negroes and males involved in homicide far exceed their proportions in the general population and rates for these two groups are many times greater than for whites and females. The rate per 100,000 by race and sex of offenders reveals the following rank order of magnitude: Negro males (41.7), Negro females (9.3), white males (3.4), and white females (.4). Although Negroes of either sex, and males of either race, are positively related to criminal slayings, the association between race and homicide is statistically more significant than that between sex and homicide. This relationship of Negroes and males to criminal homicide confirms reports and studies made elsewhere in this country, although the proportion of female offenders is reportedly much higher in England. It should be noted, however, that the whole of the British Isles has no more criminal homicides in a year than the city of Philadelphia alone (or about 125 annually).

Among offenders, the age group twenty to twenty-four predominates with a rate of 12.6 per 100,000, while the highest rate for victims is in the age group twenty-five to thirty-four. In short, victims are generally older than their offenders; the median age of the former being 35.1 years and of the latter 31.9 years. The importance of the race factor here is striking in view of the fact that the lowest five-year age specific rates for Negro males and females are similar to, or higher than the *highest* of such rates for white males and females, respectively. Although males of both races more frequently commit criminal homicide during their twenties than during any other period of life, Ne-

---

[2] For the most part, the statistical tests involved use of the nonparametric technique of chi-square (X^2) with corrections for continuity and a probability level (P) of less than .05.

gro males in their early sixties kill as frequently as do white males in their early twenties.

The race factor in criminal homicide is alarming and should be the cause of both Negro and white community leaders to examine more closely the reasons for this differential. The child is not born with homicide tendencies in his genes, so that in no way can we infer a biological explanation for this difference. Negroes are a minority group that still suffer from residential and general cultural isolation from the rest of the community, despite recent advances in integration. So long as this ethnic group is socially isolated and required to live in restricted residential areas they will continue to constitute a "subcultural" area. This subculture is characterized by poor housing, high density of population, overcrowded home conditions, and by a system of values that often condones violence and physical aggression from child-rearing processes to adult interpersonal relationships that sometimes end in criminal slayings. To a lesser degree, whites in the lower socioeconomic classes as well as Negroes become part of this *subculture of violence* and participate in criminal homicide. Only by breaking up this culturally isolated group and by integrating them into the general community of morality and values can society hope to reduce violence that results in homicide.

We have also noted significant associations between methods of inflicting death and the race and sex of both victims and offenders. In Philadelphia thirty-nine per cent of all homicides were due to stabbings, thirty-three per cent to shooting, twenty-two per cent to beatings, and six per cent to other and miscellaneous methods. There appears to be a cultural preference for particular types of methods and weapons. Males, if Negro, usually stab and are stabbed to death; and if white, beat and are beaten to death. Females generally stab their victims with a butcher knife, but are very often beaten to death.

Although homicides tend to increase during the hot summer months, there is no significant association by seasons or months of the year. But homicide is significantly associated with days of the week and hours of the day. The weekend in general, and Saturday night in particular are related to homicide, as are the hours between 8 P.M. and 2 A.M. Between 8 P.M. Friday and midnight Sunday there were, during the five years under review, 380 criminal homicides; but from the beginning of Monday morning to 8 P.M. Friday, there were only 208. Thus, on the average, sixty-five per cent of all homicides occurred during the shorter time span of fifty-two hours, while only thirty-five per cent occurred during the longer time span of 116 hours.

The time between assault and death of the victim varies according to the method employed by the offender. Relatively quick death (within ten minutes after assault) occurred for half of the victims in a shooting, for less than three-tenths in a stabbing, and for only one-sixteenth in a beating. About a third of the victims were dead within ten minutes after assault, slightly less than three-fifths after the first hour had passed, and four-fifths within a day. Only five per cent lived more than ten days after being assaulted. Probably fewer persons today die from aggravated assault wounds than was true a generation ago, for data suggest that (1) improved communication with the police, (2) more rapid transportation to a hospital (usually by the police), and (3) advanced medical technology have contributed to the decreasing homicide rates in this country during the last twenty-five years.

We do not know, of course, just how many aggravated assaults, assaults with intent to kill, and other violent assaults are today prevented from becoming classified as criminal homicides because of these three factors, but the steady increases of other crimes of personal violence, such as aggravated assaults and rapes, regularly reported in the *Uniform Crime Reports* lead us to suggest that something other than a greater repugnance to commit crimes of personal violence has entered our mores. Many factors are involved in changing rates of homicide, such as the age composition, business cycles, etc. But because crimes of violence against the person, excluding homicide, appear to have increased during the past two decades, it is logical to assume that if these gross social factors affect homicide, they should affect other crimes of violence in the same way.

Research testing the hypothesis suggested by the three

factors mentioned above might be useful in explaining the general decrease in criminal homicide over the past twenty-five years.[3] It would be valuable, for example, to know the recovery rate for those who are today grievously assaulted but who would have probably died under medical and other conditions of a generation ago. Although this type of analysis fails to account for any psychological dimensions in the phenomenon of homicide, the approach nonetheless has the virtue of mensurability in testing the validity of the explanation.

The place where the crime occurred is also important. The most dangerous single place is the highway (public street, alley, or field), although more slayings occur in the home than outside the home. Men kill and are killed most frequently in the street, while women kill most often in the kitchen but are killed in the bedroom. For victims and offenders of each race and sex group significant differences have been noted. Most cases of Negro males who kill Negro males involve a stabbing in a public street; most cases of white males who kill white males involve a beating in a public street. However, the high proportion of females who kill with a butcher knife in a kitchen, and of those who are killed in a bedroom by being beaten is associated with the fact that eighty-four per cent of all female offenders slay males and eighty-seven per cent of all female victims are slain by males.

Either or both the victim and offender had been drinking immediately prior to the slaying in nearly two-thirds of the cases. The presence of alcohol in the homicide situation appears to be significantly associated with Negroes—either as victims or as offenders—and, separately, with Negro male and female victims. Particular caution must be exercised in evaluating the presence of alcohol in these homicides, since drinking—particularly on Saturday night, the time of highest incidence of homicide—is an integral part of the mores

[3] Some recent analysis of this hypothesis has been made for Ceylon. See Cleobis Jayewardene, "Criminal Homicide: A Study in Culture Conflict," Ph.D. thesis, University of Pennsylvania, 1960.

of most groups involved in this crime.[4] A significantly higher proportion of weekend homicides than of homicides occurring during the remainder of the week had alcohol present (in either the victim, the offender, or both). An association between alcohol, weekend slayings, and the payment of wages on Friday was indicated and crudely confirmed by the available data. We have, therefore, suggested that when the socioeconomic group most likely to commit homicide almost simultaneously receives its weekly wages, purchases alcohol, and meets together socially, it is not unlikely that the incidence of homicide should also rise.

Contrary to many past impressions, an analysis of offenders in criminal homicide reveals a relatively high proportion who have a previous police or arrest record. Of total offenders, nearly two-thirds have a previous arrest record, and of total victims, almost half have such a record. Having a previous record is also associated with males both among victims and offenders, and is obvious from the fact that more *male victims* have such a record than do *female offenders*. Moreover, when an offender has a previous record, he is more likely to have a record of offenses against the person than against property; and when he has a record of offenses against the person, he is more likely than not to have a record of having committed a serious assault offense, such as aggravated assault or assault with intent to kill. A greater proportion of Negro male and female victims have a previous arrest record than do white male and female offenders, respectively. In view of these facts, it is of interest to future attempts at prevention and control of potential offenders in criminal homicide that *a larger proportion of offenders with an arrest record have a record of aggravated assault than of all types of property offenses combined.* The courts should take special care not to re-

[4] Problems of analyzing the presence of alcohol in the victim and in the offender were particularly trying. In addition to Chapter 8 in the book, the reader is referred to the author's paper (with R. Strohm) for discussion of these problems in "The Relationship Between Alcohol and Criminal Homicide," *Quarterly Journal of Studies in Alcohol* (September 1956) 17: 411–425.

lease too hastily and without proper individualized treatment those persons arrested on charges of personal assault in order to prevent later homicides.

Criminal homicide usually results from a vaguely defined altercation, domestic quarrel, jealousy, argument over money, and robbery. These five police-recorded "motives" are involved in eight out of ten cases. Most of the identified victim-offender relationships may be classified as "primary group" relations, or those that include intimate, close, frequent contacts. Close friends and relatives accounted for over half of the contacts, and the combined categories which involve primary group contacts constitute fifty-nine per cent of all victim-offender relationships among males, but significantly as much as eighty-four per cent among females. Because white males were killed more frequently than Negro males during the commission of a robbery, the former were also more frequently strangers to their slayers than the latter.

Mate slayings have been given special attention.[5] Of the one hundred husband-wife homicides, fifty-three victims were wives and forty-seven were husbands. The number of wives killed by their husbands constitutes forty-one per cent of all women killed, whereas husbands slain by their wives make up only eleven per cent of all men killed. Thus, when a woman commits homicide, she is more likely than a man to kill her mate; and when a man is killed by a woman, he is most likely to be killed by his wife. Husbands are often killed by their wives in the kitchen with a butcher knife, but nearly half of the wives are slain in the bedroom. More male than female offenders in these spouse slayings were found guilty, were convicted of more serious degrees of homicide, and committed suicide.

In ninety-four per cent of the cases, the victim and offender were members of the same race, but in only sixty-four per cent were they of the same sex. Thus, the ratio of intra- to interracial homicide is 15.2 to 1; but the ratio of intra- to intersex homicide is only 1.8 to 1. In general, it may be said that victims were homicidally assaulted most

[5] See also the author's analysis of "Husband-Wife Homicides," *The Journal of Social Therapy* (1956), 2: 263–271.

frequently by males of their own race, and least frequently by females of another race.

In thirty-two cases involving fifty-seven offenders and six victims, a felony, in addition to the killing, was perpetrated at the time of the slaying. In most cases the other felony was robbery, and white males accounted for a larger proportion of these felony-murders than they did among all homicides in general.

The term *victim-precipitated* homicide has been introduced to refer to those cases in which the victim is a direct, positive precipitator in the crime—the first to use physical force in the homicide drama. After establishing a theoretical and legal basis for analysis, the Philadelphia data reveal several factors significantly associated with the 150 victim-precipitated homicides, which is twenty-six per cent of all homicides. These factors are: Negro victims and offenders, male victims, female offenders, stabbings, victim-offender relationships involving male victims and female offenders, mate slayings, husbands who were victims in mate slayings, alcohol, victims with a previous arrest record, particularly an arrest record of assault. Thus, in most of these cases, the role and characteristics of the victim and offender are reversed, the victim assumes the role of determinant, and the victim makes a definite contribution to the genesis of his own victimization.[6]

Recently, I have extended the meaning of victim precipitated homicide to include a sociological and psychoanalytic discussion of these 150 victims as being bent on suicide.[7] Although it is impossible to verify an assumption of subconscious suicide wishes among these victims, empirical data from broad social factors combine with psychological and sociological data suggesting that victims in

[6] For more detailed treatment of this concept of victim-precipitation, which is increasingly becoming an important element in theoretical discussions of the poorly designated term, "victimology," see Chapter 14 in the book as well as "Victim-Precipitated Criminal Homicide," *Journal of Criminal Law, Criminology and Police Science,* (June 1957), 48: 1–11.

[7] "Suicide by Means of Victim-Precipitated Homicide," *Journal of Clinical and Experimental Psychopathology* (Oct.–Dec. 1959), 20: 335–349.

many cases present themselves as willing targets for violent aggression leading to homicide. It is hoped that the material presently being accumulated by John Macdonald at the Colorado Psychopathic Hospital on "The Murderer and His Victim"[8] will shed additional light on this area of analysis.

In twenty-four cases the offenders committed suicide after performing the homicide.[9] Of these, twenty-two were males, nearly half of whom were men who had killed their wives. Analysis and evaluation of these homicide-suicides indicate that half of the homicides would have been classified as first degree murder had the offender experienced a court trial. As a result, even with the low amount of suicide after homicide in this country, more offenders inflict death upon themselves than are put to death by the social sanction of legal execution. Twelve persons who committed suicide appear to have committed first degree murder. Thus the number of self-inflicted "executions" is greater than the seven offenders who were sentenced to death by a court of record. However, suicide following homicide is five to six times more frequent in England than in the United States.

Of particular importance to the police are unsolved homicides. The definition used in this study was not exactly like that of offenses not cleared by arrest, which is used for uniform crime reporting purposes, but there were similarities. Comparisons of the unsolved with solved cases reveal that the former have higher proportions of: white male and female victims, victims sixty-five years of age and over, robbery as a prelude to the slaying, victims who were strangers to their assailants, beatings, weekend slayings, and assaults that occurred in the public street.

Finally, analysis has been made of the tempo of legal procedures, of court disposition, designation of the degree

[8] A forthcoming publication by Charles C. Thomas, Publisher.

[9] In addition to Chapter 15 in the book, see also the author's "An Analysis of Homicide-Suicide," *Journal of Clinical and Experimental Psychopathology* (July–Sept. 1958), 19: 208–218.

of homicide, insanity, and sentences imposed by the court. Two-thirds of the offenders were arrested on the same day that the crime was committed, and over half appeared in court for trial within six months after the crime. Two-thirds of those taken into police custody, and over three-quarters of those who experienced a court trial were declared guilty. Proportionately, Negroes and males were convicted more frequently than whites and females; but previous analysis of the nature of these cases reveals that Negroes and males had in fact committed more serious offenses, and that a charge of unjust race and sex discrimination in court would not necessarily be correct.[10] Of the 387 offenders convicted and sentenced, thirty per cent were guilty of murder in the first degree, twenty-nine per cent of murder in the second degree, thirty-six per cent of voluntary manslaughter, and fifteen per cent of involuntary manslaughter. Less than three per cent of the offenders were declared insane by the courts, which is a proportion similar to that reported in other studies in this country, but considerably smaller than the thirty per cent or more reported insane in England.

We have only touched on some of the highlights of this analysis of criminal homicide. There are many aspects of special importance to the police that can aid them in making investigations and particularly in working on cases in which it is difficult to determine suspects, or that are listed as unsolved cases. Each city and each police department has its own peculiar problems, of course, but studies of this sort can easily be made if proper records are kept. Other types of crime need the same kind of research attention, but ultimately all such research depends on the veracity and efficiency of the police in recording and reporting their information. The greatest service the police can make to scientific research is their cooperation with the social scientist and the maintenance of valid, efficient records of their cases.

The Baltimore Criminal Justice Commission, under the

[10] Cf. Edward Green, "An Analysis of the Sentencing Practices of Criminal Court Judges in Philadelphia," Ph.D. Thesis, University of Pennsylvania, 1959.

direction of Ralph Murdy, former agent of the Federal
Bureau of Investigation, is presently engaged in a five year
study (1960–1965) of criminal homicides in Baltimore—a
study modeled on the kind of analysis made in Philadelphia. Dr. John Macdonald, Assistant Director of the Colorado Psychopathic Hospital, intends to collect similar data
for Denver over a five year period. Professor Franco Fer-
racuti, from the Institute of Criminal Anthropology at the
University of Rome, has proposed simultaneous analyses
of criminal homicide in San Juan, Puerto Rico, and in
Rome, Italy. On-going research like these that seek to du-
plicate and to expand on the Philadelphia study will confirm, reject, or modify the patterns in criminal homicide
that have thus far been described and analyzed. Only in
this way, as Albert Morris[11] has suggested, can science
produce meaningful understanding of this delimited phenomenon, leading from empirical data to a meaningful
sociopsychological theory of crimes of violence.[12]

On the basis of these findings thus far, it is obvious that
homicides are principally crimes of passion, or violent slayings that are not premeditated or psychotic manifestations.
Emerging out of the data is a theory that suggests a conflict
between the prevailing middle class values of our society
and the values of a subsocial or subcultural group. Previously we have referred to this group as constituting a
"subculture of violence." If there exists a subculture of
violence, then we must further propose that the greater the
degree of integration of the individual into this subculture
the higher the likelihood that his behavior will often be
violent; or, we may assert that there is a direct relationship
between rates of homicide and the degree of integration

[11] Albert Morris, *Homicide: An Approach to the Problem of
Crime,* Boston: Boston University Press, 1955.
[12] The most recent theoretical statement about criminal homicide, based on data from the Philadelphia study, has been
made by the author with the collaboration of Professor Fer-
racuti in "Subculture of Violence: An Interpretive Analysis of
Homicide," paper presented before the Annual Meeting of the
American Sociological Association, Section on The Sociology
of Deviation, Marshall Clinard, chairman, New York, N. Y.,
August 29–31, 1960.

of the subculture of violence to which the individual belongs. The importance of human life in the scale of values, the kinds of expected reactions to certain types of stimuli, the perceptual differences in the evaluation of the stimuli, and the general personality structure are all factors of importance in this theory. As has been pointed out,

> . . . the significance of a jostle, a slightly derogatory remark, or the appearance of a weapon in the hands of an adversary are stimuli differentially perceived and interpreted by Negroes and whites, males and females. Social expectations of response in particular types of social interaction result in differential "definitions of the situation." A male is usually expected to defend the name and honor of his mother, the virtue of womanhood . . . and to accept no derogation about his race (even from a member of his own race), his age, or his masculinity. Quick resort to physical combat as a measure of daring, courage, or defense of status appears to be a cultural expression, especially for lower socioeconomic class males of both races. When such a culture norm response is elicited from an individual engaged in social interplay with others who harbor the same response mechanism, physical assaults, altercations, and violent domestic quarrels that result in homicide are likely to be common. The upper-middle and upper social class value system defines and codifies behavioral norms into legal rules that often transcend subcultural mores, and considers many of the social and personal stimuli that evoke a combative reaction in the lower classes as "trivial." Thus, there exists a cultural antipathy between many folk rationalizations of the lower class, and of males of both races, on the one hand, and the middle-class legal norms under which they live, on the other.[13]

Highest rates of rape, aggravated assaults, persistency in arrests for assaults (recidivism) among these same groups with high rates of homicide are additional confirmations of

[13] Wolfgang, *Patterns in Criminal Homicide*, pp. 188–189.

the contention of a subculture of violence. Ready access to weapons may become essential for protection against others in this milieu who respond in similarly violent ways, and the carrying of knives or other protective devices becomes a common symbol of willingness to participate in and to expect violence, and to be ready for its retaliation. As in combat on the front lines during wartime where the "it-was-either-him-or-me" situation arises, there are similar attitudes and reactions among participants in homicide. The Philadelphia study shows that sixty-five per cent of the offenders and forty-seven per cent of the victims had a previous police record of arrests. Here, then, is a situation often not unlike that of combat in which two persons committed to the value of violence come together, and in which chance often dictates the identity of the slayer and of the slain.

We have not tried to explain the causes of this subculture of violence, but such an endeavor would involve analysis of social class and race relations that would include residential, occupational, and other forms of discrimination and social isolation as important factors. Some consideration of the groups from which the individual obtains a conception of himself and an analysis of child-rearing practices that employ punishment and promote early patterns of physical aggression would aid the search for causal factors and methods of treatment.

As we have indicated, dispersing the group that shares the subculture of violence should weaken the value. Through wider economic opportunities, freedom of residential mobility, etc., integration of the group members into the larger society and its predominant value system should function to destroy or at least to reduce the subculture of violence. The work done in New York City in breaking up delinquent gangs has demonstrated the effectiveness of this approach. Similarly in correctional institutions, the treatment program, especially when using individual or group psychotherapy, should try to counterbalance or to eliminate the allegiance of the individual to the subculture of violence and his violent perception of the world.

THE DEATH SENTENCE, 1960*

BY JAMES A. MC CAFFERTY**

A curious phenomenon in the recent use of capital punishment is the scarcity of information on capital offenders. It seems to contradict man's usual quest for knowledge beyond what is now known. In medicine, for example, an unrelenting effort is made to discover the cause of an illness or the cause of death. From these investigations, methods are developed for ameliorating or curing the ailment. Why, then, do we know so little about the capital offender? Part of the answer lies in the virtually complete withdrawal of the usual information-gathering presentence investigation service. Even in those courts where a presentence investigation is commonly conducted for the general run of cases, its use is regarded as unnecessary and wasteful when the offender's conviction leaves no alternative other than a sentence of death or commitment for a life term.

After the sentence to death is passed, the offender is returned to jail; in most states, when a proper time for appeals has elapsed or when the sentence has been reaffirmed by the state's Supreme Court, he is taken to the place where the execution will be performed. Here is the second opportunity for collecting information, but, because the capital offender is excluded from the usual admission and orientation program, he does not come under the scrutiny of the institution's classification committee and thus has no contact with its information-gathering system.

A few efforts have been made to learn something about the capital offender. Notable among them are the studies made by Elmer Johnson for North Carolina and by Frank-

* Reprinted, by permission of the author and publisher, from "The Death Sentence and Then What?", *Crime and Delinquency,* vol. 7 (October 1961), pp. 363–372.
** Chief, Research and Evaluation Branch, Division of Procedural Studies and Statistics, Administrative Office of the U. S. Courts, Washington, D.C.; formerly criminologist, U. S. Bureau of Prisons.

lin Bridge and Jeanne Mosure for Ohio,[1] and, on a some-what different basis, the recent studies on the murderer by Marvin Wolfgang in Philadelphia and Robert C. Bensing and Oliver Schroeder, Jr., in Cleveland.[2] However, in these cases, only a few of those who had been tried and con-victed of murder were sentenced to death. Doubtless more studies will be made of the pattern of disposition so that perhaps we can learn something about the differences be-tween murderers who are executed and those who have their sentences commuted to life or receive reversals upon appeal.

The phenomenon of the capital crime can be divided into three major time periods. The first is the period, some-times momentary, during which the violence is precipi-tated. The second is the time of the violent act itself and the subsequent actions of the perpetrator. Finally, there is the period following capture and disposition. The disposi-tion period can be still further divided into two categories: (1) *acquittal;* (2) *a verdict of guilty,* with the sentence set at a term of years, life, or death.

The following material is limited to the third time period and, more specifically, to those individuals whose initial disposition was simply death by legal execution.

From 1926 to 1929, in connection with its annual collec-tion of statistics on prisoners, the Bureau of the Census published fragmentary data on executions carried out in the United States. These data deal only with prisoners exe-cuted in those state institutions participating in the report-ing program; no information is given on prisoners executed in local institutions. In 1930, the Bureau of the Census cross-checked the various reports on executions with the

---

[1] Elmer Johnson, "Selective Factors in Capital Punishment," *Social Forces,* Dec., 1957, pp. 165–169, and "Capital Punish-ment in North Carolina," mimeo., North Carolina Conference for Social Service, Raleigh; Franklin M. Bridge and Jeanne Mosure, *Capital Punishment,* Research Report No. 46, Ohio Legislative Services Commission, Jan., 1961.

[2] Marvin E. Wolfgang, *Patterns in Criminal Homicide* (Phil-adelphia: University of Pennsylvania, 1958); Robert C. Ben-sing and Oliver Schroeder, Jr., *Homicide in an Urban Com-munity* (Springfield, Ill.: Charles C. Thomas, 1960).

executed prisoners' death certificates on file in its Division
of Vital Statistics. Thus, 1930 is the first year affording
complete national coverage of all executions carried out in
state institutions as well as those carried out by local sheriffs
or state executioners in local facilities.[3]

Beginning in 1950, when the prisoner statistics program
was transferred by the Bureau of the Census to the Bureau
of Prisons, the latter agency made a special effort to meet
requests for historical and current statistics on executed
prisoners. First, it concentrated on bringing the statistics up
to date by issuing an annual bulletin on executions, the first
of which covered those carried out in 1948. The 1950 publication, issued under the *National Prisoner Statistics* title,
furnished data summarizing the major characteristics of
prisoners executed under civil authority from 1937 to 1950.
This table was based on records accumulated by the Census
Bureau and corroborated by the Bureau of Prisons; it represented the first summary of data on the offense and race
of executed prisoners.

In 1951, through the cooperation of several state officials, the series was augmented by including comparable
data for the years 1930 to 1936. Each year since then, the
Bureau of Prisons has published a single historical table
which incorporates information for all years beginning with
1930.

Along with the compilation of this historical series, a
second goal was to provide, as soon as possible after the
end of the calendar year, a summary of executions carried
out in the various states. To do this it was necessary to

[3] Thorsten Sellin, "A Note on Capital Executions in the
United States," *The British Journal of Delinquency*, July, 1950,
pp. 7–8. A similar explanation appears in U.S. Bureau of the
Census, *Prisoners in State and Federal Prisons and Reformatories*, 1930, p. 49.

From time to time since 1930, Delaware, Missouri, Mississippi, Montana, and Tennessee carried out executions in counties; Louisiana carried out executions in parishes. Illinois provided places of execution at the two state prisons at Menard
and Joliet as well as at the Cook County Jail in Chicago. In
1960, only Montana permitted executions in counties and Illinois continues to maintain three places of execution.

streamline the collection and verification of execution records.

Until 1960, the method used was simply to list, on a special form, data on all executions carried out in the calendar year, together with similar information on persons held under a death sentence at the close of the year. This form was sent to those state institutions where the death sentence could be carried out. The cooperation of state officials made it possible for the Bureau of Prisons to issue annual executions statistics shortly after the end of the year.

In 1960, the participating officials were asked to fill in a special form, "Movement of Population—Sentence under Death," which provided several new bases of information. It gave, as of the first and the last day of the year, the basic data on prisoners who had been sentenced to death. In addition, it furnished information on all prisoners received from courts in 1960, on all prisoners executed during the year, and on the small group whose sentences were commuted to life or changed in some other way. This information made it possible for the *National Prisoner Statistics* series to provide a new table on the movement of prisoners who were under sentence of death in 1960. The tables appearing in this article are based on these same forms.[4]

With the historical and current executions material available on an annual basis, the next step was to bring together thirty-one years of information on executions and to transfer the details to single cards, each representing a prisoner sentenced to death. The schedule, based somewhat on the special homicide data forms developed by Marvin Wolfgang and Ralph Murdy, will be most useful in maintaining a uniform set of records on executions.[5]

[4] U.S. Bureau of Prisons, *National Prisoner Statistics,* "Executions 1960," No. 26, March, 1961.

The six tables in this paper were prepared by Mrs. Billie J. Tygrest under the direction of the author. Though the data are from official records obtained under the auspices of the *National Prisoner Statistics* program, the report represents findings made by the author and therefore does not pretend to present any official view of the U.S. Department of Justice or the Bureau of Prisons.

[5] Wolfgang, *op. cit.* Also correspondence with Dr. Wolfgang

Maintained by the Bureau of Prisons, the "Prisoners under Sentence of Death" cards will depend upon the "Movement of Population" form mentioned above for follow-up of each prisoner sentenced to death. However, because some of the items are beyond the scope of the annual collection of data, follow-up will be required for such items as criminal record, number of and basis for appeals, relationship of defendant to victim, place of offense, type of weapon used, and motive precipitating the offense. Also of great importance will be the amount of time elapsing between the significant events in the chronological history of the death sentence case. Thus, for example, for the first time data will be available on the time elapsed between date of arrest and final disposition, between sentence to death and final disposition, and so on.[6]

In summary, the Bureau of Prisons entered the 1960 decade with thirty-one years of data on prisoners executed under civil authority. With the executions bulletin issued annually without delay and the historical series completed, it is now a matter of bringing together all relevant information on each person executed and entering such data on a single card. A long and tedious process, it promises to open new horizons for the study of the prisoner under the death sentence.

In 1960, the number of prisoners executed was fifty-seven. (The record low was forty-nine, in 1958 and again in 1959.) Involved were twenty of the forty-three jurisdictions (forty-one states, the District of Columbia, and the federal government) where the statutes provide for legal execution. Five of the twenty jurisdictions accounted for thirty-seven of the fifty-seven executions. California had

and Ralph Murdy, Managing Director, Baltimore Criminal Justice Commission, concerning the proposed form. The author is indebted for their generous and useful comments.

[6] The matter of elapsed time between sentence to death and actual execution has been studied briefly, the most recent discussion being Donald M. McIntyre, "Delays in the Execution of Death Sentences," Report No. 24, American Bar Foundation, Research Memorandum Series, Dec., 1960.

nine, Arkansas and Texas had eight each, and Georgia and New York had six each.[7]

Of the fifty-seven executions, forty-five were for murder, eight were for rape, two were for kidnapping, one was for robbery, and one was for aggravated assault by a life prisoner. California and Oklahoma carried out the executions for kidnapping, the first since a federal execution for this offense in 1956. These two were the seventeenth and eighteenth executions for kidnapping since the enactment of the federal kidnapping law as well as similar laws in several states. The one for robbery was carried out in Georgia; it was the twenty-third execution for this offense since 1930, the most recent one occurring in Texas in 1958. The one execution for aggravated assault by a prisoner serving a life sentence was the fifth since 1930, all having been carried out in California.[8]

All prisoners executed in 1960 were males; they ranged in age from a nineteen-year-old in Texas to a fifty-four-year-old in Georgia. The median age of all prisoners executed was thirty. For whites the median was thirty-two years; for nonwhites, it was twenty-nine.[9]

Table 1 shows the elapsed time between sentence to death and execution of the fifty-seven prisoners. It ranged from one month and six days for a man executed for murder in Washington to eleven years and ten months for a man executed for kidnapping in California.[10]

For the fifty-seven prisoners the median period between sentence to death and actual execution was sixteen months; it was twenty months for whites and fifteen months for nonwhites. The data on median elapsed time afford detailed illustrations of how whites evaded the penalty longer than

[7] "Executions 1960," op. cit.

[8] Ibid.

[9] All medians expressed in this article are actual. That is, each represents the age or elapsed time of that person who is halfway between each end of the group when it is arrayed from lowest to highest.

The term elapsed time refers to the time, computed to the nearest month, between date of sentence to death and date of disposition, or to January 1 or December 31.

[10] "Executions 1960," op. cit.

TABLE 1

PRISONERS EXECUTED IN THE UNITED STATES: 1960

OFFENSE, AGE, SEX, RACE, AND ELAPSED TIME FROM SENTENCE
TO EXECUTION

(All males for murder except as noted)

W = White   NW = Non-White

Elapsed time (in mos.)	All ages			19-24 years		25-29 years		30-34 years		35-44 years		45 years and over	
	Total	W	NW	W	NW	W	NW	W	NW	W	NW	W	NW
Total executed..	57	22	35	2	7	6	11	6	10	7	6	1	1
Median	16	20	15										
3 and under.......	5	2	3	1	-	-	3^a	1	-	-	-	-	-
4 to 6............	3	1	2	-	-	1	-	-	1	-	1^b	-	-
7 to 12...........	10	1	9	-	2^b	-	1^b	1	2	-	3^b	-	1
13 to 18..........	17	5	12	-	4	2^c	4^b	-	4	3	-	-	-
19 to 24..........	11	6	5	-	-	3	3^b	2	1	1	1	-	-
25 to 36..........	5	3	2	-	1	-	-	1	1	1	-	1	-
37 to 48..........	3	1	2	-	-	-	-	1^d	1^b	-	1^b	-	-
49 and over.......	3	3	-	1	-	-	-	-	-	2^d	-	-	-

a Includes 1 for rape and 1 for robbery.   Source: U.S. Bureau of Prisons
b Includes 1 for rape.
c Includes 1 for assault by prisoner
   serving life sentence,
d Includes 1 for kidnapping.

nonwhites. Of the eight whites aged twenty-nine and under, four were executed after nineteen months or more; of the fourteen whites aged thirty or over, nine waited nineteen months or more. Of the eighteen nonwhites aged twenty-nine or under, only four had waited nineteen months or more; and only five of the seventeen nonwhites aged thirty or over had an elapsed period of nineteen months or more.

Table 2 shows a 1960 total of thirty-six prisoners—twenty-two white and fourteen nonwhite—who were not executed: twenty-two had their sentences commuted to life, eleven had their sentences reversed or vacated, and three were transferred to a mental hospital. Though the last group would be subject to the death sentence should they regain their sanity, the chances that the sentence would be carried out are rare; in such instances, commutation to a life sentence is generally the disposition.

Of the twenty-two whose sentence was commuted to life, nineteen had been convicted of murder and three of rape. Of the eleven with sentences reversed or vacated, ten had

TABLE 2

DISPOSITION IN 1960 OF PRISONERS UNDER
SENTENCE OF DEATH NOT RESULTING IN EXECUTION
OFFENSE, AGE, SEX, RACE, AND ELAPSED TIME FROM SENTENCE
TO DISPOSITION
(All males for murder except as noted)

W = White NW = Non-White

Offense, disposition and elapsed time (in mos.)	All ages			19 yrs & under		20-24 years		25-29 years		30-34 years		35-39 years		40-44 years		45 yrs & over	
	Total	W	NW	W	NW	W	NW	W	NW	W	NW	W	NW	W	NW	W	NW
Total other dispositions....	36	22	14	-	3	2	1	6	-	3	4	3	1	4	3	4	2
Murder....	32	20	12	-	2	2	1	5	-	2	4	3	-	4	3	4	2
Rape......	4	2	2	-	1	-	-	1	-	1	-	-	1	-	-	-	-
Commuted to life.............	22	13	9	-	3	2	-	4	-	2	3	-	-	2	2	3	1
Transferred to mental hosp.	3	3	-	-	-	-	-	-	-	-	-	1	-	1	-	1	-
Reversed or vacated........	11	6	5	-	-	-	1	2	-	1	1	2	1	1	1	-	1
Median	16	16	12														
3 and under	-	-	-	-	-	-	-	-	-	-	-	-	-	-	-	-	-
4 to 6............	2	-	2	-	1ᵃ	-	-	-	-	-	1	-	-	-	-	-	-
7 to 12...........	8	3	5	-	1	1	-	-	-	-	-	1ᵇ	1ᶜ	2ᵈ	1	1	-
13 to 18..........	10	8	2	-	1	1ᵉ	-	2ᶜ	-	1ᵉ	1	2ᶠ	-	1ᵉ	-	1ᵉ	-
19 to 24.........	4	3	1	-	-	-	-	1ᵍ	1ᵍ	1ʰ	-	-	-	1ʰ	-	-	-
25 to 36.........	5	3	2	-	-	-	-	-	-	1ᵍ	-	2ⁱ	1ᵍ	-	-	1ᶜ	-
37 to 48.........	4	3	1	-	-	-	-	-	-	1ᵃ	-	-	-	1	1	-	-
49 and over.....	3	2	1	-	-	-	-	-	-	-	-	-	-	1	-	-	1ʲ

a 1 for rape.
b 1 for rape, sentence reversed, new trial given life sentence.
c Transferred to mental hospital.
d 1 sentence vacated by court of appeals, 1 sentence commuted to life.
e 1 sentence commuted to life without parole.
f Includes 1 commuted to life without parole, 1 transferred to mental hospital.
g Sentence reversed, new trial given life sentence.
h Discharged by court order.
i Includes American Indian commuted to life. Sentence of Negro vacated by court of appeals.
j American Indian released by court order.

Source: U.S. Bureau of Prisons

been convicted of murder and the other of rape. All three of the prisoners transferred to a mental hospital had been convicted of murder.[11]

In age, the twenty-two whose sentences were commuted to life ranged from an eighteen-year-old in Ohio to a sixty-one-year-old in Florida.

11 *Ibid.*

The median age of the thirty-six death-sentence prisoners who were not executed was thirty-three years. For whites the median was thirty-three; for nonwhites, thirty-two. Compared with the median age of those executed, this group of thirty-six prisoners was somewhat older.

The range in elapsed time between date of sentence and date of disposition for this group of thirty-six death-sentence prisoners was from four months (for two prisoners, whose sentence was commuted to life) to nine years and nine months (at which time the prisoner was released by court order). The median elapsed time for the thirty-six prisoners was sixteen months; it was also sixteen months for the twenty-two white prisoners, but twelve months for the nonwhite.

In 1960, 113 persons, including one woman, were sentenced to death. Of these, ninety-four were sentenced for murder, sixteen for rape, two for kidnapping, and one, who was a lifer, was sentenced for aggravated assault. (See Table 3.)

Their median age was twenty-seven years; whites had a median of twenty-eight years and nonwhites, twenty-seven. They ranged in age from seventeen (three, sentenced for murder in Arkansas, Illinois, and New York) to seventy-two (one, sentenced for murder in Arkansas). (None of these four was executed in 1960.)

Of the 113 prisoners sentenced to death in 1960, nine were executed and one had his sentence commuted to life imprisonment. At the close of the year, 103 prisoners sentenced in 1960 to death were still being held for execution.

A study made by the author covering executions carried out in the United States from 1937 to 1952 showed an annual average of 128 executions. January accounted for the highest monthly average—fifteen; September, the lowest—seven. For the first half of each year in the sixteen-year period, the average number of executions was seventy-three; in the second half, the average was fifty-five.[12]

In 1960, the highest number of prisoners sentenced to

[12] James A. McCafferty, *Capital Punishment in the United States, 1937–1952*, M.A. thesis, Ohio State University, typescript, 1954, Table 8.

TABLE 3

PRISONERS RECEIVED FROM COURT UNDER SENTENCE OF DEATH 1960

OFFENSE, AGE, SEX, RACE, AND MONTH SENTENCED

W = White   NW = Non-White

Month sentenced and offense	All ages (See note)			19 yrs & under		20-24 years		25-29 years		30-34 years		35-39 years		40-44 years		45 yrs & over	
	Total	W	NW	W	NW	W	NW	W	NW	W	NW	W	NW	W	NW	W	NW
Total received....	113	55	58	6	5	13	17	14	14	11	9	5	2	1	8	5	2
Murder.....	94	50	44	6	5	13	10	12	11	9	7	5	2	-	7	5	2
Rape.......	16	4	12	-	-	-	6	1	3	2	1	-	-	1	1	-	-
Other.......	3	1	2	-	-	-	1	1	-	-	1	-	-	-	-	-	-
January:																	
Murder.....	9	4	5	-	1	4	-	-	1	-	1	-	-	-	2	-	-
Rape.......	1	-	1	-	-	-	-	-	-	-	-	-	-	-	1ᵃ	-	-
February:																	
Murder.....	9	6	3	1ᵃ	-	3	1	-	-	-	1	-	-	-	-	2	1ᵇ
Rape.......	1	1	-	-	-	-	-	-	-	-	-	-	-	-	-	-	-
March:																	
Murder.....	1	-	1	-	-	-	-	-	1	-	-	-	-	-	-	-	-
Rape.......	1	-	1	-	-	-	-	-	1ᵃ	-	-	-	-	-	-	-	-
Kidnapping..	1	-	1	-	-	-	1	-	-	-	-	-	-	-	-	-	-
April:																	
Murder.....	14	7	7	-	-	1	-	2ᵃ	3ᵃ	1	2ᶜ	2	1ᶜ	-	1	1	-
Rape.......	3	2	1	-	-	-	1ᵃ	1	-	1	-	-	-	-	-	-	-
May:																	
Murder.....	7	4	3	-	-	-	1	1	-	1ᵃ	-	1	-	-	2ᵃ	1	-
June:																	
Murder.....	14	8	6	1	1	2	1	4	2	1	1	-	-	-	1	-	-
Rape.......	3	1	2	-	-	-	1	-	-	-	-	-	-	1	-	-	-
July:																	
Murder.....	4	-	4	-	1	-	1	-	-	-	-	-	1	-	1	-	-
Rape.......	1	-	1	-	-	-	-	-	1	-	-	-	-	-	-	-	-
Agg. Aslt. by lifer.....	1	-	1	-	-	-	-	-	-	-	1	-	-	-	-	-	-
August:																	
Murder.....	3	2	1	1	-	-	1	-	-	1	-	-	-	-	-	-	-
Rape.......	1	-	1	-	-	-	1	-	-	-	-	-	-	-	-	-	-
September:																	
Murder.....	3	2	1	-	-	2	1	-	-	-	-	-	-	-	-	-	-
Rape.......	3	-	3	-	-	-	3	-	-	-	-	-	-	-	-	-	-
October:																	
Murder.....	8	2	6	2	2	-	3	-	1	-	-	-	-	-	-	-	-
Rape.......	2	-	2	-	-	-	-	-	1	-	1	-	-	-	-	-	-
Kidnapping..	1	1	-	-	-	-	-	1	-	-	-	-	-	-	-	-	-
November:																	
Murder.....	8	4	4	1	-	-	1	1	2	1	-	-	-	-	-	1	1
December:																	
Murder.....	14	11	3	-	-	1	-	4	1	4	2	2	-	-	-	-	-

Source: U.S. Bureau of Prisons

Note: Includes 1 non-white received in June for rape for whom age was unavailable.

a 1 executed in 1960.
b Commuted to life imprisonment.
c 1 female.

death per month—seventeen—was recorded in April and again in June. The month with the smallest number of sentences—three—was March. In the first half of the year, sixty-four persons were sentenced to death; in the second half, forty-nine. (The lower number in the latter period may be attributed to court recesses during July and August (see Table 3).

On January 1, 1960, the number of prisoners under sentence of death was 190 (see Table 4). Their median age was thirty-one years. White prisoners had a median age of thirty-three; nonwhites, twenty-nine. The fact that the cases of slightly younger prisoners received from the courts in

TABLE 4

PRISONERS UNDER SENTENCE OF DEATH JANUARY 1, 1960

OFFENSE, AGE, SEX, RACE, AND ELAPSED TIME FROM SENTENCE
TO JANUARY 1, 1960

(All males for murder except as noted)

W = White   NW = Non-White   * = 1 Female

Offense and elapsed time (in mos.)	All ages (See Note)			19 yrs & under		20-24 years		25-29 years		30-34 years		35-39 years		40-44 years		45 yrs & over	
	Total	W	NW	W	NW	W	NW	W	NW	W	NW	W	NW	W	NW	W	NW
Total under sentence of death 1-1-60....	190	90	100	2	4	9	21	23	29	17	19	18	11*	9	7	12	6
Murder....	155	81	74	2	2	8	14	20	20	15	17	16	7	8	7	12	5
Rape......	30	6	24	-	2	1	7	2	7	2	2	-	4	1	-	-	1
Other......	5	3	2	-	-	-	-	1	2	-	-	2	-	-	-	-	-
Median	12	12	10														
3 and under......	27	7	20	1	2ᵃ	1	2	1	6ᵇ	2ᶜ	4ᵃ	-	5ᵃ	1	-	1	1
4 to 6...........	26	10	16	-	1ᵃ	2ᵃ	4ᵃ	2ᵃ	4ᶠ	1	3	2	-	1	3	2	-
7 to 12...........	48	29	19	1	1	3	6ᵃ	8ᵃ	3ᵃ	8	4	5	2	2	2	2ᵃ	-
13 to 18	30	15	15	-	1	4	6	8ᶠ	-	1	3	-	3ᵃ	1	2	1
19 to 24..........	10	6	4	-	-	-	-	1	2ᵃ	2	2	1	-	1	-	1	-
25 to 36..........	26	12	14	-	1	4	4	3ʰ	-	2	4ⁱ	2ᵃ	-	1	3	1
37 to 48......:...	11	7	4	-	1	-	-	1	3ᶠ	1	1	1ᵃ	1	-	1	1ᵃ
49 and over......	12	4	8	-	-	1ᶜ	1	2	1	2ᵃ	2ⁱ	1ᵃ	-	-	-	2ᵍ

Source: U.S. Bureau of Prisons

Note: Offense and elapsed time shown for 3 non-whites for whom age was unavailable, 2 for murder (4 and 30 months), and 1 for rape (8 months.)

a Includes 1 for rape.
b Includes 1 for rape and 1 for robbery.
c Both for murder in connection with kidnapping.
d Includes 3 for rape.
e Includes 1 for rape, 1 for assault by life prisoner.
f Includes 2 for rape.
g Includes 1 American Indian.
h Includes 1 for rape, 1 for burglary.
i Includes 1 for kidnapping.

1960 were not disposed of during the year, coupled with the disposition of older prisoners by execution or other means, tended to lower the median age of the 210 reported present at the close of the year (Table 5) to twenty-nine years. (The median age was the same—twenty-nine for whites and nonwhites.)

Table 6 compares the January 1 and December 31 populations as to number of months elapsed since the day of the sentence. It shows that for the fifty-seven prisoners executed during 1960, the median elapsed time was sixteen months, identical to the median recorded for the "other disposition" group.

TABLE 5

PRISONERS UNDER SENTENCE OF DEATH DECEMBER 31, 1960
OFFENSE, AGE, SEX, RACE, AND ELAPSED TIME FROM SENTENCE
TO DECEMBER 31, 1960
(All males for murder except as noted)

W = White   NW = Non-White   * = 1 Female

Offense and elapsed time (in mos.)	All ages (See note)			19 yrs & under		20-24 years		25-29 years		30-34 years		35-39 years		40-44 years		45 yrs & over	
	Total	W	NW	W	NW	W	NW	W	NW	W	NW	W	NW	W	NW	W	NW
Total under sentence of death 12-31-60	210	101	109	6	6	18	27	26	26	18	22	12	12	9	7	12	5
Murder	172	92	80	6	5	18	15	22	20	15	16	12	11	7	7	12	4
Rape	34	8	26	-	1	-	11	3	6	3	4	-	1	2	-	-	1
Other	4	1	3	-	-	-	1	1	-	-	2	-	-	-	-	-	-
Median	12	12	13														
3 and under	37	19	18	3	2	2	7[a]	6[b]	5[c]	5	3[c]	2	-	-	-	1	1
4 to 6	19	6	13	2	1	2	6[d]	1	2[e]	1	1[e]	-	1	-	1	-	-
7 to 12	49	28	21	-	2	9	3[b]	6[c]	5	5[f]	4	3	2*	1[c]	5	4	-
13 to 18	30	9	21	-	1[c]	2	4[d]	2[a]	5[f]	1[g]	5[e]	2[g]	4	1	1	1	-
19 to 24	28	19	9	1	-	2	3[f]	6	2[c]	3	1	2	2	3	3[c]	2*	-
25 to 36	17	10	7	-	-	-	-	3	4[e]	-	1	1	1	3[c]	3	1	-
37 to 48	15	6	9	-	-	1	3	2	1	-	2[h]	1	1	1	-	1	1
49 and over	15	4	11	-	-	-	1[c]	-	2	3[e]	5[f]	1	1[c]	-	-	-	2[e]

Source: U.S. Bureau of Prisons

Note: Offense and elapsed time shown for 4 non-whites for whom age was unavailable: 2 for murder, 16 and 42 months, and 2 for rape, 6 and 20 months.

a Includes 2 for rape and 1 for murder in connection with kidnapping.
b Includes 1 for kidnapping.
c Includes 1 for rape.
d Includes 3 for rape.
e Assault by life prisoner.
f Includes 2 for rape.
g Includes 1 for murder in connection with kidnapping.
h Includes 1 for burglary.

TABLE 6
PRISONERS UNDER SENTENCE OF DEATH JANUARY 1 AND DECEMBER 31, 1960, AND EXECUTIONS AND OTHER DISPOSITIONS IN 1960
ELAPSED TIME AND OFFENSE
(* = 1 Female)

Elapsed time (in months)	Prisoners reported under sentence of death 1-1-60				Executed				Other disposition not resulting in execution				Prisoners reported under sentence of death 12-31-60			
	All	Murder	Rape	Other	All	Murder	Rape	Other	All	Commuted to life	Trans. to mental hosp.	Reversed or vacated	All	Murder	Rape	Other
Total...	190	155	30	5	57	45	8	4	36	22	3	11	210	172	34	4
Median	12	12	10	-	16	16	-	-	16	15	-	6	12	12	17	-
3 and under	27	22	4	1	5	3	1	1	-	-	-	-	37	32	4	1
4 to 6....	26	17	8	1	3	3	-	-	2	2	-	-	19	13	5	1
7 to 12...	48	42*	6	-	10	7	3	-	8	5	-	3	49	44*	4	1
13 to 18..	30	27*	3	-	17	15	1	1	10	8	1	1	30	21	9	-
19 to 24..	10	10	-	-	11	10	1	-	4	1	1	2	28	24*	4	-
25 to 36..	26	22	2	2	5	5	-	-	5	1	1	3	17	15*	2	-
37 to 48..	11	7	4	-	3	-	2	1	4	4	-	-	15	14	-	1
49 and over	12	8	3	1	3	2	-	1	3	2	-	1	15	9	6	-

Source: U.S. Bureau of Prisons

One significant increase was in the number of prisoners who had been confined for more than three years. On January 1 this group numbered twenty-three; twelve months later it had thirty.

The 210 prisoners under sentence of death on December 31 represented 0.1 per cent of the 213,143 prisoners confined on the same day in all state and federal institutions for adult offenders.[13] Collectively and singly, capital offenders appear to receive more attention than all other prisoners serving sentences in our state and federal adult correctional institutions. From the moment of violence to final disposition (whether by execution or by other means), capital cases are continuously reported to the public. But the mass of information made available about the crime and the offender contains little that is useful for scientific analysis. A comprehensive statistical picture of these cases, supported by detailed multidisciplined scientific studies of capital crime and capital offenders, would open new horizons for understanding not only the violence committed by one man against another, but also man's success in preventing that violence.

EXECUTIONS 1962*

BY BUREAU OF PRISONS, U. S. DEPARTMENT OF JUSTICE

This report covers the forty-four civil jurisdictions in the United States where capital punishment may be legally imposed. These jurisdictions include forty-two States, the District of Columbia and the Federal government.

Figures are included on all prisoners executed, or pardoned or whose sentence was otherwise modified during 1962 and all known by officials cooperating in the National Prisoner Statistics program to be under sentence of death as of December 31, 1962. The data were obtained primarily from State prison officials. Also contributing were Fed-

[13] U.S. Bureau of Prisons, *National Prisoner Statistics*, "Prisoners in State and Federal Institutions, 1960," Bulletin No. 27, Sept., 1961.

* Reprinted from *National Prisoner Statistics*, No. 32, April 1963. Washington, D.C.

eral officials and the administrators of the Cook County, Illinois, and the District of Columbia Jails (the only local institutions in this country where executions are carried out). Prisoners under sentence of death who may still be held in local or county jails ordinarily are not included in NPS figures. Exceptions would be in a few States where prisoners awaiting execution may be transferred to State prisons but subsequently returned to a local jail pending outcome of an appeal or other legal action.

The "under sentence of death" term begins when the court first pronounces the sentence of death for a capital offense and ends with the final disposition of the case, either by execution or otherwise. Many prisoners "under sentence of death" at the close of 1962 had received short stays or reprieves granted by State governors. Also, a large number had appeals before State and/or Federal courts. The remaining had their date of execution set for sometime in 1963; these prisoners, however, could still appeal or receive executive or judicial stays.

Forty-seven prisoners were executed by civil authority in the United States during calendar year 1962. This represents a twelve per cent increase over the forty-two executed in 1961. Calendar year 1962 had the second lowest number of executions on record since 1930 when this national series began.

One or more executions were carried out in eighteen of the forty-four jurisdictions whose statutes provide for legal capital punishment. Eleven of these jurisdictions also had executions in 1961. Among the other seven with executions in 1962, New Jersey (2) had had none since 1956, Illinois (2) none since 1958, Iowa (2) none since 1952, Kansas (1) none since 1954, Kentucky (1) none since 1956, Oklahoma (1) none since 1960 and Oregon (1) none since 1953.

California, with eleven, had the most executions, followed by Texas with nine and Florida with five. These three States accounted for twenty-five, or fifty-three per cent, of the forty-seven executions carried out during the year.

Among the States with no executions in 1962, but one or more in 1961, were New York with two in 1961 and Arizona, Indiana, Louisiana, Maryland, Nevada and North Carolina with one each in 1961.

Fifteen of the 1962 executions were carried out in the lethal gas chamber. This method was used thirty-two per cent of the time in 1962 as compared with forty-three per cent in 1961. Twenty-nine executions were by electrocution and the remaining three by hanging. Sixty-two per cent of the prisoners executed in 1962 were electrocuted—in 1961, fifty-seven per cent were electrocuted. There were no hangings in 1961.

Of the forty-seven executed in 1962, one was a woman —the first to be executed in this country since 1957—executed for murder in California. Of the forty-six males executed, forty were for murder, four for rape, one for assault by a life prisoner (California) and one for armed robbery (Texas).

The age of the forty-seven executed ranged from a nineteen-year-old executed in Texas for murder to the fifty-eight-year-old female executed in California for murder. The median age of the forty-seven prisoners was twenty-eight years, a drop from the 31.2 median age for the forty-two executed in 1961.

Elapsed time—the period between the first imposition of the death sentence for the instant offense and the day of execution—ranged from one month for a robbery offender in Texas to seven years, one month and twenty days for a murderer executed in Illinois. The median elapsed time was 20.5 months which is 4.3 months longer than the 16.2 months recorded in 1961.

Among the prisoners executed in 1962, only six (thirteen per cent) of the forty-seven were received that year. Fourteen (thirty per cent) were received in 1961, fifteen (thirty-two per cent) were received in 1960, eight (seventeen per cent) were received in 1959, three (six per cent) in 1958 and one (two per cent) in 1955.

There are many reasons for the wide range in elapsed time between the first sentence to death and execution.

Appeals which in a few States are automatic following the sentence of the court are made at all levels of the State courts as well as the Federal courts. These together with judicial and executive orders which grant short or long stays or reprieves account for the variation in elapsed time periods.

During calendar year 1962, a total of ninety-nine prisoners received death sentences, thirty-seven less than were reported in 1961. Of the ninety-nine, eighty-six (eighty-seven per cent) were convicted for murder, eleven (eleven per cent) for rape and one (one per cent) each for armed robbery and assault committed by a life prisoner. All were males, excepting one female convicted of murder in Florida.

At calendar year's end, eighty-seven (eighty-eight per cent) were still under the sentence of death, six (six per cent) had been executed and six (six per cent) had their cases disposed of by means other than execution—three were commuted to life, two were granted new trials and one had his sentence reversed by the Circuit Court of Appeals.

At the beginning of 1962, there were 273 prisoners under sentence of death. By including the ninety-nine received from court during the year, the grand total of prisoners under sentence of death sometime during the year was 372. Of these 372, forty-seven were executed during the year and fifty-eight cases were disposed of by means other than execution, leaving a total of 267 awaiting execution at year's end. Thus, there were six less prisoners awaiting execution at the end of 1962 than at year's end 1961 since ninety-nine were received and 105 were disposed of during the year.

Of the 267 awaiting execution at year's end, 216 were "under sentence of death" for murder, forty-six for rape, three for kidnapping (one Federal and two from New Hampshire), one for assault by a life prisoner (California), and one for burglary (Alabama).

Over half (fifty-two per cent) of the prisoners awaiting execution were distributed among five States—Florida had thirty-eight awaiting, California had thirty-five, Louisiana had twenty-seven, Maryland had twenty-two and New York had eighteen.

The age of those awaiting execution ranged from a sixteen-year-old committed for murder in Florida to a sixty-one-year-old murderer in New Jersey. One seventeen-year-old murderer was awaiting in Georgia, one eighteen-year-old murderer in Florida, and four nineteen-year-old murderers—one each in Arkansas, Kansas, New Jersey and South Carolina.

The longest period of elapsed time recorded for those awaiting execution was nine years, ten months and four days for two prisoners committed for aggravated rape in Louisiana. Elapsed time is figured from date of sentence to 12-31-62. The median elapsed time for the total group was 16.7 months.

There were fifty-eight prisoners disposed of by means other than execution in 1962. This indicates that twenty-three per cent more "other dispositions" occurred than executions in 1962. Of these fifty-eight, twenty-seven had their sentences commuted—seventeen to life, one to 199 years, five to ninety-nine years, one to eighty years and three to twenty years. Four of the fifty-nine were committed or transferred to mental hospitals and, of the remaining twenty-seven, twenty-six had their death sentence reversed or vacated by the courts (many were retried and resentenced) and one committed suicide.

Of this group, forty-three (seventy-four per cent) had been sentenced for murder, thirteen (twenty-two per cent) had been sentenced for rape and two (three per cent) had been sentenced for armed robbery. The elapsed time from sentence of death to disposition ranged from twenty-seven days for a rapist commuted to life in Texas to nine years, one month and thirteen days for a murderer commuted to 199 years in Illinois. The median elapsed time for the group was 16.8 months.

Excluded from this report are executions carried out by the armed forces. For the thirty-three year period, 1930 through 1962, the Army (including Air Force) carried out

160 executions, 148 of these during the period 1942–1950, three each in 1954, 1955 and 1957 and one each in 1958, 1959 and 1961. Of the 160 executions, 106 were for murder (including twenty-one involving rape), fifty-three were for rape and one was for desertion. The Navy has carried out no executions since 1849.

TABLE 1

MOVEMENT OF PRISONERS UNDER SENTENCE OF DEATH BY OFFENSE: 1962

| Offense | Reported under sentence of death on 1-1-62 | Received from court during 1962 | Executed | | Other disposition not resulting in execution(a) | | | Reported under sentence of death 12-31-62 | | |
| | | | Present 1-1-62 | Re-ceived in 1962 | Commu-tations (b) | Trans. to mental hosp. | Other (c) | To-tal | Year Received | |
									1962	Prior years
Total...	273	99	41	6	27	4	27	267	87	180
Murder...	214	86	37	4	16	3	24	216	77	139
Rape.....	52	11	3	1	11	1	1	46	9	37
Robbery..	2	1	-	1	-	-	2	-	-	-
Kidnapping	3	-	-	-	-	-	-	3	-	3
Assault by life prisoner	1	1	1	-	-	-	-	1	1	-
Burglary	1	-	-	-	-	-	-	1	-	1

(a) Six prisoners received in 1962 - 5 for murder and 1 for rape. Three were commuted to life (includes the rapist), two were granted new trials and one had his sentence reversed by the Circuit Court of Appeals.

(b) Seventeen commuted to life, one committed in 1953 commuted to 199 years, three committed in 1959 commuted to 20 years, five committed in 1960 - 4 commuted to 99 years and one to 80 years, one committed in 1961 commuted to 99 years.

(c) Reversals of judgment, vacated sentences and grants for new trials. Also includes one received in 1959 who committed suicide.

TABLE 2
COMPARISON OF PRISONERS EXECUTED IN 1962, DISPOSED OF BY OTHER MEANS IN 1962 AND UNDER SENTENCE OF DEATH DECEMBER 31, 1962

(Figures in parentheses show number of females included)

Item	Executed in 1962	Other disposition 1962	Under sentence of death Dec. 31, 1962
Total.......	(1) 47	58	(2) 267
Age (in years)			
Median age..	28.0	27.5	30.3
16 to 19......	1	6	8
20 to 24......	13	18·	(1) 56
25 to 29......	16	10	66
30 to 34......	5	9	55
35 to 44......	10	10	58
45 to 54......	1	2·	(1) 15
55 and over ..	(1) 1	2	8
Unknown.....	-	1	1
Marital status			
Single	20	27	(1) 112
Married	18	21	(1) 90
Separated....	4	2·	17
Divorced	(1) 4	4	20
Widowed.....	-	-	10
Common-law.	-	-	2
Unknown.....	1	4	16
Offense			
Murder	(1) 41	43	(2) 216
Rape	4	13	46
Robbery	1	2	-
Kidnapping...	-	-	3
Burglary.....	-	-	1
Assault by life prisoner	1	-	1
Elapsed time (in months)			
Median..	20.5	16.6	16.7
3 and under ..	7	2	26
4 to 6........	1	4	27
7 to 12.......	3	11	(1) 54
13 to 18......	11	20	(1) 43
19 to 24......	6	7	28
25 to 36......	11	6	47
37 to 48......	(1) 5	3	20
49 to 60......	2	2	5
61 to 72......	-	1	8
73 to 84......	-	1	6
85 to 96......	1	-	1
97 and over ..	-	1	3
Year first received sentence of death			
1953.........	-	1	3
1954.........	-	-	-
1955.........	1	-	2
1956.........	-	1	5
1957.........	-	2	8
1958.........	3	-	6
1959.........	(1) 8	9	22
1960.........	15	11	53
1961.........	14	28	(1) 81
1962.........	6	6	(1) 87

TABLE 3

PRISONERS EXECUTED UNDER CIVIL AUTHORITY IN THE UNITED STATES, BY RACE AND OFFENSE: 1930 TO 1962

(The figures in parentheses show the number of females. For years 1930–1959 excludes Alaska and Hawaii except for two Federal executions in Alaska, one in 1948 and one in 1950. For coverage see table 5.)

Year	All offenses Total	White	Negro	Other	Murder Total	White	Negro	Other	Rape Total	White	Negro	Other	Other offenses (a) Total	White	Negro
All years...	3,812	1,722	2,049	41	3,298	1,640	1,619	39	446	45	399	2	68	37	31
Percent.	100.0	-	-	-	86.5	-	-	-	11.7	-	-	-	1.8	-	-
Percent.	100.0	45.2	53.7	1.1	100.0	49.7	49.1	1.2	100.0	10.1	89.5	0.4	100.0	54.4	45.6
1962	47	28	19	-	(1)41	(1)26	15	-	4	2	2	-	2	-	2
1961	42	20	22	-	33	18	15	-	8	1	7	-	1	1	-
1960	56	21	35	-	44	18	26	-	8	-	8	-	4	3	1
1959	49	16	33	-	41	15	26	-	8	1	7	-	-	-	-
1958	49	20	28	1	41	20	20	1	7	-	7	-	1	-	1
1957	65	34	31	-	(1)54	32	22	-	10	2	8	-	1	1	-
1956	65	21	43	1	52	20	31	1	12	-	12	-	1	1	-
1955	76	44	32	-	(1)65	(1)41	24	-	7	1	6	-	4	4	-
1954	81	38	42	1	(2)71	(1)37	(1)33	1	9	1	8	-	1	2	1
1953	62	30	31	1	(1)51	(1)25	25	1	7	1	6	-	(2)4	(2)4	-

Year															
1952	83	36	47		71	35	36		12	1	11				
1951	105	57	47	1	(1)87	55	31	1	17	2	15		1		1
1950	82	40	42		68	(1)36	32		13	4	9		1		1
1949	119	50	67	2	107	49	56	2	10		10		2	1	1
1948	119	35	82	2	95	32	61	2	22	1	21		2	2	
1947	153	42	111		(2)129	40	(1)89		23	2	21		1	1	1
1946	131	46	84	1	(1)107	(1)45	(1)61	1	22		22		2	1	1
1945	117	41	75	1	(1)90	37	(1)52	1	26	4	22		1		1
1944	120	47	70	3	(3)96	45	(3)48	3	24	2	22				
1943	131	54	74	3	(3)118	(1)54	(2)63	1	13		11	2	7	6	
1942	147	67	80		(1)116	(1)57	59		24	4	20		1		1
1941	123	59	63	1	(1)102	(1)55	46	1	20	4	16		4	3	1
1940	124	49	75		105	44	61		15	2	13				1
1939	159	80	77	2	144	79	63	2	12		12		3	1	2
1938	190	96	92	2	(2)155	(2)90	63	2	25	1	24		10	5	5
1937	147	69	74	4	(1)133	67	(1)62	4	13	2	11		1		1
1936	195	92	101	2	(1)181	(1)86	93	2	10	2	8		4	4	
1935	199	119	77	3	(4)184	(2)115	66	3	13	2	11		2	2	
1934	168	65	102	1	(1)154	(1)64	89	1	14	1	13			1	
1933	160	77	81	2	151	75	74	2	7	1	6		2	1	1
1932	140	62	75	3	128	62	63	3	10		10		2		2
1931	153	77	72	4	(1)137	(1)76	57	4	15	1	14		1		1
1930	155	90	65		(1)147	(1)90	57		6		6		2		2

(a) armed robberies, 19 kidnapping, 11 burglary, 8 espionage (6 in 1942 and 2 in 1953), 6 aggravated assault.

..

TABLE 4

PRISONERS EXECUTED UNDER CIVIL AUTHORITY IN THE
UNITED STATES, BY AGE, RACE, OFFENSE, AND STATE: 1962

(The figures in parentheses show the included executions for rape.
All others were for murder except one robbery with firearms (R)
in Texas and one assault by life convict (A) in California.)

State and race		All ages	19 years only	20 to 24 years	25 to 29 years	30 to 34 years	35 to 44 years	45 and over
	Median age							
Total....	28.0	47	1	13	16	5	10	2
White...	27.8	28	-	9	9	3	5	2
Negro...	28.2	19	1	4	7	2	5	-
Alabama: Negro...		1	-	-	-	-	1	-
California: White...		8	-	2	2	2	1	1
Negro ..		3	-	1	1	(A) 1	-	-
Colorado: White...		2	-	-	-	1	1	-
Florida: White...		2	-	1	1	-	-	-
Negro ..		3	-	1	-	1	1	-
Georgia: Negro...		1	-	-	1	-	-	-
Iowa: White...		2	-	1	1	-	-	-
Illinois: White...		1	-	-	-	-	1	-
Negro ..		1	-	-	-	-	1	-
Kansas: White...		1	-	1	-	-	-	-
Kentucky: White...		1	-	-	-	-	-	1
Mississippi: Negro ..		1	-	(1) 1	-	-	-	-
New Jersey: White...		1	-	-	1	-	-	-
Negro ..		1	-	-	1	-	-	-
Ohio: White...		2	-	1	1	-	-	-
Oklahoma: White...		1	-	-	1	-	-	-
Oregon: White...		1	-	-	-	-	1	-
Pennsylvania: White...		1	-	-	-	-	1	-
Negro ..		1	-	-	-	-	1	-
South Carolina: White...		1	-	-	(1) 1	-	-	-
Negro ..		1	-	-	1	-	-	-
Texas: White...		4	-	(1) 3	1	-	-	-
Negro ..		5	1	(R) 1	2	-	(1) 1	-
Virginia: Negro ..		1	-	-	1	-	-	-

TABLE 5

PRISONERS EXECUTED UNDER CIVIL AUTHORITY IN THE UNITED STATES, BY STATE: 1930 TO 1962

(Method of Execution in 1962: E-Electrocution, G-Lethal Gas, H-Hanging, S-Shooting or hanging. For years 1930-1959, excludes Alaska and Hawaii except for two Federal executions in Alaska, one in 1948 and one in 1950)

Region and State	Total	1962	1961	1960	1959	1958	1957	1956	1955	1950-54	1945-49	1940-44	1935-39	1930-34
United States......	3812	47	42	56	49	49	65	65	76	413	639	645	890	776
FEDERAL (a)...........	31	-	-	-	-	-	2	1	-	6	6	7	8	1
NORTHEAST...........	605	4	3	7	9	4	4	9	25	56	74	110	145	155
New England:														
Maine (b)........	XX	XX	XX	XX	XX	XX	XX	XX	XX	XX	XX	XX	XX	XX
New Hampshire....H	1	-	-	-	-	-	-	-	-	-	-	-	1	-
Vermont........E	4	-	-	-	-	-	-	-	-	2	1	-	-	1
Massachusetts....E	27	-	-	-	-	-	-	-	-	-	3	6	11	7
Rhode Island (b).....	XX	XX	XX	XX	XX	XX	XX	XX	XX	XX	XX	XX	XX	XX
Connecticut......E	21	-	-	1	2	-	-	-	3	-	5	5	3	2
Middle Atlantic:														
New York......E	327	-	2	6	4	4	4	6	7	27	36	78	73	80
New Jersey......E	73	2	-	-	-	-	-	1	8	8	8	6	16	24
Pennsylvania......E	152	2	1	-	3	-	-	2	7	19	21	15	41	41
NORTH CENTRAL......	393	7	2	2	2	7	2	4	1	42	64	42	113	105
East North Central:														
Ohio..........E	170	2	1	2	1	6	1	4	-	20	36	15	39	43
Indiana........E	41	-	1	-	-	-	-	-	-	2	5	2	20	11
Illinois..........E	90	2	-	-	-	1	-	-	-	8	5	13	27	34
Michigan (b)........E	XX	XX	XX	XX	XX	XX	XX	XX	XX	XX	XX	XX	XX	XX
Wisconsin (b)........E	XX	XX	XX	XX	XX	XX	XX	XX	XX	XX	XX	XX	XX	XX

Region / State														
West North Central:														
Minnesota (b) .... H	XX	XX	XX	XX	XX	XX	XX	XX	XX	XX	XX	XX	XX	XX
Iowa	18	2	1	–	–	1	–	–	–	1	4	3	7	1
Missouri .... G	58	–	–	–	–	–	1	–	1	5	9	6	20	16
North Dakota (b)	XX	XX	XX	XX	XX	XX	XX	XX	XX	XX	XX	XX	XX	XX
South Dakota (c) ..... E	1	–	–	–	1	–	–	–	–	–	1	–	XX	XX
Nebraska .... E	4	–	–	1	–	1	–	–	–	1	2	–	–	–
Kansas (c) .... H	11	1	1	5	1	3	–	–	–	5	2	3	–	XX
SOUTH	**2,282**	**22**	**26**	**32**	**31**	**29**	**44**	**41**	**38**	**244**	**419**	**413**	**524**	**419**
South Atlantic:														
Delaware (c) .... H	12	–	1	XX	XX	XX	1	–	–	–	2	2	6	2
Maryland .... G	68	–	–	–	2	–	1	–	1	2	19	26	10	6
District of Columbia E	40	–	1	1	–	3	1	–	–	3	13	3	5	15
Virginia .... E	92	1	4	1	2	2	2	–	1	15	22	13	20	8
West Virginia .... E	40	–	1	–	1	1	1	1	–	5	9	2	10	10
North Carolina .... G	263	–	1	1	–	–	1	1	1	14	62	50	80	51
South Carolina .... E	162	2	5	6	4	6	2	4	4	16	29	32	30	37
Georgia .... E	362	1	3	2	–	3	14	6	4	51	72	58	73	64
Florida .... E	167	5	2	2	10	3	3	7	4	22	27	38	29	15
East South Central:														
Kentucky .... E	103	1	1	8	–	6	–	3	5	8	15	19	34	18
Tennessee .... E	93	–	1	–	1	–	2	–	4	1	18	19	31	16
Alabama .... E	133	1	1	3	2	1	2	1	–	14	21	29	41	19
Mississippi .... G	151	1	5	8	–	3	2	8	8	15	26	34	22	26
West South Central:														
Arkansas .... E	117	–	–	–	6	–	–	1	–	11	18	20	33	20
Louisiana .... E	133	–	1	–	–	3	7	1	2	14	23	24	19	39
Oklahoma .... E	58	1	–	3	–	–	2	1	–	4	7	6	9	25
Texas .... E	288	9	3	8	3	6	5	7	4	49	36	38	72	48

	501	14	11	15	7	9	13	10	12	65	76	73	100	96
WEST	501	14	11	15	7	9	13	10	12	65	76	73	100	96
Mountain:														
Montana ......H	6	–	–	–	–	–	1	–	–	–	–	–	4	1
Idaho ......H	3	–	–	–	–	–	–	–	–	2	–	–	–	3
Wyoming ......G	6	–	1	1	1	–	1	1	–	–	–	2	1	16
Colorado ......G	45	2	1	1	1	2	1	1	2	1	7	6	9	2
New Mexico ......G	8	–	1	1	1	1	1	–	1	2	2	–	10	7
Arizona ......G	36	–	1	1	1	–	–	2	1	2	3	3	2	–
Utah ......S	13	–	1	1	–	1	–	1	1	2	1	5	3	5
Nevada ......G	29	–	1	1	1	1	1	–	–	9	5	5	3	–
Pacific:														
Washington ......H	46	1	–	1	–	–	1	1	–	4	7	9	13	10
Oregon ......G	19	1	–	–	–	–	–	–	1	4	6	6	1	1
California ......G	290	11	8	9	6	6	9	5	9	39	45	35	57	51
Alaska	XX	XX	XX	XX	(d)	(d)	(d)	(d)	(d)	(d)	(d)	(d)	(d)	(d)
Hawaii	XX	XX	XX	XX	(d)	(d)	(d)	(d)	(d)	(d)	(d)	(d)	(d)	(d)

(a) Carried out in the following states: 1957: Georgia (2); 1956: Missouri (2), New York; 1954: New York; 1953: Missouri (2), New York (2); 1950: Alaska; 1948: Alaska, Florida, California (3); 1945: Wyoming; 1943: Tennessee; 1942: District of Columbia (2); 1938: Indiana, Illinois, Michigan, Kansas (2); 1936: Indiana, Oklahoma, Arizona; 1930: Kansas, The 3 in Kansas and the 1 in Michigan were carried out in Federal prisons; the others, in state, territorial, or local facilities.

(b) Death penalty illegal as indicated (XX), except that Michigan and North Dakota prescribe the death penalty for treason; North Dakota also permits the death penalty for first degree murder committed by a prisoner serving a life sentence for first degree murder; and Rhode Island makes the death penalty mandatory for murder committed by a prisoner serving a life sentence.

(c) Death penalty illegal: South Dakota, 1930–1938; Kansas, 1930–1934; and Delaware beginning April 2, 1958, to December 18, 1961.

(d) Alaska and Hawaii when territories abolished capital punishment in 1957. As states, Alaska and Hawaii are included in this series beginning January 1, 1960.

TABLE 6

PRISONERS EXECUTED UNDER CIVIL AUTHORITY IN THE UNITED STATES, BY OFFENSE, RACE, AND STATE: 1930 TO 1962

(The figures in parentheses show the number of females included. For years 1930–1959, excludes Alaska and Hawaii except for two Federal executions in Alaska, one in 1948 and one in 1950)

Region and State	All offenses				Murder			Rape			Armed Robbery		Kidnapping		Other offenses	
	Total	White	Negro	Other	White	Negro	Other	White	Negro	Other	White	Negro	White	Negro	White	Negro
United States	3,812	1,722	2,049	41	(18) 1,640	(12) 1,619	39	45	399	2	5	19	(1) 19	12	13	12
FEDERAL	31	27	3	1	11	3	(a) 1	2	-	-	1	-	(1) 5	-	(1)(b) 8	-
NORTHEAST	605	422	176	7	420	176	7	1	7	-	-	-	2	-	1	-
New England:																
Maine(c)	XX	XX	XX	XX	XX	XX	XX	XX	XX	XX	XX	XX	XX	XX	XX	XX
New Hampshire	1	1	-	-	1	-	-	-	-	-	-	-	-	-	-	-
Vermont	4	4	-	-	4	-	-	-	-	-	-	-	-	-	-	-
Massachusetts	27	25	2	-	25	2	-	-	-	-	-	-	-	-	-	-
Rhode Island(c)	XX	XX	XX	XX	XX	XX	XX	XX	XX	XX	XX	XX	XX	XX	XX	XX
Connecticut	21	18	3	-	18	3	-	-	-	-	-	-	-	-	-	-
Middle Atlantic:																
New York	327	233	89	5	(4) 231	(1) 89	(d) 5	1	-	-	-	-	2	-	-	-
New Jersey	73	46	25	2	46	25	2	-	-	-	-	-	-	-	-	-
Pennsylvania	152	95	57	-	(1) 95	(1) 57	-	-	-	-	-	-	-	-	-	-
NORTH CENTRAL	393	249	142	2	248	135	2	1	7	-	-	-	-	-	-	-
East North Central:																
Ohio	170	103	66	1	(2) 103	(1) 66	(f) 1	-	-	-	-	-	-	-	-	-
Indiana	41	31	10	-	31	10	-	-	-	-	-	-	-	-	-	-
Illinois	90	59	31	-	(1) 59	31	-	-	-	-	-	-	-	-	-	-
Michigan(c)	XX	XX	XX	XX	XX	XX	XX	XX	XX	XX	XX	XX	XX	XX	XX	XX
Wisconsin(c)	XX	XX	XX	XX	XX	XX	XX	XX	XX	XX	XX	XX	XX	XX	XX	XX
West North Central:																
Minnesota(c)	XX	XX	XX	XX	XX	XX	XX	XX	XX	XX	XX	XX	XX	XX	XX	XX
Iowa	18	18	-	-	18	-	-	-	-	-	-	-	-	-	-	-
Missouri	58	26	32	-	25	25	-	1	7	-	-	-	-	-	-	-
North Dakota(c)	XX	XX	XX	XX	XX	XX	XX	XX	XX	XX	XX	XX	XX	XX	XX	XX
South Dakota(g)	1	1	-	-	1	-	-	-	-	-	-	-	-	-	-	-
Nebraska	4	3	-	1	3	-	1	-	-	-	-	-	-	-	-	-
Kansas(g)	11	8	3	-	8	3	-	-	-	-	-	-	-	-	-	-
SOUTH	2,282	626	1,646	10	575	1,224	8	42	392	2	4	19	5	-	-	11
South Atlantic:																
Delaware(g)	12	5	7	-	4	4	-	1	3	-	-	-	-	-	-	-

Maryland	68	13	55		7		37		6	18			0
District of Columbia	40	17	75		3		54			21	2		
Virginia	92	31			17		8			1			
West Virginia	40	19	199	5	28		149 (a)	3		41	4		9
North Carolina	263	35	127		30	(1)	90		6	37	5	3 (b)	
South Carolina	162	55	112		63	(3)	232			58	3		
Georgia	362	66			53	(3)	77			35	1		
Florida	167	55											
East South Central													
Kentucky(i)	103	51	52		47		41		2	9			
Tennessee	93	27	66		22		44	(a)	1	22	5		2
Alabama(i)	133	26	107		24		80	3	5	20			
Mississippi	151	40	122	3	29		98	1	3	21			
West South Central													
Arkansas	117	26	90	1	25		73	(a) 1		17	1		
Louisiana	133	30	103	3	30		86	3		17			
Oklahoma	58	40	15	1	38	(1)	11	(a) 3	1	4	1		2
Texas	288	113	174		100		105	(a) 1	3	68			
WEST	501	398	83	21	388	7	81	21					1
Mountain													
Montana	6	4	2		4		2						
Idaho	3	3			3		1						
Wyoming	6	5	1	1	5		1						
Colorado	45	39	5	1	39		5	(j)	1				
New Mexico	8	6	2		6		2						
Arizona	36	26			26		10						
Utah	13	13			13		1						
Nevada	29	27	2		27		2						
Pacific													
Washington	46	39	5	2	38		5	(k) 2		5			1
Oregon	19	16	3		16		3			3			
California	290	220	53	18	209	(4)	61	(1) 18	53		6 (m)	5 (m)	1 (m)
Alaska(n)	XX	XX	XX	XX	XX	XX	XX	XX	XX	XX	XX	XX	XX
Hawaii(n)	XX	XX	XX	XX	XX	XX	XX	XX	XX	XX	XX	XX	XX

(a) American Indian(s).
(b) Espionage.
(c) Death penalty illegal during entire period, except as explained in Table 5, footnote (b).
(d) 3 Chinese, 1 Filipino, 1 American Indian.
(e) 1 American Indian, 1 Filipino.
(f) Chinese.
(g) Death penalty illegal: South Dakota, 1930–1938; Kansas, 1930–1934; and Delaware beginning April 2, 1958 to December 18, 1961.
(h) Burglary.
(i) In prior reports Kentucky was erroneously reported to have executed 1 female. Alabama, Includes 1 female previously counted as a male.
(j) Japanese.
(k) 1 American Indian, 1 Chinese.
(l) 11 Filipinos, 3 Chinese, 1 Japanese, 3 American Indians.
(m) Aggravated assault committed by prisoners under life sentence.
(n) Alaska and Hawaii when territories abolished capital punishment in 1957. As States Alaska and Hawaii are included in this series beginning January 1, 1960.

TABLE 7

MOVEMENT OF PRISONERS UNDER SENTENCE OF DEATH BY STATE AND OFFENSE: 1962

(Figures in parentheses show the number of females included)

Region and State	Prisoners reported under sentence of death 1-1-62 (a) — Offense				Received from court during 1962 — Offense				Executed in 1962 — Offense				Other disposition not resulting in execution				Prisoners reported under sentence of death 12-31-62 (b) — Offense			
	Total	Murder	Rape	Other	Total	Murder	Rape	Other	Total	Murder	Rape	Other	Total	Commuted (c)	Trans. to mental hosp.	Other (d)	Total	Murder	Rape	Other
United States	273	214	52	7	99	86	11	2	47	41	4	2	58	27	4	27	267	216	46	5
FEDERAL	1	.	.	(e)1	.	.	.	.	.	.	.	.	.	.	.	.	1	.	.	1
NORTHEAST	38	36	.	(e)2	17	17	.	.	4	4	.	.	10	4	.	6	41	39	.	2
New England	4	2	.	2	1	1	.	.	.	.	.	.	1	.	.	1	4	2	.	2
Maine(f)	XX	XX	XX	XX	XX	XX	XX	XX	XX	XX	XX	XX	XX	XX	XX	XX	XX	XX	XX	XX
New Hampshire	1	.	.	(e)1	1	1	.	.	.	.	.	.	.	.	.	.	2	1	.	1
Vermont	1	.	.	(e)1	.	.	.	.	.	.	.	.	1	.	.	1	.	.	.	.
Massachusetts	1	1	.	.	.	.	.	.	.	.	.	.	.	.	.	.	1	1	.	.
Rhode Island(f)	XX	XX	XX	XX	XX	XX	XX	XX	XX	XX	XX	XX	XX	XX	XX	XX	XX	XX	XX	XX
Connecticut(f)	1	1	.	.	.	.	.	.	.	.	.	.	.	.	.	.	1	1	.	.
Middle Atlantic	34	34	.	.	16	16	.	.	4	4	.	.	9	4	.	5	37	37	.	.
New York	14	14	.	.	10	10	.	.	.	.	.	.	6	3	.	3	18	18	.	.
New Jersey	11	11	.	.	2	2	.	.	2	2	.	.	1	.	.	1	10	10	.	.
Pennsylvania	9	9	.	.	4	4	.	.	2	2	.	.	2	1	.	1	9	9	.	.
NORTH CENTRAL	32	29	3	.	11	11	.	.	7	7	.	.	8	3	1	4	28	26	2	.
East North Central	20	20	.	.	7	7	.	.	5	5	.	.	5	1	.	4	17	17	.	.
Ohio	6	6	.	.	3	3	.	.	2	2	.	.	1	1	.	.	6	6	.	.
Indiana	3	3	.	.	3	3	.	.	.	.	.	.	.	.	.	.	6	6	.	.
Illinois	11	11	.	.	1	1	.	.	3	3	.	.	4	.	.	4	5	5	.	.
Michigan(f)	XX	XX	XX	XX	XX	XX	XX	XX	XX	XX	XX	XX	XX	XX	XX	XX	XX	XX	XX	XX
Wisconsin(f)	XX	XX	XX	XX	XX	XX	XX	XX	XX	XX	XX	XX	XX	XX	XX	XX	XX	XX	XX	XX
West North Central	12	9	3	.	4	4	.	.	2	2	.	.	3	2	1	.	11	9	2	.
Minnesota(f)	XX	XX	XX	XX	XX	XX	XX	XX	XX	XX	XX	XX	XX	XX	XX	XX	XX	XX	XX	XX
Iowa	2	2	.	.	.	.	.	.	2	2	.	.	.	.	.	.	.	.	.	.
Missouri	5	2	3	.	4	4	.	.	.	.	.	.	2	1	1	.	7	5	2	.
North Dakota(f)	XX	XX	XX	XX	XX	XX	XX	XX	XX	XX	XX	XX	XX	XX	XX	XX	XX	XX	XX	XX
South Dakota	.	.	.	.	.	.	.	.	.	.	.	.	.	.	.	.	.	.	.	.
Nebraska	.	.	.	.	.	.	.	.	.	.	.	.	.	.	.	.	.	.	.	.
Kansas	5	5	.	.	.	.	.	.	.	.	.	.	1	1	.	.	4	4	.	.
SOUTH	152	100	49	3	47	35	11	1	23	17	4	2	31	15	3	13	145	100	44	1
South Atlantic																				
Delaware(g)																				
Maryland	20	10	10	.	4	3	1	.	.	.	.	.	2	.	.	2	22	13	9	.

District of																
Columbia	8	1	1		1									4	4	4	
Virginia	4	3	1	1	2					1		1	1	1	1	3	1
West Virginia	4	1	1		1									1	1	1	1
North Carolina	5	3	1		2	2		1		1	2	3	2	1	4	2	2
South Carolina	3	1	2		5	5	1			1	1		3	3	9	6	
Georgia	10	7	6		12	13		9	1	6	3	2	1	10	4	4	
Florida	30	25	5		15	14	13	1	1	5	1	1	2	12	32	6	

East South Central:
Kentucky	7	5	2	3	1	4	1	1		1	1	3	4	4	7	
Tennessee	9	6	1		1	1		1	1	1	1	2	1	3	4	9	5
Alabama	11	4	3	2	1	1			1	1	1	1	2	1	9	4	1
Mississippi	4	8	1		1	1		1		1		1	2	4	

West South Central:
Arkansas	4	2	2	1	3	2					1	2	6	6	2	
Louisiana	26	14	12	1	3	3	1	1	1	1	2	3	27	15	12	
Oklahoma	3	3	1	3	1	3	1			1	2	1	2	2	
Texas	7	5	2	8	2	1	1	5	6	2	1	2	4	2	2	

WEST	**50**	**49**		**1**	**24**	**23**	**14**	**13**	**1**	**8**	**5**		**3**	**52**	**51**	**1**
Mountain:																
Montana																
Idaho																
Wyoming	5	5	1	1	1	1	2	1	1	4	4	
Colorado					1					1			
New Mexico	3	3	1	1	2	1	1	1	7	7	1	1	
Arizona	3	3	1	1	1		1		3	3	
Utah	2	2	1	1	1			1	1		1	1	
Nevada										1	1	
Pacific:																
Washington	1	1	1	1	1	1	3	3	
Oregon	3	3		1	1	1	1	(1) 1	(1) 1	
California	33	(1) 32	XX	18	17	11	10	XX	XX	XX	XX	35	34	XX
Alaska (J)	(1) 32	XX	XX	XX	XX	XX	XX	XX	XX	XX	XX	XX	(1)	XX
Hawaii (J)	XX	XX	XX	XX	XX	XX	XX	XX	XX	XX	XX	XX	XX	XX

(a) In a few states because of automatic appeals, as well as appeals by the defendant, prisoners sentenced to death are not immediately transferred to the place of execution. Therefore, the number of prisoners under sentence of death January 1, 1962 is higher than recorded at the close of 1961.

(b) Includes prisoners reported with appeals or other judicial or executive action pending. Excludes prisoners granted new trials.

(c) All commuted to life with the following exceptions: Illinois - 1 commuted to 199 years; South Carolina - 1 commuted to 80 years; Georgia - 3 commuted to 20 years; Tennessee - 5 commuted to 99 years.

(d) Reversals of judgment or vacated sentences. Also includes grants for new trials.

(e) Kidnapping and murder.

(f) Death penalty illegal as indicated (XX), except that Michigan and North Dakota prescribe the death penalty for treason; North Dakota also permits the death penalty for first-degree murder committed by a prisoner serving a life sentence for first-degree murder; and Rhode Island makes the death penalty mandatory for murder committed by a prisoner serving a life sentence.

(g) Death sentence reinstated December 18, 1961.

(h) Suicide.

Chapter Three

THE ARGUMENT FOR THE
DEATH PENALTY

INTRODUCTION

The five selections that follow are representative of the best current arguments for capital punishment. Not all the points heard when the subject is discussed in the state legislatures or before the general public are stated in the articles reprinted here, but the omissions are relatively insignificant. All the major considerations advanced by retentionists will be found in this chapter.[1]

As these five selections will show, retentionism may appear in any one of three major formulations. The primary support today for the death penalty comes from law enforcement groups, that is, from the police and from prosecutors. Central to their position is the belief that society has a right to exact retribution from law breakers and that the best way to do this with murderers and other vicious criminals is through capital punishment. They also defend the view that the death penalty is the only effective deterrent. The best known opponent of abolition in the United States today writes from this perspective: the Director of the

[1] For other recent examples of the case for capital punishment, see in particular California, *Senate Report on the Death Penalty* (1960), pp. 101–111, and the Minority Report in Massachusetts, *Report on the Death Penalty* (1958), pp. 64–74; and the following articles: J. A. Barkenquast, "The Case for Capital Punishment," *The Lutheran* (March 16, 1960); Randolph Childs, "Keep Capital Punishment," *Pennsylvania Bar Association Quarterly* (March 1960); Richard Gerstein, "A Prosecutor Looks at Capital Punishment," *Journal of Criminal Law, Criminology and Police Science* (July–August 1960); Ralph Murdy, "A Moderate View of Capital Punishment," *Federal Probation* (September 1961); David Smith, "The Case for the Death Penalty," *Los Angeles Bar Bulletin* (May 1957); Orvill Snyder, "Capital Punishment: The Moral Issue," *West Virginia Law Review* (February 1961); Lester Summerfield, "For the Death Penalty," *Nevada State Bar Journal* (July 1960).

Federal Bureau of Investigation, Mr. J. Edgar Hoover. All three of his recent statements on this subject have been reprinted below.[2] The selection by Chief Edward Allen is also written from this perspective.

At some point in this chapter, a plea for the death penalty from a member of the bench might also have been included. Only rarely in recent years have judges come before the public and defended the death penalty. A deliberate reticence on the subject is their more typical response. When a judge has written or spoken in favor of capital punishment, as in the vigorous lecture delivered by Samuel Leibowitz, Judge of the Superior Court, Kings County, New York, given before the meeting of the New York District Attorneys' Association in 1961,[3] the argument and tone is not significantly different from that which will be found in the remarks below by Chief Allen.

A secondary line of defense issues from some theologians of the more Bible-centered persuasion. Whereas police officers rely mainly on their personal experiences with criminals to support their claims, these theologians rest their case mainly on Biblical exegesis and dogma. Reverend Vellenga's article, though briefer than some, is representative of this outlook.[4] Only a century ago in this country, his kind of argument was dominant among those favoring

[2] It seems only fair to add, that some of the most outspoken opponents of capital punishment have a background in law enforcement or in criminal prosecution. See, e.g., the remarks of former Chief of Police Michael Reardon and of former Deputy District Attorney George Davis, in California, *op. cit.*, pp. 23–32, 97–100; the statement by Harold Langlois, formerly a Special Agent of the F. B. I., in Massachusetts, *op. cit.*, p. 39; the several statements by Governor Michael DiSalle, formerly a district attorney, cited in the Bibliography; and the statement by the late Chief of Police, August Vollmer, quoted below on p. 518.

[3] Published in *New York Law Forum* (August 1961); see also the argument which followed between Judge Leibowitz and Professor Hook, *ibid.*, pp. 296–301. A more temperate judicial defense of capital punishment will be found in Evelle Younger, "Capital Punishment," *American Bar Association Journal* (February 1956).

[4] It became the topic of a symposium, "Capital Punishment and the Bible," *Christianity Today* (February 1, 1960).

the death penalty. Orthodox Presbyterian and Congregationalist clergymen constantly advanced it against the more
humanistic theology pressed by Unitarians, Universalists
and the Quakers.[5] Because it was once so important and
has by no means disappeared today, it belongs at the head
of the selections in this chapter.

Lastly, there is a sophisticated, moderate apology for
capital punishment constructed by secular moralists who,
while they accept in the main the factual evidence cited
by abolitionists, are unwilling to take the extreme position
of opposing all recourse to the executioner. The best statements of this position are to be found in the essays reprinted here by Professors Sidney Hook and Jacques
Barzun.[6]

Probably the most famous defense of the death penalty
by a social scientist is that of the Italian criminologist,
Gabriel Tarde (1843–1904), in Chapter Nine of his *Penal
Philosophy* (1903, English tr. 1913). It will not go unnoticed that this chapter includes no comparable statement
from any American correctional authority or social scientist. Very few correctional officials have risen to defend
capital punishment in recent years. The notable exceptions
are Sanford Bates, formerly Director of the U. S. Bureau
of Prisons, and his successor, the current Director, James
V. Bennett.[7] But, as a later chapter shows, few prison
officials with responsibilities touching on the matter uphold
the need for executions. A large majority of contemporary

[5] The classic exchange of this sort was between George
Barrell Cheever, a New York Congregationalist minister, who
defended the death penalty in *Punishment By Death* (1842),
and Charles Spear, a Boston Unitarian cleric, who wrote *Essays
on the Punishment of Death* (1844). Cheever's book rapidly
went through several editions.

[6] Professor Barzun's article was extensively discussed by Jerome Natanson and others in *The American Scholar* (Summer
1962).

[7] See Part IV of the nationally syndicated series of newspaper
articles published during 1961 by Mr. Bennett and reprinted
in his pamphlet, "Of Prisons and Justice," pp. 9–12, a special
supplement distributed with the 1962 volume of *Federal Probation;* and the testimony of Mr. Bates in New Jersey, *Public
Hearings on Assembly Bills Nos. 33 & 34,* 2nd Day (1958).

psychiatrists, criminologists, penologists, and social workers seem to be opposed to the death penalty. The result is that we have not had in recent decades anything approaching a full-scale justification of the death penalty from the point of view of modern social science.

CHRISTIANITY AND THE DEATH PENALTY*

BY JACOB J. VELLENGA**

The Church at large is giving serious thought to capital punishment. Church councils and denominational assemblies are making strong pronouncements against it. We are hearing such arguments as: "Capital punishment brutalizes society by cheapening life." "Capital punishment is morally indefensible." "Capital punishment is no deterrent to murder." "Capital punishment makes it impossible to rehabilitate the criminal."

But many of us are convinced that the Church should not meddle with capital punishment. Church members should be strong in supporting good legislation, militant against wrong laws, opposed to weak and partial law enforcement. But we should be sure that what we endorse or what we oppose is intimately related to the common good, the benefit of society, the establishment of justice, and the upholding of high moral and ethical standards.

There is a good reason for saying that opposition to capital punishment is not for the common good but sides with evil; shows more regard for the criminal than the victim of the crime; weakens justice and encourages murder; is not based on Scripture but on a vague philosophical system that makes a fetish of the idea that the taking of life is wrong, under every circumstance, and fails to dis-

* Reprinted, by permission of the author and publisher, from "Is Capital Punishment Wrong?" *Christianity Today,* vol. IV, no. 1 (October 12, 1959), pp. 7–9.

** Rev. Vellenga served on the National Board of Administration of the United Presbyterian Church from 1948 to 1954. Since 1958 he has served the United Presbyterian Church in the U.S.A. as Associate Executive.

tinguish adequately between killing and murder, between punishment and crime.

Capital punishment is a controversial issue upon which good people are divided, both having high motives in their respective convictions. But capital punishment should not be classified with social evils like segregation, racketeering, liquor traffic, and gambling.

These evils are clearly antisocial, while capital punishment is a matter of jurisprudence established for the common good and benefit of society. Those favoring capital punishment are not to be stigmatized as heartless, vengeful, and lacking in mercy, but are to be respected as advocating that which is the best for society as a whole. When we stand for the common good, we must of necessity be strongly opposed to that behavior which is contrary to the common good.

From time immemorial the conviction of good society has been that life is sacred, and he who violates the sacredness of life through murder must pay the supreme penalty. This ancient belief is well expressed in Scripture: "Only you shall not eat flesh with its life, that is, its blood. For your lifeblood I will surely require a reckoning; of every beast I will require it and of man; of every man's brother I will require the life of man. Whoever sheds the blood of man, by man shall his blood be shed; for God made man in his own image" (Gen. 9:4–6, RSV). Life is sacred. He who violates the law must pay the supreme penalty, just because life is sacred. Life is sacred since God made man in His image. There is a distinction here between murder and penalty.

Many who oppose capital punishment make a strong argument out of the Sixth Commandment: "Thou shalt not kill" (Exod. 20:13). But they fail to note the commentary on that Commandment which follows: "Whoever strikes a man so that he dies shall be put to death. . . . If a man willfully attacks another to kill him treacherously, you shall take him from my altar that he may die" (Exod. 21:12,14). It is faulty exegesis to take a verse of Scripture out of its context and interpret it without regard to its qualifying words.

The Exodus reference is not the only one referring to capital punishment. In Leviticus 24:17 we read: "He who kills a man shall be put to death." Numbers 35:30-34 goes into more detail on the subject: "If any one kills a person, the murderer shall be put to death on the evidence of witnesses; but no person shall be put to death on the testimony of one witness. Moreover you shall accept no ransom for the life of a murderer who is guilty of death; but he shall be put to death. . . . You shall not thus pollute the land in which you live; for blood pollutes the land, and no expiation can be made for the land, for the blood that is shed in it, except by the blood of him who shed it. You shall not defile the land in which you live, in the midst of which I dwell; for I the Lord dwell in the midst of the people of Israel." (Compare Deut. 17:6-7 and 19:11-13.)

Deuteronomy 19:4-6,10 distinguishes between accidental killing and wilful murder: "If any one kills his neighbor unintentionally without having been at enmity with him in time past . . . he may flee to one of these cities [cities of refuge] and save his life; lest the avenger of blood in hot anger pursue the manslayer and overtake him, because the way is long, and wound him mortally, though the man did not deserve to die, since he was not at enmity with his neighbor in time past. . . . lest innocent blood be shed in your land which the Lord your God gives you for an inheritance, and so the guilt of bloodshed be upon you."

The cry of the prophets against social evils was not only directed against discrimination of the poor, and the oppression of widows and orphans, but primarily against laxness in the administration of justice. They were opposed to the laws being flouted and criminals not being punished. A vivid expression of the prophet's attitude is recorded in Isaiah: "Justice is turned back, and righteousness stands afar off; for truth has fallen in the public squares, and uprightness cannot enter. . . . The Lord saw it and it displeased him that there was no justice. He saw that there was no man, and wondered that there was no one to intervene; then his own arm brought him victory, and his righteousness upheld him. He put on righteousness as a breastplate, and a helmet of salvation upon his head; he put on garments of vengeance for clothing and wrapped himself in a fury as a mantle. According to their deeds, so will he repay, wrath to his adversaries, requital to his enemies." (Isa. 59:14–18).

The teachings of the New Testament are in harmony with the Old Testament. Christ came to fulfill the law, not to destroy the basic principles of law and order, righteousness and justice. In Matthew 5:17–20 we read: "Think not that I have come to abolish the law and the prophets; I have come not to abolish them but to fulfill them. For truly, I say to you, till heaven and earth pass away, not an iota, not a dot, will pass from the law until all is accomplished. . . . For I tell you, unless your righteousness exceeds that of the scribes and Pharisees, you will never enter the kingdom of heaven."

Then Christ speaks of hate and murder: "You have heard that it was said to the men of old, 'You shall not kill; and whoever kills shall be liable to judgment [capital punishment].' But I say to you that everyone who is angry with his brother shall be liable to judgment [capital punishment]" (Matt. 5:21–22). It is evident that Jesus was not condemning the established law of capital punishment, but was actually saying that hate deserved capital punishment. Jesus was not advocating doing away with capital punishment but urging his followers to live above the law so that law and punishment could not touch them. To live above the law is not the same as abrogating it.

The Church, the Body of Christ, has enough to do to evangelize and educate society to live above the law and positively to influence society to high and noble living by maintaining a wide margin between right and wrong. The early Christians did not meddle with laws against wrong doing. Paul expresses this attitude in his letter to the Romans: "Therefore, he who resists the authorities resists what God has appointed, and those who resist will incur judgment. For rulers are not a terror to good conduct, but to bad. . . . for he is God's servant for your good. But if you do wrong, be afraid, for he does not bear the sword in vain; he is the servant of God to execute his wrath on the wrongdoer" (13:2–4).

The early Christians suffered many injustices and were victims of inhuman treatment. Many became martyrs because of their faith. Consequently, they were often tempted to take the law in their own hands. But Paul cautioned them: "Beloved, never avenge yourselves, but leave it to the wrath of God; for it is written, 'Vengeance is mine, I will repay, says the Lord.' No, 'if your enemy is hungry, feed him; if he is thirsty, give him drink; for by so doing you will heap burning coals upon his head'" (Rom. 12: 19–21).

There is not a hint of indication in the New Testament that laws should be changed to make it lenient for the wrongdoer. Rather the whole trend is that the Church leave matters of justice and law enforcement to the government in power. "Let every person be subject to the governing authorities. For there is no authority except from God, and those that exist have been instituted by God" (Rom. 13:1). Note the juxtaposition of love to enemies with a healthy respect for government. The Christian fellowship is not to take law in its own hands, for God has government in his economy in order to take care of matters of justice.

Jesus' words on loving one's enemies, turning the other cheek, and walking the second mile were not propaganda to change jurisprudence, but they were meant to establish a new society not merely made up of law-abiding citizens but those who lived a life higher than the law, so that stealing, adultery, and murder would become inoperative, but not annulled. The law of love, also called the law of liberty, was not presented to do away with the natural laws of society, but to inaugurate a new concept of law written on the heart where the mainsprings of action are born. The Church is ever to strive for superior law and order, not to advocate a lower order that makes wrongdoing less culpable.

Love and mercy have no stability without agreement on basic justice and fair play. Mercy always infers a tacit recognition that justice and rightness are to be expected. Lowering the standards of justice is never to be a substitute for the concept of mercy. The Holy God does not show mercy contrary to his righteousness but in harmony with it. This is why the awful Cross was necessary and a righteous Christ had to hang on it. This is why God's redemption is always conditioned by one's heart attitude. There is no forgiveness for anyone who is unforgiving. "Forgive us our debts, as we forgive our debtors" (Matt. 6:12). There is no mercy for anyone who will not be merciful. "Blessed are the merciful for they shall obtain mercy" (Matt. 5:7). There is striking similarity to these verses in Psalm 18:25–26: "With the loyal thou dost show thyself loyal; with the blameless man thou dost show thyself blameless; with the pure thou dost show thyself pure; and with the crooked thou dost show thyself perverse."

Professor C. S. Lewis in his recent book *Reflections on the Psalms* deals with the difficult subject of the spirit of hatred which is in some of the Psalms. He points out that these hatreds had a good motivation. "Such hatreds are the kind of thing that cruelty and injustice, by a sort of natural law, produce. . . . Not to perceive it at all—not even to be tempted to resentment—to accept it as the most ordinary thing in the world—argues a terrifying insensibility. Thus the absence of anger, especially that sort of anger which we call indignation, can, in my opinion, be a most alarming symptom. . . . If the Jews cursed more bitterly than the Pagans this was, I think, at least in part because they took right and wrong more seriously."

Vindictiveness is a sin, but only because a sense of justice has gotten out of hand. The check on revenge must be in the careful and exact administering of justice by society's government. This is the clear teaching of Scripture in both the Old and New Testaments. The Church and individual Christians should be active in their witness to the Gospel of love and forgiveness and ever lead people to the high law of love of God and our neighbors as ourselves; but meanwhile wherever and whenever God's love and mercy are rejected, as in crime, natural law and order must prevail, not as extraneous to redemption but as part of the whole scope of God's dealings with man.

The argument that capital punishment rules out the possibility of repentance for crime is unrealistic. If a wanton killer does not repent when the sentence of death is upon him, he certainly will not repent if he has twenty to fifty years of life imprisonment ahead of him.

We, who are supposed to be Christian, make too much of physical life. Jesus said, "And do not fear those who kill the body but cannot kill the soul; rather fear him who can destroy both soul and body in hell" (Matt. 10:28). Laxness in law tends to send both soul and body to hell. It is more than a pious remark when a judge says to the condemned criminal: "And may God have mercy on your soul." The sentence of death on a killer is more redemptive than the tendency to excuse his crime as no worse than grand larceny.

It is significant that when Jesus voluntarily went the way of the Cross he chose the capital punishment of his day as his instrument to save the world. And when he gave redemption to the repentant thief he did not save him from capital punishment but gave him Paradise instead which was far better. We see again that mercy and forgiveness are something different than being excused from wrongdoing.

No one can deny that the execution of a murderer is a horrible spectacle. But we must not forget that murder is more horrible. The supreme penalty should be exacted only after the guilt is established beyond the shadow of a doubt and only for wanton, willful, premeditated murder. But the law of capital punishment must stand, no matter how often a jury recommends mercy. The law of capital punishment must stand as a silent but powerful witness to the sacredness of God-given life. Words are not enough to show that life is sacred. Active justice must be administered when the sacredness of life is violated.

It is recognized that this article will only impress those who are convinced that the Scriptures of the Old and New Testament are the supreme authority of faith and practice. If one accepts the authority of Scripture, then the issue of capital punishment must be decided on what Scripture actually teaches and not on the popular, naturalistic ideas of sociology and penology that prevail today. One generation's thinking is not enough to comprehend the implications of the age-old problem of murder. We need the best thinking of the ages on how best to deal with crime and punishment. We need the Word of God to guide us.

STATEMENTS IN FAVOR OF THE DEATH PENALTY*

BY J. EDGAR HOOVER**

I

The question of capital punishment has sent a storm of controversy thundering across our Nation—millions of spoken and written words seek to examine the question so that decisions may be reached which befit our civilization.

The struggle for answers concerning the taking of men's lives is one to which every American should lend his voice, for the problem in a democracy such as ours is not one for a handful of men to solve alone.

As a representative of law enforcement, it is my belief that a great many of the most vociferous cries for abolition of capital punishment emanate from those areas of our society which have been insulated against the horrors man can and does perpetrate against his fellow beings. Certainly, penetrative and searching thought must be given before considering any blanket cessation of capital punishment in a time when unspeakable crimes are being committed. The savagely mutilated bodies and mentally ravaged victims of murderers, rapists and other criminal beasts beg consideration when the evidence is weighed on both sides of the scales of Justice.

At the same time, nothing is so precious in our country as the life of a human being, whether he is a criminal or not, and on the other side of the scales must be placed all of the legal safeguards which our society demands.

Experience has clearly demonstrated, however, that the time-proven deterrents to crime are sure detection, swift apprehension, and proper punishment. Each is a necessary

* Reprinted from the *F. B. I. Law Enforcement Bulletin,* vol. 29 (June 1960), vol. 30 (June 1961), and *Uniform Crime Reports, 1959,* p. 14, respectively.
** Director, Federal Bureau of Investigation, since 1924.

ingredient. Law-abiding citizens have a right to expect that the efforts of law enforcement officers in detecting and apprehending criminals will be followed by realistic punishment.

It is my opinion that when no shadow of a doubt remains relative to the guilt of a defendant, the public interest demands capital punishment be invoked where the law so provides.

Who, in all good conscience, can say that Julius and Ethel Rosenberg, the spies who delivered the secret of the atomic bomb into the hands of the Soviets, should have been spared when their treachery caused the shadow of annihilation to fall upon all of the world's peoples? What place would there have been in civilization for these two who went to their deaths unrepentant, unwilling to the last to help their own country and their own fellow men? What would have been the chances of rehabilitating Jack Gilbert Graham, who placed a bomb in his own mother's luggage and blasted her and forty-three other innocent victims into oblivion as they rode an airliner across a peaceful sky?[1]

A judge once said, "The death penalty is a warning, just like a lighthouse throwing its beams out to sea. We hear about shipwrecks, but we do not hear about the ships the lighthouse guides safely on their way. We do not have proof of the number of ships it saves, but we do not tear the lighthouse down."

Despicable crimes must be dealt with realistically. To abolish the death penalty would absolve other Rosenbergs and Grahams from fear of the consequences for committing atrocious crimes. Where the death penalty is provided, a criminal's punishment may be meted out commensurate with his deeds. While a Power transcending man is the final Judge, this same Power gave man reason so that he might protect himself. Capital punishment is an instrument

---

[1] [Editor's note: For a detailed report on the Graham case, see James Galvin and John MacDonald, "Psychiatric Study of a Mass Murderer," *American Journal of Psychiatry* (May 1959).]

with which he may guard the righteous against the preda-
tors among men.

We must never allow misguided compassion to erase
our concern for the hundreds of unfortunate, innocent
victims of bestial criminals.

II

The capital punishment question, in which law enforcement officers have a basic interest, has been confused recently by self-styled agitators "against the evil of capital
punishment." A brochure released not long ago, pleading
for "rehabilitation" of murderers while passing lightly over
the plight of the killers' innocent victims and families,
charges that law enforcement officers "become so insensitized by their dealings with vicious criminals that they
go to the extreme of feeling that the death penalty is absolutely necessary."

To add to the burden of conscience borne by peace
officers, prosecutors, and jurists and to brand law enforcement officers as callous, unfeeling men "insensitized" to
the sanctity of human life are gross acts of injustice to
these servants of the public. This ridiculous allegation is
mutely refuted by the compassion which wells up in quiet
tears flowing down the cheeks of hardened, veteran officers
who too often see the ravaged bodies of victims of child
molesters.

There can be no doubt of the sincerity of many of those
who deplore capital punishment. A realistic approach to
the problem, however, demands that they weigh the right
of innocent persons to live their lives free from fear of
bestial killers against statistical arguments which boast of
how few murderers kill again after "rehabilitation" and
release. No one, unless he can probe the mind of every
potential killer, can say with any authority whatsoever that
capital punishment is not a deterrent. As one police officer
has asked, how can these "authorities" possibly know how
many people are not on death row because of the deterrent effect of executions?

Maudlin viewers of the death penalty call the most wanton slayer a "child of God" who should not be executed

regardless of how heinous his crime may be because "God created man in his own image, in the image of God created he him." (Genesis 1:27) Was not this small, blonde six-year-old girl a child of God? She was choked, beaten, and raped by a sex fiend whose pregnant wife reportedly helped him lure the innocent child into his car and who sat and watched the assault on the screaming youngster. And when he completed his inhuman deed, the wife, herself bringing a life into the world, allegedly killed the child with several savage blows with a tire iron. The husband has been sentenced to death. Words and words and words may be written, but no plea in favor of the death penalty can be more horribly eloquent than the sight of the battered, sexually assaulted body of this child, truly a "child of God."

The proponents of "rehabilitation" for all murderers quote those portions of the Bible which they believe support their lavender-and-old-lace world where evil is neither recognized nor allowed. But the Bible clearly reveals that enforcement of moral justice is nothing new to our age. In fact, in referring to man as the "image of God," the Old Testament, so freely quoted by opponents of the death penalty, also states, "Whoso sheddeth man's blood, by man shall his blood be shed: for in the image of God made he man." (Genesis 9:6) There are many passages in the Old Testament which refer to capital punishment being necessary to enforce the laws of society. Since the Old Testament was written about and to a nation while the New Testament was written to individuals and to a nonpolitical body known as the Church, there is a difference in emphasis and approach. Certainly, however, the moral laws of the Old Testament remain with us today.

Misguided do-gooders frequently quote the Sixth Commandment, "Thou shalt not kill," to prove that capital punishment is wrong. This Commandment in the twentieth chapter, verse 13, of Exodus has also been interpreted to mean: "Thou shalt do no murder." Then the twenty-first chapter, verse 12, says, "He that smiteth a man, so that he die, shall be surely put to death." We can no more change the application to our society of this basic moral

law in the Old Testament than we can change the meaning
of Leviticus 19:18: "thou shalt love thy neighbor as thyself," which Jesus quoted in the New Testament.

To "love thy neighbor" is to protect him; capital punishment acts as at least one wall to afford "God's children"
protection.

III

Most states have capital punishment; a few do not. For
the most part, capital punishment is associated with the
crime of murder. Some states have high murder rates; some
do not. Of those states with low murder rates, some have
capital punishment; some do not. The number of murders
that occur within a state as indicated by rates is due to a
wide range of social, human and material factors.

It would be convenient for a study of the effects of
capital punishment as a deterrent if states fell neatly into
two groups: (1) those with low murder rates and capital
punishment; and (2) those with high murder rates and no
capital punishment. Or, if the user of these statistics is
making a case against capital punishment, he would prefer
to demonstrate that the states with low murder rates are
those that do not have capital punishment. But to expect
such an oversimplification of a highly complex subject is
to engage in wishful thinking or a futile groping for proof
that is not there.

Some who propose the abolishment of capital punishment select statistics that "prove" their point and ignore
those that point the other way. Comparisons of murder
rates between the nine states which abolished the death
penalty or qualified its use and the forty-one states which
have retained it either individually, before or after abolition, or by group are completely inconclusive.

The professional law enforcement officer is convinced
from experience that the hardened criminal has been and
is deterred from killing based on the prospect of the death
penalty. It is possible that the deterrent effect of capital
punishment is greater in states with a high murder rate
if the conditions which contribute to the act of murder
develop more frequently in those states. For the law en-

forcement officer the time-proven deterrents to crime are sure detection, swift apprehension, and proper punishment. Each is a necessary ingredient.

CAPITAL PUNISHMENT: YOUR PROTECTION AND MINE*

BY EDWARD J. ALLEN**

In our own times the people of California have repeatedly (sixteen times from 1933 to 1960) turned back the constantly recurring repeal attempts of a militant minority and their malinformed minions. Yet, the present governor, with a seeming fixation, has vowed that he will foist the matter upon the California Legislature at succeeding sessions . . . and the same old tired arguments will be trotted out again:

1. Capital punishment does not deter crime.
2. It "brutalizes" human nature.
3. The rich and powerful often escape the death penalty.
4. Swift and certain punishment is more effective.
5. Society is to blame for the criminal's way of life, so we ought to be more considerate of him.

Let us, then, apart from the demands of pure justice, which should be the only determining factor, examine the above claims for validity and provability.

Capital Punishment Does Not Deter Crime?

If this be true, then why do criminals, even the braggadocian Chessman type, fear it most? Why does every criminal sentenced to death seek commutation to life imprisonment? Common sense alone, without the benefit of knowledge, wisdom, and experience, convinces that we are influenced to the greatest degree by that which we love, respect or fear to the greatest degree—and that we cling

* Reprinted, with minor omissions, by permission of the publisher and author, from *The Police Chief*, vol. 27 (June 1960), pp. 22 ff. *The Police Chief* is the official publication of the International Association of Chiefs of Police, Washington 6, D. C.
** Chief of Police, Santa Ana, California.

most tenaciously to our most valued possessions. Life is indisputably our greatest possession. Additionally, there is no definitive proof anywhere that the death penalty is not a deterrent. There are merely the gratuitous statements of wishful thinkers, some of whom, because of the responsible duties of their positions, ought not be making unprovable or misleading statements.

Parole and probation people, an occasional governor, prison wardens (some prefer to be called penologists), criminal defense attorneys, and oftentime prison chaplains advance this "no deterrent" point of view. None doubts their sincerity, but they are hardly qualified to speak on the matter authoritatively or with pure objectivity. How can they *possibly* know how many people are *not* on death row because of the deterrent effect of the death penalty? Neither do they see the vicious, often sadistic despoiler or the cold-blooded professional killer plying their murderous trades. They encounter these predatory creatures after their fangs have been pulled; after they have been rendered harmless, deprived of the weapons and the opportunities to commit additional crimes. Naturally, in their cages they behave more like sheep than ravenous wolves.

Prison wardens are housekeepers, custodians of criminals after they have been convicted under our system of justice; hence, they see them when they are docile by compulsion but certainly cunning enough to know that to "spring" themselves they must "make friends and influence people" of power and authority *inside* the prison walls, since their own criminal lives on the outside have deservedly brought upon them the judgment of society. It is neither the duty nor the prerogative of wardens or chaplains to decide matters of criminal justice. This has already been accomplished by the people, and their jobs, respectively, are to keep the gate locked, to feed, to clothe, and to guard—and to counsel, console, and convert. True, it is altogether human to develop sympathy for even a depraved and chronic criminal. I suppose a zoo keeper develops a fondness for the wild animals which the taxpayers pay him to feed and guard. Yet, what kind of a zoo keeper would he be if he opened the cage doors and released the voracious beasts to prey upon the public? This very act would throw a community into terror and alarm. Even so, if a wild beast attacked a human being, there would be less guilt attached, since such an animal acts from instinct and not malice aforethought. Not so, a rational human being who deliberately murders or defiles his fellowman. It might serve a good purpose if these "bleeding hearts" could accompany those whose duty it is to examine first-hand, at the scenes of their crimes, the gruesome handi-work of those for whom they intercede. This might give them pause to properly weigh the public interest in their private scales of justice.

It is also put forth by those who would weaken our laws and, perforce, our ability to protect the innocent, that many murderers on death row claim they did not think of the death penalty when they committed their crimes. This is undoubtedly true. That is precisely the point. If they had thought of it, they would not have committed their crimes. Here we have the spectacle of a minute minority of con-victed murderers convincing intelligent people that capital punishment is wrong because of their own failure to realize the consequences of their murderous conduct. Are we then to base our laws on this reasoning? What of the countless others who *were* deterred from murder through fear of the penalty? The implication is clear: even those murder-ers who didn't think of the death penalty would have been deterred had they given it consideration. Our laws are made for reasonable creatures, not to satisfy an abnormal handful. It is hardly the part of wisdom to be guided by the counsel and advice of an infinitesimally small band of bestial criminals. Further, the cunning individual and conspiratorial group who plot murder always imagine themselves too clever to get caught, or if caught, convicted.

It Brutalizes Human Nature?

But the opposite is true. Wanton *murder* brutalizes hu-man nature and cheapens human life, not the penalty for its perpetration. Capital punishment is the guarantee against murder and the brutalization of human nature. It places an inestimable value on human life—the forfeiture of the life of the despoiler. To allow heinous criminals to commit their crimes without the commensurate reparation of the death penalty would surely brutalize and degrade human nature and reduce society to a state of barbarism. True Christian charity is based upon justice, the proper concern for the weak and innocent, not upon a soft-headed regard for despicable and conspiratorial killers. Let us resort to right reason and view retribution and reparation in proper perspective.

The Rich and Powerful Generally Escape?

There is truth in this statement and it is equally applicable to other penalties, not the death penalty alone. No one decries this discrimination more than law enforcement. The deals which allow criminals to escape justice are consummated by courts and attorneys. Attorneys present evidence to the courts and judges hand down sentences. Responsibility also devolves upon citizen jurors to return proper verdicts. If some citizens, courts, and lawyers fail in their duty, is the law itself to blame? Rather it is their administration of it. Surely, bribery, social position, or political pull ought not to influence the administration of justice, but admittedly they often do. Since this is so, it would be as logical to advocate the repeal of the entire criminal code. If one person escapes justice, is it unjust that another does not? Since justice does not *always* prevail, ought we abandon our striving for its attainment? Who would advocate the abolition of the Ten Commandments because they are honored more in their breach than in their observance? Justice is still justice if no man is just! The defect, in this instance, lies in men, not in the law! Law enforcement firmly believes that all men should be treated equally at the bar of justice. There are attorneys, judges, governors, parole boards and that peculiar phenomena called "Adult and Juvenile Authorities" who decree otherwise.

Jurors and Governors and Judges

Let us take the matter of justice, including capital punishment, a step further. In selecting a murder jury each prospective juror is asked if he has a conscientious objection to returning a death penalty verdict. If so, such a person is summarily excused as unqualified. No injustice obtains from this practice, since a private citizen has a right to his own opinion.

But this does not apply to judges and governors who have the duty of sentencing and the right of commutation, since their consciences must be guided by the law which they have sworn to uphold. Therefore, if a judge or state governor has such a conscientious objection to the death penalty that he "creeps through the serpentine windings of utilitarianism to discover some advantage that may discharge him from the justice of punishment or even from the due measure of it," then such a judge or governor has disqualified himself, and ought, in all justice to the commonwealth he serves, to vacate his lofty position and return it to the people to whom it belongs. Then, as a private citizen, he can campaign to his heart's content for the abolition of whatever law he doesn't happen to like. In the meantime, however, he ought not attempt to substitute the minority decisions of our Supreme Courts for majority decisions or be persuaded by the opinions of condemned criminals on murderer's row. Further, to incessantly inveigh from high office against the law of the land, particularly a law ingrained in the tradition of our Judeo-Christian culture, smacks of arbitrary dictation. The business of government is justice, not pity—however self-consoling.

Life Imprisonment

In most of our states life imprisonment simply does not exist. In truth and justice the term ought to be discarded since it does not mean what it says. In the State of California, for example, the State Constitution provides that the governor, under his commutation powers, may set aside the words "without parole" with respect to life imprisonment. It would take a constitutional amendment to abolish that power. In other states life imprisonment means merely a varying number of years.

Death Penalty Seldom Used

The argument that the death penalty is seldom used argues for its retention, not its abolition. It proves that juries and courts are exercising extreme leniency, even with vicious murderers. Yet, there are certain heinous crimes regarding which the very stones would cry out for the death penalty were it abolished. Therefore, it should be retained as just punishment and reparation for these and as a deterrent for other malignant criminals. It would be a better argument for the abolitionists if they could say that the death penalty was capriciously or routinely being returned for every homicide.

Specious Arguments

Two of the reasons advanced for the abolition of the death penalty have no validity whatsoever. One is an attempt to equate human slavery with capital punishment. The argument is this: slavery was once rampant, but now an enlightened society favors its abolition; therefore, we ought to do away with capital punishment, since we "moderns" are more "enlightened" than our forebears.

Firstly, slavery never was, or never will be, morally right or justifiable or just. The death penalty *is* morally right and justifiable and just. So these sophists are merely advancing a completely false and odious comparison. Here is another "beaut" from a university psychiatrist: the death penalty could be society's way of "projecting its own crime into the criminal." Now, I submit that the longer we permit this type of nonsense to be spread abroad, the more ridiculous our nation is going to appear in the eyes of the world. I understand that there is a growing resentment among those in the medical profession against this type of gobble-de-gook, and about time.

It is obvious to anyone who believes in the moral and natural law (as clearly stated in the law of the land) that first degree murder requires personal premeditation and the full consent of the will, hence, its punishment should be meted out to the criminal or criminals personally responsible. To argue otherwise is to argue the unnatural, but admittedly, this is the day of the unnatural logician.

We argue that the unnatural in sex is natural and point to fables for proof. Thus, we have the Oedipus and Electra complexes, situations culled from Greek drama and foisted upon us as Freudian truisms. No use talking about free will, we just can't help ourselves. So today there is no crime, really, and no criminals—just "complexes." And these "complexes" are so "complex" we must all eventually succumb to their "complexity"—and employ a psychoanalyst. (Physician, heal thyself!) Truly, it is possible for people, even with exceptionally high IQ's, to be nuttier than fruitcakes, or vice versa, as the case may be. We had better be careful in these "modern" times (which condone the criminal immorality of ancient Greece and Rome) or we, too, will abandon our reason altogether. Mainly because of their sexual excesses, aberrations and perversions, St. Paul told the Romans (First Epistle to the Romans) that they had gone blind and no longer knew the difference between right and wrong. Neither does this generation in many respects, and we will degenerate further if we continue to give ear to certain types of psychoanalytical professors and their automorphic automatons who impute to all of us (including themselves?) the guilt for the personal crimes of individual criminals.

Swift and Certain Punishment

Swift and certain punishment is assuredly a crime deterrent, but only when coupled with commensurate severity, otherwise the statement is an absurdity. Suppose a bank robber was very swiftly and very surely sentenced to five days in the county jail; or a rapist swiftly and certainly given a $25 fine. Would such punishment (?) be a deterrent to either the bank robber or the rapist? Surely, the deterrent value is in the severity as well as the swiftness and the certainty. However, if one had to choose but one of the three, then the severity of the punishment must needs be selected.

Once again, we must reiterate that some lawyers and courts and the criminals themselves have caused the "swiftness and certainty" of justice to have almost vanished from the American scene. The same sources would now abolish the severity. Yet, those lawyers who, through capricious, dilatory tactics continually postpone justice are the very ones who prattle about swiftness and certainty as a substitute for severity. The Chessman case is a prize example of how lawyers, judges and a governor can foul up "swift and certain" punishment. The irony of it is that Chessman and his attorneys and the present governor, who were responsible for the seemingly interminable postponements, now cry to the high heavens that such postponements are "cruel and unusual punishment." No wonder Hamlet cited the "law's delay" as one of the problems that was driving him nuts. Chessman himself became so disgusted with the publicity-seeking antics of one lawyer who injected himself into the case that he fired him, publicly. However, this did not delay the redoubtable attorney, and he is still trying to make a career of the case. Wonder what further "deterrent" he needs?

Individual States and Capital Punishment

A study of the statistics on murder in the forty-eight states in 1958 produced some interesting results with respect to the capital crime. The proponents for abolition make much of the fact that there were seven states in 1958 (nine since the admission of Alaska and Hawaii) which have abolished capital punishment. These proponents make no mention of the fact that eight other states in the Union once abolished capital punishment and have returned to it.

The states which abolished capital punishment and after an unhappy experience restored it are: Kansas, Iowa, Colorado, Washington, Oregon, Arizona, Missouri, and Tennessee. It is noted that three of these states border on California: Arizona, contiguous to the southeast; Oregon, contiguous to the north on the coast; and Washington, further north and also on the west coast. Since these comprise the area surrounding and abutting California, it is the most revealing and significantly important statistic for California residents. Of the states which have abolished capital punishment, two are now in New England: Maine and Rhode Island. Maine had one of the highest murder rates in New England in 1958, with an average of 2.5 per 100,000 population (all averages are quoted using this population figure). The six New England states have an average of 1.6, the lowest murder rate of any section of the country, yet only two of the six states have abolished the death penalty, and one of them has a rate half again as high as the average. New Hampshire, which has the death penalty, compares with the lowest, 0.7.

Seven midwestern states: Iowa, Kansas, Minnesota, Nebraska, North Dakota, South Dakota and Missouri, have an average of 2.2 murders for 1958. It is noted that three of these states returned to capital punishment after having abolished it, and two of the seven still have no capital punishment.

In the eleven far western states, the average percentage in 1958 was 3.7, oddly enough the exact percentage for the State of California. Four of these states returned to the death penalty. The other seven states have always had capital punishment.

Eleven northeastern states had an average of 3.1 murders in 1958.

The highest murder rate of the geographical groups of states was the southern group of thirteen states. They had the exceptionally high rate of 9.0. Admittedly, the South has a problem, but the removal of the death penalty would only aggravate it. Of these states only Tennessee ever tried to get along without capital punishment and has since returned to it.

It would appear that the permeance of racial, ethnic and religio-political cultures influence crime rates, including murder, in the various geographical sections of our country. Common sense dictates that more severe punitive sanctions are necessary in those states or sections where serious crime is more prevalent. Conversely, where the crime is minimal because of the law-abiding nature of the people, murder is less frequent. Thus it is that the New England states have a low murder rate while the South has an unusually high rate. It would be the height of folly therefore to advocate the removal of the death penalty throughout the Southern states where the crime of murder is a serious threat.

Where crime and murder are at a low level and where community life is governed by respect and reverence for law, rather than by its enforcement, then severe punitive measures may be relaxed, but not abolished. (Such a state presages the millennium.) On the other hand, where crime and murder are a serious problem, then the removal of stringent punitive measures further aggravates it. The eight states which re-enacted the death penalty after a trial period without it, discovered this to their own dismay.

The seven states within the corporate United States which do not have the death penalty are among the smallest, in territory and/or population: Delaware, Maine, Michigan, Minnesota, North Dakota, Rhode Island, and Wisconsin. There is among them only one really large state, Michigan, whose 1958 population of 7,865,547 exceeds by more than a half-million the combined total of the six other states. Michigan's 1958 murder rate per 100,000 population was 3.1, not only the highest of these seven states, but higher than both Pennsylvania and New York, two of the three most populous states in the Union—with over eleven to sixteen million respectively. California, in the top three, has approximately twice the population of Michigan. New York has a 2.8 rate and Pennsylvania 2.5. The experience has been that the larger states with crime problems have found it necessary to return to the death penalty. And to re-emphasize, three of these states either border on California, or are on the west coast, or both.

California Officers Murdered on Duty

I do not have the figures for the other states, but in California a review of the number of police officers killed in line of duty during the past ten years is of significance. From 1950 through 1959 there have been thirty-five law enforcement officers shot and killed while performing law enforcement duties, i.e., protecting the lives and property of California citizens. Even more alarming is the fact that of the thirty-five, approximately twice as many were murdered during the latter half of the decade than were killed during the first half. Twelve were killed from 1950 through 1954 and twenty-three from 1955 through 1959. In the last three years seventeen of these twenty-three were murdered while on duty.

At a time in our national and state history when crime is increasing alarmingly and when the murder of police officers in the State of California is reaching new heights, we have powerful figures and groups advocating the abolition of capital punishment—almost an invitation for murderous thugs to kill more police officers whose duty it is to protect (even at the expense of their own lives) the very citizens who advocate leniency for their murderers. Where is the reciprocal regard for the life of a police officer in the minds and hearts of these paragons of Christian charity, in or out of the governor's office, in or out of our courtrooms, on or off our judicial benches, or in or out of the Humpty-Dumpty (egghead) claque in politics, entertainment, television, journalism, and education? (By "eggheads" I do not mean authentic intellectuals, but the poseurs.)

Perhaps we are arriving at a governmental philosophy which considers the lives of police officers expendable, but not so the lives of the vicious criminals who murder them. Rather, we must protect the latter, since to punish them too severely would be "projecting society's crime into the criminal." Would it not be more sensible and accurate to state that "society" is to blame for the murder of its police officers unless it insists upon the retention of the death penalty as a protection for its own protectors, ergo, society itself? Unmistakably, without militant police protection the whole of society would overnight become a criminal jungle.

Conclusion

Of course, the overwhelming statistic (for those who wish to decide on statistics alone) is that forty-one of the fifty states and the majority of the nations in the world have the death penalty.

However, even though statistics, per se, unquestionably

favor the retention of the death penalty, mere numbers, pro and con, ought not be the deciding factor. The deciding factor should be the consideration of justice—the primary, if not the sole business of government. All of the erudition, wisdom, experience, and knowledge of history reveals that the death penalty is morally and legally just. For the just man or nation this should be sufficient. Even so, justice is still justice, if no man is just—were it not so, God would have told us.

THE DEATH SENTENCE*

BY SIDNEY HOOK**

Is there anything new that can be said for or against capital punishment? Anyone familiar with the subject knows that unless extraneous issues are introduced a large measure of agreement about it can be, and has been, won. For example, during the last 150 years the death penalty for criminal offenses has been abolished, or remains unenforced, in many countries; just as important, the number of crimes punishable by death has been sharply reduced in all countries. But while the progress has been encouraging, it still seems to me that greater clarity on the issues involved is desirable: Much of the continuing polemic still suffers from one or the other of the twin evils of vindictiveness and sentimentality.

Sentimentality, together with a great deal of confusion about determinism, is found in Clarence Darrow's speeches and writings on the subject. Darrow was an attractive and likeable human being but a very confused thinker. He

* Reprinted, with three new paragraphs added, by permission of the author and publisher from *The New Leader,* vol. 44 (April 3, 1961), pp. 18–20. Cf. the original version which appeared in *The New York Law Forum* (August 1961), pp. 278–283, as an address before the New York State District Attorneys' Association.

** Professor of Philosophy and Chairman of the Graduate Philosophy Department at New York University. Author of *Heresy, Yes—Conspiracy, No* (1953), *Common Sense and the Fifth Amendment* (1957), *Political Power and Personal Freedom* (1959), and *The Paradoxes of Freedom* (1962).

argued against capital punishment on the ground that the murderer was always a victim of heredity and environment —and therefore it was unjust to execute him. ("Back of every murder and back of every human act are sufficient causes that move the human machine beyond their control.") The crucifiers and the crucified, the lynch mob and its prey are equally moved by causes beyond their control and the relevant differences between them is therewith ignored. Although Darrow passionately asserted that no one knows what justice is and that no one can measure it, he nonetheless was passionately convinced that capital punishment was unjust.

It should be clear that if Darrow's argument were valid, it would be an argument not only against capital punishment but against all punishment. Very few of us would be prepared to accept this. But the argument is absurd. Even if we are all victims of our heredity and environment, it is still possible to alter the environment by meting out capital punishment to deter crimes of murder. If no one can help doing what he does, if no one is responsible for his actions, then surely this holds just as much for those who advocate and administer capital punishment as for the criminal. The denunciation of capital punishment as unjust, therefore, would be senseless. The question of universal determinism is irrelevant. If capital punishment actually were a deterrent to murder, and there existed no other more effective deterrent, and none as effective but more humane, a case could be made for it.

Nor am I impressed with the argument against capital punishment on the ground of its inhumanity. Of course it is inhumane. So is murder. If it could be shown that the inhumanity of murder can be decreased in no other way than by the inhumanity of capital punishment acting as a deterrent, this would be a valid argument for such punishment.

I have stressed the hypothetical character of these arguments because it makes apparent how crucially the wisdom of our policy depends upon the alleged facts. Does capital punishment serve as the most effective deterrent we have against murder? Most people who favor its retention believe that it does. But any sober examination of the facts will show that this has never been established. It seems plausible, but not everything which is plausible or intuitively credible is true.

The experience of countries and states which have abolished capital punishment shows that there has been no perceptible increase of murders after abolition—although it would be illegitimate to infer from this that the fear of capital punishment never deterred anybody. The fact that "the state with the very lowest murder rate is Maine, which abolished capital punishment in 1870," may be explained by the hypothesis that fishermen, like fish, tend to be cold-blooded, or by some less fanciful hypothesis. The relevant question is: what objective evidence exists which would justify the conclusion that if Maine had not abolished capital punishment, its death rate would have been higher? The answer is: no evidence exists.

The opinion of many jurists and law enforcement officers from Cesare Beccaria (the eighteenth century Italian criminologist) to the present is that swift and certain punishment of some degree of severity is a more effective deterrent of murder than the punishment of maximum severity when it is slow and uncertain. Although this opinion requires substantiation, too, it carries the weight which we normally extend to pronouncements by individuals who report on their life experience. And in the absence of convincing evidence that capital punishment is a more effective and/or humane form of punishment for murder than any other punishment, there remains no other reasonable ground for retaining it.

This is contested by those who speak of the necessity for capital punishment as an expression of the "community need of justice," or as the fulfillment of "an instinctive urge to punish injustice." Such views lie at the basis of some forms of the retributive theory. It has been alleged that the retributive theory is nothing more than a desire for revenge, but it is a great and arrogant error to assume that all who hold it are vindictive. The theory has been defended by secular saints like G. E. Moore and Immanuel Kant, whose dispassionate interest in justice cannot reasonably be challenged. Even if one accepted the retributive theory or believed in the desirability of meeting the community need of justice, it doesn't in the least follow that this justifies capital punishment. Other forms of punishment may be retributive, too.

I suppose that what one means by community need or feeling and the necessity of regarding it, is that not only must justice be done, it must be seen to be done. A requirement of good law is that it must be consonant with the feeling of the community, something which is sometimes called "the living law." Otherwise it is unenforceable and brings the whole system of law into disrepute. Meeting community feeling is a necessary condition for good law, but not a sufficient condition for good law. This is what Justice Holmes meant when he wrote in *The Common Law* that "The first requirement of a sound body of law is that it should correspond with the actual feelings and demands of the community, whether right or wrong." But I think he would admit that sound law is sounder still if in addition to being enforceable it is also just. Our moral obligation as citizens is to build a community feeling and demand which is right rather than wrong.

Those who wish to retain capital punishment on the ground that it fulfills a community need or feeling must believe either that community feeling *per se* is always justified, or that to disregard it in any particular situation is inexpedient because of the consequences, *viz.*, increase in murder. In either case they beg the question—in the first case, the question of justice, and in the second, the question of deterrence.

One thing is incontestable. From the standpoint of those who base the argument for retention of capital punishment on the necessity of satisfying community needs there could be no justification whatsoever for any *mandatory* death sentence. For a mandatory death sentence attempts to determine in advance what the community need and feeling will be, and closes the door to fresh inquiry about the justice as well as the deterrent consequences of any proposed punishment.

Community need and feeling are notoriously fickle.

When a verdict of guilty necessarily entails a death sentence, the jury may not feel the sentence warranted and may bring in a verdict of not guilty even when some punishment seems to be legally and morally justified. Even when the death sentence is not mandatory, there is an argument, not decisive but still significant, against any death sentence. This is its incorrigibility. Our judgment of a convicted man's guilt may change. If he has been executed in the meantime, we can only do him "posthumous justice." But can justice ever really be posthumous to the victim? Rarely has evidence, even when it is beyond reasonable doubt, the same finality about its probative force as the awful finality of death. The weight of this argument against capital punishment is all the stronger if community need and feeling are taken as the prime criteria of what is just or fitting.

What about heinous political offenses? Usually when arguments fail to sustain the demand for capital punishment in ordinary murder cases, the names of Adolf Hitler, Adolf Eichmann, Joseph Stalin and Ilse Koch are introduced and flaunted before the audience to inflame their feelings. Certain distinctions are in order here. Justice, of course, requires severe punishment. But why is it assumed that capital punishment is, in these cases, the severest and most just of sentences? How can any equation be drawn between the punishment of one man and the sufferings of his numerous victims? After all, we cannot kill Eichmann six million times or Stalin twelve million times (a conservative estimate of the number of people who died by their order).

If we wish to keep alive the memory of political infamy, if we wish to use it as a political lesson to prevent its recurrence, it may be educationally far more effective to keep men like Eichmann in existence. Few people think of the dead. By the same token, it may be necessary to execute a politically monstrous figure to prevent him from becoming the object of allegiance of a restoration movement. Eichmann does not have to be executed. He is more useful alive if we wish to keep before mankind the enormity of his offense. But if Hitler had been taken alive, his death would have been required as a matter of political necessity, to prevent him from becoming a living symbol or rallying cry of Nazi die-hards and irreconcilables.

There is an enormous amount of historical evidence which shows that certain political tyrants, after they lose power, become the focus of restoration movements that are a chronic source of bloodshed and civil strife. No matter how infamous a tyrant's actions, there is usually some group which has profited by it, resents being deprived of its privileges, and schemes for a return to power. In difficult situations, the dethroned tyrant also becomes a symbol of legitimacy around which discontented elements rally who might otherwise have waited for the normal processes of government to relieve their lot. A *mystique* develops around the tyrant, appeals are made to the "good old days," when his bread and circuses were used to distract attention from the myriads of his tortured victims, plots seethe around him until they boil over into violence and bloodshed again. I did not approve of the way Mussolini was killed. Even he deserved due process. But I have no doubt whatsoever that had he been sentenced merely to life imprisonment, the Fascist movement in Italy today would be a much more formidable movement, and that sooner or later, many lives would have been lost in consequence of the actions of Fascist legitimists.

Where matters of ordinary crime are concerned these political considerations are irrelevant. I conclude, therefore, that no valid case has so far been made for the retention of capital punishment, that the argument from deterrence is inconclusive and inconsistent (in the sense that we do not do other things to reinforce its deterrent effect if we believe it has such an effect), and that the argument from community feeling is invalid.

However, since I am not a fanatic or absolutist, I do not wish to go on record as being categorically opposed to the death sentence in all circumstances. I should like to recognize two exceptions. A defendant convicted of murder and sentenced to life should be permitted to choose the death sentence instead. Not so long ago a defendant sentenced to life imprisonment made this request and was rebuked by the judge for his impertinence. I can see no valid grounds for denying such a request out of hand. It may sometimes be denied, particularly if a way can be found to make the defendant labor for the benefit of the dependents of his victim as is done in some European countries. Unless such considerations are present, I do not see on what reasonable ground the request can be denied, particularly by those who believe in capital punishment. Once they argue that life imprisonment is either a more effective deterrent or more justly punitive, they have abandoned their position.

In passing, I should state that I am in favor of permitting *any* criminal defendant, sentenced to life imprisonment, the right to choose death. I can understand why certain jurists, who believe that the defendant wants thereby to cheat the state out of its mode of punishment, should be indignant at the idea. They are usually the ones who believe that even the attempt at suicide should be deemed a crime—in effect saying to the unfortunate person that if he doesn't succeed in his act of suicide, the state will punish him for it. But I am baffled to understand why the absolute abolitionist, dripping with treacly humanitarianism, should oppose this proposal. I have heard some people actually oppose capital punishment in certain cases on the ground that: "Death is too good for the vile wretch! Let him live and suffer to the end of his days." But the absolute abolitionist should be the last person in the world to oppose the wish of the lifer, who regards this form of punishment as torture worse than death, to leave our world.

My second class of exceptions consists of those who having been sentenced once to prison for premeditated murder, murder again. In these particular cases we have evidence that imprisonment is not a sufficient deterrent for the individual in question. If the evidence shows that the prisoner is so psychologically constituted that, without being insane, the fact that he can kill again with impunity may lead to further murderous behavior, the court should have the discretionary power to pass the death sentence if the criminal is found guilty of a second murder.

In saying that the death sentence should be *discretionary* in cases where a man has killed more than once, I am *not* saying that a murderer who murders again is more deserving of death than the murderer who murders once. Bluebeard was not twelve times more deserving of death when he was finally caught. I am saying simply this: that in a sub-class of murderers, i.e., those who murder several times, there may be a special group of sane murderers who, knowing that they will not be executed, will not hesitate to kill again and again. For *them* the argument from deterrence is obviously valid. Those who say that there must be no exceptions to the abolition of capital punishment cannot rule out the existence of such cases on *a priori* grounds. If they admit that there is a reasonable probability that such murderers will murder again or attempt to murder again, a probability which usually grows with the number of repeated murders, and still insist they would *never* approve of capital punishment, I would conclude that they are indifferent to the lives of the human beings doomed, on their position, to be victims. What fancies itself as a humanitarian attitude is sometimes an expression of sentimentalism. The reverse coin of sentimentalism is often cruelty.

Our charity for all human beings must not deprive us of our common sense. Nor should our charity be less for the future or potential victims of the murderer than for the murderer himself. There are crimes in this world which are, like acts of nature, beyond the power of men to anticipate or control. But not all or most crimes are of this character. So long as human beings are responsible and educable, they will respond to praise and blame and punishment. It is hard to imagine it but even Hitler and Stalin were once infants. Once you *can* imagine them as infants, however, it is hard to believe that they were already monsters in their cradles. Every confirmed criminal was once an amateur. The existence of confirmed criminals testifies to the defects of our education—where they can be reformed—and of our penology—where they cannot. That is why we are under the moral obligation to be intelligent about crime and punishment. Intelligence should teach us that the best educational and penological system is the one which prevents crimes rather than punishes them; the next best is one which punishes crime in such a way as to prevent it from happening again.

IN FAVOR OF CAPITAL PUNISHMENT*

BY JACQUES BARZUN**

A passing remark of mine in the *Mid-Century* magazine has brought me a number of letters and a sheaf of pamphlets against capital punishment. The letters, sad and reproachful, offer me the choice of pleading ignorance or being proved insensitive. I am asked whether I know that there exists a worldwide movement for the abolition of capital punishment which has everywhere enlisted able men of every profession, including the law. I am told that the death penalty is not only inhuman but also unscientific, for rapists and murderers are really sick people who should be cured, not killed. I am invited to use my imagination and acknowledge the unbearable horror of every form of execution.

I am indeed aware that the movement for abolition is widespread and articulate, especially in England. It is headed there by my old friend and publisher, Mr. Victor Gollancz, and it numbers such well-known writers as Arthur Koestler, C. H. Rolph, James Avery Joyce and Sir John Barry. Abroad as at home the profession of psychiatry tends to support the cure principle, and many liberal newspapers, such as the *Observer*, are committed to abolition. In the United States there are at least twenty-five state leagues working to the same end, plus a national league and several church councils, notably the Quaker and the Episcopal.

The assemblage of so much talent and enlightened goodwill behind a single proposal must give pause to anyone who supports the other side, and in the attempt to make clear my views, which are now close to unpopular, I start

* Reprinted, by permission of author and publisher, from *The American Scholar*, vol. 31, no. 2 (Spring 1962), pp. 181–191. Copyright © 1962 by the United Chapters of Phi Beta Kappa.
** Dean of Faculties and Provost of Columbia University. Author of *The House of Intellect* (1959) and *Classic, Romantic and Modern* (1961).

out by granting that my conclusion is arguable; that is, I am still open to conviction, *provided* some fallacies and frivolities in the abolitionist argument are first disposed of and the difficulties not ignored but overcome. I should be glad to see this happen, not only because there is pleasure in the spectacle of an airtight case, but also because I am not more sanguinary than my neighbor and I should welcome the discovery of safeguards—for society *and* the criminal—other than killing. But I say it again, these safeguards must really meet, not evade or postpone, the difficulties I am about to describe. Let me add before I begin that I shall probably not answer any more letters on this arousing subject. If this printed exposition does not do justice to my cause, it is not likely that I can do better in the hurry of private correspondence.

I readily concede at the outset that present ways of dealing out capital punishment are as revolting as Mr. Koestler says in his harrowing volume, *Hanged by the Neck*. Like many of our prisons, our modes of execution should change. But this objection to barbarity does not mean that capital punishment—or rather, judicial homicide—should not go on. The illicit jump we find here, on the threshold of the inquiry, is characteristic of the abolitionist and must be disallowed at every point. Let us bear in mind the possibility of devising a painless, sudden and dignified death, and see whether its administration is justifiable.

The four main arguments advanced against the death penalty are: *1.* punishment for crime is a primitive idea rooted in revenge; *2.* capital punishment does not deter; *3.* judicial error being possible, taking life is an appalling risk; *4.* a civilized state, to deserve its name, must uphold, not violate, the sanctity of human life.

I entirely agree with the first pair of propositions, which is why, a moment ago, I replaced the term capital punishment with "judicial homicide." The uncontrollable brute whom I want put out of the way is not to be punished for his misdeeds, nor used as an example or a warning; he is to be killed for the protection of others, like the wolf that escaped not long ago in a Connecticut suburb. No anger, vindictiveness or moral conceit need preside over the removal of such dangers. But a man's inability to control his violent impulses or to imagine the fatal consequences of his acts should be a presumptive reason for his elimination from society. This generality covers drunken driving and teen-age racing on public highways, as well as incurable obsessive violence; it might be extended (as I shall suggest later) to other acts that destroy, precisely, the moral basis of civilization.

But why kill? I am ready to believe the statistics tending to show that the prospect of his own death does not stop the murderer. For one thing he is often a blind egotist, who cannot conceive the possibility of his own death. For another, detection would have to be infallible to deter the more imaginative who, although afraid, think they can escape discovery. Lastly, as Shaw long ago pointed out, hanging the wrong man will deter as effectively as hanging the right one. So, once again, why kill? If I agree that moral progress means an increasing respect for human life, how can I oppose abolition?

I do so because on this subject of human life, which is to me the heart of the controversy, I find the abolitionist inconsistent, narrow or blind. The propaganda for abolition speaks in hushed tones of the sanctity of human life, as if the mere statement of it as an absolute should silence all opponents who have any moral sense. But most of the abolitionists belong to nations that spend half their annual income on weapons of war and that honor research to perfect means of killing. These good people vote without a qualm for the political parties that quite sensibly arm their country to the teeth. The West today does not seem to be the time or place to invoke the absolute sanctity of human life. As for the clergymen in the movement, we may be sure from the experience of two previous world wars that they will bless our arms and pray for victory when called upon, the sixth commandment notwithstanding.

"Oh, but we mean the sanctity of life *within* the nation!" Very well: is the movement then campaigning also against the principle of self-defense? Absolute sanctity means letting the cutthroat have his sweet will of you, even if you have a poker handy to bash him with, for you might kill.

And again, do we hear any protest against the police firing at criminals on the street—mere bank robbers usually—and doing this, often enough, with an excited marksmanship that misses the artist and hits the bystander? The absolute sanctity of human life is, for the abolitionist, a slogan rather than a considered proposition.

Yet it deserves examination, for upon our acceptance or rejection of it depend such other highly civilized possibilities as euthanasia and seemly suicide. The inquiring mind also wants to know, why the sanctity of *human* life alone? My tastes do not run to household pets, but I find something less than admirable in the uses to which we put animals—in zoos, laboratories and space machines—without the excuse of the ancient law, "Eat or be eaten."

It should moreover be borne in mind that this argument about sanctity applies—or would apply—to about ten persons a year in Great Britain and to between fifty and seventy-five in the United States. These are the average numbers of those executed in recent years. The count by itself should not, of course, affect our judgment of the principle: one life spared or forfeited is as important, morally, as a hundred thousand. But it should inspire a comparative judgment: there are hundreds and indeed thousands whom, in our concern with the horrors of execution, we forget: on the one hand, the victims of violence; on the other, the prisoners in our jails.

The victims are easy to forget. Social science tends steadily to mark a preference for the troubled, the abnormal, the problem case. Whether it is poverty, mental disorder, delinquency or crime, the "patient material" monopolizes the interest of increasing groups of people among the most generous and learned. Psychiatry and moral liberalism go together; the application of law as we have known it is thus coming to be regarded as an historic prelude to social work, which may replace it entirely. Modern literature makes the most of this same outlook, caring only for the disturbed spirit, scorning as bourgeois those who pay their way and do *not* stab their friends. All the while the determinism of natural science reinforces the assumption that society causes its own evils. A French jurist, for example, says that in order to understand crime we must first brush aside all ideas of Responsibility. He means the criminal's and takes for granted that of society. The murderer kills because reared in a broken home or, conversely, because at an early age he witnessed his parents making love. Out of such cases, which make pathetic reading in the literature of modern criminology, is born the abolitionist's state of mind: we dare not kill those we are beginning to understand so well.

If, moreover, we turn to the accounts of the crimes committed by these unfortunates, who are the victims? Only dull ordinary people going about their business. We are sorry, of course, but they do not interest science on its march. Balancing, for example, the sixty to seventy criminals executed annually in the United States, there were the seventy to eighty housewives whom George Cvek robbed, raped and usually killed during the months of a career devoted to proving his virility. "It is too bad." Cvek alone seems instructive, even though one of the law officers who helped track him down quietly remarks: "As to the extent that his villainies disturbed family relationships, or how many women are still haunted by the specter of an experience they have never disclosed to another living soul, these questions can only lend themselves to sterile conjecture."

The remote results are beyond our ken, but it is not idle to speculate about those whose death by violence fills the daily two inches at the back of respectable newspapers— the old man sunning himself on a park bench and beaten to death by four hoodlums, the small children abused and strangled, the middle-aged ladies on a hike assaulted and killed, the family terrorized by a released or escaped lunatic, the half-dozen working people massacred by the sudden maniac, the boatload of persons dispatched by the skipper, the mindless assaults upon schoolteachers and shopkeepers by the increasing horde of dedicated killers in our great cities. Where does the sanctity of life begin?

It is all very well to say that many of these killers are themselves "children," that is, minors. Doubtless a nine-year-old mind is housed in that 150 pounds of unguided muscle. Grant, for argument's sake, that the misdeed is "the fault of society," trot out the broken home and the slum environment. The question then is, What shall we do, not in the Utopian city of tomorrow, but here and now? The "scientific" means of cure are more than uncertain. The apparatus of detention only increases the killer's anti-social animus. Reformatories and mental hospitals are full and have an understandable bias toward discharging their inmates. Some of these are indeed "cured"—so long as they stay under a rule. The stress of the social free-for-all throws them back on their violent modes of self-expression. At that point I agree that society has failed—twice: it has twice failed the victims, whatever may be its guilt toward the killer.

As in all great questions, the moralist must choose, and choosing has a price. I happen to think that if a person of adult body has not been endowed with adequate controls against irrationally taking the life of another, that person must be judicially, painlessly, regretfully killed before that mindless body's horrible automation repeats.

I say "irrationally" taking life, because it is often possible to feel great sympathy with a murderer. Certain *crimes passionnels* can be forgiven without being condoned. Black-mailers invite direct retribution. Long provocation can be an excuse, as in that engaging case of some years ago, in which a respectable carpenter of seventy found he could no longer stand the incessant nagging of his wife. While she excoriated him from her throne in the kitchen—a daily exercise for fifty years—the husband went to his bench and came back with a hammer in each hand to settle the score. The testimony to his character, coupled with the sincerity implied by the two hammers, was enough to have him sent into quiet and brief seclusion.

But what are we to say of the type of motive disclosed in a journal published by the inmates of one of our Federal penitentiaries? The author is a bank robber who confesses that money is not his object:

My mania for power, socially, sexually, and otherwise can feel no degree of satisfaction until I feel sure I have struck the ultimate of submission and terror in the minds and bodies of my victims. . . . It's very difficult to explain all the queer fascinating sensations pounding and surging through me while I'm holding a gun on a victim, watching his body tremble and sweat. . . . This is the moment when all the rationalized hypocrisies of civilization are suddenly swept away and two men stand there facing each other morally and ethically naked, and right and wrong are the absolute commands of the man behind the gun.

This confused echo of modern literature and modern science defines the choice before us. Anything deserving the name of cure for such a man presupposes not only a laborious individual psychoanalysis, with the means to conduct and to sustain it, socially and economically, but also a re-education of the mind, so as to throw into correct perspective the garbled ideas of Freud and Nietzsche, Gide and Dostoevski, which this power-seeker and his fellows have derived from the culture and temper of our times. Ideas are tenacious and give continuity to emotion. Failing a second birth of heart and mind, we must ask: How soon will this sufferer sacrifice a bank clerk in the interests of making civilization less hypocritical? And we must certainly question the wisdom of affording him more than one chance. The abolitionists' advocacy of an unconditional "let live" is in truth part of the same cultural tendency that animates the killer. The Western peoples' revulsion from power in domestic and foreign policy has made of the state a sort of counterpart of the bank robber: both having power and neither knowing how to use it. Both waste lives because hypnotized by irrelevant ideas and crippled by contradictory emotions. If psychiatry were sure of its ground in diagnosing the individual case, a philosopher might consider whether such dangerous obsessions should not be guarded against by judicial homicide *before* the shooting starts.

I raise the question not indeed to recommend the prophylactic execution of potential murderers, but to introduce the last two perplexities that the abolitionists dwarf or obscure by their concentration on changing an isolated penalty. One of these is the scale by which to judge the offenses society wants to repress. I can for example imagine a truly democratic state in which it would be deemed a form of treason punishable by death to create a disturbance in any court or deliberative assembly. The aim would be to recognize the sanctity of orderly discourse in arriving at justice, assessing criticism and defining policy. Under such a law, a natural selection would operate to remove permanently from the scene persons who, let us say, neglect argument in favor of banging on the desk with their shoe. Similarly, a bullying minority in a diet, parliament or skupshtina would be prosecuted for treason to the most sacred institutions when fists or flying inkwells replace rhetoric. That the mere suggestion of such a law sounds ludicrous shows how remote we are from civilized institutions, and hence how gradual should be our departure from the severity of judicial homicide.

I say gradual and I do not mean standing still. For there is one form of barbarity in our law that I want to see mitigated before any other. I mean imprisonment. The enemies of capital punishment—and liberals generally—seem to be satisfied with any legal outcome so long as they themselves avoid the vicarious guilt of shedding blood. They speak of the sanctity of life, but have no concern with its quality. They give no impression of ever having read what it is certain they have read, from Wilde's *De Profundis* to the latest account of prison life by a convicted homosexual. Despite the infamy of concentration camps, despite Mr. Charles Burney's remarkable work, *Solitary Confinement,* despite riots in prisons, despite the round of escape, recapture and return in chains, the abolitionists' imagination tells them nothing about the reality of being caged. They read without a qualm, indeed they read with rejoicing, the hideous irony of "Killer Gets Life"; they sigh with relief instead of horror. They do not see and suffer the cell, the drill, the clothes, the stench, the food; they do not feel the sexual racking of young and old bodies, the hateful promiscuity, the insane monotony, the mass degradation, the impotent hatred. They do not remember from Silvio Pellico that only a strong political faith, with a hope of final victory, can steel a man to endure long detention. They forget that Joan of Arc, when offered "life," preferred burning at the stake. Quite of another mind, the abolitionists point with pride to the "model prisoners" that murderers often turn out to be. As if a model prisoner were not, first, a contradiction in terms, and second, an exemplar of what a free society should not want.

I said a moment ago that the happy advocates of the life sentence appear not to have understood what we know they have read. No more do they appear to read what they themselves write. In the preface to his useful volume of cases, *Hanged in Error,* Mr. Leslie Hale, M.P., refers to the tardy recognition of a minor miscarriage of justice—one year in jail: "The prisoner emerged to find that his wife had died and that his children and his aged parents had been removed to the workhouse. By the time a small payment had been assessed as 'compensation' the victim was incurably insane." So far we are as indignant with the law as Mr. Hale. But what comes next? He cites the famous Evans case, in which it is very probable that the wrong man was hanged, and he exclaims: "While such mistakes are possible, should society impose an irrevocable sentence?" Does Mr. Hale really ask us to believe that the sentence passed on the first man, whose wife died and who went insane, was in any sense *revocable?* Would not any man rather be Evans dead than that other wretch "emerging" with his small compensation and his reasons for living gone?

Nothing is revocable here below, imprisonment least of all. The agony of a trial itself is punishment, and acquittal wipes out nothing. Read the heart-rending diary of William Wallace, accused quite implausibly of having murdered his wife and "saved" by the Court of Criminal Appeals—but saved for what? Brutish ostracism by everyone and a few years of solitary despair. The cases of Adolf Beck, of Oscar Slater, of the unhappy Brooklyn bank teller who vaguely resembled a forger and spent eight years in Sing Sing only to "emerge" a broken, friendless, useless, "compensated" man—all these, if the dignity of the individual has any meaning, had better have been dead before the prison door ever opened for them. This is what counsel always says to the jury in the course of a murder trial and counsel is right: far better hang this man than "give him life." For my part, I would choose death without hesitation. If that option is abolished, a demand will one day be heard to claim it as a privilege in the name of human dignity. I shall believe in the abolitionist's present views only after he has emerged from twelve months in a convict cell.

The detached observer may want to interrupt here and say that the argument has now passed from reasoning to emotional preference. Whereas the objector to capital punishment *feels* that death is the greatest of evils, I *feel* that imprisonment is worse than death. A moment's thought will show that feeling is the appropriate arbiter. All reasoning about what is right, civilized and moral rests upon sentiment, like mathematics. Only, in trying to persuade others, it is important to single out the fundamental feeling, the prime intuition, and from it to reason justly. In my view, to profess respect for human life and be willing to see it spent in a penitentiary is to entertain liberal feelings frivolously. To oppose the death penalty because, unlike a prison term, it is irrevocable is to argue fallaciously.

In the propaganda for abolishing the death sentence the recital of numerous miscarriages of justice commits the same error and implies the same callousness: what is at fault in our present system is not the sentence but the fallible procedure. Capital cases being one in a thousand or more, who can be cheerful at the thought of all the "revocable" errors? What the miscarriages point to is the need for reforming the jury system, the rules of evidence, the customs of prosecution, the machinery of appeal. The failure to see that this is the great task reflects the sentimentality I spoke of earlier, that which responds chiefly to the excitement of the unusual. A writer on Death and the Supreme Court is at pains to point out that when that tribunal reviews a capital case, the judges are particularly anxious and careful. What a left-handed compliment to the highest judicial conscience of the country! Fortunately, some of the champions of the misjudged see the issue more clearly. Many of those who are thought wrongly convicted now languish in jail because the jury was uncertain or because a doubting governor commuted the death sentence. Thus Dr. Samuel H. Sheppard, Jr., convicted of his wife's murder in the second degree is serving a sentence that is supposed to run for the term of his natural life. The story of his numerous trials, as told by Mr. Paul Holmes, suggests that police incompetence, newspaper demagogy, public envy of affluence and the mischances of legal procedure fashioned the result. But Dr. Sheppard's vindicator is under no illusion as to the conditions that this "lucky" evader of the electric chair will face if he is granted parole after ten years: "It will carry with it no right to resume his life as a physician. His privilege to practice medicine was blotted out with his conviction. He must all his life bear the stigma of a parolee, subject to unceremonious return to confinement for life for the slightest misstep. More than this, he must live out his life as a convicted murderer."

What does the moral conscience of today think it is doing? If such a man is a dangerous repeater of violent acts, what right has the state to let him loose after ten years? What is, in fact, the meaning of a "life sentence" that peters out long before life? Paroling looks suspiciously like an expression of social remorse for the pain of incarceration, coupled with a wish to avoid "unfavorable publicity" by freeing a suspect. The man is let out when the fuss has died down; which would mean that he was not under lock and key for our protection at all. He *was* being punished, just a little—for so prison seems in the abolitionist's distorted view, and in the jury's and the prosecutor's, whose "second degree" murder suggests killing someone "just a little."[1]

If, on the other hand, execution and life imprisonment are judged too severe and the accused is expected to be harmless hereafter—punishment being ruled out as illiberal

[1] The British Homicide Act of 1957, Section 2, implies the same reasoning in its definition of "diminished responsibility" for certain forms of mental abnormality. The whole question of irrationality and crime is in utter confusion, on both sides of the Atlantic.

—what has society gained by wrecking his life and damaging that of his family?

What we accept, and what the abolitionist will clamp upon us all the more firmly if he succeeds, is an incoherence which is not remedied by the belief that second degree murder merits a kind of second degree death; that a doubt as to the identity of a killer is resolved by commuting real death into intolerable life; and that our ignorance whether a maniac will strike again can be hedged against by measuring "good behavior" within the gates and then releasing the subject upon the public in the true spirit of experimentation.

These are some of the thoughts I find I cannot escape when I read and reflect upon this grave subject. If, as I think, they are relevant to any discussion of change and reform, resting as they do on the direct and concrete perception of what happens, then the simple meliorists who expect to breathe a purer air by abolishing the death penalty are deceiving themselves and us. The issue is for the public to judge; but I for one shall not sleep easier for knowing that in England and America and the West generally a hundred more human beings are kept alive in degrading conditions to face a hopeless future; while others—possibly less conscious, certainly less controlled—benefit from a premature freedom dangerous alike to themselves and society. In short, I derive no comfort from the illusion that in giving up one manifest protection of the law-abiding, we who might well be in any of these three roles—victim, prisoner, licensed killer—have struck a blow for the sanctity of human life.

Chapter Four

THE ARGUMENT AGAINST THE DEATH PENALTY

INTRODUCTION

Does the Bible, or at least the Old Testament, obligate Jews and Christians to support the death penalty, as Reverend Vellenga and others have argued? What is the authoritative theological and historical interpretation of the Noahic commandment of Genesis 9:6, and of the *lex talionis*—"eye for eye, tooth for tooth, . . . life for life" (Exodus 21:23–24)? Whether or not one believes that sound contemporary social policies can be inferred directly from ancient religious texts, it is necessary to study these questions to understand the full range of current debate on capital punishment. Two of the following selections, by representative Protestant and Jewish theologians, should be of assistance here.

The excerpt from Rabbi Kazis reprinted below casts a different light on some of these issues than that suggested in the previous chapter by Reverend Vellenga. Rabbi Kazis has remarked elsewhere,

> In seeking to ascertain what Judaism has to say on a certain subject it is imperative to study not only what the Bible provides but also the Rabbinic interpretation of the Biblical provisions . . . One cannot go by the Bible alone with reference to the law of retaliation. It must be remembered . . . that it was the Rabbinic interpretation of the Biblical Law which became the law in the Jewish religious tradition.[1]

The effect of heeding this admonition is a significant humanization of the retributive ordinances in the early books of the Bible.

[1] Quoted by permission of Rabbi Kazis from the extension of his remarks, in reply to Rt. Rev. Thomas Riley, delivered before the Massachusetts Special Commission Investigating the Death Penalty, 1958.

But what sort of positive argument do Jewish and Christian theologians direct against the death penalty? No one supposes that either the Biblical or the Rabbinic traditions contains an explicit prohibition of killing as a punishment. How much, then, must one rely on humanitarian convictions and scientifically grounded hypotheses from sociology and psychology to eke out the strictly theological materials? Some have defended the death penalty on religious grounds without taking into account whether murderers could be rehabilitated, terrible risks of injustice reduced, and the public deterred in some other equally effective way. Similarly, there have been those whose religious principles apparently allowed them to oppose the death penalty without having to consider the social consequences of their stand. The selection below from Reverend Charles Milligan shows that his opposition to the death penalty is not given so unconditionally. The way his analysis interweaves theological and sociological considerations is fairly typical. Most of the many essays by Jewish and Christian theologians and all the resolutions adopted by churches and their spokesmen against the death penalty show that on this social issue, purely theological conceptions are usually supplemented with empirical hypotheses. For example, in 1958, the Central Conference of American Rabbis released the following statement:

> The question of capital punishment is now under official study in several states. The Central Conference of American Rabbis urges the abolition of the death penalty where it is still in effect. We are convinced that it does not act as an effective deterrent to crime.[2]

Two years later, the American Baptist Convention adopted the following resolution:

> Because the Christian believes in the inherent worth of human personality and in the unceasing availability of God's mercy, forgiveness, and redemptive power, and

[2] Quoted in Friends' Conference on Crime and the Treatment of Offenders, *What Do the Churches Say on Capital Punishment?* (1961), p. 24.

Because the Christian wholeheartedly supports the emphasis in modern penology upon the process of creative, redemptive rehabilitation rather than on punitive and primitive retribution, and

Because the deterrent effects of capital punishment are not supported by available evidence, and

Because the death penalty tends to brutalize the human spirit and the society which condones it, and

Because human agencies of legal justice are fallible, permitting the possibility of the executing of the innocent,

We, therefore, recommend the abolition of capital punishment and the re-evaluation of the parole system relative to such cases.[3]

These two statements against capital punishment are typical of those issued during the past decade by Jewish and Protestant churches and by their theologians.[4]

The position of the Roman Catholic theologian or layman who favors abolition is somewhat more complex. There is, to date, no official Roman Catholic position on the issue of capital punishment. The most recent papal pronouncement on penology, by the late Pius XII, "Crime and Punishment" (1954), avoids any direct discussion of this controversial question. Nor have the Roman Catholic Bishops, or any other national Catholic organization in this country, taken a stand on this question, as they have on other policy issues of the day. *L'Osservatore Romano,* the official Vatican newspaper, protested the Rosenberg and

[3] *Ibid.,* pp. 2–3. The full text of several dozen similar statements in recent years from church groups is available in this pamphlet. For a partial list of these groups, see the article below by Sara Ehrmann, note 52. A few churches have commissioned pamphlets explaining their opposition to the death penalty. See Ruth Leigh, *Man's Right to Life* (1960); Trevor Thomas, *This Life We Take* (1959); John Howard Yoder, *The Christian and Capital Punishment* (1961); and Richard Werkheiser and Arthur Barnhart, *Capital Punishment* (1961).

[4] For abolitionist arguments in which extra-doctrinal considerations play only a small part, see in particular Karl Herz, "Let Justice Serve the Law of Love," *The Lutheran* (March 23, 1960), and Yoder, *ibid.*

Chessman executions, but it is doubtful whether the paper maintains an editorial policy against the death penalty as such. No more than a handful of Roman Catholic diocesan newspapers in this country have taken such a stand, either. Nevertheless, Reverend J. D. Conway, in *The Catholic Digest*, has argued that "the Church is naturally inclined, by history, doctrine, spirit and example, to favor abolition of the death penalty in our modern society."[5]

The remaining articles in this chapter present a predominantly secular outlook in favor of ending the death penalty. It has been argued, though without much persuasion, that the campaign to abolish the death penalty today is based on theories acceptable only to socialists, atheists and other irreligious radicals.[6] It is true that two hundred years ago, many of the most outspoken opponents of the death penalty were free thinkers, and that a century ago the most vigorous defenders of the gallows were fundamentalist Protestant clergymen. But today no such ideological cleavages exist. Just as few clerics attempt to attack the death penalty unless armed with supporting sociological evidence, few secular thinkers strip their argument against capital punishment of every appeal to religious doctrine and belief.

The article below by Dean Donal MacNamara illustrates this, and it is an example of the best kind of comprehensive statement against the death penalty tendered to the legislatures during the past few years. In his capacity as President of the American League to Abolish Capital Punishment,[7] Dean MacNamara has personally delivered similar statements before a Congressional and several state

[5] J. D. Conway, "What Would You Like to Know About the Church? How She Feels About Capital Punishment?" *The Catholic Digest* (May 1959), p. 122. For criticism of the death penalty by other Roman Catholics, see Donald Campion, "Should Men Hang?" *America* (December 5, 1959); Robert Hovda, "The Death Penalty," *Commonweal* (July 17, 1959); and J. D. Nicola, "The Case Against the Death Penalty," *Information* (June 1959).

[6] See E. L. H. Taylor, "Secular Revolution in Christian Disguise," *Canadian Bar Journal* (August 1958).

[7] See Note, "MacNamara Heads Foes of Death Penalty," *Journal of Criminal Law, Criminology and Police Science* (May–June 1959).

legislative committees charged with investigating the abolition of capital punishment.

The essay by Mr. Gerald Gottlieb is unusual in the literature against the death penalty in that it mounts a purely
constitutional argument for abolition. Our nation was
founded on the notion that there are constitutional boundaries arising from the inherent rights of a free people
against certain forms of state action. Among these limitations is the notion, embodied in the Eighth Amendment to
the federal Constitution, that there shall be "no cruel and
unusual punishments." It has occurred to more than one
lawyer since Jefferson that if anything is "cruel and unusual," it is the death penalty. But Mr. Gottlieb is the first
to spell out an entire argument organized around this point.
It remains to be seen whether his criticism of capital punishment will take the form of a courtroom plea or an appellate brief in an actual criminal case.

One obstacle preventing many persons from opposing the
death penalty is their uncertainty about the alternative.
Should the punishment of death be replaced by literal life
imprisonment? Or should the possibility of parole for all
convicts at least be theoretically envisaged? Difficulties of a
different sort may arise from the failure to distinguish between capital punishment, which is the state's right to kill
persons for the crimes they have committed, and laws that
would give to the state the right to kill criminals in the name
of mercy, or in the name of eugenics. I have concluded
this chapter with an essay in which I attempt to formulate
an acceptable alternative to the death penalty and to draw
the above distinctions. Both are needed, especially if we are
to understand (and rebut) the arguments of Professors
Barzun and Hook in the previous chapter.[8]

[8] Besides the books and articles opposing the death penalty
which are listed in the notes above, the following also deserve
special mention: Curtis Bok, *Star Wormwood* (1959); Fred
Cook, "Capital Punishment," *The Nation* (March 10, 1956);
Clinton Duffy, *88 Men and 2 Women* (1962); Herbert Hart,
"Murder and the Principles of Punishment," *Northwestern
University Law Review* (September–October 1957); Giles Play-
fair and Derrick Sington, *The Offenders* (1957); and William
Styron, "The Death-in-Life of Benjamin Reid," *Esquire* (Feb-

JUDAISM AND THE DEATH PENALTY*

BY ISRAEL J. KAZIS**

In order to understand the Jewish attitude toward capital punishment it is not sufficient to consult the Old Testament on this subject. It is necessary also to consult the Mishnah and the Gemara, which represent the codes of Jewish law compiled after the completion of the Bible. This is necessary because Jewish law was not static. It was dynamic and developmental, undergoing modifications through the centuries in terms of the requirements of different periods and places. This legal evolution had to proceed within a given framework; namely, that Biblical law, because it was divinely revealed, could not be abrogated. Consequently the Rabbis had to resort to legal techniques, which, while not abrogating the law technically, nevertheless made it practically unenforceable. The following two examples will illustrate this procedure:

The Prosbul. According to Biblical law all debts were canceled in the Sabbatical or seventh year (Deut. 15:1–3). Hillel, who lived during the first century, B.C.E., saw that this Biblical law worked a hardship on the commercial economy of his time. Those who had money refused to lend it to those who needed money because these loans would be forfeited in the Sabbatical year. Consequently, Hillel introduced an enactment whereby the creditor could turn over the promissory note to the court which in turn would collect the debts from the debtors. While this enactment did not technically abrogate the Biblical law, inasmuch as the creditor himself did not do the collecting of the debt, it did make the Biblical law unenforceable because, by this en-

ruary 1962), and "Aftermath of Benjamin Reid," *Esquire* (November 1962).

* Reprinted, with permission of the author and publisher, from Ruth Leigh, *Man's Right to Life* (1959), pp. 31–36, one of the pamphlet series, "Issues of Conscience," issued by the Commission on Social Action of Reform Judaism. © 1959 by the Union of American Hebrew Congregations.

** Rabbi, Temple Mishkan Tefila, Newton, Massachusetts.

actment, debts were not canceled in the seventh year. (See the *Jewish Encyclopedia*, Vol. 10, pp. 219–220)

The Law of Retaliation. The Bible provides for "an eye for an eye, a tooth for a tooth" (Lev. 24:20), etc. This law of retaliation was interpreted by the Rabbis in terms of monetary compensation for damages, and hence, physical retaliation was unenforceable.

Capital Punishment. The Bible prescribes capital punishment for fifteen different crimes (see the *Jewish Encyclopedia*, Vol. 3, pp. 554–558). However, an investigation of the many provisions and restrictions instituted by the Rabbis in the Mishnah and the Gemara in cases involving capital punishment will show that it became virtually impossible to enforce the death penalty.

Some of these provisions and regulations are:

1. Cases involving capital punishment had to be tried before a court of twenty-three qualified members.

2. Trustworthy testimony had to be presented by two qualified *eye-witnesses*. This requirement was most difficult to meet because the commission of such crimes is not usually attended by so much publicity.

3. Circumstantial evidence was not admitted. The Talmud gives the following example: "I saw a man chasing another into a ruin; I ran after him and saw a sword in his hand dripping with the other's blood and the murdered man in his death agony. I said to him, You villain! Who killed this man? Either I or you. But what can I do? Your life is not delivered into my hand, for the law says, at the mouth of two witnesses shall he that is to die be put to death." (Sanhedrin 37b)

4. The testimony of those related by blood or marriage is not admissible.

5. Men who were presumed to be lacking in compassion were not to be appointed to the court of twenty-three. In this regard the Talmud says: "We do not appoint to a Sanhedrin (court) an old man, a eunuch and a childless man." R. Judah adds, "One who is hard-hearted." (Sanhedrin 36b)

6. Witnesses were warned not to testify to anything that

was based on their own inference, or that they know only second-hand.

7. Witnesses were interrogated separately about the exact time, place, and persons involved in the crime. If any material discrepancy was discovered in their testimony, the accused was acquitted.

8. Witnesses were asked whether they had warned the accused that he was about to commit a crime for which the penalty was death. Such warning was required.

9. The accused was presumed to be innocent until proven guilty, and every reasonable effort was made in the cross-examination to bring out grounds for finding for the accused.

10. In order to prevent witnesses from conspiring to place the guilt on the accused, they were warned that if they testified falsely they would be liable to the same penalty which the accused would suffer if he were convicted on the basis of their testimony.

11. The contrast between procedures in civil cases and criminal cases as shown in the following provisions indicates the kind of restrictions that were imposed upon the deliberations of the court in cases involving criminal offenses:

A. In civil cases a majority of one was sufficient to find for the defendant or the plaintiff. In criminal cases a majority of one was sufficient to find for the accused, but a majority of two was needed to find against the accused.

B. In civil cases the judges could change their judgment in favor of either party. In criminal cases they could reverse their judgment in order to find *for* but not *against* the convict.

C. In civil cases all the judges could argue for either party. In criminal cases they could all argue to find *for* but not *against* the accused.

D. In civil cases a judge who argued against one party could later argue for the other, and vice versa. In criminal cases a judge who argued to convict could later argue to acquit but not vice versa.

E. In civil cases the opinions of the senior judges were expressed first. In criminal cases the opinions of the junior judges were expressed first to prevent them from being influenced by the opinion of their seniors. (For the procedure at the trial, see A. Cohen, *Everyman's Talmud*, N.Y., 1949, pp. 310 ff.)

12. If the accused was found guilty and was being led to the place of execution, there still was a provision on his behalf. As he was led to the place of execution a herald preceded him, calling out his name, his crime, when and where it was committed, and the names of those upon the basis of whose testimony he was condemned. The herald proclaimed that anyone who possesses any evidence favorable to the condemned should hasten to produce it. Should such evidence be forthcoming or should the condemned man declare that he can prove his innocence a stay of execution was granted. If the convict's testimony proved to be ineffective, he was still allowed to make another attempt at proving himself innocent, since two scholars walked along with him for the purpose of judging whether any further testimony that he might offer would justify a delay in execution.

13. If the accused was acquitted he could not be placed in jeopardy a second time regardless of what new evidence might be forthcoming.

It is quite clear that the many restrictions and provisions imposed by the Rabbis made it very difficult to inflict capital punishment. George Foot Moore, an eminent authority on Judaism, wrote in this connection: "It is clear that with such a procedure conviction in capital cases was next to impossible, and that this was the intention of the framers of the rules is equally plain." (See George Foot Moore, *Judaism,* Harvard University Press, 1927, Vol. II, p. 186.) The sentiment against capital punishment is expressed in the Mishnah in an opinion which maintains that a court which executes one man in seven years is a destructive one. R. Eleazar ben Azariah maintained that a court is destructive if it executes one man in seventy years. R. Tarfon and R. Akiba said, "If we had been in the Sanhedrin, no man would ever have been put to death." (Mishnah Makkot 1, 10)

From our discussion of the provisions and restrictions

imposed by the Rabbis upon the procedure in the trial of capital cases, we believe that it is reasonable to maintain that they did not look with favor upon capital punishment.

A PROTESTANT'S VIEW OF
THE DEATH PENALTY*

BY CHARLES S. MILLIGAN**

There is great diversity in the thinking of Christians on the question of capital punishment. Among the views commonly encountered among us are the following: (1) that capital punishment should be abolished as soon as possible; (2) that abolition is right, but not very important; (3) that abolition may be the Christian position, but in a world of evil men we cannot as a practical matter afford it; (4) that the death penalty is right and necessary from a Christian point of view; (5) that the state has the theoretic right to execute men, but it is seldom desirable to carry out execution.

This last view is a typical Roman Catholic position. The Vatican State retains the death penalty but no longer carries out executions; indeed the Pope frequently appeals for clemency elsewhere. This is quite different from the view (No. 4) that the death penalty ought to be carried out even more frequently, which is found occasionally in fundamentalist publications.

Most Protestant church bodies have called for abolition of capital punishment (No. 1). This is also the view usually supported by individual Roman Catholics writing on the subject, and is generally the official view of Jewish organizations. However, it is important to recognize that all the above viewpoints will be found among thoughtful and conscientious Christians of every denomination. Evidently we need to clarify our thinking about a Christian approach to this question.

* Reprinted, with some additions and revisions, by permission of the author and publisher, from "Capital Punishment: A Christian Approach," *Social Action* (April 1961), pp. 16–22. Copyright 1961 by the Council for Christian Social Action, United Church of Christ.
** Professor of Christian Ethics, Iliff School of Theology.

Several Old Testament passages call for the death penalty. In Exodus the following are capital crimes: murder, striking or cursing one's parent, slave procurement, fatal attack by an ox, witchcraft, sodomy, and sacrifice to any god other than Jahweh. To these Leviticus adds adultery. Deuteronomy holds responsible both parties involved in criminal assault in the city, a rebellious son, and an unchaste bride.[1] The remarkable thing is that punishment by death is as rare as it is and that there are so many restraints placed upon it, as if to curb its wanton use. Nevertheless, if the Bible is used legalistically to support capital punishment, only the crimes specifically listed would be punished with death, and all of them would be under that requirement. Also, where the method of execution is specified—usually stoning—that would be required. If we are going to proceed on an absolutized proof-text method, there is no way to underscore one verse and erase the next.

There are other difficulties involved for those who use selected Old Testament texts to justify capital punishment today. If these texts are legislatively binding on us, on what basis do we reject equally clear rules against wearing wool and linen at the same time (Deut. 22:11), requiring a man to have children by his brother's widow (Deut. 25:5), and setting forth innumerable food requirements and taboos? There are many other passages in the Old Testament that ought to caution against elevating the rules cited into a universal approval of capital punishment for all time. For example, "if any one slays Cain, vengeance shall be taken on him sevenfold" (Gen. 4:15). The strictly legalistic application of selected laws in the Old Testament is a tragic misuse of the Bible, as the Salem execution of witches, based upon Exodus 22:18, should remind us.

The New Testament nowhere deals explicitly with this subject. There are, however, three events that relate to it. One is that of the woman taken in adultery, whose guilt was not questioned, and who should have been executed according to a legalistic application of the law. It is of interest not only that Jesus brought about her release, but

[1] Ex. 21:12–29, 22:18–20; Lev. 20:10; Deut. 22:24, 21:21, 22:21.

that the legalists threw him into the situation to entrap him. There would have been no point in questioning Jesus about the execution had he not impressed them as the sort of person who might disapprove of capital punishment (John 8:1–11). A second event is Paul's effort to save the life of the escaped slave, Onesimus, who under Roman law was liable to execution (Philemon). The third event is the crucifixion: the supreme case in which malice, cruelty, and injustice combined forces so that even those who found no crime in this man participated in and gave consent to his execution.

It is a sad thing that it is necessary to go into such elemental matters, but one runs into such distorted arguments seriously proposed: for instance, that had there been no capital punishment there would have been no crucifixion or salvation. But bribery, betrayal, and mob justice figured also in the crucifixion. Shall we urge continuance of these practices by the strange logic which thus justifies capital punishment? That God can and does redeem evil does not mean that men should deliberately pursue evil and perpetuate its instruments.

What we are called upon to do is to strive for that mind which was in Christ Jesus and to bring it to bear upon the issues of our time. The New Testament gives much guidance in this; but, far more than a set of answers, it gives us a burden of concerns. It is our responsibility to find the ways and means to love God with our whole being and our neighbor as ourselves. The issue of slavery will serve as a clarifying illustration. By the proof-text method there is no direct biblical warrant for the abolition of slavery. Numerous passages assume the propriety of slavery. Yet it is clear to us that when we take the Bible as a whole and strive to walk by the Spirit, slavery is unjust and evil. It is an interesting academic question whether slavery was necessary in 1000 B.C., but Christians did not begin to be fully Christian on that issue until they began to ask whether it was right in their own time and place. So with capital punishment. We should not approach these issues by asking what this or that verse says, but by bringing an enlightened and compassionate conscience to the issues. It is not what

the Bible says in a *specific verse,* but what it says to us
through its total message, interpreted in terms of our own
conditions, that is relevant.

It may be of interest to Christians to note that Jews in
modern times do not hold to the blood vengeance principle
of Genesis 6:9 in a literal way. The ancient belief seems to
have been that innocent blood contaminates the land, which
can be cleansed only by more blood (Deut. 21:1–9). This
has been reinterpreted and symbolically explained by rabbinic tradition. It may be argued that views advanced
within Judaism have no bearing on what Christians are to
think, but it is curious to find some Christians more firmly
attached to Old Testament vengeance passages than Jews,
when supposedly the Christian's New Testament is claimed
to have brought freedom from "bondage" to laws of vengeance and retribution. It remains that Christians who use
the Bible most literally and who most stress "the blood of
Christ" have not characteristically held that the blood of
Christ cancels the blood vengeance principle. (See He-
brews 9:18–22) It is, from their view, a *new* covenant only
in cancelling blood sacrifices, but not blood vengeance. It
appears that such a view stems not from biblical study but
from social convictions derived from other sources, which
hide behind selected Bible verses, views that seem to exercise selective inattention when they encounter such clear
statements as: "Render to no man evil for evil. . . .
avenge not yourselves." (Romans 12:17–19)

To take a Christian approach we must find out what the
situation is. This amounts to saying that the good Samari-
tan must use his eyes and his head as well as have compassion. He must see what is wrong and use his best reasoning to deal helpfully and effectively with the problem,
using the means available. As Reinhold Niebuhr says:

A community may believe, as it usually does, that reverence for life is a basic moral attitude, and yet rob a
criminal of his life in order to deter others from taking
life. It may be wrong in doing this; but if it is, the error
is not in taking the life but in following a policy which
does not really deter others from murder. The ques-

tion cannot be resolved on *a priori* grounds but only by observing the social consequences of various types of punishment.[2]

Although I would not agree wholly with this, considerations of effectiveness must certainly be included in decisions of a responsible Christian social ethic. Therefore a necessary part of a Christian approach is to discover how capital punishment works out. For this there are numerous sociological and psychological studies. With remarkable unanimity they show that neither the presence of the death penalty in a state's laws nor the frequency of execution lowers the homicide rate.[3] Execution is such a drastic medicine and crime such a serious problem that conscientious people cannot remain indifferent to society's continued dependence upon so demonstrably ineffective a medicine. If it worked for the good of society—effectively lowering the homicide rate or resulting in greater safety for police officers or if executing a murderer restored his victim to life —Christians would face a different problem and sometimes a very cruel dilemma. But we are not concerned with how it might be on some other planet or in another age. And it so happens that on this issue the humane and the pragmatic criteria lead to the same conclusion.

That Christianity places emphasis on mercy, compassion and redemption does not mean that it is indifferent to the base of justice on which these "higher" values function. When a nation has around 8,000 homicides and less than fifty executions a year, it is obvious that "as it is now applied the death penalty is nothing but an arbitrary discrimination against an occasional victim," as the House Committee report to the Eighty-sixth Congress put it. Under these circumstances the victims will tend to be selected on a

[2] *Moral Men and Immoral Society* (Scribner's, 1932), Chap. 7.

[3] E.g., "Murder and the Penalty of Death," *The Annals of the American Academy of Political and Social Science,* vol. 284 (Nov. 1952); Massachusetts Commission Report (House Document 2575, 1958); Royal Commission Report (Great Britain, 1953); Gregory Zilboorg, *The Psychology of the Criminal Act and Punishment* (London: Hogarth Press, 1955).

very emotional basis in which the prejudices of the society will find expression and poverty will exclude for some the superior legal defense available to others. Instead of dealing responsibly with the question of insanity, it inevitably becomes a legal game. The mere possibility of execution results in endless appeals, hearings and complications in the judicial process. Public cynicism, unwarranted in fact and unhealthy for the body politic, is thus fed. No one of these items taken singly may be of decisive importance, but taken together the cumulative side effects of capital punishment are important as they affect the administration of justice.

Without minimizing justice, the distinctive witness of the Christian is found in compassionate concern. This is not a sentimental romanticizing over the criminal but a recognition that he is a human being. It means that the Christian asks: What can be done, if anything, to redeem this man and to restore his maimed or brutalized humanity? It means that Cain as well as Abel is made in the image of God. It means that the overriding purpose of correctional institutions must be corrective. It is not a question of tough or soft methods, but of intelligent and effective methods. Nor does it mean any lack of feeling for the family of a murdered person, but quite the contrary. Not infrequently it is not such heartbroken families but professional purveyors of hate and fear that cry for blood. It is in this tragic dimension of our life in community that the Christian brings his witness of informed compassion and humane wisdom.

The Christian has a continuing task of interpreting to the community the fact that it is not fundamentally because of a man's "value" to the community or how well he has used his capabilities that he merits justice before the law and depth of concern from us, but because he is a human being and our brother, under one God and Father of us all. There is an authentic Christian note in Eugene Debs' statement to the court:

> Your Honor, years ago I recognized my kinship with all living beings, and I made up my mind that I was not one bit better than the meanest on earth. I said then, and I say now, that while there is a lower class, I

am in it, while there is a criminal element I am of it, and while there is a soul in prison, I am not free.

Capital punishment is not the most crucial issue before us. The importance it has stems first from a conviction that no man ought to die needlessly, and that if but one man in all the world were involved, and that man a vicious pathological murderer, it would still be a matter of importance. This is an issue which reminds us that the sacredness of the individual is not man-conferred or state-enacted but God-given and inherent.

Additional importance comes from the relationship with other questions. Because it is highly charged with emotion, the issue of capital punishment can become a powerful stimulus for action on behalf of improved criminal laws and correctional methods. It is most unfortunate if a state abolishes capital punishment at the price of regressive parole procedures. Social actionists should be vigilant to see that this issue is understood in relation to the whole pattern of law and custody.

Capital punishment has also a symbolic importance. It is a symbol of an approach to crime that has been tried in the balance of history and found wanting. It stands for the very passions that contribute to crime. We of this age have, like Macbeth, "supp'd full with horrors," and many brutalizing influences continue to play upon our spirits. Any concern that has a humanizing influence and that renews sensitivity where the daily battering of brutal fact, rumor and phantom has left us calloused and unfeeling, is important for the health of our own souls as well as for the atmosphere of the community. This does not threaten civilization; it is saving health unto it. It was amid the deep horror and brutality in the world of 1941 that Winston Churchill wrote these words:

The mood and temper of the public with regard to the treatment of crime and criminals is one of the most unfailing tests of the civilization of any country. A calm dispassionate recognition of the rights of the accused, and even of the convicted criminal against the state; a constant heart-searching by all charged with

the duty of punishment; a desire and an eagerness to
rehabilitate . . . ; tireless efforts toward the discovery
of creative and regenerative processes; unfailing faith
that there is a treasure, if you can only find it, in the
heart of every man. These are the symbols which . . .
mark and measure the stored-up strength of a nation
. . . proof of the living virtue in it.[4]

STATEMENT AGAINST CAPITAL PUNISHMENT*

BY DONAL E. J. MACNAMARA**

The infliction of the death penalty is becoming less frequent and the actual execution of the sentence of death
even more rare, both in the United States and in foreign
countries. Not only is this trend apparent in those nations
and states which have formally repudiated the *lex talionis*
and have eliminated capital punishment from their penal
codes[1] but it is almost equally clear in many of the jurisdictions which still retain the ultimate sanction for from

[4] *Probation*, Dec. 1941; quoted by W. E. Hocking, *The Coming World Civilization* (Harper 1956).

* Reprinted, by permission of the author and publisher,
from "The Case Against Capital Punishment," *Social Action*
(April 1961), pp. 4–15. Copyright 1961 by the Council for
Christian Social Action, United Church of Christ.

** President, American League to Abolish Capital Punishment, and Dean, New York Institute of Criminology.

[1] Michigan, Rhode Island, Wisconsin, Maine, Minnesota,
North Dakota, Delaware, Alaska, Hawaii, Puerto Rico, and the
Virgin Islands in the United States. Many nations have abolished capital punishment outright; others retain it in restricted
application (e.g., Israel for war criminals; Guatemala for men
but not for women or children; USSR for treason and certain
atrocious murders; England for murders with firearms or explosives and for killing a police or prison officer in escaping
custody); still other nations have just stopped using the death
penalty (Luxemburg's last execution was in 1822 and Belgium's
in 1863). Only fifteen of the forty-three death penalty jurisdictions in the United States actually executed anyone during 1958
and four states (California, Georgia, Ohio and Texas) accounted for half the total executions. Canada, which retains
the death penalty despite an aggressive campaign by the abolition forces, actually commuted thirty-two of its last forty death
sentences.

one to fourteen crimes. This diminished frequency is a reflection of the popular distaste for executions and of the recognition by many criminologically and psychiatrically oriented judges, juries, prosecutors, and commuting and pardoning authorities that capital punishment is as ineffective as a special capital crimes deterrent as it is ethically and morally undesirable.

The case against the death penalty is supported by many arguments—with the order of their importance or precedence dependent upon the orientation of the proponent or the composition of the audience to whom the argument is being addressed. The late Harold Laski, in opening his series of lectures to one of my graduate seminars in political theory, suggested that a lecturer or writer was under obligation to his audience to define both the articulate and inarticulate basic premises upon which his theoretical structure, and its practical application to the matters under discussion, rested. This writer, then, is a practicing criminologist with both administrative and operational experience in police and prison work over a period of more than two decades; he was brought up in a Catholic household, went to parochial schools for twelve years, and then took degrees from two non-sectarian institutions. He is a "convert" to abolition, for during his active police and prison career he not only accepted the death penalty pragmatically as existent, necessary, and therefore desirable but participated in one or another formal capacity in a number of executions.

The case against capital punishment is ten-fold:

1. *Capital punishment is criminologically unsound.* The death penalty is the antithesis of the rehabilitative, non-punitive, non-vindictive orientation of twentieth century penology. It brutalizes the entire administration of criminal justice. No criminologist of stature in America or abroad gives it support. And those "arm-chair" and so-called "utilitarian" criminologists who plead its necessity (never its desirability or morality) do so in terms of Darwinian natural selection and/or as a eugenics-oriented, castration-sterilization race purification technique, an economical and efficient method of disposing of society's jetsam. Those

who advance these arguments are probably not aware that they are rationalizing a residual lust for punishment or propagating an immoral, virtually paganistic, philosophy.

2. *Capital punishment is morally and ethically unacceptable.* The law of God is "Thou shalt not kill," and every system of ethics and code of morals echoes this injunction. It is well recognized that this Commandment (and the laws of man based upon it) permit the killing of another human being "in the lawful defense of the slayer, or of his or her husband, wife, parent, child, brother, sister, master or servant, or of any other person in his presence or company"[2] when there is "imminent danger" and in "actual resistance" to an assault or other criminal act. It is equally well recognized that society, organized as a sovereign state, has the right to take human life in defending itself in a just war against either internal or external unjust aggression. But the individual citizen has no right in law or morals to slay as punishment for an act, no matter how vile, already committed; nor has he legal or moral justification to kill when—his resistance to an attempted criminal act having proved successful short of fatal force—the imminent danger is eliminated and the criminal attack or attempt discontinued.

Individuals in groups or societies are subject to the same moral and ethical codes which govern their conduct as individuals. The state, through its police agents, may take human life when such ultimate measure of force is necessary to protect its citizenry from the imminent danger of criminal action and in actual resistance to felonious attempts (including attempts forcibly to avoid arrest or escape custody). Once, however, the prisoner has been apprehended and either voluntarily submits to custody, or is effectively safeguarded against escape (maximum security confinement), the right of the state to take his life as punishment, retribution, revenge, or retaliation for previously committed offenses (no matter how numerous or heinous) or as an "example" to deter others, or as an economical expedient, does not exist in moral law.

[2] Section 1055, New York State Penal Code.

I argue this despite the fact that it is a position which is contrary to that expounded by a number of eminent theologians, notably Thomas Aquinas. Writing in times long past and quite different, and expressing themselves in terms of conditions, logic and experiences of those times, such theologians have defended the right of the state to take human life as a punishment "when the common good requires it." Moreover, they have held that, under certain conditions, the state is morally bound to take human life and that not to take it would be sinful. Although I am philosophically opposed to war whether as an extension of diplomacy or an instrument of national policy, I recognize the right of a nation, through its armed forces and in accord with the rules of civilized warfare, to take human life in defense of its sovereignty, its national territory, and its citizens. Such recognition is in no way inconsistent with my views anent the death penalty, for the Geneva Convention makes it clear that the killing of one's enemy (no matter how many of one's troops he has slaughtered in battle) after he has laid down his arms, surrendered, or been taken prisoner, will not be countenanced by civilized nations.

3. *Capital punishment has demonstrably failed to accomplish its stated objectives.* The proponents of the death penalty base their support largely on two basic propositions: (1) that the death penalty has a uniquely deterrent effect on those who contemplate committing capital crimes; and (2) that the provision of the death penalty as the mandatory or alternative penalty for stated offenses in the statute books removes for all time the danger of future similar offenses by those whose criminal acts have made them subject to its rigors.

Neither of these propositions will stand logical or statistical analysis. Proposition 1 is dependent upon acceptance of the repudiated "pleasure-pain" principle of past-century penology. This theory presupposes a "rational man" weighing the prospective profit or pleasure to be derived from the commission of some future crime against the almost certain pain or loss he will suffer in retribution should he be apprehended and convicted. That many persons who commit crimes are not "rational" at the time the crime is committed is beyond dispute. Avoiding the area of psychiatric controversy for the moment, let it be sufficient to report that Dr. Shaw Grigsby of the University of Florida in his recent studies at the Raiford (Florida) State Penitentiary found that more than seventy-five per cent of the males and more than ninety per cent of the females then in confinement were under the influence of alcohol at the time they committed the offenses for which they were serving sentence; and that Dr. Marvin Wolfgang's studies of the patterns in criminal homicide in Philadelphia in large measure lend support to Dr. Grigsby's findings.

While perhaps the theological doctrine of "sufficient reflection and full consent of the will" as necessary prerequisites to mortal sin is somewhat mitigated by the mandate to "avoid the occasions of sin" in the determination of moral responsibility, we are here discussing rationality in terms of weighing alternatives of possible prospective deterrence rather than adjudicated post-mortem responsibility. Proposition 1 further presupposes knowledge by the prospective offender of the penalty provided in the penal code for the offense he is about to commit—a knowledge not always found even among lawyers. It further assumes a non-self-destructive orientation of the offender and, most importantly, a certainty in his mind that he will be identified, apprehended, indicted, convicted, sentenced to the maximum penalty, and that the ultimate sanction will indeed be executed. When one notes that of 125 persons indicted for first degree murder in the District of Columbia during the period 1953–1959, only one (a Negro) was executed despite the mandatory provision of the law;[3] and further that, despite the fact that more than three million major felonies were known to the police in 1960, the total prison population (federal and state) at the January 1961 prison census (including substantially all the convicted felons of 1960 and many from prior years) stood at a miniscule 190,000, the rational criminal might very well elect to "play the odds."

The second part of the proposition assumes that all or a high proportion of those who commit crimes for which the

[3] Section 22, D. C. Code 2404.

death penalty is prescribed will in fact be executed—an assumption, rebutted above, which was false even in the hey-day of capital punishment when more than two hundred offenses were punishable on the gallows. It shows no awareness that the mere existence of the death penalty may in itself contribute to the commission of the very crimes it is designed to deter, or to the difficulty of securing convictions in capital cases. The murderer who has killed once (or committed one of the more than thirty other capital crimes) and whose life is already forfeit if he is caught would find little deterrent weight in the prospect of execution for a second or third capital crime—particularly if his victim were to be a police officer attempting to take him into custody for the original capital offense. The suicidal, guilt-haunted psychotic might well kill (or confess falsely to a killing) to provoke the state into imposing upon him the punishment which in his tortured mind he merits but is unable to inflict upon himself.

Prosecutors and criminal trial lawyers have frequently testified as to the difficulty of impanelling juries in capital cases and the even greater difficulty of securing convictions on evidence which in non-capital cases would leave little room for reasonable doubt. Appeals courts scan with more analytical eye the transcripts in capital cases, and error is located and deemed prejudicial which in non-capital cases would be overlooked. The Chessman case is, from this viewpoint, a monument to the determination on the part of American justice that no man shall be executed while there is the slightest doubt either as to his guilt or as to the legality of the process by which his guilt was determined. Criminologists have pointed out repeatedly that the execution of the small number of convicts (fewer than fifty each year in the United States) has a disproportionately brutalizing effect on those of us who survive. Respect for the sanctity and inviolability of human life decreases each time human life is taken. When taken formally in the circus-like atmosphere which unfortunately characterizes twentieth century trials and executions (both here and abroad), emotions, passions, impulses and hostilities are activated which may lead to the threshold of murder many who might never have incurred the mark of Cain.

4. *Capital punishment in the United States has been and is prejudicially and inconsistently applied.* The logic of the retentionist position would be strengthened if the proponents of capital punishment could demonstrate that an "even-handed justice" exacted the supreme penalty without regard to race or nationality, age or sex, social or economic condition; that all or nearly all who committed capital crimes were indeed executed; or, at least, that those pitiful few upon whom the sentence of death is carried out each year are in fact the most dangerous, the most vicious, the most incorrigible of all who could have been executed. But the record shows otherwise.

Accurate death penalty statistics for the United States are available for the thirty-year period, 1930–1959. Analysis of the more than three thousand cases in which the death penalty was exacted discloses that more than half were Negroes, that a very significant proportion were defended by court-appointed lawyers, and that few of them were professional killers. Whether a man died for his offense depended, not on the gravity of his crime, not on the number of such crimes or the number of his victims, not on his present or prospective danger to society, but on such adventitious factors as the jurisdiction in which the crime was committed, the color of his skin, his financial position, whether he was male or female (we seldom execute females), and indeed oftentimes on what were the character and characteristics of his victim (apart from the justifiability of the instant homicidal act).

It may be exceedingly difficult for a rich man to enter the Kingdom of Heaven but case after case bears witness that it is virtually impossible for him to enter the execution chamber. And it is equally impossible in several states to execute a white man for a capital crime against a Negro. Professional murderers (and the directors of the criminal syndicates which employ them) are seldom caught. When they are arrested either they are defended successfully by eminent and expensive trial counsel; or they eliminate or intimidate witnesses against them. Failing such advantages, they wisely bargain for a plea of guilty to some lesser degree of homicide and escape the death chamber. The homicidal maniac, who has massacred perhaps a dozen, even under our archaic M'Naghten Rule, is safely outside the pale of criminal responsibility and escapes not only the death penalty but often even its alternatives.

5. *The innocent have been executed.* There is no system of criminal jurisprudence which has on the whole provided as many safeguards against the conviction and possible execution of an innocent man as the Anglo-American. Those of us who oppose the death penalty do not raise this argument to condemn our courts or our judiciary, but only to underline the fallibility of human judgment and human procedures. We oppose capital punishment for the guilty; no one save a monster or deluded rationalist (e.g., the Captain in Herman Melville's *Billy Budd*) would justify the execution of the innocent. We cannot however close our minds or our hearts to the greater tragedy, the more monstrous injustice, the ineradicable shame involved when the legal processes of the state, knowingly or unknowingly, have been used to take the life of an innocent man.

The American Bar Foundation, or some similar research-oriented legal society, might well address itself to an objective analysis of the factors which led to the convictions of the many men whose sentences for capital crimes have in the past few decades been set aside by appellate courts (or by executive authority after the courts had exhausted their processes), and who later were exonerated either by trial courts or by the consensus of informed opinion. Especial attention should be directed to the fortunately much smaller number of cases (e.g., the Evans-Christie case in England and the Brandon case in New Jersey) in which innocent men were actually executed. Perhaps, too, a re-analysis would be profitable of the sixty-five cases cited by Professor Edwin Borchard in his *Convicting the Innocent*, the thirty-six cases mentioned by U. S. Circuit Court of Appeals Judge Jerome Frank in *Courts on Trial*, and the smaller number of miscarriages of justice outlined by Erle Stanley Gardner in *Court of Last Resort*.

6. *There are effective alternative penalties.* One gets the impression all too frequently, both from retentionist spokesmen and, occasionally, from the statements of enthusiastic but ill-informed abolitionists, that the only alternative to capital punishment is no punishment; that, if the death penalty does not deter, then surely no lesser societal response to the violation of its laws and injury to its citizens will prove effective.

The record in abolition jurisdictions, some without the death penalty for more than one hundred years, both in the United States and abroad, in which imprisonment for indeterminate or stated terms has been substituted for the penalty of death, is a clear demonstration that alternative penalties are of equal or greater protective value to society than is capital punishment.

In every instance in which a valid statistical comparison is possible between jurisdictions scientifically equated as to population and economic and social conditions, the nations and states that have abolished capital punishment have a smaller capital crimes rate than the comparable jurisdictions that have retained the death penalty. Further, the capital crimes rate in those jurisdictions which, while retaining the death penalty, use it seldom or not at all is in most instances lower than the capital crimes rates in the retentionist jurisdictions which execute most frequently.

And, finally, comparing the before, during, and after capital crimes rates in those jurisdictions (nine in the United States) which abolished capital punishment and then restored it to their penal codes, we find a consistently downward trend in capital crimes unaffected by either abolition or restoration. Startling comparisons are available. The United States Navy has executed no one in more than 120 years; yet it has maintained a level of discipline, effectiveness, and morale certainly in no sense inferior to that of the United States Army which has inflicted the death penalty on more than 150 soldiers in just the last three decades.

Delaware, most recent state to abolish the death penalty, experienced a remarkable drop in its capital crimes rate during the first full year of abolition. No criminologist would argue that abolition will necessarily reduce capital crimes; nor will he attempt to demonstrate a causal connection between absence of the death penalty and low capital crimes rates. In point of fact, homicide is the one major felony which shows a consistent downward trend in both capital punishment and abolition jurisdictions—indicating to the student of human behavior that the crime of murder, particularly, is largely an irrational reaction to a concrescence of circumstances, adventitiously related, wholly independent of and neither positively nor negatively correlatable with the legal sanction provided in the jurisdiction in which the crime actually took place. Dr. Marvin Wolfgang has pointed out with some logic that our decreasing murder rate is probably in no small part due to improved communications (ambulance gets to the scene faster), improved first aid to the victim, and the antibiotics, blood banks, and similar advances in medicine which save many an assault victim from becoming a corpse—and of course his assailant from being tagged a murderer. The consistent upward trend in assaultive crimes gives support to Dr. Wolfgang's thesis.

7. *Police and prison officers are safer in non-death penalty states.* The studies of Donald Campion, S.J., associate editor of *America,* and others indicate (albeit with restricted samplings) that the life of a police officer or a prison guard is slightly safer in the non-death penalty states, although the difference is so slight as to be statistically insignificant. Prison wardens overwhelmingly support abolition but large segments of the police profession support the retention of the death penalty both as a general crime deterrent (which it demonstrably is not) and as a specific safeguard to members of their own profession. Significantly, few of the police officers who serve in non-death penalty states are active in the fight to restore capital punishment and most of those who oppose abolition in their own jurisdictions have never performed police duties in an abolition state. It is a criminological axiom that it is the certainty, not the severity, of punishment that deters. Improvements in the selection, training, discipline, supervision, and operating techniques of our police will insure a

higher percentage of apprehensions and convictions of criminals and, even without the death penalty, will provide a greater general crime deterrent and far more safety both for the general public and for police officers than either enjoys at present.

8. *Paroled and pardoned murderers are no threat to the public.* Studies in New Jersey and California, and less extensive studies of paroled and pardoned murderers in other jurisdictions, indicate that those whose death sentences have been commuted, or who have been paroled from life or long-term sentences, or who have received executive pardons after conviction of capital crimes are by far the least likely to recidivate. Not only do they not again commit homicide, but they commit other crimes or violate their parole contracts to a much lesser extent than do paroled burglars, robbers, and the generality of the non-capital crimes convicts on parole. My own study of nearly 150 murderers showed that not a single one had killed again and only two had committed any other crime subsequent to release. Ohio's Governor Michael DiSalle has pointed out (as Warden Lewis Lawes and other penologists have in the past) that murderers are by and large the best and safest prisoners; and he has demonstrated his confidence by employing eight convicted murderers from the Ohio State Penitentiary in and about the Executive Mansion in Columbus in daily contact with the members of his family.

9. *The death penalty is more costly than its alternatives.* It seems somewhat immoral to discuss the taking of even a murderer's life in terms of dollars and cents; but often the argument is raised that capital punishment is the cheapest way of "handling" society's outcasts and that the "good" members of the community should not be taxed to support killers for life (often coupled with the euthanasian argument that "they are better off dead"). The application of elementary cost accounting procedures to the determination of the differential in costs peculiar to capital cases will effectively demonstrate that not only is it not "cheaper to hang them"; but that, on the contrary, it would be cheaper for the taxpayers to maintain our prospective executees in the comparative luxury of first-rate hotels, with all the

perquisites of non-criminal guests, than to pay for having them executed. The tangible costs of the death penalty in terms of long-drawn-out jury selection, extended trials and retrials, appeals, extra security, maintenance of expensive, seldom-used death-houses, support of the felon's family, etc., are heavy.

10. *Capital punishment stands in the way of penal reform.* Man has used the death penalty and other forms of retributive punishment throughout the centuries to control and govern the conduct of his fellows and to force conformity and compliance to laws and codes, taboos and customs. The record of every civilization makes abundantly clear that punishment, no matter how severe or sadistic, has had little effect on crime rates. No new approach to the criminal is possible so long as the death penalty, and the discredited penology it represents, pervades our criminal justice system. Until it is stricken from the statute books, a truly rehabilitative approach to the small percentage of our fellowmen who cannot or will not adjust to society's dictates is impossible of attainment. That there is a strong positive correlation between advocacy of the death penalty and a generally punitive orientation cannot be gainsaid. Analysis of the votes for corporal punishment bills, votes against substitution of alternative for mandatory features in the few mandatory death penalty jurisdictions,[4] votes against study commissions and against limited period moratoria,[5] and comparison with votes for bills increasing the penalties for rape, narcotics offenses, and other felonies discloses a pattern of simple retributive punitiveness, characterizing many of our legislators and the retentionist witnesses before legislative committees.

Many church assemblies of America and individual churchmen of every denomination have underscored the moral and ethical non-acceptability of capital punishment. Church members have the responsibility to support the campaign to erase this stain on American society. Capital punishment is brutal, sordid, and savage. It violates the

[4] New York and the District of Columbia, notably.
[5] Massachusetts, New Jersey, Connecticut, Illinois, New York, California, Canada and England.

law of God and is contrary to the humane and liberal
respect for human life characteristic of modern democratic
states. It is unsound criminologically and unnecessary for
the protection of the state or its citizens. It makes miscarriages of justice irredeemable; it makes the barbaric *lex
talionis* the watchword and inhibits the reform of our prison
systems. It encourages disrespect for our laws, our courts,
our institutions; and, in the words of Sheldon Glueck,
"bedevils the administration of criminal justice and is the
stumbling block in the path of general reform in the treatment of crime and criminals."

IS THE DEATH PENALTY
UNCONSTITUTIONAL?*

BY GERALD H. GOTTLIEB**

On the frontiers of public law are to be found issues with
special characteristics. The issues hinge on certain ambiguous phrases found in constitutions, treaties and statutes.
The meanings of the phrases depend upon changing and
dynamic realities of society. These dynamic realities consist, among other things, of the formation and decay of
values, the advance of education, increases in knowledge
of the human mind and motivations, the continuing evolution of the American economic system, and our developing
national self-consciousness vis-à-vis the image of our nation in a world society.

Potentially the issues are thus latently governed by the
leverages of social change. The courts, on rare occasions,
have redefined the ambiguous phrases.[1] The changed rules

* Reprinted, by permission of the author and publisher, from
"Testing the Death Penalty," *Southern California Law Review,*
vol. 34 (Spring 1961), pp. 268–281.
** Member of the Bar, Los Angeles, California.
[1] See, Brown v. Board of Education, 347 U.S. 483 (1953);
Muller v. Oregon, 208 U.S. 412 (1908); Durham v. United
States, 237 F.2d 760 (D.C. Cir. 1956); Fujii v. State, 38 Cal.
2d 718, 242 P.2d 617 (1952).
It has been argued that ambiguous terms in statutes or constitutional provisions are often used purposely by legislatures;
they are in effect delegating powers to the courts. See Miller,

of law each time have in turn crystallized new standards and new values for society.

When these changed standards are recognized and understood by society, through pronouncement and enforcement, the realities of society are in turn affected. A churning action operates; the issues communicate between the basic notions of the law and the basic realities of society. Ultimately, the philosophies of the citizenry are thereby modified. Those legal issues which thus deeply affect and are affected by the philosophies, conditions and values of mankind can be referred to as the "issues-with-leverage."

Within the field of crime and punishment resides one of these "issues-with-leverage." The issue hinges on the phrase, "cruel and unusual punishment," which the federal constitution's Eighth Amendment prohibits the federal government from inflicting. This phrase also may apply to state governments, since there is substantial authority to the effect that the Eighth Amendment is deemed incorporated within the due process clause of the Fourteenth Amendment, and that, through the impact of the Fourteenth Amendment upon the states, the states are thereby, albeit indirectly, to a great extent subject to the same inhibitions against cruel and unusual punishment as is the federal government.[2] Also, many states are subject to this limitation because of express prohibitions in their state constitutions similar to the Eighth Amendment.

The Eighth Amendment uses "cruel and unusual," speaking in the conjunctive. However, there is indication in court

---

Statutory Language and the Purposive Use of Ambiguity, 42 Va. L.R. 23, 39.

[2] Mr. Justice Douglas has stated that: "The infliction of 'cruel and unusual punishments' against the command of the Eighth Amendment is a violation of the Due Process Clause of the Fourteenth Amendment, whether that clause be construed as incorporating the entire Bill of Rights or only some of its guarantees. . . . For despite Hurtado and Twining, this Court has now held that the Fourteenth Amendment protects from State invasion the following 'fundamental' rights safeguarded by the Bill of Rights . . . at the very least, certain types of cruel and unusual punishment. . . ." Sweeney v. Woodall, 344 U.S. 86, (1952) (dissent). See also NAACP v. Williams, 359 U.S. 550, 551 (1959) (separate opinion).

decisions that this phrase is intended as disjunctive.[3] The California Constitution is expressly in the disjunctive, enjoining "cruel or unusual" punishment.[4]

I. Capital Punishment: A Measure for Cruel and Unusual Punishment

The phrase "cruel and unusual" is profoundly ambiguous. It refers to certain dynamic realities of society and of men's states of mind. Although those realities have been changing during the many centuries since the phrase was coined, judicial definition of the phrase in terms of contemporary society has only recently begun and is incomplete.

One of the punishments yet fully to be tested under the Eighth Amendment, within the context and findings of modern penology, psychology, morals and social requirements, is the death penalty. To proceed with such a test would seem important, if for no other reason than that this penalty is practiced by the federal government and forty-one of our states.[5]

[3] "Generally viewing the action of the States in their bills of right as to the prohibition against inhuman or cruel and unusual punishments, it is true to say that these provisions substantially conform to the English bill of rights and to the provisions of the Eighth Amendment we are considering, some using the expression cruel and unusual, *others the more accurate expression 'cruel or unusual,'* and some cruel only. . . . It is true that when the reasoning employed in the various cases is critically examined a difference of conception will be manifested as to the occasion for the adoption of the English bill of rights and of the remedy which it provided. Generally speaking, when carefully analyzed, it will be seen that this difference was occasioned by treating the provision against cruel and unusual punishment as *conjunctive* rather than *disjunctive, thereby overlooking the fact, which I think has been previously demonstrated to be the case,* that the term unusual, as used in the clause, was not a qualification of the provision against cruel punishments, but was simply synonymous with illegal, and was mainly intended to *restrain the courts,* under the guise of discretion, from indulging in an unusual and consequently illegal exertion of power. . . ." Weems v. United States, 217 U.S. 349, 401 (1910) (dissent). (Emphasis added.)
[4] Cal. Const. art. 1, §6.
[5] Nine states have abolished the death penalty: Alaska, Dela-

The constitutionality of the death penalty in the present social setting comprises a substantial and justiciable question and it may tenably be urged that capital punishment is unconstitutional. Capital punishment may, on a sufficient factual showing, be found violative of the Eighth Amendment, since death by means of the gas chamber, gun, rope or electric chair may now with good reason be alleged to be "cruel and unusual" punishment and within the reach of the Eighth Amendment and its state counterparts. An issue of law dependent upon judicially noticeable facts awaits its day in court.

The thesis that the constitutionality of capital punishment is now a substantial question rests in part on decisional law that has defined and explored the notion of cruelty in the Eighth Amendment and the notion of due process in the Fourteenth Amendment in relation to punishment. This thesis is also partially supported by the observations of society from the sixteenth century onward. These observations assist in showing changes in man's consciousness and morality relevant to the concepts expressed in court opinions.

Does the death penalty constitute such cruelty as violates the United States Constitution? What measurement shall determine this? Who shall take the measurement? Has the measurement been changed? Does it change?

In past rulings of the United States Supreme Court and state courts, the judges have declined to hold the death penalty to be illegal. However, careful review of the opinions and close analysis of the language of the decisions support the view that the constitutionality of capital punish-

---

ware, Hawaii, Maine, Michigan, Minnesota, North Dakota, Rhode Island and Wisconsin. Of the others twenty-two and the District of Columbia practice electrocution, twelve use lethal gas, six use hanging, and in Utah the condemned man has his choice of hanging or shooting. Hanging is the method of execution in the territories of American Samoa, Guam, and the Canal Zone. The federal courts use the method of execution followed by the state in which the sentence is imposed, and if the state does not have a death penalty, the federal judge may prescribe the method for carrying out the death sentence. *Information Please Almanac* 335 (1960).

ment depends on questions of judicially noticeable fact. The evidence, responding to the language and opinions of the judges, has not heretofore been presented in any of our courts.

A number of alternate criteria may be applied in a test of the death penalty as a "cruel and unusual" punishment. The judges from time to time have given various definitions to the phrase. Any one of the definitions may become the hinge on which the ultimate question of unconstitutional cruelty may turn. The succeeding sections of this article deal each with one of those hinging definitions and frame one of those testing questions.

II. Decency as a Measure

The sentence of death violates the Eighth Amendment to the United States Constitution if the sentence and its execution are repugnant to the evolving standards of decency that mark the progress of our maturing society.

Although expressions by intellectual and moral leaders on criminal punishment have gradually changed over the centuries, the law has only recently begun to reflect those changes. In one line of cases the phrase "cruel and unusual" in the Eighth Amendment had been defined against the context of the practices carried on several centuries ago. Alongside that static view, today a new view has grown in the law.

The former view is exemplified by an 1890 case, *Ex parte Kemmler*.[6] In that case the United States Supreme Court affirmed that New York's electric chair could be used in administering the death penalty and that the electrocution process did not violate the United States Constitution. The Court held that only such extreme penalties as "burning at the stake, crucifixion, breaking on the wheel, or the like"[7] were within the constitutional prohibition. As recently as 1947, the Supreme Court followed the static view of "cruel and unusual." In the *Resweber* case,[8] the Court sanctioned the return of a condemned man to

[6] *In re* Kemmler, 136 U.S. 436, 446–47 (1890).
[7] *Id.* at 447.
[8] Louisiana *ex rel.* Francis v. Resweber, 329 U.S. 459 (1947).

the electric chair after two abortive attempts at electrocution had failed. In its decision the Court mentioned that the phrase "cruel and unusual punishment" came from the English Bill of Rights of 1688.

However, it should be noted that the period prior to the adoption of our Bill of Rights was marked by a catalogue of cruelties that were unspeakable and disgusting. For example, the philosopher Michel de Montaigne writing of a Roman execution at the end of the sixteenth century stated that the convicted robber was strangled and then cut in quarters before the populace.[9] Blackstone has referred to drawing and quartering, disemboweling, beheading, public dissection, burning at the stake, dismembering, and branding.[10] To define, as the United States Supreme Court seemed to do in the *Kemmler* and *Resweber* cases, "cruel and unusual" by a mere repudiation of the grosser aspects of torture and of the manifest cruelties of past centuries is to give a poor standard of measurement for contemporary society, to thwart and blunt the phrase and to destroy the protective purpose of our Eighth Amendment.

The advent of the dynamic and contemporary view of the meaning of "cruel and unusual punishment" first came in a 1910 case, *Weems v. United States.*[11] The United States Supreme Court decided that sentence of a defendant to a term of years coupled with the requirement that the defendant must carry a chain hanging from his ankle and wrist, and that he be employed at hard and painful labor and suffer permanent loss of civil rights, constituted the infliction of "cruel and unusual" punishment. Yet that sentence and punishment would have been considered mild in old England both before and after the enactment of the English Bill of Rights. Thus, the Supreme Court in the *Weems* case departed from the rule earlier stated in *Kem-*

[9] 2 Michel de Montaigne, 112–13 (1913).

[10] 2 Blackstone, *Commentaries* 2620–23 (Jones' ed. 1916). These punishments were carried out after, as well as before, the English Bill of Rights was enacted, but Blackstone asserted that the post-1688 penalties were mild compared with the shocking apparatus of death and torment to be found in the criminal codes of many European countries at that time.

[11] 217 U.S. 349 (1910).

mler, and instead held that the context of old England must not be allowed to determine the meaning of the words "cruel and unusual." Justice McKenna, speaking for the Court, stated that:

> Legislation . . . should not, therefore, be necessarily confined to the form that evil had theretofore taken. Time works changes, brings into existence new conditions and purposes. Therefore, a principle to be vital, must be capable of wider application than the mischief which gave it birth. This is peculiarly true of constitutions. They are not ephemeral enactments, designed to meet passing occasions. They are, to use the words of Chief Justice Marshall, "Designed to approach immortality as nearly as human institutions can approach it." The future is their care, and provision for events of good and bad tendencies of which no prophecy can be made. In the application of a Constitution, therefore, our contemplation cannot be only of what has been, but of what may be. . . .[12]

The *Weems* case did not condemn, nor has any case condemned in principle, the death penalty. It did, however, establish a primary concept that the definition of cruelty shall be fashioned in terms of the present and future needs of society, rather than the public's inclination, or standards regarding cruelty of medieval Europe.

In 1958 the dynamic view of *Weems* received express ratification when the Supreme Court cited that case with approval in its opinion in *Trop v. Dulles.*[13] In the latter case the Court held that excommunication and deprivation of citizenship, as a punishment for desertion, was "cruel and unusual" punishment, and thus, illegal. The Court recognized that "the words of the Amendment are not precise, and . . . their scope is not static. The Amendment must draw its meaning from the evolving standards of decency that mark the progress of a maturing society."[14]

Is the death penalty unconstitutional today within the

[12] *Id.* at 369–73.
[13] 356 U.S. 86 (1958).
[14] *Id.* at 99–101.

context of the social and cultural conditions of this nation and of the world? The *Trop* and *Weems* cases hold that the concept of cruelty is a dynamic one. Necessarily, those holdings cause the constitutional question of the validity of capital punishment to be a combined question of law and fact. The facts to be adduced refer to the injuries done to society and to the family of the executed man, the extent of pain, both physical and psychological,[15] and generally the social context in such aspects as are relevant to the problem of crime, crime prevention, punishment and the developing culture and humanity of our country. The issue of constitutionality then requires the judges to be acute observers of the times and of the imperatives which spring from an "evolving standard of decency." If the death penalty is now repugnant to our evolved standards "that mark the progress of a maturing society," then it seems that capital punishment ought to be struck down by judicial action.

III. The Test of Necessity

Whether capital punishment and the processes and proceedings necessarily associated therewith violate the Eighth Amendment can be said to depend upon whether the processes are cruel by definition. Cruelty is properly definable

---

[15] A century-old passage from Dostoevksy's *The Idiot* gives a towering yet touching indication of the cruelty of capital punishment: "But the chief and worst pain may not be in the bodily suffering but in one's knowing for certain that in an hour and then in ten minutes, and then in half a minute, and then now, at the very moment, the soul will leave the body and that one will cease to be a man and that that's bound to happen; the worst part of it is that it's certain. . . . To kill for murder is a punishment incomparably worse than the crime itself. Murder by legal sentence is immeasurably more terrible than murder by brigands. Anyone murdered by brigands, whose throat is cut at night in a wood, or something of that sort, must surely hope to escape till the very last minute. . . . But in the other case (execution) all that last hope, which makes dying ten times as easy, is taken away for certain. There is the sentence, and the whole awful torture lies in the fact that there is certainly no escape, and there is no torture in the world more terrible. . . ." Dostoevsky, *The Idiot* 19–21 (1958).

as "the infliction of pain or loss without necessity[16] or justification."[17]

Blackstone considered necessity to be a prerequisite of the death penalty and noted that the necessity must be great and overriding:

> . . . But, indeed were capital punishments proved by experience to be a sure and effectual remedy, that would not prove the necessity . . . of inflicting them upon all occasions when other expedients fail. I fear this reasoning would extend a great deal too far. For instance, the damage done to our public road by loaded wagons is universally allowed, and many laws have been made to prevent it; none of which have hitherto proved effectual. But it does not therefore follow that it would be just for the legislature to inflict death upon every obstinate carrier who defeats or eludes the provisions of former statutes. . . .[18]

The courts have verged on, but have not expressly embraced the common sense definitions and doctrine that turns on necessity. In *Resweber,* though upholding the punishment, the majority admitted that: "The traditional humanity of modern Anglo-American law forbids the infliction of unnecessary pain in the execution of the death sentence. . . ."[19] The dissent in which Justices Burton, Douglas, Murphy and Rutledge joined, appeared to take a further step toward the literal application of the test of necessity: "Taking life by unnecessary cruel means shocks the most fundamental instincts of civilized man. It should

---

[16] "Cruelty: 1. Quality or state of being cruel, disposition to inflict or enjoy unnecessary pain or suffering; inhumanity. . . ." Webster, *New International Dictionary* 636 (unabr. 2d ed., 1954).

[17] "Cruelty in the law, has no narrowly defined or technical meaning, but is a generic term applicable to all categories of wilful mistreatment, particularly the infliction of *unjustifiable* physical pain or suffering. . . ." 8 *Encylopedia Americana* 254 (1956). (Emphasis added.)

[18] 2 Blackstone, *Commentaries* 2164–65 (Jones' ed. 1916).

[19] Louisiana *ex rel.* Francis v. Resweber, 329 U.S. 459, 463 (1947).

not be possible under the constitutional procedure of a self-governing people. Abhorrence of the cruelty of ancient forms of capital punishment has increased steadily, until, today, some states have prohibited capital punishment altogether."[20]

At least as a philosophical criterion, unnecessary pain and loss in-the-method is not a far cry from unnecessary pain and loss in-the-prescription of punishment. Yet the writer has not been able to find any case where the facts have been placed before any court regarding the necessity for the death penalty itself. An issue of judicially noticeable fact looms as to the necessity or non-necessity for the institution of capital punishment in view of the alternative and available programs including, but not limited to, sentence of imprisonment for a term of years or for life. If there is no necessity for the death penalty, then the death penalty, under the definition stated above, becomes unconstitutional and cannot be imposed legally.

The definition of cruelty as *unnecessary* pain or loss finds support in the comments of the early writers on republican government. Montesquieu, whose writings constitute to a great extent part of the heritage of republican theory, commented:

> The severity of punishment is fitter for despotic governments, whose principle is terror, than for a monarchy or republic, whose spring is honor and virtue.
>
> In moderate governments, the love of one's country, shame, and the fear of blame, are restraining motives, capable of preventing a multitude of crimes.
>
> Mankind must not be governed with too much severity; we ought to make a prudent use of the means which nature has given us to conduct them; let us follow nature, who has given shame to man for his scourage; and let the heaviest part of the punishment be in infamy attending it. . . .[21]

[20] *Id.* at 473.
[21] 4 Montesquieu, *The Spirit of Laws,* book 6, ch. IX (1900).

The wisdom of the common sense definition is attested not only by the use of the concept of necessity by the Supreme Court of the United States, albeit within a limited framework, but also by reference to ethical concepts. The ethics of republican government lead us to the conclusion that punishment shall not be meted which inflicts pain or loss without necessity. Jefferson and Locke extolled those who are "willing to part with only so much power as is *necessary* for their good government. . . ."[22]

From the standpoint of governmental morality, if we agree with Jefferson, we would deny to the governments such powers as are not necessary for a government to have. And the power to inflict the death penalty is qualitatively different and vastly greater today than any other punitive power in practice.

The criteria of necessity has also been supported as an ethical position by many eminent philosophers. For example, Albert Schweitzer believes that "to a man who is truly ethical all life is sacred, including that which from the human point of view seems lower in scale." In deciding when such life must be taken, Schweitzer would make distinctions only as each case arises, and under the pressure of *necessity*.[23]

As against life imprisonment, and other penological programs, is the death penalty necessary? If it is not, then under several tests, common sense, ethical and legal, the punishment of death constitutes cruelty.

IV. A Proper Function for Punishment

Some recent decisions of our state courts suggest another criterion. Under this view capital punishment may be said to comprise unconstitutional cruelty if that institution cannot secure a proper function of society within civilized standards.

The California Supreme Court was called upon to decide whether, among other things, it had been improper for the trial judge to allow the jury to hear a certain tape re-

---

[22] Longman's *Jefferson,* presented by John Dewey 54 (1948). (Emphasis added.)
[23] Schweitzer, *Out of My Life and Thoughts* 233 (1949).

cording. It seems the police had recorded the dying murder victim's pain, groans, and failing voice. The court, with Justices Schauer and McComb dissenting, reversed and remanded the case to the trial court. After holding that the evidence had no probative value other than showing the victim died in unusual pain, the court discussed the principle of criminal penalties:

> . . . Proof of such pain is of questionable importance to the selection of penalty unless it was intentionally inflicted. . . . Pain unintentionally inflicted is relevant only to the extent that criminal penalties are designed to exact retribution for the evil done by criminals. Whatever may have been the facts historically, retribution is no longer considered the primary objective of the criminal law . . . and is thought by many not ever to be a proper consideration (see M. R. Cohen, *Law and the Social Order*, 310; Holmes, *The Common Law*, 42, 46; Michael and Wechsler, *Criminal Law and its Administration*, 10–11) granted, however, that retribution may be a proper consideration, it is doubtful that the penalty should be adjusted to the evil done without reference to the intent of the evildoer. Modern penology focuses on the criminal, not merely on the crime. . . .[24]

Three of the seven Justices of the California Supreme Court collaterally advanced the position indicated above in a subsequent case, *People v. Harmon*,[25] decided in April 1960. The defendant, a life prisoner, had attacked a fellow prisoner. At the time of the offense the California Penal Code[26] made the death penalty mandatory for the assault. Just before Harmon's trial, the Penal Code had been amended to make the death penalty optional. The Supreme Court of California had the task of deciding whether the amendment should be deemed retroactive to favor the de-

[24] People v. Love, 53 Cal. 2d 843, 856–57, 350 P.2d 705, 3 Cal. Rptr. 665 (1960).

[25] People v. Harmon, 54 Cal. 2d 9, 351 P.2d 329, 4 Cal. Rptr. 161 (1960).

[26] Cal. Pen. Code § 4500.

fendant. The majority held that the death penalty remained mandatory as to the crime committed prior to the amendment. Chief Justice Gibson and Justice Traynor joined with Justice Peters in dissenting, concluding that the defendants should be given the benefit of the amendment:

> . . . There is no logical or rational reason to presume, as does the majority opinion, that the Legislature, in such cases intended the old law to apply. Such a presumption can only be predicated on the theory that *punishment is intended as vengeance against the wrongdoer. This violates all* the modern theories of penology.[27]

Recently, the New York Court of Appeals held that a defendant was entitled to the benefit of mitigated punishment and asserted that:

> This application of statutes reducing punishment accords with the best modern theories concerning the functions of punishment in criminal law. According to these theories, the punishment or treatment of criminal offenders is directed toward *one or more of three ends*: (1) to discourage and act as a deterrent upon future criminal activity, (2) to confine the offender so that he may not harm society, and (3) to correct and rehabilitate the offender. *There is no place in the scheme for punishment for its own sake, the product simply of vengeance or retribution.* (See Michael and Wechsler on *Criminal Law and its Administration* [1940], Pages 6–11; Note 55 Col. L.R., Pages 1039, 1052). . . .[28]

There is reason to believe that the above concept is potentially the majority rule of the California Supreme Court and of the United States Supreme Court. Can the death penalty be shown to have a proper function? Certainly its function cannot be that of rehabilitation, nor

[27] People v. Harmon, 54 Cal. 2d 9, 32, 351 P.2d 329, 343, 4 Cal. Rptr. 161, 175 (1960) (Peters, J., dissenting).
[28] People v. Oliver, 1 N.Y.2d 152, 160, 134 N.E.2d 197, 201, 151 N.Y.S.2d 367, 373 (1956).

can it be that of confinement, a function which is thoroughly and efficiently served by imprisonment. The burden is to show that the death penalty constitutes, as compared to life imprisonment, and differentially, a deterrent upon future criminal activities. Unless the death penalty has such a proper function in our society, it would seem to be cruel by definition.

V. The Comparative Test

Another test, somewhat more mechanical, should be included in the constitutional review. If a penalty is more cruel than another punishment already held to violate these constitutional provisions, then the death penalty is unconstitutional as a matter of simple logic. Thus, comparison becomes the relevant factor.

In *Trop v. Dulles,* the Supreme Court held that a punishment generally considered *less* than death, the punishment of deprivation of citizenship, was nevertheless "cruel and unusual" and violative of the Eighth Amendment:

. . . There may be involved no physical mistreatment nor primitive torture. There is instead the total destruction of the individual's status in organized society. It is a form of punishment more primitive than torture, for it destroys for the individual the political existence that was centuries in development. . . . In short, the expatriate has lost the right to have rights.

This punishment is offensive to cardinal principles for which the Constitution stands. It subjects the individual to a fate of ever-increasing fear and distress. . . . The civilized nations of the world are in virtual unanimity that statelessness is not to be imposed as punishment for crime. . . .[29]

If *Trop v. Dulles* is now the standard, does the death penalty constitute cruelty as a matter of law, based on comparison to the *Trop* case? And in considering the cruelty of the death penalty we must consider the antecedent and auxiliary processes as inflicted in California, the total

[29] Trop v. Dulles, 356 U.S. 86, 101–02 (1958).

experience of the courts and the executioner with respect thereto, and all the facts referable to pain, loss and torture. An issue of fact is tendered, even though the opinion suggests that the punishment attempted in the *Trop* case might be worse than death. The fact issue relates to the comparative pain and loss as between the death penalty with its antecedent waiting period following conviction, on the one hand, and the penalty in *Trop* on the other.

VI. The Context of Man's Dignity

Repeatedly the courts advert to still another touchstone of cruelty. Under this test the question whether capital punishment violates the Eighth Amendment is to be answered affirmatively if the punishment violates conscience, morality, humanity, or the dignity of mankind.

In *Trop v. Dulles,* the Court stated: "The basic concept underlying the Eighth Amendment is nothing less than the dignity of man. While the State has the power to punish, the Amendment stands to assure that this limit be exercised within the limits of civilized standards."[30]

A close reading of this decision,[31] and other opinions, particularly the dissenting opinions in the *Resweber* case,[32] leave a reader with a strong impression that a majority of the Justices of the United States Supreme Court disfavor capital punishment, and find it repugnant to their own respective consciences.[33]

[30] *Id.* at 100.

[31] The majority opinion in *Trop,* in which Justices Black, Douglas and Whittaker joined with Chief Justice Warren, contains this gentle aside: "Whatever the arguments may be against capital punishment, both on moral grounds and in terms of accomplishing the purposes of punishment—and they are forceful . . ." *Id.* at 99.

[32] Justices Douglas, Murphy and Rutledge joined Justice Burton in referring to capital punishment as "cruelty" at least as it was there to be inflicted. Louisana *ex rel.* Francis v. Resweber *supra* note 8, at 474 (dissent).

[33] Justice Frankfurter stated that: "A lifetime preoccupation with criminal justice, as prosecutor, defender of civil liberties and scientific student, naturally leaves one with views. Thus I disbelieve in capital punishment. . . ." Haley v. Ohio, 332 U.S. 596, 602 (1948) (concurring opinion).

The courts have announced that the measurement is to be made in terms of man's dignity. When the judges decide that judgment is to be made on the basis of a determination by the judges, applying their own knowledge, understanding, and historical and social perspective, then it seems capital punishment will be deemed illegal.

There is, as Montesquieu indicated in the eighteenth century, a reciprocal effect of crime and punishment.[34] It might be shown to the courts that historically, the more harsh and the more severe is the scale of punishment, the more degraded is the society as a correlative thereof. It further might be shown that the very act of the sovereign, descending in his majesty upon an offender to vengeful or unnecessarily severe punishment, a punishment that has been prepared by the sovereign with premeditation, coldness and infinite planning, has a symbolic effect upon society far beyond the fact that a life is then taken. This act by the state tends to cheapen the very values that refer to humanity itself, to lower the opinion of humanity regarding itself and to diminish its standards of decency, of conscience and of culture. The practice of capital punishment might be proven to violate the dignity of mankind.

VII. Intent of the Framers

Story has expressed the view that the provision against cruel and unusual punishment is unnecessary in a free government and was adopted only as an admonition to all departments to warn them against such violent proceedings as had taken place in England under the arbitrary reigns of some of the Stuarts.[35] The Supreme Court's opinion in

[34] Montesquieu pointed out that "experience shows that in countries remarkable for the lenity of their laws the spirit of the inhabitants is as much affected by slight penalties as in other countries by severer penalties. . . . Mankind must not be governed with too much severity. . . . If there are other [countries] where men are deterred only by cruel punishments, we may be sure that this must, in a great measure, arise from the violence of the government which has used such penalties for slight transgressions." Montesquieu, *op. cit. supra,* note 21, at ch. IX.

[35] 2 Story, *Commentaries on the Constitution* (5th ed. 1903).

the *Weems* case asserted that Story's citations[36] did not sustain the theory that the provision was intended to be so limited. The Court's opinion asserted that the framers of our Bill of Rights had something else in mind than merely to add verbiage to our Bill of Rights.

The framers were greatly influenced by the views of Blackstone and Montesquieu.[37] One can, with some force, urge that Montesquieu's and Blackstone's views regarding severity of punishment were shared by the framers and that it was their inclination to eliminate the practices summarized and condemned by Blackstone and ultimately the death penalty, when no longer necessary for the public safety.

The provision against cruel and unusual punishment received very little debate in Congress. According to the Congressional Record there were two primary objections to the adoption of this prohibition in the Eighth Amendment. Mr. Smith felt the phrase "cruel and unusual" was too indefinite. Mr. Livermore contended: "It is sometimes necessary to *hang a man,* villains often determine whipping and perhaps having their ears cut off; but are we in the future to be prevented from inflicting these punishments because they are cruel?"[38] In the *Weems* case, the Court based its reasoning and conclusion in part upon the fact that the Congress adopted the Eighth Amendment in the face of these objections and must be deemed to have intended to abolish certain cruelties.[39] However, Mr. Livermore also raised a point with regard to the death penalty. Can we not, therefore, conclude that the *Weems* decision is persuasive as to the emergent unconstitutionality of the death penalty?

If the "cruel and unusual" provision is interpreted in a strict manner, as Story suggested, the provision would be virtually a dead letter today. However, under the *Weems* view this prohibition is a vital provision of the Consti-

---

[36] Weems v. United States, 217 U.S. 349, 368–73 (1910).

[37] 1 Bryce, *The American Commonwealth* 274, 375 (1889).

[38] Cong. Reg. 225 (1910). This was referred to in Weems v. United States, 217 U.S. 349, 368–69 (1910).

[39] *Ibid.*

tution and is available as a weapon to strike down cruelty in any form, and possibly in the form of capital punishment.

VIII. Judicial Self-Restraint or Nullification

The guarantee against cruel punishment is fundamental. The weapon of the Eighth Amendment is made to be wielded, and such wielding is the job of the judiciary. Thus, when the pertinent facts regarding the cruelty of the death penalty are compiled and presented the judges ought to notice them; they should not be tabled as legislative matters.

Neither in *Weems* nor in *Trop*, where the United States Supreme Court had the burden to determine whether the Eighth Amendment was violated, did the Court deem the matter of cruelty to be merely a legislative and/or political question. Having found cruelty, the Court struck down the punishments.

In *Trop* the Court pointed out that:

> In concluding as we do that the Eighth Amendment forbids Congress to punish by taking away citizenship, we are mindful of the gravity of the issue inevitably raised whenever the constitutionality of an act of a national Legislature is challenged. . . . When the constitutionality of an act of Congress is challenged in this Court, we must apply those rules. The basic concept underlying the Eighth Amendment is nothing less than the dignity of man.[40]

In *Weems*, the Court applied the Eighth Amendment and a similar provision in the Philippine Bill of Rights to that island territory. The provision against "cruel and unusual punishment" was deemed "essential to the rule of law and the maintenance of individual freedom."[41] Since the Philippines were not incorporated at the time of the *Weems* case, only the most fundamental provisions of the American Bill of Rights applied.[42] Thus, it appears

[40] Trop v. Dulles, 356 U.S. 86, 103 (1958).
[41] Weems v. United States, 217 U.S. 349, 367–68 (1910).
[42] Dorr v. United States, 195 U.S. 138 (1904) held that the Philippines were not incorporated into the United States, and that the constitutional right of trial by jury did not apply to

clear that the prohibition against cruel and unusual punishment was deemed by the Court in the *Weems* case to
be of a fundamental character, as compared, for example,
to the less important guarantee of right to trial by jury.[43]

Although the legislature has the power to define crimes
and their punishment and to determine the expediency of
such laws, the Court has a legal duty to consider the
law when it encounters a constitutional prohibition. The
Court must then comprehend all that the legislature did
or could take into account, considering the mischief and
the remedy.[44]

A limited example of judicial consideration of the cruelty
of a penalty as a question of fact is *Territory v.
Ketchum*,[45] where the penalty of death was sustained in
the New Mexico territory after a factual review, albeit superficial. In that case a statute imposed the death penalty
upon any person who should make an assault upon any
railroad train, for the purpose and with the intent to commit murder, robbery, or other felony upon passengers. The
supreme court of the territory discussed the purpose of
the Eighth Amendment, and rested its decision upon the
conditions which existed in the territory, and the circumstances of terror and danger which accompanied the crime
denounced. To take note, as in *Ketchum,* of the "conditions of the territory" is, in a sense, to receive evidence
under the several tests suggested herein for testing the
death penalty for cruelty. If in a subsequent case the evidence of the "condition of the territory" (state) and of the
people, and relevant to the factual issues referable to the
definitions of cruelty, establish that the death penalty is
in fact cruel, then a court should strike down the penalty.

To ask a court to consider the cruelty of the death penalty as a question of fact is to ask the court to do what it

---

judicial procedure in the Philippines. Subsequently, and six
years after the *Weems* opinion, Congress provided that certain
of these "non-fundamental" constitutional privileges be secured
to persons in the Philippines, 39 Stat. 546 (1916), 48 U.S.C.
§ 1008 (1958).

[43] See note 42 *supra.*

[44] Weems v. United States, 217 U.S. 349, 378–79 (1910).

[45] Territory v. Ketchum, 10 N.M. 718, 65 Pac. 169 (1901).

is required to do by law. And if the death penalty is found to be unnecessary or unconscionable, and thus in fact cruel, the court must wield the Eighth Amendment to strike down this penalty.

IX. Conclusion

The term "cruel and unusual" is latently ambiguous to a profound extent. The cruelties and depravities of the middle ages and the Stuart period should to a degree be considered as a background for this constitutional prohibition. However, to exclusively consider past cruelties and fail to notice the present contents and standards perpetrates an anachronism. The phrase is a dynamic intendment and the courts must notice and consider the facts and resulting changed standards of decent conduct marked by our great penologists, wardens, social philosophers, and psychologists.

The same point, the need to consider changing standards, may be made as to the other suggested tests for determining the cruelty and, thus, unconstitutionality of the death penalty. What is necessary, under the test of necessity, changes with the changed knowledge, increased skills and improved facilities for incarceration, rehabilitation and for public education. Equally, necessity is to be judged by each era based on the scientific facts, such as factors of motivation and deterribility known to the judges of that era.

The ambiguity of the phrase "cruel and unusual" is latent and the latency resides in contemporary society and in the new facts which it harbors. To bring the artifacts and evidence of those facts to the courtroom is to fill out the dimensions of the question in the public law.

In terms of historical fact and tendency, the advances of man's liberty and of man's culture and civilization is accompanied by lessening of severity of punishment. It is also accompanied by an increasing appreciation and valuation of life itself.

The courts should seriously consider the changed and advanced standards of our civilization in determining if the death penalty is unconstitutional as cruel and unusual punishment.

DEATH AS A PUNISHMENT

I

Before turning to the main issues, one or two comments on the structure of the abolitionist's argument are in order. It is important for us to grant that the evidence supporting our position could be stronger and more complete than it is. But to admit this is not to confess that the evidence is weak or insufficient. Defenders of the death penalty frequently fail to realize that what evidence there is consistently favors abolition. More than that, too many retentionists complacently talk as if the burden of proof were not on them—as though somewhere it was once proved that the death penalty was a social, moral, or theological necessity, or as though the long history of executing our fellow-man was a sufficient justification for continuing the practice indefinitely, or as though compelling reasons for killing people no longer need to be given once this policy has become the law. Actually, the arguments offered today for retaining the death penalty, as I believe this book shows, are little more than dogmas, confusions and evasions. In particular, I know of very few instances where retentionists have earnestly tried to support their convictions by conducting an investigation into some area where the facts are in dispute, and none in which they have come up with convincing supporting evidence.[1]

It also should be admitted that those who oppose the death penalty from a moral position of absolute non-violence and respect for human life have it somewhat easier when they justify their position as abolitionists than do those of us whose position is based on more complex considerations. Professor Barzun, however, is nothing if not misleading when he argues *ad hominem* (in his essay reprinted in Chapter Three) that abolitionists betray their professed ideal of the "absolute" sanctity of human life by advocating the living death of life imprisonment and by failing to oppose with equal vigor various other forms

[1] The one instance I can think of I have discussed below in the Introduction to Chapter Six.

of disrespect for human life: by nations in warfare, by private citizens in self-defense, by policemen in restraining or apprehending a felon. Abolitionists I have known who profess to believe in the "absolute" sanctity of human life do in fact oppose these other forms of legalized killing. But those who don't take this extreme view are still entitled to appeal to the sanctity of human life, and they suffer no inconsistency if they do, as I shall explain below.

Likewise, I find nothing inconsistent in those who disturb Professor Hook, because they oppose the death penalty on the ground that it isn't punishment enough (" 'Death is too good for the vile wretch!' "). The moral convictions from which they oppose the death penalty are not mine, any more than they are his. I am consoled by the knowledge that very few abolitionists hold such convictions. But what if the contrary were true? As a point of logic and as a matter of fact, opposition to the death penalty is consistent with a wide variety of moral and social (or even immoral and anti-social) principles. Here as elsewhere, politics makes strange bedfellows, among retentionists as well as abolitionists. It is only simpler, perhaps not wiser and certainly not necessary, to oppose the death penalty from a moral principle of absolute non-violence.

II

Let me now turn to the case for the death penalty that Professors Barzun and Hook have made out, for it deserves the closest attention. (I should say from the onset that I am quite aware of the several differences between Hook's and Barzun's arguments; and I know there is some risk of misrepresenting their views by allying them as closely as I have at several points. The reader will have to judge whether I have been unfair to one in the course of objecting to the other.)

It will not go unnoticed that, unlike many retentionists, they concede a great deal to the opposition. They understand that the question is not one of capital punishment or no punishment. They share our doubts about the social utility of the motives that usually animate the defenders of the death penalty. They admit that the doctrine of general deterrence cannot any longer be the lynch-pin of a reasonable man's defense of capital punishment in America. They implicitly recognize that the burden of proof is on them as advocates of killing certain types of persons, not on those who would let even the worst convicts live. As Professor Barzun rather wistfully comments, his concessions almost make him happier with the abolitionist than against him.[2] Almost, but not quite. What remains of the case for the death penalty that he and Professor Hook are able to construct would crumble if several crucial distinctions were drawn, distinctions that would clarify their arguments and enable us to see the full consequences of the principles they espouse.

For example, one distinction of importance, neglected by Professor Barzun, is between a man's killing someone else when there is a clear and present danger that he will otherwise be the victim of some violent act, and the state's killing a man as a punishment, i.e., between a man's right to defend himself and society's right to punish criminals. It is because Barzun fails to make this distinction that he thinks abolitionists are inconsistent in appealing to the sanctity of human life. So far as law and the prevailing morality of Western civilization have been concerned, respect for human life has never been an obstacle to the use of force in self-defense; indeed, it has always been thought to be its justification. It has, however, obligated anyone who pleads self-defense in justification of a killing to satisfy society that the force he used really was necessary in the circumstances and was motivated solely by a desire to ward off imminent harm to himself. But to kill a person who in fact is not at the time dangerous (because he is in prison), on the possibility that he might at some later date be dangerous, would be to use unjustifiable force and thus to flout the respect human life is due. Were it to be shown that there is a threat to society, or to any of its members, in allowing a criminal in prison to remain there, comparable to the danger a man invites in a dark alley if he turns his

---

[2] Likewise Professor Hook; at least, his remarks in reply to Judge Samuel Leibowitz, in *New York Law Forum* (August 1961), pp. 296–300, strongly suggest this.

back on a thug who has a weapon in his hand and violence on his mind, then—but *only* then—would it be inconsistent for the abolitionist to tolerate force sufficient to kill the thug in the alley but to refuse to kill the prisoner. It may be that the pacifist, with his commitment to the absolute sanctity of human life, would in theory and in practice have to tolerate the slaughter of innocent lives (including his own). But if such a disaster were a likely consequence of abolishing the death penalty, or of extending parole at least in principle to all capital offenders, few of us who favor both would advocate either. The facts here, in terms of which the degree of risk can alone be measured, happen to be on our side.[3]

On the issue of whether abolition of the death penalty would improve the lot of persons unjustly convicted, I think both Professor Hook and Professor Barzun are misled and confusing. Barzun is unquestionably right when he points to cases where men have been exonerated after years in prison, only to find that their lives have been destroyed. Of course, abolishing the death penalty is no remedy for the injustice of convicting and punishing an innocent man. It is obviously as *wrong* to imprison an innocent man as it is to kill him. But I should have thought it is just as obviously *worse* for him to be killed than for him to be imprisoned. This point must not be blurred by speculating whether it is worse from the convict's point of view to be dead than to be imprisoned and perhaps never vindicated or released. If an innocent convict thinks he is better off dead than alive, this is for *him* to determine, not us. What we must decide is the less metaphysical question of what general penal policy the state should adopt, on the understanding that the policy will in practice be applied not only to the numerous guilty but also to a few who are innocent. No one can deny, even if Hook and Barzun neglect to stress it, that the *only* way the state is in a position to do something for the victim of a miscarriage of justice is if it has refused as a matter of principle to kill *any* of its

[3] See Chapter Seven, "Parole of Capital Offenders, Recidivism, and Life Imprisonment."

convicts. Executing an innocent man is not impossible,[4] and it is a great risk to run for the questionable advantage of executing a few guilty ones.

Nor am I impressed by the "humanitarian" concern for the agony of a man erroneously convicted which, in claiming to deliver him from the greater evil, would take not only his freedom but his life as well. I cannot believe in point of fact that Tom Mooney would have been better off had he been hanged in 1917 for a crime he did not commit, rather than pardoned as he was more than twenty years later. I know of no evidence that he came to the opposite conclusion. I leave it for anyone acquainted with the case of James Fulton Foster to judge whether he would have been better off dead than as he is: alive, exonerated, and free.[5] Are these cases as exceptional as Professor Barzun evidently believes? Even if they were, how could putting a Mooney or a Foster to death ever be justified on *humanitarian* grounds?

These reflections suggest a general point. There is a fundamental distinction to be made between choosing the death penalty for yourself and choosing it for someone else. Both Hook and Barzun seem to believe that imprisonment, even for a guilty man (and certainly for themselves, were *they* in prison, innocent or guilty), may be a far worse punishment than execution, and that abolitionists deceive themselves in believing that they advocate the lesser penalty. I doubt that this is so: but even if it were, I am certain that their argument is a deception.

Just as most abolitionists would agree that if the death penalty must be kept then less gruesome modes of execution ought to be adopted than those currently in use, many of us would also agree that we ought to consider allowing our penal authorities, under proper judicial and medical supervision, to cooperate with any long-term prisoner who is too dangerous to be released and who would honestly and soberly prefer to be dead rather than endure further imprisonment. That there are such convicts I am willing

[4] See Chapter Eight, "Murder, Errors of Justice, and Capital Punishment."

[5] See Chapter Nine, "The Question of Identity."

to concede. The question here is this: is it wisest for the state to allow a convict to take his own life if he decides that it would be better for him to be dead than to suffer any more imprisonment? Can a person in good physical health, in a tolerable prison environment, and who professes to want to die be of sound mind? (or isn't that important?) Does not civilized society always have a fundamental interest, if not an obligation, to try to provide even for its most incompetent members in that most oppressive of environments, a prison, some opportunity to make their lives worth living? Wouldn't a policy that amounts to euthanasia for certain convicts run counter to this interest and sap the motive to satisfy it?

These questions are not new, for they arise whenever "mercy killing" as a social policy is advocated. But they are instructive, for they indicate how the issue under discussion has subtly changed. No longer are we considering how we ought to punish crimes. Instead, we are asking whether we ought to allow a convict, if he so wishes, to be painlessly put to death for no other reason than so that his imprisonment and his despair may come to an end— as if there were no better alternatives! This question, and the other questions above, has little to do with the one posed by capital punishment: is it wisest for the state to impose death or imprisonment as the punishment for certain crimes, irrespective of what the convicts in question may prefer? To give an affirmative answer to the former is not to decide the latter at all. In arguing, as Hook and Barzun do, that convicts should have the right to obtain from their custodians the means for a decent suicide, they have not argued for capital punishment. They have not even shown that any convict who chooses death rather than imprisonment has made the wiser choice. It is a great misfortune, and shows the confusion I have imputed to him, that Professor Hook raises this whole issue as (in his words) one of several "exceptions" to his general disapproval of capital punishment. Supervised suicide for those convicts who want it, irrespective of their crime, is not an "exception" in which capital punishment would remain as part of a penal system; supervised suicide is an entirely different matter, as we have seen, with questions all its own.

It is essential in weighing their viewpoint to notice that Professors Hook and Barzun judge the crucial facts very differently than does Chief of Police Allen (cf. his article in Chapter Three). One reason why Hook and Barzun want to keep the death penalty is because they believe in mercy killings and the right of suicide even for the worst criminals, because they believe that a lifetime behind bars, with its endless humiliations, frustrations and utter wretchedness, is a far greater misery than a few moments of violent pain followed by eternal oblivion. But Allen wants the death penalty retained because he believes that a condemned man invariably prefers to have his sentence commuted to life imprisonment, which proves that the threat of the death penalty must be the greater terror and thus the better deterrent. It turns out that the death penalty cannot be replaced by imprisonment, as Arthur Koestler ironically remarked, because it is at once too cruel and not cruel enough.

Quite independently of the foregoing considerations Hook and Barzun advance what is by far their strongest argument for the death penalty, namely, that there is no other solution for the very worst criminals, those whose sole instinct is Kill, Kill, Kill. Having agreed on this, they disagree on everything else. Professor Hook plainly thinks these criminals are the *sane* unreformable twice-guilty murderers, for this is the class of criminals he expressly and repeatedly specifies. But it is just as clear that it is the "escaped lunatic," the "sudden maniac," the criminally *insane* killer (or rapist, or mugger), whether reformable or not, whom Professor Barzun is anxious to see executed. Moreover, whereas Hook insists that *mandatory* death penalties are unjustifiable, Barzun's preference must run the other way. For if our insistence on parole looks to him too much like "an expression of social remorse for the pain of incarceration," what must he think of a life sentence in the first place but that it is an expression of the jury's remorse for convicting the man at all? And it is just such sentimental nonsense, whether in a Parole Board or a jury, that is out of place when your safety and mine is at stake. Finally, whereas Professor Hook's argument presupposes that he regards the execution of a sane murderer as a *punishment,* it is very doubtful whether this is how Professor Barzun views the executions of those whom he would have put to death. Whether or not it was his intention, he makes it clear that it is "judicial homicide" he favors, and so far as he defends the death penalty it is mainly because it accomplishes much the same thing, namely, eugenic executions.[6] I think Professor Hook has come to the defense of the death penalty on behalf of a small if not non-existent class of criminals. Whether or not we make the "exception" he advises, it appears that in practice it will make little difference (though, if my argument below is correct, this may not be so). Professor Barzun, however, has altogether ceased to defend the death penalty, and a great deal both in theory and practice depends on understanding why this is so.

What conception of insanity Professor Hook would accept, he does not indicate. Yet any defense of the death penalty for *sane* unreformable murderers turns on this point. He contends that there is no "*a priori* ground" to rule out the possibility of sane murderers murdering again after a term of imprisonment. He infers that the death penalty is necessary to prevent such criminals from repeating their crimes. But is there really no such *a priori* ground? Any murderer who murders again, after a term of imprisonment and under at least somewhat different circumstances—ought he not by definition to be classified as criminally irresponsible? Must he not be suffering from some mental or emotional defect, whether or not it has been identified by psychiatrists, which warrants the label, "insanity"? It is more than a mere possibility.

Of course, the classic Anglo-American definition of "in-

[6] Not only a critic is bound to understand Barzun's position in this way, as is proved by the noted scholar who found himself in "complete agreement" with Barzun and construed his views exactly as I have; see *The American Scholar* (Summer 1962), pp. 446 f.

222 THE DEATH PENALTY IN AMERICA

sanity," in terms of the M'Naghten Rules of 1843, would never yield any such result. But these Rules are slowly giving way to others that might provide this.[7] For all that Professor Hook or I know, it may be that a careful study of the psychopathology of unreformed murderers would show a set of symptoms that would entitle them without exception to be treated as insane. If no such set of symptoms were located, or even hypothesized, I admit it would be arbitrary to stretch "insane" so as to describe every such murderer for no other reason than that he repeated his offense. But arbitrariness and the *a priori* with it lie all around us in this area. It must not be forgotten that the term, "insane," unlike "paranoid," has never been a description of any set of symptoms. It has never been related to forms of mental illness via empirical hypotheses contributed by psychopathology. It is simply the term employed by the law when a court wishes to hold an accused not accountable for his criminal acts by reason of his "unsoundness of mind." The kinds and causes of his "unsoundness of mind" are not legal but medical questions. The legal questions concern how to frame and to apply a general rule that will specify as insane all and only those persons whose acts are traceable to their mental ill-health and who, on that account, are to be excused from criminal responsibility and its consequences.

Professor Hook's confidence that in theory at least there may be sane multiple murderers must derive from *his* definition of "insane"; and such a definition is itself an *"a priori* ground." Depending on where we want to come out, we can make assumptions in the form of a definition of "insane" which will have the result that all, or some, or no unreformed murderers are insane. The trouble is not, as Hook asserts, that there is no *"a priori* ground" for ruling out the possibility of such criminals, but that such a ground, being only an *a priori* one, in the sense

[7] See the essays collected by Richard Nice (ed.), *Crime and Insanity* (1958); and also the bibliography prepared by Dorothy Campbell Tompkins, *Insanity and the Criminal Law* (1960).

that it consists of a definition, has other alternatives equally
a priori but with very different consequences.

What this shows is that if one's purpose is really to execute unreformable murderers, it is best to ignore the incidental facts of their sanity. Otherwise, one's purpose may
be frustrated by nothing more than a change in the legal
definition of "insanity." Professor Barzun, who does not
scruple on this question, has all the advantages, and hard-
core retentionists would be well advised to ally themselves
with his position rather than Hook's.

It is also necessary to argue with Professor Hook on
empirical grounds. What is the probability that there are
any "sane" persons knowledgeable and imaginative enough
to know what might be in store for them if they commit
another murder, vicious enough to kill with cool deliberation, and still stupid enough to risk years of imprisonment after having already experienced it (for we are
hypothesizing that our murderers are repeaters)? The probability is apparently so slight that competent authorities
agree it is negligible.[8] But we do not need to settle for the
educated guesses of the authorities. Five states (Michigan,
Minnesota, Wisconsin, Rhode Island, Maine) have long
been without capital punishment for murder. If they have
suffered from the problem of the sane unreformable murderer (as their courts define "sanity"), there has been
plenty of time to remedy it by adopting just such a statute
as Professor Hook recommends. Is their failure merely
proof of public apathy? Or is it perhaps proof that in these
states, the most vindictive have become abolitionists, and
that their vindictiveness has gone to their heads: they relish
the knowledge, shared with Professor Barzun, that in their
jurisdictions the murderer suffers the ultimate punishment,
literal life imprisonment; and public satisfaction in this
knowledge more than compensates for the risk that one
of the unreformables might sometime be paroled?

I have yet to mention my strongest objection to Professor
Hook's argument. It arises from what may be only a casual
comment. Professor Barzun, it will be recalled, asks why

8 See below, Introduction to Chapter Six.

society must wait until a man has killed several times before he may be executed, given that we are willing to have
murderers executed at all. Elsewhere, Hook has said what
amounts to his reply: because "the first time a man murders
we are not sure that he is a mad dog."[9] (Let us merely
note the curious turn of phrase which has him eventually
defending the execution of sane "mad dogs.") This is reasonable enough. But Hook now expresses the doctrine, in
his essay in Chapter Three, that second-time murderers
ought to be executed where there is "a reasonable probability" they "will murder again or attempt to murder again."
This is a somewhat unsettling idea, and a revealing one as
well. Would Hook consider allowing a court to sentence
a person to death even if he had not yet committed a second murder, and had not even attempted one, so long as
it was "reasonably probable" that he would? Suppose we
had a delinquency diagnostic test which would tell us with
"reasonable probability" that a given person would attempt
to commit his *first* murder and that he would not respond
to subsequent imprisonment. What would Professor Hook
allow us to do with such knowledge? If he would allow us
to execute a man after he has twice murdered, or after
one murder and an attempted second murder, on the
ground that there is no "reasonable probability" of rehabilitating him in prison, why should he not allow us to
execute the man when he has killed but once? Or, indeed,
before he has killed or attempted to kill at all? Is it the
risk that even "reasonable probabilities" may in fact not
lead to valid predictions? Then by the same token, executing a man no matter how many murders he has committed and no matter how often he has failed to respond
to rehabilitation must also be rejected. Thus, the line Professor Hook attempts to draw between murderers deserving execution and those deserving imprisonment, which began by appearing firm and clear, turns out, thanks to the
way one can manipulate the notion of "reasonable probabilities," to be no line at all.

Professor Barzun, unlike Professor Hook, directs his

[9] See *New York Law Forum* (August 1961), p. 297.

putative defense of the death penalty toward the class of criminals that, because of its number and danger, is of somewhat greater significance: the class inclined to violent and brutal acts, whether or not they are insane, whether or not they are reformable, and whether or not they have already committed any crimes. Barzun seems willing to embrace the "prophylactic execution of potential murderers," though only on the admittedly speculative assumption that the courts had a reliable test to predict future violence. Except for reservations about the sanity of those to be executed, Professor Hook's position, if I am right, leads to a similar conclusion. So this is the end of their line of argument purportedly advanced on behalf of the death penalty. The only way we can regard the desirability of such executions as relevant to the issue is if we ignore the fact that a system of capital punishment is, after all, a system of *punishment,* and that in such a system death can be inflicted on a person only for what he has done. A system of judicially sanctioned homicide, in which people are executed (at least in theory) *before* they have committed any crime at all, and thus are "punished" for what they will do and for the sort of person they will become, is not a system of punishment at all.

It is not a novel idea, either. In 1922, George Bernard Shaw, inspired both by genuine distress over the plight of men imprisoned for life and by pseudo-Darwinian eugenics, defended just such a system in his provocative essay, "The Crime of Imprisonment." But at least he recognized that in taking the position he did, he was *not* advancing an argument in favor of capital punishment or any other sort of punishment. Shaw defended the remarkable position that "we have no right to punish anybody." His conclusion that "persons who give more trouble than they are worth will run the risk of being . . . returned to the dust from which they sprung,"[10] was expressly offered as a reasonable man's alternative to every known system of punishment. On such a view the actual commission of a crime would be nothing but an incontrovertible symptom of a social disease

[10] *The Crime of Imprisonment* (1946), pp. 97–98.

which, whether or not it might be curable or might have been avoided, can be controlled only by exterminating the sick man. Were there some sure way of identifying the crime-prone before they break out with the fatal (to us) symptoms, there is every reason to put them out of the way. The medical analogy, to be sure, is not very apt. We are in effect advised to exterminate the sick and, if possible, the disease-prone, whereas analogy to public health measures suggests that we should bend every effort to immunize everyone with a suitable vaccine. Be that as it may, as Shaw well understood, to adopt such a system would certainly result in executions. But they would not be punishments, and the system would not be a system of capital punishment.

To take the line I have is not merely to quibble evasively. I do not want it thought that whereas I object to Barzun's defense of eugenic killings because he implies they are capital punishments, I would welcome them as readily as he and Shaw do if only they were called what they are. For I have serious reservations about the Shaw-Barzun position even when properly described and candidly defended for what it is. But each social question in its own time and place. One ought to be prepared to debate the merits of "judicial homicide" as a eugenic policy, for the very same reason one ought to be prepared to discuss euthanasia and abortion.[11] These practices, like capital punishment itself, consist essentially in ending or preventing someone else's life, presumably for good reasons, and thus they pose variations on a theme of incomparable moral importance. But these issues are clearly independent of each other. Just as nothing has prevented us in the past from having capital punishment without also having euthanasia or eugenic killings, there is nothing to prevent us in the future from abolishing the death penalty and introducing executions in the name of mercy and social hygiene. It will be time enough to discuss these proposals when they are up for serious debate. Meanwhile, it does not take a philosopher to see that

[11] In this connection, one might read Joseph Fletcher, *Man, Morals and Medicine* (1954), and Glanville Williams, *The Sanctity of Life and the Criminal Law* (1957).

the death penalty can no more be defended by an argument for eugenic killings than it can be defended by an argument for suicide.

Yet the problem of the "incurables" does exist, and Professors Barzun and Hook have performed a service in forcing everyone to face this terrible fact. There is little doubt that some who have been executed fall into this category. One thinks of Albert Fish in New York,[12] Gordon Northcott in California,[13] and Charles Starkweather in Nebraska,[14] to name only a few. In the light of our present knowledge about psychopathology and the actual methods of therapy and the personnel at our disposal, it would have been unreasonable to have hoped to cure and eventually release these men. But what does this prove? Not that it was theoretically impossible to cure them. Not that other men just as sick have never been known to get well. Not that such men cannot be safely incarcerated, for life if necessary. Apparently Professor Barzun is convinced that it is not worth our trouble to imprison such criminals possibly for life and that (as Professor Hook also believes) it is worse for them to be *made* to stay alive in prison rather than to be put to death; and that, regrettable as it may be, capital punishment ought to be preserved in America because it is a system that even now fairly well achieves the result he desires.

On the other hand, I am convinced that anyone who takes this view has thoroughly confused the possible merits of a utopian society, in which a hypothetically infallible system of "social defense" operates to eradicate all and only the unpreventable and incurable killers, with the very real evils of every known system of criminal justice which uses the death penalty. There is no doubt that a large number of the more than 7,000 persons capitally punished since 1900 in this nation were far from incurable. Fish, Northcott, and Starkweather are the much-publicized exceptions, not the rule. At the present time, no one has any idea how

12 See Francis Wertham, *The Show of Violence* (1949).
13 See Clinton Duffy, *88 Men and 2 Women* (1962).
14 See James Reinhardt, *The Murderous Trail of Charles Starkweather* (1960).

to work out a system of capital punishment that would be applied only to such persons, assuming for the sake of the argument that it would be desirable to execute them. In the end, there seems to me to be an enormous distance between Barzun's and Hook's implicit factual assumptions about society, crime, and the administration of justice, in terms of which they find their conclusions persuasive, and the actual circumstances in which the death penalty exists in this country. While they cannot be held responsible for what they have not defended, it is regrettable that the present system of capital punishment will reap the benefit of their argument.

III

In any serious discussion of the death penalty, those who are opposed to it should be ready to offer some alternative with detailed provisions that could be adopted with a minimum overhaul of the rest of the criminal code and penal system. In 1929, Lewis E. Lawes, then Warden of Sing Sing Prison and one of America's leading abolitionists, proposed the following model legislation for the punishment of murder:

> Upon conviction of murder in the first degree, the defendant shall be sentenced to life imprisonment.
>
> Prisoners serving life sentence shall receive no time allowance for commutation, or compensation until commuted to a definite term.
>
> No prisoner serving a life sentence shall be pardoned or commuted by the Governor until he has served at least twenty years actual time, unless the Court of Appeals shall make an order or decree, in which the majority of its members concur, to the effect that
>
> (a) Evidence which was not known at the time of the trial or which was not presented to the court or jury creates a probable doubt of the guilt of the accused; or,
>
> (b) Facts or circumstances exist which in the opin-

ion of the court make a case for executive clemency consideration.

After a prisoner shall have served twenty years actual time he shall be eligible for pardon or for commutation to a lesser term than life, and if commuted to a definite term of years, may thereafter earn commutation and compensation.

A substantial percentage of the earnings of the prisoner shall be applied to the support of his dependents and to the support of the dependents of the person killed, to be apportioned in the discretion of the Superintendent of Prisons.[15]

This model statute, conservative though it may be at several points, is in fact much more radical than any abolition bill actively discussed in an American legislature during the past decade. Most contemporary abolitionists have compromised the principle of parole as a theoretical possibility for all murderers, and have supported bills that would replace the death penalty with a flat term of imprisonment for life. Other proposed bills have compromised by retaining the death penalty for the murder of a police officer or prison guard, and/or for any murder committed while on parole from a conviction for murder. Warden Lawes may have rejected these compromises, as I would, on the ground that optimum deterrence does not require them.

Nevertheless, to arrive at the wisest alternative to the death penalty, we should have to alter Warden Lawes's model statute in three major respects. The twenty-year minimum sentence which he would allow a court to impose should be reduced by half. Neither deterrence nor rehabilitation requires more. (The American Law Institute, as I have noted in Chapter Seven, has gone so far as to recommend a term of from one to ten years as the minimum court-imposed sentence. The Institute was able to do this, however, only because their proposal was part of a

---

[15] Lewis Lawes, *Man's Judgment of Death* (1924), pp. 28–29; reprinted in Julia Johnson (ed.), *Capital Punishment* (1939), p. 59.

complete Model Penal Code.) The ten-year minimum I suggest could be adopted with few or no changes elsewhere in the system of punishments. Even ten years would be an unnecessarily long imprisonment in a few cases, but the widespread desire for Draconian punishments and the anxiety over premature release of murderers may require some such concession. The twenty-year minimum Warden Lawes proposed may have been tendered in a similar spirit of compromise.

Secondly, I think it is best not to introduce the principle of compensation by the criminal as part of the punishment for murder. There is no doubt that compensatory punishments are more useful to the injured party (and to his dependents), to society, and even to the criminal than are retaliatory ones. But a convicted murderer could provide no more than a token compensation if it is to be obtained from his prison earnings, another portion of which may have to go to support his own dependents. The attractive idea that through deductions from his prison earnings the murderer may expiate his guilt at least to some degree (something that his rehabilitation alone could never accomplish) is probably an illusion, so long as the restitution is not of his own choice but is required by law. A cynical criminal might come to look upon the payments being exacted from him as nothing but part of the cost of his crime and without any moral significance. These are among the reasons why compensation by murderers is not to my knowledge practiced in any American abolition jurisdiction. A more practical proposal, if special indemnification for victims of criminal violence really seems desirable, would be for the government to offer assistance to the victim's dependents over and above their usual social security benefits.[16]

Finally, Warden Lawes formulated his model statute in terms of the punishment for murder, thereby leaving it

[16] This has been suggested by several of the contributors to "Compensation for Victims of Criminal Violence: A Round Table," *Journal of Public Law* (1959), pp. 191–253. On this subject see also Stephen Schafer, *Restitution to Victims of Crime* (1960).

open whether other crimes should still be punished by death. In my view, his statute or something like it ought to be adopted as the punishment for *all* crimes that currently permit or require the punishment of death. Furthermore, whereas many states have written the death penalty for certain crimes (usually treason) into their constitutions, I should like to see a universal constitutional prohibition against capital punishment.

The formulation of an optimum alternative to the death penalty is a subject that few abolitionists ever thoroughly discuss. No doubt they would if they thought there was some hope of enacting such ideal legislation in the near future. As it is, however, abolitionists in America during the past decade have found themselves at one time or another defending almost every conceivable alternative. This has been confusing to the general public and has encouraged our opponents to view us as more desperate than we are. Whether the three revisions of Warden Lawes's model statute proposed here would command general assent among American abolitionists, I do not know. But I am convinced that if they became part of the criminal law throughout the country, we would have made a great step toward the ideal.

Chapter Five

WHAT DO AMERICANS THINK OF THE DEATH PENALTY?

INTRODUCTION

The attitudes of Americans today toward the death penalty obviously govern the likelihood of retaining, extending, or abolishing it in our time. Sociologists have often gone so far as to claim that when the public no longer wants the death penalty, it will be removed no matter what happens to the crime rate. The retention or abolition of capital punishment, they say, depends almost completely on the way people *feel*.[1] The implication is that what people feel on an issue such as this is not a function solely of what they know or consciously think.

What our legislative representatives think in the two score states which still have the death penalty may be inferred from the fate of the bills to repeal or modify the death penalty filed during recent years in the legislatures of more than half of these states. In about a dozen instances, the bills emerged from committee for a vote. But in none except Delaware did they become law. In those states where these bills were brought to the floor of the legislatures, the vote in most instances wasn't even close. In 1959, for instance, an abolition bill in California was defeated forty-three to thirty-five, and a similar bill lost in New Jersey thirty to nineteen; but in Massachusetts the abolition bill that year was crushed 168 to fifty. Likewise, in 1961, abolition was defeated in Vermont 155 to sixty-two, in Arkansas fifty-six to twenty-eight, and again crushed, this time in Pennsylvania, 173 to thirty-two. It may be, of course, that such votes do not reflect the private opinions of the legislators on the merits of abolition. There are many reasons why a legislator will not vote according to his convictions on an "issue of conscience" such as this. The fact remains, however, that over the past few years in the country at large, the legislative attitude toward abolition has been consistently and fairly definitely negative.

One naturally wonders whether this negative attitude reflects public opinion (and one also wonders how much, on a question such as this, a legislative decision *should* reflect public opinion). No opinion surveys were made in any of the states when and where the issue was voted in the legislature, so we are unable to make any direct comparison between the public and the legislative attitudes. One seldom hears of capital punishment as an election issue, and it is doubtful whether very many members of state legislatures were returned to office, or defeated for reelection, because

[1] See Professor Sellin's testimony before the British Royal Commission, *Minutes of Evidence* (1951), p. 656; and also *The Nation* (December 1, 1956), p. 478, reporting on testimony from another sociologist in Connecticut.

of their record on this question. It may be, as Warden Clinton Duffy has recently said,[2] that "the public doesn't care" either way, except when some dramatic crime or trial inflames passions.

We do have some inconclusive evidence of public opinion on capital punishment in states where the issue has been contested. In recent years only in Oregon (in 1958 and again in 1964) and in Colorado (1966) has the public voted directly on abolition. The earlier Oregon referendum was defeated in a close vote; six years later, abolition carried, 455,654 to 302,105. In Colorado, the retentionists easily won, 389,707 to 193,245. In California, television station KTTV of Los Angeles conducted a poll on the death penalty in 1955. Fifteen thousand people responded to the invitation to send in a postal card ballot for or against abolition. The result was a three to two defeat for the death penalty. Shortly thereafter, the legislature itself surveyed the opinions of several dozen judges, district attorneys, sheriffs, clergymen and professors. By a wide margin, the clergymen (and by a narrow margin, the professors) favored abolition. But the total result was almost two to one for retention. Almost exactly the same proportion opposed even a moratorium. In 1957, an abolition bill in the legislature was not reported out of committee, while a moratorium bill that easily passed in the Assembly died in a Senate committee.[3]

We also have several published and unpublished studies which attempt nationwide measures of the attitudes of the public and of some special interest groups on this subject. Five of the most important of these studies—Gallup Polls and a Harris Survey measuring national public opinion,

2 Clinton Duffy, *88 Men and 2 Women* (1962), p. 258.
3 See California, *Assembly Report on the Death Penalty* (1957), pp. 38, 48–51, and *Senate Report on the Death Penalty* (1960), p. 3. During 1962 the Maryland Legislature investigated abolition, and an opinion poll conducted by the Legislative Committee on Capital Punishment showed fifty-three per cent of the sample (1,458 residents of the state) in favor of, forty-seven per cent against, retaining the death penalty. The Committee voted five to two in favor of abolition. See Maryland, *Report on Capital Punishment* (1962), pp. 19, 37–38.

Professor Paul Thomas's survey in 1951 of state and federal prison wardens, and Father Donald Campion's poll in 1955 on the attitudes of state police—are reprinted in their entirety here.

The studies most in need of interpretation are the six polls, stretching over the thirty-year period from 1936 to 1966, attempting to sample national public opinion. Four are by the Gallup organization (1936, 1953, 1960, 1965), one is a Roper Poll (1958), and one is a Harris Survey (1966). If all are reliable, public opinion has undergone considerable fluctuation during the period studied. Abolition sentiment was at its lowest in 1953 (twenty-five per cent) and at its height in 1958 (fifty per cent), retentionist sentiment at its peak in 1953 (sixty-eight per cent) and at its ebb in 1966 (thirty-eight per cent). The major obstacle to a smooth pattern of waning retentionism and waxing abolitionism is the Roper Poll of February 9, 1958, which already showed abolitionists with a bare majority on their side, a strength they have been unable to sustain. Only the "don't knows" show a steady growth over this span of years in all six polls, from a negligible five per cent in 1936 to a significant fifteen per cent in 1966. Inquiries addressed to the Gallup and Roper organizations, inviting their explanations of the erratic results reported in the polls of 1953, 1958, and 1960, have gone unanswered. In any event, we should notice that only once in four polls (1960) has retentionism emerged with a majority (fifty-one per cent) on its side.

There are a few other published studies that may be noted briefly. In one which was conducted in 1951 by Dr. Philip Q. Roche of the University of Pennsylvania Medical School, 150 American psychiatrists were questioned. Of the eighty-six who responded (all but four of whom lived in death penalty states), "one-third to one-half stated their experience did not enable them to make either yes or no replies."[4] Of the remainder who thought it did, "only one out of seven believed that abolition would increase the

[4] Philip Roche, "A Psychiatrist Looks at the Death Penalty," *The Prison Journal* (October 1958), p. 47.

frequency of murder, and four out of five stated that the effect would be indifferent." In another poll, reported in 1961, the attitudes of state Governors were studied. Of the fifty inquiries sent, thirty-three replies were received. They were sorted out as follows: "sixteen were opposed to capital punishment, eight favored executions, and six indicated that their support for the death penalty was predicated on existing statutes in their states. Three formally declined comment." The governors of all the abolition states responded, and all favored abolition.[5] Still another poll, in Iowa during 1959, showed that out of a total of 1,142 persons questioned (including 817 students, 200 prison inmates and 125 prison guards), 61.6 per cent favored the death penalty, 26.7 per cent opposed it, and the remainder, 11.7 per cent, were undecided. Those favoring the death penalty included two-thirds of the students, nearly three-fourths of the guards, but almost no prisoners.[6]

In addition to these published surveys summarized above, there are three others, conducted in 1960, and unpublished at the time of this writing, by Professor Joseph Balogh of Bowling Green State University in Ohio. Using one fairly sophisticated questionnaire in all three of his studies,[7] Professor Balogh obtained the following results. In his study of public opinion in forty-six urban areas across the nation, he found that fourteen favored the death penalty, twelve opposed it, but no consistent attitudinal pattern emerged in the remaining twenty. These results do not seem too inconsistent with the Gallup and Roper results, given the very different testing methods used. In his second study, of sixteen urban police departments, he found that thirteen favored and two opposed the death penalty, while in only one department was the response indeterminate. His third

5 W. V. Levy, "The Rights and Wrongs of Capital Punishment," *Pageant Magazine* (September 1961), p. 119.

6 Walter Lunden, *The Death Penalty* (1960), pp. 23–25; see also his *The People, Their Prisons and Prisoners* (1961), pp. 11–12.

7 See Joseph Balogh and Mary Mueller, "A Scaling Technique for Measuring Social Attitudes Toward Capital Punishment," *Sociology and Social Research* (October 1960).

survey was addressed to wardens across the nation. Of the fifteen who responded, six opposed and four favored capital punishment, while five registered no opinion. Here, again, Professor Balogh's results, though not identical with those obtained by Father Campion and Professor Thomas, are not inconsistent with them.[8]

Can one hazard any generalizations from these several public opinion and attitude surveys? It seems fairly probable that: (1) psychiatrists, penologists and possibly social scientists and social workers generally, as well as higher government officials, tend to oppose the death penalty in this country at this time; (2) law enforcement officers tend to favor it. The strength of these divergent attitudes is about equally pronounced. (3) The general public shows a steadily growing trend to doubt the death penalty and to favor abolishing it. What principally accounts for these attitudes —first-hand exposure to the phenomena of criminal and penal violence, scientific and moral argument of the sort included in this volume, or deep-seated and relatively permanent unconscious desires—is impossible to estimate at present.[9]

PUBLIC OPINION AND THE DEATH PENALTY

THE AMERICAN INSTITUTE OF PUBLIC OPINION[*]
and THE HARRIS SURVEY

I

March 22, 1960. The case of Caryl Chessman, the convicted kidnapper sentenced to die May 2, has renewed a

[8] These data are cited by permission of Professor Balogh from his forthcoming study, *Capital Punishment, A Study of Social Attitudes.*

[9] The only attempt to measure change in attitudes on capital punishment is in several articles by Mapheus Smith, beginning with "Spontaneous Change of Attitude Toward Capital Punishment," *School and Society* (March 5, 1938).

[*] Reprinted, with minor omissions, through the permission of the American Institute of Public Opinion, Princeton, N.J., of the "Gallup Poll" reports dated March 22, 1960, and February 5, 1965.

worldwide debate: *should capital punishment be abolished?*

The latest Gallup Poll survey finds fifty-one per cent of the American public is in favor of the death penalty for persons convicted of murder. This marks a sharp drop from a previous measurement in November 1953, which showed sixty-eight per cent approving of capital punishment for murder. In April 1936,[1] when the Gallup Poll first sought the opinion of the American public on this issue, it was found that sixty-two per cent believed persons convicted of murder should be sentenced to death.

Across the nation, Gallup Poll reporters in the latest survey sought to determine how typical citizens line up today on the issue of capital punishment for murder. Here is the question asked of people in all walks of life: "Are you in favor of the death penalty for persons convicted of murder?" Following are the results of the latest survey, compared with the findings from the surveys in 1953 and in 1936:

FAVOR DEATH PENALTY FOR MURDER?

	Today	1953	1936
Yes	51%	68%	62%
No	36	25	33
Undecided	13	7	5

Among men, a considerably greater number in the latest survey favor the death penalty for murder than oppose it. Among women the margin of difference between those who favor and those who oppose invoking the supreme penalty is substantially less. Following are the figures by men and women:

FAVOR DEATH PENALTY FOR MURDER?

	Men	Women
Yes	58%	45%
No	33	39
Undecided	9	16

[1] [Editor's note: This survey is reported in Hadley Cantril, ed., *Public Opinion 1935–1946* (1951), p. 94.]

The number of executions in the United States has been decreasing over the last several years. In 1947 there were 152 executions. In 1959 there were forty-nine. On the other hand, the number of states where capital punishment is practiced has been on the rise. At present, forty-one of the fifty states now invoke the death penalty as a standard form of punishment for major crimes. . . .

II

February 5, 1965—The ranks of those who oppose capital punishment have swelled tremendously over the last twelve years. In 1953 the proportion in favor of the death penalty for convicted murderers was sixty-eight per cent. Twenty-five per cent were opposed. Today, Americans are virtually split on the issue—forty-five per cent in favor and forty-three per cent opposed.

The issue of capital punishment has long been debated in this country. A gradual state-by-state abolishment of the death penalty has been in evidence in recent years. Although only nine states have actually removed the statute from the law books, there has been a marked decline in the number of persons executed. To find out the views of people in this country, this question was asked: "Are you in favor of the death penalty for persons convicted of murder?" The results, and the trend since 1954:

FAVOR DEATH PENALTY?

	Latest	1960	1953
Yes	45%	51%	68%
No	43	36	25
No opinion	12	13	7

Much of the opposition to capital punishment comes from women, as the following table shows:

	Men	Women
Yes	54%	37%
No	37	49
No opinion	9	14

Since 1950 there has also been a marked trend of opinion away from capital punishment in Canada. The views of Canadians today closely parallel attitudes of Americans, as seen in a recent Canadian Gallup Poll. In 1950 nearly seven out of ten Canadians were for retention of the death penalty for murderers. Six years later, in 1956, belief in capital punishment had dropped, with only a slight majority endorsing it. Today, forty-five per cent of Canadians are opposed to capital punishment. Forty-six per cent favor the death penalty for both men and women. Another two per cent favor it for men but not for women. Seven per cent express no opinion.

Views in Great Britain and West Germany—according to recent surveys by Gallup affiliates in those countries—differ markedly from opinions held by Americans and Canadians. In Great Britain, only twenty-one per cent think the death penalty should be abolished. Seventy-nine per cent either take the opposite position or express uncertainty about the issue. Little change in views is noted from an earlier survey in that country, in July 1962. In West Germany, opinion is heavily in favor of capital punishment for murder, where extenuating circumstances cannot be proven. But opposition has been on the increase, as in Canada and the U. S. Eighty per cent of West Germans in 1958 opposed capital punishment. Today, sixty-five per cent do so.

Persons in favor of the death penalty are divided on whether or not persons under twenty-one years of age should pay the supreme penalty. The question asked, and the results: "Are you in favor of the death penalty for persons under twenty-one?"

FAVOR DEATH PENALTY FOR MINORS?

Yes	21%
No	20
No opinion	4
TOTAL:	45%
Opposed to death penalty	43
No opinion	12

III*

Revenge against the offender has a low priority in the attitudes of Americans toward the "National Crime Problem."

Many are anxious about their personal safety and many city dwellers harbor uneasy feelings about their police departments. But most Americans believe that crime can be curbed better by positive measures that attack the environmental and psychological roots of criminal activity than by great employment of police force.

The latest Harris Survey on attitudes toward crime was made amid increasing anti-crime activity in Washington and across the country. A presidential crime commission is studying the problem "from arrest to rehabilitation." More Federal money is going to local enforcement officials trying to find new crime-fighting techniques. Ability to put more rehabilitation facilities into the battle against drug traffic is sailing through Congress. The Justice Department has come out against capital punishment.[2]

Contrary to the punitive attitudes many experts have expected to find, people express these specific opinions: By more than five to one, people believe better programs for young persons will do more to reduce crime than merely a beefing up of local police forces. By seven to one, people think prisons should be more corrective than punitive, with heavy emphasis on rehabilitating criminals to re-enter society. By four to three, most Americans reach the same conclusion about capital punishment that the Justice Department has. A carefully drawn cross-section of the adult public was asked: . . . "Some states have abolished capital punishment—executing persons who commit a murder

* Reprinted, with omissions, from the Harris Survey, July 3, 1966, Copyright © 1967, The Washington Post Company, and by permission of Louis Harris & Associates, Inc.

[2] [Editor's note: See New York *Times,* July 24, 1965, p. 1; *Proceedings of the American Correctional Association* (1966), pp. 57–59; and *Capital Punishment Quarterly* (Austin, Texas, March 1966), p. 2.]

—and have substituted life imprisonment instead. Do you favor or oppose capital punishment?"

	Favor	Oppose	Not sure
Nationwide	38%	47%	15%
By education:			
8th grade or less	32	52	16
High school	28	46	16
College	44	44	12
By size of place:			
Cities	37	46	17
Suburbs	48	37	15
Towns	30	56	14
Rural	33	52	15
By sex:			
Men	44	43	13
Women	31	51	18

It is surprising that the less well-educated, more rural and small-town residents—women especially—carry the day against capital punishment. The more affluent parts of society, especially among men and suburban dwellers, are more in favor of continuing capital punishment . . .

ATTITUDES OF WARDENS TOWARD
THE DEATH PENALTY*

BY PAUL A. THOMAS**

Penologists, criminologists, jurists, philosophers, social scientists and correctional officials are well acquainted with the body of literature devoted to the history of capital punishment. The questions of its efficacy and of its retention or abolition have been argued at length on the religio-ethical plane, on an academic level, in highly emotional terms, and from the statistical approach. In view of the current British action relative to the death penalty,[1] and the fact that a recent issue of *The Annals* pertained to "Murder and the Death Penalty,"[2] it seems appropriate to present the following data for consideration by persons in the general field of correctional work.

The issue of *The Annals* referred to covered many aspects of the question. In this paper, however, specifically the questions of the deterrent effect of the death penalty, of the abolition of the death penalty, and of the murderer's considering the consequences (penalty) of his act are reviewed. The official views presented and analyzed here were collected from the responses to inquiries mailed to all state-prison wardens and superintendents and to four federal prison wardens in the United States: a total of fifty-five.[3] Such first-hand ideas pertinent to murder and the

* Reprinted, with permission of the author and publisher, from "Murder and the Death Penalty," *American Journal of Correction*, vol. 19, no. 4 (July–August 1957), pp. 16 ff.

** Professor of Sociology, DePauw University, and formerly member of Governor's Commission on Criminal Sexual-Psychopath Legislation, Indiana.

[1] "Britain Abolishes Death Penalty; Vote Is 293–262," *N. Y. Times*, February 17, 1956, p. 1. The British Commons, by the above vote, supported the Labor Party's amendment to abolish or suspend capital punishment.

[2] The American Academy of Political and Social Science, November, 1952.

[3] Originally collected in 1951–52 by David E. Gates, former DePauw student, and submitted to the writer. Acknowledgment is made to Mr. Gates.

death penalty would appear to be valuable because prison officials' opinions are often discussed without foundation or given otherwise distorted publication (*e.g.*, in the movies), and because relatively few statements from such sources are available to the public. One might at least suggest that these individuals are best qualified to judge the effects and utility of the death penalty. Prison officials have the opportunity to know, better than others, why convicts commit their crimes; are acquainted with their backgrounds and the conditions under which the crimes were executed; are able to inquire into the question whether or not convicts consider the consequence of their acts prior to commission; and must carry out the death penalty in each case. To these persons three questions were submitted:

1. Do you consider capital punishment a deterrent for murder?

2. Taking into consideration the state of mind of the offender at the time of the murder, do you think that the offender actually thinks about the consequences which his criminal act might bring upon himself?

3. (a) Does the fact that innocent persons have been executed create, in your estimation, a fallacy in the use of capital punishment, and (b) is this enough to abolish it in the United States?[4]

Thirty-two replies were received: twenty-nine state, three federal (thirty-one men, one woman) from all regions of the United States. They are summarized in the tables below.

First it will be noted that six of the thirty-two wardens and superintendents did not answer any of the questions. Some of the refusals were blunt, but others were more explanatory: *e.g.*, the fact that they carry out executions caused two wardens to make no comment; another replied that "any statement on the questions posed by you would be purely speculative." The last response is of interest be-

[4] The original question was not divided into parts (a) and (b). The writer made the division for purposes of tabular presentation, and because the total question could not be answered with "yes" or "no". For instance, one might favor abolition of the death penalty but not on account of the execution of innocent (convicted) persons.

TABLE 1: *Question 1*

Replies	Yes (%)	No (%)
26	3 (11)	23 (89)

TABLE 2: *Question 2*

Replies	Yes (%)	No (%)	No Answer (%)
26	1 (4)	24 (92)	1 (4)

TABLE 3: *Question 3*

Replies	Yes (%)	No (%)	No Answer (%)
26	16 (62)	6 (23)	4 (15)
(b)			
26	8 (31)	14 (54)	4 (15)

cause it might be *assumed* that wardens, in the face of their experiences, are the best informed on the questions posed, and because certain research data on these and related questions are available to them. Furthermore, the tables indicate that one official did not reply to Question 2, four did not reply to (a) of Question 3, and four did not reply to (b) of Question 3.

Question 1 was answered simply with yes or no by most of the respondents. Some statistical evidence was referred to in support of the negative reply. One warden said, "Harsh, brutal, or excessive punishment has never in penal history proven effective as a deterrent for any kind of crime."[5] Two others stated that, in their opinions, only in the case of organized crime does the penalty of death act as a deterrent. The writer believes, however, that the history of organized crime in the United States does not substantiate this opinion, nor does he believe that it has been established that organized criminals act on a pleasure-pain basis to any greater extent than do other persons in society. If they do, then it may rest upon an ability to avoid apprehension and conviction through some type of fix—a calculated risk?

[5] A similar point is made by R. G. Caldwell, "Why Is the Death Penalty Retained?", *The Annals,* November, 1952, 45–53. See p. 51.

Another state superintendent put it as follows:

"Of course, any punishment tends to deter the commission of crime; but I am not altogether persuaded that capital punishment is worth the price we pay for it. For instance, during my tenure as Superintendent there has not been a single pardon of a man sentenced to death nor have there been any death sentences commuted. There have been appeals to the Supreme Court which have led to retrial and a lessening of the sentence. But it has been generally understood, and such things get around among the criminal classes, that pardons are not easy to get in——————. In spite of that fact, we have now at the Penitentiary twelve men under sentence of death. This does not prove to me that capital punishment really deters very many people."

One affirmative reply to Question 1 also discloses the recognition of social-psychological factors involved in the matter of deterrence:

"Capital punishment unquestionably is a deterrent which probably prevents a good number of murders. There are other deterring factors involved when a person considers killing another person—fear of retaliation other than through legal processes; fear of the guilt or remorse which might result; loss of friendship, respect of others, and of social status generally; and so on. I don't think it is possible to isolate the relative deterrent values of all the various 'risks' involved in committing a murder.[6]"

The last observation merits attention because it acknowledges the complexity of any single act of human behavior as well as the complexity of the question posed, a point not made in the balance of the comments on this given item.

Another statement provides a basis for debate: "If capital punishment does not deter, it certainly should not encourage crime." This viewpoint, of course, might be expressed toward any form of punishment, mild or severe, and although it can be argued that it is difficult or impos-

[6] Caldwell also refers to "a growing recognition that it is the desire to find love, respect, and security among relatives, friends, and business associates rather than the fear of legal penalties that keeps the majority of persons from violating the law. This is the principal form of social control . . ." *Ibid.*, pp. 52–53.

sible to measure the deterrent effect of the death penalty, a stronger case might be made against the measurement of a penalty's encouragement of crime. The social-psychological elements bearing upon human behavior, referred to above, can not be ignored in the attempts to evaluate a penal sanction.

Considerable comment was made in answer to Question 2. There was consensus that murder is committed by a person under emotional strain, in sheer rage or anger, or while apprehended in another felony, *i.e.,* conditions or situations militating against concern about the future. One warden replied:

"We do know that at least the majority of these murders are committed on the impulse of the moment, while under the influence of liquor, or in a fit of passion, and a great many of our men at this institution serving life sentence for murder are first offenders. It is difficult, however, to know what to do with a man or woman who premeditates a crime and carries it out according to schedule. However, I believe that such cases are in the minority."

Where a murder is committed on the impulse of the moment, the fact that there is capital punishment in the state where such murder is committed, is given little, if any, consideration by the one committing the murder. In other words, it is pretty difficult to believe that one of normal mind wants to take the life of another, regardless of cause or consequence.

Other officials noted the possibility that premeditated murder (the minority of cases) is accompanied by some thought of its consequences, but one only took a definite stand:

"I believe that most offenders actually think about the consequence which his criminal act may bring upon himself. The capital punishment is usually inflicted upon premeditated crimes, and I do feel that the person involved does consider the consequences, but no doubt builds up the feeling that he has a right to commit the crime, and thus extradite himself from the situation, or possibly, he plans not to be apprehended."

Even in this case the warden reveals the significant view

that persons who commit premeditated murder frequently expect to beat the rap; that is, to defeat the principle of certainty of punishment. Thus, a severe penalty may not deter. However, we can not lay this to an intrinsic weakness of the death penalty *per se*, but instead attention must be directed to other processes (*e.g.*, the fix) which nullify the potential deterrence of the death penalty.

Another warden wrote, "I have talked with almost every man who has been on condemned row since 1929, and have yet to have a man tell me he has given any thought to the consequences of his crime at the time it was committed."[7] So, with the possible exception of premeditated murder, in these replies there is little to give meaningful support to hedonistic theories of behavior with respect to murderers, particularly in regard to the penalty.

Responses to Question 3 showed a rather surprising fact; namely, that some of the officials had never heard, or had heard but were not convinced, that innocent persons have been executed in the United States.[8] Table 3 reveals that sixteen (sixty-two per cent) of the officials agreed that errors in execution had been or may have been made, in contrast to six (twenty-three per cent) who denied it or strongly doubted the fact. In regard to Part (b) of the question, eight (thirty-one per cent) officials believed that such errors do justify the abolition of the death penalty, but fourteen (fifty-four per cent) did not accept this point of view. The writer found the following statements especially illuminating on this third question:

A. I feel that the deterring effect of capital punishment outweighs the possibility of an innocent victim being executed.

B. I do not know of any innocent person who has been executed. Quite often a man claims innocence, but actual

[7] See K. F. Schuessler, "The Deterrent Influence of the Death Penalty," *The Annals,* November, 1952, pp. 61–62, for comparable statements.

[8] Officials might consult C. Kirkpatrick, *Capital Punishment,* Philadelphia, 1925, and E. M. Borchard, *Convicting the Innocent,* New Haven, 1932. Recent cases in England are cited by Woodrow Wyatt, "Again the Issue of Capital Punishment," *New York Times Magazine,* January 8, 1956, pp. 17, 44.

proof of innocence has not been established. I do believe that capital punishment should be abolished, but many men convicted of atrocious murders, however, should be confined for life.

C. I feel, however, with the abolishment of capital punishment that wherever a man or woman is confined and serving a life sentence, the population of that institution deserves protection from the individual, and in the event that he commits another murder while serving his sentence, there should be no choice in the matter—either execution or confined in solitary where he can harm no one but himself.

D. If the fact that innocent persons have been executed indicated enough fallacy in the use of capital punishment to abolish it in the United States, then it would necessarily follow that punishment for all crimes should be abolished in as much as innocent persons undoubtedly have been convicted of all crimes.

E. This reminds me of the question "When did you stop beating your wife?" I'm not at all sure that the execution of innocent persons has to do with the type of punishment to be used. It has much to do with judicial processes. For example, I certainly would not say that correctional institutions should be done away with because innocent persons have been sent to prison. I do not believe that this argument would be sufficient, in itself, to justify abolishing capital punishment.

F. Certainly, the rights of individuals concerning due process of law, gives every opportunity for every legal means to be executed in proving innocence and I would be reluctant to agree that capital punishment should be abolished on the assumption that innocent persons have been executed. This is not to say that I either oppose or condone capital punishment as it exists in the laws of the various states.

G. If our courts function properly, a person's guilt is assumed to be established before the person is sentenced. Undoubtedly, the utmost care should be taken to insure a fair and impartial trial.

H. I do not believe that the fallacy of innocent people being executed for murder is enough to abolish capital punishment in the United States. It is, however, a good point to use in the fight, but I believe that most trouble lies in bringing to the public the understanding that the philosophy "an eye for an eye and a tooth for a tooth" is wrong and that treatment rather than punishment is progress.

I. The occasional miscarriage of justice in the execution of an innocent person is of course tragic; but this fault is not of itself sufficient reason for abolishing capital punishment. A more cogent reason would come from the fallacy of the old requirement of "an eye for an eye," etc.

J. All of our religious training and humanitarian instincts convince us that it is better that many of the guilty be allowed to go free rather than that we punish one innocent person and of course this is especially true where the irrevocable death penalty is involved. However, in considering the abolishment of the death penalty in the United States I would rate the fact that an occasional innocent person is executed as secondary and supplemental to the premise that the death penalty is ineffective as a deterrent. Since Society long ago abandoned, or should have abandoned, the motive of revenge in its penal thinking it is absurd to continue a policy which has been proven ineffective and which also violates our instincts against the punishment of the innocent.

K. It is probably true that some innocent persons have been executed, which in itself presents a sordid situation, but in my estimation the practice of capital punishment belongs to the dark ages, and is not in step with modern civilization . . . I certainly do not feel that murderers should not be punished, however, I do not feel that capital punishment alleviates the situation. In fact, for most, it is the easy way out. Too, I do not think it was ever intended by our Supreme Ruler for one man to designate the termination of another.

L. I would say that the fact that innocent persons have been executed is no more argument against capital punishment than that innocent persons have suffered the blighting experience of confinement. Death to me is not nearly so distressing as the slow spiritual death of unjust confinement. I am opposed to capital punishment, but I am also opposed to nearly every other form of punishment that has been meted out in our modern age.

M. While only a minute fraction of one per cent of murderers convicted have been found to be innocent, that factor does have a bearing on the public mind and its attitude towards capital punishment.

The thirteen quotations display, in general, the historic bases of argument concerning the death penalty and the desirability of its retention: its utility or disutility as a deterrent is cited; academic and theoretical comments are offered relative to punishment, to the judicial process, and to the justification of punishment; religio-ethical arguments are presented; and the role of the public is suggested in the final excerpt.[9] Sociologically, the claims that the death penalty does not coincide with the times (statements H through K) recognize that punitive policies are not immutable but rather are cultural phenomena, capable of adjustment in line with new knowledge of human nature and with changing demands of different periods of society. It is interesting to note this same emphasis in the British Labor Party's amendment to the present law in England:

. . . the House "believes that the death penalty for murder no longer accords with the needs of the true interests of a civilized society and calls upon her majesty's Government to introduce forthwith legislation for its abolition or for its suspension for an experimental period."[10]

The doubt indicated with respect to the execution of innocent persons, coupled with the faith expressed in due process of law, to some readers may be the crux of the entire question. There is little doubt that the entire reaction to crime must be strong and just, but weaknesses in the legal process may be the reasons why some officials do not know that innocent individuals have been convicted and executed. The problem of obtaining accurate statistics and of underreporting in such cases has been described in this way:

"Such cases will not arouse law enforcement officers to

[9] This is also in evidence in the recent debates on the abolition of the death penalty in England. See Wyatt, *op. cit.*

[10] *New York Times, op. cit.,* February 17, 1956, p. 4.

great effort, because that would mean enthusiasm for professional self-indictment. Obviously, they cannot ensure the co-operation of the victim. Furthermore, the impossibility of reparation to the victim of the error will probably weaken the effort also of those who were interested in him as long as there was hope. Finally, the efforts of the actual killer to remain undetected together with the fact that the case has been decided and led to the punishment demanded by the law, tends to conceal a miscarriage of justice rather than leave public traces of its occurrence.[11]"

We can conclude that the officials raised traditional arguments on the death penalty and murder. The evidence (replies to Questions 1 and 2) appears to support the belief that capital punishment should be abolished. However, replies to Question 3 make it clear that, although execution of innocent persons constitutes a fallacy in capital punishment to sixty-two per cent of the respondents, only thirty-one per cent were convinced that *this* feature justifies abolishing the death penalty. On the basis of the fact that there was such an admission of a chance for miscarriage of justice, and the fact that eighty-nine per cent of the officials denied the deterrent effect of capital punishment, one might expect that the officials would favor the abolition of the death penalty in view of the errors of justice. But logic is not the point in question.

Furthermore, the concern expressed (1) about the proper functioning of the machinery of justice, (2) about the fact retaliation still is a powerful *public* reaction to crime, and (3) about the ineffective influence of the death penalty as a deterrent shows thoughtful opinions. If widespread publicity were given to these views, possibly public opinion would be altered. Perhaps precedent plays an important role here: capital punishment has a long history—it is traditional—and is retained largely for that reason. In addition, does society want complete abolition of the death penalty? There are premeditated murderers, hired murderers, and, some claim, habitual murderers. If it is established that such persons are guilty, the officials believe that such

11 Otto Pollak, "The Errors of Justice," *The Annals*, November, 1952, 115–123. See p. 123.

persons must be removed from society. Some states, after abolishing the death penalty, appear to have controlled satisfactorily the problem with life imprisonment. Perhaps this policy can become traditional throughout the United States. It is a matter of public education, with official leadership, first, and then public support: that is, social organization about a principle.

ATTITUDES OF STATE POLICE TOWARD THE DEATH PENALTY *

BY DONALD R. CAMPION, S.J.**

In view of the negative conclusion drawn from a survey of state police officers killed by criminals,[1] some interest attaches to the question of the extent of police support of the death penalty as a source of protection. How universal is such support? Does this support vary in some observable relation to actual experience? Through the cooperation of state police respondents some information pertinent to these questions has been gathered in the course of the present study.

Together with a request for completion of the blank described in the first section of this study, the following request was also addressed to the directors of the twenty-seven state police forces:

Please give me your personal opinion of the accuracy of the claim made in the opening paragraph of this letter.

The claim, as stated in the letter was: "that the existence of the death penalty in a given state gives the police a certain amount of protection, which would be lost if the death penalty were abolished".

* Reprinted from "The State Police and the Death Penalty," Appendix F, Part II, *Minutes of Proceedings and Evidence*, no. 20, Joint Committee of the Senate and the House of Commons on Capital Punishment, Corporal Punishment and Lotteries, 1955, pp. 735–738. Available from The Queen's Printer, Ottawa, Canada.

** Associate Editor, *America*.

[1] [Editor's note: See Chapter Six.]

Statements in response to this request were received from eighteen of the twenty-four respondents. No expression of opinion was forthcoming from the responding officials of the Georgia, Illinois, Nebraska, North Dakota, Pennsylvania, and South Dakota state police forces. It will be noted that one of the six, North Dakota, is a non-death penalty state.

Since the request asked for expressions of personal opinion, it has not been possible to classify the responses under exact categories. A study of the opinions expressed, however, furnishes the following summary:

Respondents from eight states, California, Connecticut, Indiana, Iowa, Maryland, New York, Oregon, and Texas, favored the view that the existence of the death penalty provides a certain protection for police officers;

Respondents from three states, Maine, Massachusetts, and Wisconsin, rejected the claim;

Respondents from two states, Minnesota and West Virginia, expressed the opinion that the existence of the death penalty probably did not provide greater protection;

Respondents from the remaining five of the eighteen states replying to this request, Michigan, Missouri, Ohio, Rhode Island, and Washington, indicated in their replies that they had no fixed opinion on the claim.

From this summary it can be seen that no one opinion prevails throughout police circles. In some instances, respondents from neighboring states have expressed opposing sentiments on the question of the death penalty as a protection to the police. Though not all replies from the non-death penalty states showed fixed opposition to the claim, explicit replies in favor of the claim were all from states having the death penalty in existence within their jurisdictions.

In conclusion, a brief analysis of the replies from some states will be made by way of a comparison between opinions expressed and the corresponding data on killings reported from the state forces. For this purpose we select three groups within the regional divisions utilized in the first section of this study.

From the New England region, Commissioner John C. Kelly, of the Connecticut State Police, stated:

I personally agree with the supporters of the death penalty that the existence of such a penalty in a given state gives the police a certain amount of protection which would be lost if the penalty were abolished. With the death penalty existing it is only common sense to believe that criminals are less likely to carry lethal weapons for fear that they might be tempted to use them when coming in contact with the police.

On the other hand, from the same area Colonel Robert Marx, Chief of the Maine State Police, replied:

Both the record and experience in this State would indicate that the lack of a death penalty in no way influences the element of protection to the police in this State.

In the neighboring Commonwealth of Massachusetts, Commissioner of Public Safety Otis M. Whitney, is of the view that the existence of the death penalty gives the Public a certain amount of protection, but he adds:

I do not think criminals would be less likely to carry lethal weapons because of the threat of the death penalty, but they might be less likely to use them while committing a crime . . . They do not give much thought to the possibility that they might be tempted to use them in a brush with the police.

And from a fourth New England state, Colonel John T. Sheehan, Superintendent of the Rhode Island State Police remarked:

Relative to your specific inquiry concerning the comparative values in the retention or abolition of the death penalty, it is my thought that the question is based on the knowledge of laws entertained by the criminal. Since this is such a speculative estimation no conclusive opinion can be formed or expressed.

Over against the opinions thus expressed, we may consider the number of police officers killed in the ranks of the state police forces of this region:

For	2	Against		No fixed opinion	
Connecticut		Maine	0	Rhode Island	1
		Massachusetts	1		

From the states in the East North Central region, we find that Superintendent Frank A. Jessup, of the Indiana State Police, favors the view that the existence of the death penalty gives police a certain amount of protection. In support of his opinion he writes:

During the past twenty years of police experience many criminals have told me that the presence of the death penalty on the Indiana statutes acts as a deterrent in the carrying of firearms. These people were not too concerned over serving time for burglary or larceny, but were concerned in the penalty for shooting a police officer.

Commissioner Joseph A. Childs, of the Michigan State Police, however, presents a somewhat different view on the protective value of the death penalty:

With respect to the protection such a penalty would or does afford police officers, I do not feel as qualified to speak as are chiefs of police in the larger cities where there is more of a concentration of the vicious type of criminal and lethal weapon attacks on police officers are more frequent . . . Our own experience does not provide a broad enough basis for definite conclusions . . . Granting that the intent of penalty is to deter crime as well as punish it, the death penalty should be the greatest deterrent of all, but this logic is open to many counter arguments and is certainly not supported in its entirety by the records.

A third state in this area, Ohio, has a police force with limited jurisdiction. Colonel George Mingle, Superintendent of the Ohio State Highway Patrol, reports that in discussing the question at issue with members of his staff, he found that they were divided in their opinions. On the matter of criminals carrying lethal weapons, he remarks:—

> How often . . . criminals have been tempted or refrained from using them because Ohio has a capital punishment law, we do not know. There is a limited number of cases where our Patrol officers have been injured by lethal weapons in the hands of criminals. In our more than twenty-one years of existence as a law-enforcement agency in this state, we have had one officer murdered. We are not able to say that these results would have been different if this state did not have capital punishment.

Once again, for purposes of comparison, we recall the respective numbers of killings for members of the state police forces and the opinions expressed from these states:—

	For		*No fixed opinion*	
Indiana	3		Michigan	5
			Ohio	1

Just as in the New England region, so we find here that the range of police experience with killings by criminals is wide and police opinion on the death penalty seems to vary independently of any observable relation to this experience.

A final comparison may be made of three states in the West North Central region. In support of the claim for the death penalty is the statement of Chief David Herrick, of the Iowa Highway Safety Patrol:

> I am inclined to believe that the existence of the death penalty does give the police a certain amount of protection.

An opposite position on the question is taken by L. E. Beier, Director of Enforcement of the Wisconsin Motor Vehicle Department:

> It is my belief that a deterrent effect is not achieved by the retention of the death penalty. It is my further belief that very few criminals take into consideration

at the moment when a crime is committed whether or not apprehension would result in the death penalty being imposed.

And from another non-death penalty state in the same region, we find the following statement by E. T. Mattson, Assistant Superintendent of the Bureau of Criminal Apprehension, Department of Highways, Minnesota:

It is our belief that the certainty of apprehension and punishment is the greatest deterrent force in our society today. However, it is doubtful that capital punishment such as the death penalty, is a greater deterring force than punishment in a lesser degree, by imprisonment.

The data on killings of members of the state police for these West North Central states will be recalled:

For		*Against*	
Iowa	1	Minnesota	0
		Wisconsin	0

It is to be noted that the replies from these states exhibit the same variations in opinion and experience found in the other regions examined.

In summary of this section of the study, then, we may say that the opinions held by police officials on the claim that capital punishment is a source of greater protection to the police, varies widely, though the more common view supports that claim. From our survey of opinions it would seem that the record of killings of police in a particular police force does not of itself determine police opinion for or against the death penalty as a protection. Though most support for the death penalty came from rather populous, urbanized states, having the death penalty on their statutes, and all reporting some killings of officers in their state police forces, we find dissenting opinions held by police officials from states possessed of these same characteristics. Whether grouped with respect to geographical proximity, similarity of crime rates, population distribution, or compared on the basis of numbers of police officers killed, the different states manifested no fixed pattern of opinion among police officials on the value of the death penalty as a protection to the police.

Chapter Six

THE QUESTION OF DETERRENCE

INTRODUCTION

In order to understand the complex question of capital punishment as a deterrent, it is necessary to place it within the context of the nature and purposes of punishments in general. Punishments under law are usually framed with a two-fold purpose—retribution and prevention. A punishment is imposed on someone because of a crime he has committed (the law does not punish someone for something he hasn't done). But the penal code authorized the punishment in the first place mainly in the hope of discouraging anyone from committing such acts (the class of acts a society punishes under law is the class of acts it most desires to prevent). Undoubtedly, other factors once played a larger role than these two. Expiatory punishments, for example, are familiar in the literature of most ancient peoples, though they have little or no role in modern penology.

Even retribution no longer plays the predominant role it once did. What remains behind every penal system, of course, is the public's demand for vengeance against criminals and, at a more elevated level, the expression of moral indignation for the offenders' effrontery. In a memorable passage in the literature on capital punishment, Sir James Fitzjames Stephen wrote:

> It is highly desirable that criminals should be hated, that punishments inflicted upon them should be so contrived as to give expression to that hatred, and to justify it so far as the public provision of means for expressing and gratifying a healthy natural sentiment

can justify and encourage it . . . When a man is hung, there is an end of our relations with him. His execution is a way of saying, "You are not fit for this world, take your chance elsewhere."[1]

Vengeance, unredeemed by any higher sentiments or lofty rhetoric, is unmistakable in this statement for newsmen from the mother of a boy killed in New York when it was announced that the death sentence of her son's killer had been commuted to life imprisonment: "Agron will live on our tax which we must pay, but I wish he never has a good day for the rest of his life. May he die a thousand deaths a day."[2] No one can study the testimony offered at legislative hearings on abolition bills, or listen to the debates when such bills are up for consideration, and have any doubt that the right to vengeance is believed to justify capital punishment. Nor is it likely that anyone will dispute that capital punishment is an excellent form of retributive punishment, at least for the crime of murder.

But the main focus of discussion, whether in the legislature, before popular audiences, or in scholarly reports, is the efficacy of the death penalty as a preventative of crime. There are four ways in which a punishment may be used to prevent crime. First, it may be used to incapacitate known offenders, either absolutely (by killing them) or relatively (by incarcerating them), thereby preventing them from committing any more offenses. No more need be said as to the merits of the death penalty as a preventative of crime by means of incapacitation.[3] Second, a punishment may be intended to prevent known offenders from committing further crimes by correcting them through a program of detention, education and therapy—what is popularly called "reformation" or "rehabilitation." Obviously, the death penalty has never been used in this fashion. The most ever

---

[1] James Fitzjames Stephen, *A History of the Criminal Law of England* (1883), II, p. 81; and "Capital Punishment," *Fraser's Magazine* (June 1864), p. 763.

[2] *New York Times* (February 8, 1962).

[3] It is a common mistake to call this "deterrence," a mistake, because to deter is to prevent by *threatening* the would-be offender with consequences he prefers to avoid.

claimed for it in this respect was that there is nothing like awaiting a date with the hangman to make a man's heart properly contrite and, in this sense, to "reform" him.

Not all punishments aimed at preventing crime, of course, are aimed solely at individual offenders already in custody. Indeed, most penal sanctions designed to prevent crimes are directed at the general public. One way a punishment may be used to prevent the general public from committing a crime is by underlining the gravity of those acts which society wishes to discourage. If the state promises that its coercive force will be brought to bear against anyone who commits a certain act, the enormity and gravity of the act from a moral point of view are effectively emphasized. Some students of the principles of punishment have pointed to the death penalty as the natural and necessary means to the end of inculcating respect for human life, liberty and property.[4] But by far the most common way to employ a punishment as a preventative of crime is to adopt a sufficiently severe penalty so as to compel general obedience out of fear of the consequences of disobedience—the classic doctrine of deterrence. Even though deterrence cannot override every other concern in formulating a rational penal philosophy, there is no doubt that the death penalty's efficacy as a deterrent is the major factual issue in dispute between abolitionists and retentionists.

Exactly what the issue is, however, is oftentimes needlessly confused. (1) A minority among abolitionists defends extreme views on the subject, asserting that punishment in any form is never a deterrent, or, at least, that capital punishment is no deterrent. Either of these propositions is difficult to believe. Fortunately, the majority of abolitionists are not required by the logic of their position to defend them. Only those who favor *no* punishment for capital crimes

---

[4] Though one may believe that the primary purpose of the criminal law is to reflect society's condemnation of certain acts, one need not believe that the death penalty is the proper punishment for the gravest crimes; see Henry Hart, "The Aims of the Criminal Law," *Law and Contemporary Problems* (September 1958), p. 426.

have anything at stake in these extreme views, and their defense will have to be left to them. (2) Retentionists also make an excessive demand when they expect abolitionists to show that imprisonment is a superior deterrent to execution. From the point of view of deterrence, it ought to be enough to prefer imprisonment over executions, if, all other things being equal, imprisonment is less cruel and if it is as good a deterrent as execution. (3) Sometimes, it is argued that the dispute is over whether or not the death penalty is a uniquely effective deterrent. Even this formulation is inaccurate. If some mode of unspeakably brutal torture should prove to be an even more effective deterrent than the death penalty, few retentionists and no abolitionists would be interested in adopting it. So the question of which mode of punishment is the most effective deterrent may be left to one side also.

There is only one question we need to answer: (4) Is long term imprisonment (on the assumptions that it is less savage and more easily administered by the judicial system than capital punishment) as good a deterrent for the major crimes currently punished by death? This formulation leaves open, as it should, the question of how close either penalty is to a completely effective deterrent; and it does not raise the further question, as it shouldn't, whether death might be a better deterrent for certain crimes (e.g., against property) that no one would think of punishing in this way. To put it another way, the real dispute over deterrence is this: how many capital crimes, if any, have been (or might be) prevented by the threat of execution, which would not have been (or would not be) prevented by the threat of imprisonment? We know that every year about half a dozen in every 100,000 of the population are not deterred by capital punishment from committing a homicide; what we want to know is whether another half a dozen, or a dozen, or hundreds or thousands are deterred by it, who wouldn't be deterred by the threat of a prison sentence.

No social scientist has directly studied this question of *differential deterrence;* indeed, it is almost impossible to do so. It has been studied indirectly, however, and the five research studies reprinted in this chapter represent all the major original work of this sort published in recent years. Each of these investigations is addressed to the alleged deterrent efficacy of the death penalty for murder.

In principle, differential deterrence can be studied in several different ways. For instance, the homicide (or even where available, the murder) rates of all death penalty jurisdictions can be compared for a given year, or preferably for a period of years, with the homicide (or murder) rates of all abolition jurisdictions. Whenever this has been done, it has turned out that the abolition jurisdictions have much the lower average rate. In fact, a rank order of states according to annual homicide rate correlates very closely with the rank order of states according to the annual number of executions.[5] But criminologists generally recognize that this sort of comparison is quite superficial and inconclusive. The obvious socio-cultural differences between the abolition states and the states in the South, where homicide rates are several times higher and where executions are fairly frequent, almost certainly obliterates whatever effects are attributable to the relevant variable, the different mode of punishment for murder. Hence, no study of this sort is included in the present volume. Notice, however, that to the degree one accounts for the low murder rate in certain death penalty states, such as Oregon, for example, as opposed to the high rate in Georgia, by appeal to socio-cultural differences between the two states, to that degree one is tacitly conceding that the rate of murder itself is *not* primarily a function of the mode of punishment. Indeed, if in this light one consults the murder rates for different states in recent years, one sees that the retentionist faces a serious dilemma: either he admits that imprisonment (in Alaska and Maine, for example) is as good or even a better deterrent than death (in Kansas and Geor-

[5] For full details, see Massachusetts, *Report on the Death Penalty* (1958), pp. 15–16, 43; and also Karl Schuessler, "The Deterrent Influence of the Death Penalty," *The Annals* (November 1952), p. 57. The interested reader may easily construct such correlations for himself from the crime and execution statistics supplied in Chapter Two of this book.

gia); or he admits that factors having little or nothing to do with the mode of punishment account for differences in murder rates in different states (the murder rate in Alaska is thrice that in Maine, and the rate in Georgia is four times that in Kansas). On either alternative, he must give up his conviction that the *main* factor in controlling the rate of murder is using, or threatening to use, the death penalty.

The studies that are included below proceed along three different lines. (1) Homicide rates of contiguous jurisdictions, one (or more) of which has the death penalty for murder, and one (or more) of which has imprisonment, have been compared. The studies reprinted below by Professor Thorsten Sellin and Father Donald Campion are of this sort. The cornerstone of the case against the deterrent superiority of the death penalty over imprisonment rests on these investigations of Professor Sellin, and I shall consider below what they seem to prove. (2) Homicide rates in a given jurisdiction where the death penalty was abolished for a brief time have been studied for the years before, during, and after abolition. Several short term studies of this sort from among the few states where it is possible to make such a study have been included in Chapter Seven. (3) Lastly, there are comparisons of homicide rates in a given jurisdiction where the death penalty is used for murder, over the periods before, during, and after a capital trial and/or execution. The articles by Professor Leonard Savitz and Dr. William Graves adopt this approach. Their studies are not, of course, attempts to study differential deterrent efficacy. What they attempt to establish is whether there is any proximate reduction in the volume of murder traceable to the imposition of death sentences or executions.

Three of the six selections in this chapter are of special interest for other reasons. Father Campion's study and the second of Professor Sellin's two essays are not concerned with the general protection given to society by the death penalty, but with the special protection it supposedly affords law enforcement personnel. All those who are inclined to accept the views of Chief Allen, presented in Chapter Three, ought to give these two essays in the present chapter the closest attention. Dr. Graves's work is suggestive because it appears to confirm the theory, hitherto supported only by anecdotes,[6] that executions, far from operating solely as a deterrent, actually incite some persons to criminal violence. Although this possibility is often greeted with derision, it receives some support from current psychiatric theory.[7]

What do all these studies, taken together, seem to show? The results are negative; there is no evidence to support the theory that the death penalty is a deterrent superior to imprisonment for the crime of murder. The significance one assigns to this negative result depends entirely upon the credence one gives to the possibility that further research might, after all, support the theory that the death penalty is the superior deterrent. Professor Sellin has on occasion gone so far as to assert positively that there is evidence for the view that imprisonment is as good a deterrent as the death penalty; and either the negative or the positive conclusion has been accepted (with a few notable exceptions) by all of the official governmental reports so

[6] Several are given in Thorsten Sellin, *The Death Penalty* (1959), pp. 65–69; G. Ryley Scott, *A History of Capital Punishment* (1950), p. 246; Massachusetts, *op. cit.*, pp. 27–28; and Ohio, *Report on Capital Punishment* (1961), p. 49.

[7] On the phenomenon of "suicide-by-murder," Dr. Isadore Ziferstein, a psychiatrist practicing in Los Angeles, writes: "A couple of fairly recent cases come to mind. One, the case of a disc jockey from Las Vegas who shot a complete stranger on the streets of Los Angeles in broad daylight. On being arrested, he stated that he had been despondent for some time but did not have the courage to commit suicide. He therefore chose murder as an indirect route to his own destruction. A similar case occurred a couple of years ago in Los Angeles, where a man, after several unsuccessful attempts at suicide, killed his landlady and turned himself in. As I recall, the State eventually obliged him by executing him. For every case where this mechanism of suicide-by-murder is conscious and is verbalized, there are probably several where the same mechanism is unconscious and not manifestly verbalized, although it can be deduced from a careful study and interpretation of the material. In these cases, obviously, the death penalty is not a deterrent, but has quite the opposite effect of motivating the sick person to commit murder." (Quoted, with permission, from a letter of May 13, 1962.)

far published on capital punishment in the past decade.[8]
This is not so surprising when it is realized that every one
of these reports relied on the statistical studies conducted
by Professor Sellin. The fact remains, however, that his
evidence has managed over the past decade to convince a
wide variety of legislative committees throughout the
English-speaking world, and not in every case were the
members of these committees initially receptive to his conclusions.[9]

Nevertheless, some objections do remain to be considered. First of all, the statistical studies reprinted here (except Professor Savitz's) rely on inferences from homicide
rates to capitally punishable murder rates. We have already
seen in Chapter Two how sketchy the known connection is
between the two rates. To whatever degree the former is
an unreliable guide to the latter—which we have no way of
directly measuring at all—to that degree all the studies reprinted here are unreliable at the crucial point: is the death
penalty an effective deterrent for those kinds of homicides
punishable by death? Here is one kind of difficulty that
arises when one expects homicide statistics to provide a
conclusive answer to this question. Data reported below in
Professor Sellin's article shows that the ten-year average of
annual homicide rates in Ohio fell during the 1920's from

[8] See Royal Commission on Capital Punishment, *Report*
(1953), § § 65, 65, 67–68; California, *Assembly Report on the
Death Penalty* (1957), p. 30; Massachusetts, *op. cit.*, pp. 43–44;
Ohio, *op. cit.*, pp. 31, 37; Pennsylvania, *Report on Capital Punishment* (1961), pp. 20–24; Ceylon, *Report on Capital Punishment* (1959), pp. 45, 52. The main exceptions are Florida,
Report . . . [on] Abolition of Death Penalty (1965), pp. 13–
19; New Jersey, *Report . . . [on] Capital Punishment* (1964),
pp. 7 ff.; and Canada, *Report on Capital Punishment* (1956),
pp. 12–15. The argument of the latter is analyzed in the text
below, pp. 267–269. In each case, the conclusions submitted by
Professor Sellin were rejected in favor of the *ad lib.* testimony
of law enforcement spokesmen.

[9] The most dramatic and best known change of opinion is
that of Lord Gowers, the Chairman of the British Royal Commission on Capital Punishment. His book, *A Life for a Life?*
(1956), tells the story of his conversion to the cause of
abolition.

that studied capital punishment in 1956, the only governmental body exposed to Professor Sellin's statistical researches that refused to accept his interpretation, wrote in
part:

> One measure of its [the death penalty's] deterrent
> effect was afforded by an analysis of murders which
> indicated that a considerable proportion, probably in
> excess of half, are committed under the compulsion of
> overwhelming passion or anger where no deterrent
> could have been effective. This would seem to demon-
> strate that the death penalty, coupled with the excel-
> lent standards of law enforcement prevailing in Can-
> ada, has been successful in deterring the commission
> of deliberate, premeditated murders and reducing
> their incidence to minimum proportions. The deterrent
> effect may also be indicated by the widespread associa-
> tion of the crime of murder with the death penalty
> which is undoubtedly one reason why murder is re-
> garded as such a grave and abhorrent crime.[14]

Several of these points, including the last one, are undoubtedly true. But there is little or no evidence in favor of
the Committee's view that a crime ceases to be regarded as
grave and abhorrent if it is not punished by death; killing
a person will remain exactly what it is, no matter how it is
punished. Grading punishments according to the severity
of the crime does not require that the upper limit of severity
be the death penalty. As to the main point, the Committee
overlooks its tacit admission that approximately half of all
the murders analyzed were deliberate and premeditated,
and that not even the excellence of law enforcement plus
the death penalty could deter a certain portion of the general public from committing these murders! The Committee also assumes that all the possible murders that did *not*
occur, did not occur because the potential murderers were
deterred. This is very doubtful. Whereas it is trivial to say
that all the murders that *did* occur were committed by

[14] Canada, *Report on Capital Punishment* (1956), p. 14, § 53.

persons who were not deterred, it is not trivial but quite false (and in no way logically derivable from the prior trivial proposition) to say that all the murders that did *not* occur did not take place because their potential authors were deterred. There is no reason to attribute the failure of the vast bulk of the population to commit or even to contemplate murder to the efficacy of the deterrent capacity of *any* penal sanctions. What the Committee must have assumed is that (1) everyone who did contemplate murder but who did not go through with it, plus everyone who did not contemplate murder at all, behaved as he did because of the deterrent powers of capital punishment, and (2) in the face of the penalty of imprisonment, some of this group would have been undeterred and would have either committed murder, or tried to commit murder, or at least would have contemplated it seriously enough so that there was a real risk of their murdering someone, whether they would have done so deliberately or not. The Committee had no evidence, and purported to offer none, regarding these two propositions. But unless these propositions are true, the Committee's argument falls far short of its purpose. Although it is absurd on its face to believe that *all* the possible murders that might have occurred were still-born instead, because of the deterrent power of capital punishment, it is not absurd and one must admit that probably *some* murders did not occur for this reason. But what would be a reasonable estimate of their number? One gets the impression from police spokesmen that the number must run into the hundreds or even thousands each year. The comparative statistics offered by Professor Sellin strongly suggest, on the contrary, that the number must be quite small and might be zero.

The confusions to which the doctrine of deterrence leads are not confined to retentionists alone. Warden Clinton Duffy, a prominent spokesman for abolition, has on several occasions stated that, to his knowledge, none of the men on Death Row in San Quentin Prison ever thought of the death penalty before they committed their crimes. He seems to conclude that the death penalty is vastly overrated as a deterrent.[15] If so, he apparently assumes that the men *not* on Death Row (because they didn't commit any capital crimes) don't think of the death penalty, either. This may be true, but it cannot very well be confirmed by interviewing men on Death Row. Indeed, the opinions of men under sentence of death probably have almost no relevance one way or the other on the question of deterrence.

Unquestionably of more importance to abolitionist thinking than interviews with condemned men or even statistical inferences from homicide rates are two general arguments against the special deterrent efficacy of the death penalty. Since the time of Beccaria, Bentham, Rush and Livingston, most penologists have agreed that for any punishment to have optimum efficacy as a deterrent, the penalty must be imposed consistently, immediately and inexorably; that is, on all offenders, promptly after their crime, and in such a way that the general public expects exactly this. But in practice, not one of these conditions is satisfied by the way capital punishment is administered. Only a small proportion of first degree murderers are sentenced to death and even fewer are executed. The delay in convicting and executing those who do get a death sentence is increasing and notorious. So, almost anyone who contemplates some horrible crime can see some chance in getting away with it, or at least in not having to pay the supreme penalty. If, in practice, the death penalty is no more effective a deterrent for murder, rape and kidnapping than imprisonment is, this may be the reason. One must either admit it, and keep capital punishment on other grounds, in the knowledge that it cannot be made a better deterrent than it is; or else abandon the jury system, the right of appeal, and deprive the accused of most of his basic constitutional rights in all capital cases, in the hopes of improving the deterrent efficacy of the death penalty; or else get rid of the death penalty itself in the confidence that imprisonment is on the evidence as good a deterrent and considerably simpler to administer.

There is another classic argument, in the form of a di-

[15] Clinton Duffy, *88 Men and 2 Women* (1962), p. 22.

lemma, which abolitionists have always offered to those who believe in the special deterrent efficacy of the death penalty for murder. Persons who are likely to commit murder (so the argument runs) either premeditate it or they don't. If they don't, then it is difficult to see how *any* punishment, no matter how severe or promptly administered, could deter them; hence, imprisonment cannot be any less effective for them than death. When one considers that most of the undeterrables are likely to be suffering from one or another form of mental illness, and that considerable evidence exists to show that murderers and condemned men generally include a large proportion who are sick, it seems pointless to threaten such offenders with death. Unless, of course, one wishes to inflict suffering on the insane, as some do, without any reference to their capacity to control their own behavior and to respond to threats.

But if, on the other hand, the offender does weigh his crime beforehand and then decides to go ahead with it, he does so either expecting to get away with it, or not. In the latter case, there is nothing whatever gained (so far as controlling his behavior is concerned) by threatening to kill him as his punishment; for he is as likely to try to kill himself (just as he is likely to surrender to the police right after his crime). Such cases are by no means rare.[16] But if the criminal does intend to try to escape detection and believes he can succeed, then it is again impossible to see how the mere threat of a severe punishment might deter him, since he expects never to have to suffer it. Gangland killings, kidnappings for ransom, and a large proportion of all serious crimes are committed by those who think they will never be caught. The obvious, and probably the only, way to deter such persons is by increasing the effectiveness of law enforcement and criminal prosecution in the courts. There is no real need to have recourse to maximally severe

16 "Analysis of these homicide-suicide cases leads to the conclusion that more persons inflict death upon themselves as punishment for their crimes than are legally executed by the state." Marvin Wolfgang, *Patterns in Criminal Homicide* (1958), p. 283, and see also pp. 326–327.

penalties; and there is no use whatever in them unless
police effectiveness is already at a fairly high level. This
seems to be the major lesson that the history of kidnapping
in this country teaches. It was probably the incessant war
waged on kidnapping by the F. B. I., with all the resource-
fulness of modern police methods, beginning in the summer of 1932 (when Congress authorized them to investigate every kidnapping almost immediately after it was
reported to the police), and not the threat of the death
penalty (which already existed in six states by 1931, though
not under federal law until 1934), that accounts for the
way this crime has all but completely disappeared during
the past generation.[17]

There remains but one class of persons whose deterrence
is still in question: those who are sane and cautious enough
to weigh the risk of punishment against the anticipated
gain from crime, and who would decide that the risk is
too great if the threatened punishment is death, but not
great enough to deter them if it is only imprisonment. How
many such persons are there in the total population? On
this point, the authors of the Ceylon *Report on Capital
Punishment* are unequivocal:

> It would be most exceptional for a man to be in-
> sufficiently sane and normal to be deterred by the
> risk of a sentence of protracted imprisonment but yet
> sufficiently sane and normal to be deterred by the risk
> of his own execution, when both risks are at a level
> of contingency which he is doing his utmost to
> avoid.[18]

The dilemma posed for the retentionists who want capital
punishment mainly for its unique deterrent efficacy has
considerable force.

Arguments over the differential deterrent efficacy of the

---

[17] See the remarks of J. Edgar Hoover in the annual *Report*
of the Attorney General of the United States, for the years beginning with 1932, and especially the 1933 *Report*, p. 105. On
kidnapping in general, see "A Rationale of the Law of Kidnapping," *Columbia Law Review* (April 1953), pp. 540–558.
[18] Ceylon, *Report on Capital Punishment* (1959), p. 50.

death penalty and imprisonment for crimes *other than murder* have little statistical basis and seem to find the abolitionists and retentionists at a standoff. In favor of capital punishment, it is often argued that the death penalty must have at least a marginal deterrent superiority over imprisonment, because if armed robbery or armed burglary (or felony murder) is a capital crime robbers and burglars will be less likely to arm themselves. Against capital punishment, it is argued that if rape or kidnapping is made into a capital offense along with murder, the criminal has every reason to kill his victim, since in this way he removes at a stroke the best possible witness against him without appreciably increasing the severity of his punishment if he is caught.[19] On these hypotheses, one would expect that felony murders in abolition states would form a considerably larger percentage of all murders than their percentage in death penalty states; and that in states where several crimes are capital there would be more felony murders than in states where only premeditated murder is capital. Unfortunately, no one seems to have attempted to gather statistics to test either of these hypotheses.

There are other gaps in our knowledge of the deterrent effectiveness of the death penalty. Warden Duffy has told the story of how one of the men who built the first gas chamber at San Quentin Prison ended up several years later as one of its victims.[20] Yet if the death penalty is a more effective deterrent than imprisonment, one would expect that it would show this effect particularly on those most intimately exposed to it, the convicts who have served terms in prisons, or in the prisons of states, in which executions occur. A retentionist might hypothesize that convicts released from such prisons have a lessened tendency to commit capital crimes, when compared with convicts released from prison in abolition states. Abolitionists would

19 See Herbert Wechsler, in *New York Law Forum* (August 1961), pp. 257–258.

20 Clinton Duffy, *op. cit.,* pp. 155–159. A United Press International story in *New York Times* during 1962 reported that Charles Justice, builder of the Ohio electric chair, died in it some forty years ago after he committed murder while on parole.

probably predict there would be no discernible patterns of
post-release behavior in the two groups. But the question
has not been put to the test.

It is difficult enough to determine the facts, and far more
difficult to weigh them against one another and decide the
fundamental question: should capital punishment be kept
for its deterrent efficacy, or for some other reason; or
should the death penalty be abandoned? Abolitionists have
gone to considerable lengths to justify their convictions that
it is vastly overrated as a deterrent. Retentionists have
made almost no efforts to justify their belief that capital
punishment is a superior deterrent. I cannot do better than
to conclude by quoting the final judgment a decade ago
by the British Royal Commission: "It is important . . .
not to base a penal philosophy in relation to murder on
exaggerated estimates of the uniquely deterrent force of
the death penalty."[21]

DEATH AND IMPRISONMENT AS DETERRENTS TO MURDER*

BY THORSTEN SELLIN**

When we think of deterrence, restraint or prevention—
these terms are used interchangeably—we usually think of
the effect which a punishment has (1) on the future conduct of the person punished and (2) on the future conduct
of others. Some writers distinguish these two effects by
calling the one individual and the other general prevention.

[21] Great Britain, Royal Commission on Capital Punishment,
Report (1953), p. 24. For other discussions of the question of
deterrence, see Johs Andenaes, "General Prevention—Illusion
or Reality?", *Journal of Criminal Law, Criminology and Police Science* (May–June 1952); John Ball, "The Deterrence
Concept in Criminology and the Law," *ibid.*, (September–
October 1955). On capital punishment and deterrence, see especially Ohio, *op. cit.*, pp. 31–50.

* Reprinted, by permission of the author and publisher, from
The Death Penalty (Philadelphia: The American Law Institute, 1959), pp. 19–24, 62–63.

** Professor of Sociology, University of Pennsylvania, and
Editor of *The Annals* of the American Academy of Political
and Social Science.

In the case of the executed death penalty individual prevention is, of course, completely effective. This is the one executed punishment in connection with which general prevention alone can be studied.

The process of deterrence is obviously a psychological one. It presumes in this connection that life is regarded by man as a precious possession which he wishes to preserve more eagerly, perhaps, than any other of his attributes. He would therefore defend it to the utmost against every threat, including the threat of capital execution. Every such threat, it is assumed, arouses his fear and as a rational being he would try to conduct himself in such a manner that the threat would be avoided or that, once materialized, it would be nullified. It is further assumed that the potential threat is made vivid to him by the fact that he knows that the death penalty exists.

If the death penalty carries a potential threat which has a restraining influence on human conduct, we may assume that the greater the threat the more effective it would be. Now, the term "death penalty" as used in discussions concerning its deterrent power may mean many things. First, we have the death penalty defined by law as a mandatory or discretionary punishment for crime. Then we have the death penalty that looms as a possible threat to a person arrested for, or accused of a capital offense, and the death penalty pronounced but not yet executed. Finally, we have the death penalty actually applied to the offender. Presumably, the potential power of deterrence of the death penalty is not the same at all these levels of manifestation. Were it present in the law alone it would be completely robbed of its threat. Death is still the legal punishment for murder in Belgium, but it has, except for one "accident" so to speak and after World War II against collaborators with the enemy, never been applied since 1863. Under such circumstances even the knowledge that persons are still arrested and prosecuted for murder and even sentenced to death in Belgium would contain no threat of death to potential murderers in that country. We arrive then at the conclusion that if the death penalty is to have any restraining effect there must be an adequate threat of execution, but no one has ventured to calculate how great the risk of possible execution must be in order to constitute an adequate threat.

It seems reasonable to assume that if the death penalty exercises a deterrent or preventive effect on prospective murderers, the following propositions would be true:

(a) Murders should be less frequent in states that have the death penalty than in those that have abolished it, other factors being equal. Comparisons of this nature must be made among states that are as alike as possible in all other respects—character of population, social and economic condition, etc.—in order not to introduce factors known to influence murder rates in a serious manner but present in only one of these states.

(b) Murders should increase when the death penalty is abolished and should decline when it is restored.

(c) The deterrent effect should be greatest and should therefore affect murder rates most powerfully in those communities where the crime occurred and its consequences are most strongly brought home to the population.

(d) Law enforcement officers would be safer from murderous attacks in states that have the death penalty than in those without it.[1]

Prior to any analysis of available data we are compelled to make certain assumptions. First we must decide what element in the death penalty gives it a maximum of deterrent power. We can assume—those who debate the issue do it generally speaking—that it is the execution which by its finality is the strongest agency of deterrence. We should therefore examine the effect of executions on murder rates.

This brings us to a second necessary assumption. We

[1] The most extensive, recent and well documented discussion of deterrence is found in the *Report* of the Royal Commission on Capital Punishment, 1949–53 (506 pp. London: Her Majesty's Stationery Office, 1953), Appendix 6, pp. 328–380, "The Deterrent Value of Capital Punishment."

do not know with any great degree of accuracy how many murders *punishable by death* occur. In the United States, for instance, where only murders in the first degree or similar murders are subject to the death penalty, no accurate statistics of such offenses exist, yet this is the only type of murder which people are presumably to be deterred from committing. Most deaths are no doubt recorded, but among deaths regarded as accidental or due to natural causes or suicide there are no doubt some successful murders. Where the killer never becomes known it is often impossible to determine if the death was the result of a capital murder. This is, of course, a problem which exists in all countries. We are everywhere compelled to use other statistics than those of strictly *capital* homicides.

Most advanced countries today possess statistics of reported deaths classified by cause of death. One of these is homicide, i.e., deaths wilfully caused by others. Students of criminal statistics have examined these data with some care and have arrived at the conclusion that the homicide death rate is adequate for an estimate of the trend of murder. This conclusion is based on the assumption that the *proportion* of capital murders in the total of such deaths remains reasonably constant. Accepting this assumption, we shall examine the relationship between executions and the rates of deaths due to homicide. One may challenge the assumption, but the fact remains that there are no better statistical data on which to base arguments about deterrence. Other statistics, such as conviction statistics, have greater defects.

Homicide death rates[2] vary enormously in the United States from state to state. In 1955, for instance, Vermont showed a rate of .5 per 100,000 estimated population, and New Hampshire and Wisconsin 1.1, while Georgia and Alabama had 11.4 and 12.6, respectively. It is not uncommon to see in the writings of the opponents of the death penalty comparisons made between the homicide rates of

---

[2] Homicide death rates used in this report, in text or tables, unless otherwise noted, have been taken from the *Vital Statistics—Special Reports,* published by the National Office of Vital Statistics, Washington, D.C.

death penalty states and those of abolition states, but such comparisons must be made with discretion. The abolition states in the Union have always had lower homicide rates than the others, not because they were without the death penalty but because they differed from the others in social organization, composition of population, economic and social conditions, etc. The only comparison that is at all defensible is one of states, some with and others without the death penalty, which are closely similar in the above respects.

In Tables 6–8 there are presented data on crude homicide rates and executions in various American states. Table 6 and Charts 1 and 2[3] permit comparisons among the New England states of Maine, New Hampshire, Vermont, Massachusetts, Rhode Island and Connecticut, belonging to the same culture area. Two of these states, Maine and Rhode Island, have no death penalty. The great similarity in the rates of these states is obviously noticeable.

Table 7 presents homicide rates and executions in the Middle Western states of Michigan, Ohio and Indiana; Minnesota, Wisconsin and Iowa; and North Dakota, South Dakota and Nebraska (Charts 3, 4, and 5). The states have been grouped in the diagrams so as to place contiguous states together, each group having at least one state in which the death penalty does not exist: Michigan, Minnesota and Wisconsin, and North Dakota and South Dakota (until 1939). Again, each group presents fundamentally similar rates and basic trends. The important thing to be noticed is that whether the death penalty is used or not and whether executions are frequent or not, both death penalty states and abolition states show rates, which suggest that these rates are conditioned by other factors than the death penalty.

Table 8 and Chart 6 present data for Colorado, Kansas

---

[3] [Editor's note: The graphs (Charts 1–6) are taken from the versions published in *Capital Punishment,* by the Ohio Legislative Service Commission, (1961) pp. 40–42, based on those found in Sellin, *op. cit.,* pp. 25–33. The tables to which Professor Sellin refers in the text, and on which his graphs are based, have been omitted.]

and Missouri, contiguous states, somewhat farther to the south of those mentioned above. All these states have the death penalty, but Kansas introduced it only in 1935. The general picture is the same, a rise in the rates of the early 'twenties and a downward trend since then.

The data examined reveal that

1. The *level* of the homicide death rates varies in different groups of states. It is lowest in the New England areas and in the northern states of the middle west and lies somewhat higher in Michigan, Indiana and Ohio.

2. Within each group of states having similar social and economic conditions and populations, it is impossible to distinguish the abolition state from the others.

3. The *trends* of the homicide death rates of comparable states with or without the death penalty are similar.

The inevitable conclusion is that executions have no discernible effect on homicide death rates which, as we have seen, are regarded as adequate indicators of capital murder rates.

Students of the problem of homicide rarely ever discuss the death penalty. They do not think of it as a factor worth mentioning. They are usually interested in finding the relationship between homicide and social and economic conditions under which the offender lives or the personality characteristics which he possesses. Even in personality studies of murderers it is rare to find any mention of the role which the potential threat of execution is assumed to play. It is only those who are primarily concerned with the social policy of penal treatment who in considering the death penalty wonder what purpose it may serve and debate the issue of its retention or abolition. . . .

In preceding pages, one of the aspects of this issue has been considered, namely, the question of whether or not the death penalty appears to have any effect on homicide death rates. We have examined comparatively such rates in selected states that do and those that do not have the death penalty; we have compared the rates of capital crimes in specific states or countries that have experimented with abolition in order to observe the effect of the aboli-

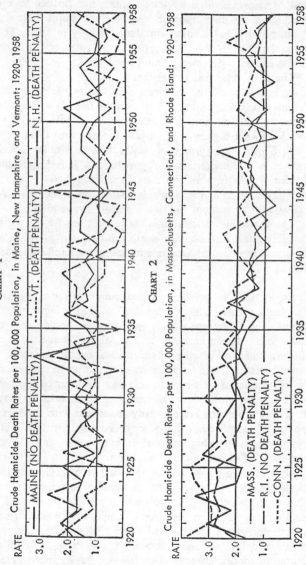

CHART 1

Crude Homicide Death Rates per 100,000 Population, in Maine, New Hampshire, and Vermont: 1920–1958

MAINE (NO DEATH PENALTY) ——— VT. (DEATH PENALTY) ‑‑‑‑‑ N.H. (DEATH PENALTY) — —

CHART 2

Crude Homicide Death Rates, per 100,000 Population, in Massachusetts, Connecticut, and Rhode Island: 1920–1958

MASS. (DEATH PENALTY) ——— R.I. (NO DEATH PENALTY) — — CONN. (DEATH PENALTY) ‑‑‑‑‑

RATE

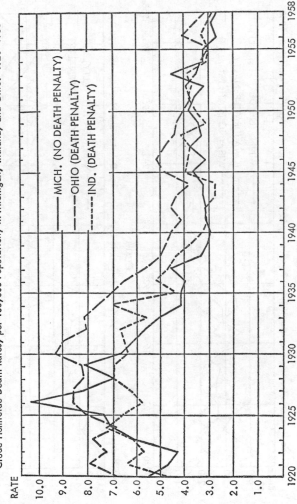

CHART 3

Crude Homicide Death Rates, per 100,000 Population, in Michigan, Indiana, and Ohio: 1920–1958

MICH. (NO DEATH PENALTY)
OHIO (DEATH PENALTY)
IND. (DEATH PENALTY)

RATE

10.0
9.0
8.0
7.0
6.0
5.0
4.0
3.0
2.0
1.0

1920 1925 1930 1935 1940 1945 1950 1955 1958

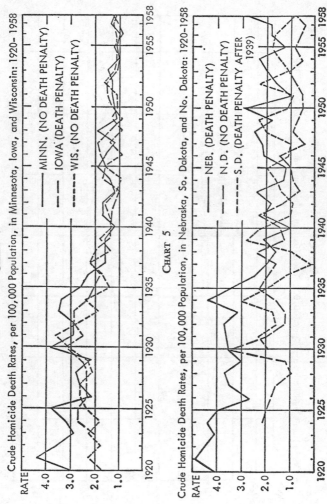

CHART 4

Crude Homicide Death Rates, per 100,000 Population, in Minnesota, Iowa, and Wisconsin: 1920–1958

MINN. (NO DEATH PENALTY)
IOWA (DEATH PENALTY)
WIS. (NO DEATH PENALTY)

CHART 5

Crude Homicide Death Rates, per 100,000 Population, in Nebraska, So. Dakota, and No. Dakota: 1920–1958

NEB. (DEATH PENALTY)
N.D. (NO DEATH PENALTY)
S.D. (DEATH PENALTY AFTER 1939)

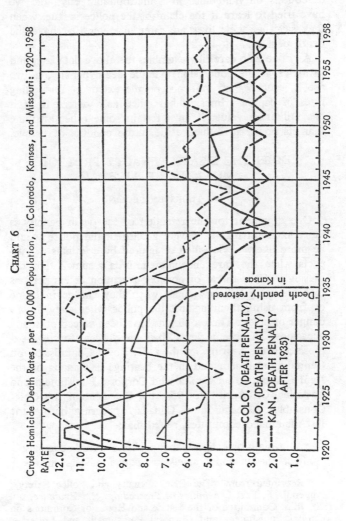

CHART 6

Crude Homicide Death Rates, per 100,000 Population, in Colorado, Kansas, and Missouri: 1920–1958

RATE

Death penalty restored
in Kansas

—— COLO. (DEATH PENALTY)
— — MO. (DEATH PENALTY)
- - - - KAN. (DEATH PENALTY
        AFTER 1935)

tion or the introduction of capital punishment on such rates; we have noted the specific effect of highly publicized executions on homicides in a metropolitan city; and we have tried to learn if the claim of the police is true, when they say that their lives are safer in states that have the death penalty.

Any one who carefully examines the above data is bound to arrive at the conclusion that the death penalty, as we use it, exercises no influence on the extent or fluctuating rates of capital crimes. It has failed as a deterrent. If it has utilitarian value, it must rest in some other attribute than its power to influence the future conduct of people.

DOES THE DEATH PENALTY PROTECT MUNICIPAL POLICE?*

BY THORSTEN SELLIN

One argument for the retention of the death penalty is the contention that if it were abolished, the police would be more likely to be killed or injured by criminals or suspects when they are encountered. It is assumed that the presence of the threat of possible execution deters persons from carrying lethal weapons when they engage in crime or from using them against the police when they are in danger of arrest. These opinions have been voiced on many occasions. In recent years they have been forcibly expressed in the hearings of the U.K. Royal Commission on Capital Punishment and in the hearings in Canada of the Joint Committee on Capital and Corporal Punishment and Lotteries. On April 27, 1954, the President of the Chief Constables Association of Canada, appearing before the last mentioned committee, stated that:

Our main objection is that abolition would adversely affect the personal safety of police officers in the

* Reprinted from "The Death Penalty and Police Safety," Appendix F, Part I, *Minutes of Proceedings and Evidence*, no. 20, Joint Committee of the Senate and House of Commons on Capital Punishment and Corporal Punishment and Lotteries, 1955, pp. 718–728. Available from the Queen's Printer, Ottawa, Canada.

daily discharge of their duties. It would be interesting to know, and if time had permitted I would have tried to obtain this vital information as to the number of policemen murdered in the execution of their duty in those parts of the world where capital punishment has been abolished. I submit that it will be found the number is much higher than in those countries where the death penalty is still in effect, and this point is the main one in our submission that our government should retain capital punishment as a form of security.

It should be noted that in this statement the witness not only voiced the belief that threat of the death penalty afforded protection to the police; he also voiced a claim that were data available they would show that more police are killed in abolition countries than in death penalty countries. And, finally, he implied that were it discovered that this would not be the case, the main argument of the police against abolition would be invalidated. The testing of the validity of the argument would therefore seem to be useful, especially since up to now neither the proponents or the opponents of capital punishment have made any effort to do so, relying instead on general assumption believed to have a factual basis.

There are great obstacles in the way of making a conclusive study of this problem. From a *theoretical point of view* what one should like to know is first of all whether or not a larger proportion of criminals actually *carry* lethal weapons in abolition states. This is probably impossible to discover with any degree of accuracy. Failing this, one would like to know if criminals in these states *use* such weapons in encounters with the police more frequently than in the death penalty states, whether or not a wounding or killing of a policeman occurs. In reading police reports one sometimes finds a notice that a policeman has been commended for bravery because after an exchange of shots, he succeeded in wounding the criminal or disarming him, although he himself was not injured. To secure reliable statistics of such attacks would, however, be virtually impossible. One is, therefore, compelled to seek data on the number of police killed or wounded. There is an *a priori* likelihood that records of such occurrences are kept in police departments. Although in discussions of the relationship of the death penalty to police safety references are generally made only to policemen killed, it is obvious that woundings are equally important, for every wounding can be regarded as a killing that was avoided merely by chance, because the bullet or the knife failed to strike a vital spot, or medical aid was so promptly given that an otherwise possible death did not occur.

In brief, one should have data on the number of attacks on the police by criminals or suspects, whether the police are hurt or not, since the use of a lethal weapon (gun or knife) indicates a disregard for the consequences and since such a weapon is potentially fatal to life. If such data cannot be secured, we should have data on actual woundings and killings resulting from such attacks or encounters. *At the very least* we should have data on police killed by lethal weapons.

There are not only theoretical but also practical difficulties in making a comparative study of police safety in states with and those without the death penalty. These difficulties arise from the fact that many police departments possess unsatisfactory record systems and have, in some instances, evidently failed to keep information on the events here under discussion. Another problem is that of securing the cooperation of the police even when they undoubtedly possess records. This particular problem will become quite clear when in later pages we note the extent of cooperation in the study which will be reported on presently.

In the author's seminar in criminology at the University of Pennsylvania during the academic year 1954–55, several studies have been carried on relating to various aspects of capital punishment. One of these studies was specifically designed to secure data on the comparative risk of a policeman's being injured or killed by a criminal or suspect using a lethal weapon. It was hoped that by securing data of this nature from cities in capital punishment states and in abolition states, some idea might be gained of the extent to which the police might be better protected in states with the death penalty. In other words, an attempt was made to discover the validity of the assumption so boldly stated by the witness before the Joint Committee to whom reference has already been made.

During the middle of December, 1954, a letter was mailed to police departments in all cities with more than 10,000 population according to the Census of 1950. This letter asked for data to be supplied on two schedules. One of these requested information, year by year beginning with 1919 and ending with 1954, on each case of a wounding or a killing of a member of the police department by a lethal weapon in the hands of a criminal or a suspect. A brief description of each incident was requested indicating, if possible, the nature of the offence involved. Furthermore, in each case information was asked about the kind of weapon used and whether or not the offender was insane. The part of the letter pertaining to this schedule read:

Dear Sir: In discussions about the retention or abolition of the death penalty, it has sometimes been claimed that the threat of this punishment in a state gives the police a certain amount of protection, which would be lost if that penalty were abolished and which the police do not have in states without capital punishment . . . Therefore, I would be much indebted to you, if you would at the earliest opportunity (1) have a responsible person in your department fill out and return to me the schedule enclosed; (2) give me your personal opinion on whether or not you feel that the presence or absence of the death penalty in your state has any effect on the practice of carrying and using lethal weapons by criminals. Since I am sending this questionnaire to all cities with more than 10,000 inhabitants in a large number of states, I would be glad to send you a copy of the results of the study, if you would find it of interest.

Seventeen states were selected for the study. All the six states which have no death penalty and had abolished it before 1919 were included and eleven states bordering on the abolition states. Knowing the great variations in the homicide rate in the United States, a problem already touched upon in the author's evidence before the Joint Committee in June 1954, it was assumed that states from about the same culture areas would afford the best basis for comparison.

Altogether 593 letters were sent out in the first mailing and after two months a follow-up letter was sent to departments that had not responded. As a result of this procedure 274 schedules were returned. Of these 266 proved to be adequate; those that were not used offered data for only a few years or reported that the data could not be compiled. The distribution of the schedules mailed out is found in Table 1, as follows:

1. Of the 593 cities 397 fell into the smallest population group, with populations of between 10,000 and 30,000. One hundred and fourteen (114) had between 30,000 and 60,000 inhabitants; 38 had between 60,000 and 100,000 inhabitants; 33 had from 100,000 to half a million, but all but two—one city in Indiana and one in Ohio—had fewer than 350,000. Finally, six cities had over half a million, including New York City, Buffalo, Cincinnati, Cleveland, Boston and Chicago in capital punishment states and Milwaukee, Detroit and Minneapolis in abolition states.

2. 44.8 per cent of the cities returned usable schedules, but the percentage was higher for the abolition states— 55.4 per cent—than for the capital punishment states—41 per cent.

3. The smaller the city, the better the response. In abolition states, 60.4 per cent of the cities under 30,000 inhabitants returned usable schedules; so did half of the cities between 30,000 and 100,000 population. In the capital punishment states, 42.4 per cent of the smallest class of cities replied and 41.7 and 30 per cent respectively of the next two classes in size.

4. No replies were received from Detroit and Minneapolis, nor from New York City, Cleveland or Boston. The largest cities represented in the returns were Chicago, Milwaukee, Cincinnati and Buffalo.

TABLE 1

NUMBER OF CITIES WITH POPULATION OF 10,000 OR OVER,
NUMBER OF REPLIES RECEIVED, NUMBER OF USABLE
REPLIES AND PERCENTAGE OF SUCH REPLIES OF TOTAL
RECEIVED FROM SEVENTEEN STATES.

Abolition States	Number of Cities	Number of Returns	Usable Returns Number	Usable Returns Percentage
Maine	13	6	6	46.2
Michigan	57	33	31	54.4
Minnesota	22	14	14	63.6
North Dakota	5	4	3	60.0
Rhode Island	17	6	6	35.3
Wisconsin	34	22	22	64.7
Total	148	85	82	55.4
Capital Punishment States				
Connecticut	44	19	19	43.2
Illinois	72	22	21	29.2
Indiana	39	18	15	38.6
Iowa	23	10	10	43.5
Massachusetts	88	38	38	43.2
Montana	7	2	1	14.3
New Hampshire	10	6	6	60.0
New York	73	37	36	49.3
Ohio	78	34	34	43.6
South Dakota	6	2	2	33.3
Vermont	5	1	1	20.0
Total	445	189	183	41.0
Grand Total	593	274	266	44.8

5. The percentage of cities replying in the various abolition states ranged from 64.7 and 63.6 per cent in Wisconsin and Minnesota to 35.3 per cent in Rhode Island; in the capital punishment states the range was from 60 per cent in New Hampshire to 20 per cent in Vermont. Of the largest capital punishment states—New York, Illinois, Ohio and Massachusetts, New York had the best percentage (49.3) and Illinois the lowest (29.2). On the other hand, Chicago submitted the best report and the only one from a truly metropolitan center.

In the analysis which follows, Chicago will be dealt with in a separate section for during the period 1919–54 that city had 177 casualties, or thirty-nine more than all the other 265 cities put together. We shall take these 265 cities first.

It will be recalled that the schedule asked for information both on woundings and on killings of police, in the belief that this would yield more probative results. However, an inspection of the schedules returned made it clear that the data on woundings were so incomplete that there was no possibility of using them. All the largest cities reporting (except Chicago) reported only the policemen killed; many others stated that figures on woundings were available only for the most recent years, etc. Hence, only the information on the killing of policemen can be utilized. Since, however, this is the kind of information which always seems to be brought forward in discussions of police safety in capital punishment states, it should suffice for our purposes.

We shall analyze, then 128 instances or attacks or encounters in which policemen were killed during 1919–54 in 266 cities in seventeen states, six of which are abolition states. In these 128 encounters 138 police were actually killed; in one instance, three policemen were casualties and in each of nine of them, two were killed. It is assumed a priori that it is something of an accident that more than one is shot in an encounter and that the important fact is that the criminal shot at the policeman or policemen, whether one or more happened to confront him. Four of these instances occurred in Michigan and one in Minnesota, one in Ohio, one in Connecticut and two in Massachusetts.

We have not included in the 128 cases the following:

(1) Seven cases in which the killer was insane: Minnesota, 1; Wisconsin, 1; Connecticut, 1; Iowa, 1; New York, 2; Ohio, 1. Two then, occurred in abolition states and five in capital punishment states.

(2) One case in Wisconsin (abolition state), where the offender struck the officer with a flash light; one in New York, where the offender struck the officer with the gun without firing it, and one in Ohio where the offender

backed a motor vehicle into the officer in such a manner that he was crushed against another vehicle. It is assumed that these attacks were chiefly meant to disable the officer in each case. These offenders either did not carry guns or did not use them as firearms.

On the other hand we have included three occurrences, one each in Connecticut, New York and Ohio, when a suspect during or after arrest, although he was himself unarmed, succeeded in seizing the policeman's own gun and shooting him with it.

Table 2 gives, state by state and by size of city, the number of cities whose schedules have been used, the number of cases reported during the entire period 1919–54 and the rate per 100,000 population for each state and group of cities based on the 1950 census. Abolition states and capital punishment states have been separately treated. It might be argued that it is improper to use the 1950 population as the base for the computation of rates that involve cases scattered over a thirty-six year period preceding. It would undoubtedly be possible to arrive at some population figure which would on the surface appear more defensible, but which would on close analysis be found to have equally great defects, for it must be remembered that all the cities involved have undergone the effect of considerable migratory changes due to a depression and a world war and that no one can determine with any real accuracy what population basis is preferable. It is believed that the rates reflect with reasonable faithfulness the *comparative* size of the problem in the different states and in the two types of states. Whatever categories are compared, these comparisons are, of course, more useful the larger the number of cities and populations involved. If one city alone is found in a particular class and if it has a small population, a single case of police homicide would give it a rate which could be very high and yet meaningless.

Let us first compare the *rate* of fatal attacks on police in six abolition state cities (82) with a total population of 2,804,757, with the corresponding rate for eleven capital punishment state cities (182) except Chicago with a total population of 7,147,216 in 1950. The rate per

TABLE 2

CASES OF POLICE HOMICIDE, BY CITIES GROUPED ACCORDING TO SIZE; AND RATES PER 100,000 POPULATION IN EACH GROUP OF CITIES, BY STATE.

A. Abolition States	10,000—30,000				30,000—60,000				60,000—100,000			
	No. Cit.	No. Cases	Popu-lation	Rate	No. Cit.	No. Cases	Popu-lation	Rate	No. Cit.	No. Cases	Popu-lation	Rate
Maine	4	.....	54,280	0.0	1	.....	31,558	0.0	1	.....	77,634	0.0
Michigan	24	8	419,904	1.9	4	1	189,609	0.5	2	3	187,912	1.6
Minnesota	14	4	259,461	1.5								
North Dakota	3	1	51,369	1.9								
Rhode Island	3	.....	46,084	0.0	3	1	116,463	0.9				
Wisconsin	13	2	207,940	0.9	7	4	252,580	1.6	1	3	96,056	3.1
Total	61	15	1,039,038	1.3	15	6	590,210	1.0	4	6	361,602	1.6

A. Abolition States	100,000—350,000				500,000—650,000				All Cities			
	No. Cit.	No. Cases	Popu-lation	Rate	No. Cit.	No. Cases	Popu-lation	Rate	No. Cit.	No. Cases	Popu-lation	Rate
Maine									6	.....	163,472	0.0
Michigan	1	1	176,515	0.6					31	13	973,940	1.3
Minnesota									14	4	259,461	1.5
North Dakota									3	1	51,369	1.9
Rhode Island									6	1	162,547	0.6
Wisconsin					1	5	637,392	0.8	22	14	1,193,968	1.2
Total	1	1	176,515	0.6	1	5	637,392	0.8	82	33	2,804,757	1.2

Top panel

B. Capital Punishment States	10,000—30,000				30,000—60,000				60,000—100,000			
	No. Cit.	No. Cases	Population	Rate	No. Cit.	No. Cases	Population	Rate	No. Cit.	No. Cases	Population	Rate
Connecticut	11	....	190,746	0.0	5	1	212,213	0.5	1	....	74,293	0.0
Illinois	14	4	206,214	1.9	6	1	225,701	0.4	1	1	92,927	1.1
Indiana	10	3	170,785	1.7	4	7	171,048	4.1				
Iowa	6	....	85,429	0.0	2	2	64,244	3.1	1	....	72,296	0.0
Massachusetts	31	6	499,841	1.2	5	1	221,877	0.4	1	1	66,112	1.5
Montana	1	1	17,581	5.7								
New Hampshire	4	....	59,809	0.0	1	1	34,469	2.9	1	....	82,732	0.0
New York	24	3	426,631	0.7	7	....	290,304	0.0	2	4	171,546	2.3
Ohio	21	7	371,623	1.9	7	3	223,303	1.3	2	1	146,379	0.7
South Dakota	2	....	24,920	0.0								
Vermont	1	....	12,411	0.0								
Total	125	24	2,065,990	1.2	37	16	1,443,159	1.1	9	7	706,285	1.0

Bottom panel

B. Capital Punishment States	100,000—350,000				500,000—650,000				All Cities			
	No. Cit.	No. Cases	Population	Rate	No. Cit.	No. Cases	Population	Rate	No. Cit.	No. Cases	Population	Rate
Connecticut	2	3	263,186	1.1	...	...	....	...	19	4	740,438	0.5
Illinois	...	...	....	...	...	...	....	...	21	6	524,842	1.1
Indiana	1	1	133,607	0.7	...	...	....	...	15	11	475,440	2.3
Iowa	1	6	177,965	3.3	...	...	....	...	10	8	399,934	2.0
Massachusetts	1	....	203,486	0.0	...	...	....	...	38	8	991,316	0.8
Montana	...	...	....	...	...	...	....	...	1	1	17,581	5.7
New Hampshire	...	...	....	...	1	8	580,132	1.4	6	1	177,010	0.5
New York	2	3	434,019	0.7	1	13	503,998	2.6	36	18	1,902,632	0.9
Ohio	3	14	635,389	2.2	...	...	....	...	34	38	1,880,692	2.2
South Dakota	...	...	....	...	...	...	....	...	2	....	24,920	0.0
Vermont	...	...	....	...	...	...	....	...	1	....	12,411	0.0
Total	10	27	1,847,652	1.5	2	21	1,084,130	1.9	183	95	7,147,216	1.3

100,000 population in the former is 1.2 and in the latter 1.3. They prove to be the same, for the difference is hardly significant.

If we take the cities of the smallest class—those between 10,000 and 30,000 inhabitants—and use only rates from states with at least ten such cities reporting, we find the following comparative rates:

Abolition States		*Capital Punishment States*	
Michigan	1.9	Ohio	1.9
Minnesota	1.5	Illinois	1.9
Wisconsin	0.9	Indiana	1.7
		New York	0.7
		Connecticut	0.0
		Massachusetts	1.2

In the group of cities with populations between 30,000 and 60,000, the abolition cities have a total rate of 1.0 and the capital punishment cities 1.1, but there are considerable variations among the states ranging from a high of 4.1 in Indiana to a low of .4 for Massachusetts. In the third to fifth groups of cities the number reporting is, of course, small but it may be observed that compared with Milwaukee's (Wisconsin) rate of .8 the rate for Cincinnati, Ohio—2.6—and Buffalo, New York—1.4—are somewhat higher.

It is obvious from an inspection of the data that it is impossible to conclude that the states which have abolished the death penalty have thereby made the policeman's lot more hazardous. It is also obvious that the same differences observable in the general homicide rates of the various states are reflected in the rate of police killings. This can be readily observed by comparing the middlewest states with and without the death penalty with corresponding states in the eastern part of the country, as is done in the following, where the appropriate rates of police homicides are presented.

Another interesting comparison is afforded by the material, namely the trend of the killings. Table 3, in which the cases for the thirty-six year period have been grouped

EASTERN STATES

Abolition States		*Capital Punishment States*	
Maine	0.0	New Hampshire	0.5
Rhode Island	0.6	Massachusetts	0.8
		Connecticut	0.5
		New York	0.9

MIDDLE WEST STATES

Abolition States		*Capital Punishment States*	
North Dakota	1.9	Iowa	2.0
Minnesota	1.5	Illinois	1.1
Michigan	1.3	Indiana	2.3
Wisconsin	1.2	Ohio	2.2

into six year periods, show clearly that the 1925–36 periods were the most hazardous and that the hazards have greatly declined.

In only two of the killings was a knife the weapon used; the others were committed by firearms, usually described

TABLE 3

TRENDS IN CASES OF POLICE KILLINGS, 1919–54, AS REPORTED BY 266 CITIES IN SEVENTEEN STATES.

	Cases		Police Killed		Both Combined	
Years	Abol. States	C.P. States	Abol. States	C.P. States	Cases	Police Killed
1919–1924	8	25c	12	25	33	37
1925–1930	8a	31e	9	31	39	40
1931–1936	5a	24a	5	26	29	31
1937–1942	4	9	4	11	13	15
1943–1948	5b	5a, d	5	5	10	10
1949–1954	3	1	4	1	4	5
Total	33	95	39	99	128	138

a Excluding a case in which the killer was insane.

b Excluding a case in which officer was struck by flashlight.

c Excluding three cases in which the killer was insane; excluding a case in which killer used gun as club.

d Excluding a case in which officer was crushed by car operated by the killer.

e Including three cases, in which killer seized the officer's gun and killed him.

merely as a gun, a pistol, or a revolver. In one case, a rifle was used and in three cases a shotgun. A machine gun was used in a single instance—in connection with a bank robbery in Needham, Massachusetts, in 1934, when two police officers were killed, one during the robbery and the other during his pursuit of the criminals.

It will be recalled that the letter which asked for data also requested that the reporter indicate whether or not he believed that the existence of the threat of possible execution gave the police a certain amount of protection which was lacking in the abolition states. Only sixty-nine replies to this request were received from cities in capital punishment states and twenty-seven replies from abolition states, i.e. 36.5 per cent of the responding cities in the capital punishment states and 31.7 per cent of the cities in the abolition states gave an opinion. In the death penalty states, the police officer reporting believed in the added protective force of the death penalty in sixty-two out of sixty-nine cities, or 89.8 per cent. In the abolition states, twenty out of twenty-seven, i.e. 74.1 per cent did *not* believe that there was any connection between the possible threat of the death penalty and the likelihood of a criminal using a lethal weapon in encounters with the police. In view of the results from this study, this opinion seems to be the correct one.

The Chicago Data

The largest cities, which presumably would have the best records and the most accessible ones generally failed to return the schedules, as has already been mentioned. One prominent exception is Chicago, a city which in 1950 had a population of 3,620,962. Due to the courtesy of Commissioner Timothy Connor O'Regan and the work of Mr. Edward C. Erickson, Director of Records and Communications of the Chicago Police Department, rather complete data were returned for the period 1919–1954, both on the number of police killed each year and on those wounded in encounters with criminals. These data made it possible to discover in what connection the killings occurred—the crime or situation involved—and for a brief span of years, 1923–1931, this information could also be secured in relation to the woundings. Injuries were not recorded before 1923 nor after 1931. The following table (Table 4) contains, in summarized form, the information given about each death. Unlike the preceding presentation, each police officer killed is counted rather than cases.

A study of Table 4 and the diagram based upon it shows that in a general way the experience in Chicago follows the same trend shown in Table 3. The decade of 1920 and the first half of the decade of 1930 were especially hazard-

NUMBER OF POLICE KILLED OR WOUNDED IN CHICAGO, ILL., AND NUMBER OF EXECUTIONS IN COOK COUNTY, 1920–1954

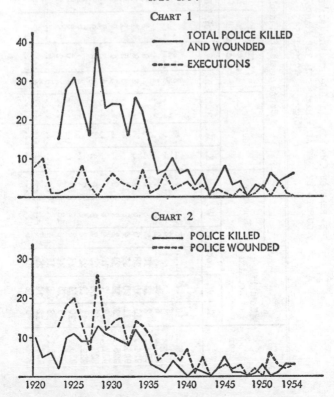

CHART 1

TOTAL POLICE KILLED AND WOUNDED
----- EXECUTIONS

CHART 2

POLICE KILLED
----- POLICE WOUNDED

MEMBERS OF CHICAGO, ILL., POLICE DEPARTMENT KILLED OR
WOUNDED BY LETHAL WEAPONS IN THE HANDS OF CRIMINALS
OR SUSPECTS, 1920–1954

| Year | Total killed or wounded | | | Crime or situation involved | | | | | | | | | | | | | | | | Number of executions in Cook County |
| | | | | Robbery | | | Murder | | | Attempted arrest or escape | | | Investigation or search | | | Other crimes | | | |
	K.	W.	Tot.	K.	W.	Tot.	K.	W.	Tot.	K.	W.	Tot.	K.	W.	Tot.	K.	W.	Tot.	
1920	10	...	...	5	...	...	...	...	...	3	...	...	...	...	...	2	...	...	8
1921	5	...	...	2	...	...	...	...	...	1	...	...	1	...	...	1	...	...	10
1922	6	...	...	2	...	...	...	...	...	1	...	...	...	...	...	3	...	...	1
1923	2	13	15	...	3	3	...	1	1	...	9	9	2	...	2	...	1	1	1
1924	10	18	28	6	5	11	...	...	...	2	9	11	1	...	1	1	4	5	2
1925	11	20	31	4	9	13	...	...	...	6	5	11	1	1	2	...	5	5	3
1926	9	14	23	2	7	9	...	...	...	3	4	7	1	...	1	3	3	4	8
1927	9	7	16	4	3	7	2	1	3	4	3	7	...	...	...	1	1	2	3
1928	13	26	39	7	9	16	...	...	...	3	16	19	2	...	2	1	...	1	...
1929	11	12	23	3	4	7	...	...	...	2	7	9	3	...	3	4	1	5	4ᵃ
1930	10	14	24	3	7	10	...	...	...	2	6	8	1	...	1	2	1	3	6
1931	9	15	24	6	13	19	1	...	...	2	2	4	...	...	...	...	...	...	4
1932	8	8	16	4	...	...	...	...	...	3	...	...	...	...	...	1	...	...	3
1933	12	14	26	7	...	...	...	...	...	2	...	...	...	...	...	2	...	...	2
1934	9	13	22	5	...	...	...	...	...	...	...	...	...	...	...	4	...	...	7

Year																				
1935	3	10	13	3									1			1				1
1936	2	4	6																	2
1937	1	6	7	1						1						1				6
1938	4	6	10	2																2
1939	2	4	6	2												1				3
1940		7	7																	4
1941	2	1	3	2																2
1942	1	5	6	1																3
1943							2			3										1
1944	2	2	4	1			1			1										2
1945	5	3	8							1										1
1946	1	2	3																	
1947	1	3	4	1						1										2[b]
1948													1							
1949	1	2	3																	1
1950	2		2	1																3
1951		6	6																	
1952	1	3	4	1																4
1953	3	2	5	1						2										1
1954	3	3	6							3										
Total	168	243	411	75			6			46			16			25				100

a First executions by electricity in Cook County.
b National execution statistics published by U.S. Bureau of Prisons reports only one execution in Illinois in 1947.
  Warden of Cook County Jail, where electric chair for County is found, reports two.

ous to the police in Chicago, peaks in the number of killed
and wounded being reached in 1925 and 1928 and gradually reaching a fairly stable and comparatively low level
after 1938. The table also gives the annual number of executions in Cook County, which has its own electric chair.
These executions were not necessarily for the murder of
police officers, such cases not having been segregated. However, the curve of executions follows generally the trend
of the homicide curve. There is nothing to suggest that
there is any other relation between the two than that when
there are more homicides there are more executions and

TABLE 5
POLICE KILLED OR WOUNDED

Year	Chicago, Illinois			Detroit, Michigan		
	Killed	Wounded	Total	Killed	Wounded	Total
1928	13	26	39	4	11	15
1929	11	12	23	4	13	17
1930	10	14	24	3	7	10
1931	9	15	24	2	5	7
1932	8	8	16	1	3	4
1933	12	14	26	1	–	1
1934	9	13	22	–	4	4
1935	3	10	13	1	–	1
1936	2	4	6	1	4	5
1937	1	6	7	1	–	1
1938	4	6	10	2	–	2
1939	2	4	6	1	2	3
1940	–	7	7	–	–	–
1941	2	1	3	–	–	–
1942	1	5	6	–	–	–
1943	–	–	–	2	–	2
1944	2	2	4	–	–	–
1945	5	3	8	(not compiled)		
1946	1	2	3	–	–	–
1947	1	3	4	2	–	–
1948	–	–	–	–	–	–

The population of these two cities was
in 1930 for Chicago 3,376,438 and for Detroit 1,568,662
in 1940 for Chicago 3,396,808 and for Detroit 1,623,452
in 1950 for Chicago 3,620,962 and for Detroit 1,849,568

when there are fewer homicides there are fewer executions.

The table, furthermore, indicates that most of the killings of policemen occurred in encounters with robbers. All but twenty-six of the 168 cases occurred either when police officers interfered with hold-ups, were trying to arrest a person or search him or were investigating some complaint, which brought them into contact with a suspect.

Although the Detroit police department failed to reply to our request, the annual reports of that department have been examined for the years 1928–1944 and 1945–1948. Fortunately these reports contain complete data on both woundings and killings of policemen, so that a comparison can be made with Chicago for the years mentioned.

In 1930, Chicago had some 200,000 inhabitants more than double Detroit's population, but by 1950 Chicago was not quite twice the size of Detroit. If this is kept in mind, the table above is distinctly in Detroit's favour.

Conclusion. The claim that if data could be secured they would show that more police are killed in abolition states than in capital punishment states is unfounded. On the whole the abolition states, as apparent from the findings of this particular investigation, seem to have fewer killings, but the differences are small. If this is, then, the argument upon which the police is willing to rest its opposition to the abolition of capital punishment it must be concluded that it lacks any factual basis.

DOES THE DEATH PENALTY PROTECT STATE POLICE?*

BY DONALD R. CAMPION, S.J.

Testifying before a Joint Committee of the Senate and the House of Commons of the Canadian Parliament, on

* Reprinted from "The State Police and The Death Penalty," Appendix F, Part II, *Minutes of Proceedings and Evidence,* no. 20, Joint Committee of the Senate and House of Commons on Capital Punishment and Corporal Punishment and Lotteries, 1955, pp. 729–735. Available from the Queen's Printer, Ottawa, Canada.

April 27, 1954, Mr. Walter H. Mulligan, President of the Chief Constables' Association of Canada and Police Chief of Vancouver, stated with respect to policemen killed in the execution of their duty in those parts of the world where capital punishment has been abolished:

> I submit that it will be found that the number is much higher than in those countries where the death penalty is still in effect and this point is the main one in our submission that our government should retain capital punishment as a form of security.[1]

Elsewhere in his testimony in support of the claim that the death penalty is a deterrent, Mr. Mulligan remarked:

> That is my opinion as a police officer, and over the years in speaking with other police officers in this country and in the United States I have found that it seems to be a general opinion amongst police officers on the North American continent.[2]

Further proof of the popularity of this viewpoint in police circles came from testimony of several other Canadian police officials as reported in the same *Evidence*. Similar sentiments, in fact, are found expressed wherever discussion arises on the value of capital punishment.

In view of current public interest concerning the retention of capital punishment in the United States and Great Britain, as well as in Canada, a test of the empirical validity of this claim made in support of the death penalty would seem of some practical value. Such a test, it is here assumed, may be made by comparing the actual number of police officers killed in jurisdictions having and those not having the death penalty. For as Mr. Mulligan implies, if

[1] Joint Committee of the Senate and the House of Commons on Capital and Corporal Punishment and Lotteries, *Minutes of Proceedings and Evidence*, No. 8, Tuesday, April 27, 1954. Ottawa: Queen's Printer and Controller of Stationery, 1954; p. 331.

[2] *Ibid.*, p. 333.

this claim is valid, where other factors are equal the number of officers killed in areas retaining the death penalty should prove to be lower than the number killed in areas where this penalty has been abolished.

For purposes of such a test selected states in the United States of America suggest themselves, since several of these states have abolished the death penalty, while others have not. In each of these states a number of separate police forces are found. The present study is restricted to forces organized and maintained by the state governments, as distinguished from municipal and other agencies. In the absence of adequate information on killings of state police officers in public records, it was necessary to seek data for the proposed comparison from the selected police forces. Requests were mailed to the directors of twenty-seven state police forces for information on the number of deaths or woundings of officers, by lethal weapons in the hands of criminals, for the period since the organization of their respective departments. Included in the twenty-seven states from which information was sought were all six of the United States which do not have the death penalty in their statutes and a group of other states selected primarily on the basis of geographical proximity and cultural similarity.

The mailed request read:

> In discussions about the retention or abolition of the death penalty, the claim of the supporters of that punishment, especially in police circles, has often been made that the existence of the death penalty in a given state gives the police a certain amount of protection which would be lost if the death penalty were abolished. The reasoning behind this belief is that, where the death penalty exists criminals are less likely to carry lethal weapons for fear that they might be tempted or forced to use them in a brush with the police.

1. Please complete the enclosed blank as accurately as possible.

The accompanying blank was headed:

Name of Department: Date Organized:
Extent of jurisdiction (i.e. full police authority; limited to highway patrol, etc.):
Please fill in the information requested in the columns below, for any instances of death or wounding, by lethal weapon in the hand of a criminal, of a member of the state police force; since the department was organized.

Date of incident	Rank of member	Killed or wounded: specify which	Check, if criminal was insane	Type of weapon used	Brief description of circumstances of death or wounding

Response to the mailed requests was very satisfactory. Replies were received from twenty-four of the twenty-seven state police forces queried. Among the respondents were the six non-death penalty states. In every instance the reply furnished basic information about killings, though in one instance the date of an incident was not reported. In several replies no details were reported on the circumstances of the killing.

For an understanding of the data reported by the state police forces, it must be noted that these forces vary from state to state in several respects. An index to some of these variations is provided in Table 1 furnishing the date of organization of the state police force in each state, the size of the forces in the last reported year, the extent of jurisdiction conferred on the different forces. Study of this table shows, for instance, that the Connecticut Department of State Police was organized as early as 1903, whereas the California Highway Patrol came into existence in its present form only in 1947. Again, the range of size extends from the Pennsylvania State Police with 1900 uniformed members in 1954, to the thirty-seven uniformed officers of the South Dakota force for the same year.

Jurisdiction, it will be noted in Table 1, is described as limited or full. Limited jurisdiction, though the precise limits may vary slightly from state to state, implies that the state police force exercises power only on highway patrol and that its primary duty involves "enforcement of

Vehicle Code and related acts respecting the use of vehicles on highways."[3]

Full jurisdiction, on the other hand, signifies that the state police possess all general police powers enjoyed by sheriffs, constables, municipal police, or other peace officers, and the exercise of this power is territorially limited only by the state's boundaries. In some states, state police officers may also act as fire, fish or game wardens.

The nature and scope of police activities and, presumably, the consequent risk of exposure to criminals willing to use lethal weapons, will also vary to some extent in accordance with such factors as the demographic or cultural pattern of the different states. Table 1 accordingly includes some statistical information about the states as an aid to a comparison of them on the basis of size and distribution of population in urban and rural areas, and on the basis of the crime rate per 100,000 population, for murder and non-negligent manslaughter, for the urban areas in each state reporting to the Federal Bureau of Investigation of the United States Department of Justice, and published annually by the F.B.I. in the *Uniform Crime Reports*. The crime rate for murder and non-negligent manslaughter will represent, it is assumed, at least roughly the prevailing cultural pattern in a given state with respect to criminalty involving deeds of ultimate violence.[4]

[3] The quotation is from a report furnished by the California Highway Patrol. For information on the history and present status of state police in the United States, cf. Bruce Smith, *Police Systems in the United States,* xiii, 351 pp. New York: Harper and Brothers, 1949; pp. 164–90.

[4] "Crime rates . . . are the number of crimes reported by the police expressed in terms of crimes per unit of population in the areas represented by the reporting law enforcement agencies. The unit of population used is 100,000 inhabitants." Federal Bureau of Investigation. *Uniform Crime Reports for the United States,* Vol. XXV, No. 2, 1954. Washington: Government Printing Office, 1955; p. 90. "Murder and nonnegligent manslaughter includes all wilful felonious homicides as distinguished from deaths caused by negligence. Does not include attempts to kill, assaults to kill, suicides, accidental deaths, or justifiable homicides." p. 119.

TABLE 1
DATA RELATING TO THE STATE POLICE FORCE, POPULATION DISTRIBUTION, AND CRIME RATE FOR TWENTY-FOUR STATES

State	Date of organization, State Police(a)	Size of police force(b)	Total population, 100,000's(c)	Urban population, 100,000's(c)	Rural population, 100,000's(c)	Average of Crime Rates(d)
California(e)	1947(g)	1,526	10,856	8,539	2,046	3.53
Connecticut	1903(h)	365	2,007	1,558	448	1.78
Georgia	1937	308	3,444	1,559	1,885	18.13
Illinois	1919	501	8,712	6,759	1,952	5.45
Indiana	1935	446(i)	3,934	2,357	1,577	4.65
Iowa	1935	225	2,621	1,250	1,370	1.44
Maine(f)	1925	128	913	472	441	1.31
Maryland	1935	251	2,343	1,615	727	7.66
Massachusetts	1921	336	4,690	3,959	731	1.10
Michigan(f)	1917	680	6,371	4,503	1,868	4.28
Minnesota(e) (f)	1927	216	2,982	1,624	1,357	.99
Missouri	1931	320	3,954	2,432	1,521	7.41
Nebraska(e)	1937	132	1,325	621	703	1.84
New York	1917	1,201	14,830	12,682	2,147	2.52
North Dakota(e) (f)	1935	42	619	164	454	—

Ohio(e)	1933	562	7,946	5,578	2,368	4.29
Oregon	1931	391	1,521	819	702	2.40
Pennsylvania	1905	1,900	10,498	7,403	3,094	2.41
Rhode Island(f)	1925	84	791	667	124	1.03
South Dakota	1939	37	652	216	436	.69
Texas	1930	796	7,711	4,838	2,873	11.28
Washington	1921	259	2,378	1,503	875	2.79
West Virginia	1919	220	2,005	694	1,311	4.95
Wisconsin(e) (f)	1939	70	3,434	1,987	1,446	1.47

(a) Information supplied by State Police Departments.

(b) Number of uniformed members, as of July, 1953; *The Book of the States*, Vol: X, 1954–55. Chicago: The Council of State Governments, 1954, pp. 282–83.

(c) As of April 1, 1950; source: *Seventeenth Decennial Census, 1950*. Washington: United States Bureau of the Census.

(d) Average of crime rates, for murder and non-negligent manslaughter, for urban areas reporting to the Federal Bureau of Investigation, per 100,000 inhabitants in areas reporting, for 1951–52–53; *Uniform Crime Reports for the United States*, Vols. XXII–XXIV.

(e) Indicates limited jurisdiction exercised by State Police; unless indicated, the State Police exercise full police powers within the state.

(f) Indicates death penalty illegal in state, except that Michigan and North Dakota prescribe the death penalty for treason; North Dakota also permits the death penalty for first-degree murder committed by a prisoner serving a life sentence for first-degree murder; and Rhode Island makes the death penalty mandatory for murder committed by a prisoner serving a life sentence.

(g) Present force reorganized, 1947; report covered 1946 activity of previous force.

(h) Present study covers 1905–54; no deaths report for period prior to 1905.

(i) Estimated number, as reported in *The Book of the States*, Vol. X., p. 283.

TABLE 2

NUMBER OF STATE POLICE OFFICERS KILLED BY LETHAL
WEAPONS IN THE HANDS OF CRIMINALS, FOR
TWENTY-FOUR STATES

State	Records Kept	Deaths by Year		Total
California[a]	1946–1954	1946	2	3
		1954	1	
Connecticut	1903–1954	1928	1	2
		1953	1	
Georgia	1937–1954	1940	1	2
		1948	1	
Illinois	1920–1954	1927	2	6
		1932	1	
		1939	1	
		1946	1	
		1951	1	
Indiana	1935–1954	1937	1	3
		1938	1	
		1946	1	
Iowa	1935–1954	1936	1	1
Maine	1925–1954			0
Maryland	1935–1954	1950	1	1
Massachusetts	1921–1954	1951	1	1
Michigan	1917–1954	1921	1	5
		1927	1	
		1930	1	
		1937	1	
		1950	1	
Minnesota	1927–1954			0
Missouri	1931–1954	1932	1	3
		1941	2	
Nebraska	1937–1954	1953	1	2
		1954	1	
New York	1917–1954	1923	1	8
		1927	2	
		1928	1	
		1931	1	
		1945	1	
		1948	1	
		1951	1	
North Dakota	1935–1954			0
Ohio	1933–1954	(no date given)	1	1

State	Period	Year	Count	Total
Oregon	1931–1954	1931	1	7
		1933	1	
		1937	1	
		1945	1	
		1947	1	
		1950	2	
Pennsylvania	1905–1954	1906	2	16
		1907	1	
		1909	2	
		1918	2	
		1919	1	
		1924	1	
		1927	1	
		1928	1	
		1929	1	
		1930	1	
		1937	3	
Rhode Island	1925–1954	1934	1	1
South Dakota	1939–1954	1946	1	1
Texas	1930–1954	1934	2	4
		1954	2	
Washington	1921–1954	1942	1	1
West Virginia	1919–1954	1920	1	9
		1921	3	
		1922	1	
		1923	1	
		1924	1	
		1926	1	
		1946	1	
Wisconsin	1939–1954			0
		Total		77

a The present California Highway Patrol was organized in 1947; data reported covers one year of duty by the previous force.

Table 2 records the total number of state police officers killed by lethal weapons in the hands of sane criminals for the twenty-four state police forces reporting. To the total of seventy-seven officers thus killed may be added nine reported killed by persons identified as insane. These nine deaths are not included in our study since the possible deterrent value of the death penalty cannot be presumed to have been in question under such circumstances. Deaths resulting from automobile accidents or other accidents in the line of duty are likewise excluded from consideration.

Of the seventy-seven deaths tabulated, six were reported from two out of the six non-death penalty states. The remaining seventy-one deaths were distributed among the eighteen death penalty states. Thus, of the twenty-four states reporting, four reported no officers killed. These four were all non-death penalty states.

Of the eighteen states in which the state police exercise full police power, seventeen reported a total of seventy-one officers killed. The eighteenth state in this group reported no killing; this state is likewise one of the three in this group that do not have the death penalty.

Of the six states which grant only limited power to their state police forces, three reported a total of six killings. These three states likewise have the death penalty. The three non-death penalty states in this group reported no killing of a police officer in their histories.

In summary form, the totals reported are:

Number killed in 18 death penalty states	71
Number killed in 6 non-death penalty states	6
Number killed in 18 full jurisdiction states	71
Number killed in 6 limited jurisdiction states	6
Number killed in 15 death penalty, full jurisdiction states	65
Number killed in 3 non-death penalty, full jurisdiction states	6
Number killed in 3 death penalty, limited jurisdiction states	6
Number killed in 3 non-death penalty, limited jurisdiction states	0

Information on woundings of state police officers was less complete than that on killings. Twelve of the twenty-four respondents gave no information under this heading. In some instances the respondent indicated that a record of woundings was either not available or incomplete. Because of this incomplete response no attempt has been made to compare data on woundings. . . .

In summation it may be noted that of the twelve states offering some data on woundings, nine were death penalty states and three were non-death penalty states. A total of seventy-one woundings of state police officers, by lethal weapons in the hands of sane criminals, were reported; sixty-five from death penalty states, six from non-death penalty states.

With respect to the nature of the weapons used in the seventy-seven killings reported by the State Police forces, in three instances the nature of the weapon was not recorded. The seventy-four remaining killings involved the use of firearms of various types.

Information concerning the circumstances of the killings was incomplete in twenty-one of the seventy-seven killings reported. Thirty killings of police officers are reported to have occurred while the officer was attempting to arrest criminals wanted for such crimes as murder, robbery, and the like. In eight instances the officer met death while investigating premises or serving warrants. In seven instances a killing resulted when an officer attempted to stop a stolen car on the highway. Of the remaining eleven killings reported, five occurred when an officer attempted to disarm unruly persons, three took place in the course of investigations of traffic violations, two occurred while police attempted to disperse mobs, and one took place while an officer was transporting a prisoner.

Since the data recorded in Table 1 on the police force, population distribution, and crime rate of the twenty-four states here studied indicate considerable diversity among the states, three groups of states have been selected from the entire number for the purpose of making more meaningful comparisons among them. The first basis for selection was geographical proximity. With the exception of Wisconsin, which here has been assigned to the West North Central group, all the states now to be considered are grouped according to the standard regional divisions used by the United States Bureau of the Census: New England, East North Central, West North Central. Wisconsin, in fact, borders on states in both the North Central regions, but in other respects its affinity to the West North Central region is marked. Such are its population distribution and crime rate for murder and non-negligent manslaughter in urban areas. Inspection of Table 1 under the appropriate headings will show that the states in each group are roughly similar in these respects.

The first group selected includes four New England states; two of these are non-death penalty states, Maine and Rhode Island. All four states grant full jurisdiction to their police forces. The state forces have all been in existence since 1925, the year in which Maine and Rhode Island organized their departments. Of the four states, three are heavily urbanized in population. The average crime rate for murder and non-negligent manslaughter in urban districts reporting to the F.B.I. for 1951–53, is reasonably close for the four states.

TABLE 3

NUMBER OF STATE POLICE KILLED BY LETHAL WEAPONS IN THE HANDS OF CRIMINALS, FOR 4 NEW ENGLAND STATES

State	Killings, 1925–54	All Killings
Connecticut	2	2
Maine	0	0
Massachusetts	1	1
Rhode Island	1	1

Though the two non-death penalty states, as seen in Table 2, report less killings, it may be argued that the lower number reflects their smaller population and smaller state police forces and thus that the rate of killings for the death penalty states is not proportionately higher. On the other hand, it cannot be said that this data supports the claim of the proponents of the death penalty as a protection to the police.

The four East North Central states which make up our second group are all relatively populous states which are predominantly urban in population distribution. The crime rate average selected for comparison shows similarity, though the rate for Illinois is somewhat higher than the rates for the other three states. All four states have had state police forces since 1935 and, with the exception of Ohio, grant full jurisdiction to these forces. Michigan is the only non-death penalty state in this group.

TABLE 4

NUMBER OF STATE POLICE KILLED BY LETHAL WEAPONS IN THE HANDS OF CRIMINALS, FOR 4 EAST NORTH CENTRAL STATES

State	Killings, 1935–54	All Killings
Illinois	3	6
Indiana	3	3
Michigan	2	5
Ohio	?a	1

a Report from the Ohio State Highway Patrol did not indicate the date of the single killing reported.

In interpreting the data presented in Table 4, some allowance must be made for the fact that Ohio is the only state in the group limiting the jurisdiction of its force. It may be argued that police work concerned primarily with traffic violations involves less risk of contact with potential killers than work which of its nature brings the police officer into contact with a greater range of criminal activities. The Michigan State Police, for instance, during the Prohibition era were faced with great risk from smugglers operating across the U.S.-Canadian border. This circumstance must be allowed for here, since two out of the five deaths reported by the Michigan State Police were killings by rum runners during the period in which the Volstead Act was in force. In the light of the differences noted, therefore, it would appear misleading, despite the lower number of killings in Ohio, to conclude from a comparison of the Ohio and Michigan reports that greater protection came to the Ohio police simply by reason of the retention of the death penalty in that state. The data from four East North Central states cannot be said to furnish any conclusive support to the claim that the death penalty provides greater protection to the police.

Of the six states making up the third group to be studied further, five are designated by the United States Bureau of the Census as part of the West North Central region; the sixth state, Wisconsin, borders on this region. In contrast with the states of the two previous groups, these states are less populous and generally more rural in population distribution. The crime rates reported for urban areas in these states are uniformly low. Three of the states, Minnesota, North Dakota, and Wisconsin, are non-death penalty states; these states, and Nebraska, restrict the jurisdiction of their state police to highway patrol, or as the report of the Wisconsin force states: "Authority is limited to traffic patrol and enforcement of certain truck regulations, automobile dealer license laws, certain finance laws, and laws governing the regulation of circuses, peddlers and transient merchants." All six states have had state police forces since 1939.

TABLE 5

NUMBER OF STATE POLICE KILLED BY LETHAL WEAPONS IN THE HANDS OF CRIMINALS, FOR 6 WEST NORTH CENTRAL STATES

State	Killings, 1939–54	All Killings
Iowa	0	1
Minnesota	0	0
Nebraska	2	2
North Dakota	0	0
South Dakota	1	1
Wisconsin	0	0

While it is true that the three non-death penalty states in this group grant only limited jurisdiction to their police, the same holds true for Nebraska. Thus, we cannot disallow the killings reported by the Nebraska Safety Patrol on any grounds of greater exposure to risk from the nature of its work. Study of the data presented in Table 5 reveals that the record of killings for death penalty and non-death penalty states in this group lends no support to the claim of death penalty proponents.

In summary, therefore, of this section of the study, we conclude that the data available to us after a survey of half the state police forces of the United States do not lend empirical support to the claim that the existence of the death penalty in the statutes of a state provides a greater protection to the police than exists in states where that penalty has been abolished.

THE DETERRENT EFFECT OF CAPITAL PUNISHMENT IN PHILADELPHIA*

BY LEONARD D. SAVITZ**

While a great deal has been written concerning deterrence and capital punishment, there have been exceedingly few empirical studies. Robert Dann in his monograph, "The Deterrent Effect of Capital Punishment,"[1] studied deterrence and the death penalty by analyzing the homicide rate of Philadelphia sixty days before and sixty days after five highly publicized executions of Philadelphia murderers, on the assumption that if capital punishment does indeed deter, ". . . deterrence should be most in evidence in the days immediately following the execution and in the locality where the crimes were committed and where the criminal is known. That is to say, it should be possible to notice periods of reduction in the homicide and murder rate, if not an absolute cessation of murders, mostly after executions."[2]

Though this study takes some of its basic assumptions and theoretical orientation from Dann's article, there are major differences from it as regards methodological approach, units of measurement, and the analysis of data.

A preliminary investigation which aimed at getting some insight into the extent and type of publicity attendant on a few selected capital cases resulted in the following methodological decision: while it is obvious that the point of

* From "A Study in Capital Punishment," reprinted by special permission of the author and the *Journal of Criminal Law, Criminology and Police Science* (Northwestern University School of Law), vol. 49, no. 4, 1958, pp. 338–341.

** Department of Sociology and Anthropology, Temple University.

[1] Robert Dann, *The Deterrent Effect of Capital Punishment*, Bulletin 29, Friends Social Service Series, Committee on Philanthropic Labor and Philadelphia Yearly Meeting of Friends, Third Month 1935.

[2] *Ibid.*, p. 4.

greatest deterrence, all things being equal, would be the day of execution of the criminal, the aforementioned investigation indicated that all things were not equal. This study is predicated on the assumption that at the point of maximum publicity, through the various media of mass communication, the greatest deterrence occurs, and in capital cases since 1944 at least, the greatest publicity came with the trial, conviction, and sentencing to death. The execution itself, in recent years, usually takes place a year or more after the sentencing and receives rather perfunctory notice in the newspapers; it lacks the sustained public attention that a continuing trial occasions and apparently the great time lag between the formal sentence and the actual execution has led to an editorial belief that public interest has all but vanished by the time the prisoner is put to death. Hence the execution receives relatively little "play" in the newspapers. As a case in point, George Gatlin raped and strangled a young girl in what was described as "the most atrocious crime in Pennsylvania history"; he was executed some eight months after receiving the death sentence and his execution was noted in one inch of space on page 18 of the *Philadelphia Inquirer*.

After a list of all twenty convicted felons who had received a death sentence in Philadelphia from 1944 to 1954 was secured, examination of the individual cases made it apparent that sixteen could not be utilized either because:

1. In some cases, immediately after conviction (and before sentencing) various appeals to the appellate courts were made, so that the formal sentencing to death, coming many months after the trial received minimal newspaper publicity; or

2. It was considered necessary that in eight week periods prior and subsequent to any particular sentencing to death no other death penalty should be imposed, or else considerable "masking" of deterrent effect might take place; a number of cases did not meet this desideratum because their sentences were too closely bunched.

The four remaining capital offenders were all "felony-murderers" whose trial and sentencing received from thirty to seventy-five inches of print in the *Philadelphia Inquirer*. They were:

1. Raymond Pierce who was sentenced to death on November 4, 1944, and who committed suicide shortly before he was to be executed.

2. William Chavis, who was sentenced to death on June 9, 1946, and who was executed a year and a half later.

3. Aaron "Treetop" Turner, who was sentenced to death September 27, 1946 and who subsequently had his sentence commuted to life imprisonment.

4. William Ramage, who was sentenced to death on September 24, 1947, and who was executed about a year later.[3]

Once the above-listed "Dates of Greatest Deterrence" was determined, it was necessary to determine the number of murders committed in an eight week period prior and an eight week period subsequent to each of those four dates. With the cooperation of the Philadelphia Police Department, the "Murder Books" of the Homicide Squad, which contained a listing and short resume of every homicide known to the police, were examined for the various time periods under consideration.

It was obvious that care had to be taken to select from those records only first degree murder cases, for in Pennsylvania the death penalty can be applied only for that crime, which is defined as, ". . . murder . . . perpetrated by means of poison, or lying in wait or by any other kind of willful, deliberate and premeditated killing, or which shall be committed in the perpetration or attempt to perpetrate any arson, rape, robbery, burglary or kidnapping."[4]

The "Murder Books," of course, did not list the killings specifically as first degree, second degree, manslaughter,

---

[3] It will be noted that all four of the offenders were not actually executed but this in no way affects our underlying assumption that the greatest deterrence occurs at the point of greatest publicity, *i.e.*, the day of the imposition of the death penalty (and not its actual execution).

[4] Act of June 24, 1938, 18 Purd Pa Stat. Ann (1945) Sec 4701.

etc., which meant that there was a crucial problem of determining which of the homicides were first degree murders.

There were, first of all, those offenses which were patently capital crimes either because of a subsequent conviction for first degree murder, or the crime was of such a nature—*e.g.*, a "felony-murder"—as to be certainly murder in the first degree even though there were no convictions because of the police's inability to identify, arrest or convict the perpetrator. These were classified as Definite Capital Crimes (DCC).

There were, in addition, however, a considerable number of murders that leave one doubtful as to the specific degree of the offense. These were cases in which the jury returned a verdict of "guilty of murder in the second degree," but the descriptions of the crimes were such as to suggest the possibility that, except for jury leniency, they may have been first degree murders. In Pennsylvania, the offender is prosecuted for "Murder in General," and the determination as to the precise degree of the killing rests with the court or the jury. In some cases, it was found that the prosecuting attorney specifically told the court that the offense involved only second degree murder, and the court (or jury), while still legally required to choose between first and second degree murder, never actually exceeded the "suggested" degree. The possibility then arose that where the prosecution did not declare the crime to be less than first degree murder, it felt there was at least some possibility of a conviction in the first degree; thus, in many instances the jury may have brought in a verdict of guilty of second degree murder, whereas some other jury, judging the same case, might well have returned a finding of guilty of first degree murder. Using as a guide Professor Schwartz's "Memorandum on the Punishment of Murder in Pennsylvania,"[5] particularly as it discussed

[5] Louis Schwartz, *Memoranda: Punishment of Murder in Pennsylvania, Royal Commission on Capital Punishment, Memoranda and Replies to a Questionnaire received from Foreign and Commonwealth Countries, Part II, United States of America,"* pp. 776–778, London, 1952.

TABLE 1

NUMBER OF DEFINITE CAPITAL CRIMES, POSSIBLE CAPITAL CRIMES AND TOTAL CAPITAL CRIMES IN EIGHT-WEEK PERIODS PRIOR AND SUBSEQUENT TO FOUR DAYS IN WHICH THE DEATH PENALTY WAS IMPOSED

		Pre-Sentence Period (Period I)									Date of Sentence	Weeks	Post-Sentence Period (Period II)								
	Weeks	8	7	6	5	4	3	2	1	Total			1	2	3	4	5	6	7	8	Total
Pierce	DCC	0	0	2	0	2	0	0	1	5	11/4/44	DCC	2	0	1	0	1	0	1	1	6
	PCC	0	0	1	0	1	1	2	0	5		PCC	0	0	0	1	0	0	1	0	2
	TCC	0	0	3	0	3	1	2	1	10		TCC	2	0	1	1	1	0	2	1	8
Chavis	DCC	1	1	1	1	1	2	0	1	8	6/9/46	DCC	1	0	0	2	0	2	1	1	7
	PCC	0	1	0	0	1	0	1	1	4		PCC	0	1	0	0	0	1	1	0	3
	TCC	1	2	1	1	2	2	1	2	12		TCC	1	1	0	2	0	3	2	1	10
Turner	DCC	0	1	0	1	0	0	1	1	4	9/27/46	DCC	2	0	2	0	1	4	1	0	10
	PCC	0	0	3	1	0	0	0	2	6		PCC	2	1	1	0	1	1	0	0	6
	TCC	0	1	3	2	0	0	1	3	10		TCC	4	1	3	0	2	5	1	0	16
Ramage	DCC	0	0	2	0	0	1	1	2	6	9/24/47	DCC	0	0	2	0	2	1	0	0	5
	PCC	0	1	0	0	0	0	2	2	5		PCC	1	0	0	0	0	1	0	0	2
	TCC	0	1	2	0	0	1	3	4	11		TCC	1	0	2	0	2	2	0	0	7
Total	DCC	1	2	5	2	3	3	2	5	23		DCC	5	0	5	2	4	7	3	2	28
	PCC	0	2	4	1	2	1	5	5	20		PCC	3	2	1	1	1	3	2	0	13
	TCC	1	4	9	3	5	4	7	10	43		TCC	8	2	6	3	5	10	5	2	41

$\overline{X}$ DCC 2.86; $\overline{X}$ PCC 2.5; $\overline{X}$ TCC 5.37 $\overline{X}$ DCC 3.5; $\overline{X}$ PCC 1.63; $\overline{X}$ TCC 5.13

the meaning of the concept of "wilful, deliberate and pre-meditated," and the effect of mental defectiveness and drunkenness on the degree of the offense in the courts of Pennsylvania, an intensive examination was made of all second degree murder convictions in which the prosecution had not suggested to the court that this be the true degree of the murder, for the four sixteen-week periods in question.

Those cases which might be classified as first degree murder were classified as Possible Capital Crimes (PCC). They constituted approximately twenty-five per cent of all the second degree murder convictions for the periods under examination.

Examination of Table 1 reveals that with the sentencing to death of Raymond Pierce on November 4, 1944, there were ten Total Capital Crimes (combining Definite and Possible Capital Crimes) in Period I (the eight weeks prior to 11/4/44), of which five were Definite Capital Crimes and five were Possible Capital Crimes. In Period II (the eight weeks after 11/4/44) there were eight Total Capital Crimes of which six were Definite and two were Possible. There was, thus, a twenty per cent decrease from Periods I to II in Total Capital Crimes, but this was caused in a sixty per cent decrease in the Possible crimes.

William Chavis had the death penalty imposed on him on June 9, 1946, and for Period I there were twelve Total Capital Crimes of which eight were Definite and four were Possible Capital Crimes. In Period II, there were ten Total crimes of which seven were Definite and three were Possible. This represented a sixteen per cent decrease in Total Capital Crimes from Period I to Period II, with one less Definite and one less Possible Capital Crime in the latter period.

With the sentencing to death of Aaron Turner on September 27, 1945 we have by far the largest number of murders of all the periods under examination. In Period I, there were ten Total Capital Crimes (four Definite and six Possible) while in Period II there were no less than sixteen Total Capital Crimes (ten Definite and six Possible) which represented an increase of sixty per cent, with a

250 per cent increase in Definite Capital Crimes. It may be noted in passing that in the three days following Turner's sentencing (9/28/45 to 9/30/45) there were two Definite and two Possible Capital Crimes committed.

William Ramage received the death penalty on September 24, 1947 and the table reveals eleven Total crimes in Period I (six Definites and five Possibles) in contrast to seven Total Capital Crimes in Period II (five Definites and two Possibles).

When data relative to all four cases were combined, it was found that in the four eight week periods prior to separate sentencings to death (the total of the four Period I's) there were forty-three Total Capital Crimes, of which twenty-three were Definite and twenty were Possible Capital Crimes. The combined total for Period II was forty-one Total Capital Crimes (twenty-eight Definite and thirteen Possible Capital Crimes). There was, thus, a total decrease of about four per cent in Total Capital Crimes, but this was caused by a sharp decline in Possible Capital Crimes (from twenty in Period I to thirteen in Period II).

While aware that the numbers involved are minute and not susceptible to any rigorous statistical manipulation, it is interesting to note that the weekly mean ($\overline{X}$) of Definite Capital Crimes was 2.86 in Period I, which rate was exceeded by the Definite Capital Crimes in the first, third, fourth and fifth weeks in Period II. The weekly mean of Possible Capital Crimes in Period I was 2.5, which was exceeded or equalled only by the Possible Capital Crimes in the first and sixth week of Period II. The weekly mean of Total Capital Crimes is 5.37 in Period I, which figure is equalled or exceeded by the Total Capital Crimes in the first, third, fifth, sixth and seventh week of Period II.

There emerges, therefore, no pattern that would indicate deterrence. Certainly the first idea that comes to mind, that the deterrent effect of the imposition of the death penalty might be felt shortly after the date of sentencing is not borne out by the data. The first, third and fifth week in Period II exceeded or equalled the average Total and Definite Capital Crimes rates in Period I. The second and fourth weeks in Period II are considerably lower in Total,

Definite and Possible Capital Crimes than the average in Period I.

Summary

It can be said in summary, that the author is aware that the short period of time under analysis and the extremely small number of murders dealt with prevent conclusive findings, but we must conclude from the data at hand that there was no significant decrease or increase in the murder rate following the imposition of the death penalty on four separate occasions.

It will be admitted that any decrease in the Total Capital Crimes from Period I to Period II is due to the Possible Capital Crime figures; cases that were somewhat arbitrarily selected, albeit within the desiderata listed by Professor Schwartz. Utilization of only Definite Capital Crimes disclosed a substantial *increase* (twenty-two per cent) from Period I to Period II.

THE DETERRENT EFFECT OF CAPITAL PUNISHMENT IN CALIFORNIA*

BY WILLIAM F. GRAVES, M.D.**

My greatest concern in the presentation of this paper is that it may be thought that I have looked too closely at capital punishment. I would not wish to delude anyone with the notion that I am without prejudice on the general issue of the death penalty. My judgment, however, is based on considerations of justice and morality, and is entirely aside from another very important issue having to do with this penalty. I refer now to the relationship, if any, of the death penalty to the incidence of the particular crime for which it is applied.

* Reprinted, by permission of the author and publisher, from "A Doctor Looks at Capital Punishment," *Medical Arts and Sciences,* journal of the Loma Linda University School of Medicine (formerly College of Medical Evangelists), vol. 10, no. 4 (Fourth Quarter, 1956), pp. 137–141.

** Chairman, Subcommittee on Penal Problems of the Friends Committee on Legislation, Pasadena, California, and formerly on the medical staff of San Quentin Prison, California.

The vast majority of those who oppose abolition of the death penalty share, I am sure, my concerns regarding questions of justice and morality, but feel that these considerations are superseded by the need for a deterrent to restrain the potential murderer; and for this they feel that only the death penalty will suffice.

Therefore, without entering into the serious philosophical and legal arguments that surround the use of this "sharp medicine," I would like to present a study of its effectiveness against the disease for which it is administered—murder.

I have tried to approach the problem very much in the same manner one would follow in evaluating the effectiveness of any medicine or procedure in the treatment of any disease. Mine, of course, is not the first such effort. Many studies have been conducted in numerous countries. Probably the most extensive of these was the one conducted from 1949 to 1953 by the British Royal Commission on Capital Punishment. In this report all aspects of the death penalty and its administration as carried out in England and in much of the world were investigated. A great number of statistics were collected and presented.

In this study, however, as in others that have been honestly undertaken, it has not been possible to reach, from the mass of statistics, any definite conclusions with respect to the effectiveness of the death penalty as a deterrent to murder. To illustrate the problem, we may compare the homicide rates of the U.S. abolition states with the U.S. states retaining the death penalty. It will be found that the homicide rates in the abolition states (all of which are northern states) is only about one third as great as it is in the capital punishment states (which include the South and nearly all the large metropolitan areas).[1] An untrained person might conclude that capital punishment in some way caused the homicide rate to be much higher in the states where it was used. But it would also be true that there is much more sunshine in the capital punishment states. Could it be that this, too, is a cause of murder?

[1] Karl F. Schuessler: *Annals of American Academy of Political and Social Science* (Nov.), 1952, p. 57.

TABLE 1

HOMICIDES IN ALAMEDA, LOS ANGELES, AND SAN FRANCISCO COUNTIES, AND PRISONERS EXECUTED IN CALIFORNIA, BY MONTH: 1946 THROUGH 1955[a]

Item	1946	1947	1948	1949	1950	1951	1952	1953	1954	1955
Total										
Homicides	287	310	231	229	200	210	239	245	242	220
Executions	6	7	8	11	7	6	9	8	9	9
January										
Homicides	25	24	24	13	14	15	20	14	14	20
Executions	—	—	1	2	—	—	—	—	1	—
February										
Homicides	18	32	21	11	22	13	27	18	24	17
Executions	—	2	1	2	1	—	1	2	1	2
March										
Homicides	27	29	22	16	16	15	22	19	23	16
Executions	—	1	—	—	1	2	2	—	2	—
April										
Homicides	14	25	25	23	9	18	18	16	13	21
Executions	—	1	2	2	—	—	1	1	1	—
May										
Homicides	32	27	32	20	16	18	17	18	29	16
Executions	2	—	1	—	—	—	1	2	—	—

June	Homicides	22	25	15	21	13	12	16	15	18	15
	Executions	—	1	—	—	1	—	1	—	—	3
July	Homicides	25	36	21	23	18	19	20	30	19	17
	Executions	—	—	—	2	—	—	1	—	3	3
August	Homicides	19	24	9	19	14	18	20	26	13	23
	Executions	—	1	—	—	1	1	—	—	—	—
September	Homicides	23	21	16	15	22	26	28	22	26	19
	Executions	2	—	—	—	—	—	—	—	1	1
October	Homicides	19	16	16	29	22	21	16	28	25	15
	Executions	1	—	2	—	2	—	1	3	—	—
November	Homicides	21	20	13	21	14	16	14	11	13	20
	Executions	1	1	—	—	—	2	—	—	—	—
December	Homicides	42	31	17	18	20	19	21	28	25	21
	Executions	—	—	1	3	1	—	1	—	—	—

a Homicide figures based on reports furnished by coroner's office of respective counties. Execution figures furnished by California State Department of Corrections.

Of course the difficulty lies in the fact that we are comparing geographic areas differing in a vast number of respects: economically, socially, racially, et cetera. They are, therefore, not comparable. Comparisons are also made of homicide statistics in the same areas before and after abolition or restoration of capital punishment. This technique is hardly any better, since we live in a society that is anything but static. Therefore, time intervals cannot be compared, any more than can geographical areas.

To get at the problem one must find some means of deriving a comparison in which, for practical purposes, there is only one variable, and that variable must be the impact or influence of capital punishment on the social organism. One such effort was that conducted in 1935 by Robert H. Dann, of Oregon State College. Homicide statistics preceding and following a selected group of executions in Pennsylvania were analyzed. It was concluded from this study that no deterrent effect could be demonstrated. Mr. Dann, at about the same time, conducted a similar study on the West Coast, and for his pioneering of this approach I am in debt.

California, with its habit of carrying out executions on Friday at 10 A.M., provides a peculiar opportunity for such a study. Anyone studying homicide trends will soon note that for any one area the incidence of homicide varies with the day of the week. Thus with a fairly large number of weeks to consider, it is easily possible to construct a curve, the points on which would represent the average homicide incidence of the days of an average week of this group of weeks. This can be done for any group of weeks that one chooses, and depending on the choice, the height and shape of the curve will greatly vary. This is due to the wide and chaotic variations in the homicide rate from month to month. Indeed, a glance at this wildly fluctuating rate (see Table 1) makes the isolation of the effect of a single variable seem a nearly hopeless task. However, since nearly all executions occur at the same point in the week, the detection of their effect, if any, on the weekly homicide curve is greatly facilitated. The problem, as I see it, is simply to compare this curve as it occurs on the average week during which there is an execution, to the same curve as it appears on weeks similar in every other respect to the execution weeks except that they contain no execution.

To do this, I have arbitrarily selected for this study, on the one hand, all the weeks during which there was an execution in the state of California during the years 1946 through 1955; and on the other hand, all the weeks either immediately preceding or immediately following an execution week, or falling between two execution weeks. For the purpose of this study I have considered the week to start with Tuesday and end with Monday, thereby placing the execution day in the middle of the execution week.[2]

The homicides that I have considered are those listed by the coroners' offices of Los Angeles, San Francisco, and Alameda counties for the years 1946 through 1955. The execution dates for the same period were kindly supplied to me by the California State Department of Corrections. The statistical material is summed up in Table 2. When the incidence figures are expressed graphically, the curves seen in Chart 1 appear.

The weekend rise in homicide incidence is apparent in all weekly groups. The total weekly incidence is not seen to vary significantly with respect to the relationship of the week to the execution. However, when one compares the curve representing nonexecution weeks studied with that representing execution weeks studied, the curves are seen to be strikingly different. (See Chart 2.) The difference lies in the elevation of the Thursday-Friday homicide incidence and the depression of the Saturday-Sunday incidence in weeks that include executions. Admittedly the size of the sample is limited. Nevertheless a statistical analysis of this variation from the expected curve shows it to be probably significant. There is less than one chance in twenty that such a variation is due to chance alone.

I should like now to be permitted a few words of speculation. It would seem that the execution, or more precisely the publicity surrounding it, results in part of the peak homicide incidence being moved to an earlier part of the week.

[2] This applies except with respect to six executions, which occurred on days other than Friday (see Table 2).

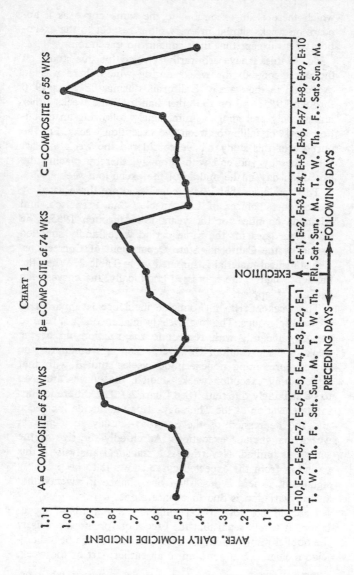

CHART 1

A = COMPOSITE of 55 WKS   B = COMPOSITE of 74 WKS   C = COMPOSITE of 55 WKS

AVER. DAILY HOMICIDE INCIDENT

E-10, E-9, E-8, E-7, E-6, E-5, E-4, E-3, E-2, E-1   FRI.   E+1, E+2, E+3, E+4, E+5, E+6, E+7, E+8, E+9, E+10
T. W. Th. F. Sat. Sun. M. T. W. Th.   EXECUTION   Sat. Sun. M. T. W. Th. F. Sat. Sun. M.

PRECEDING DAYS ← → FOLLOWING DAYS

CHART 2

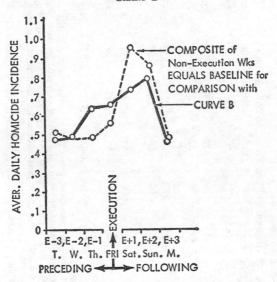

This is to me a very intriguing finding. May it be that minds already burdened with conscious or subconscious homicidal intent are stimulated by the example of the state's taking of life to act sooner? Is it possible that this is a statistical representation of the diminution of respect for human life that some feel executions entail? Or alternatively does the early rise represent these effects while the latter depression of the curve represents an actual deterrent effect of an execution? If this latter is true, then it would seem that the deterrent effect of a typical execution is almost exactly canceled out by its earlier "brutalizing" effect. In any case there would seem to be no evidence in this study of any over-all deterrent value in the death penalty.

Now I presume it will be contended that other variables are at work here as well as in the studies in which different areas and different times are compared. I have considered this, but I can conceive of none that might have a consistent effect.

However, in any case, because of the smallness of the

TABLE 2

HOMICIDES BY DAY OF WEEK PRECEDING AND FOLLOWING WEEK OF EXECUTION AND HOMICIDES DURING WEEK OF EXECUTION: 1946 TO 1955

(Covers homicides occurring in Alameda, Los Angeles, and San Francisco counties only)

Weekly Groups	[a]Tues. 28	Wed. 27	Thu. 26	Fri. 29	Sat. 46	Sun. 47	Mon. 29
1. Weeks prior to execution week (covers 55 weeks) E–10 through E–4	.509 26	.491 29	.473 28	.528 32	.837 57	.855 47	.528 24
2. Weeks following execution week (covers 55 weeks) E+4 through E+10	.473 59	.528 56	.509 56	.582 64	1.037 110	.855 99	.437 55
3. Sum of 1 and 2, plus 6 weeks that fell between execution weeks (covers 116 weeks)	.508 35	.483 36	.483 47	.552 48	.948 54	.854 59	.474 34
4. Weeks of execution (covers 74 weeks) E–3 through E+3	.473	.486	.635	.649	.729	.797	.459

NOTE: The whole figure in each column represents the total number of homicides occurring on the particular day during the entire weekly group. The decimal figure represents the mean daily number of homicides occurring on the same day during the entire weekly group. Thus, on line 1 the 28, under Tuesday, represents the total number of homicides that occurred on Tuesday during the entire 55 single weeks that preceded the week of execution. The .509 is the mean daily average for each Tuesday of the 55-week period.

There were 80 California prisoners executed during the 74 weeks of execution, and there were 3 Federal executions, making a total of 83 herein considered.

[a] Days of the week apply except with respect to 6 executions, which occurred on days other than Friday.

sample (711 homicides and eighty-three[3] executions— seventy-four execution dates), these findings cannot be considered conclusive. Further studies with much larger samples will be needed if firm conclusions are to be drawn. It is my hope that this limited work may inspire such a further study.

For their kind help in obtaining for me the statistical material necessary for this report, may I express my appreciation to the following persons:

E. A. Winstanley, Coroner, and Victor Cefalu, M.D., Chief Deputy Coroner, Los Angeles County.

Henry W. Turkel, M.D., Coroner, San Francisco County.

E. M. Lundegaard, M.D., Coroner, Alameda County.

Clinton Duffy, Member State of California Adult Authority, and former Warden, California State Prison, San Quentin, California.

A. LaMont Smith, Executive Officer, Board of Corrections, State of California, Department of Corrections.

[The following addendum to Dr. Graves's article is from a letter of his dated June 22, 1959, and is printed here with his permission.]

In an effort to make a little more clear the results of this study, I have prepared another chart in which I have simply straightened out the homicide curve occurring on non-execution weeks. If this "curve" is taken as a baseline and if the deviations from it on execution weeks are expressed as percentiles of this baseline, it is apparent that an approximately thirty per cent increase in homicides occurs on the day before executions. On the day of executions an almost twenty per cent increase occurs; and on the day after executions, an approximate twenty-five per cent decrease occurs in the homicide rate.

As I have pointed out, the study is not on a large enough scale to be statistically conclusive. According to my calculations, such a variation could occur slightly less than one time in twenty due to chance timing alone.

[3] Included in the number are three Federal executions.

If the effects noted, however, are not due to chance, it seems to be difficult to attribute them to any other factor than the executions and their attendant publicity. I should probably leave it to the psychiatrists and psychologists to account for the exact nature of the effects.

CHART 3

HOMICIDES ON COMPOSITE EXECUTION WEEKS EXPRESSED AS PERCENTILES OF HOMICIDE RATES FOR NON-EXECUTION WEEKS, 1946 TO 1955

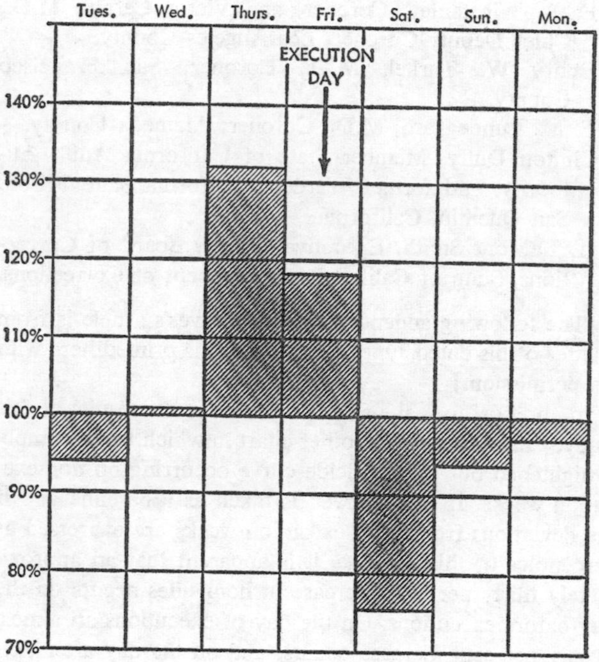

Chapter Seven

ABOLITION: SUCCESS OR FAILURE?

INTRODUCTION

Defenders of capital punishment have often claimed that three of the strongest reasons in favor of keeping the death penalty are the failure of abolition where it has been tried, the public's refusal to accept it, and the dangers in imprisoning and later paroling murderers. Each of these allegations has a basis in fact. If by the failure of abolition is meant the willingness of state legislatures to reintroduce the death penalty after, in many cases, no more than a very brief period without it, then this is true in one-half of the states where abolition has been tried. If by public rejection is meant the absence of sufficient pressure on the legislatures to force repeal of the death penalty for murder, then this claim is correct for two-thirds of the jurisdictions in the country (though the remaining one-third has, at one time or another, tried abolition for crimes). If by the danger of imprisonment and parole is meant that some killers who were caught and convicted, but not executed, later committed other crimes of violence, then this must be conceded as well.

But it would be misleading to leave it at this, and the purpose of the six selections in this chapter is to develop a fuller answer on all these issues.[1] The selection by Professor Sellin shows that in every abolition state, whether or not it later restored capital punishment, there is no correlation between the status of the death penalty and the homicide rate. This strongly suggests that in the ten states that abolished the death penalty and later restored it the reasons

[1] It would have been desirable to include in this chapter an account of the experiment with abolition in at least one state which has been without capital punishment for a long time (particularly Michigan or Rhode Island). My researches failed, however, to disclose the existence of any such study and I was unsuccessful in arranging to have one prepared in time for publication in this volume.

had nothing to do with the measurable effects of death vs. imprisonment as a deterrent to murder. Conjecture of such effects, however, very likely played a considerable role in justifying an end to abolition. These suggestions are supported in some detail by three studies of this phenomenon in three different states: Oregon, Missouri, and Delaware. Mr. Herbert Cobin's study was written especially for this book and the case of Sergeant Mulrine, which he reports, is unusually tragic and instructive.

What seems to account for the reintroduction of the death penalty in the other former abolition states—Washington, Tennessee, Kansas, South Dakota, Iowa, Colorado, and Arizona? Careful studies comparable to those printed here are not available at this time (except for Washington). What evidence there is suggests that allegations of a crime wave aroused segments of the press, the public and the legislature into virtually a hysterical demand for restoration of the death penalty. In almost every case, one or two particularly violent and revolting crimes caught the public's eye, arousing emotions that easily smothered a cooler appraisal of the relation between crime and punishment. For instance, the precipitating event in Washington seems to have been public outrage when, in 1917, the murderer of a leading business man openly "boasted that he would be sent to the pen for life to be fed and cared for" at public expense.[2] In Colorado, it was three crimes in 1900, two by Negroes, which led directly to lynchings. In one case, a twelve-year-old white girl was raped and murdered; her attacker was burned at the stake by a lynch mob.[3] This complete breakdown of law and order in Colorado was reenacted in 1917 in Georgia, when Leo Frank was taken out of jail and lynched shortly after his death sentence had been voided, and it gave rise to the myth that to abolish the death penalty is to provoke lynching. As Raymond Bye later showed, ten other states had at least one lynching prior to abolition of the death penalty, but only six of the ten had

[2] Norman Hayner and John Cranor, "The Death Penalty in Washington State," *The Annals* (November 1952), p. 101.

[3] J. E. Cutler, "Capital Punishment and Lynching," *The Annals* (May 1907), p. 184.

any after abolition; and in only one state did the incidence of lynching rise after abolition.[4] Reliable statistics now pretty definitely show that the states that have had the most homicides and the most legal executions have also had the most illegal executions, in the form of lynchings.

An invariably disturbing question often raised in estimating the wisdom of abolition is whether it is safe for one state to abolish the death penalty when its immediate neighbors retain it. At a public hearing in the New Jersey Assembly on abolition bills in 1958, Sanford Bates made headlines when he warned of "the risk of abolishing the [death] penalty here in this little corridor state which is between two large metropolitan areas, both of which have the death penalty."[5] The image immediately comes to mind of killers pouring across the Delaware and Hudson Rivers, from Philadelphia and New York, carrying their helpless victims into the Garden State and turning it into a vast abattoir, even as they mocked the electric chairs they had left behind, secure in the knowledge that the worst they could suffer was a mere "life" term in prison. The picture is graphic enough, but is it a likely forecast of what would happen?

No special research has been undertaken on the question, but what evidence there is suggests the danger is overrated. According to Warden Lewis Lawes:

> About six years ago [1934] a band of gunmen invaded a small Kansas bank and in their getaway murdered the cashier. The killers were captured and convicted . . . and sentenced to life imprisonment. This punishment failed to soothe many Kansans who felt that murderers, in escaping the chair, had avoided a fate rightfully due them.[6]

More recently, in testimony before the Royal Commis-

[4] Raymond Bye, *Capital Punishment in the United States* (1919), pp. 64–67.

[5] New Jersey, *Public Hearing on Bills to Abolish Capital Punishment* (1958), 2nd day, p. 81.

[6] Lewis Lawes, *Meet the Murderer* (1940), p. 176.

sion on Capital Punishment, the then Attorney General of
Kansas reported that:

> One of the contributing factors leading to the re-enact-
> ment of the death penalty for first degree murder was
> the fact that shortly prior thereto numerous deliberate
> murders were committed in Kansas by persons who
> had previously committed murders in states surround-
> ing Kansas, where their punishment, if captured, could
> have been the death penalty. Such murders in Kansas
> were admittedly made solely for the purpose of secur-
> ing a sentence to life imprisonment in Kansas if cap-
> tured.[7]

According to Professor Sellin's testimony before the Royal
Commission:

> South Dakota reintroduced the death penalty because
> a couple of Illinois convicts, who had finished serving
> their terms, tramped across the state and killed a cou-
> ple of filling-station attendants, if I remember cor-
> rectly—they were robbery murders.[8]

No suggestion of this phenomenon seems to have occurred
in several other states, however. In particular, during the
nearly four years Delaware was without the death penalty,
there was no intimation that anything of this sort happened.
Yet Delaware is just across the river from Maryland, Pennsylvania, and New Jersey, all of which have capital punishment. A similar case is Rhode Island, situated between
Massachusetts and Connecticut. Testimony presented to the
Massachusetts Commission on Capital Punishment showed
that in the one known case in over a century where criminals from Massachusetts killed their victim in Rhode Island, "the criminals did not come across the state line for
the purpose of being in Rhode Island when the killing was
done. They were not paying much attention to which side
of the line they were on."[9] How little attention criminals

---

[7] Great Britain, Royal Commission on Capital Punishment,
Report (1953), p. 375.

[8] Great Britain, *loc. cit.*, p. 375.

[9] Massachusetts, *Report on the Death Penalty* (1958), p. 18.

pay to which side of the state line they are on is revealed by another case. Although New Hampshire has not had an execution since the 1930's, murder is officially punishable by death in that state if the jury so wishes. Yet on February 9, 1959, two men kidnapped a Rhode Island business man, took him to Nashua, N. H., and killed him. They were sentenced to death in New Hampshire for a crime which if they had committed it in Rhode Island would have got them at most a life sentence.[10]

As for the killings in Kansas mentioned above, restoration of the death penalty in 1935 probably did prevent such murders from happening. It is also true that Kansans may have had a legitimate complaint against Missouri during the 1920's and early 1930's, because abolition in their state coupled with restoration of the death penalty in Missouri in 1919 evidently created a strong inducement to some criminals to murder Kansas residents. But if abolition in Kansas created this inducement, this was as much a reason for Missouri to reabolish the death penalty as it was for Kansas to reintroduce it. Either way, the inducement to murder Kansas residents would have disappeared. As for the felony murders in South Dakota mentioned by Professor Sellin, they probably would have occurred whatever the punishment for murder. This is also true of a case Judge Marcus Kavanaugh of Chicago cited many years ago, in which a man confessed to taking his wife into Wisconsin from Iowa so he could kill her without risking the death penalty (in another case, a man confessed to taking his wife for the same reason from Pennsylvania into Michigan).[11] Judge Kavanaugh did not consider whether in such cases the husband is not likely to murder his wife in any event, and that the only consequence of abolishing the death penalty in one state and not in another is to change the scene of the crime. What is constantly overlooked when

---

[10] See State v. Nelson et al., 103 N. H. 178 (1961). The sentence was not immediately carried out, however, and as of August 1, 1963, the two were half way through a six-month stay of execution.

[11] Cited in Julia Johnson (ed.), *Capital Punishment* (1939), p. 175.

such cases are cited and when (more likely) the mere possibility of such crimes is imagined is how little relation there seems to be between the state laws punishing murder and the volume and frequency of the crime.

One is probably safe from contradiction, by the facts, at least, if he holds to the view that very few persons from death penalty states who deliberately chose to kill someone in a neighboring abolition state were induced to do so solely by the fact of abolition in that state; and that what crimes such persons do intend to commit will be committed at home, without the bother of transporting their victims deliberately into abolition jurisdictions, unless the level of law enforcement under abolition becomes noticeably lax.

Let us turn now to the second argument to be considered here, that the public would not accept abolition even if the state legislatures could somehow be persuaded to approve it. Data cited in Chapter Five of this book shows that considerable support already exists among the general public for punishing the worst criminals with imprisonment rather than with death (despite the fact that the emotions tending to support the death penalty are far more easily and regularly aroused by crime reporting in the mass media), and that many people exhibit considerable reluctance to serve on a jury that is to try a capital case.

The failure to achieve statutory repeal of the death penalty is not really attributable to the attitude of the public on the question, anyway. It is attributable to the votes of a few thousand elected state representatives. Exactly why these political representatives have not enacted abolition legislation in recent years (except briefly in Delaware) is not really understood. Certainly the failure to enact abolition in California, Massachusetts, Ohio and Pennsylvania is not attributable to the absence of suitable research by the legislatures themselves on the subject, nor to indifference or active opposition from offices of the various Governors, nor to the failure of abolitionists to present their point of view vigorously and persistently. Part of the answer surely lies in the fact that many legislators have not been convinced by the evidence and argument marshalled against capital punishment. Nor have all or even most of their constituents. Yet these facts do not in themselves provide a sufficient description of the obstacles to abolition, much less a satisfactory explanation of why abolitionists are still a considerable distance from their goal. As a step toward providing the kind of political and sociological analysis needed, I have included in this chapter my own account of the abolition campaign in New Jersey over the past several years.[12]

The third argument, that imprisonment and eventual parole of capital offenders is fraught with disaster, is directly examined in a brief article at the end of this chapter. The data it presents strongly suggests that incarceration of *all* convicted capital offenders is a practical alternative to the death penalty, one which could be adopted tomorrow across the land without any administrative upheavals or expenses; and that except in a very small percentage of cases, where for one reason or another literal "life" imprisonment might turn out to be necessary, all such convicts could eventually be returned to society without endangering themselves or the public, exactly as it has proved to be possible to release such convicts in dozens of other civilized nations throughout the world.[13] Whether it is desirable to do what penologists know is feasible, is a question of social policy that answers itself.

EFFECT OF REPEAL AND REINTRODUCTION OF THE DEATH PENALTY ON HOMICIDE RATES*

BY THORSTEN SELLIN

Since a few American states have abolished the death penalty either permanently or temporarily it would be im-

[12] A state by state summary of the abolition movement in the United States since 1957 is available in Eugene Block, *And May God Have Mercy* (1962), pp. 123–135.

[13] See Giles Playfair and Derrick Sington, *The Offenders* (1957).

* Reprinted from *The Death Penalty* (Philadelphia: The American Law Institute, 1959), pp. 34–38, by permission of the author and publisher.

portant to know what effect the policy has had on homicide rates. Most of the states that removed the death penalty for murder permanently did so, however, many years ago, (Michigan in 1846, Rhode Island in 1852, Wisconsin in 1853, and Maine in 1887) long before adequate mortality statistics were compiled. Some information about these states, is nevertheless available. In Michigan, the number of prisoners received in the state prison after conviction for murder in the first degree totaled thirty during 1847–1858 or an average of 2.5 per year, and twenty-one during 1859–1867, or an annual average of 2.3.[1] During the seventeen years, 1852–1868, a total of sixteen prisoners were received in the Rhode Island state prison on life sentences for murder, or an average of one per year.[2] During the six years, 1854–1859, following the repeal of the death penalty in Wisconsin, twenty prisoners arrived in the state prison after convictions for murder, or an annual average of 3.3; during 1860–1867, twenty-one were received, an average annually of 2.6.[3] Bovee cites these declines as evidence of the beneficial effect of abolition but fails to take into account the transfer of some of the male population into the armed services.

Maine abolished the death penalty in 1876, re-introduced it in 1882 and abandoned it again in 1887. Some statistical data are available for the period 1862–1901.[4] The source of the data before 1877 is not given, but figures for later years have been drawn from the reports of the attorney general of Maine. In the following table, the years when the state had the death penalty have been bracketed.

The experience of states which temporarily abolished the death penalty should give us some idea of the effect of this policy.

Arizona had no such punishment between December 8, 1916 and December 5, 1918. The Governor reported that forty-one murderers were convicted during the two years

[1] Marvin H. Bovee, *Reasons for Abolishing Capital Punishment* (328 pp. Chicago, 1878), pp. 256, 260.

[2] *Ibid.*, p. 235.

[3] *Ibid.*, p. 266.

[4] Ohio State Library, *Monthly Bulletin* I, pp. 7–8, Jan. 1906.

TABLE 1

Average annual number of

	Homicides	Murder convictions
[1862–66]	17.8	1.8
[1867–71]	11.2	3.4
[1873–76]	11.6	1.4
	Prosecutions for homicide	Sentences for homicide
1877–81	8.0	4.2
[1882–86]	6.8	5.8
1889–91[a]	6.0	3.8
1892–96	8.0	4.8
1897–1901	6.4	3.4

[a] No report issued for 1887 and 1888.

prior to abolition, forty-six during the abolition period, and forty-five during the following two years.[5]

Colorado abolished the death penalty on March 29, 1897 and re-introduced it in 1901. The annual average number of convictions for murder was 16.3 during 1891–1896, eighteen during 1897–1900, and nineteen during 1901–1905.[6] In a report to the International Prison Commission, Mr. C. L. Stonaker, Secretary of the State Board of Charities and Corrections, wrote: "Capital punishment has been abolished in this state without any apparent increase in number of murders committed, but with a better showing for speedy trials and convictions. Since the establishment of the law abolishing capital punishment fifty per cent of murder trials have resulted in convictions."[7]

Iowa abolished the death penalty in 1872 and restored it in 1878. The annual average number of convictions for

[5] *Report from the Select Committee on Capital Punishment* (London, His Majesty's Stationery Office, 1931), p. 552.

[6] M. Liepmann, *Die Todesstrafe* (220 pp. Berlin, 1912), p. 69, citing Ohio State Library, *Monthly Bulletin* I, No. 10, p. 14.

[7] S. J. Barrows, *Prison Systems of the United States*. Reports prepared for the International Prison Commission (59th Congress, 1st Session, House of Representatives, Document No. 566), 157 pp. Washington: Government Printing Office, 1900; p. 40.

murder during the seven years prior to abolition was 2.6; during abolition, 8.8, and during the next seven years, 13.1.[8]

Missouri voted to abandon the death penalty on April 13, 1917 but restored it at a special session in July, 1919.[9] The homicide death rates during the five years prior to abolition rose from 7.8 in 1912 to 10.0 in 1916. The rates for 1917–1919 were 12.3, 10.1 and 9.7, respectively, followed by rates of 7.9, 10.1, 11.4, 12.3 and 13.2 during the next five years.

Tennessee abolished the death penalty in 1915 for murder and restored it in 1919. Homicide death rates are available only since 1918. These rates were, for the white and the colored populations separately:

Year	Whites	Colored
1918	6.9	29.2
1919	8.8	41.3
1920	7.0	42.4
1921	11.4	39.5
1922	10.7	45.9
1923	10.5	49.8
1924	10.8	52.5

Oregon had no death penalty during 1915–1920. It is reported that fifty-nine murderers were received in the state prison during 1910–1914 and thirty-six during the five years of abolition.[10] The homicide death rate of 1918, the first annual rate available, was 4.0 and in 1919 and 1920, it was 4.9 and 4.1, respectively. The 1921 rate rose to 7.7, followed during the next five years by rates of 5.9, 3.9, 3.5, 4.1 and 4.3.

Washington abolished the death penalty on March 22, 1913, and restored it on March 14, 1919. From 1902 to 1951, the rates of first degree murder convictions in the

[8] Liepmann, *op. cit.,* p. 69.

[9] Ellen Elizabeth Guillot, "Abolition and Restoration of the Death Penalty in Missouri." *The Annals of the American Academy of Political and Social Science,* 284:105–109, Nov., 1952.

[10] *Report from the Select Committee on Capital Punishment,* p. 552.

state, per 100,000 estimated population at the mid-decade, were:

1902–1911	3.56
1912–1921	5.57
1922–1931	5.99
1932–1941	6.66
1942–1951	2.58[11]

The annual homicide death rate averaged 6.5 during 1908–1912. In 1913 it was 6.5 but it rose in 1914 to 10.0 and then gradually fell to 8.9, 5.5, 5.5, and 4.2 (1918). The year the death penalty was again introduced the rate rose to 7.5, but during the next five years, 1920–1924, it was 5.1, 5.9, 5.2, 4.7 and 6.2. The average annual rate was 6.8 during the period of abolition, and 5.8 during the first six years after the re-introduction of the death penalty.

Kansas and *South Dakota* went back to the death penalty in 1935 and 1939, respectively. In Kansas the annual average homicide death rate dropped from 6.5 during the five years prior to 1935 to 3.8 during the next five years. In South Dakota the rate for the corresponding periods before and after 1939 remained the same, 1.4.

ABOLITION AND RESTORATION OF THE DEATH PENALTY IN OREGON*

BY ROBERT H. DANN**

Capital punishment was mandatory in Oregon until 1914, when, by a very narrow margin of voter expression, the state substituted life imprisonment for the death penalty. In 1920 capital punishment was re-established, but made subject to the discretion of the jury.

Prior to 1903, executions were more or less public dem-

[11] Norman S. Hayner and John R. Cranor, "The Death Penalty in Washington." *The Annals,* 284:101–4, Nov., 1952, p. 102.

* Reprinted, by permission of Mrs. Dorothy D. Bower and the publisher, from "Capital Punishment in Oregon," *The Annals,* vol. 284 (November 1952), pp. 110–114.

** Late Professor of Sociology, Oregon State College.

onstrations, carried out in the yards of the county jails or in public squares. In that year Governor George E. Chamberlain, in his inaugural address to the legislature, recommended that "all executions should take place within the wall of the penitentiary." In the same year a law was passed requiring that all executions take place at the State Penitentiary at Salem, and two years later Governor Chamberlain said he was sure this law would "be most beneficial in its results."

Governor Oswald West, in his first message to the legislature in 1911, opened the campaign to abolish capital punishment. He denied the validity of the doctrine of an eye for an eye, and called attention to the unreliability of circumstantial evidence and to the reluctance of juries to demand the death sentence. He concluded that the "desperate criminal, relying on the reluctance of the average juror and the caution of the court, in the imposition of the capital sentence, is more willing to take a gambler's chance with death . . . than he would be to face the greater certainty of life spent behind the bars." He also recommended that restriction be placed on the pardoning power of the governor.

TABLE 1
RECORD OF VOTING ON CAPITAL PUNISHMENT IN OREGON

Year	Number Voting	For Capital Punishment	Against Capital Punishment	Majority		Did Not Vote
				For Capital Punishment	Against Capital Punishment	
1912	144,113	64,578	41,951	22,627		37,584
1914	259,868	100,395	100,552		157	58,921
1920	171,592	81,756	64,589	17,167		25,247

In 1912 an initiative petition to abolish capital punishment appeared on the ballot in the November election but failed to secure a majority vote.

A second attempt, led by Governor West, was made in 1914, against the judgment of many, who felt that it was too soon following a defeat. There were thirty-one items on the ballot, but the abolition of capital punishment received a majority of 157.

In 1915 the necessary legislation was passed, repealing three sections of Lord's Oregon Laws and amending the state constitution. The repealed sections, which had been adopted in 1903, were Section 1598, "Warrant to Enforce Judgment of Death"; Section 1599, "Death Sentence, How and Where Executed"; and Section 1600, "Warrant Issued to Sheriff Where Action Commenced." The amendment to the constitution became Section 36 of Article I, and read: "The death penalty shall not be inflicted upon any person under the laws of Oregon. The maximum punishment which may be inflicted shall be life imprisonment."

In his address to the legislature in 1915, Governor West said, "the old barbarous system of capital punishment has been abolished." He proposed that pardons should be granted only upon the recommendation of the court in which the case originated.

The matter rested only until 1917, when a House Joint Resolution was introduced with the proposal that it be referred to the people in the election of 1918. The resolution was to amend the constitution to read: "The death penalty shall be inflicted upon any person under the laws of Oregon, who is convicted of the crime of murder in the first degree." The proposal was referred to the Committee on Resolutions and was indefinitely postponed.

In 1919 Governor James Withycombe, in his address to the legislature, called attention to the fact that since the repeal of capital punishment the state was without any punishment for treason. He hoped the legislature would remedy the situation, even though treason was a concern of the federal government. He was worried about "I.W.W.ism and other forms of disloyalty." He died shortly after his reelection, and the Secretary of State, Ben W. Olcott, succeeded him.

Governor Olcott called a special session of the legislature in 1920, and in his address he said:

Since the adjournment of the regular session in 1919 a wave of crime has swept over the country. Oregon has suffered from this criminal blight, and during the past few months the commission of a number of cold-blooded and fiendish homicides has aroused our people to a demand for greater and more certain

protection. . . . Because of a series of dastardly homicidal offenses a distinct public sentiment has developed that the people of the state should once more be
given an opportunity to pass upon the question of the
restoration of capital punishment and that there should
be no unnecessary delay in bringing this question before the electorate.

At the special session, the legislature passed for reference
to the people an amendment designed to re-establish capital punishment. The proposed Section 37 of Article I was to
read: "The penalty for murder in the first degree shall be
death, except when the trial jury shall in its verdict recommend life imprisonment, in which case the penalty shall be
life imprisonment." Section 38 was to re-establish the former sections 1598, 1599, and 1600 as found in Lord's Oregon Laws.

Prior to each election the state publishes what is known
as The Voters Pamphlet, in which candidates set forth
their claims to office, and bills initiated by or referred to
the public are explained. In the pamphlet issued for the
1920 special election, which was also the primary election,
pro and con articles regarding the death sentence appeared.

The article supporting its restoration was sponsored by
Senators B. L. Eddy of Douglas, K. K. Kubli of Multnomah, and David E. Lofgren of Clackamas counties.
They argued that "to punish cold-blooded murder with
death naturally has a tendency to deter" even the hardened
criminal, while a term in prison "is no serious hindrance."
The death penalty marks murder as a "heinous offense,"
and the psychological effect on the young must be of
"greatest deterrent value." "We naturally come to rate an
offense as serious in proportion to the weight of the penalty."

The article recognized that crime waves are associated
with other factors in the social situation, but pressed the
issue of the dangerous criminal who is beyond hope,
"whose restraint amounts to no more than holding in leash
dangerous beasts who may at any time break away." The
authors quoted the Old Testament to support their position,

and concluded: "Let us not be weakly sentimental. . . . Sentiment should not outweigh Justice. . . . A person who willfully commits murder writes his own doom—the state merely executes the judgment."

The negative argument was prepared by W. H. Strayer of Baker, and Mrs. Alexander Thompson and Eugene E. Smith of Multnomah counties. They argued that changing the constitution was a serious matter, and that the forthcoming election was designed for other matters. They doubted the wisdom of leaving much discretion to juries, because they are subject to influence. And they regretted that space did not allow a full discussion of the weakness of capital punishment as a deterrent. "A person seldom kills another with the expectation that he will be punished at all, and if he does kill with a knowledge that he will be punished, the condition of the murderer's mind is such, and his passions are so aroused, that no punishment will act as a deterrent." The article did not carry enthusiasm or show deep conviction.

The Oregon Voter is a weekly publication, edited by C. C. Chapman, which has considerable political influence. In the issue of May 8, 1920, a letter appeared from Rev. W. J. McElven, in opposition to the death penalty. His position was that restoration of the death penalty would be a step backward for Oregon, from its place as a progressive state to the demand for revenge; that criminologists are opposed to the death penalty; that figures do not support the contention that it is deterrent; that there is a tendency to punish those who cannot afford an adequate legal battle; that the executed man is likely to become a hero; that the requirement of death often prevents conviction when the jury has no choice; that capital punishment is unchristian, and a sin is no less a sin when committed by the whole state. He commented on a recent "heinous" murder. A man had been sponsored on parole from the penitentiary by a woman whom he subsequently murdered, and he was reported to have said he would not have committed this murder had there been capital punishment in the state. McElven doubted the value of this man's testimony. He concluded that Oregon needed strict and impartial law enforcement and a limitation on the pardoning power of the authorities.

The next issue of *The Oregon Voter*, May 15, 1920, contained a reply from Senator B. L. Eddy, in much the same language as that of the positive article in *The Voters Pamphlet*. He said: "More sophistry and misinformation could hardly be combined in a single article." He criticized McElven for failure to quote criminologist authorities, and then quoted Baron Raffaele Gorofalo, the Italian criminologist, who said: "The death penalty is a defensive measure and based on analogy of the operation of the Darwinian principle of natural selection." Punishment should either eliminate the offender or make reparation for the harm done. He accused McElven of neglecting the Old Testament and espousing theories of human progress. He claimed to be an understanding Christian who believed both Old and New Testaments to be the Word of God.

The issue of *The Oregon Voter* for May 22, 1920, circulated just prior to the election, contained a strong article against the proposed constitutional amendment, preceded and followed by strong editorial comment. The editor compared a murderer to a rattlesnake that should be killed to defend mankind. He wrote: "And if the duty were upon us [the editor] we would not hesitate to slay a human rattlesnake to protect innocent human beings from murder."

Space was then given to an article prepared under the sponsorship of Norman F. Coleman—listed as president of the Loyal Legion of Loggers and Lumbermen, but not as a professor at Reed College, of which he later became president—Ben Selling a prominent Portland businessman, Bishop Sumner of the Episcopal Church, George Rebec the revered professor of philosophy at the University of Oregon, Sarah H. Evans, Millie R. Turnbull, Frederic K. Howard, and C. S. Kohs.

This article, bounded "fore and aft" by editorial comment, argued against restoration of capital punishment. To the proposition that the jury should have power to decide in favor of hanging, the authors replied that juries more often gave the life sentence when given a choice. They referred to the problem of circumstantial evidence and unjust convictions. They held that the certainty of punishment was more deterrent than severity, and that the Biblical quotations so often used did not fit in with the spirit and teachings of Jesus. They referred to psychological evidence that criminals are sick but that coddling is not the best method of dealing with them. "Sound psychology is not against the death penalty, if it is the best method . . . but it denies that hanging and electrocution are the best methods, but they are the easiest." They advocated individual treatment of each case, and were opposed to classification until a complete diagnosis had been made. They believed that "weakly sentimentality" did not agree with the idea that "brutality begets brutality," and raised the question why we did not execute all misfits. They concluded that the fact that one man had stained his soul with murder was no reason why the whole state should do the same.

This article was followed by quotation of an editorial by George Putnam, editor of the *Capital Journal* of Salem, Oregon. With reference to the famous "California Bluebeard" who under pressure had confessed and saved himself from the death penalty, the editorial commented: "Had this modern bluebeard been apprehended in Oregon, the confession would not have been forthcoming, for there would have been no fear of the gallows to extort it." The editor concluded: "As long as society breeds bluebeards and degenerates of this type, just so long will the gallows be needed as a protection to society. While not a preventive of crime the noose is certainly a deterrent." He failed to comment that California, where the bluebeard operated, had the death penalty, and it did not deter him from his crimes.

At the election held in May 1920, the voters adopted the constitutional amendment proposed at the special legislative session. Table 1 gives the details of the election returns.

There is a dearth of reference to the death penalty in the biennial reports of the wardens to the Secretary of State. Superintendent C. W. James reported in 1910 that eighteen men had been executed in Oregon in the last seven and a half years, "the greatest number ever executed in any similar period in this state." He said: "It does not appear, however, that the increasing number of executions in this state has operated as a deterrent to the crime of homicide; . . . I am fully convinced that capital punishment should be abolished." During his administration, capital punishment was the only sentence for first degree murder.

The next reference in the biennial reports appears in 1925, when three men are listed as being executed. The following years show a constant change in wardens, none of whom make any reference to the death penalty.

The only reference to our topic in the chaplains' reports occurs in the report of Protestant Chaplain Carl H. Bryan in 1923, when he wrote: "I have visited death row as often as I thought wise and rendered what assistance I could to the condemned men, which was always appreciated by them."

TABLE 2
POPULATION OF OREGON STATE PENITENTIARY

Year	Man-slaughter	Murder	First Degree Murder	Second Degree Murder	Executions
1907	15			24	1903–10, 18
1909	14			32	
1911	20			40	
1913	15			33	
1915	12	7		44	
1917	7	14			
1919	7	16			
1921	10	15			
1923	12	7		7	
1925	7		7	3	3
1927	11		3	5	4
1929	12		12	3	4

The statistical records of the penitentiary reporting the population of the institution offer very little information, and do not reflect the changes that took place in the law. Table 2 gives the data as presented in the biennial reports.

Conclusion

The evidence presented here does not warrant much conclusion, except perhaps that a majority of 157 is not sufficient on which to stabilize a constitutional change, and the further comment that there is need for objective data that can be presented to the voting public in clear and convincing terms.

ABOLITION AND RESTORATION OF THE DEATH PENALTY IN MISSOURI*

BY ELLEN ELIZABETH GUILLOT**

Throughout the nineteenth century and up to the present time, there has been in the state of Missouri a more or less academic interest in the subject of capital punishment. Various articles for or against the practice have made their appearance in the press from time to time. The matter was, however, of crucial importance in the spring of 1917 when the legislature abolished the death penalty, and again in 1919 when it was restored. As far as Missouri is concerned, the most significant interest in this subject is confined neatly within this period. It is possible, therefore, to present a fairly comprehensive account of the history of capital punishment in Missouri within the limitations of those two years.

In connection with the act abolishing capital punishment passed by the Missouri Legislature in 1917, it is to be remembered that the movement for the reform of prison life and the reformation of individual criminals was at that time nation-wide. It is therefore natural to believe that the Missouri act was a part of this greater movement.

The basic idea was that capital punishment forestalled the possibility of reformation. In addition, it had become increasingly difficult to get properly qualified jurors to serve

* Reprinted, by permission of the author and publisher, from *The Annals,* vol. 284 (November 1952), pp. 105–109.
** Associate Professor of Medical Social Work, University of North Carolina, and formerly Assistant Professor of Social Work, University of Missouri.

in cases of capital crime, because of their conscientious scruples against the infliction of the death penalty. For example, Judge Nick T. Cave,[1] now of the Kansas City Court of Appeals, told the writer that in 1914, while he was Prosecuting Attorney for Callaway County, he prosecuted, for first degree murder, a colored man who was accused of shooting and killing a white boy. The case was opened on Monday and went to the jury on Wednesday afternoon. The jury did not report until Saturday afternoon, when it was called into court by the presiding judge. It was learned later that on the first ballot the jury was unanimous in its verdict of first degree murder, but on the question of inflicting capital punishment the jurors failed to agree; seven were for hanging and five for life imprisonment. A decision by the jury regarding punishment was therefore impossible.

The movement for the abolition of capital punishment is described as gradual and as characterized by a sensible approach. A good many reforms in the treatment of prisoners had already been carried out, such as establishment of night classes at the penitentiary, exercises out of doors, dedication of a new playground for prisoners with facilities for playing baseball, elimination of the contract labor system, and the purchase of a prison farm along the rich Missouri River bottoms where quantities of fruits and vegetables were raised and the prisoners given opportunity for work in the out-of-doors; severe punishments (such as hanging up by the thumbs) had been done away with, and the parole system had been rewritten.[2]

The bill for the abolition of capital punishment in Missouri was introduced in the Forty-ninth General Assembly in 1917 by Representative O. B. Whitaker of Hickory County. Whitaker was a man of importance in the state; he had been president of three small colleges, and had written a number of books on Christian fellowship and so-

---

[1] The writer is indebted to Judge Cave for much of the material for this article. Judge Cave was a member of the Judiciary Committees of both houses of the Legislature during this decade.

[2] *Kansas City Star*, April 4, 1917, p. 2.

cial problems.[3] The revised statute as adopted read as follows:

An Act to Abolish Capital Punishment in the State of Missouri. From and after the taking effect of this act it shall be unlawful in this state to take human life as a punishment for crime, and no court shall enforce capital punishment as a penalty for crime. All acts and parts of acts inconsistent or in conflict with this act are hereby repealed.

The act was approved on April 13, 1917. It never appeared in the Revised Statutes of Missouri, since it was repealed before the codification of 1919.

It will be noticed that this important enactment was made just when this country was entering the First World War. There was probably little opposition to the law; so occupied were the people and the newspapers with the war that the enactment was hardly noticed in the press. There were, however, some brief comments expressing satisfaction that the spectacle of public execution, with its attendant debauchery, would no longer take place.[4]

The matter was perhaps exaggerated, since the number of criminals put to death was certainly not large. The *Kansas City Star* reported that there were in Jackson County nine victims in twenty-six years,[5] and the *St. Louis Post-Dispatch* noted that not a single execution had taken place in St. Louis County during the fourteen years previous to the passage of the act.[6]

There were certain serious misgivings and difference of opinion as to what would result from the repeal of the law inflicting the death penalty. Hunt C. Moore, then prosecuting attorney of Jackson County, declared that the new statute was a humane law and that the abolition of capital punishment would have no effect on the spread of crime. It

---

[3] *Missouri Historical Review*, Vol. XXXVI, No. 4 (July 1942), p. 310.

[4] William M. Reedy, "Hanging is a Lost Art," *Kansas City Star*, April 19, 1918.

[5] *Kansas City Star*, April 15, 1917, p. 8A.

[6] *St. Louis Post-Dispatch*, July 5, 1919, p. 14.

would also, he thought, make it possible to secure better juries in first degree crime cases.

Judge Ralph S. Latshaw of the same county, however, was bitterly opposed to the new enactment. He thought it had been made by softhearted legislators who allowed their sympathies to overpower their reason. He believed that the penitentiary held no terror for the rapist, the robber, or the murderer, and that life sentences were a joke. He said that there was but one man in the State Penitentiary at that time who had been there over ten years, and that he was a poor, unknown, friendless Hawaiian who would also have been free if he had had a single friend. Judge Latshaw also said that kidnapping and train robbery were so rare since they had been punishable by death that not a single instance had come to his attention. He quoted the Bible as his authority: "Whosoever sheddeth the blood of man by man shall his blood be shed."[7]

Dissatisfaction among law enforcement agencies with the new law abolishing capital punishment seems to have grown during the two years following its enactment, for we find that Prosecuting Attorney McDaniels of St. Louis County issued early in January 1919 an appeal for the re-enactment of the older statute.[8]

This was possibly in some measure provoked by a situation described by Judge Cave, who records the commission of a serious crime shortly before the abolition act was repealed. Men from St. Louis came to Fulton, in Callaway County, where copper wire was stored preparatory to the construction of certain electrical installations. Copper wire was very valuable at that time. The robbers cut the wire into short lengths and loaded it into their truck. They carried it to St. Louis, and it was reported to the police that the truck was to be stored in a garage behind an apartment building. Police officers were stationed at the garage to await the arrival of the robbers. The men drove the truck into the alley leading to the garage, and when officers attempted to put them under arrest, a battle followed. Two

[7] *Kansas City Star*, April 15, 1917, p. 8A.
[8] *St. Louis Post-Dispatch*, Jan. 26, 1919, p. 2 Editorial Section.

policemen were killed. Later the men were caught and came to trial. They were sentenced to the penitentiary for life.

There was a hysterical reaction to these murders. People who had been previously opposed to capital punishment were outraged, and newspapers that had supported its abolition now advocated the restoration of the death penalty for murder. It was argued that the criminal element had no fear of the law and that criminals could "shoot their way out." If they surrendered to the police, they would be sent to the penitentiary; if they murdered the police, they would also merely be sent to the penitentiary. The law thus gave no protection to the police. Law enforcement officers throughout the state urged the restoration of capital punishment.

The consequence of McDaniel's appeal and of the situation just described was the introduction in the Missouri Senate, Fiftieth General Assembly, by Senator Mayes of Penobscot County, on January 20, 1919, of Senate Bill 84, entitled

> An Act to repeal an Act of the Forty-ninth General Assembly, approved April 13, 1917, entitled "An Act to Abolish Capital Punishment in the State of Missouri" and to enact a section reviving all former laws providing for capital punishment.

The bill went through the ordinary routine of legislative procedure in the Senate and, on April 3, 1919, was passed by a vote of twenty-six yeas, eight nays, absent three. However, when the bill came up in the House, at a time when it was next to impossible to keep more than a bare quorum in their seats, it lacked three votes to pass that body.[9]

One does not know how long the bill abolishing capital punishment in Missouri might have remained on the statute books had it not been for a series of crimes that greatly disturbed the public mind. In the jail at Lamar, in Barton County, there was confined a man ominously named Jay

[9] *Journal of the Missouri Legislature,* 50th General Assembly, Regular and Extra Sessions, Senate, p. 50; *Kansas City Times,* July 3, 1919, p. 13.

Lynch. It is believed that his wife or mother or both of them delivered to him a package containing a pistol. Lynch, so equipped, made his dash for liberty and in so doing killed the sheriff and the sheriff's son. He seems to have been tried and sentenced to life imprisonment. A mob broke into the jail and seized and lynched him early in June 1919.[10] Representative Chancellor of Barton County told his fellow legislators that this lynching would not have occurred had it not been for the law of two years previous abolishing capital punishment.[11] Also, at the same time, peace officers of Lafayette County were murdered.[12]

But the most disturbing event of this kind was in connection with the robbery of the Meramec Trust Company in St. Louis County, June 12, 1919, on which occasion one patrolman was killed and another wounded. A number of "Letters from the People" appeared in the *Post-Dispatch,* some of which are extremely interesting in their reflection of public sentiment. On June 17 one correspondent quotes from a recent editorial in the *Post-Dispatch,* "the stolen money was speedily recovered, and two desperate principals were by arrest permanently removed from the class of those who prey on the community." He then goes on:

The *Post-Dispatch* is slightly mistaken. First, they were not desperate. Desperate men fight to the last. Secondly, they will not be permanently removed, at least so long as there is a workable parole board. They will probably be at liberty in three or four years as is usual in such cases. A short time ago I read in your esteemed paper where five hundred or so murderers were let loose in society. All paroled by the board. Will they commit murder again? . . . It is truly marvelous that we do not have more lynching than we do. The people of Missouri deserve credit for it. If the law don't protect, who will? Shall we have to go back to the day when every man carried his own legislature and his justice strapped to his belt?

[10] *St. Louis Post-Dispatch,* June 18, 1919, p. 17.
[11] *Kansas City Star,* July 3, 1919, p. 13.
[12] *Ibid.*

Another letter writer on June 28, however, declaring himself opposed to capital punishment, quotes Genesis 9:6, as given above, and adds, "This would exterminate the race."

Significant action connected with the settlement of the issue came from the Tenth Ward Improvement Association of St. Louis.[13] It happened that a special session of the Missouri Legislature had just been called by Governor Frederick G. Gardner to convene July 2 to consider and ratify the amendment to the federal Constitution granting suffrage to women. The Tenth Ward Improvement Association joined in the current demand on the Governor to issue a supplemental message to the legislature calling upon it to consider a bill restoring capital punishment in Missouri. The association complained that St. Louis had been overrun with crime during the past year, and said that crime had been violent because criminals knew that capital punishment was no longer law in Missouri.

Governor Gardner, in his reply to the Tenth Ward Improvement Association, stated that he had not included the question of the restoration of capital punishment in his call because the legislature meeting in regular session had opposed restoration. A new legislature would be chosen in eighteen months, and it might view the matter differently. He added that he had been in communication with the governors of eleven states in which capital punishment had been abolished, and they had been asked if crime had increased. "None said that it had increased, and eight declared that it had not." The Governor was thus reluctant to have the matter of the restoration of capital punishment considered at the special session of the legislature.[14]

A petition was circulated by Representative Chancellor of Barton County that requested the Governor to send a special message to the legislature submitting the question of restoring capital punishment. This petition was quickly signed by seventy-eight members of the House, six more than a constitutional majority. The Governor was anxious to hold down the expenses of the special session and to

[13] *St. Louis Post-Dispatch,* June 16, 1919, p. 12.
[14] *St. Louis Post-Dispatch,* June 24, 1919, p. 14.

confine the members to action on the issue they had been
summoned to consider. However, he met with four or five
petitioners, discussed the matter with them, and demanded
of them statistics. In spite of the fact that none of them had
any statistics, he yielded to their argument that public sentiment among their constituents was most decidedly in favor
of restoring the capital punishment law for the purpose of
discouraging highway robberies, bank robberies, and attendant murders.

The Governor thus gave his consent, but the session that
restored capital punishment in Missouri was a stormy one.
The friends of the Governor resorted to obstructive tactics
to prevent the matter from coming to a vote, and the debate was complicated by the proposal of an amendment to
substitute the electric chair for the noose.[15]

The legislature at this special session repealed the act of
1917 and re-enacted sections of the revised statutes of
1909, so that treason, rape, kidnapping for ransom, perjury committed in the trial of any indictment for a capital
offense, train robbery of certain sorts, and murder in the
first degree remained punishable by death at the discretion
of the jury.

Conclusion

The abolishment of capital punishment in Missouri thus
came about as part of a general movement for the amelio-
ration of the lives of the condemned that was nation-wide,
and capital punishment was restored by an urgent public
sentiment of fear and indignation brought about by crimes
following the First World War.

It has been said that the race question entered into the
matter of the re-enactment, but this seems not to be true.
Indeed, Judge Cave assures the writer—and his assurance
is supported by examination of the press of the state—
that the race question did not enter into the issue of capital
punishment as it arose in Missouri, since the crimes were
those of whites against whites and were not reflective of
race prejudice.

[15] *Kansas City Times,* July 6, 1919, p. 1.

By way of completion it may be said that it was not until 1937 that the administration of lethal gas was substituted for hanging, and the place of execution transferred from the counties to the State Penitentiary at Jefferson City. Since that time there have been twenty-seven executions, distributed as follows: Colored: rape, three; murder first, fifteen. White: murder first, nine.[16]

ABOLITION AND RESTORATION OF THE DEATH PENALTY IN DELAWARE

BY HERBERT L. COBIN*

In the early history of Delaware, the penal code reflected the influences of England and Pennsylvania and the use of the death penalty fluctuated with these influences:[1]

Crimes Punishable by Death

1676	8	
1682	1	(Pennsylvania Quaker influence)
1719	13	(reactionary laws of England)
1829	6	
1935	5	

As of April 1, 1958, the death penalty could be invoked for five crimes: treason, murder in the first degree, kidnapping, rape and wilful or malicious wounding or poisoning where death ensued within one year.

Actually, by 1917, in a death penalty case, upon a recommendation of mercy by the jury, the Court could impose a life sentence.[2] This was made mandatory in rape cases in 1949, after such a recommendation had once been ignored by the Court.[3]

[16] Letter dated June 23, 1952, from R. N. Edson, warden of Missouri State Penitentiary.

* Chairman, Governor's Committee for a State Correctional Program; Chairman, Board of Directors of the Prisoners Aid Society of Delaware; and formerly Chief Deputy Attorney General of Delaware.

[1] Robert G. Caldwell, "Penology in Delaware", in C. Reed, ed., *A History of the First State,* II, p. 851.

[2] Rev. C. 1935, Sec. 5330, 29 Del. L. 266.

[3] 47 Del. L. Ch. 402, 11 Del. C. 1953, sec. 781.

Since 1902, twenty-five persons have been legally hanged under these laws, nineteen for murder and six for rape. All but one were male. All were unskilled workers, and none had more than a limited education (many were illiterate). Five of those executed for rape and thirteen of those for murder were Negroes. The last execution in Delaware was that of a thirty-four-year-old Negro, in Sussex County in 1946, for the crime of murder.[4] In 1945, a twenty-three-year-old Negro was executed in New Castle County for rape. In Kent County, the last execution took place in 1935, a Negro for murder. Evidence that the death penalty was visited more regularly upon Negroes than whites resulted in the commutation of a death sentence in 1947 by the Republican Governor J. Caleb Boggs (now U. S. Senator), and the practice has continued in all cases.

In April 1955, Elwood F. Melson, Jr. (R., New Castle County), a lawyer, introduced in the state Senate a bill to abolish the death penalty for all crimes and to substitute life imprisonment. Senator Melson's bill was voted on several times during 1955 and 1956 in the Senate, but it did not pass in that session. On one occasion, it was defeated by only one vote, although it had no particularly vigorous support from any citizen during this period.

Five months after the new legislature convened in 1957, Senator Melson, with co-sponsors, introduced a similar bill. Because of the Senator's persistence and of the ground work he had laid in previous months, this bill was reported out of committee favorably after only three days, and three weeks later it passed the Senate by a vote of ten to one (six absent or not voting).

The bill went over to the House, to be immediately referred to the Judiciary Committee on June 18 and reported out of that Committee six days later. Despite fairly general expectations that it would die in the House, as many Senate bills did, nothing had been done about it when the

---

[4] For a fuller analysis, see I. M. H. Bradner, "Legal Executions in Delaware", a mimeographed report distributed by the Prisoners Aid Society of Delaware in 1958.

Legislature took a recess in the early part of July, and the matter rested until the following year.

As President of the Prisoners Aid Society of Delaware, which had for years been on record as opposing capital punishment, I took an active interest in the bill and spent some months in absorbing the various governmental studies that had been made in England, Canada and California on the subject. I read a great amount of material, going back to the early 1800's. To present the basic facts in a simplified manner, the Society prepared a brochure, the so-called "Cobin Report". During the early months of 1957, it was sent to each member of the Legislature, to the Governor, the Attorney General, State Judges, the Director of Corrections, the Superintendent of the State Police, the Chiefs of Police of Wilmington and other cities, the Superintendent of Mental Institutions, certain political leaders, church councils, newspaper editors and columnists and radio commentators.[5] Conferences were arranged with many of these people. The newspapers gave great support in news articles, feature stories and editorials. There was not, however, sufficient time to appeal on a more individual basis to various citizen groups with an interest in this legislation. In addition, not many members of our Prisoners Aid Society were intimately acquainted with all the details and the merits of our position in favor of abolition. Thus, partly out of choice and partly out of necessity, our efforts were directed mainly toward members of the General Assembly and to others of immediate importance in securing passage of the bill. However, key citizens, including public officials and ministers, were brought into the picture and made themselves effective in special ways. Some raised their voices on behalf of abolition in public; others contacted those members of the House who had some questions or doubts about the bill's merits.

The "Cobin Report", which was the focus for discussion in these conferences, presented 198 pages of material (much of it then not otherwise available) on the issue of

[5] See Herbert L. Cobin, "Citizen Action for Abolishing Capital Punishment", *Journal of Criminal Law, Criminology and Police Science*, vol. 52, no. 1 (May–June 1961), p. 90.

abolishing the death penalty. As a preface, I set out nine
arguments that this information demonstrated and that,
taken together, made a strong case for abolition. They
were:

1. The evidence clearly shows that execution does not
   act as a deterrent to capital crimes.
2. The serious offenses are committed, except in rare
   instances, by those suffering from mental disturbances; are impulsive in nature; and are not acts of the
   "criminal" class. (Of those executed in Delaware,
   fifty per cent had no previous conviction.)
3. When the death sentence is removed as a possible
   punishment, more convictions are possible with fewer
   delays.
4. Unequal application of the law takes place because
   those executed are the poor, the ignorant, and the
   unfortunate, without resources.
5. Conviction of the innocent does occur and death
   makes a miscarriage of justice irrevocable. Human
   judgment cannot be infallible.
6. The state sets a bad example when it takes a life. Imi-
   tative crimes, including murder, are stimulated by
   executions.
7. Legally taking a life is useless and demoralizing to
   the general public. It is also demoralizing to the public officials who, dedicated to rehabilitating offenders,
   must callously put a man to death. The effect upon
   fellow prisoners can be imagined.
8. A trial where a life may be at stake is given sensational publicity, adversely affects the administration
   of justice, and is bad for the community.
9. Society is amply protected by a sentence of life imprisonment.

On March 11, 1958, the House began its consideration
of the Melson bill. On that day, a public hearing was conducted before the entire House, called by Representative
Sherman W. Tribbitt (D., New Castle County), Chairman
of the Judiciary Committee. This public hearing, which set
the pattern for such hearings in many other states in subse-

quent years, was one of the most significant single episodes in the campaign for abolition.[6]

Among the speakers at the hearing were: Dr. Thorsten Sellin, Professor and Chairman of the Department of Sociology at the University of Pennsylvania and the leading American researcher on the subject of capital punishment; James A. McCafferty, criminologist with the U. S. Bureau of Prisons and one of those responsible for preparing the Bureau's annual study of executions in this country; Trevor Thomas, formerly executive secretary of the Friends Committee on Legislation in California and one of the leaders of the abolition movement there; Dr. M. A. Tarumianz, State psychiatrist and Superintendent of Delaware's mental health institutions; Rev. Henry N. Herndon, rector of Calvary Episcopal Church, Wilmington, and representative of the Wilmington Council of Churches; and Rev. Robert W. Duke, of Dover, representing the State Council of Churches. The hearing lasted for two hours, and the speakers offered support, from various points of view, for the nine arguments presented earlier to the legislature in the "Cobin Report". Impressed by this evidence, the House weighed the bill over the next few weeks.

During this period it became known that generally the judges, as individuals, favored abolition. The police, impressed by the evidence that the death penalty had no deterrent value and that abolition created no increased hazard to law enforcement, agreed not to oppose it. The Director of Corrections and the Superintendent of Mental Institutions were known to be in favor of abolition. The two largest newspapers in Delaware, the *Wilmington Morning News* and the *Wilmington Journal-Every Evening,* both with a long history of favoring improvements in the administration of justice and rehabilitation of offenders, endorsed abolition, and their columnists supported it with great vigor.[7]

[6] See: James V. Bennett, "A Historic Move: Delaware Abolishes Capital Punishment", *American Bar Association Journal,* vol. 44 (November 1958) pp. 1053–1054; and Ernest Havermann, "Capital Punishment Is Not The Answer", *Reader's Digest* (May 1960).

[7] See: The *Morning News* of March 12 and 25, 1958, and the *Journal-Every Evening* of March 26, 1958.

On March 24, when the bill came up for vote, the House passed it by a vote of eighteen to eleven (with seven absent or not voting), the minimum necessary margin.

The incumbent Attorney General had some hesitancy about the Governor's signing it, because the bill made no distinction between the sentence for first and second degree murder, because there was no exception for a second homicide committed during a prison break, and because of the belief that any repeal of the current law would result in a heavier murder trial list or in more frequent acceptance by the state of a plea of guilty to a manslaughter charge. Nevertheless, the Attorney General did favor the principle of abolition because of humane considerations and because juries are disinclined to convict defendants where the punishment is death without recommendation of mercy.

On April 2, 1958, Governor J. Caleb Boggs signed the bill, thereby abolishing capital punishment in Delaware. This was the first time that any state in the nation had abolished the death penalty since Missouri did so in 1917. Two weeks earlier, the *Wilmington Morning News* had editorialized:

> . . . Now, we believe, the people and the state are ready for this historic step. But the innovation will still be on trial. One particularly revolting crime during the next few years, or a wave of the sort of crimes to which the death penalty formerly applied, could bring an outcry for the restoration of capital punishment.[8]

Subsequent events were to prove this observation prophetic.

During the rest of 1958, Delaware's abolition of capital punishment received national attention,[9] almost all favorable, and constituted an enormous inspiration to those in other states opposing the death penalty. In Delaware, largely due to the persistence of the Prisoners Aid Society,

[8] *Wilmington Morning News*, March 26, 1958, p. 22.

[9] Largely on account of a much reprinted article by James V. Bennett. See above, footnote 6.

the change in the law was acclaimed by the bar, the churches and throughout the professional and business community.[10] Some indication of the popular acceptance of abolition can be found in Senator Melson's remark that "those legislators who supported the bill to abolish capital punishment in April, who ran again in November, ran with their ticket. There is no indication that the people held it against them."[11]

The capital crime rate seemed to show—just as experts had predicted—no fluctuations traceable to abolition. In Wilmington, for example, which is the largest city in Delaware and contains approximately one-third of the state's population, there were seven murders during the twelve month period immediately prior to abolition, from April 1957 through March 1958. For the twelve months following abolition (i.e., from April 1958, through March 1959) there was only one murder.[12] In the state generally, whereas the population increased some 40.3 per cent between 1950 and 1960, murders and non-negligent manslaughters over the latter part of this period were as follows:[13]

Year	State Outside Wilmington	Wilmington	Total
1956	18	13	31
1957	12	11	23
1958	12	1	13
		(abolition April 2, 1958)	
1959	7	8	15
1960	14	10	24
1961	9	7	16

[10] See, e.g., the editorial "One More Plus for the State of Delaware", *Delaware State Medical Journal*, August 1958, p. 225.

[11] Communication from Senator Melson quoted in the *Report* of the Joint Legislative Committee on Capital Punishment, General Assembly of Pennsylvania (June 1961), p. 30.

[12] Source: Official Reports of the Bureau of Police of the City of Wilmington, Delaware; cf. the release from the Prisoners Aid Society of Delaware in March 1959.

[13] Source: Division of Criminal Statistics, State of Delaware, as reported by Governor Elbert N. Carvel on Dec. 14, 1961.

An analysis of the killings for the year 1960 shows the typical pattern familiar to criminologists. Of the fourteen killers in the State, one committed and one attempted suicide. No murders by parolees occurred nor were there any in connection with attempts to rape or kidnap, though two did come about in the course of attempted robbery or theft. Two others were cases of parents' killing their children.[14]

In April 1960, on the second anniversary of abolition, Attorney General Januar D. Bove, Jr. ended an address on "Capital Punishment" before the Overseas Press Club of New York by saying:

> We in Delaware are proud that our State has abolished capital punishment and has taken this forward step in the field of criminology. We do have need for many other laws to aid law enforcement and probation and parole officers in their work and we are hopeful of obtaining them. . . . There is no evidence whatsoever that attacks on the police or prison guards or threats to public safety have increased because of abolishment and, although Delaware has had at least one sensational vicious murder since abolishment, there has been no effort to restore the death penalty.

Fourteen months later, however, on Saturday, June 10, 1961, an eighty-nine-year-old woman was badly beaten and stabbed to death in Georgetown, Delaware, the rural county seat in the southern part of the State. The victim was a well-known, well-liked and highly respected church-going widow.

On June 13, Russell Leon Purnell, a twenty-five-year-old Negro confessed to the crime. He was transferred on June 14 to the custody of the New Castle County Correctional Institution for safety. Purnell had been released on April 9 from the Sussex Correctional Institution where he had been sentenced to three years on a burglary charge. As he was indigent, the Court appointed an attorney for him on Au-

[14] Source: See note 12.

gust 3. On September 27 he was arraigned and pled guilty to first degree murder and was immediately sentenced to life imprisonment, which he is now serving.

The case recalled the still unsolved murder of the prominently known Mrs. Leland Money, killed by a shotgun blast while preparing food in her kitchen near Middletown, Delaware.[15]

On Monday, June 12, a bill (SB 192) to restore the death penalty, supported by the son of the victim, was introduced in the Senate by Senator Harvey B. Spicer (R., Georgetown), who was also the Mayor of Georgetown. The bill was immediately sent to the Judiciary Committee and was reported out of the Committee five minutes later. No hearing was held and no opportunity was afforded citizens to oppose it. It was passed two days later, June 14, on a vote of twelve to three (two members absent or not voting). Senator James H. Snowden (R., Wilmington) minority leader, branded the bill as "panic legislation" based upon emotion and revenge.[16]

The bill made the death penalty applicable only to murder in the first degree—murder done with express malice aforethought or committed in perpetrating or attempting to perpetrate "any crime punishable with death". Obviously the hastily drawn bill was badly drafted, as there were no crimes then punishable with death. It took a House amendment to redefine the crime to mean "with express malice aforethought, or in perpetrating or attempting to perpetrate the crime of rape, kidnapping or treason" and also to avoid a constitutionally doubtful retrospective application of the law to Purnell.

The Senate bill reached the House on June 16 and was assigned to the Judiciary Committee on the 20th. In its haste the Senate had forgotten that a sentence of death also requires legislation on how the sentence is to be carried out. On June 21 the House sent the bill back to the Senate for clarification and amendment, but the Senate refused to accept it and remedied the situation by introducing a bill

15 *Wilmington Morning News,* June 14, 1961.
16 *Wilmington Morning News,* June 15, 1961.

(SB 215) to make hanging the punishment. This was expediously handled by having it introduced, reported in and out of committee and passed all on the same day, June 22. A House member, thinking that death by gas would be nicer, introduced an amendment to so provide and, with deference to local pride, suggested that a gas chamber be constructed in each of the three counties although the distance between the two most widely separated institutions could not have been more than eighty miles.

As soon as the bills reached the House, they were actively fought by the Prisoners Aid Society, the Councils of Churches and other supporters of abolition. A public hearing was requested, but Representative Glenn Busker (D., Smyrna), the Chairman of the Judiciary Committee, who alone could hold back or bring up the bill for a vote, said it would be a "waste of time"[17] to hold a hearing. Mr. Busker was an outspoken proponent of the death penalty bill (and the whipping post, too) and was unmoved by any of the facts and arguments against it.

Considerable literature on the subject was once again sent to the members of the Legislature, the Governor, and to other officials. The two Wilmington newspapers opposed restoration while the Dover newspaper favored it. Despite growing pressure for a hearing, Chairman Busker continued to refuse to hold one. In the late summer agitation for restoration simmered down and the Legislature recessed on September 20, to reconvene on November 27. By the fall, there was some hope the bill, in one way or another, would be defeated.

In July, at a special meeting, it was approved "that the Delaware Bar Association is opposed to the restoration of capital punishment in the State of Delaware." The Delaware Psychiatric Society stated that "the restoration of capital punishment is not in the public interest." The Wilmington and State Councils of Churches very actively opposed restoration.

On October 31, however, on a farm seven miles from the small town of Laurel, Delaware, (and not too far from

17 *Wilmington Morning News,* June 20, 1961.

Georgetown) Kermit West, a twenty-five-year-old Negro, killed an elderly couple, Lorenzo and Marmie Whaley, with a shotgun. West had been released from the Sussex Correctional Institution about four months previously after having served three years of a four-year sentence for a brickbat assault on Mr. Whaley. West, who lived near the Whaleys, had been behaving strangely in front of their home. The Whaleys had complained to the police who said they "couldn't arrest him for walking on the road." West, like Purnell, was indigent and the Court appointed counsel for him on December 26, 1961. He was arraigned on September 14, 1962, pled guilty to first degree murder on each of two charges and was sentenced to life imprisonment.

The Whaleys' three sons at first asked only that West be kept in custody for the rest of his natural life, saying in part, "We are Christians, and our families are Christians. We have never believed that life was man's to take.—We do not feel that capital punishment is a definite remedy." Considerable newspaper and radio publicity made the sons the center of much attention. What change took place within them is not known, but later their persistent presence in the legislature no doubt contributed to the passage of the restoration bills. Fuel was added to the fire when on November 7, Senator Spicer claimed that restoration was delayed by Governor Carvel's reluctance to act on such a measure. The Legislature convened on November 27 and on December 4, without a hearing, passed the two bills to restore the death penalty by a vote of twenty-three to twelve. Speaker of the House Sherman W. Tribbitt (D., Odessa), on a motion to table, ruled the yeas had it. After another bill had been acted upon, he permitted a roll call to lift the bill from the table. Mr. Tribbitt, who had been Chairman of the Judiciary Committee and a supporter of abolition in 1958, voted for restoration. It is interesting that he has since become a staunch supporter of correctional improvement recommended by a Governor's Committee.

When the bill was sent to Governor Elbert N. Carvel on

December 12, he promptly vetoed it. In his veto message he carefully reviewed the whole question of the death penalty and criminal law reform, and said in part:

"The news of the recent brutal, deplorable slayings which occurred in the lower part of our State was received by me with deep emotions of revulsion and despair. My sincerest sympathy goes out to the relatives and friends of the victims of these unspeakable crimes.

In view of the fact that the two men charged with the slayings referred to were products of our prisons, we as Delaware citizens must shamefully share part of the responsibility for our apathy in refusing to improve and modernize our correctional, rehabilitation and parole systems . . .

Senate Bill No. 192 provides for the death penalty in the case of murder. . . . I repeatedly urged members of the Legislature to hold public hearings on this measure since the public suffers from grave misapprehension and misconceptions regarding the areas of criminology and penology. I believe that had such a public hearing been conducted you would have been convinced, as I am, that the real facts do not support the need for this bill . . .

It is highly significant that of the many careful and thoughtful studies which have been made throughout the world in recent years by official bodies, they have all reached the same conclusion that the presence or absence of the death penalty has no effect on the homicide rate.

This lack of useful purpose of the death penalty has been the basis for the almost universal condemnation of its use by the church bodies in the United States and throughout the world upon the ground that revenge and brutality can have no place in a morally oriented society and that society can be protected by other means than the taking of a human life.

Our Delaware society is deeply rooted in the religious traditions and teachings of our community churches. We may, in the heat of passion, momentarily stray from these teachings—that human life is God given and not for man to take away. But in the cold light of reason, who among us wishes to face our Maker with the blood of our brother on our hands . . .

It is important to bear in mind, as I have stated at the beginning, that the persons charged with the tragic slayings committed in May and November [sic] of this year in the lower part of our State were both recent products of our prison system and, clearly, no benefits of parole supervision was given them following their release from the prisons. The citizens of this State are partly at fault as to what occurred, as society is partly at fault with regard to criminality in general. It was because of the inadequacies and defects in our entire correctional system and related areas that I appointed the Committee . . . to make a complete survey of our corrections system, including probation and parole, and to make its report to the next session of the General Assembly . . .

The function of the criminal law is to protect the law-abiding and not to fulfill a lust for revenge. Anything that tends to associate the law with the idea of vengeance impairs its dignity and subtracts from the respect that intelligent people accord it. It is our function to build and to create and not to destroy. Only by moving in that direction do we move ahead and in accordance with a high sense of ethics and morality.

In the light of these facts, I respectfully return to you Senate Bill No. 192 without my approval . . .

Despite this careful, reasoned defense, the Senate overrode the veto two days later by a vote of twelve to two (three not voting or absent). On December 18, the House joined the Senate and by the margin of one vote made Senate Bill No. 192 the law. Thus, after three years, eight months and sixteen days capital punishment returned in Delaware.

Why did it return? One reason seems to be, of course, the occurrence of the "particularly revolting crimes" described above, which the *Wilmington Morning News* had warned of at the time capital punishment was abolished. But this hardly seems sufficient, for there were murders in each of the years 1958, 1959 and 1960, as there had been in the past and will be in the future. Certainly an important factor, suggestive for further study, was the impact of these two crimes involving the killing of three elderly white persons, two of them women, by young Negroes at the very time when racial tension was high for several reasons: the desegregation movement in the school systems; a strong demand from Negroes for anti-discrimination and civil rights laws, which were introduced in the Legislature but did not pass; and "action" and "sit-in" groups seeking to desegregate restaurants in lower Delaware and Maryland and along Route 40 to Washington, D.C. From June through December hardly a day passed without numerous newspaper headlines and articles on these anti-discrimination problems. Did this atmosphere account for legislators voting for restoration, even when they were personally opposed to the death penalty and generally in favor of humanitarian measures?

There is also another reason, stated by the *Wilmington Morning News* in its editorial, "The Right Name is Tyranny":

> . . . It is a shock to realize that senators representing only 45.1 per cent of the people passed the bill restoring capital punishment over the opposition of senators representing 54.9 per cent of the people. It is a shock to realize that the same thing happened in both branches of the General Assembly—except that the twenty-three who voted to bring back hanging came from districts containing only forty per cent of the population. . . . When this can happen, we in Delaware are not enjoying democratic government. We are getting something else.[18]

Legislative representation fixed by the Constitution of 1897 gave the more rural, southern counties of the state a dis-

[18] *Wilmington Morning News,* December 28, 1961, p. 16.

proportionate voting strength in the Legislature. That a fairly apportioned Legislature would have upheld abolition seems reasonably certain.

The first murder case after the reintroduction of capital punishment was a sobering and tragic anti-climax. On December 28, 1961, just ten days after restoration of the death penalty, Detective Sergeant William J. Mulrine, III, white, forty-nine years of age, killed his wife with a single revolver shot, and was immediately charged with first degree murder. Detective Mulrine had twenty years service on the Wilmington Police Force. In a discussion with a prominent local minister a few weeks before the murder, he had expounded at great length his reasons for favoring restoration of the death penalty. It was, he said, a real deterrent and murderers ought to be punished; many members of the police force, he said, believed as he did. He became the first possible candidate for the reinstated hangman's noose, a classic example of why there is no deterrent in the death penalty. Fortunately, that punishment was not for him. He personally engaged two lawyers who represented him energetically. His trial began on June 11, 1962. During the presentation of the State's case, it appeared, among other things, that the police had taken no statement from Mulrine until the day after his apprehension, which evoked some comments from the trial judge. Mulrine's son testified that his father had called it an "accident". So, on the third day of the trial, a plea of guilty to a manslaughter charge ended the matter. On July 13 Mulrine was sentenced to five years imprisonment, but in January 1963, he applied through the same lawyers to the Board of Pardons for commutation of sentence. The Board reduced the term to four years, which makes him eligible for parole after having served two years from the commencement of the original sentence.

THE STRUGGLE OVER CAPITAL PUNISHMENT IN NEW JERSEY*

Beginning in the late 1950's, a wave of opposition to the death penalty has swept across the United States, much as it did on two earlier occasions, in the 1840's and the 1910's. Whether the present movement will achieve significant changes in the direction of complete abolition, as those earlier efforts did, remains to be seen. Meanwhile, few first hand accounts of the current movement have been published, and it is my intention here to remedy this by giving an admittedly partisan analysis of the abolition movement between 1956 and 1961 in one state, New Jersey. From what I know of the experiences of abolitionists in California, Massachusetts, New York, Pennsylvania, and Ohio, our experience in New Jersey is indicative of what has been happening all over the nation.

I

It is convenient to begin by examining the proposals affecting the death penalty that were placed before the 1961 session of the New Jersey Legislature. There were four such measures, rather more than usual. The only one to have bi-partisan sponsorship was a bill filed in the Senate as a Joint Resolution (SJR-1) to create a commission of nine members, to be appointed by the Governor and the Legislature, to study the problem of capital punishment and to make appropriate recommendations. The history of this proposal began in 1957, when C. Williams Haines (R., Burlington) introduced a bill in the Assembly to create a similiar study commission. In each of the following years, paralleling Assemblyman Haines's efforts to get an abolition bill passed, John Waddington (D., Salem) introduced in the Senate a Resolution for a study commission. Not once, however, was his bill released for a floor

* A revised version of an essay originally written for *New Jersey State Bar Journal;* the whole of section II appeared in the Winter 1962 issue under the title, "The Struggle for Law Reform."

vote, even though it authorized no expenditures and carefully avoided providing for a moratorium on executions during the period of the study. Several times during the past two years, many Senators implied that they would vote for the bill if it were released, and it was thought their number included enough Republicans to get it through the party caucus and onto the floor. Evidently not, for the bill has died annually in the Judiciary Committee.

Since the bill's sponsors were obviously abolitionists (the preamble to their Resolution read like a lay sermon against the death penalty), it may be that their bill was viewed as the entering wedge of an issue Senate leaders had no desire to see erupt in their chamber. Perhaps many Senators also believed that New Jersey did not need a study commission on this subject because the lengthy hearing and floor debate on abolition bills in the Assembly during 1958–1959 had served much the same purpose. Anyway, there was no legislation during 1961 authorizing a study commission on capital punishment in New Jersey.

All the rest of the proposed legislation on capital punishment was filed in the Assembly. Of these three bills, certainly the most important was A-518, which would have abolished all four of New Jersey's capital crimes and substituted an irreducible thirty-year prison sentence, except in those cases where the jury recommends "mercy," in which instance "life" would be meted out (as it is now). A-518 was not released from the Judiciary Committee during 1961, and so, once again, for the fifth time in the past six years, the Assembly turned its back on abolition.

A-518 is identical with the Haines-Stepacoff bills on which a two-day public hearing was held in 1958 and a floor vote in 1959. The initial bill of this series was introduced by Assemblyman Haines late in the 1956 session, largely at the urging of a small group of his co-religionists in the Society of Friends. Although hitherto he had had no special interest in such issues, Assemblyman Haines not surprisingly felt the force of their arguments, and he had a bill drafted. His bill, so far as my research has disclosed, was the first abolition bill in the New Jersey legislature since the 1937 session.

It was not until the next year, however, that Assembly-man Haines began to work vigorously on behalf of this measure. Early in 1957, a public hearing was arranged on his bill before the Committee on Institutions, Public Health and Welfare. Like its predecessor, the bill that year pro-vided for complete abolition and the substitution of an ir-reducible life sentence, in the literal sense of that term. This stringent alternative to capital punishment was pro-posed partly on the ground that the Legislature would never vote for a lesser alternative and partly because Haines him-self did not altogether relish the idea of first degree mur-derers on parole.

The transcript of the hearing is available for study in the State Law Library. It is a pretty meager record. The hearing had been poorly publicized and was attended ac-cordingly. Only ten persons testified, and the entire testi-mony took no more than a couple of hours. Neither the bill's advocates nor its opponents managed to offer very much in the way of compelling evidence to the Committee. Toward the end of the hearing, Assemblyman William Oz-zard (R., Somerset) suggested that the witness then testify-ing try to offer the Committee "something other than the emotional and religious view which had been expressed so far on both sides of the issue." Assemblyman Ozzard asked, "Are facts and figures and information available that can be laid on the table and discussed and considered, at least to attempt to evaluate the social effect of abolition of the death penalty?" The witness lamely replied, "I'm sorry, I personally couldn't say." As if this weren't enough of an anti-climax, a spokesman for the State Bar Associa-tion reported that its Criminal Law Committee had given the bill careful study. However, he said, "At this time the State Bar is not in a position to express itself affirmatively on any issue." So in 1957, neither the moralists nor the lawyers apparently had anything useful to lay before the New Jersey Legislature on the problem of capital punishment.

To everyone at the hearing, it must have been obvious that except for a few members of the Society of Friends and of the Womens International League for Peace and Freedom, there was no organized support behind the

Haines bill. Moreover, even these two groups could muster no more than a handful of their small membership at the Hearing, and the testimony of their witnesses, as Assemblyman Ozzard correctly implied, left every important question unanswered. It could hardly have come as a surprise to anyone that the Haines bill never reached the floor during the 1957 session.

Beginning in the spring of 1958, however, three different and largely uncoordinated efforts got underway in support of Assemblyman Haines. One newspaper in New Jersey that for years has given favorable coverage to the cause of abolition is the *Bergen Evening Record,* which has made Bergen County the main stronghold of abolitionist sentiment in the state. During the spring of 1958, Mr. William Oriol, the *Record* reporter on the State House beat, conducted several interviews in Trenton in preparation for a series of articles on capital punishment. At the same time, he served as an informal liaison man between Assemblyman Haines, various officials elsewhere in the state government, and the public at large who favored abolition. When his series of articles appeared in June, they immediately became the best source of information generally available on the subject. The *Record* even went so far as to print ten thousand additional copies for general distribution. Later that summer, both the *New Brunswick Daily Home News* (July 6–11) and the *Red Bank Register* (August 7, 15, 21) ran similar series, indicating considerable interest and some sentiment for abolition.

Meanwhile, the Society of Friends' Social Order Committee, borrowing the technique of Herbert Cobin in Delaware, prepared an excellent source-book on the whole problem of the death penalty, summarizing the many religious, moral, scientific and administrative considerations favoring abolition. The Friends arranged for a copy of their pamphlet to be delivered to every New Jersey legislator. At the same time, under the direction of Mr. Edmund Goerke, Jr., the chairman of the Committee, they were rounding up several national authorities in penology, criminology, psychiatry and social work to appear at the public hearing it was expected would again be held that year on the Haines bill.

The other handful of abolitionists in the state consisted of an ad hoc group called the Citizens Committee in Princeton for the Abolition of Capital Punishment. My wife and I and a few friends were the nucleus. Our main concern was to get some publicity and public support throughout the state for the Haines bill, to urge the State Department of Institutions and Agencies to send a representative to testify at the public hearing, and to conduct some research on the sociology of homicide and executions in New Jersey. Our first job, we discovered to our surprise, was to insure that there would be a hearing at all. None had been scheduled, and the Judiciary Committee Chairman, David Stepacoff (D., Middlesex), who had custody of A-33, as the Haines bill was numbered in 1958, made it clear that there would be no hearing unless his Committee had some evidence very soon that somebody in New Jersey really cared about the issue of capital punishment.

After a frantic scramble to get a token of public sentiment on record before the Judiciary Committee, the hearing was finally scheduled and held for two full days on June 5 and 19. Scores of people attended the proceedings in the Assembly chamber. Twenty-four witnesses testified before the Committee. All but two were in favor of abolition. The entire content of the hearing on A-33 is preserved in a bulky two-volume mimeographed transcript, copies of which are available in many state libraries. Probably the most significant testimony at the hearing was supplied by members of the Department of Institutions and Agencies, especially by the Commissioner, John Tramburg, and by the late Parole Board Chairman, Homer Zink. Commissioner Tramburg announced, "I want to say I am against capital punishment . . . If you can prove to me, or if anybody can, conclusively, that capital punishment is a deterrent, I'll buy it . . . but I haven't been able to convince myself that it is a deterrent to crime." Chairman Zink took the opportunity to explain the excellent parole record maintained by New Jersey's "lifers." He reported that since the parole board had been reorganized in 1949, "it has paroled

117 men and women sentenced to life imprisonment . . . Only ten of these persons or about 8½ per cent violated parole; none committed a new murder." (This last fact, by the way, still stands.) In the course of his testimony he also expressed unqualified support for abolition.

The statements of these two officials were well received in the local and metropolitan press, which gave fairly wide coverage to the hearing. But it was more than offset by the remarks given at some length ad lib by two other witnesses. One was the former Chief of Police of Bergen County, speaking for the State Chiefs of Police Association. The other was an internationally known penologist, and former Institutions and Agencies Commissioner, Sanford Bates, probably the only major figure in American penology today who gives even qualified support for the death penalty. Naturally, the newspapers headlined their remarks. Nevertheless, by the end of the hearing, an enormous amount of information of the very sort Assemblyman Ozzard had wanted the year before had been placed into the record.[1]

A-33 did not become law, however. In fact, it did not get released from Committee for a vote, even though Assemblyman Stepacoff later joined Assemblyman Haines as a co-sponsor of the bill. The reasons for the 1958 defeat were several, and it is instructive to examine them because they point up the obstacles in the way of grass-roots citizen reform movements. First of all, the hearings were not scheduled until so late in the year that they had to be held after the regular session had adjourned. Most of the Judiciary Committee was never directly approached at any time by any constituent who wanted the Haines bill released. These facts help explain the absence from the hearing of five of the Committee's seven members, the attendance only of Chairman Stepacoff at all the sessions, and the presence of only two or three of the eighty-one Senators and Assemblymen at any of the testimony.

Furthermore, the only state-wide organizations that lent their support were, once again, the Womens International League and the Friends, hardly the biggest or the most in-

[1] See, e.g., *New York Times* and *Newark News* of June 6 and 20, 1958.

fluential political bodies. Except for the Greater Red Bank
Council of Churches and the Friends, no church groups
and few churchmen showed any awareness that the issue
of capital punishment even existed. As Murray Kempton
described it in the *New York Post,* after the first day of the
hearing, "The old State House was conspicuous for the
turned collars of the clergy. But such is the condition of
organized religion that these deputations of the cloth turned
out to be there for another hearing, by the Senate, to consider the alleged oppression of ecclesiastical lotteries by
the State Bingo Commission." The excellent testimony on
behalf of abolition offered by several officials from the
Department of Institutions and Agencies was somewhat
undercut by the fact that their governing body, the Board
of Control, made no statement in favor of abolition on the
ground that they were unable to speak unanimously. Several months after the hearing, in December, Lloyd Wescott,
the Chairman, finally announced that he, at least, strongly
favored abolition. But only the *Bergen Record* seemed interested enough in the news to print it; the other papers
ignored it.

Increasing local opposition was offered by the Police
Chiefs Association and the Patrolmans Benevolent Association. During the months after the hearing they saw to it
that the newspapers served up to the public such gems as
this forecast by the State P. B. A. President: "Without
capital punishment there would be a 100 per cent increase
in the crime rate."[2] Besides the *Bergen Evening Record,*
the only daily newspaper in the state to come out against
the death penalty was the *Daily Home News.* The *Hudson
Dispatch,* in a series of editorials during November that
can only be described as irresponsible, bemoaned New
Jersey's "Be Kind To Criminals Laws," and shrieked that
the obvious remedy for the complete "Breakdown of Law
Enforcement" in the state was constant use of the electric
chair. (How criminals were to be executed when, if the

---

[2] *Newark News,* Feb. 9, 1959. See also the editorial, "Capital Punishment," in *New Jersey's Finest* (the State P. B. A.
monthly) for May 1960; and also the *Trenton Times* of March
12, 1961.

editorials were to be believed, they weren't being convicted, or even caught, was not explained.) As for the *Newark News,* the leading daily in New Jersey, an editorial observed with some apprehension that support for Haines' bill "seems to be increasing." Finally, although a few public debates and lectures were hastily set up here and there, none was arranged in the major urban centers of Newark, Paterson, Jersey City, Elizabeth, Trenton or Camden. The nearest thing to a state-wide public discussion of the subject took place during July on two successive Sunday afternoons over WNTA-TV in Newark. Governor Robert Meyner moderated a very brief debate between Sanford Bates and me, and a few weeks later a full hour was given over to a mock rerun of the June public hearing in the Assembly.[3] No one at any time tried to find out what the bulk of the public really thought on the issue of abolishing the death penalty.

The resulting pressure on the New Jersey Legislature during 1958 to face squarely the problem of capital punishment was wholly inadequate. In retrospect, it may have been naive of us, but we really thought that the evidence and argument we presented at the hearings gave us an airtight case which no one in his right mind could ignore. Whether or not it did, we did not get the reform we wanted and our experience was at least a sobering baptism into the realities of state politics.

In an effort to avert future defeats, those who arranged for the June hearings joined forces and in October 1958, decided to form a New Jersey Council to Abolish Capital Punishment as the state branch of the American League to Abolish Capital Punishment. The retiring Chairman of the Parole Board, Homer Zink, agreed to be Honorary Chairman of the new group. The day-to-day leadership was to remain in the hands of the Executive Committee, consisting of Mr. Goerke and me. To our great loss, Mr. Zink was almost immediately taken ill and shortly thereafter died, and the contribution he undoubtedly would have made was lost. We could call, however, for some help and advice on

[3] See *Newark Star Ledger, New Brunswick* and *Daily Home News* of July 14, 1958.

an impressive and diverse group, acting as a Board of
Sponsors: F. Lovell Bixby, then Director, State Division of
Correction and Parole; Donald Borg, Editor and Publisher, *Bergen Evening Record;* Gunnar Dybwad, Executive
Director, National Association of Retarded Children; Emil
Frankel, formerly Director, State Bureau of Social Research; Assemblyman Haines; Robert Knowlton, Professor
of Law at Rutgers; Geraldine Thompson, formerly member,
State Board of Control; Jackson Toby, criminologist, Rutgers University; and Senator Waddington.[4] As everyone
knows, however, the amount of actual service performed
by such advisory boards is severely limited. In our own
case, it was no different. The direction of the movement
against capital punishment in New Jersey remained very
largely a two man operation.

Our main efforts, through the Council, were propagandis-
tic and legislative. The results of our research were succinctly stated in a pamphlet, *Twenty Questions on Capital
Punishment in New Jersey.* Throughout the next three
years, Council members appeared on television and radio
programs, and lecture and debate platforms in every part
of the state, before many kinds of groups. Press releases
and numerous "Letters to the Editor" frequently appeared
in all the major New Jersey newspapers. High school and
college students were supplied with material for themes
and debates. These activities of the Council helped to ele-
vate the tone of public discussion on capital punishment to a
responsible level. And all this was done on annual operating
expenses of about $300, and with an active membership
never in excess of a hundred!

On the legislative front, the Council's success was to remain far less complete. During the winter of 1958–1959,
every effort was directed toward lobbying in the Assembly
on behalf of the Haines-Stepacoff bill. By this time, William
Oriol had left the *Bergen Evening Record* for the office of
Senator Harrison Williams in Washington, D. C. This loss,
however, was more than offset by the work of Mr. Arnold

[4] See *The Trentonian* and *The Bergen Evening Record* for
October 22, 1958.

Feldman, then Executive Director of New Jersey's Americans for Democratic Action, who spent much of his time during his weekly visit to Trenton effectively lobbying for abolition.

Thanks to patient work inside and outside the Assembly chamber, the friends of abolition were finally rewarded on April 6, 1959, when the Haines-Stepacoff bill, A-355, was at last brought to the floor for debate and vote. The debate, later described by reporters as "emotion-packed" and even "torrid," was thoroughly covered by the local and metropolitan newspapers. Since I have elsewhere already analyzed at length the issues as they were raised in the floor debate that afternoon,[5] I shall not review them here. Suffice to say that the vote was at least historic. Not since 1915 had the Assembly voted directly on an abolition bill, when the Senate passed it by a vote of eleven to one, only to have it defeated in the Assembly, twenty-nine to twenty.

When the Haines-Stepacoff bill was finally ready for a vote, after more than two hours of debate before a full gallery of hushed observers, it was 1915 all over again. Abolition was defeated, thirty to nineteen, with eleven not voting (about half were absent, and the rest abstained). Neither the debate nor the vote went along party lines; both sponsors, plus three others, spoke for it; six, some from each party, spoke against it. Although a greater proportion of Republicans than Democrats voted for it (nine of the former for, six against; ten of the latter for, twenty-four against), it was the Democrats who maneuvered the bill through Committee and Conference and onto the floor. The vote takes a clearer pattern only if it is analyzed geographically. Of the twenty-two votes from the northern metropolitan industrial counties (Essex, Hudson, Union), A-355 received exactly two. Had these counties, where we were the weakest, not benefitted from malapportionment of the Assembly (which was not corrected until two years

[5] "The Case Against the Death Penalty," *The New Leader*, (August 17–24, 1959), pp. 19 ff. See also *Newark News* for March 10 and 22 and April 7, 1959; and *Newark Star Ledger*, *Elizabeth Daily Journal* and *Bergen Evening Record* of April 7, 1959.

later), the vote would probably have been even closer. Counties with a growing suburban population gave us a much better ratio of support. Even so, it was a fairly close defeat, as is shown by the fact that if only half those who didn't vote, plus four of those who voted "Nay," had cast their votes for the bill it would have carried.

A week later, the *Newark News* wrote the epitaph for A-355. After complimenting the Assembly for its "wise decision" in defeating the Haines-Stepacoff bill, the editorial added, for the benefit of any doubting readers, "The death penalty should be kept, for whatever beneficial effect it may have, until we have much more conclusive evidence that its abandonment would not encourage the homicidal."

At the end of the 1959 session, Assemblymen Haines and Stepacoff retired from the legislature. From that time the abolition movement languished noticeably. In 1960, no abolition bill was even introduced. In 1961, as stated earlier, a bill was introduced, but it died in committee without a murmur. The substance of the difficulty in 1961, as in 1958, was that too many obstacles remained to be overcome and the modest resources of the New Jersey Council to Abolish Capital Punishment were unequal to the task.

One of the factors in the defeat of A-355 in 1959 was the pull exerted by another bill, A-440, introduced that year by the Union County delegation. This bill was designed to make "carnal abuse" of a female by any male sixteen years or older a capital crime. This bill and the Haines-Stepacoff bill tended to polarize the Assembly, and while the former did not draw much direct support, it muted enthusiasm for the latter. As a diversionary thrust, in short, A-440 was a success. In 1961, another version of this bill was again put into the hopper. It was modified, however, so as to limit the death penalty to "carnal knowledge" by means of "brutal force," or "together with unnatural acts," or where a pregnant woman was the victim. But the Assembly was no more in a mood for this version than for its predecessor. In taking no action in this case, the Assembly acted wisely. It is generally known that every one of the twenty-one states that permit rape to be punished by death does so in order to retain one of the worst forms of racial discrimination. Of the 455 men executed for rape since 1930, all were executed in southern states, and 405 were Negroes. It is unthinkable that New Jersey would take this backward step, now or in the foreseeable future. The irrationality of the whole idea is sufficiently revealed by the fact that the bill's advocates have yet to attempt to give the public a coherent account of its alleged merits,[6] and that no one in the Departments of Institutions and Agencies takes the bill seriously.

The last of the four bills in the New Jersey legislature affecting capital punishment during 1961 would have introduced a procedure recently adopted in California and Pennsylvania whereby in first degree murder cases the jury holds two separate sessions, one, on the question of guilt, and another, upon a conviction and "after hearing such additional evidence as may be submitted," on the question of sentence. This proposal first appeared in New Jersey in 1960, in the Senate. The statement of purpose appended to the bill is thoughtfully worded and deserving of study. The aim of this bill (A-675) was to rationalize the decision in *State v. Mount*, 30 N. J. 195 (1959), which held that the defense in a murder trial may introduce such "background evidence" as may serve to assist the jury in its task, not of finding guilt, but of assessing the penalty. The American Law Institute has recently devoted considerable discussion to this proposal, and has concluded that if capital punishment must be kept, this modification of the traditional jury trial should be adopted. Moreover, the Institute has given detailed proposals for the criteria on which the jury, so instructed by the judge, should find aggravating or mitigating circumstances in the crime in order to modify its sentence accordingly.[7] The New Jersey State Bar Association's Criminal Law Committee, however, dis-

[6] See, for instance, the running discussion among correspondents in *The Elizabeth Daily Journal* during February–April 1959.

[7] See American Law Institute, *Model Penal Code Proposed Official Draft* (1961), pp. 128–133, and also the Institute's *Proceedings* (1959), pp. 147–216, and *Proceedings* (1962), pp. 118–134.

approved of A-675 on the ground that its recommendations were too drastic.[8]

Were this bill adopted, it would very likely take some of
the wind out of the abolitionist's sails (retentionists might
want to bear this in mind). But it would also free defense
counsel in every capital case to plead before the jury certain mitigating circumstances, with the real likelihood that
the death sentence would become a rarity even if it would
not altogether disappear. In 1960, the Union County prosecutor stated that in his opinion this would be the eventual
consequence anyway of the decision in *Mount*.[9] There is,
no doubt, both some support for this bill and some opposition to it, though the legislature so far seems uninterested.

One merit of A-675 is that it would go toward meeting
the need for "due process" which capital punishment raises
in an acute form. But, I suggest, it would not go far enough.
Even if its provision were adopted, there would still remain
the inequities that result from the common law heritage
whereby courts automatically deny jury service in a capital
trial to anyone who has conscientious scruples against the
death penalty. When such scruples had a direct relation to
the capacity of a juror to find guilt, as they did when capital
punishment was the mandatory penalty for murder (and
given the doctrine that the jury must reach a unanimous
verdict), the procedure of excluding such jurors was a
practical necessity. But this no longer applies, and the result is a problem, perhaps a constitutional one, which ought
to be faced. It is not clear how it can be resolved except by
a return to mandatory capital punishment (which even the
prosecutors would oppose) or by an advance to complete
abolition.[10] As everyone familiar with the administration

[8] See the Committee's memorandum as reported in *New
Jersey Law Journal* (May 19, 1960), p. 255.

[9] *Newark News*, February 17, 1960, and also the editorial of
July 24, 1959. In general, see Joel Handler, "Background Evidence in Murder Cases," *Journal of Criminal Law, Criminology and Police Science* (1960), pp. 317 ff.

[10] See the leading article by Walter Oberer, "Does Disquali-
fication of Jurors for Scruples Against Capital Punishment
Constitute Denial of Fair Trial on Issue of Guilt?" *Texas Law
Review* (1961), pp. 545 ff.

of the criminal law knows, the question takes on growing practical importance because of the increasing difficulty in impanelling a capital jury. The magnitude of the problem prosecutors sometimes face here is hard to overstate. Frederick A. Siegel, thirty, pled no defense to a first degree murder indictment in Freehold during October 1961. The prosecutor urged the court to accept the plea, "reluctant" though he was to do so, because "two days of interrogation of thirty-seven prospective jurors failed to seat even one." The prosecutor added that "a general reluctance on the part of all talesmen to ask for the death penalty prevented them from being seated."[11] A return to mandatory capital punishment for first degree murder would almost certainly bring the present system for administering criminal justice to a grinding halt.

This completes the survey of the four bills dealing with capital punishment before the last session of the legislature. The variety of these proposals is not unusual. In 1959, for instance, A-626 would have reversed the provisions of the Haines-Stepacoff bill, giving a mandatory thirty-year prison term for all capital crimes unless the jury recommended death. In 1960, A-219 would have provided that persons convicted of first degree murder would either suffer death or a minimum twenty-year prison term, without possibility of parole or commutation. In this connection, it ought to be realized that, according to Mr. Zink's testimony at the 1958 hearings, the "lifer" in New Jersey already serves an average of nineteen years before he is paroled, even though his parole eligibility occurs five years earlier. Both A-626 and A-219 went the way of the bulk of the bills we have examined here: no vote, no debate, no release to the floor.

Is there any lesson in the common fate of all these bills in this area of the criminal law? Perhaps just one. The legislature has been very reluctant to overhaul New Jersey's capital laws, either by way of augmenting or diminishing their number, or by way of altering procedure or substance. One explanation for this inertia is the conviction, evidently held by many legislators, that if there is any vital

11 *Newark News* of October 19, 1961.

public interest at stake in the whole controversy, it is best served by preserving the status quo.

II

Not all the forces at work in the struggle over reform of capital laws have been confined to the arena where statutes are up for enactment or repeal. Despite the failure of abolitionists to have their way in the legislature, there is no doubt that they have had the best of it at the prison. No one has been executed in New Jersey since August 1956, over five and one-half years ago, the longest period without an execution in the state in this century (and perhaps since 1691, when William Lutherland was hanged in Salem for murder, the first recorded execution in New Jersey).

Of the fifteen men received at Trenton State Prison under sentence of death since the last execution, every one has received at least one stay of execution, and seven have obtained them through the Federal courts. Ten of the fifteen are still awaiting final disposition of their cases! Of the five who have left "Death Row" during this period, all received life sentences, four through retrial and one through executive clemency. Only in the last of these cases was the discovery of some substantive injustice at the trial court level the basis of the reversal. In all the others, purely procedural questions, hardly reaching to the issue of guilt, sufficed to obtain the order for a new trial. Whatever else this record shows, it amply confirms the fact that a man sentenced to death is not certain to be put to death.

This disposition of capital cases in New Jersey since August 1956, stands in striking contrast to the practice earlier in the century.[12] In the five-year period beginning in 1907 (when electrocution replaced hanging in this state) through 1911, thirty-one men (no women) were received in State Prison under sentence of death. Of these, twenty-one were executed during this period, twelve of them without any record of a stay, reprieve or appeal.[13] Of those

[12] The data reported in this and the next two paragraphs are drawn from my article, "Death Sentences in New Jersey, 1907–1960," *Rutgers Law Review* (Fall 1964), pp. 1–54.

[13] By the phrase, "No record of stay, reprieve or appeal," I

who did receive a stay or reprieve, none was issued by a Federal court. These facts are interesting when it is recalled that during this period, the death sentence was still mandatory upon a conviction of first degree murder; it became optional in New Jersey only in 1916. Of the ten men not executed during this period, only three were permitted a retrial. Four received executive commutation of sentence. Notice that during this five-year period, all the cases were finally disposed of except three (and of these two were disposed of by execution during the next three months).[14]

Compare now the five-year period between 1933 and 1937, only a generation ago. During those years, twenty-five men were received under sentence of death. Of these, eleven were executed within the period, and all but one had at least one stay, reprieve or appeal. Of the remaining ten, all eventually received life sentences, half through retrial and half directly by executive clemency. But out of the total of twenty-five cases, seven were not finally disposed of until after the end of the five-year period (though all were disposed of by execution within the next eight months).

The significance of these data is unequivocal. The trend in capital cases in New Jersey has been toward fewer death sentences at the trial level and fewer executive commuta-

---

mean that no such record is to be found in the inmate records of the State Prison or in the record of cases decided by the old Court of Errors and Appeals. Under New Jersey law, there has never been any "automatic" appeal of a death sentence. What alone is now "automatic," according to *R. R.* 1: 4–3 (a), is that if an appeal is brought it automatically goes before the Supreme Court, and when it is filed a stay automatically issues. For a genuine "automatic" appeal, i.e., the issuance of a writ of error to the trial court automatically upon a death sentence, without any action on the defendant's part, one must look elsewhere; see e.g. California Penal Code § 1239 (b).

14 The remaining case is the fantastic one of Archibald Herron. Herron was sentenced to death by hanging in 1908, although the statute required that death be inflicted by electrocution. Before Herron could be properly resentenced, the trial judge died; but the statutes then required that only the sentencing judge could resentence! In this anomolous situation, Herron remained in State Prison until 1948, when he died of old age. See 77 N.J.L. 523 (1908).

tions. The trend has also been toward lengthening the time required for final disposition of capital cases and toward involving more and more cases in this lengthening process. Studying the last point more closely, we find that in New Jersey as elsewhere, the period of time required for final disposition has lengthened because of the growing tendency to contest state court decisions in the Federal courts.[15]

It would be a great mistake to conclude that all these changes over the decades must be attributed to the operation of social forces over which neither the courts, the legislature, the bar nor the general public has any control. There is a definite, assignable set of causes for New Jersey's recent *de facto* moratorium on executions. Aside from the eagle-eye scrutiny with which higher courts are increasingly more willing to examine the capital cases brought to them, the most important single factor in this phenomenon lies in the brief but noteworthy career of a unique organization known as New Jersey Citizens Against the Death Penalty.

During the period in the spring of 1960 when the world was briefly distracted from the "cold war" by the Caryl Chessman case in California, an obscure paragraph in the *Newark News* mentioned that three men were to be electrocuted in Trenton State Prison immediately after Easter. At the time, these executions looked inevitable. The death sentences had been confirmed on appeal to the State Supreme Court. The Governor had refused to extend executive clemency. The condemned men were young unskilled Negro laborers, penniless, seemingly guilty beyond a doubt, and undeserving of special sympathy. Their lawyers considered the cases closed. Their future seemed hopeless. No one seemed to know or to care about what was soon to happen to them.

As a gesture of moral protest against these impending executions, simply because they were executions and were the first in the state for over three years, a dozen people from an upstate rural area along the Delaware River met together and decided to conduct a poster demonstration in Trenton during Holy Week. They called themselves "The Hunterdon County Committee to Abolish Capital Punishment." The nucleus was provided by a group of neighbors connected with publishing the pacifist monthly, *Liberation*. With cooperation from several of us who had worked for abolition in the legislature during the previous two years, the demonstration started on Tuesday before Easter, under the leadership of a Clinton school teacher, Michael Ciavolino, Jr. The group walked, silently and orderly, in front of the State House all day every day through Saturday. Never more than half a dozen marchers were involved at any one time. On Easter morning, under the anxious and occasionally hostile eyes of church-going crowds, a final demonstration was held opposite the Governor's mansion in Princeton.

The newspapers and wire services, diverted by the solemnity of the season from other local news, gave continuous front-page coverage to the demonstration throughout the week.[16] Despite the value of the publicity in informing an hitherto indifferent public, the hopelessness of the effort seemed beyond doubt. The marchers distributed a statement, urging that the executions be delayed in order to give the Senate time to consider SJR-2 (the death penalty study commission bill of 1960). But most of us knew that such a bill had been under consideration for three years already and that even if SJR-2 were somehow to be passed, in its present form it had no provision for a moratorium on executions. Executive clemency, though already once denied, seemed the only hope. But Governor Meyner was then in Caribbean waters, on his annual cruise with the Naval Reserve, and no date for his return had been made public.

Saturday morning, a young attorney in Levittown, Edward Kent, read of our demonstration in the *Philadelphia Inquirer* and learned, as we had told the reporters, that

---

[16] For further details, see *Philadelphia Inquirer*, April 16, 1960; *New York Post*, April 20, 1960; and *Hunterdon County Democrat*, April 21, 1960.

the condemned men no longer had legal counsel. Kent telephoned us immediately and volunteered to examine the court record on the chance that there might be some reasonable basis for a new appeal in state or federal courts. After studying the record of the case over the rest of the Easter weekend, he sought and obtained a stay of the executions, with only ten hours to spare. The executions have yet to take place. From this beginning, the New Jersey Citizens Against the Death Penalty was formed.

To all of those who participated in that modest but memorable public protest of Holy Week, 1960, it became obvious that there are many legal remedies for those under a death sentence. But they cannot be pursued without the money to pay lawyers' expenses and the costs of preparing, printing and filing the necessary legal papers. It seemed, therefore, a legitimate step for us to pursue a double aim—securing equal justice and opposing the death penalty—by creating an organization whose sole task would be to obtain legal counsel for appeal in capital cases involving indigent defendants. Accordingly, in May 1960, the New Jersey Citizens Against the Death Penalty was chartered as a non-profit organization with this express purpose declared in its incorporation papers. So far as has been determined, there is not and never has been any similar organization anywhere in the country.[17]

As in other cases where appeals of a death sentence are undertaken,[18] our efforts to obtain a remedy on behalf of these three condemned men were occasionally stigmatized as a thinly disguised dilatory maneuver. We, on the contrary, acted from the conviction that the attempt to establish one's legal rights is never dilatory, no matter

[17] For a description of the appellate work undertaken by the Clemency Committee of the N. Y. Committee to Abolish Capital Punishment, see Harold Lavine, "Last Chance on Death Row," *Saturday Evening Post* (June 29–July 6, 1963).

[18] This problem, among others, as it arose in the Chessman case is discussed from different points of view in Note, "The Caryl Chessman Case: A Legal Analysis," *Minnesota Law Review* (1960), pp. 892 ff., and in A. L. Wirin and Paul M. Poser, "A Decade of Appeals," *U. C. L. A. Law Review* (1961), pp. 768 ff.

how often one tries. Our adversary system of criminal justice requires it. This attitude seemed wholly justified because human life was at stake, and because it is so hard to get equal justice for rich and poor, white and black, the innocent and the guilty.

In its report of April 1961, the chief executive officer of the group, Steven Sieverts, stated that the New Jersey Citizens had disbursed nearly $6000 in expenses on behalf of four of the eight men then under sentence of death. (Subsequent to the filing of this report, the organization has taken several additional cases under its wing.) Two attorneys, Kent and Chester Apy, of Red Bank, had offered their services to the Citizens to pursue these appeals. The report also pointed out that the Citizens had played a role in persuading the Governor to grant executive clemency to a condemned man in May 1961, the first executive commutation of a death sentence in New Jersey since 1945.

The founders of this unique group initially conceived their purpose to be a sharply limited one. But as the group began to take more and more cases on appeal, it became apparent that there were difficulties ahead unless the legislature showed some sign of willingness to abolish the death penalty. If *every* death sentence were to be appealed to the extent that money and ingenuity allowed, many observers would certainly conclude that it had become our business to exploit the resources of the law simply in order to delay justice. Were this to happen, it would not be excused by the immorality of capital punishment. These possibilities, which loomed in the future, crossed not only the minds of some county prosecutors; they became matters of concern to the members of the Citizens and to their counsel as well.

So far, at least, it would be unreasonable to suggest that anything of this sort has happened. One is encouraged in making this judgment by the fact that the argument on appeal before the U. S. Supreme Court, requesting a writ of certiorari on the issue of federal jurisdiction, in *Johnson et al. v. New Jersey* (S. Ct. October Term, 1961, No. 347 Misc.)—the latest stage of the case involving the three Negroes scheduled to die after Easter, 1960—has raised a question, perhaps for the first time,[19] bearing on the very possibility of achieving "due process" under a system of capital punishment such as New Jersey's. Appellants contended that the New Jersey statutes (and, by implication, similar statutes in other death penalty states) violate the "due process" clause of the Fourteenth Amendment, since they permit the jury "in its unbridled discretion to impose either the death penalty or life imprisonment without providing standards or principles to guide it." For some this may be an idle contention, sown in the barren ground of interstices in the Constitution. But for others, it is a serious attempt to face up to the actual implications of current procedure (or, rather, the lack thereof) in capital trials. Should the Supreme Court grant a reversal in *Johnson* on the strength of this argument, its effects on capital punishment would be incalculable. It would not, of course, amount to judicial repeal of the death penalty, any more than the adoption of A-675 last year would have amounted to statutory repeal. But it would require either a return to mandatory death sentences or an explicit statement in capital statutes of the criteria the jury is to follow in distinguishing those cases deserving of "mercy" from those undeserving of it. It would be more than interesting to see what those criteria would be. The alternative is to allow the present haphazard jury practices, which abuse the good name of "discretion," to continue.

I have gone into substantial detail on the whole history of capital punishment in New Jersey since 1956, into the background of events in earlier years, and into an account of the origin of the two citizens' organizations in New Jersey active in these matters, because it is useful that there

[19] An "original" question, according to the N. J. Supreme Court; see *State v. Johnson*, 34 N. J. 212, 229, (1961). The U. S. Supreme Court subsequently denied jurisdiction; 82 S. Ct. 247 (1961). According to *The New York Times* of December 22, 1961, appeals in several other states are currently exploring the same question, all apparently influenced by the argument in *Johnson*. The argument in the brief is based on research by Edwin D. Wolf, in his published article, "Jury Sentencing in Capital Cases: New Jersey, 1937–1961," *Rutgers Law Review* (Fall 1964), pp. 56–64.

be a full record somewhere of these facts. Law reform, especially when it is almost entirely in the hands of the general public, as has been true of the movement to abolish capital punishment in New Jersey, is a volatile enterprise. One obvious way to reduce the inherent risks is for lawyers and the Bar Associations to play a more active role (as, for instance, the State Bar Association has done in Delaware). After all, it is lawyers more than any one else who have a professional, and thus a permanent and fundamental interest in shaping the path of the law. The public is not well served when it feels (as many did in New Jersey for several years) that it must grope for that path largely by itself.

Postscript

Four developments in the months since this article was originally written deserve a brief mention. First, to the list of New Jersey newspapers which have run series on capital punishment the *Newark Star-Ledger* may now be added; see the issues for the week of June 3–10, 1962. Second, the New Jersey Citizens Against the Death Penalty has suffered the loss of its energetic director, Steven Sieverts, whose career has taken him out of the state. Coming at a time when the organization has paid out all its resources in the form of expenses, this loss has placed the future of the group in considerable doubt. Third, on July 3, 1962, Fred Sturtivant was executed by the State of New Jersey, one month less than six years after the last previous execution, and with this the informal moratorium on the death penalty has come to an end. Lastly, SJR-3, a bill to provide a study commission on capital punishment, was passed on May 5, 1964. The report of the Commission, filed six months later, showed a majority of the members in favor of retaining the death penalty without any important modifications in the present law.

PAROLE OF CAPITAL OFFENDERS, RECIDIVISM, AND LIFE IMPRISONMENT

There are, unquestionably, cases where convicts and ex-convicts have committed capital crimes. "A report by the

Pennsylvania Board of Parole concerning parole violations
from June 1, 1946 to May 31, 1956, in that State . . .
indicates that of sixty-four parolees convicted of homicide,
five committed another homicide. One of these was first
degree murder. During this same period of time, forty-four
homicides were committed by parolees who had previously
been convicted of other offenses."[1] The vast majority of
such cases, however, as in this instance, are cases of ordinary recidivism; that is, these homicides are not committed
by ex-convicts whose original conviction was for homicide.
Only five of the forty-nine Pennsylvania homicides fell into
this category. If we confine our attention, then, only to
those cases where both the original and the subsequent
conviction is for homicide, it still must be admitted that
crimes of this sort do occur. There are even cases of first
degree murder by convicts (either in prison or escaped)
or ex-convicts who were under a life sentence for a previous murder. In Michigan, capital punishment was almost
restored in 1931 after "Gypsy" Bob Harper, originally
convicted of murder, escaped and killed two persons and
then, after recapture, killed the prison warden and his
deputy.[2] In 1936, J. Edgar Hoover cited the case of
"a prisoner in Florida [who] committed two murders,
received clemency for each, then committed a double murder to show how much he was reformed."[3] In the summer
of 1960, Frederick Wood, paroled only a month after
serving seventeen years of a twenty-year sentence for second degree murder, killed a man in a New York hotel
room and confessed to four other killings as well.[4] Every
metropolitan police department and every state parole
board probably has similar cases in its files.

Such crimes raise two main questions that must be an-

[1] Massachusetts, *Report on the Death Penalty* (1958), pp.
31–32.

[2] Michigan State Bar Association, Committee on Capital Punishment, "Report," *Michigan State Bar Journal* (November
1928), pp. *283–284*.

[3] Quoted in Julia Johnson (ed.), *Capital Punishment* (1939),
p. 64.

[4] See *The New York Times,* July 6, 1960, p. 1, and July 7,
p. 22.

swered if their significance for the issue of capital punishment is to be rationally appraised. How often do such crimes occur? (or, how likely is it that any particular murderer would sometime later in his life kill again?) How much importance should we attach to guaranteeing that crimes of this sort shall not happen? Only the first question permits a scientific answer, and the following paragraphs attempt to sketch such an answer to it.

Despite the wealth of anecdotes which suggest that such crimes flourish, their frequency is surprisingly low. Whether it would be higher if all the capital offenders so far executed had been given prison sentences instead is doubtful. The general position of American penologists on the matter of pardoning (or paroling) murderers was stated succinctly a decade ago by the retired Director of the Federal Bureau of Prisons, Sanford Bates, when he informed the Royal Commission on Capital Punishment: "Cases of murder committed by persons pardoned from the death penalty are rare if not almost unknown."[5] This is almost as true of all murderers, whether sentenced to death and commuted by the governor or sentenced to life imprisonment by the jury, and whether kept in prison or released, as the following records show.

California. Between 1945 and 1954, 342 first degree murderers were released on parole; thirty-seven were declared violators during this period, including one who committed second degree murder and one who committed assault with intent to murder. No other group of parolees had nearly as low a recidivist rate.[6] A more recent report from California indicates that between 1945 and 1960, five persons on parole from a life sentence for murder were returned to prison after conviction for some form of criminal homicide.[7]

Connecticut. Between 1947 and 1960, sixty first and

[5] Great Britain, Royal Commission on Capital Punishment, *Report* (1953), p. 489.

[6] California, *Assembly Report on the Death Penalty* (1957), pp. 12–13.

[7] California, *Senate Report on the Death Penalty* (1960), p. 109.

second degree murderers serving life sentences were paroled, after serving an average of over fifteen years in
prison. The group included five whose death sentences had
been commuted to imprisonment. Seven were returned to
prison during this period, some for a crime of violence,
none for another homicide.[8]

Maryland. Between 1936 and 1961, 225 persons were
sentenced to life imprisonment for first degree murder (and
fifty-nine for rape). Of these, thirty-seven were paroled
during that period (plus four of those convicted for rape),
after serving an average prison term of sixteen years. Nine
of these murderers (and two of the rapists) violated their
parole, two by a crime of assault (plus one convicted on
two counts of assault to rape), but none for another
homicide.[9]

Massachusetts. Between 1900 and 1958, out of 101
convictions for first degree murder, thirty-five persons received life sentences of which ten were released after serving an average of twenty-two years. Two were returned to
prison during this period "for indiscreet behavior," none
for a crime of violence.[10]

Michigan. Between 1938 and 1959, 164 first degree
murderers have been paroled. Four were returned during
this period, one for a felony (not homicide).[11] Another
report, for the years 1937 to 1951, states that of sixty-eight
first degree murderers paroled after serving an average of
over twenty-two years, two violated their parole during
this period though neither committed another homicide.[12]

Ohio. Between 1945 and 1960, 169 first degree murderers have been paroled after serving an average of
twenty-three years. Ten have been returned during this

[8] Richard Donnelly and Carroll Brewster, "Capital Punishment in Connecticut," *Connecticut Bar Journal* (March 1961),
pp. 50–51.

[9] Maryland, *Report on Capital Punishment* (1962), p. 15.

[10] Massachusetts, *op. cit.,* p. 29, and cf. pp. 118–120.

[11] Ohio, *Report on Capital Punishment* (1961), p. 82.

[12] Arthur Wood, "The Alternatives to the Death Penalty,"
The Annals (November 1952), p. 71.

period, two for the commission of a felony, in neither case another homicide.[13]

New York. Between 1950 and 1959, 357 murderers were paroled. One committed another murder.[14] Another report, for the period 1943 to 1960, states that thirty-six "lifers" were paroled, most of whom originally had a death sentence. Two were returned during this period, one on a non-murder felony charge.[15] Still another New York report, for the years 1943 to 1958, concerning the twenty-three murderers released directly through the Governor's use of his clemency powers, states that only one has been returned during this period, for a minor parole violation.[16]

Rhode Island. Between 1915 and 1958, nineteen murderers were paroled. Two violated parole during this period, but neither committed another "capital" offense.[17]

In these eight states, cited here only because of the availability of their parole data, we find that of some 1,158 murderers paroled, six committed another murder and nine others committed a crime of personal violence short of murder, or a felony. The record of success shown by the two abolition states (Michigan and Rhode Island) is certainly equal to that of the six states which retain the death penalty. Indeed, of the eight states, California is the only one with several cases where a murderer was released and killed again. Notice, too, how long on the average were the prison sentences served by these men before their release.[18]

---

[13] Ohio, *op. cit.*, pp. 81–82.

[14] Gertrude Samuels, "Parole—The Issue and the Promise," *New York Times Magazine* (September 18, 1960), reprinted in McClellan (ed.), *Capital Punishment,* p. 158.

[15] Ohio, *op. cit.*, p. 82.

[16] Averell Harriman, "Mercy Is a Lonely Business," *Saturday Evening Post* (March 22, 1958), p. 84.

[17] Massachusetts, *op. cit.*, p. 32.

[18] A survey of some 197 convicts from twenty-two states paroled from a "capital" offense showed that these persons had served an average prison term of twenty-one years. Twenty-three, or twelve per cent, were involved in parole violation: seven infringed the parole rules, five absconded, and eleven perpetrated a new offense. No information was given as to whether any of these new offenses included any homicides or crimes

If we turn to the question of how safe it is to incarcerate a convicted murderer, our data is far less complete, though the inference seems to be that such men, with very few exceptions, can be safely incarcerated without danger to prison guards or to other inmates. According to research conducted by Professor Albert Morris, criminologist at Boston University,

> . . . of 121 assaults with intent to kill, committed in the penal institutions of twenty-seven of our states between 1940 and 1949 inclusive, none were committed by prisoners sentenced to be executed for murder whose sentences had been commuted to life imprisonment; ten were committed by prisoners committed to life imprisonment for murder; and 111 were committed by prisoners for other offenses . . . It is of some interest also to note that four out of the six states which do [not] have capital punishment for murder were among those having no assaults with intention to kill during this ten year period.[19]

These figures show that one-third of the abolition states during this period had assaults by prisoners with intent to kill; but during the same period, well over half of the death penalty states also had such assaults. The figures do not indicate, however, whether there was any difference between abolition and death penalty states in the ratio of life term prisoners who committed such assaults to those who did not.

It is easy to create some doubts about the value of these statistics. They are incomplete, as they cover only a few of the states incarcerating and paroling capital offenders. Other states may have a much less favorable record. Even for the eight states whose parole records have been reported, not all the paroled murderers are covered in the reports, nor are all the years for each parolee between

---

against the person. See G. I. Giardini and R. G. Farrow, "The Paroling of Capital Offenders," *The Annals* (November 1952), pp. 90–91. See also Pennsylvania, *Report on Capital Punishment* (1961), pp. 13, 19.

[19] Massachusetts, *op. cit.*, pp. 21–22.

his release and his death surveyed. Any one of the hundreds of released murderers mentioned above may kill again at any time. We cannot be certain that serious parole violations have not already occurred without detection. It is also possible that if none of these ex-convicts has committed a second homicide, at least, in the death penalty states, it is because they have been effectively deterred by the death penalty. Having escaped it once, they are not anxious to bet their lives again.

Should we give much credence to these speculations? We must avoid the error here, as at so many other places, of impugning what we do know concerning the successful incarceration and parole of hundreds of capital offenders by mere possibilities which we can easily imagine but for which there is no evidence. There is evidence that abolition states have a safety record for murderers in prison and on parole equal to that of death penalty states. There is evidence that if a parolee doesn't commit a crime of violence within the first few months or years after his release, he is very unlikely to do so later. The confidence with which so many wardens and even governors use the services of convicted murderers in running their households, graphically illustrated recently in the book by Governor Michael DiSalle of Ohio,[20] suggests the soundness of these generalizations. The fundamental fact is that thousands of convicted murderers are safely incarcerated in prisons and that others are being released every day without endangering the public.

At the present time, the opportunity for parole of life term prisoners is far from uniform across the nation. One gets the impression from some authorities that every state in the nation does permit parole of these prisoners if in the judgment of the state parole board the man can be safely released. But this is incorrect. In California, a commuted death sentence often results in a life sentence "without possibility of parole," and release for anyone under this sentence is possible only if his sentence is again com-

[20] Michael DiSalle, *The Power of Life or Death* (1965).

muted, this time to an ordinary "life" term.[21] In Minnesota, which has no death penalty, a life term prisoner
can be released only after twenty-five years of his term
has been served (though with good conduct time this can
be lowered to seventeen years). But if he has a previous
felony conviction, this adds a minimum of another seven
years. Prior to 1951, the Minnesota parole law was so
stringent that only two lifers, on an average, were paroled
each decade.[22] According to a recent survey of parole
and release procedures, there are thirteen states (Arizona,
Arkansas, Indiana, Iowa, Louisiana, Massachusetts, Nebraska, New Hampshire, New York, Ohio, Oklahoma,
Pennsylvania, Wyoming) in which "some or all life prisoners appear ineligible for parole."[23] Thus, the chance for
a man to be paroled in these states bears no relation to
what he now is and what his prospects are for the future;
it is determined solely by his past.

As an example of the waste in human values that such
harsh prison terms yield, Giles Playfair pointed to the case
in Minnesota State Prison of Joseph Redenbaugh, who in
1956 had already served thirty-nine years of a life-plus-
thirty-years sentence. Playfair commented:

> . . . if reform was the chief aim of the penal system
> in the abolition state of Minnesota, or even a sub-
> sidiary aim, this, in Redenbaugh's case, was a mock-
> ery. He had done two murders of the kind which only
> "mad dogs" commit; of the kind which a quickly
> aroused public wishes to see avenged, irrespective of
> the perpetrator's age or mental state or degree of
> responsibility. Accordingly, the sentence that had been
> passed on young Redenbaugh was purely retributive
> in purpose. It meant that, regardless of what he might
> strive to become or succeed in becoming, regardless

[21] See "Criminal Law—Commutation of Sentence," *Southern
California Law Review* (December 1952).

[22] Douglas Rigg, "The Penalty Worse Than Death," *Saturday Evening Post* (August 31, 1957), reprinted in McClellan
(ed.), *op. cit.*, pp. 151–152.

[23] American Law Institute, *Model Penal Code, Tentative
Draft No. 9* (1959), p. 131.

of what he was, he would continue to be punished, year after year after year, for what he had been.[24]

Warden Rigg, in whose prison at Stillwater, Minnesota, Redenbaugh is held, has himself cited this case as an outstanding example of the hardships actually worked by rigid penal statutes, which make a mockery of the whole philosophy of rehabilitation and parole.

Such examples are by no means rare. What they prove is clear. If literal life imprisonment is required for any convict, out of concern for the public safety, it is certainly wisest that the determination of who shall serve such a sentence should not rest in the hands of a judge or a jury, which determines his guilt shortly after the crime, but should be in the hands of the parole or pardon board which supervises him once he is behind bars. The Model Penal Code of the American Law Institute recommends that all major crimes ("felonies of the first degree") should be punished with a maximum sentence of life and a minimum from one to ten years.[25] This is a complete rejection of the idea that a judge or a jury should have the authority to impose a life sentence on anyone.

If the only alternative to capital punishment were life imprisonment without possibility of parole, indeed, without the strong likelihood of release from prison after some years, except in a few cases, it is far from clear that abolition of the death penalty should be greeted as much of an improvement. Joseph Redenbaugh himself once wrote:

> Based on inquiries made in this prison, I am inclined to believe that few prisoners would object to capital punishment if they knew there was absolutely no chance of their ever being released.[26]

This, of course, is no argument for capital punishment, since if it is retained solely on this basis, it is not being used simply as a punishment. Instead, it has become an

[24] Giles Playfair and Derrick Sington, *The Offenders* (1957), pp. 104–105.
[25] American Law Institute, *op. cit.*, pp. 79–80.
[26] Playfair and Sington, *op. cit.*, pp. 140–141.

alleviation of punishment, a form of mercy killing. The only possible reason for adopting a system of rigid life sentences without parole as the alternative to the death penalty is that the public is generally unaware of the success with which capital offenders can be paroled, or else that the public is allowed to believe that the purpose of the penal system is blind retribution. Even if some few convicts must remain behind bars for life, no one can say for certain who they will be until after many years have passed.

It remains indisputable that some men have avoided a death sentence with tragic consequences to society. Probably as bad a case as one could find is that of Joseph Taborsky in Connecticut. Taborsky, with a criminal record from early youth, was sentenced to death for murder in 1951. He protested his innocence and, in 1955, obtained a new trial, when the courts held that the chief prosecution witness, Taborsky's own brother, was incompetent to give evidence by reason of his insanity. Without this witness available, the prosecution had to drop the case, and Taborsky was released from Death Row, a free man. He returned almost immediately to his old ways, and after terrorizing the Connecticut countryside for several days in 1957, he was taken into custody on a charge of murder. Found guilty again and again sentenced to death, he was electrocuted in May 1960. Shortly before his execution, he confessed that he had committed the 1951 murder as well.[27]

Taborsky was not a parolee and his death sentence was not commuted by the governor but was voided by the courts, and for no frivolous reason. Nothing short of radical changes in the rules of criminal procedure could have prevented his release. The possibility, though not the likelihood, of another such horrible sequence of events as happened in this case remains. But commutation of death sentences and parole of capital offenders should not get a black eye from the Taborsky episode. Cases such as his draw attention to the danger, which no one denies, of re-

[27] Ruth Reynolds, "The Murderer Who Wanted No Leniency," *New York Sunday News* (June 12, 1960), pp. 124–125.

leasing certain persons not ready for parole. But this is not an argument for capital punishment. There is no correlation between the type of crime committed by a person and the chances of his being safely incarcerated and later paroled. Therefore, if the purpose of punishment is the protection of society with a minimum of restraint and severity against those who have proved to be a public menace, there is no sense in stipulating that certain kinds of crimes shall be punishable by death.

Chapter Eight

CRIMINAL JUSTICE: THE GENERAL ASPECTS

INTRODUCTION

The distance between the commission of a capital crime and the legal execution of the criminal is bridged by the institutions that administer criminal justice.[1] The usual sequence is as follows: a capital crime is reported, an accused is brought into custody; he is interrogated and arraigned before a grand jury or magistrate, tried by judge and jury, convicted and sentenced to death, and the execution date is set by the judge; the conviction is appealed to the state Supreme Court (appeal denied), a new execution date is set, a hearing for executive clemency is held (clemency denied), and the final date of execution is set; the convict is executed. Very often, however, this last stage is never reached. We have already seen statistics that show that during the past decade, only one in one hundred homicides and one in ten murders resulted in an execution. In 1955 in California, for instance, some 417 non-negligent homicides were reported; these crimes led to the indictment for murder of 234 persons; these indictments resulted in

[1] On this topic in general, see Lester Orfield, *Criminal Procedure from Arrest to Appeal* (1940), Ernst Puttkammer, *Administration of Criminal Law* (1953), and Marshall Houts, *From Arrest to Release* (1958).

fifty-two convictions of first degree murder; but only eight persons were sentenced to death.[2] In the same state, between 1942 and 1956, 180 death sentences resulted in 119 executions: twenty-five were reversed on appeal, eleven were commuted to a lesser sentence by the Governor, six committed suicide, one was declared insane, one was killed in an attempted escape, one died awaiting execution, and the fate of eight had yet to be finally determined.[3]

What effect does the final stage of the process—the execution itself—have on the several proceedings up to that point? How does it affect selection of the jury, and the care given to reviewing the conviction when (and if) it is appealed to a higher court? What are the criminals like around whom the process revolves? What determines whether they will be nol prossed (not prosecuted, *nolle prosequi*), or permitted to plead *non vult* or *nolo contendere* before a judge (no defense, tantamount to a plea of guilty), or be taken before a jury on trial for life? What determines whether a person will be found guilty of something less than first degree murder if he is accused of killing someone? Or if found guilty, not sentenced to death but to life imprisonment? Or if sentenced to death, granted executive clemency and a commutation of sentence? Or granted an acquittal or a new trial by a higher court? These are some of the questions that need to be answered, and what evidence is available will be presented in this and the next chapter.[4]

Once a capital crime has been committed and someone

[2] California, *Assembly Report on the Death Penalty* (1957), p. 9.

[3] Note, "Post-Conviction Remedies in California Death Penalty Cases," *Stanford Law Review* (December 1958), p. 99. Cf. California, *Senate Report on the Death Penalty* (1960), p. 12.

[4] Considerable legal and criminological research remains to be done on every aspect of these questions. Literature has been cited elsewhere in this book on the problems in the law of sentencing discretion in capital cases and on the sociology of delays in execution of death sentences. On the executive power to commute death sentences and the procedure therein, see Austin Scott, "The Pardoning Power," *The Annals* (November 1952), and Thomas Yager, "Executive Clemency," *California State Bar Journal* (May–June 1958).

apprehended and arraigned, the spectre that constantly haunts the judicial process in every further step toward the electric chair or gas chamber is the possibility of executing the wrong person, or of executing the right person but for the wrong reason (someone whose guilt has mitigating features, or someone not criminally responsible—which is all that "insane" legally implies—or someone deprived of a fair trial). All these possibilities create genuine risks. Heading the list is the error of convicting an innocent man and sentencing him to death. I have included below a compilation of such cases, and they constitute a sobering array. It is well to realize that the hanging of innocent men is said to have led to the abolition of the death penalty during the last century in Wisconsin, Rhode Island and Maine.[5]

Unjust death sentences, in the sense of a death sentence resulting from an unfair trial, are not unusual. Nor are they happily a thing of the past. Between 1936 and 1961, the United States Supreme Court reversed convictions in sixteen capital cases, solely on grounds of coerced confessions.[6] For these excesses, the police are largely responsible. But withholding evidence from the defense, subornation to perjury, and inflammatory practices by overzealous prosecutors, though they seldom constitute grounds for a reversal by a higher court, do occur and are attributable directly to the practices of too many district attorneys. In addition to the police and the prosecution, there is the effect of the frequent "trial by newspaper," which transpires before the case ever reaches the jury. The incapacity of American newspapers to exercise self-restraint in reporting details of sensational murder cases has led many reflective jurists, most notably, Mr. Justice Felix Frankfurter, to wish an end to the death penalty if for no other

[5] On Wisconsin, see Wisconsin, *Capital Punishment in the States* (1962), p. 2; on Rhode Island, see Lamar Beman (ed.), *Selected Articles on Capital Punishment* (1925), pp. 355–356; on Maine, see the letter of March 20, 1958 by the then Governor Edmund S. Muskie of Maine, in Society of Friends, *Materials: New Jersey Assembly Bills 33 and 34* (1958).

[6] U. S. Commission on Civil Rights, *Justice* (1961), pp. 256–262.

reason than to prevent our free press from upsetting fair judicial procedure in murder trials.[7]

A further obstacle in the pursuit of justice under the shadow of the death penalty is the vexing problem of determining whether the accused is sane: sane enough to stand trial, sane enough at the time of the crime to be found guilty, and sane enough at the time of execution to be put to death. Despite this three-fold assessment of sanity, there is ample evidence to show that many of those legally executed each year in the United States are sufficiently sick that had they come to the attention of the proper authorities before they committed a capital crime, they undoubtedly would have been diagnosed as in need of institutionalization and treatment. A study of all the one hundred persons executed in California between 1938 and 1953 turned up case after case of mental defectiveness, amnesia, chronic alcoholism, psychoneurosis, hysteria, brain damage, even psychosis.[8] The public ought to know that a very large number of the persons actually executed fall into this category, and that these persons are as incapable of preventing their criminal acts as the normal person would be of deliberately committing similar acts himself.

It is, of course, not necessary that moral responsibility,

[7] See Felix Frankfurter, "The Problem of Capital Punishment," in his *Of Law and Men* (1956), pp. 81, 84; also Irvin v. Doud, 366 U. S. 717 (1961).

[8] Robert M. Carter, *Capital Punishment in California* (1953), abstracted in California, *Assembly Report on the Death Penalty* (1957), pp. 16–21. See also the cases of Solesbee v. Balkcom, 339 U. S. 9 (1950), and Caritativo v. Dickson, 357 U. S. 549 (1958). Valuable discussions showing the relation of the death penalty to the law of insanity will be found in Stanley Cobb, "The Death Penalty," *American Journal of Psychiatry* (December 1958); Philip Roche, "Dr. Woodhouse Meets Daniel McNaghten," *Pennsylvania Bar Association Quarterly* (March 1958); and Frederick Wiseman, "Psychiatry and Law," *American Journal of Psychiatry* (October 1961). The law on execution of the insane is discussed in Solesbee v. Balkcom, *op. cit.*, pp. 16–32, and considerable detail on California law will be found in Geoffrey Hazard and David Louisell, "Death, the State and the Insane," *U. C. L. A. Law Review* (March 1962).

involving the capacity to control one's own conduct, be a precondition of criminal punishment; indeed, in some areas of the law where so-called "strict liability" reigns, this view has largely been abandoned. And an argument can be made for the theory that if anyone is to be executed it should be the criminally insane. But this theory is not the foundation of our present criminal law nor of our whole attitude toward mental illness. Yet if people are to be executed irrespective of their capacity to control their own behavior, then the public ought to face that policy decision for what it is. All these points, and more besides, in the administration of criminal justice are discussed with a plenitude of illustration in this chapter by Herbert B. Ehrmann (and in the next chapter by Mrs. Sara R. Ehrmann).

The presence of the death penalty in America today seems to have primarily two results for the administration of the criminal law. First, capital punishment makes the whole process unnecessarily wasteful of time and money. Starting with the selection of the trial jury, the capital trial is notoriously a long drawn out affair. Although the subject still awaits thorough research, it appears that in many states with the death penalty, it is exceedingly difficult to get a trial jury impanelled for a murder case, and then almost impossible to get the jury to award a death sentence even when there is no doubt that the defendant is guilty. For instance, several of the most brutal murders in New Jersey during the past decade resulted in the court accepting either a plea of *nolo contendere* because a jury simply could not be impanelled, or a life sentence despite the prosecutor's urging in the strongest language for the death penalty.[9]

Second, although the number of persons executed annually continues to decline, the number under sentence of death increases slightly each year, as does the average length of time spent under sentence of death. The "Executions" bulletins of *National Prisoner Statistics* show that

[9] See State v. Wolak (Passaic County, 1959), State v. Driver (Mercer County, 1961), State v. Siegel (Monmouth County, 1961), and State v. Maxey and Parks (Union County, 1961).

the prisoners under sentence of death at the end of 1959 numbered 190, and that they increased to 210 at the end of 1960, to 257 at the end of 1961, and to 267 at the end of 1962. This same source shows that of the 113 condemned men dispatched from the courts to the prisons during 1960, only nine were executed that year; and although during 1961 a total of 136 men were sentenced to death, again only nine of them had been executed by the end of the year. During 1962, when ninety-nine persons were received under sentence of death, only six had been executed by January 1, 1963. These delays in carrying out the death sentence very largely result from the growing practice of appealing every death sentence to some higher court. Critics have been quick to complain that "the great majority of the petitions filed [in appeal of a death sentence] are frivolous and instituted solely for the purpose of delay."[10] But it is obvious from the number of reversals that many appeals have merit; and the courts cannot weed out the frivolous appeals from the meritorious without examining them all. Capital punishment without the right of appeal to higher courts, though it was once the rule, cannot now be seriously proposed. Yet capital punishment with appeal is often a seemingly endless process of litigation.

Certainly, a striking feature of the present system is the glaring inequality with which the death sentence is awarded and carried out. The whole pattern of treatment of capital convictions by the higher courts seems devoid of rhyme or reason. Thus, a man proven guilty is saved from execution by the striking ingenuity of his counsel on appeal to the Supreme Court (Green v. U. S., 355 U. S. 184 [1957]). But another man goes to his death purely because his attorney neglected to raise a point of procedure at the trial, thereby barring the higher courts from touching the issue (Williams v. Georgia, 349 U. S. 375 [1955]). One man is literally taken from the electric chair, after his

---

[10] *Stanford Law Review*, loc. cit., p. 100. In general, see Donald M. McIntyre, *Delays in the Execution of Death Sentences* (1960).

counsel had the good luck to find a Supreme Court Justice who would issue a temporary stay of execution; upon re-hearing, the conviction was reversed (Vernon v. Alabama, 313 U. S. 547 [1941]). But another man is executed be-cause the notice of stay of execution arrived seconds too late to halt the flow of lethal gas into the execution cham-ber (People v. Abbott, 47 C.2d 362 [1956]). This is the sort of luck-of-the-draw justice actually dispensed in capi-tal cases by the highest courts in the land, as though human lives were nowhere in the balance, and as though no better system were conceivable or feasible.[11]

These irrationalities do not end when the courts have washed their hands of a capital case. The studies, reprinted below, by Elmer Johnson and by Marvin Wolfgang and his associates, show that executive clemency is also influenced by several irrational factors. Among them is racial preju-dice. Nor is there much to choose in this regard, it would seem, between southern and northern states.

The degree of racial prejudice in the disposition of capi-tal cases is difficult to determine. It is hardly surprising that executive clemency in capital cases falls less frequently on non-whites than on whites, and that more non-whites than whites are sentenced to death in the first place. But these facts are not necessarily a consequence of racial prejudice, as the following parallel shows. One of the con-tentions of abolitionists in this country, popularized by the late Warden Lawes, is that "only the poor, the friendless and the foreign-born" are sentenced to death and executed. As a description of the class of persons executed, this is probably fairly accurate (though, with the virtual curtail-ment of immigration, the place of the foreign-born has been taken by native non-whites). But if it is meant to imply deliberate discrimination by trial courts, appellate courts and boards of pardons, it remains unproved. The vast majority of all prisoners throughout our country's his-tory probably have been the poor, the friendless and the foreign-born (or non-white). It has yet to be shown that

[11] Several of the cases cited above are discussed in detail in Barrett Prettyman, Jr., *Death and the Supreme Court* (1961).

murderers or prisoners under death sentence differ significantly in these respects from other criminals.[12]

For many decades, there has been ample evidence that Negroes in this country commit three to six times more crimes than their population ratio to whites would lead one to expect.[13] To be sure, given the kind of subculture in which Negroes are forced to live in the United States, there is every reason to expect that the volume of crime Negroes commit ought to be far in excess of their proportion of the total population. Otherwise, crimes of violence would not fit into the kind of sociological frustration-aggression pattern that they seem to. One would therefore expect to find that Negro convicts have a comparably higher ratio than white convicts of all kinds of severe prison sentences, including death penalties.

It may be, of course, that a study of criminal, penal, and parole statistics for all criminals would show that abolitionists are right after all, and that the disposition of Negroes and whites convicted of murder and sentenced to death shows that the Negro convict receives an unusually high ratio of severe treatment. If this were established, the most natural way to explain it would be in terms of racial prejudice. No such statistical investigation has yet been undertaken, but there are two features of capital punishment in certain areas which do strongly suggest that its administration is affected by racial prejudice. Not until recently have Negroes even been allowed to serve on criminal juries in many states.[14] It almost goes without saying that a racially-mixed jury would have had a harder time bringing in a death sentence against a Negro defendant in

[12] See the discussion in California, *Senate Report on the Death Penalty* (1960), p. 106.

[13] See Thorsten Sellin, "The Negro Criminal," *The Annals* (November 1928); Hans von Hentig, "The Criminality of the Negro," *Journal of Criminal Law, Criminology and Police Science* (January–February 1940); Guy Johnson, "The Negro and Crime," *The Annals* (September 1941); and Herbert Block and Gilbert Geis, *Man, Crime and Society* (1962), pp. 262–263.

[14] See U. S. Commission on Civil Rights, *op. cit.*, pp. 89–103.

at least some cases than did the all-white jury.[15] Also, as *National Prisoner Statistics* shows, of the nineteen jurisdictions that have executed men for rape since 1930, a third of them have executed only Negroes. In these six states, the very existence of rape as a crime with an optional death penalty is, in the light of the way it has been used, strong evidence of an original intent to discriminate against non-whites. This was probably the purpose behind the decision in Tennessee in 1915 to abolish capital punishment for murder and treason, but to retain it for rape.

It is comforting to be told that in some communities, "on the whole, there is no significant differences with respect to the disposition of the cases of white and Negro persons accused of felonious homicide. Certainly, there is no statistical evidence of racial discrimination."[16] Despite the absence of careful investigations, however, one is left with the overall impression that racial discrimination in the United States makes the death penalty weigh more heavily, proportionally, on Negroes than on whites and that one desirable consequence of its abolition would be to lessen this inequality.

What, it may well be asked, has all this to do with the dispute between retentionists and abolitionists? No one so enthusiastically supports the death penalty that he would refuse to deplore a wrongful death sentence. Surely, retentionists as well as abolitionists are entitled to regret the increasing delays and mounting costs which result from the trial and appeal of capital cases. No defender of the death penalty needs to apologize for the "third degree," perjured testimony from prosecution witnesses, withheld evidence, nor any of the other perversions of justice documented in

[15] William Bradford Huie has argued that even an all-Negro jury in Mississippi would have sentenced "Mack" Parker to death for the rape of a white woman (he was lynched before trial). But Huie ignores the fact that in modern times in Mississippi, no Negro has served on a capital trial jury and no white man has been executed for rape. See "A Tale of Two Lynchings," reprinted in Huie, *The Hero of Iwo Jima and Other Stories* (1962), p. 152.

[16] Robert Bensing and Oliver Schroeder, Jr., *Homicide in an Urban Community* (1960), p. 56.

this and the next chapter. Consequently, many retentionists have complained that it is both irrelevant and unfair
to cite the maladministration of criminal justice as an argument for abolishing the death penalty. It is unfair, because
it implies they have no right to protest these corruptions
of justice, which is not so; and it is irrelevant, because
abolishing the death penalty would not necessarily correct
a single one of these evils. Trials might be a bit cheaper
and faster, but they would still be quite expensive and
lengthy. Not death sentences, but life sentences would be
appealed endlessly in the higher courts. The innocent and
the insane would no longer be executed; instead, they would
be sent to rot in prison for life. Accordingly, many retentionists have complained that this is a classic instance where
the right problems are attacked with the wrong remedy.

Nevertheless, Professor Edmund Cahn of New York
University Law School speaks for many when he writes
that "the inveterate fallibility of penal administration constitutes a *sufficient* reason" for ridding ourselves of the
death penalty.[17] No one can deny that capital punishment, whatever its virtues, is an expensive complication
in an already complex process, and that it aggravates every
tendency toward uneven-handed criminal justice. One must
wonder whether the electric chair, the gas chamber and
the gallows are worth the endless extra trouble they impose
on our judicial system. At the very least, these difficulties
suggest that the death penalty ought to have substantial
and uncontroversial virtues at some point, in order to com-
pensate for its demonstrable vices in the administration of
criminal justice and the constant jeopardy in which it places
our ideals.[18]

[17] Preface to Arthur Koestler, *Reflections on Hanging*
(1957), p. xix. Italics in original.
[18] Among other discussions which shed light on points raised
above, see "Criminal Law—Capital Punishment," *University of
Kansas City Law Review* (Summer 1960); Lindley McClelland,
"Conscientious Scruples Against the Death Penalty in Pennsylvania," *Pennsylvania Bar Association Quarterly* (March 1959);
Averell Harriman, "Mercy Is a Lonely Business," *Saturday Evening Post* (March 22, 1958); and Charles Larrowe, "Notches
on a Chair," *The Nation* (April 14, 1956).

THE DEATH PENALTY AND THE
ADMINISTRATION OF JUSTICE*

BY HERBERT B. EHRMANN**

Armchair criminology is among the least reliable of the social sciences. It is, however, one of the most popular. To qualify as an expert on crime one needs only to be a legislator, a lawyer, a prosecutor, or a judge. Such persons may actually be authorities in the field. Generally, however, they have had no scholastic preparation and no special experience beyond a few sporadic episodes. All too often the opinions of individuals in such positions are accorded a factitious authority merely because of the office which they hold. Unfortunately, the public does not understand the meagerness of experience and inadequacy of data on which such views are so frequently based.

Discussions concerning the death penalty have been especially confused by the voices of unqualified "authorities." For nearly a century and a half change has been delayed and the acquisition of real knowledge hampered by sonorous pronouncements of the eminent, but uninformed. When in 1810 Sir Samuel Romilly introduced a bill in Parliament to abolish capital punishment for stealing five shillings or more from a shop, it was unsupported by a single judge or magistrate.[1] Speaking for the unanimous opposition to the bill by his judicial colleagues in the House of Lords, Lord Ellenborough, Chief Justice of the King's Bench, predicted that the repeal of this law would lead to abolition of the death penalty for stealing five shillings from a dwelling house, in which case no man could "trust himself for an hour without the most alarming apprehensions that, on his return, every vestige of his property will be swept away by the hardened robber."[2]

* Reprinted, by permission of the author and publisher, from *The Annals,* vol. 284 (November 1952), pp. 73–84.
** Member of the Bar, Boston, Massachusetts, author of *The Untried Case* (1960) and co-author of *The Criminal Courts of Cleveland* (1921).

[1] *Hansard,* May 1, 1810.
[2] *Ibid.,* May 30, 1810.

These and similar laws were eventually repealed without any increase in the number of offenders in the particular class of crime. In fact, the absolute number of such offenders diminished.[3] As lawyer and judge, Lord Ellenborough was no fool. Although inclined to be harsh in criminal cases, he did much to bring the civil law into harmony with mercantile practice. He was a profound legal scholar. He knew the value of evidence. Yet, when it came to the death penalty, he felt qualified to pronounce an authoritative judgment without the aid of any evidence whatsoever other than his own emotional reflexes. His contemporaries accorded his words the respect due his high position; but history has proved that the great Lord Ellenborough, in discussing capital punishment, was talking nonsense.

The efforts to remove or modify the death penalty for the crime of murder have run a similar course. Fortunately, there has now been enough experience with abolition and curtailment to establish as a fact that the repeal of capital punishment is not followed by an increase in the number of murders, nor does its restoration result in a diminution. Whatever other purpose the death penalty may serve, it is now obvious that, in a settled community, it is not needed to protect society from murderers.

Nevertheless, even in this narrow area where data are abundant and easy to obtain, pronouncements of the Ellenborough variety continue to confuse the public. As late as 1950, the legislative halls of Massachusetts still rang with dire predictions that the passage of a bill to give juries a chance to designate life imprisonment as a penalty for murder in the first degree would result in loosing upon the people of the commonwealth a horde of savage murderers. This was at a time when thirty-eight other states and the federal government already had some form of the alternate penalty and six states had abolished capital punishment!

A similar disregard of experience frequently marks discussion of the effect of the death penalty on the administration of justice. For instance, it was claimed that the

[3] Second Report on the Criminal Law by His Majesty's Commissioners, 1836, p. 21.

giving of the power to impose the alternate penalty of life imprisonment would result in the complete disuse of capital punishment. Those making the claim seemed to think that this would be very bad indeed. In 1948 the then governor of Massachusetts vetoed the proposed bill granting juries the right to choose life imprisonment instead of death on conviction in murder cases, stating in his veto message that such a law would abolish capital punishment by "indirection"; that it pays "lip service to capital punishment" and then "effectively proceeds to destroy it."

Coming from the governor, the veto message was treated with respect;[4] but it was only another example of armchair criminology. For the ten years ending with 1946, Massachusetts, under a law making death a mandatory punishment for first degree murder, had twelve executions. For the same period, alternate-penalty states had the following record: New Jersey, with a slightly smaller population, sixteen executions; Pennsylvania, with something more than twice the population, fifty executions; and New York, with about three times the population, 118 executions. For the same period, North Carolina, a mandatory state, had 118 executions, and its neighbor, Georgia, somewhat smaller in population, under the alternate penalty, had 102.

There are too many variables—such as homicide rates, population characteristics, police efficiency, prosecution standards, jury attitudes, executive clemency—for any quantitative comparison of states within these groups, but the figures indicate clearly that capital punishment continues to flourish in states which provide the alternate penalty.

On the other hand, the residents in certain areas have, in practice, virtually abolished capital punishment in both mandatory and alternative penalty jurisdictions. Vermont, a mandatory state, has had only two executions in twenty-eight years; New Hampshire, an alternate state, has had only one execution in twenty-eight years; South Dakota, an alternate state, has had only one in the ten years since it restored the death penalty; Nebraska, an alternate state,

---

[4] Not, however, by the dean of the Harvard Law School, who commented on the fact that the message ignored available data.

has had only two in twenty-eight years.[5] In Massachusetts during a period of fifty years under the mandatory penalty, Worcester County, with a half-million population, had only two executions; Bristol, a sizable county, only one; Berkshire County, of moderate size, none; and some of the smaller counties, none. The failure to use the death penalty in certain counties of Massachusetts is dramatically shown in Table 1.

The counties named in the table have about one and a half million population, well over a third of the people in Massachusetts. A conviction rate of about sixty-four per cent of murder indictments indicates an effective administration of justice, but only three of those accused were convicted of first degree murder (requiring the death penalty), and only two were executed. Here, under a mandatory law, there was a pretty effective abolition of capital punishment.

A closely related problem is presented by the claim that the mandatory sentence of death upon a finding of guilty of murder in the first degree results in more acquittals. Some of those who express this opinion are extremely well informed penologists.[6] The reason given is that the infliction of death is so repugnant to most people that juries tend to avoid a conviction if possible. Curiously enough, proponents of the death penalty seem to confirm this tendency in a backhanded sort of way. In arguing that the danger of a miscarriage of justice is slight in a capital case, they frequently urge that the evidence must be overwhelming before a jury would vote to consign a fellow being to his death.

Convincing data on this subject are not available. We may, however, accept the reasoning and observations that

[5] Data from *Memorandum on Capital Punishment*, prepared by Thorsten Sellin for the Royal Commission on Capital Punishment, 1951, pp. 657–60.

[6] For instance, Lewis E. Lawes, former warden of Sing Sing Prison, *Man's Judgment of Death* (New York: G. P. Putnam's Sons, 1925), p. 58; Austin H. MacCormick, formerly Commissioner of Corrections, New York City, then executive director of the Osborne Association, in *Boston Sunday Herald*, December 11, 1949.

TABLE 1

CONVICTIONS ON MURDER INDICTMENTS, CERTAIN MASSACHUSETTS COUNTIES, 1925–41

County	Indictments for Murder	Convictions		Manslaughter	Executions for Murder
		1st Degree	2nd Degree		
Berkshire	11	0	5	1	0
Bristol	36	0	16	3	0
Essex	26	1	12	2	1
Hampden	27	1	12	9	1
Hampshire	8	1 (commuted)	1	4	0
Plymouth	21	0	10	4	0
Total	129	3	56	23	2

Data compiled from records in State Prison and reports of the Attorney General by Sara R. Ehrmann, executive secretary Massachusetts Council for the Abolition of the Death Penalty.

the reluctance of jurymen to convict, where death is the penalty, leads, in some cases, to acquittal. Nevertheless, one may well question the conclusion that the net over-all result is a larger percentage of acquittals. There are complicating factors working in the opposite direction. For instance, numbers of prospective jurors are frequently excused from serving in capital cases because of opposition to the death penalty. Sometimes the numbers are so great that the judges assail the veniremen for "jury dodging," and these denunciations reach the newspaper headlines.[7]

This process of weeding out jurors who will not serve because of the death penalty tends to produce an unbalanced jury. Those most likely to lean emotionally toward the defendant are eliminated. No doubt the great majority of those who remain view the death penalty with considerable distaste, but their emotional attitude is likely to be negative. Inevitably, however, on some juries there will be those who favor the use of the death penalty. These people are occasionally forcefully articulate and capable of swaying jurors with less positive attitudes. They are not counterbalanced by those most reluctant to inflict death. Thus hostility toward the death penalty may actually, in some cases, produce juries which are most likely to convict the accused.

There are other factors which work for conviction rather than acquittal in a capital case. Of all crimes, murder is most likely to produce a violent emotional public reaction, a demand for vengeance, a feeling that the perpetrator "deserves" to be put to death. Jurymen cannot help sharing this feeling. The idea that a jury "weighs" the evidence in a criminal case to decide whether the accused is guilty beyond a reasonable doubt, conveys a wrong picture of the process. In many cases it is merely a question of what evidence the jury chooses to believe. If the government's case rests largely on identification testimony and the defense is an alibi, the jury does not "weigh" one

[7] See for instance the quoted remarks of Chief Justice Higgins in the *Boston Daily Record,* November 5, 1942; those of Judge Warner in the *Boston Herald,* June 7, 1933; and those of District Attorney Foley in the *Boston Herald,* April 10, 1930.

against the other. If it believes the identification testimony, the alibi is thrown out of the scales of justice entirely, and vice versa. Where there is conflict of testimony, people tend to believe that which they would like to believe. The emotional drive to punish someone for an atrocious murder frequently plays an important part in conditioning a jury for believing the evidence which proves the guilt of the accused.

In a recent Massachusetts case the only issue was the criminal responsibility of the defendant, who had killed his wife. According to the opinion of the Supreme Judicial Court, the evidence portrayed "the sudden destruction, while in apparent good health, of one member of a harmonious and cultured household by the only other member, in a series of acts paradoxically done, it is confessed, solely in kindness to benefit the victim, yet revoltingly achieved in the grossest barbarity with the crudest of weapons."[8] Two eminent psychiatrists testified that the defendant was not criminally responsible at the time of the killing. There was no medical testimony that he was responsible. Nevertheless, the jury returned a verdict of guilty. The conclusion that the accused was sane beyond a reasonable doubt can be explained only on the ground of emotion aroused by the sheer horror of the deed itself. Although there was no error of law, the Supreme Judicial Court ordered a new trial under a statute passed in 1939 for the review of capital cases.[9] The defendant was tried a second time, found insane, and committed to a mental institution.

When prejudice is added to the emotional reactions induced by a slaying, the jury finds even greater difficulty in believing evidence offered for the accused.[10] If the jury is composed of the dominant or "in-group" and the defendant and his witnesses belong to an "out-group"—as

[8] Mr. Justice Wilkins in Commonwealth v. Cox, 1951 A. S. 857; 100 N. E. 2d 14.

[9] Mass. St. 1939, Sec. 341; G.L. (Ter. Ed.) C. 278, Sec. 33E. This case was an unusual one for Massachusetts, where, under the Briggs law, so-called, insanity is usually determined before trial. G.L. (Ter. Ed.) C. 123, Sec. 100A.

[10] See Arthur Garfield Hays, *Trial by Prejudice,* New York: Covici Friede, 1933.

they frequently do—the defendant's evidence is often discounted to zero. The jury tends to believe that foreigners, Negroes, or members of any minority group will lie for one another and "stick together" under all circumstances.

The United States Supreme Court has recognized this human failing, in holding that the exclusion of Negroes from a jury trying a Negro is a denial of equal protection of the laws.[11] Massachusetts had a case where a Chinese, arrested and tried with others for a tong killing, was convicted of murder although no witness identified him or implicated him in the affair.[12] In Kentucky it used to be said that if a Negro killed a white man it was murder, if a white man killed a Negro it was unfortunate, but if a white man killed a white man it was self-defense, unless the affray was over a woman, in which case the cause of death was apoplexy.

If to a brutal killing and prejudice there is added the element of public hostility against the accused, the jury listens to the defendant's evidence with ears that are stone-deaf. This is the combination which produces most of our *causes célèbres* subsequently believed by many to be miscarriages of justice, such as the cases of Leo Frank, Tom Mooney, and Sacco and Vanzetti. In the last-named case, the jury, after thirty-five days of trial, received the case in the afternoon and returned a verdict of guilty in the evening. According to one of the jurymen, his colleagues were ready to vote a guilty verdict immediately at the close of the case, but he forced an hour's discussion because he thought such precipitate action was improper.

Regardless of the eventual verdict, the jury could not possibly have considered the mass of testimony in favor of the defendants or weighed the improbabilities in the government's case in so brief a time. Even without the benefit

[11] Smith v. Texas, 311 U. S. 128, 61 S. Ct. 164, 85 L. Ed. 84 (1940); Pierre v. Louisiana, 306 U. S. 354, 59 S. Ct. 536, 83 L. Ed. 760 (1939); Strauder v. W. Virginia, 100 U. S. 303, 25 L. Ed. 664 (1879).

[12] Related by Wendell Murray, Esq., of the Boston Bar, called in as counsel for Wong Duck after the trial. Three of the defendants were executed, but Wong Duck was among those granted a new trial.

of the subsequent revelations which threw new doubt on the defendants' guilt, a relaxed and unprejudiced jury would have debated at great length the validity of the fleeting and even silly identifications and would not have lightly assumed that a large number of reputable Italian alibi witnesses were perjurers.

Strip the case of the then current antiradical hysteria, change the defendants into Massachusetts veterans of World War I, the identifying witnesses into Italians, and the alibi witnesses into native New Englanders, and it becomes inconceivable that the weaknesses of the prosecution and the massive evidence for the defense would have received such brief consideration by the jury.

Whether or not the mandatory death penalty results in more acquittals, there seem to be some general data indicating that it produces a smaller proportion of convictions for first degree murder and a larger proportion for second degree murder.[13] Opponents of capital punishment claim that this is due to the fact that juries shy away from the infliction of death; proponents allege that the possibility of the extreme penalty produces more pleas of guilty to murder in the second degree, for which the sentence is imprisonment. Without further and more precise research, it is impossible to draw any general conclusions. People and conditions differ. Doubtless both theories are valid, but it is not known to what extent.

How difficult it is to generalize about these questions may be seen in the contrasting experience with the death penalty of the two most populous counties in Massachusetts—Suffolk and Middlesex. These two counties are contiguous, being separated, for the most part, only by the Charles River. During the test period they were approximately the same size in population[14] (Middlesex was actually about five per cent more populous). The criminal courts han-

[13] Royal Commission on Capital Punishment, Minutes of Evidence taken before the Royal Commission on Capital Punishment, Thirtieth Day, Thursday, 1st February, 1951. Witness: Professor Thorsten Sellin. [Pp. 647–678] London: H. M. Stationery Office, 1951.

[14] The 1940 Census gave Middlesex, 958,855; Suffolk, 912,-706.

dling murder cases are presided over by judges who rotate their sittings in the various counties, so they are not indigenous to either Suffolk or Middlesex. Nevertheless, respective records of the two counties for disposing of murder cases are strangely different.

State Prison records for the years 1900 to 1949 inclusive show that twenty-three individuals were executed for murder in Middlesex, and only ten for the crime in Suffolk. More detailed reports of the Attorney General for the years 1925 to 1941 inclusive indicate that of 113 indictments for murder in Middlesex, nineteen were convicted of first degree (of whom seventeen were executed), twenty-three of second degree, and thirty of manslaughter; of those not guilty, eighteen were insane, ten received a verdict of not guilty, and thirteen were nol-prossed, meaning that the district attorney refused to prosecute. For the same period in Suffolk, three were convicted of first degree (of whom two were executed), sixteen of second degree, and twenty-four of manslaughter; of those not guilty, ten were insane, twenty-two received a verdict of not guilty, and four were nol-prossed. The approximate percentages are shown in Table 2.

The period covered by Table 2—seventeen years—and the number of cases involved are sufficient to smooth out any substantial distortions due to unusual cases. From these figures it appears that one indicted for a capital offense in Middlesex stood nearly a seventeen per cent chance of being convicted of first degree murder and a fifteen per cent chance of being executed; whereas if the murder were committed in Suffolk, he would stand only a four per cent chance of being so convicted, and only a 2.5 per cent chance of being executed. Those guilty of second degree murder, whether by plea or after trial, were approximately the same in percentage in both counties, as were those guilty of manslaughter. The accused had three times the chance of being acquitted after trial in Suffolk that he would have had in Middlesex, but in the latter county the district attorneys may have nol-prossed weak cases more freely than their opposite numbers in Suffolk.

Explanations may be offered for these startling differ-

TABLE 2
DISPOSITION OF CAPITAL CASES MIDDLESEX AND SUFFOLK
COUNTIES, MASSACHUSETTS 1925–41
By Percentage of All Cases

MIDDLESEX COUNTY

Convicted

First degree	16.8
Executed	15.0
Second degree	20.4
Manslaughter	26.4
Total	64.0

Not convicted

Not guilty	9.0
Nol-prossed	11.4
Not guilty and nol-prossed	20.4
Insane (not tried)	16.0
Total	36.0

SUFFOLK COUNTY

Convicted

First degree	3.9
Executed	2.55
Second degree	20.2
Manslaughter	30.4
Total	54.0

Not convicted

Not guilty	27.8
Nol-prossed	5.0
Not guilty and nol-prossed	32.8
Insane (not tried)	12.65
Total	46.0

Compiled from data collected by Sara R. Ehrmann.

ences. Suffolk contains a larger percentage of more recent immigration; its racial, religious, and ethnic proportions of population vary substantially from those in Middlesex; its residents, on the whole, are on a lower economic level; they are less suburbanite; there is a tradition of "hanging" prosecutors in Middlesex. The very nature of these explanations, however, indicates the complexity of the problem. If citizens of the same state, living in adjoining counties, operating under the same administration of justice, differ so drastically in their attitude toward the death penalty, how is it possible to generalize for an entire state or nation?

Again, it is claimed that fewer trials are required in abolition states because obviously guilty defendants are more likely to plead guilty where they do not have to battle for their lives. There are, indeed, some instances where this appears to be the fact. On the other hand, there are those who claim that it is harder to secure pleas of guilty in abolition states because the prosecutor has less inducement to offer the guilty defendant. The answer necessarily depends upon the attitude of prosecutors in a death penalty state. If, for instance, the prosecutor insists on first degree with death as the penalty, the accused has nothing to lose by trial; if the prosecutor is willing to trade for a plea of guilty in the second degree, the defendant has much to gain by not risking a trial. How do we know, however, what prosecutors will do?

The application of armchair psychology to forecast the conduct of prosecutors—or any other public authority— is no easier than the Ellenborough method of predicting the reaction of criminals. For instance, as early as 1900, Hosea M. Knowlton, then attorney general of Massachusetts, recommended the commutation of the death sentence of a seventeen-year-old murderer whose crime was particularly vicious, on the ground that Massachusetts public sentiment would not tolerate the execution of so young a boy.

In 1942, after forty years' development in the field of handling juvenile delinquency, another Massachusetts prosecutor insisted on the death penalty for a seventeen-year-old offender despite the suggestion of the judge that the case was a proper one for a plea of guilty to murder in the second degree. The boy's previous record had been good, and there was a conflict of medical testimony as to whether the cause of the victim's death was the wound or a heart ailment, since the victim lived for seven weeks and his injuries had apparently healed. Nevertheless, the lad was allowed by the governor to be electrocuted, with the assent of the parole board acting in an advisory capacity.

A few years later, in another case involving a seventeen-year-old boy, another Massachusetts judge took the initiative and accepted a plea of guilty to second degree on the ground that no Massachusetts governor would ever allow so youthful an offender to be electrocuted!

A very conscientious district attorney will sometimes secure a conviction which the facts require, in the belief that the governor will take care of mitigation. Such a case was *Commonwealth v. Desatnick*,[15] where the father of an illegitimate child, plagued by accusing parents and a religious sense of guilt, murdered the infant. Instead of commuting, however, the governor sent for clerics of the defendant's faith and asked them whether illegitimacy was a more serious offense than murder. On the basis of the obvious answer, the young man was electrocuted. Within a short time, however, another Massachusetts district attorney, regarded by many as more hard-boiled than the one who prosecuted Desatnick, nol-prossed the case of a mother who had abandoned her illegitimate child to die, on the ground that, although the crime would ordinarily be murder, "society needs no penalty for this, unfortunate as it is."

These instances are sufficient to indicate the futility of generalizing on insufficient data. Research alone, in a wide area and covering a period of years, could establish what prosecutors tend to do in the death penalty states by way of accepting pleas of guilty to second degree murder.

Degrees of murder present such a confusing problem that they create a further obstacle to predictability in the administration of criminal justice. In states where capital punishment has been abolished, the situation is not too serious. An intelligent parole board may ultimately adjust any gross errors in the jury's verdict or in the pleas. But where the penalty is death, a confused jury may eternalize its mistakes.

The principal variety of "first degree" murder is generally defined as including "malice aforethought," and involves "premeditation" and "deliberation." However, judi-

15 262 Mass. 408 (1928).

cially defined "malice" does not necessarily involve malice against the victim in the ordinary dictionary sense. Moreover, the courts have explained "deliberation" and "premeditation" in such a way that these words also have lost their usual meaning. Under judicial definition, "premeditation" and "deliberation" can both occur within a few seconds of the killing itself. In the now rather celebrated case of *Fisher v. United States*,[16] a Negro of low-grade intelligence, suddenly feeling that he was insulted by his victim, struck her, and then killed her "to stop her from hollering." The jury by its verdict found deliberation and premeditation, essential to first degree murder.

Mr. Justice Frankfurter, in his dissenting opinion in the United States Supreme Court, referred to the judge's charge on the subject as the "dark emptiness of legal jargon." According to Mr. Justice Frankfurter, the insult "pulled the trigger of Fisher's emotions." We shall never know how many defendants have been hanged or electrocuted for a "deliberate" and "premeditated" killing where some unexpected incident "pulled the trigger" of the accused's emotions.

"Is it possible," asked Sir Ernest Gowers of Mr. Justice Frankfurter at hearings held by the Royal Commission on Capital Punishment in 1950, "to express premeditation clearly and logically without mumbo-jumbo entering into it?" Mr. Justice Frankfurter thought that it was possible, but conceded that "the charges given by trial judges in the United States are often not very helpful." The Royal Commission appeared to think this observation to be an understatement.[17]

Another type of first degree murder is usually defined as a homicide occurring in the act of committing a serious felony. Here again the situation may be far from clear. If the jury believes that the accused, at the time of the killing, had given up all intention of committing the felony, and killed the victim because of fear for his own safety, the crime is not first degree murder. In a close case, how is the

16 328 U. S. 463, 66 S. Ct. 1318, 90 L. Ed. 1382 (1946).
17 See Testimony of Mr. Justice Frankfurter before the Royal Commission on Capital Punishment, 1950, pp. 580–82.

jury to read the defendant's mind in order to apply the instructions of the judge?

It would be unfair, however, to blame the judges for their inability to explain clearly the different degrees of murder. The fact that so many do not succeed suggests that the real blame rests with the rather fanciful distinctions between first degree and second degree murder. Mr. Justice Cardozo himself found it difficult, if not impossible, to draw a satisfactory line:

> I think the distinction is much too vague to be continued in our law. . . . The statute is framed along the lines of a defective and unreal psychology. . . . The present distinction is so obscure that no jury hearing it for the first time can fairly be expected to assimilate and understand it. I am not at all sure that I understand it myself after trying to apply it for many years and after diligent study of what has been written in the books. Upon the basis of this fine distinction with its mystifying psychology, scores of men have gone to their deaths.[18]

Degrees of murder were introduced into the law originally in order to give juries an opportunity to mitigate the harshness of the death penalty. No doubt in many cases they have accomplished their purpose. Some juries find second degree despite the facts and the judge's instructions; other juries, more conscientious than merciful, find first degree where warranted; still others muddle through the "mystifying psychology" to a bewildered finish. In conjunction with the death penalty, these degrees of murder have created a combination which tends to produce a most haphazard application of the criminal law in capital cases. Once the death penalty has been abolished, however, the criminal law may safely drop such metaphysical distinctions and relate the period of imprisonment to modern penology for the protection of society and the rehabilitation of the convicted.

18 Benjamin N. Cardozo, *Law and Literature* (New York: Harcourt, Brace & Co., 1931), pp. 99–101.

Another cause for the haphazard application of the death penalty is the submission of the issue of mental responsibility to juries under legal definitions of insanity which are completely at variance with medical science. Most jurisdictions still apply the century-old rule in M'Naghten's case, namely: Did the defendant know that his act was morally and legally wrong? The rule has been somewhat qualified by such exceptions as the "irresistible impulse" test, but on the whole, M'Naghten still dominates judicial charges and decisions.

Under this definition of insanity, the lowest-grade morons and the most disturbed psychopaths are repeatedly convicted because they "knew the difference between right and wrong." It has also provided astute defense counsel with a handy means of getting guilty clients off without any penalty whatever, through a verdict of "not guilty by reason of insanity," and a subsequent speedy cure of a nonexistent mental disease.

In Massachusetts, under the Briggs law, the issue of insanity in capital cases is now usually decided before trial by the report of two impartial psychiatrists. In most states, however, the juries must continue to choose between contending alienists who are paid for their opinions by the side which calls them to the stand. Since there can be no reconciliation between the legal test for insanity and a conscientious psychiatrist's ideas about mental disease, the expert testimony from the witness stand is given under conditions which often confuse rather than assist a jury in reaching a verdict.

If imprisonment or confinement were the result in any event, then a finding of either sanity or insanity would provide opportunity for further study and possible treatment. Under the present system, a mistaken finding of guilty or not guilty where insanity is pleaded may result in irrevocable error. It is the presence of the death penalty that hinders a new approach to the entire question of mental responsibility.

Whether there is actually a larger proportion of pleas of guilty without trial where capital punishment has been abolished is also largely unexplored territory. The trial of murder cases is an expensive process. The ordinary murder trial may cost the county thousands of dollars, and some of the more bitterly contested cases may run high up in five figures. In Massachusetts, the trial of the Millen brothers and Abraham Faber in 1934 for murder in the commission of robberies ran for nearly eight weeks at very great cost to the county. These criminals and their lawyers knew that the government's case was overwhelmingly strong and that public feeling ran high against them. Slim as their chances were, however, they went to trial because no prosecutor in a mandatory death penalty state, on the facts of their outrageous crimes, would have accepted a plea of second degree. Under the same conditions in an abolition state, would the accused have pleaded guilty?[19]

California was put to a great expense in the trial of the sensational Hickman case involving the fiendish sex killing of a child. Would the defendant have pleaded guilty in an abolition state? Shortly after the Hickman trial, Michigan had a murder case almost exactly the same in its gruesome details, apparently induced by the lurid press treatment of the California crime. The accused, one Hoteling, promptly pleaded guilty, thereby sparing the state much expense and the public a recital of the macabre details.

The money spent on the trial of capital cases would pay the salaries of a substantial number of additional parole officers, badly needed in a constructive effort to reduce

[19] Cf. *Boston Globe,* October 14, 1930. "Battle Creek, Michigan [an abolition state]. Only a little more than twelve hours following their capture after the killing of a state policeman and the robbery of a bank, Thomas Martin and James Gallagher were sentenced to life imprisonment in Jackson Prison." The Millen-Faber cases are notable for reasons other than great expense. At the time of the arrest of these criminals, two innocent men, Berrett and Molway, were being tried for one of the murders committed by the Millen gang. The trial was nearing a conclusion, and eight reputable witnesses, with good opportunity to observe, had identified Berrett and Molway as the robbers, when the real criminals were apprehended, bringing confessions and ballistic evidence to the rescue. No one familiar with the Berrett-Milway trial has ever doubted that these men would have been convicted—and executed—but for this timely occurrence.

crime. It might repay any state to investigate the probability of saving the cost of these expensive murder trials through repeal of the death penalty.[20]

Whether or not capital punishment increases the expense of administering justice by forcing to trial a greater number of murder cases, there can be no doubt that the cost of cases actually tried is greatly increased because of the reluctance of jurors to serve where they may feel compelled to decree death to the accused. This is a universally observed phenomenon. Where the cases are notorious, the delay in securing a jury may be fantastic. In the trial for the murder of "King" Solomon in Boston, only one of ninety veniremen failed to disqualify himself on the ground that he was opposed to capital punishment. After 160 had been interrogated, there still were not enough to make up a jury.[21] In the case of Sacco and Vanzetti, four days were consumed in impaneling a jury.[22] These instances may be extreme, but they underscore a fact which should properly be considered in any evaluation of the death penalty in the administration of justice.

Expert observers also agree that the trial of murder cases where death may be the penalty tends to be more sensational than where imprisonment is the only punishment. The spectacle of a human being fighting for his life is stirring drama inside and outside of the courtroom. Frequently, in order to sway a jury toward the fatal verdict—and possibly to reassure his own conscience—a prosecutor will inflame the jurors against the accused by playing upon every prejudice and ghastly detail. It is generally recognized that some prosecutors, because of political ambition or

[20] Commenting on the execution of Irene Schroeder by the State of Pennsylvania in 1931, Dr. Harvey M. Watkins, of Reading, a social worker, is quoted in a bulletin issued by the American League to Abolish Capital Punishment as saying: "It cost the State of Pennsylvania $23,658 to prosecute, convict and electrocute Irene Schroeder at the Western Penitentiary. If one twentieth of this sum had been spent ten years ago by any social workers on that twenty-two-year-old girl, that electrocution would have been prevented."

[21] *Boston Herald,* June 7, 1933.

[22] Record published by Henry Holt & Co., 1928.

simple vanity, are not above deliberately seeking the head-lines.

Of course, noncapital cases may also tend toward sensationalism; but where this occurs, it is because of reasons other than the penalty involved. Generally speaking, the trial of cases where the penalty may be death is surcharged with an emotional tension not present in other prosecutions. Defense counsel, witnesses, judges, and even prosecutors have been visibly affected by the strain. This atmosphere, created by invoking the specter of death to destroy the life in the dock, is hardly a help to calm consideration of the evidence.

Indeed, the one conclusion on which practically all criminologists agree is that the death penalty tends to distort the course of the criminal law. In the phrase of Professor Sheldon Glueck, it "bedevils the administration of justice."[23] Data may indicate that in some instances it may result in acquittals or findings not merited by the accused; in others, in convictions and executions not justified by an unemotional consideration of the evidence. In either case, the normal is deflected. The penalty is erratically inflicted at different times in different places. It retards progress in the criminal law by maintaining concepts which should have little to do with the process of ascertaining guilt, innocence, or responsibility.

Just as the death penalty is a paradoxical block in a modern system of penology, so does the fear of its finality hinder reform in the administration of criminal justice. Professor Sam Bass Warner, then on the faculty of the Harvard Law School, declared to the Joint Judiciary Committee of the Massachusetts Legislature in 1935 that "the existence of the death penalty for first degree murder is one of the principal reasons, if not the main reason, why it is extremely difficult to get judges and legislators to remove procedural barnacles from our law."

It may be said that all human processes are imperfect, and that those of justice are no different; but the fact of human fallibility is not a good reason for increasing it. If

[23] Minutes of Faculty Meeting on Capital Punishment, Twentieth Century Club, January 18, 1936.

to err is human, then it becomes all the more important to reduce the probability of errors—especially fatal ones. On the massive evidence now available dealing with the use and disuse of the death penalty, there would seem to be no sufficient compensating advantage in retaining it. Its disappearance could only improve the administration of justice.

MURDER, ERRORS OF JUSTICE, AND CAPITAL PUNISHMENT

In 1912, wardens across the country were asked whether they knew of any cases where someone who was probably innocent was nevertheless legally executed. Only one warden claimed to know of "one or two" such cases; no identification was given of when or where these errors of justice occurred.[1] Most of the retentionists in law enforcement today appear to believe that there is little chance for an innocent man to be sentenced to death. Readers of Edwin Borchard's *Convicting the Innocent* (1932), Erle Stanley Gardner's *Court of Last Resort* (1952), and Jerome and Barbara Frank's *Not Guilty* (1957), may remember that none of these books includes a case of an innocent man having been put to death. It is no wonder, then, that retentionists are sceptical when they are told that one of the most important arguments against the death penalty is the risk of executing an innocent man; even if the possibility is there, the risk cannot be very great when there are no documented cases of its occurrence, especially in recent years.

It must be acknowledged that on this question, abolitionists tend to argue as inconclusively as do retentionists on the question of deterrence. Roy Calvert, the leading figure in the English abolition movement during the 1930's, has written, "The fact that few errors of justice come to light in connection with capital offenses should not lead us to suppose that such mistakes do not occur."[2] This is exactly like

[1] *Journal of Criminal Law, Criminology and Police Science* (May 1912), p. 131.

[2] Roy Calvert, *Capital Punishment in the Twentieth Century* (1936), p. 125.

advising unqualified belief in the unique deterrent efficacy of the death penalty after having admitted that few cases of such deterrence have been verified. Jerome Frank has stated, "No one knows how many innocent men, erroneously convicted of murder, have been put to death by American governments."[3] This is, of course, true, but as a forensic tactic it is deceptive. Were a retentionist to say, "No one knows how many persons have been deterred from crimes by the threat of capital punishment," either he would be stating a platitude or he would be making a fallacious appeal to ignorance, i.e., begging the question by assuming from the start that the death penalty is known to be a superior deterrent and that the only thing not known is the exact number of persons deterred. Judge Frank's remark suffers from precisely the same defect.

The parallel between abolitionists and retentionists here does not end with their use of the same fallacious reasoning. Much as there are stories of how someone didn't carry a gun during a planned robbery, or didn't shoot his victim, because he was afraid of the death penalty, so there are stories every now and then of innocent men who have been executed. But neither side turns its allegations into carefully researched case histories which prove all that is claimed for them. For instance, *Time* magazine recently carried an interview with a Texas newspaper editor who claimed to have witnessed 158 executions. He was a "firm opponent of capital punishment," partly because he was "sure there have been at least six or seven executions for crimes they did not commit, and Lord only knows how many people died for crimes they did commit but whose punishment was too severe."[4] *Time* gave no particulars on these cases, and this serious charge against the Texas courts has not, to my knowledge, been substantiated. It may be true, but unless the necessary research and documentation is published, we will probably never know.

Even on those rare occasions when a wrongful conviction for homicide has been established beyond a reasonable doubt, and where an execution was averted, very little pub-

[3] Jerome and Barbara Frank, *Not Guilty* (1957), p. 248.
[4] *Time* (June 8, 1959), p. 60.

licity usually attends such dramatic events. Or else the publicized cases are of such antique vintage that one complacently assumes such blunders don't happen any more.
Everyone who studies this subject eventually reads of the
Boorne brothers in Vermont, who confessed to killing their
brother-in-law and were sentenced to hang, only to have a
friend discover hardly more than a few days before the
scheduled execution that the alleged deceased was alive and
healthy—in New Jersey![5] But the moral can be dodged,
since nobody was executed in this case and it occurred in
1820. It is not so easy to pass this off as an isolated judicial
error once it is realized that *five* other cases of exactly this
same sort, incredible though it may seem, have been documented: in the Philippine Islands in an American court
some sixty years ago,[6] in 1907 in Alabama and in the
Oklahoma Territory, the next year in Virginia, in Kentucky
in 1925, and again in Alabama in 1928. If all the cases of
wrongful convictions in which the death penalty was, or
might have been, invoked, could be brought together, their
collective impact would jar anyone's complacency.

In this essay, I have abstracted seventy-four cases occurring in the United States since 1893, in which a wrongful
conviction of criminal homicide has been alleged and, in
most cases, proved beyond doubt. These cases represent
the bulk of this sort of judicial error so far brought to my
attention. In many instances, it has been possible to provide
citations to the law reports for readers who may wish to
check into certain details. But in many other cases, there
seems to be no law report of the case, and the imputation
of trial court error rests entirely on extra-judicial evidence.
Since the law reports contain, with rare exceptions, only
appellate court opinions, information on a case that was
not appealed will be available only in the unpublished court
house records. Though it is customary now for a death
sentence to receive at least a perfunctory appeal in the
higher state courts, this was much less common a genera-

[5] See, e.g., Edmund Pearson, *Studies in Murder* (1924), pp.
265–285.
[6] See James Jenkins, "A Most Extraordinary Case," *Case and
Comment* (August 1917).

tion ago. In a few other instances, there is no law report because the indictment was quashed before the case even went to the jury (e.g., the 1924 Connecticut case of Harold Israel).

It may seem incredible that in no more than a small percentage of these seventy-four cases did the state or federal appellate courts play a decisive role in correcting the miscarriage of justice. On the contrary, in almost every case in which an appeal was taken, and error was later established, the appellate court had sustained the conviction and usually unanimously! The main reason for this is that the scope of review of a criminal conviction, even where a death sentence is involved, is exceedingly narrow in almost all American jurisdictions. Usually, only "rulings of law" (e.g., the judge's instructions to the jury on the law of homicide), in contrast to "findings of fact" (e.g., the jury's decision on the credibility of conflicting evidence), are subject to review by a higher court. Never is the substantial issue of the convicted man's guilt or innocence squarely before the appellate court. More often than not, the case is decided on review by reference to some point of law barely relevant to the culpability of the defendant. In the last decade, reversals based on rather broader grounds have been granted in many capital cases because the federal judiciary has become increasingly sensitive to violations of "due process of law" by the state criminal courts.[7] Perhaps if the federal courts had exercised this supervisory control in earlier decades, many more reversals would have issued. As it is, almost every one of the judicial errors in the cases reported below was rectified by fact-finding of a type insufficient at the time to warrant a reversal and a new trial, and perhaps even insufficient to get an acquittal at a second trial had one been granted.

For purposes of classification by the original sentence of

[7] Curtis Reitz, "Federal Habeus Corpus," *University of Pennsylvania Law Review* (February 1960), p. 484, cites seventeen capital cases, nine involving death sentences, in which the federal courts reversed state court convictions. Upon retrial in two of the nine death sentence cases, acquittals resulted (p. 497).

the trial court, the seventy-four cases abstracted here
may be broken down as follows:

Death sentence executed	8
Death sentence not executed	23
Life sentence	30
Less than life sentence	10
Conviction averted	3
Total	74

It is important to realize that eleven of the thirty life sentences were meted out in abolition states. Had the death
penalty not been abolished in these states, it is likely that at
least some of these eleven men would have received a death
sentence and been executed.

Although the cases come from two dozen different states,
the Army, the federal government, and the District of Columbia, a large percentage come from the Atlantic seaboard and the Pacific coast. The reason is not that these
regions have a weakness for judicial error, but that interested persons (Warden Lawes in New York, Mrs. Ehrmann in Massachusetts, and Erle Stanley Gardner in California) have been in a position to investigate many leads
there and to keep a close record of such cases as they
turned up.

Although the cases span the years from 1893 to 1962,
and thus average about one per year, and though the chronological order in which they are presented shows at a
glance that there are many recent cases, most of them date
back several decades. This is because a large number come
from the research of the late Professor Borchard, and all
his cases date from before 1930. In light of all the cases
discovered since Borchard published his book, it is not improbable that future investigators will be able to point to
several wrongful convictions of homicide during the 1960's.

The wonder is, with more than 7,000 persons executed in
this century, that only eight probably erroneous executions
and an additional twenty-three erroneous death sentences
have been discovered. Is this nearly all, or merely a few, of
the wrongful executions and death sentences in recent dec-

ades? How is it that nearly ninety per cent of the cases reported here did not result in a death sentence and execution? There are several reasons. Occasionally, when the jury has some doubts it will convict of murder in the first degree and award life imprisonment rather than death (e.g., the 1933 Illinois case of Joseph Majczek), or perhaps the jury will even bring in only a second degree murder or a manslaughter conviction (e.g., the 1958 California case of John Fry). Very rarely, the real culprit comes forward in the nick of time and the innocent man is dramatically freed (e.g., the 1957 Georgia case of James Foster). But what usually happens is that a lawyer or relative who believes in the condemned man's innocence convinces the governor to grant a reprieve and, after further investigation, a commutation of sentence and, still later, a full pardon and perhaps even indemnification (e.g., the 1925 New York case of Edward Larkman). Discovery of error in such cases, not to mention success in persuading those with the power of life and death to admit that a mistake had been made, almost always rests on tireless persistence and luck. It seems very probable that there have been other cases in which poverty, faint-heartedness or lack of ingenuity allowed judicial error in homicide convictions to go unchallenged, unproved, or uncorrected (e.g., the 1918 New Jersey case of George Brandon).

Perhaps the most alarming fact which the cases below reveal is that once a man is found guilty, he cannot easily have his innocence established without cooperation from the very prosecuting authorities who convicted him in the first place. Erle Stanley Gardner, whose work with the Court of Last Resort has made him America's foremost authority on wrongful convictions, pointedly charged, "In virtually every case that we have investigated, we have found that the attitude of the prosecutor's office has been one of either active or passive resistance."[8] The only exceptions he mentions in his book occurred when the origi-

---

[8] Erle Stanley Gardner, *Court of Last Resort* (1952), p. 178. See also Marshall Houts, *From Arrest to Release* (1958), pp. 160–167, and Richard Donnelly, "Unconvicting the Innocent," *Vanderbilt Law Review* (December 1952).

nal prosecutor had long been out of office—and the innocent man long behind bars.

No one should be surprised at the resistance Gardner
describes, unless one is unaware of forced confessions,
denials of counsel, subornation to perjury, withheld evidence, and racially-biased juries, which so many of the
cases below involve, in which the police, the prosecutor, or
the judge (or even all three) are guilty of having subverted
justice to gain a conviction. If such methods were used to
secure a conviction and an execution resulted, the motive
for preventing exoneration of the dead man is obviously
even stronger. Many investigators have noticed how officials close ranks and cut off further investigation by a solid
wall of non-cooperation. Confronted with such resistance, it
is no wonder that the efforts to exonerate the deceased
weaken and that the lingering suspicions of his innocence
are never fully confirmed;[9] usually the case is forgotten
(e.g., the 1937 New York case of Everett Applegaite).
Whether any of the eight cases below really deserve to be
classified as wrongful executions remains in some doubt.
No doubt, however, attaches to the fact that nearly two
dozen men have been sentenced to death for crimes they
demonstrably did not commit.

* * * * *

1893. Mississippi. Will Purvis. 71 Miss. 706 (1893).
Purvis was sentenced to death for murder; eye-witness
testimony convicted him. He survived his hanging when
the knot slipped. Pardoned in 1898, he was cleared by the
death-bed confession of the guilty man in 1917 and indemnified by the State legislature in 1920. Source: Borchard, *op. cit.*, pp. 210–217.

1898. Massachusetts. Jack O'Neil. Executed. For de-

---

[9] A death-bed confession by the real culprit is often an important factor in deciding that an innocent person has been convicted (e.g., the 1931 New York case of Pietro Matera). A
generation ago, Edmund Pearson, *op. cit.*, pp. 266–267, insin-
uated that there never had been a genuine death-bed confession.
The existence, if not the reliability, of such confessions is now
beyond doubt.

tails, see Sara Ehrmann, "The Human Side of Capital Punishment," reprinted in the next chapter.

1898. Massachusetts. John Chance. 174 Mass. 245 (1899). Convicted of murder and sentenced to life imprisonment. Pardoned in 1911 after a friend admitted to the killing. Conviction based on perjured testimony and Chance's own lies on the witness stand. Source: Borchard, *op. cit.*, pp. 332–337.

1900. Illinois. Michael Synon. 188 Ill. 609 (1901). Sentenced to death for murder. Reversed on appeal for prejudicial remarks of the trial judge. At second trial, witnesses testified Synon was several miles away from the scene of the crime; he was acquitted. Source: Raymond Bye, *Capital Punishment in the United States* (1919), p. 84.

1901. Florida. J. B. Brown. 44 Fla. 28 (1902). Sentenced to death for murder. Hanging averted at the gallows on the ground that the execution warrant listed the jury foreman's name! Brown's sentence commuted to life. His "accomplice" gave a death-bed confession in 1913 that he had falsely implicated Brown. He was released and indemnified in 1929. Source: Borchard, *op. cit.*, pp. 33–39.

1907. Alabama. Bill Wilson. 191 Ala. 7 (1915). Convicted of first degree murder and sentenced to life. After nearly four years in prison, he was fully pardoned by the Governor and indemnified by the Legislature when the victim turned up alive. Source: Borchard, *op. cit.*, pp. 309–316.

1907. Oklahoma Territory. Millard Vaught and Will Stiles. After a mistrial from a hung jury, Vaught and Stiles were convicted in Federal court of manslaughter. In 1917, the supposed victim was accidentally discovered in Los Angeles, and the two prisoners were released. Conviction based on perjured testimony and the jury's refusal to accept the defendants's perfect alibi. Source: Borchard, *op. cit.*, pp. 294–303.

1907. New Jersey. John Schuyler. 75 N. J. L. 487 (1907). Sentenced to death for murder, Schuyler was pardoned and indemnified eight years later when the real murderer confessed. Conviction based wholly on circumstantial evidence. "Had it not been for the persistent efforts of ex-

Governor Stokes and of the New York banker, Mr. C. Ledyard Blair, for whom Schuyler formerly worked . . . the death chamber would have had him as its victim." Source: *New Jersey Law Journal,* 38 (1915), p. 1.

1908. Virginia. Ernest Lyons. Negro. Sentenced to eighteen years for second degree murder. Released three years later when his supposed victim turned up alive in North Carolina. Convicted on mistaken identification of a corpse. Source: Borchard, *op. cit.,* pp. 148–152.

1908. New York. Edward McGrath. 202 N. Y. 445 (1911). Sentenced to death for murder, conviction reversed on appeal, and reconvicted of second degree murder and sentenced to twenty years. Claimed he was innocent; paroled in 1925. Source: Edward McGrath, *I Was Condemned to the Chair* (1934).

Ca. 1910. California. James Donnelly. 228 U. S. 243 (1913). Sentenced to life for first degree murder. Claimed he was innocent. Death-bed confession by another person not allowed as admissible evidence, under the hearsay rule, and conviction affirmed. Source: Bye, *op. cit.,* pp. 83–84.

1911. Wisconsin. John Johnson. Sentenced to life imprisonment for murder. Released in 1922 after someone else was shown to have committed the crime. Johnson, who had a neurotic fear of being lynched, confessed when he was told a mob was about to break into his cell and string him up. "There was no reason at all to connect Johnson with the crime; but the need for a scapegoat seemed to furnish the necessary motive for pinning the crime on the poor fellow." Source: Borchard, *op. cit.,* pp. 112–122.

1911. Michigan. Robert MacGregor. 178 Mich. Rep. 436 (1914). Sentenced to life imprisonment for murder. Granted full pardon in 1916, though the grounds on which MacGregor's innocence was established have never been disclosed. Source: Borchard, *op. cit.,* pp. 153–157.

1913. Georgia. Leo Frank. 141 Ga. 243 (1914) and 237 U. S. 309 (1915). Sentenced to death for murder. Conviction obtained on perjured testimony from the person who was the real culprit. After the Governor commuted his death sentence in 1915, Frank was lynched. Source: Francis Busch, *Guilty or Not Guilty?* (1952), pp. 15–74.

1913. Kansas. Anon. Governor Hodges reported paroling a man under life sentence (?) after twenty-one years in prison. Believed to be innocent and, in any case, convicted in an unfair trial and "would undoubtedly have been hanged" had he not been lucky. Source: Bye, *op. cit.,* p. 78.

1915. New York. "Dago" Frank. Sentenced to death and executed for the murder of one Rosenthal. According to a statement by Warden Clancy of Sing Sing Prison, Frank's accomplices later admitted in prison that he was not even at the scene of the crime. Source: Bye, *op. cit.,* pp. 77–78.

1915. New York. Charles Stielow. 217 N. Y. Rep. 641 (1916) and 161 N. Y. S. 559 (1916). Sentenced to death for murder, Stielow received a stay forty minutes before his scheduled execution. After three years, he was exonerated and released when the real culprit confessed. Conviction obtained by a coerced confession. Source: Borchard, *op. cit.,* pp. 245–256.

1916. California. Tom Mooney. 177 Cal. 642 (1918). Sentenced to death for murder. At the instigation of President Wilson, the sentence was commuted to life, and in 1939 Governor Olson pardoned Mooney. A political conviction based on perjured eye-witness testimony and falsification of other evidence. Source: Brad Williams, *Due Process* (1960), pp. 13–18, 21–38, 91–111.

1916. Illinois. Earnest Wallace. Negro. 279 Ill. 139 (1917). Sentenced to death for murder. Reversed on appeal. Source: James Barbour, "Efforts to Abolish the Death Penalty in Illinois," *Journal of Criminal Law, Criminology and Police Science,* (February 1919), p. 508.

1918. West Virginia. Payne Boyd. Negro. Convicted of murder, and at a second trial in 1925 he was reconvicted and sentenced to life imprisonment. At a third trial, he was acquitted through new evidence showing that not he, but Cleveland Boyd (no relation) was guilty. Source: Borchard, *op. cit.,* pp. 23–28.

1918. New Jersey. George Brandon (alias Harold Lamble). 96 N. J. L. 23 (1924). Sentenced to death for murder and executed. Widely believed to be innocent; his attorney later disbarred for mishandling the defense. Testimony of an accomplice, who turned state's evidence, and Brandon's admission on the witness stand of his previous felony convictions led to his conviction. Source: New Jersey, *Public Hearing on Assembly Bills 33 & 34* (1958), Second Day, p. 29 A (testimony of J. G. Deardorff, Jr.).

1918. New Jersey. Raffaelo E. Morello. A native Italian, convicted of murdering his wife, and sentenced to life imprisonment. At the coroner's inquest, he had admitted he was "responsible" for her death. No appeal taken. Pardoned in 1926 after he had learned enough English to explain that his wife committed suicide when he told her that he was to be drafted into military service. "A fatally wrong meaning was given to his testimony through misunderstandings of his interpreter." Source: Felix Frankfurter, *The Case of Sacco and Vanzetti* (1927), pp. 109–110; and files of the New Jersey State Library (courtesy Mrs. Herta Prager, Head, Bureau of Law and Legislative Reference).

1919. Michigan. Alexander Ripan. Convicted of first degree murder and sentenced to life. Escaped in 1929, recaptured in 1935. In 1939, the original prosecutor of Ripan helped him obtain a new trial; released when the court dismissed the charges. Source: Frank and Frank, *op. cit.*, chapter 7.

1919. Michigan. Lloyd Prevost. 219 Mich. 233 (1922). Convicted of first degree murder and sentenced to life. Pardoned in 1930. Conviction obtained by unscrupulous methods of prosecution, perjury, and mistaken expert ballistics testimony. "Prevost's refusal to talk before trial . . . certainly did not help him . . . On the whole, the case may be deemed to show that the supposed privilege against self-incrimination is of but little, if any, help to an innocent man." Source: Borchard, *op. cit.*, pp. 201–209.

1919. District of Columbia. Zian Sung Wan. 266 U. S. 1 (1924). A native Chinese, convicted of murder and sentenced to death. Conviction reversed on appeal to the U. S. Supreme Court on grounds of coerced confession. Juries in two later trials refused to reconvict, and the indictment was dropped. Wan was released after seven years in prison. Source: Frankfurter, *op. cit.*, pp. 108–109.

1920. Alabama. Cleo Staten and John Murchison. Negroes. Sentenced to life imprisonment for murder. After hearing evidence implicating someone else for the crime, the Board of Pardons released Murchison in 1927 and four years later he was awarded a compensation. Staten died in prison a few days before he received a full pardon. Convicted mainly on perjured testimony. Source: Borchard, *op. cit.*, pp. 165–169.

Ca. 1920. New York. "Stephen, Max and Allen." All were convicted of felony murder and sentenced to death and executed. Allen insisted that neither Stephen nor Max were involved in the crime, and had been mistakenly identified by witnesses. Source: Lawes, *op. cit.*, pp. 314 ff.

Ca. 1920. New York. "Russell." Convicted of murdering a police officer, sentenced to death and executed. Claimed to be innocent from the moment of his arrest to his death; his "accomplice" admitted his own guilt and denied Russell's. Source: Lawes, *op. cit.*, pp. 337–339.

1922. Ohio. Clarence McKinney. Sentenced to life imprisonment for first degree murder. Appeal pending when another man confessed to the crime. In 1923, McKinney was given a new trial and the indictment was nol prossed. McKinney had a previous criminal record, and his conviction was obtained by circumstantial evidence and mistaken identification. Source: Borchard, *op. cit.*, pp. 158–164.

1924. Michigan. Vance Hardy. Convicted of first degree murder and sentenced to life. Perjured eye-witness testimony was the basis of the conviction. A new trial was granted in 1951, and when the main witness at the earlier trial repudiated his testimony, Hardy was acquitted. Source: Gardner, *op. cit.*, chapter 8.

1924. Connecticut. Harold F. Israel. Confessed to murder, and the ballistics expert testified that Israel's gun was the murder weapon. District Attorney Homer S. Cummings, dissatisfied with the testimony, entered a *nolle prosequi* after he discovered that the expert witness was unreliable and that the confession was coerced. "Without question, Israel would have hanged if it had not been for

the conscientiousness of the Connecticut prosecutor."
Source: Lewis Lawes, *Meet the Murderer* (1940), pp.
336–337; also William Kunstler, *The Case for Courage,*
(1962), pp. 275–311.

1925. Kentucky. Condy Dabney. Convicted of murder
and sentenced to life imprisonment. A year later, the supposed victim turned up alive and Dabney was immediately
pardoned. An appeal was pending at the time. The conviction was obtained on false testimony. Source: Borchard,
op. cit., pp. 51–58.

1925. New York. Edward Larkman. 244 N. Y. Rep.
503 (1926). Convicted of murder and sentenced to death.
In 1927 the sentence was commuted to life, and in 1929
another convict confessed to the crime. Governor Lehmann
unconditionally pardoned Larkman in 1933. Source: Frank
and Frank, *op. cit.,* chapter 7.

1926. New Jersey. James Sweeney. Convicted of felony
murder and sentenced to life. Sweeney had a previous
criminal record. He was exonerated in 1928 when the real
culprits confessed, and was then freed by the Board of
Pardons. Conviction obtained by mistaken identification,
perjury and circumstantial evidence. Source: New Jersey,
loc. cit.

1926. Texas. Anastarcio Vargas. Death sentence. For
details, see Ehrmann, *op. cit.*

1927. California. Harvey Lesher, Mike Garvey, Phil
Rohan. Convicted of felony murder and sentenced to life.
Full pardons granted by Governor Young in 1930, and
Rohan indemnified. Unsavory background of Lesher and
Garvey, plus "some perjury" and mistaken identification by
a ten-year-old boy, contributed to the conviction. Source:
Borchard, *op. cit.,* pp. 141–147.

1927. Massachusetts. Gangi Cerro and Samuel Gallo.
264 Mass. 264 (1928). Death sentences for murder. For
details, see Ehrmann, *op. cit.*

1927. Illinois. Henry Olson. After one trial ending in a
hung jury, Olson was convicted of murder at a second trial
and sentenced to life. He vanished after being released on
bond pending decision on a motion for a third trial. Later,
two youths confessed to the crime and were given long

terms of imprisonment. Olson was eventually located, returned, and ordered acquitted. Mistaken eye-witness testimony was the basis of the conviction. Source: Borchard, *op. cit.*, pp. 176–180.

1928. Alabama. Louise Butler and George Yelder. Negroes. Convicted of murder and sentenced to life. Both were released two months later when the supposed victim was discovered alive and well in another county. Louise Butler at first confessed to the crime, but denied it in court. The main witnesses for the prosecution were two children, her daughter and niece. Source: Borchard, *op. cit.*, pp. 40–45.

1929. Missouri. Walter Hess and Alvin Craig. Convicted of second degree murder and sentenced to ten years in prison. Shortly after the conviction, the real culprits confessed, and Hess and Craig were pardoned by the Governor. "The Hess and Craig case exemplifies the danger of conviction for first degree murder on circumstantial evidence; only the prosecutor's belief that he might not be able to sustain that charge induced his request for the alternative second degree charge, which under the circumstances was equally erroneous." Source: Borchard, *op. cit.*, pp. 94–99.

1929. Mississippi. Thomas Gunter. Convicted, mainly on the testimony of his seven-year-old granddaughter and of the deceased's wife, of murdering his son; sentenced to five years in prison. In 1930, his daughter-in-law admitted killing her husband; she was given a suspended sentence. Gunter, released on a suspended sentence, fled the state after refusing to return to prison. Source: Borchard, *op. cit.*, pp. 342–344.

1929. Michigan. Gerald Crowden. Convicted of murder and sentenced to life. In 1932, another man then under arrest confessed to the murder, and Crowden was released. Source: Frank and Frank, *op. cit.*, chapter 7.

1929. Georgia. Robert Coleman. Convicted of murder and sentenced to life. The evidence at the trial was wholly circumstantial. In 1933, he was granted an unconditional pardon and indemnified by the Legislature. Source: Frank and Frank, *op. cit.*, chapter 7.

1931. New York. Pietro Matera. 258 N. Y. Rep. 563

(1932). Death sentence. For details, see Ehrmann, *op. cit.*

1932. Michigan. Louis Gross. Convicted of murder and sentenced to life. In 1943, evidence of a "frame-up" by the police was produced; in 1948, the prosecutor obtained a new trial for Gross and he was nol prossed. Gross had a prior criminal conviction. Source: Gardner, *op. cit.*, chapter 7.

1932. Minnesota. Leonard Hankins. 193 Minn. 375 (1935). Convicted of murder and sentenced to life. Obtained a new trial, on grounds of false testimony, but was reconvicted and resentenced as originally. In 1953, he was released and indemnified, and his sister was reimbursed by the Legislature for her expenses in exonerating him. Source: Marshall Houts, *From Arrest to Release* (1958), pp. 160–162; also Leonard Hankins, *Nineteen Years Innocent* (1956).

Ca. 1930. New York. George Chew Wing. Convicted of murder, sentenced to death and executed. He convinced several observers while he was in the prison awaiting execution that he had been falsely identified by an eye-witness and that perjured testimony had been used against him. Source: Lawes, *op. cit.*, pp. 323–326.

1932. Washington. Clarence Boggie. Convicted of murder and sentenced to life. Boggie had a previous criminal record. In 1948, he was conditionally pardoned when considerable evidence pointed to another person as the guilty party. Perjured testimony suborned by the prosecution was used to obtain the conviction. Source: Gardner, *op. cit.*, chapter 2.

1933. Illinois. Joseph Majczek. 360 Ill. 261 (1935). Convicted of murder and sentenced to life. In 1945, he obtained a new trial and was acquitted. Perjured testimony, with the collusion of the police, had secured the conviction. Source: Frank and Frank, *op. cit.*, chapter 1.

1934. Massachusetts. Louis Berrett and Clement Molway. Conviction of murder averted. For details, see Ehrmann, *op. cit.*

1935. Missouri. Joseph Huett. Convicted of manslaughter and sentenced to five years in prison. Five months later, the chief prosecution witness confessed to perjury and admitted that the killing was in self-defense. Huett was released. Source: Frank and Frank, *op. cit.,* chapter 7.

1936. California. Coke Brite and John Brite. 9 C. 2d 666 (1937). Convicted of murder and sentenced to death. Their death sentences commuted to life, and in 1952 they were paroled after evidence was produced that the prosecution's case had been based on perjured testimony and had proceeded on a false theory of the crime. Source: Gardner, *op. cit.,* chapter 5.

1937. Maine. Paul Dwyer. 154 Me. 179 (1958). Convicted of murder and sentenced to life. The main evidence against Dwyer, in addition to his own confession, was testimony from the arresting officer, a deputy sheriff, who was also later convicted of the same crime and sentenced to prison. Dwyer claimed his confession was coerced by the deputy; he was released in 1959. Source: Bulletin of the American Civil Liberties Union dated December 7, 1959.

1937. New York. Everett Applegate. He and Frances Creighton were executed for the murder of Applegate's wife. Some evidence that he was falsely implicated by his "accomplice," though a few weeks after the execution all investigation of his innocence stopped. "Even if we proved he was innocent, we couldn't bring him back to life, could we?" Source: Lawes, *op. cit.,* pp. 333–335.

Ca. 1937. Michigan. "Paget." Convicted of murdering a policeman and sentenced to life. Granted a new trial in 1943 and again convicted and sentenced. Ca. 1951 (after fourteen years in prison), Paget was given a "truth serum" injection; on the basis of the results from this test, and on other evidence, the Parole Board released him with a full pardon. Source: California, *Senate Report on the Death Penalty* (1960), pp. 60–61.

1939. Pennsylvania. Rudolf Sheeler. 367 Pa. 152 (1951). Convicted of murder and sentenced to life. In 1951, a new trial granted, with a directed verdict of acquittal. Sheeler was held incommunicado, tortured and forced by the police to confess. "One of the most shameful cases ever brought to public notice." Source: Frank and Frank, *op. cit.,* chapter 6.

Ca. 1940. California. Anon. Mexican-American. Convicted of murder and sentenced to life. The trial jury was given incontrovertible evidence that the defendant was in prison in Mexico at the time of the crime, but they convicted him anyway. Source: Coleman Blease, "Abolition of the Death Penalty in California," *Lawyers Guild Review* (Summer 1959), p. 60.

1940. New York. Louis Hoffner. 288 N. Y. Rep. 552 (1942). Convicted of murder and sentenced to death. Sentence commuted by Governor Dewey; in 1955, Hoffner was released and indemnified for false imprisonment by the New York Legislature. Source: Massachusetts, *Report on the Death Penalty* (1958), p. 26.

1943. California. William Keys. Convicted of voluntary manslaughter; the prosecution sought a first degree murder conviction and Keys pled self-defense. In 1948, he was paroled after further evidence convinced the Adult Authority that Keys' plea was correct. Source: Gardner, *op. cit.*, chapter 4.

1943. Virginia. Silas Rogers. 183 Va. 190 (1944). Death sentence. For details see Ehrmann, *op. cit.*

1943. California. William Lindley. 26 C. 2d 780 (1945). Convicted of murder and sentenced to death. Execution averted by last-minute correspondence between Erle Stanley Gardner and the California State Supreme Court. The sentence was commuted to life, but Lindley was not released or pardoned. Eye-witness testimony, later shown to be mistaken, was the basis of the conviction; the real killer was identified but never located. "I know of no case which gives a better example of the dangers inherent in capital punishment." Source: Gardner, *op. cit.*, chapter 1.

1945. U. S. Army. Pvt. A. B. Ritchie. Death sentence. For details, see Ehrmann, *op. cit.*

1945. Michigan. Willie Calloway. Convicted of second degree murder. In 1953 a new trial was ordered and a *nolle prosequi* entered after the prosecution was convinced of his innocence. Source: Massachusetts, *op. cit.*, p. 26.

1947. Pennsylvania. Gerard Wentzel. 260 Pa. 137 (1948). Convicted of murder and sentenced to life. Conviction based wholly on circumstantial evidence; the jury refused to believe Wentzel's alibi that he was out of town at the time of the crime. In 1950 Wentzel was released after another man's confession convinced the Board of Pardons that the wrong man had been convicted; Wentzel's sentence was commuted to his time served. Source: Frank and Frank, *op. cit.*, chapter 5 and Gardner, *op. cit.*, chapter 6.

1949. Connecticut. Frank Smith. 141 Conn. 202 (1954). Death sentence. For details, see Ehrmann, *op. cit.*

1950. California. Ernest Woodmansee. Convicted of murdering a special police officer and sentenced to life. The major evidence at the trial was the testimony of a self-confessed participant in the murder. After this testimony was impeached and six years after Woodmansee entered prison, he was released on parole. Source: Fred Cook, "Capital Punishment: Does it Prevent Crime?" *The Nation* (March 10, 1956), pp. 196–197.

1954. Pennsylvania. Paul Pfeffer. Second degree murder. For details, see Ehrmann, *op. cit.*

1954. Massachusetts. Santos Rodriguez. Second degree murder. For details, see Ehrmann, *op. cit.*

1956. California. Remmel Brice. Convicted of murder and sentenced to death. Sentence commuted to life by Governor Knight. Source: Erle Stanley Gardner, "The Impossible Murder," *Argosy* (June 1958) and "The Murder Case Which Kept Contradicting Itself," *Argosy* (October 1958).

1957. Georgia. James Foster. 213 Ga. 601 (1957). Death sentence. For details, see below, Chapter Nine, "The Question of Identity," and the book by his attorney, James Horace Wood, *Nothing But the Truth* (1960).

1958. California. John Fry. Convicted of manslaughter and sentenced to prison. After seven months, he was pardoned by Governor Brown when another man's confession was verified. Fry himself had originally confessed also. The State Board of Control voted him $3,000 compensation. Source: California, *op. cit.*, pp. 8, 11–12, and Block, *And May God Have Mercy* (1962), pp. 64–65.

1962. U. S. Air Force. Gerald M. Anderson. Confessed, according to Air Force authorities at the Mountain Home Air Force Base, Idaho, to the murder of a neighbor and her young son. Kept in jail ten months, although there was no evidence against him except his own confession which, it became apparent, was coerced. Meanwhile, another man confessed. Charges against Anderson were finally dropped, he was released and discharged. At the time of this writing his attorney was bringing a suit for false imprisonment. Source: *Portland Reporter*, April 8, 1963, and Jack Foisie, "The Air Force Murder Case," *The Nation* (April 6, 1963), pp. 285–287.

1933. District of Columbia. Charles Bernstein. Convicted of murder and sentenced to death. Notified of his commutation of sentence minutes before the scheduled time of execution. Two years later, police proved he was innocent and he was released and pardoned by the President. Source: *Federal Probation* (March 1965), p. 70, and Edward Radin, *The Innocents* (1964), pp. 107–110.

19 ? ? New York. Tommy Bambrick. Convicted of murder, sentenced to death and executed. Efforts to contact the governor the night of the execution failed. Evidence was discovered which convinced Warden Thomas Mott Osborne that another man committed the crime. Bambrick refused to implicate anyone else. Source: Bye, *op. cit.*, pp. 82–83.

EXECUTIONS AND COMMUTATIONS IN NORTH CAROLINA*

BY ELMER H. JOHNSON**

Lack of appropriate and accurate information handicaps objective analysis of capital punishment as a means of meeting the crime problem. This paper will meet some of this need by drawing on a study of the 660 convicted capital offenders who have entered death row in Central Prison,

* Reprinted, by permission of the author and publisher, from "Selective Factors in Capital Punishment," *Social Forces*, vol. 36, no. 2 (December 1957), pp. 165–169. Copyright 1957, by the University of North Carolina Press (by assignment of the Williams & Wilkins Company, Baltimore).

** Associate Professor of Sociology, North Carolina State College.

Raleigh, since 1909 when the State of North Carolina assumed responsibility for executions from local government.

Capital punishment is the expression of laws which select out certain criminal acts as appropriate for exaction of the death penalty. The nature of the offense and of the offender influences the final outcome even after a capital offender has been committed to death row. The implementation of the capital laws occurs within a social environment which can create selective factors not visualized when the laws were formulated. This discussion is restricted to such selected factors.

It is probable that only a fraction of the capital offenders are committed to death row. Although judicial statistics are known to suffer from incomplete reporting, they show in an approximate manner that the four major capital offenses of North Carolina differ in both commitment and execution rates. Table 1 indicates such rates for July 1, 1938, to December 31, 1953, a period determined by the time covered by the data offered by the Biennial Report of the Attorney General of the State of North Carolina. Only 21.8 per cent of the first degree murderers whose conviction was

TABLE 1

COMPARISON OF NORTH CAROLINA SUPERIOR COURT
CONVICTIONS OF MALE CAPITAL OFFENDERS WITH DEATH
ROW ADMISSIONS AND EXECUTIONS, JULY 1, 1938–
DECEMBER 31, 1953

Capital Offense	Number Convicted in Superior Court[a] (A)	Number Admitted to Death Row (B)	Number Executed (C)	Percentages	
				B ÷ by A	C ÷ by A
First degree murder	742	162	102	.218	.137
Rape	382	52	30	.136	.079
First degree burglary	201	12	4	.060	.020
Arson	272	3	—	.011	.000

a Source: *Biennial Reports of the Attorney General of the State of North Carolina.* Period covered by these reports determined choice of period for comparisons.

reported, 13.6 per cent of the convicted rapists, six per cent of the first degree burglars, and one per cent of the arsonists were commited to death row. Only 13.7 per cent of the convicted first degree murderers, 7.9 per cent of the rapists, two per cent of the first degree burglars, and none of the arsonists were executed. It would appear that arson and even first degree burglary do not qualify in actuality as a capital offense according to the mores as held by the citizens of North Carolina and as expressed through action of their state.

Although differences between offenses in the disposition of capital offenders probably function to the greatest extent before sentencing, the differences are to be found even after the offender has been committed to death row. Table 2 shows data on all offenders committed to North Carolina's death row since 1909. Again we find first degree murderers and rapists with the highest execution rates. Only 23.9 per cent of the forty-one first degree burglars entering death row were executed, compared with 56.3 per cent of the 490 murderers and 55.6 per cent of the 126 rapists.

The execution rates differed for various types of murder, rape, and burglary. Three were executed of the four burglars who were classified by responsible officials as professional criminals. This was the highest execution rate. In contrast, only one of the twenty-one "common" burglars was executed; these committed crimes which did not include elements of violence, systematic burglary techniques, nor an acceptance of criminal norms. Among murderers, the highest execution rate (72.0 per cent) was exhibited when a crime for economic gain was involved. Murders of law officers (prison guards and law enforcement officers) resulted in an execution rate of 64.1. In contrast, "passion" murders had a rate of only 46.3. Among the passion murders, crimes stemming from sundry types of quarrels had an execution rate of 42.1; of the slayers of wives 49.3 per cent were put to death. Murders involving an illicit love relationship had the highest execution rate, 55.8 per cent, among the types of passion murder. The execution rate among rapists was highest when the rape victim was a white female.

TABLE 2
EXECUTION RATES BY TYPE OF CRIME, NORTH CAROLINA,
1909–1954

Type of Crime	Number of Capital Offenders Admitted to Death Row	Number of Death Row Inmates Executed	Pct. of Death Row Inmates Executed
Total committed	660	356	53.9
Murder	490	276	56.3
Rape	126	70	55.6
Burglary	41	10	23.9
Arson	3	0	0.0
Type of Murder			
Murder-Gain	161	116	72.0
Murder-Passion	285	132	46.3
Law officer killed	39	25	64.1
Type of Passion-Murder			
Quarrel-Murders	164	69	42.1
Wife-Murders	69	34	49.3
Profane Love-Murders	52	29	55.8
Type of Victim of Rape			
White adult	78	50	64.1
White minor	28	15	53.6
Negro adult	14	2	14.3
Negro minor	6	3	50.0
Type of Burglary			
Professional	4	3	75.0
Attack on female	12	5	41.7
Attack on male	4	1	25.0
Common	21	1	4.8

Of course, the legal aspects of the capital case would be the chief selective factor in determining whether the offender would be executed. However, could extra-legal factors also be present? The governors granted commutations in case of 229 of the 304 death sentences which were not carried out. The justifications they offered for commuta-

TABLE 3

MAJOR THEMES RECURRING IN GOVERNORS' STATEMENTS IN JUSTIFYING COMMUTATIONS OF DEATH SENTENCES FOR
MURDERERS AND RAPISTS, NORTH CAROLINA, 1909–1954[a]

Themes in Commutation Statements	Percentage of Commutation Statements Which Expressed Given Theme, by Type of Crime					
	Rape	Total murder	Murders for gain	Slayings of law officers	Passion murders	
Responsible officials and/or jury urged commutation	52.3	56.0	46.7	66.7	56.9	
Community urged commutation	13.6	16.4	10.0	25.0	17.2	
Age of offender or his underprivileged status	11.4	13.8	23.3	41.7	8.6	
Victim contributed to crime or was disreputable	29.5	17.6	6.7	16.7	20.7	
Mental condition of offender	20.5	32.7	33.3	16.7	34.5	
Crime was not premeditated	4.5	24.5	16.7	50.0	24.1	
Evidence does not justify death penalty or is of doubtful nature	50.0	24.5	36.7	—	23.3	
Number of cases	44	159	30	12	116	203

[a] Because several themes could be expressed in one statement, the percentages do not total 100.

tions throw some light on this question. Table 3 summarizes the most frequent themes found in the commutation statements for murderers and rapists. As would be expected, the governors often cited the failure of the case to meet legal requirements. Mental abnormality was noted in a third of the statements involving murders and a fifth of the statements involving rapists. Lack of premeditation was cited for a quarter of the murderers but for only two of the rapists. The evidence was deemed doubtful or otherwise inappropriate for capital punishment in half of the rapist commutations but only in a quarter of the murderer commutations.

Other themes move beyond the bounds of written law. Over half the statements cite the requests for commutation by court and other officials and/or by the jurors. Presumably legal aspects of the case are involved here, but often the requests appeared to reflect opinions that characteristics of the offender or the victim made the infliction of the supreme penalty inappropriate. For rapists, thirty per cent of the statements cited the bad reputation of the victim or the victim's contribution to the crime. This was true for eighteen per cent of the commuted murderers. For eleven per cent of the rapists and fourteen per cent of the murderers, the governors pointed to the extreme youth or elderliness of the offender and/or his socially underprivileged status. The governors called attention to the appeals for extension of mercy to the convict from citizens of the affected community in fourteen per cent of the commuted rapists and sixteen per cent of the commuted murderers.

The use of commutations for death sentences has declined in North Carolina because of revision of the state's statutes and perhaps because of more rigorous sifting out of questionable cases before commitment to death row. The 1941 General Assembly amended the law so that a jury could recommend life imprisonment in first degree burglary and arson convictions. The 1949 Legislature extended this to murder and rape convictions. The 1953 Legislature made it possible for defendants to obtain life imprisonment if their plea of guilty is accepted by the state.

As shown by Table 4, there has been a decline in proportion of commutation statements which question the evi-

TABLE 4
CHANGES OVER TIME PERIODS IN MAJOR
THEMES RECURRING IN GOVERNORS' STATEMENTS
IN JUSTIFYING COMMUTATIONS OF DEATH SENTENCES
FOR MURDERERS AND RAPISTS, NORTH CAROLINA[a]

Themes in Commutation Statements	Percentage of Commutation Statements which Expressed Given Theme During Given Years:		
	1909–1923	1924–1938	1939–1954
Responsible officials and/or jury urged commutation	69.6	52.5	44.4
Community urged commutation	31.9	11.3	5.6
Age of offender or his underprivileged status	11.6	8.8	22.9
Victim contributed to crime or was disreputable	21.7	16.3	25.9
Mental condition of offender	27.5	30.0	31.5
Crime was not premeditated	21.7	20.0	27.8
Evidence does not justify death penalty or is of doubtful nature	36.2	30.0	22.9
Number of cases	69	80	54

a Because several themes could be expressed in one statement, the percentages do not total 100.

dence in the case as justifying the death penalty, which cite the support of responsible officials and/or jurors, and which note requests from citizens for extension of mercy. On the other hand, an increasing proportion of commutation statements point to the age or underprivileged status of the offender. It would appear that, with improved communication and the expanding resources of the Paroles Commission available for the obtainment of information directly, the governors have had to depend less upon the officials and citizens of the local community for information. At the same time, there appears to be a growing awareness of the importance of environmental factors in criminal causation. It must be remembered that such an awareness would more likely be expressed before commitment to death row. Therefore, the statement of this theme in application to an already selected population is more remarkable than it might appear at first glance.

Now we turn to selective factors involving social and personal characteristics of the offender. First of all, capital punishment appears to be directed largely at the economically and socially underprivileged. Educational attainment and occupational data on death row population offer a possibility for testing this assumption.

The male capital offenders admitted to death row, Central Prison, had a mean educational attainment of 4.7 years compared with an average of 6.6 years for all male con-

TABLE 5

MEAN YEARS OF SCHOOLING COMPLETED BY MALES 15 YEARS AND OLDER, FOR SPECIFIED POPULATIONS COVERING PERIOD JULY 1, 1940 TO JUNE 30, 1954[a]

Total North Carolina[b]	7.47
Central Prison Admissions[c]	6.59
Death Row Admissions	4.65
Not Executed	4.78
Executed	4.54

[a] To test the significance of the differences in educational attainment, chi-square values were computed from the distribution of these three populations. The chi-square value of 1947 is significant at less than the one per cent level. When the Central Prison admissions and Death Row admissions were compared, a chi-square value of 152 was obtained. This was significant at less than the one per cent level. When the "executed" population was compared with the "not executed" population, the chi-square value of 5.45 was not significant statistically.

[b] Data of U. S. Census for 1940 and 1950 were combined to approximate period covered by reports of North Carolina Prison Department.

[c] Based on annual reports of North Carolina Prison Department; the period covered by these reports determined the choice of period for comparisons in this paper.

victs admitted to Central Prison and 7.5 years for all North
Carolina males aged fifteen years or more. The sources of
this data are shown in Table 5. Because the differences between these averages are statistically significant, it appears
that the socially underprivileged are heavily represented in
the death row population.

Occupational data on death row inmates are shown in
Table 6. Comparisons with, first, the total male population
of North Carolina and, second, the total admissions to
Central Prison reveal capital offenders were more heavily
representative of the laboring class, but to a definitely
less extent of the professional, managerial, proprietorial,
clerical, and craft occupations. There was relatively little
difference between the three populations in terms of proportion of farmers; however, the death row records often
reported the occupation as "farming," which could include
farm laborers as well as farm owners and farm tenants.
Therefore, it is likely that some of the "farmers" in death
row should be included among the farm laborers to increase further the occupational inferiority of the capital offenders.

A common assumption is that the death row population
is composed of the most hardened criminals. Our data do
not support this. We define as "hardened criminals" those
convicts who have served at least three prison sentences,
each of at least six months' duration, previous to their present prison term. Reports of the North Carolina Prison Department offer pertinent data for the period July 1, 1940
to June 30, 1954 on males admitted to Central Prison. Of
15,812 such male admissions, 21.1 per cent had served at
least three previous sentences and 45.6 per cent were serving their first prison sentence. During this same period, 189
males were committed to Death Row. Of these, 11.6 per
cent qualified as hardened criminals, but 52.9 per cent had
no previous prison sentence of six months or more. Of
these 189 males, 113 were put to death. Of the men executed, 15.9 per cent were hardened criminals and 49.6
per cent had no previous prison record.

It would appear that the hardened criminal is less characteristic of the capital offenders than of the general prison

TABLE 6
PERCENTAGE DISTRIBUTION OF NORTH
CAROLINA MALES, 15 YEARS AND OLDER,
JULY 1, 1940 TO JUNE 30, 1954a

Occupational Groups as Defined by U. S. Census	North Carolinab	Central Prison Admissionsc	Death Row Admissions
Total per cent	100.0	100.0	100.0
Professional, technical and kindred workers	3.6	0.2	—
Farmers and farm managers	23.8	17.2	24.2
Managers, officials, and proprietors, except farm	7.3	0.3	2.2
Clerical, sales, and kindred workers	8.3	1.5	0.5
Craftsmen, foremen, and kindred workers	12.2	14.8	5.4
Operatives and kindred workers	19.8	18.2	12.9
Private, household, and service workers	4.7	12.7	4.8
Farm laborers, foremen, and other laborers	20.3	35.1	50.0
Total Reported	959,144	12,468	186

a When the occupational distribution of total North Carolina males was compared with that of males admitted to Death Row, the chi-square value was 118.3. Comparison of the occupational distributions of males admitted to Central Prison and of males admitted to Death Row resulted in a 39.3 chi-square value. Both values were statistically significant at less than the one per cent level.

b Data of U. S. Census for 1940 and 1950 were combined to approximate period covered by reports of North Carolina Prison Department.

c Based on annual reports of North Carolina Prison Department.

population, even when we consider only those capital offenders who are executed.

Capital punishment is directed almost exclusively toward males. Of the 660 admitted to death row, only six were females; one white and five Negro women, of which two Negro women were executed. The chivalry implied in this differential treatment was expressed by Governor Locke Craige on March 21, 1916, when he commuted the death sentence of a white woman accused of chloroforming her husband, with the aid of her lover who strangled the husband:

> I cannot contemplate with approval that this woman, unworthy and blackened by sin though she be, shall be shrouded in the cerements of death, dragged along the fatal corridor and bound in the chair of death. . . . Humanity does not apply to women the inexorable law that it does to men. . . .

Another important selective factor is the race of the offender. Not considering the seven Indians who entered

TABLE 7

PERCENTAGE OF CAPITAL OFFENDERS
COMMITTED TO DEATH ROW WHO WERE EXECUTED,
BY OFFENSE AND RACE, NORTH CAROLINA, 1909–1954

Offense by Race	Number of Offenders on Death Row	Pct. of Offenders Executed			Pct. Change in Execution Rates Between Periods
		All Years	1909–1933	1934–1954	
Murderers					
Whites	153	43.8	29.3	52.6	79.5
Negroes	332	62.0	55.0	67.8	23.3
Rapists					
Whites	14	42.9	33.0	50.0	51.5
Negroes	110	56.4	53.5	58.2	8.8
Burglars					
Whites	3	0.0	0.0	0.0	0.0
Negroes	38	26.3	35.7	20.8	41.7

death row, Negroes represented 73.8 per cent of all death row inmates, 92.7 per cent of the first degree burglars, 88.7 per cent of the rapists, and 68.5 per cent of the murderers. Since Negroes tend to be heavily represented in the lower socio-economic class, the relationship between race and the functioning of capital punishment is affected by all of the other factors already discussed. The racial mores would appear to be a major influence in first degree burglary and rape cases, and to a lesser extent murder cases. However, some of the differences in application of the death penalty to the races can be explained in terms of class differences in likelihood of an individual to commit a capital crime and in ability to evade the maximum penalty once the crime had been perpetrated. Furthermore, the execution rates shown in Table 7 indicate that the difference between the races is being narrowed.

Summary

We have tried to demonstrate that capital punishment operates differentially on the basis of the type of crime and type of offender. It is doubtful that sufficient attention has been given this matter by those who defend the death penalty as one of the means of solving the crime problem. The deterrent and eugenic arguments in support of capital punishment rest on a consistent and certain application of the penalty according to carefully formulated principles. It would appear that consistency, certainty, and principles are lacking.

EXECUTIONS AND COMMUTATIONS IN PENNSYLVANIA*

BY MARVIN E. WOLFGANG, ARLENE KELLY, AND
HANS C. NOLDE**

The Basis for This Study

The purpose of this study is to analyze statistically the social characteristics of those persons who have been sentenced to death for the crime of murder since the introduction of the electric chair in Pennsylvania. The basic data consist of the case records of 439 persons sentenced to death for first degree murder[1] and detained under custody on death row between 1914 and 1958.[2] These records are

---

* An unrevised version of "Comparison of the Executed and the Commuted Among Admissions to Death Row," *Journal of Criminal Law, Criminology and Police Science,* vol. 53 (September 1962), pp. 301–311. Reprinted by special permission of the authors and the *Journal of Criminal Law, Criminology and Police Science.* Copyright ©, 1962, by Northwestern University School of Law.

** Miss Kelly and Mr. Nolde are graduates in sociology from the University of Pennsylvania. Miss Kelly has been doing social work for the past two years; Mr. Nolde is a law student at the University of Pennsylvania Law School.

[1] "All murder which shall be perpetrated by means of poison, or by lying in wait, or by any other kind of wilful, deliberate and premeditated killing, or which shall be committed in the perpetration of, or attempting to perpetrate any arson, rape, robbery, burglary, or kidnapping, shall be murder in the first degree." (From Article VII, Section 701 of the Pennsylvania Penal Code.)

The first statute to divide the crime of murder into degrees was enacted in Pennsylvania on April 22, 1794. Many other states of the union adopted this model with slight changes in the substantive law but with considerable variations in judicial interpretations. See, for example: Edwin R. Keedy, "History of the Pennsylvania Statute Creating Degrees of Murder," *University of Pennsylvania Law Review* (1949), 97:759–777; E. R. Keedy, "A Problem of First Degree Murder: Fisher v. United States," *ibid.* (1950), 99:267–292; E. R. Keedy, "Criminal Attempts at Common Law," *ibid.* (1954), 102:464–489.

[2] A recent review of data in the archives of the State Correctional Institution at Rockview, furnished by W. W. Thomas to

filed at the State Correctional Institution at Rockview, Pennsylvania, the only place in the state where the death penalty is administered. Because an offender sentenced to die is transported there only as his date of execution approaches, there are a number of offenders who were sentenced to die during the 1914–1958 period who do not appear in the present study because their sentences were commuted before being placed on death row at Rockview. Of those who did reach Rockview, 341 were executed and seventy-one were commuted; the remaining twenty-seven included persons who either died of natural causes on death row or for whom it has not been possible to determine the final disposition.

Although the amount and kind of information on individual cases varies greatly, most records provide sufficient data for analysis of the following major attributes of the convicted offender: age, sex,[3] race, nativity, occupation, and marital status. Additional information usually obtainable and secured from examination of the original bill of indictment and of the Pennsylvania Legislative Journal includes: type of counsel for the defendant (private or court-appointed); type of murder (felony or non-felony); reasons for commutation of the death sentence.

There is a growing body of literature concerned with differential treatment of offenders who have committed similar offenses, but discussion usually centers around the sentencing problem and judicial caprice in sentencing is contrasted with the need for individual treatment.[4] It is a

---

the Bureau of Corrections, indicates that there were 433 total dispositions from death row in that institution between 1915 and 1959; of these, 347 were executed (eighty per cent), and eighty-six were commuted (twenty per cent). (*Populations in the Bureau of Correction During August 1960,* Camp Hill, Pennsylvania: Directorate of Research and Statistics, Department of Justice, Bureau of Correction, p. 3.)

[3] The number of females sentenced to die is too small to analyze separately, so that for all intents and purposes we are referring to males throughout the study. In only four cases during the entire period were females detained on death row; and of these, two were executed and two were commuted.

[4] For a cogent discussion of these matters, see: Sheldon Glueck, "The Sentencing Problem," *Federal Probation* (Dec.,

widely held belief that minority groups, particularly Negroes, suffer discrimination in the courts, but there are few studies that examine this hypothesis empirically.[5] Because there are always many difficulties encountered when seeking to hold constant a variety of factors in the personal and social background of offenders who appear before the courts, carefully controlled research in this area of differential judicial treatment is still in its nascency.

The present study does not pretend to overcome these difficulties. We are required to assume, in the absence of detailed psychological analyses and other kinds of data regarding the specific character of the murder, the offender, and his victim, that there has been some randomness in the distribution of known factors. Hence, we are able to work only with the accessible gross social variables in the records. However, there is one common underlying factor, it must be remembered, that is socially and legally visible and that permits us to examine the present cases as a homogeneous group already controlled for the most significant attribute: all of these persons have been convicted—justly or unjustly—of having committed first degree murder and have been sentenced to death. There are, of course, many social and legal forces that function selectively prior to this stage and that have produced many differences in the conditions surrounding commission of the crime. Age, race, sex, social status and other factors have long been recog-

1956), 20:15–25; Edward Green, "An Analysis of the Sentencing Practices of Criminal Court Judges in Philadelphia," Ph.D. dissertation, University of Pennsylvania, 1959; Albert Morris (ed.), "What's New in Sentencing," Correctional Research (October, 1957), Bulletin No. 7.

[5] F. J. Gaudet, G. S. Harris, and C. W. St. John, "Individual Differences in the Sentencing Tendencies of Judges," Journal of Criminal Law and Criminology (1933), 23:811–818; Harold E. Lane, "Illogical Variations in Sentences of Felons Committed to Massachusetts State Prison," ibid. (1941), 32:171–190; E. Frankel, "The Offender and the Court: A Statistical Analysis of the Sentencing of Delinquents," ibid. (1940), 31:448–456; Edwin M. Lemert and Judy Rosberg, "The Administration of Justice to Minority Groups in Los Angeles County," University of California Publications in Culture and Society, Vol. II, No. 1, 1948, pp. 1–28; Edward Green, op. cit.

nized as functioning selectively in the commission of this and other types of crime.[6] Moreover, the youthful first offender even though having committed a heinous murder is rarely sentenced to death. The reasons and emotions involved in court decisions that refrain from legally permitted use of the death penalty are so numerous that research has only scratched the surface of these phenomena. There are no official public national statistics on the number of capital crimes committed in the United States each year, but good estimates suggest that not more than fifteen per cent of all criminal homicides are capital crimes. In any case, the *Uniform Crime Reports* for 1959 reveal that there were 8,583 murders and non-negligent manslaughters throughout the country.[7] For the same year *National Prisoner Statistics* reported only forty-nine executions for the nation.[8] In 1959 there were 285 murders and non-negligent manslaughters in Pennsylvania, and the state executed three persons during that year. Because only nine states presently have abolished the death penalty by statute, it is obvious that executions are disappearing de facto if not de jure and that a variety of factors in concatenation function to spare most convicted murderers from execution.

We are not here analyzing the factors that determine whether a penalty of death or some lesser penalty is more likely to be the sentence of the court. We recognize that from the total population capable of committing murder selective forces are operating to "cause" some persons rather than others to commit the crime of murder, to be detected, to be prosecuted, to be convicted, to be sentenced to death and to be held in custody on death row. The cases presently under analysis are taken from this last level of the whole cultural and judicial process of selectivity. We begin with all persons who have been sentenced to die and who have been detained on death row. We then dichoto-

[6] Marvin E. Wolfgang, *Patterns in Criminal Homicide,* Philadelphia, University of Pennsylvania Press, 1958.

[7] *Uniform Crime Reports*—1959, Washington, D.C.: United States Department of Justice, 1960, p. 33.

[8] "Executions 1959," *National Prisoner Statistics,* Washington, D.C.: Federal Bureau of Prisons, Number 23, Feb., 1960.

mize this group into (a) those persons who actually were executed (or those whose sentences were in fact carried out) and (b) those whose sentences of death were commuted to a lesser penalty (usually life imprisonment).[9] Whether there was legal or moral justification for the sentences of death is not our immediate concern. We may even assume (for lack of primary evidence upon which to base any other assumption) that all of those persons were equally guilty of first degree murder and were given equal treatment by the courts. At any rate, all of these offenders received identical sentences for their crimes. This element of homogeneity is one of the most severe that our society can place upon its citizens, but our judicial machinery permits reconsideration of the sentence in the form of a pardon or commutation. It is important, therefore, for us to know something about any differences that may exist between those persons who suffer the full extent of the law through death and those who have enjoyed the privilege of administrative reconsideration and retraction of the original sentence.

Comparison of the Executed and the Commuted

Because our political institutional machinery does provide a means for mitigating the severity of a death sentence pronounced in the judicial process, we should expect some differences to be apparent between offenders who have been executed and those who were commuted. However, assuming that this legal machinery functions on the basis of rational and legal principles and discriminates among convicted offenders only in these ways, any class or racial differences that are noted between the executed and commuted cast doubt on the basic principles. Only a minimal number of factors can presently be examined in this kind of comparison because of the paucity of data available to the

[9] For discussion and research on pardons and commutations, see: "Pardons and Commutations," *The Prison Journal* (Philadelphia: The Pennsylvania Prison Society), April, 1959, Vol. 39; also, Marvin E. Wolfgang, "Murder, the Pardon Board, and Recommendations by Judges and District Attorneys," *Journal of Criminal Law, Criminology and Police Science*, (1959), 50:338–346.

researcher. But statistical analysis even on a macroscopic level is useful for it provides a point of departure for more intensive examination of the refined differentials that are placed in focus in this way.

To assure elimination of spurious associations due to chance operation we have employed common devices for testing the data. These include the chi-square (X^2) with correction for continuity and the test of significance of differences between proportions, both with a probability level (P value) of less than .05. The total N, or number of cases possible for comparison among each of the variables under analysis, differs from one table to another because not all of the same information was available for all 439 cases. Among these cases for which data are available, we have used test statistics to determine whether statistically significant differences occur between the executed and commuted, and where the P value is less than .05 we are in effect saying that the difference is not due to chance factors, or that some selectivity is functioning that differentiates those who were put to death from those who were spared the ultimate penalty.

Type of Murder. Although all of these cases are defined in Pennsylvania as first degree murder, an important legal and social difference is whether the death occurred in conjunction with, or as a result of, commission of another type of felony.[10] In Pennsylvania any death that occurs during the commission of arson, burglary, robbery, rape or kidnapping is by statute prosecuted as a first degree murder, whether or not the felon committed, intended or premeditated the slaying. This type of slaying is referred to as "felony murder," and all other types of murder are "non-felony murder." While there may be many extenuating circumstances involved in commission of a non-felony murder, there can be little doubt that the court nonetheless found the defendant guilty of a premeditated, intentional

[10] Leonard D. Savitz, "Capital Crimes As Defined in American Statutory Law," *Journal of Criminal Law, Criminology and Police Science* (1955), 46: 355–363. See also, *Patterns in Criminal Homicide,* Chapter 13, "Homicide During Commission of Another Felony."

killing. A felony murder may involve deliberate killing concomitant to another felony, but usually this type of slaying occurs incidental and peripheral to the principal purpose of another crime, which most commonly is some form of theft or crime for financial profit.[11]

Relative to these two types of murder a null hypothesis states: among felony and non-felony murderers sentenced to death and detained on death row there are no significant differences in the proportions who are subsequently executed or commuted. Table 1 presents the distribution of these cases and a test for significance of difference reveals that there is an association between conviction of a felony murder and being executed for the crime. Not only are there absolutely more felony murders (184) than non-felony murders (125) among the total cases for which information has been available, but proportionately more felony murderers than non-felony murderers actually suffer the death penalty; contrariwise, more non-felony cases have their sentences commuted. We shall later examine these relationships by holding constant the factor of race.

TABLE 1

TYPE OF MURDER BY FINAL DISPOSITION

Final Disposition	Felony Murder		Non-Felony Murder		Total	
	N	%	N	%	N	%
Executed	159	86.4	92	73.6	251	81.2
Commuted	25	13.6	33	26.4	58	18.8
Total	184	100.0	125	100.0	309	100.0

$X^2 = 7.14$; P less than .01

These findings are interesting simply as descriptive statistics of the disposition of capital crimes, but they take on important meaning because of wide state variations in the definition of felony murder.[12] Moreover, recent suggestions have been made to eliminate from the penal code an automatic charge of first degree murder in felony homicide cases. The felony murder rule has also been subjected to

[11] *Patterns in Criminal Homicide*, pp. 238–244.
[12] Savitz, *op. cit.*

some criticism in England from which country our own use of this rule has evolved.[13] An act that is by statute labeled "first degree murder" is consequently a capital crime and subjects the offenders, whether principals in the first or second degree, to the maximum penalty. Thus, all other things being equal a state such as Kansas that considers as a felony murder a death occurring during *any* felony proportionately has a greater number of capital offenders involved in the administration of justice than does a state as Massachusetts that considers as felony murder a death occurring only during a crime punishable by death or life imprisonment. On the basis of the experience in Pennsylvania, an offender categorized as having been convicted of a felony murder, regardless of the kind of felony in which he participated concurrent to the death and irrespective of how the death occurred (by accident, by a police officer, or by the offender directly), has less probability of having his death sentence commuted. Although we cannot speak conclusively about experience in other states, it would appear that states with felony murder statutes so broad in scope as to include a death during any felony would have an even higher proportion of executions than we have found in Pennsylvania. This assumption leads to a generalization requiring further study; namely, that the more inclusive the definition of felony murder, the higher the proportion of executions and the greater will be the differential in final disposition between felony and non-felony murderers.

We cannot know what would have been the fate of the 184 felony murderers sentenced to death had there been no statutory definition of felony homicide as first degree murder; but it is probably safe to say that more than a few of the 159 defendants who were executed under this ruling would have been convicted of less serious forms of criminal homicide and consequently would not have received sentences of death and would not have been executed.[14] It

13 *Royal Commission on Capital Punishment 1949–1953 Report,* London: Her Majesty's Stationery Office, 1953, p. 29.

14 Especially would this statement be valid for at least twenty persons executed who were not directly responsible for the deaths which occurred.

appears, then, that abolition of the felony murder rule
would reduce the number of executions if the past proportion of commutations for non-felony cases should continue.
At any rate, nearly half a century of Pennsylvania history
indicates that a significantly higher proportion of felony
murder than of non-felony murder cases were carried to
the full extent of society's negative reaction to homicide.

Age of the Offender. Table 2 shows the distribution of
407 cases for whom age at time of arrival on death row
was known. As might be expected, the polar ends of the
age groups (fifteen–nineteen years, and those fifty-five
years and over) have the lowest frequency of execution
and consequently the highest frequency of commutation. As

TABLE 2
FINAL DISPOSITION BY AGE OF OFFENDER

Age of Offender	Executed N	Commuted N	Per Cent Executed	Total N
15–19	7	7	50.0	14
20–24	96	8	92.3	104
25–29	71	21	77.2	92
30–34	58	12	82.9	70
35–39	48	9	84.2	57
40–44	26	6	81.3	32
45–49	18	2	90.0	20
50–54	7	1	87.5	8
55 +	5	5	50.0	10
Total	336	71	82.6	407

a matter of fact, an equal number in each of these age
groups were executed as were commuted. The highest frequency (ninety-two per cent) of execution occurs in the age
group twenty–twenty-four years. Although it is true that the
highest rate of criminal homicide occurs in this same age
group,[15] this fact does not explain their highest proportion
of executions. The answer seems to lie in the fact that this
age group contributes most disproportionately to felony
murders.[16] Of the 160 felony murderers executed, only

[15] *Patterns in Criminal Homicide*, pp. 65–78.
[16] Among those cases for whom information was available

sixteen, or ten per cent, were aged twenty–twenty-four. Although persons in the youngest (fifteen–nineteen years) and the oldest (fifty-five years and over) age groups may be treated differentially because of age, it appears that within the age range from twenty through fifty-four age per se has little or no influence on final disposition. Rather, it is the higher frequency of felony murders that most directly affects the final disposition, as is indicated by the association between felony murder, execution, and the age class twenty–twenty-four years. This age group constitutes the highest frequency among all felony murderers; consequently, any change in the statutes regarding felony murder would most directly affect homicide offenders in their early twenties. Non-felony murders appear to be more evenly distributed throughout the age groups from fifteen–nineteen to age fifty-five and over. Finally, the median age for executed felony murderers is 27.5 years, and the median age for executed non-felony murderers is 35.7 years. The interrelationship therefore is strikingly obvious between the proportion of persons convicted of murder who (a) are executed, (b) are young adults, and (c) committed felony murder.

Race of the Offender. Much previous research in criminal homicide, which includes murder in the first degree, has demonstrated the fact that a disproportionate contribution to the homicide rate is made by Negroes.[17] It is no surprise, therefore, that as many as thirty-six per cent of persons placed on death row are Negro. Consistent with independent research and the *Uniform Crime Reports,* Negroes comprise between three and four times more of the criminal homicide cases (either as offenders or as victims) than they do of the general population.

What interests us in the present analysis, however, is not

for both age and type of murder (N = 317), there are 185 felony murderers and 132 non-felony murderers; of the felony murderers, 160, or eighty-seven per cent, were executed compared to ninety-nine, or seventy-five per cent, of non-felony murderers.

[17] For an analysis of criminal homicide rates by race both in Philadelphia and in other community studies, see *Patterns in Criminal Homicide,* pp. 31–46.

the rate of criminal homicide but the ratio of executed-to-commuted Negroes compared to this same ratio among whites. Using the null hypothesis again, we may assert that there is no significant difference between Negroes and whites in the proportionate distributions of capital offenders who are ultimately executed and those who are commuted. Table 3 indicates that this hypothesis is rejected and that there is an association between race and type of disposition. The probability value resulting from the X^2 reveals in this table that compared to whites a significantly higher proportion of Negroes are executed instead of commuted.

TABLE 3
RACE OF THE OFFENDER BY FINAL DISPOSITION

Final Disposition	Negro		White		Total	
	N	%	N	%	N	%
Executed	130	88.4	210	79.8	340	82.9
Commuted	17	11.6	53	20.2	70	17.1
Total	147	100.0	263	100.0	410	100.0

$X^2 = 4.33$; P less than .05

Although there may be a host of factors other than race involved in this frequency distribution, something more than chance has operated over the years to produce this racial difference. On the basis of this study it is not possible to indict the judicial and other public processes prior to the death row as responsible for the association between Negroes and higher frequency of executions; nor is it entirely correct to assume that from the time of their appearance on death row Negroes are discriminated against by the Pardon Board. Too many unknown or presently immeasurable factors prevent our making definitive statements about the relationship. Nevertheless, because the Negro/high-execution association is statistically present, some suspicion of racial discrimination can hardly be avoided. If such a relationship had not appeared, this kind of suspicion could have been allayed; the existence of the relationship, although not "proving" differential bias by the Pardon Boards over the years since 1914, strongly suggests that such bias has existed.

Within the confines of the data available examination has been made of race and type of final disposition by holding constant the factor of age. Of the total number of cases for which there is information for each of these variables (N = 308), no significant differences emerged. When tests were run to determine association only between race and type of murder (excluding final disposition), both among Negroes and among whites a little over six out of ten had been convicted of felony murder.[18] (See Table 4.) No significant differences occurred in this comparison; hence, the previously noted significant association between felony murder and a high proportion of executions could not account for the proportionately greater number of Negro offenders who are executed. Furthermore, there are no important differences in the distributions of Negro and white offenders among non-felony murder cases according to the type of disposition (Table 4). In short, although among non-felony cases a higher percentage of Negroes (seventy-nine per cent) than of whites (seventy-one per cent) are executed, it is not a statistically significant difference and could be due to chance.

But, as Table 4 indicates, it is among felony murder cases that major differences may be noted when type of disposition is examined: ninety-four per cent of Negro felony murderers are executed compared to eighty-three per cent of white felony murderers. Thus, we see that the earlier statistical association between executions and felony murder is principally due to the fact that proportionately a much greater number of Negro felony murderers are executed. In terms of final disposition, no significant differences occur when Negro felony murder is compared with Negro non-felony murder; and no significant differences occur when white felony murder is compared with white non-felony murder.

Here, then, is a point at which the lack of statistical significance carries important meaning when placed side by side with a relationship that is significant. Thus, the fact

18 Of 207 whites, 121, or fifty-nine per cent, had been convicted of felony murder; of 101 Negroes, sixty-three, or sixty-three per cent, had been convicted of felony murder.

TABLE 4

RACE OF OFFENDER BY TYPE OF MURDER AND FINAL DISPOSITION

| Final Disposition | Negro | | | | White | | | | Total | |
| | (A) Felony Murder | | (B) Non-Felony Murder | | (C) Felony Murder | | (D) Non-Felony Murder | | | |
	N	%	N	%	N	%	N	%	N	%
Executed	59	93.7	30	79.0	100	82.6	61	70.9	250	81.2
Commuted	4	6.3	8	21.0	21	17.4	25	29.1	58	18.8
Total	63	100.0	38	100.0	121	100.0	86	100.0	308	100.0

For columns (A) and (C): $X^2 = 4.27$; P less than .05
For columns (B) and (D); (A) and (B); (C) and (D): not significant

that Negroes on death row do not comprise a significantly higher proportion of felony murderers than do whites, combined with the fact that a significantly higher proportion of Negro felony murderers are executed than are white felony murderers focuses the direction of differential treatment. It is the Negro felony murderer more than any other type of offender who will suffer the death penalty. Especially is this finding striking when we note that nearly three times more white (17.4 per cent) than Negro (6.3 per cent) felony murderers have their sentences commuted.

Nativity. Although differentials between the native-born and the foreign-born have been noted relative to the commission of certain types of crime[19] our point of reference once again is executions and commutations among those who have been sentenced to death and have been held in custody on death row. A null hypothesis states: there is no significant difference between native-born and foreign-born in the proportions executed and commuted. (Negro males have been eliminated from this particular analysis for obvious reasons.) Table 5 presents data by nativity and disposition and shows that the hypothesis generally is not rejected. Too many national groups are involved to analyze these cases statistically by country of origin.

TABLE 5
NATIVITY OF OFFENDER BY FINAL DISPOSITION

Final Disposition	Native Born		Foreign Born	
	N	%	N	%
Executed	127	80.9	83	79.8
Commuted	30	19.1	21	20.2
Total	157	100.0	104	100.0

X^2 test not significant

In order to determine whether there are interrelationships obscured by the factor of type of murder, Table 6 is presented below.

[19] For a general survey of nativity and crime, see Donald R. Taft, *Criminology,* 3rd edition, New York: Macmillan Co., 1956, pp. 152–166; also, E. H. Sutherland and D. Cressey, *Principles of Criminology,* 5th edition, Philadelphia: J. B. Lippincott, 1955, pp. 143–150.

TABLE 6
NATIVITY BY TYPE OF MURDER

Type of Murder	Native Born		Foreign Born	
	N	%	N	%
Felony	83	67.5	38	46.3
Non-Felony	40	32.5	44	53.7
Total	123	100.0	82	100.0

$X^2 = 8.25$; P less than .01

Among those on death row, proportionately and significantly more native-born than foreign-born offenders committed felony murder. Of the 123 native-born offenders two-thirds had committed felony murder; whereas, among the eighty-two foreign-born offenders less than half had committed felony murder. We should expect, on the basis of our previous finding of a relationship between felony murder and higher frequency of executions, that significantly more native-born than foreign-born offenders would be executed. Therefore, the observed absence of any significant association between nativity and final disposition (as shown in Table 5) is meaningful and Table 6 indicates that proportionately fewer native-born than foreign-born felony murderers are executed.

Table 7 should help to clarify the relationships among these various attributes. As it indicates, nearly ninety per cent of foreign-born felony murderers are executed compared to slightly less than eighty per cent of native-born felony murderers. However, the difference does not quite reach the level of statistical significance. It is important to recognize what cannot be asserted statistically from this table. We cannot say, for example, that compared with the native-born significantly more foreign-born felony murderers are executed (columns A and C); nor that more foreign-born non-felony murderers are executed (columns B and D); nor that among the native-born more felony murderers than non-felony murderers are executed (columns A and B). The only statistically significant difference that emerges from this particular analysis is that among the foreign-born more felony murderers (ninety per cent) than

TABLE 7

NATIVITY OF OFFENDER BY TYPE OF MURDER AND FINAL DISPOSITION

	Native Born				Foreign Born			
	(A)		(B)		(C)		(D)	
	Felony Murder		Non-Felony Murder		Felony Murder		Non-Felony Murder	
Final Disposition	N	%	N	%	N	%	N	%
Executed	66	79.5	30	75.0	34	89.5	30	68.2
Commuted	17	20.5	10	25.0	4	10.5	14	31.8
Total	83	100.0	40	100.0	38	100.0	44	100.0

For columns (C) and (D): $X^2 = 4.14$; P less than .05
For columns (A) and (B); (A) and (C); (B) and (D): not significant

non-felony murderers (sixty-eight per cent) are executed (columns C and D). A statement about commutations is, of course, equally true; that is, among the foreign-born significantly more non-felony murderers (thirty-two per cent) than felony murderers (eleven per cent) have their sentences commuted. This finding suggests that there may have been some kind of conflict between the communal mores of the foreign-born who committed non-felony murder and the legal codes of the host culture to which the immigrants came, and that the Pardon Boards (if not the courts) recognized this culture conflict as a basis for mitigation of the severity of the sentence.[20]

Race and Nativity Compared. At this point in our analysis we can make some interesting generalizations about the various sets of attributes consisting of ethnic status (Negro, white, native-born, foreign-born); types of murder (felony, non-felony); and type of final disposition (execution, commutation).

1. If an offender commits a first degree murder, he is more likely to be executed than commuted (in a ratio between three and four to one) regardless of his ethnic affiliation.

2. Negroes (in a ratio of five to one) more than whites (in a ratio of four to one) are more likely to be executed than commuted.

3. If the offense is a non-felony first degree murder, there are no statistically significant differences among ethnic groups in the proportions that are executed, although a higher proportion of foreign-born (thirty-two per cent) than of native-born (twenty-five per cent) or of Negroes (twenty-one per cent) have their sentences commuted.

4. If the offense is a felony murder, a significantly higher proportion of Negroes (ninety-four per cent) than of whites (eighty-three per cent) are executed.

5. If the offense is a felony murder, there is no significant difference in the proportion of offenders executed when Negroes (ninety-four per cent) are compared with the foreign-born whites (ninety per cent), nor when the

[20] Thorsten Sellin, *Culture Conflict and Crime,* New York: Social Science Research Council Bulletin No. 41, 1938.

foreign-born whites are compared with the native-born whites (eighty per cent).

6. If the offense is a felony murder, there is a significant difference between the proportion of Negroes (ninety-four per cent) and of native-born whites (eighty per cent) executed.

7. The statistically greatest likelihood of being executed occurs among Negro felony murderers (ninety-four per cent).

8. The statistically greatest likelihood of being commuted occurs among foreign-born white non-felony murderers (thirty-two per cent).

Occupation and Marital Status. Our null hypothesis again states that there are no significant differences in the distribution by occupational status of capital offenders who have been executed, compared to capital offenders who have been commuted. Table 8 presents these distributions, and analysis does not reject this hypothesis. Moreover, no significant differences occur when the table is compressed into

TABLE 8
FINAL DISPOSITION BY OCCUPATION OF OFFENDER[a]

Occupation of Offender	Executed	Commuted	Total
Professional	5	0	5
Farmers and farm managers	0	2	2
Managers, officials, proprietors	7	0	7
Clerical, sales	5	1	6
Craftsmen, foremen	60	9	69
Operatives, kindred workers	75	20	95
Laborers, incl. farm	122	21	143
Service workers, household	51	15	66
Total	325	68	393

[a] Adapted from occupational categories in *Alphabetical Index of Occupations and Industries,* United States Department of Commerce, Bureau of Census, Washington, D. C., 1950, p. vi.

relatively similar occupational groupings, or when race or type of murder is held constant. It cannot be said, therefore, on the basis of these data, that differential application of the death penalty among those persons who ultimately reach death row is due to social class variation as represented by occupation. The race differential previously noted remains therefore unaffected by the factor of social class.

Similarly, no important differences appear between the executed and commuted when examined in terms of marital status. One interesting feature is that there are five times as many widowers among the commuted as among the executed, even though the executed outnumbered the commuted nearly five to one. The major reason appears to be that many of the commuted had slain their wives in non-felony murders.

Counsel. An a priori assumption suggests that a private counsel will devote more attention and energy to his client's case than will a court-appointed attorney. A variety of reasons may be offered to explain why this assumption appears to be valid, although we are not necessarily casting any aspersion on capable court-appointed attorneys. However, the expenses incurred in pursuing a murder case through the judicial process from indictment to petition for commutation would seem to handicap the court-appointed counsel in preparation of his case. If incentive to work diligently on the case is present, expenses usually are not; and lack of the latter may sometimes reduce the former. Moreover, it is suggested that younger lawyers eager or willing to accept these cases for experience are often appointed by the courts to act as counsel for persons indicted for murder. More thorough analyses of the system of court-appointed counsel, the methods of selection of counsel, and the qualification of the appointed attorneys are needed before any valid assertions can be made that the defendant with a court-appointed counsel is at a definite disadvantage.

However, the data presented in Table 9 indicate that there is a significant relationship between type of counsel and final disposition, for less than fifteen per cent of the death-row offenders with a court-appointed counsel received commutation of sentence compared to over twenty-five per cent of those offenders with private counsel. Refined examination of the data leads us to conclude that race is the major factor influencing this association. Among whites, no significant differences are noted in the final dis-

TABLE 9

RACE OF OFFENDER AND TYPE OF COUNSEL BY FINAL DISPOSITION

	Negro				White			
	(A) Court-Appointed Counsel		(B) Private Counsel		(C) Court-Appointed Counsel		(D) Private Counsel	
Final Disposition	N	%	N	%	N	%	N	%
Executed	93	91.2	9	69.2	121	81.2	53	75.7
Commuted	9	8.8	4	30.8	28	18.8	17	24.3
Total	102	100.0	13	100.0	149	100.0	70	100.0

For columns (A) + (C) and (B) + (D): $X^2 = 4.14$; P less than .05

For columns (A) and (B): $X^2 = 5.40$; P less than .05

For columns (A) and (C): $X^2 = 4.04$; P less than .05

For columns (C) and (D); (B) and (D): not significant

position according to whether the defendant had a private or a court-appointed counsel; but among Negroes, a decided relationship is discernible. It appears that if a Negro offender has a private counsel he is much more likely to have his death sentence commuted than if he has a court-appointed attorney. The number of cases (thirteen) of Negroes on death row having a private attorney is so small that statistical analysis must be viewed with much caution. If the counsel is private, no significant differences are noted between whites and Negroes in the final disposition; hence, the race differential under private counsel disappears. But if the counsel is court-appointed, the race differential is again evident, for proportionately twice as many whites (nineteen per cent) have sentences commuted as do Negroes (nine per cent).

Reasons for Commutation

Of the total seventy-one commutations over the period examined, information was available regarding the reasons for commutation in sixty-two cases. The number is too small for more refined analysis than the frequencies presented in Table 10. (Overlapping in these commutation themes means that the total percentage is more than one hundred.) The seventy-one cases represent over seventeen per cent of the total 407 persons sent to death row between 1914 and 1958. Thus, in nearly one out of six cases in which a court had pronounced the death sentence and the defendant had moved as close to the electric chair as being in custody at the center for executions, a politically designated body—the Board of Pardons—found legally justifiable reasons to impose limits on the courts' decisions.

It is especially interesting to note that of the eleven reasons given for commuting sentences, four involve serious doubts about the circumstances of the slaying so that the status of first degree murder is legally in question. These items include: lack of premeditation (twenty-six per cent), provocation by victim (eleven per cent), not directly responsible for the death (eight per cent), and the possibility of mistaken identity (five per cent). All told, these items (under "A" in Table 10) related to the crime itself ac-

TABLE 10

NUMBER AND PER CENT COMMUTED ACCORDING TO REASON
FOR COMMUTATION[a]

Reason for Commutation	Number Commuted	Per Cent Commuted
A. *Relative to Crime:*		
Lack of premeditation	16	25.8
Provocation by victim	7	11.3
Not directly responsible for death	5	8.0
Possibility of mistaken identity	3	4.8
	31	49.9
B. *Relative to Defendant:*		
Previous good record	9	14.7
Mentally deficient or diseased	9	14.7
Intoxication at time of crime	8	12.9
Comparative youth	7	11.3
Lacking (or poor) family background	3	4.8
	36	58.4
C. *Relative to Court Trial:*		
Accomplices received lesser sentences	13	20.9
Deprivation of right to fair trial	4	6.4
	17	27.3

a More than one reason was given for some of the 62 persons commuted; hence, the per cent commuted on the table totals more than one hundred. Our interest, however, is in the frequency with which each reason for commutation occurred among the total persons commuted.

count for fifty per cent of the reasons for commutation.[21] Another fifty-nine per cent of the commutation themes ("B" in Table 10) are related to the character of the defendant rather than to aspects of the crime and include such items as the comparative youthfulness of the offender, his previous good record, poor family background, mental condition and intoxication at the time of the crime. Finally,

21 It is conceivable that "intoxication at time of crime" could be added to this list of items that relate to the crime instead of being listed under items related to the defendant. However, drunkenness is not generally a legally justifiable basis for reduction of the seriousness of the crime nor for mitigation of the penalty.

in twenty-seven per cent of these commutation statements ("C" in Table 10) the reason given was most directly related to the conduct of the trial, for in twenty-one per cent it was noted that accomplices had received lesser sentences and in six per cent the defendants had been considered as having been deprived of fair trials.

Summary and Conclusion

An attempt has been made in the foregoing analysis to examine the application of the death penalty in Pennsylvania since introduction of electrocutions in 1914. The original group studied consisted of 439 cases of persons who were held in custody awaiting final disposition at the state center for execution. This number was reduced as additional variables were introduced for analysis, for all data were not available for each case. The major focus of attention has been on the proportion of persons whose sentences were executed and those whose sentences were commuted. Significant relationships (P less than .05) were found to exist between the type of final disposition and several attributes summarized under A and B below. The numbered item under A was compared with the same numbered item under B relative to final disposition.

A Attributes Associated With Execution	B Attributes Associated With Commutation
1. Felony murder	1. Non-felony murder
2. Offenders 20–24 years of age	2. Offenders 15–19 or 55+ years
3. Negro offenders	3. White offenders
4. Negro felony offenders	4. White felony offenders
5. Foreign-born white felony offenders	5. Foreign-born white non-felony offenders
6. Offenders with court-appointed counsel	6. Offenders with private counsel
7. Negro offenders with court-appointed counsel	7. Negro offenders with private counsel
8. Negro offenders with court-appointed counsel	8. White offenders with court-appointed counsel

No significant differences in distributions were noted when the following were analyzed:

Age and race with type of murder
Race and felony murder
Race and non-felony murder
Among Negroes, type of murder and final disposition
Among whites, type of murder and final disposition
Among native-born whites, type of murder and final disposition
Non-felony murder, by nativity and final disposition
Occupation and final disposition
Occupation, by race and type of murder
Marital status and final disposition
Among whites, type of counsel and final disposition
Among offenders with private counsel, race and final disposition

The quality and quantity of data which were available for research do not permit more refined analysis, but on the basis of what we have, it appears that the three significant findings are intricately interrelated: type of murder, race of the offender, and type of counsel. The one factor that links each of the others together is that of race; for while more offenders convicted of felony murder and offenders with court-appointed counsel are executed than offenders convicted of non-felony murder and offenders with private counsel, respectively, these differences are produced by the fact that significantly more Negroes than whites are executed. This race differential bears no relationship to the fact that the homicide rate (or perhaps even the murder rate) is higher for Negroes than for whites in the general population. We have consistently posed the question: after the pre-death-row factors have selectively functioned to produce a group possessing the major element of homogeneity characterized by being convicted of first degree murder and held in custody at the center for execution, what measurable factors differentiate those who are executed from those who are commuted? While the present study has not been able to draw any conclusions regarding differential treatment of Negroes in the courts, and although there may be many factors obscured by the available gross data, there is reason to suspect—and statistically significant evidence to support the suspicion—that Negroes have not received equal consideration for commutation of the death penalty.

Thus, although differences in the disposition of capital offenders probably function to the greatest extent before sentencing, differences may be found even after offenders have been committed to death. This study of the Pennsylvania data has discovered nothing new; Johnson's analysis in North Carolina has many similarities and also used death-row data.[22] But any empirical verification of previously assumed differences among persons who received society's ultimate sanction should be of value in understanding the operation of our legal principles. The fact that race is one of these significant differences is a social and political violation of the principle of equal justice and is an obvious argument for those who favor abolition of the death penalty.

Chapter Nine

CRIMINAL JUSTICE: CASE HISTORIES

INTRODUCTION

It is doubtful whether any one dominant belief or feeling motivates all opponents of the death penalty. No doubt many abolitionists rest their case on the incontrovertible fact that this method of punishment consists in deliberately killing human beings, and that the better one gets to know them as persons, the quicker one loses his stomach for executing them. This is what Mrs. Sara Ehrmann rightly calls "the 'human' side of capital punishment." It is fitting, therefore, that this volume should conclude with a series of case histories illustrating in some depth what the contro-

[22] Elmer Johnson, "Selective Factors in Capital Punishment," *Social Forces* (1957), 36:165–169.

versy over the death penalty in the United States is really about.

The four cases related here date from the past decade. All involved the crime of murder. The criminal in each case was male. The first occurred in Texas, the next in Georgia, the third in New York, and the last in Illinois. In one, the accused was a Mexican-American; in another, a Puerto Rican; in another, a Negro. Only in one case was the criminal a white American. In terms of geographic region, racial origin, sex and type of crime, these four cases are a fair sample of the crimes that result in a capital indictment and of the men currently being sentenced to death in this country.

But in none of these cases was the death penalty carried out! Thus, in the disposition of these four convicts, it is possible to see in capsule form what abolitionists are striving for. Each case illustrates the risks in capital punishment as well as whatever is problematic and imprudent in imprisoning and possibly later releasing, rather than executing, men found guilty of brutal crimes.

James Fulton Foster, of course, did not commit the murder for which he was sentenced to death. His case, ably described by John Bartlow Martin,[1] has often been cited in recent years to show that innocent men even now can be sentenced to death, and that an erroneous execution can sometimes be averted only if the guilty man is willing to confess.

Alvaro Alcorta's misfortune was the not uncommon one of being prosecuted for a graver crime than he actually committed, and of being convicted through illegal suppression of evidence by the prosecution. The United States Supreme Court came to Alcorta's rescue—a rare thing, as we have seen—and ordered a new trial. He was again found guilty, but this time his sentence was a prison term which let him become eligible for release in 1961.

Abolishing capital punishment will not prevent other Fosters and Alcortas from unjust convictions. Nothing can

[1] A considerably fuller account of the case will be found in the book by Foster's attorney; see James Horace Wood, *Nothing But the Truth* (1960).

do that except greater care on the part of the courts to guarantee that defendants, whoever they are and whatever their crimes, are given a fair trial. But so long as the grim game of criminal justice must be played, and played without any certainty that ghastly errors will not occur, it is arguable whether the stakes should be as high as they are when the loss of life itself is one of the penalties available. This is the relevance of these two case histories to the debate over the death penalty.

In Salvador Agron and Paul Crump, we have ideal illustrations of two of the most important arguments advanced by abolitionists: no one like Agron should be executed, because he was too young, too emotionally impoverished from birth to bear full responsibility for his acts, and because he would never have received a death sentence in the first place had it not been for New York's anachronistic mandatory death penalty for first degree murder. No one like Crump should be executed, because there was some lingering doubt about his guilt[2] but almost no doubt that the "illiterate, beastly animalistic criminal," as he was described in 1953, had been transformed during nine years imprisonment into a truly reformed and rehabilitated inmate. Agron's case illustrates the ever present danger of executing a legally sane but emotionally helpless adolescent boy, Crump's, the absurdity of killing a man because of something he did in the past when there is ample evidence that he has become, in effect, a different person, one who can perform a valuable role in society (and not only in prison society, though that is where Crump is likely to remain).

When all the Agrons and Crumps are put together, it should be distressing to the defenders of the death penalty to see how few of the actual candidates for the executioner consist of the "professional" killers or even of the "uncurable" psychopaths. The fifty or so men executed each year in this country include few if any of the Public Ene-

---

[2] On this aspect of the Crump case, see particularly William Friedkin, "Eight Years on Death Row," *The Californian* (October 1961). See also Fr. Dismas Clark, "The Case of Paul Crump," *Catholic Digest* (January 1963).

mies No. 1, such as John Dillinger and "Pretty Boy" Floyd (both killed by police in gun battles) or Al Capone and Alvin Karpis (both sentenced to prison terms on Alcatraz). Rather, the vast majority were the young men who live on the other side of the tracks and in the shadows caused by parental and social neglect. These are the men actually sentenced to death and executed in the United States today. For every execution of a Louie Lepke (crime king of New York when he headed "Murder, Inc.") or a Charles Starkweather (paranoiac killer of eleven men, women and children in eight days), a dozen like the four men described in this chapter are put to death. To approve of the death penalty in the middle of the twentieth century is to approve of a system that, whomever in theory it may be aimed at, usually nets men like Alcorta, Foster, Agron, and Crump, men no worse and, as it turned out, in some cases considerably better than thousands of others in and out of prisons across the land. This, I suggest, is the inhuman side of capital punishment in America.[3]

[3] For other recent case histories involving capital punishment, see: James Galvin and John MacDonald, "Psychiatric Study of a Mass Murderer" [John Gilbert Graham], *American Journal of Psychiatry* (May 1959); Joe Henry, "Tennessee v. Wash Jones," *American Bar Association Journal* (January 1960); William Bradford Huie, *The Execution of Private Slovik* (1954); Peter Maas, "The Man Who May Break Chessman's Death-Cell Record" [Edgar Labat], *Look* (July 19, 1960); Gene Marine, "The Jury Said 'Death'" [Burton Abbott], *The Nation* (May 19, 1956); Barrett Prettyman, Jr., *Death and The Supreme Court* (1961); Tabor Rawson, *I Want To Live* [Barbara Graham] (1958); James Reinhardt, *The Murderous Trail of Charles Starkweather* (1960); Frederick Wiseman, "Psychiatry and Law" [Jack Chester], *American Journal of Psychiatry* (October 1961).

THE HUMAN SIDE OF CAPITAL PUNISHMENT*

BY SARA R. EHRMANN**

The recent articles in FEDERAL PROBATION by Professor Thorsten Sellin and James A. McCafferty give excellent statements of the general sociological data which show that capital punishment is much overrated as a deterrent to murder[1] and that the prevailing trend in the United States today is toward gradual abolition.[2] Mr. Ralph G. Murdy deals realistically with some of the practical problems involved in passing legislation.[3] But the "human" side of capital punishment has hardly been discussed at all.

In this article, I shall attempt to give some of this much needed information concerning the nature of the offenders who are convicted of capital crimes. . . .

*Reprinted, with omissions, by permission of the author and publisher, from "For Whom the Chair Waits," *Federal Probation,* vol. 26 (March 1962), pp. 14–25.

**Executive Director, American League to Abolish Capital Punishment, and President, Massachusetts Council to Abolish the Death Penalty.

[1] Thorsten Sellin, "Capital Punishment," *Federal Probation,* September 1961, pp. 3–11.

[2] James A. McCafferty, "Major Trends in the Use of Capital Punishment," *Federal Probation,* September 1961, pp. 15–21.

[3] Ralph G. Murdy, "A Moderate View of Capital Punishment," *Federal Probation,* September 1961, pp. 11–15. Mr. Murdy's suggestion of "compromise" is not necessarily a solution. The Massachusetts Council for the Abolition of the Death Penalty campaigned twenty-five years on legislative proposals to modify the mandatory capital punishment law (finally enacted 1951) and for the appointment of an impartial investigating commission (enacted 1957). In 1959 the group led a powerfully backed public campaign for an abolition bill, favorably reported and amended by the Joint Judiciary Committee, the provisions of which are somewhat similar to Mr. Murdy's suggested compromise. In 1961 the abolition group again campaigned for a measure which would provide the penalty of life imprisonment unless the jury recommended death. All of these measures to modify the capital punishment statute or to study it have been opposed (almost solely) by the Massachusetts Chiefs of Police Association who conduct an opposition lobby.

In 1958, for instance, forty-eight prisoners were legally executed in the United States, the lowest recorded number of executions. Since I have been engaged for over thirty years in attempting to collect facts about capital punishment, I tried to obtain information concerning these forty-eight persons who suffered the extreme penalty—who they were and something of their personal histories. The only reliable information available about them was reported in the "Executions" Bulletin prepared by the Federal Bureau of Prisons.[4] The Bulletin showed that the executions had taken place in fifteen states, as follows: six each in California, Georgia, Ohio, Texas; four in New York; three each in Florida, Mississippi, Virginia; two each in Arizona, Louisiana, North Carolina, West Virginia; one each in Alabama, Illinois, Utah. There were no executions in the other thirty-three states (including the six which had abolished capital punishment). The Bulletin also showed that of the forty-eight, none was a woman, nineteen were Negroes, one was a Filipino. We knew that their ages ran from twenty years to fifty-four. Seventeen were between twenty and twenty-four when they were executed. Forty were executed for murder, seven for rape (all Negroes), and one prisoner was executed in Texas for robbery with a firearm. Elapsed time between sentence to death and execution ranged from three months and under (six prisoners) to forty-nine months and over (six prisoners).

Beyond these data nothing further could be learned. So we are left with no knowledge of the personal histories of these forty-eight persons who were executed, the events which led to their crimes, or their mental state or social or economic status. Yet such information is vital to the public assessment of capital punishment as it actually exists in our society today. This situation illustrates one of the difficulties confronting those who wish to bring the facts about capital punishment to the American public. There is no central bureau of information to collect or to publish these and other important facts. The result is that the public gets its impressions on the value of the death penalty from the ut-

[4] *National Prisoner Statistics,* No. 20, *Executions, 1958,* Federal Bureau of Prisons, Washington, D. C., February 1959.

terances of public officials as quoted in the press, and from news reports on crimes of violence and on prison disturbances.

These opinions are often erroneous. For instance, advocates of capital punishment frequently brand prisoners who are condemned to die as "ruthless killers," "wild beasts," "mad dogs," and the like, as if they were not individual human beings at all but belonged to a special class of dangerous criminals engaged in the practice of murder. Many newspapers constantly encourage this opinion in their reports of sensational crimes.

Actually, among those who incur death sentences, very few could be so-called "professional killers." Such men are either not caught, or, if apprehended and convicted, frequently manage to get lesser sentences through astute criminal representation. As for the wild beasts, they are usually adjudged insane and are committed. Some are executed. The careful study by Professor Reinhardt of Charles Starkweather,[5] the Nebraska slayer of eleven men, women, and children, should provide greater understanding of this "ruthless" killer because it tells the full story that never got into the newspapers.

The need for this usually unavailable information can be seen from the importance that is attached to it in debates over whether to retain or to abolish capital punishment. . . . In the rest of this article I shall illustrate some of these facts, particularly those bearing on the conduct of life-term prisoners, on the opinions of those most closely acquainted with abolition of the death penalty, and on the sentencing and execution of innocent and mentally ill persons.

Twenty-five years ago Warden Lewis E. Lawes found that the chief objection to abolishing capital punishment was the fear that the condemned prisoners would be released if they were not executed, but he found no validity in these fears. He said, "As a matter of fact, pardons for 'natural lifers' are very rare. In the seven years I have been warden of Sing Sing only one commutation has been granted to

[5] James Reinhardt, *The Murderous Trail of Charles Starkweather*. Springfield, Ill.: Charles Thomas Co., 1961.

a lifer, and this man had been in prison over nineteen years."[6] More recently, Warden Lawes had this to say about the general problem of incarceration and subsequent release of life-term prisoners:

> Lifers, contrary to popular belief, are model prisoners. I have been in contact with hundreds of them during my years in penal work. They are industrious, as a rule, and give a warden the least trouble. Many of them are first offenders. Some committed murder during a moment of blind fury and have never ceased repenting their misdeeds. I have found, too, that lifers seldom, if ever, violate their parole. Granted freedom, they have become hard-working normal citizens. . . . There is need for remedial legislation concerning lifers.[7]

These views of the late Warden Lawes are definitely supported by the facts.

In order to illustrate the general situation involving the postconviction conduct of life-term prisoners, it is useful to look at the data available from Massachusetts. Before the Massachusetts Legislature's hearing in 1961, an inquiry was made concerning the conduct of prisoners at Walpole Correctional Institution whose death sentences have been commuted to life. The following reply was received from the office of the superintendent: "None of these men whose death sentences were commuted to life imprisonment have been any greater disciplinary problem than any of the other inmate population."

Professor Zechariah Chafee, Jr., of the Harvard Law School, wrote:

> It is not the occasional pardon to a murderer that endangers society but rather the fact that indictments of first degree so often lead to acquittal. Undoubtedly ten murderers are free on our streets due to lack of

---

[6] Lewis E. Lawes, *Life and Death in Sing Sing.* New York: Garden City Publishing Co., 1928.

[7] Official report to the Governor of Massachusetts, 1946.

apprehension and conviction to every one who is pardoned after careful consideration.[8]

In January 1936, at a parole hearing, Warden Lanagan (of the Charlestown Prison) complained, "They moved the best prisoners, the lifers, to Norfolk. This is one cause of unrest at Charlestown." Five years earlier, Charlestown Prison Warden Hoggsett had said to me, "The life prisoners at Charlestown Prison are the best prisoners, as a class. They are the most trustworthy. Very few of them were ever arrested before for any offense. . . ."

An unpublished study in my files of paroled lifers is especially revealing.[9] Between 1911 and 1940, seventy-five (out of a total of approximately 242) Massachusetts prisoners serving life sentences were released on parole. All (except one—convicted as "habitual criminal" in 1933) were serving convictions for murder, and four had been commuted from a death sentence. The reasons cited for granting the paroles by the governors and executive councillors were as follows: thirteen committed murder under great provocation (including sex), twelve were intoxicated at the time of the crime and under great provocation (two of these attempted suicide), eleven were either acting in self-defense or were possibly erroneously convicted, eleven pleaded to murder where the indictment should have been for manslaughter, two were accessories, twelve were being deported to their native land, seven were quite old and had records of excellent conduct, six were insane, and one was released at the request of the sentencing judge. These reasons show that in many cases a serious miscarriage of justice was rectified only many years after conviction. This would have been impossible if these prisoners had been executed.

Governor Joseph B. Ely, who was responsible for most of these releases, stoutly defended his exercise of executive clemency for prisoners serving life sentences and for

---

[8] "Abolish the Death Penalty," Massachusetts Council for the Abolition of the Death Penalty, 1928, p. 8.
[9] Data taken from Massachusetts Senate Documents and Department of Correction Reports.

shorter sentences. Upon assuming office in 1931, Governor
Ely found many cases of men who had been in jail twenty-
five, thirty, and thirty-five years. In a statement published
in the *Boston Herald,* October 26, 1932, Governor Ely
said that, "In practically every instance the prisoner had
but one bad day in his whole life. . . . His previous record
was in almost every case without blemish. . . ." Governor
Ely said that in the sixty-five cases of clemency granted
during his first two years in office, "not one has broken the
terms and the conditions upon which release was given—not
a single solitary instance. . . . I shall exercise the pardon
power in order that justice may be finally tempered with
mercy.". . .

The advocates of the death penalty lay great stress on
the imaginary viciousness of those who would remain behind bars if executions were discontinued. But authoritative
opinions from abolition states do not support their view at
all.

In 1955 Donald E. Currier, M.D., surgeon general of the
Commonwealth of Massachusetts, sent a questionnaire to
prison administrators in states where capital punishment
had been abolished, asking the following questions:

1. Do you consider "lifers" a special morale problem in your correctional institution? If so, please describe.

2. Have any guards been murdered by "lifers" in
your institution in recent years?

3. Have any guards been murdered by other prisoners?

4. Have persons other than guards been murdered
by "lifers" in prison?

5. What has been the conduct of "lifers" who have
been released from prison through pardon or otherwise?

6. In your opinion is capital crime more prevalent
in your state as a result of the abolition of capital punishment?

7. In your opinion are the police in any greater

danger in your state than in neighboring states which
have retained capital punishment?

Replies were received from all abolition states (except
Michigan). The excerpts cited below show unanimous
agreement as to the safety with which lifers may be imprisoned and in many cases eventually released.

Harold V. Langlois, assistant director of correctional
services for Rhode Island, replied:

> In my opinion capital punishment is no more or less
> prevalent in the State of Rhode Island as a result of
> the abolition of capital punishment. I do not believe
> the presence of capital punishment in law serves as a
> deterrent to the crime of murder in the first degree.
> . . . I believe in Rhode Island, the police are not in
> any greater danger than the police in neighboring
> states which have retained capital punishment. I be-
> lieve such a conclusion is absurd. . . . The conduct
> of "lifers" released from prison through pardon or pa-
> role has been generally very good to excellent. . . .
> So-called "lifers" are no more or no less a morale
> problem than any other prisoner serving a lengthy sen-
> tence. . . . A Rhode Island law provides that anyone
> serving a life sentence for the crime of murder com-
> mitting a second murder while incarcerated shall be
> punished by hanging, upon conviction. This statute has
> never been invoked.

A. C. Gillette, acting director of corrections for Minnesota, said:

> I will be interested in knowing if the State of Massa-
> chusetts moves in the direction of abolition of capital
> punishment, as it is my feeling that it meets no con-
> structive end and is a definite handicap to effective law
> enforcement. . . . If you will refer to the national
> statistics on crime, you will note that Minnesota has a
> comparatively low rate of murder. There is no indica-
> tion that the abolition of capital punishment resulted
> in an increased rate of murder. . . . The conduct
> of most lifers who have been released from prison

through pardon or parole has been generally satisfactory and they have adjusted much more satisfactorily than other types of offenders. . . . I would like to point out that our experience has been that "it" would serve no useful purpose in solving our correctional problems in the State of Minnesota.

C. J. Myzaard, warden, North Dakota State Penitentiary, replied:

"Lifers" are not a special morale problem in the institution. No guard or any other persons have been murdered by lifers. . . . Conduct of lifers, upon release—satisfactory, one returned on burglary charge. . . . Capital crime is not more prevalent as a result of the abolition of capital punishment in North Dakota. The police are not in any greater danger in North Dakota than in neighboring states which have retained capital punishment.

Allan L. Robbins, warden, Maine State Prison, reported:

Lifers are not a special morale problem. No guards or other persons have been killed by lifers. Conduct of lifers who have been released—very good. No complaints whatsoever. Capital crime is not more prevalent in Maine as a result of the abolition of capital punishment. The police are not in any greater danger in Maine than in neighboring states which have retained capital punishment. . . . I do feel that capital punishment certainly has its advantages for killings in certain categories. Police guards and others in a law enforcement category should be protected in every way possible. If an inmate kills a guard or prison employee "or perhaps other prisoners" I believe he could well be exterminated.

John C. Burke, warden, Wisconsin State Prison, stated:

I have a notion that if we had capital punishment in this State it would be far more difficult to get a jury to vote a man guilty than it is now. When a jury finds a man guilty under the present set-up, they must be unconsciously aware of the fact that if by any chance of making a mistake in finding the man guilty and if he were committed to the prison for life, any mistakes made could be corrected in years to come. On the other hand, if we had capital punishment, they might be so reluctant in taking a man's life that they might hesitate in cases where there was just a speck of a question, to find the man guilty. . . . My notion is that the police in this State are not in any more danger than are the police in those states that don't have capital punishment. . . . I have a notion that in states where there is capital punishment, a man, seriously involved in a crime, might be more apt to try to kill a policeman so that he would not be available to testify against him. . . . I am certainly of the opinion that we do not have any more murders in Wisconsin than do other states that have capital punishment. I am pretty sure that the Uniform Crime Reports put out by the Federal Government indicate that those states that do not have capital punishment have a lot less murder than the others. . . . Lifers have never created any special morale problem in this institution. I would say that they have had a good effect on the morale of the institution because usually they have been the best behaved and have made the greatest effort to help themselves while in the institution. . . . I have been warden here since 1938 and no guard, other civilian employee or prisoner has been murdered by anyone. . . . The general impression I get from parole officers in the State is that generally speaking the lifers are some of their most successful parolees.

These opinions seem to be supported by such facts as are available. . . .

Erle Stanley Gardner, famous attorney-author, wrote in *Federal Probation* in March 1959: "I have seen guilty persons who have been wrongfully acquitted. I have seen innocent persons who have been wrongfully convicted. . . ." Although this statement did not refer to any particular crime, it is true of murder as of other crimes. And somewhere Mr. Gardner is quoted as follows: ". . . when a prisoner protests his innocence to the end the probabilities are that he is, in fact, innocent."

The claim is frequently made that innocent persons are not executed, but no one denies that many innocent persons are sentenced to death. The assumption seems to be made that their innocence is always discovered by the courts or their sentences commuted by the governor. Nevertheless, this does not always happen and it is a fact that innocent people have been put to death. In a brief submitted by the Province of Saskatchewan to the Canadian Parliamentary Commission, 1955, this statement was made:

> Miscarriages of justice have occurred in Canada. . . . Ronald Powers, Paul Cachia, both were imprisoned many months (for robbery) before the error of the court was discovered. If a person had been killed in the course of the robberies, they may have been executed, although they had no connection with the offense. [The authors of the brief added]. . . . This would not have been the first time that innocent people have been executed.

It is, however, almost impossible to secure evidence of innocence *after* a person is put to death. Even a confession by someone else may not be acceptable as actual proof of innocence.

For instance, in England it is now generally believed, although it cannot be "proved," that Timothy John Evans was innocent when he was hanged in 1950 for murdering his child. His wife had been killed also. Evans first confessed to killing his wife, and then later denied it. He never admitted to killing his child. The chief witness against Evans was his neighbor, John R. Christie. Four years after the hanging of Evans, Christie confessed that he himself had murdered at least seven women whose bodies were found walled up in his home, among them Evans' wife and child. Christie was then hanged also. In reference to the death of Evans, Mr. Chuter Ede, former Home Secretary, said, "I hope no future Home Secretary will feel that although he did his best—in fact, he sent a man who was not guilty as charged to the gallows."[10]

Earlier, in England, Walter G. Rowland had been hanged in 1947, protesting his innocence, although another man, David John Ware, made three confessions of guilt. In 1951, Ware committed another murder, under much the same circumstances as the crime for which Rowland was hanged.[11]

Much less famous than these two English cases are several in this country which deserve closer attention. In Virginia, one Rogers was convicted and sentenced to death in 1943. He served nine years before being given his freedom. The fight for his freedom was led by a New York newspaper editor. Governor Battle stated he was a "victim of a gross miscarriage of justice."[12]

In Massachusetts, Santos Rodriguez, a penniless Puerto Rican bus boy, was freed after thirty-nine months in prison for a murder he never committed. In 1954 he had been found guilty of second degree murder for killing a woman. In January 1957 another prisoner confessed his guilt in the murder. He had withheld his confession until after the death of his mother. Rodriguez was released and given $12,500 compensation.[13] . . .

In the U. S. Army, Private A. B. Ritchie had been convicted of murder by a court martial and was sentenced to hang July 1, 1945. Another man confessed guilt. Mrs. Ritchie reached President Harry S. Truman at a "homecoming" celebration in Independence, Missouri. Ritchie's death sentence was commuted and he was pardoned in 1947.[14]

In Texas, Anastarcio Vargas was sentenced to die in 1926. His head had been shaved for execution. A man who re-

---

[10] *Manchester Guardian,* February 17, 1955. For details on the Evans-Christie case, see Ludovic Kennedy, *Ten Rillington Place.* London: Victor Gollancz, Ltd., 1961.

[11] Arthur Koestler, *Reflections on Hanging.* New York: The Macmillan Company, 1957.

[12] Letter to Mrs. Herbert B. Ehrmann from Morton L. Wallerstein, March 22, 1957.

[13] *Boston Globe,* April 10, 1957.

[14] *Boston Traveler,* February 14, 1947.

sembled Vargas confessed. The judge himself made an investigation which cleared Vargas. The death sentence was commuted to life. He was pardoned in 1930 and compensated by the State ($26,500).[15]

In Connecticut, Frank Smith had been in the death house four years. Eight times his date of execution was set. He had received reprieves from Governors Chester Bowles and John Lodge. He was finally saved June 7, 1954 when a police official offered new evidence. Smith's sentence was commuted to life by the State Board of Pardons two hours before the execution was to have taken place. The *Hartford Courant* carried a front page full account on June 8, 1954.

In Pennsylvania, David Almeida was granted a second trial after six years because the prosecutor had withheld evidence at the first trial. Almeida had had thirty execution dates! In the same State, Paul A. Pfeffer was serving a sentence of twenty years to life when John F. Roche, who had taken at least three other lives and who wanted to die, confessed his guilt.[16]

The *New York Journal-American* of July 24, 1961, reported that Pietro Matera had been released from New York prisons after serving thirty years for murder. Originally sentenced to death, Governor Franklin Roosevelt commuted his sentence. Then, in the winter of 1960, the real culprit's wife, Adalgisa Lo Cascio, confessed on her deathbed that she had "fingered Matera to save her husband."

Massachusetts has had several dramatic capital cases in which grave doubt of guilt exists. The Sacco-Vanzetti case is the most famous. Most students of the case believe there is grave doubt of guilt. Efforts are still being made to unearth evidence. At the time, another prisoner's confession confirmed by a mass of corroboration might have exonerated the defendants, but the court refused to grant a new trial.[17]

[15] "Brighter Days Loom," San Antonio (A.P.)—date missing.
[16] *New York Herald Tribune* series, July 20, 1954, "The Ever-Present Possibility of Executing an Innocent Man."
[17] For details see Herbert B. Ehrmann, of defense counsel, *The Untried Case*. New York: Vanguard Press, 1961.

Then there is the strange Cero-Gallo case. Cero Gangi, a young Italian seaman, had been found guilty of murder and sentenced to die in September 1928. His employer, Samuel Gallo, provided his own lawyer to defend Cero. On the night of the execution a witness identified Gallo as the murderer. Cero was reprieved. Gallo was then indicted. Both men were then tried together in an unprecedented capital trial. Cero was acquitted; Gallo was convicted. Finally, after the main witness had left the country and after still another trial, Gallo was also acquitted.[18]

The Berrett-Molway Taxi Cab case in Lynn, Massachusetts, involved two men who almost went to the electric chair for a crime they did not commit. Their case was tried in Superior Court of Salem in February 1934. Eight undisputed eye witnesses had identified the two defendants, Clement Molway and Louis Berrett, Boston taxi drivers, as the two men who murdered an employee of the Paramount Theatre in Lynn. Just before final arguments by counsel, Abraham Faber, who with the Millen brothers had been found guilty of the Needham Bank murders, confessed they had murdered the Paramount Theatre employee and that Berrett and Molway were entirely innocent. Berrett and Molway were exonerated and freed and granted compensation. The foreman of the jury, Hosea E. Bradstreet, said:

> Those witnesses were so positive in their identification that it was only natural that we should be misled. While I sat at the trial I somehow hated the thought of sending those two men to the electric chair; but we were sworn to perform our duty and we would have done it—to the best of our ability. I don't say we would have returned a guilty verdict—but it certainly didn't look like anything else for a time. This trial has taught me one thing. Before it I was a firm believer in capital punishment. I'm not now.[19]

[18] Dr. Winfred Overholser, former commissioner, Department of Mental Diseases, Massachusetts, wrote an article on this case, printed in a leaflet by the American League to Abolish Capital Punishment.

[19] *Boston Globe,* March 1, 1934.

The *Boston Post,* Monday, June 26, 1950, reported the following account of the hanging of an innocent man:

Jack O'Neil was hanged on Friday, January 7, 1898 for the murder of Hattie McCloud, at Buckland, near Shelburne Falls. O'Neil denied the killing and charged that he was the dupe of racial bigotry when this prejudice was still widespread. . . . He said calmly, as he went to his death, "I shall meet death like a man and I hope those who see me hanged will live to see the day when it is proved I am innocent—and it will be, some time."

This was the last hanging in Massachusetts. (Electric chair was installed in 1900.) A few months later a dying Shelburne Falls soldier, fighting the Spaniards in Cuba as a member of the old Sixth Massachusetts Militia confessed to the murder and cleared O'Neil.

Eddie Collins, an ace newspaper reporter, was correspondent in Cuba interviewing the soldier and arranged for a signed confession. He flashed the news to Dan W. Gallagher, of East Boston, ace reporter for the *Boston Post* who covered O'Neil's execution in Greenfield.

Many persons are judged legally sane who are medically insane or mentally ill. Judge Evelle J. Younger, of the Los Angeles Municipal Court, said:

A compelling reason which cries out for abolition of the death penalty is the new view furnished by "medical knowledge and experience" that a person may be declared legally sane even where the problem is one of mental illness or "diminished responsibility."[20]

The draftsmen of the Model Penal Code said:

No problem in the drafting of a penal code presents larger intrinsic difficulty than that of determining when individuals whose conduct would otherwise be criminal ought to be exculpated on the ground that they are

[20] *Christian Science Monitor,* August 13, 1955.

suffering from mental disease or defect when they acted as they did.[21]

Three recent Massachusetts cases will illustrate the truth of these two statements. Jack Chester, a mentally ill youth who killed his sweetheart, was sentenced to die in 1957. He had made several suicide attempts, had pleaded with the jury for death in the electric chair. Addressing the jury, he said, "It is my opinion that any decision other than guilty of murder in the first degree with no recommendation for clemency is a miscarriage of justice." When he was sentenced to die he thanked the judge. He refused to request commutation. Before the final execution date, September 15, 1957, further examination made by the Department of Mental Health, revealed that Chester had "suicidal tendencies" and could not "appropriately be executed." Commutation was about to be recommended by the Governor on Monday, December 1, but on November 29th Chester hanged himself with his sweater in his cell.[22]

In 1956, Kenneth Chapin, eighteen years old, was sentenced to die for savagely slaying a teenage baby sitter and the boy in her charge. According to technical legal definitions the defendant was sane. Yet his act was the deed of a maniac. A reprieve came a few hours before execution. After further medical testimony the death sentence was commuted to life. Former Governor Christian A. Herter recommended commutation, stating:

My own views are that society would not be benefited by the execution of Chapin because of his abnormal characteristics and questionable personality condition, as well as his youth and complete lack of prior criminality.

A letter published later by defense counsel and the Com-

[21] American Law Institute, Model Penal Code, Draft No. 4, p. 156, quoted in *Commonwealth* v. *Chester,* 150 N.E.2d 914.
[22] "Killer Chester, Denied Death Chair He Sought, Ends Life," *Boston American,* November 28, 1958, p. 1. [Editor's note: See also Frederick Wiseman, "Psychiatry and Law: Use and Abuse of Psychiatry in a Murder Case," *American Journal of Psychiatry* (October 1961).]

missioner of Mental Health stated that the Chapin jury had not had a complete account of Chapin's mental state.[23]

In 1961, Tucker Harrison, a Negro and former waste collector in Springfield, Massachusetts, killed his estranged wife and was found legally sane and sentenced to die. He is an epileptic and was a chronic alcoholic. After shooting his wife he tried to kill himself. He managed to shoot away a large portion of the frontal lobe of his brain. The Supreme Judicial Court found no error in his trial and denied his appeal for a second trial. The Supreme Court decision states in part:

> We conclude that it was not error to decide that the defendant, notwithstanding his illnesses, weaknesses and injury, was sufficiently a human being to be brought to trial, with ability, although impaired, to co-operate in his own defense.[24]

On September 27, 1961, Harrison's death sentence was commuted to life imprisonment by Governor John Volpe and the Executive Council.

These last three cases are all too typical. A study of the dispositions of capital cases during seventeen years in Massachusetts, 1925 to 1941 inclusive, revealed that out of 238 cases, sixty-eight defendants were found insane and two committed suicide.

A sampling of cases from across the United States proves that this problem is a national one. In California, the *Sacramento Bee* and the *Oakland Tribune* reported on March 29, 1961 that Erwin Walker, forty-three, a former Army officer, "cop killer," had had his death sentence commuted to life without the possibility of parole by Governor Brown (after nearly fifteen years in the shadow of death in the gas chamber). In 1949 the execution had been called off hardly one hour before it was scheduled. Walker has since been judged insane and is now confined in a state mental hospital. Clinton Duffy, recently retired member of the California Adult Authority and former warden at San Quentin

[23] *Boston Herald*, December 16, 1956.
[24] *Springfield News*, March 27, 1961.

who had seen at least 150 men go to their death, said Walker's case was the "worst ever." Walker attempted suicide the morning before he was to die. Dr. David Schmidt, chief psychiatrist at San Quentin, said Walker had lost his personality as a human being and "had almost become a vegetable."[25]

In Lansdale, Pennsylvania, George L. Derbyshire, now legally sane, faced trial February 22, 1960 for strangling his wife seven years ago. Most of the time since his crime Derbyshire had been in a state hospital for the criminally insane.[26]

In Kentucky, Henry R. Anderson was tried three times before a jury agreed on the death penalty. The cause of disagreement was whether Anderson knew what he was doing when he shot the doctor. The Assistant Attorney General told the Court of Appeals that Anderson was a schizophrenic paranoid when he was tried, but that he was "not insane."[27]

In Iowa, Governor Herschel Loveless commuted to life imprisonment the death penalty for first degree murder imposed on Lee Hawkins. Hawkins is illiterate and there is reason to believe he may have misunderstood the statements he signed prior to the trial admitting his guilt.[28]

In Illinois, Charles Townsend, a Negro, was sentenced to die for a crime in 1953. The defense claimed that his confession was improperly obtained by police when he was under the influence of a "truth drug." Townsend said he committed the crimes to get money for narcotics. Townsend has undergone the tension of an execution date being set fourteen times. The *Illinois Daily News* of April 4, 1961 reported that the defense attorney sought an early clemency hearing because of Townsend's "mental and physical deterioration."

In California, Governor Brown commuted Vernon Atch-

[25] [Editor's Note: see also *Newsweek,* March 20, 1961, pp. 29–30.]

[26] *North Pennsylvania Reporter,* February 22, 1960 (Lansdale, Pa.).

[27] *Louisville Times,* June 16, 1961.

[28] *Des Moines Register,* December 29, 1960.

ley's death sentence to life without possibility of parole because of new medical evidence.[29]

In Washington, D. C., James J. Clark twice was scheduled to face the electric chair for first degree murder, but was recently sentenced to the maximum five to fifteen years for manslaughter. There was testimony at both trials that Clark was drunk, and expert witnesses said he had an "emotionally unstable personality" but that the crime was not a product of his mental condition.[30]

In Pennsylvania, Norman Moon, twenty-five, was sentenced to die for shooting a judge in the courtroom. He attempted suicide as an officer arrested him. The Pittsburgh *Post-Gazette* of October 22, 1954 commented as follows:

> A three-man sanity commission, in accordance with the mental health act, has held that Moon "is not a mental defective" although he is a "proper subject for commitment to a mental hospital." His mental illness is that of dementia praecox of the paranoid type. The finding that Moon, for legal purposes, including electrocution, is sane while for most practical purposes he is off his rocker is bound to open further avenues for delay in pronouncement of the death sentence recommended by the jury last May 25.

William F. (Billy) Rupp was executed in California on November 7, 1958 for slaying a fifteen-year-old baby sitter in 1952. He was a mental defective suffering from a schizoid type of mental disorder, but he "knew right from wrong"—according to some physicians, government witnesses. Another government witness disagreed, "He had a damaged brain, couldn't think for more than a few seconds a minute and conceivably didn't know right from wrong on August 8th." Defense medical testimony claimed Billy "was legally and medically insane at the time of the crime." It took the jury twenty-two minutes to decide he was sane. By 1957 at least six of his jurors had signed petitions to spare his life.

[29] *San Francisco Examiner,* August 23, 1961.
[30] *Washington Daily News,* February 24, 1961.

Dr. Henry Sjaarjems, head of the electroencephalograph (brain testing) departments of three Los Angeles institutions and of Camarillo State Hospital, had tested Billy's brain when he was fourteen. The substance of his findings was that Billy's thought processes "diffused and degenerated" at fourteen, and could not have improved at eighteen.[31]

Austin H. MacCormick, at that time professor of criminology at the University of California, at Berkeley, had urged clergymen "as a Christian duty" ". . . and on the grounds of justice in its truest sense—to society as well as the individual"—to try to get the death sentence commuted. He wrote the following statement:

Even if I believed in the death penalty, I would not believe it should be inflicted on this mentally defected young man, penniless and practically friendless whose own sister asks only that his sentence be commuted to life imprisonment without possibility of parole.[32]

It is difficult to find cases where persons of means or social position have been executed. Defendants indicted for capital offenses who are able to employ expert legal counsel throughout their trials are almost certain to avoid death penalties.[33] In the famous Finch-Tregoff case in California, there were three trials, two hung juries, and finally verdicts of guilty but *without* the death penalty. It is estimated that the cost of these trials was over $1 million. But in the trials of some defendants without funds, juries have deliberated for as little as nineteen minutes, or an hour more or less, and then returned verdicts of guilty and death.[34]

Almost all of the persons eventually executed were represented by court-appointed counsel. Although many such

[31] *Sunday News,* New York, January 4, 1959.
[32] *Register,* Santa Ana, California, May 18, 1955.
[33] See John Bartlow Martin, "Who Killed Susan Hansen?" *Saturday Evening Post,* August 6, 1960; and John Mulligan, "Death, the Poor Man's Penalty," *The American Weekly,* May 15, 1960, p. 9.
[34] *New York Journal-American,* February 14, 1960, and *New York Times,* March 28, 1961.

attorneys are able and devoted, they are often severely hampered by the lack of funds needed for research and investigation on behalf of their clients. Lawrence Cowan, attorney, was appointed by the court to defend Louis Franklin Smith and John Allen, who were sentenced to die in California in March 1951. He was convinced the two men were not guilty. But he had spent $1,200 of his own money, and could not finance the cost of appealing to the United States Supreme Court.[35]

In Delaware all of the persons executed since 1902 were from the unskilled laboring class and poorly educated.[36] Every person executed in Oregon for the last twenty-one years has been defended by a court-appointed lawyer.[37] Yet many first-degree murderers escape the maximum penalty (see footnote 33).

Likewise, most of the defendants sentenced to die and those executed are from minority racial groups, especially Negroes. In Delaware, of the twenty-five persons executed, seventeen were Negroes. During the years 1930 to 1959,[38] a total of 3,666 prisoners were put to death. Of these, 1,972 were Negroes, 1,653 were white, and forty-one were from other groups.[39]

Fifty-seven prisoners were executed in 1960. Of these, thirty-five were Negroes and twenty-two were white. Of the forty-five persons executed for the crime of murder, twenty-six were Negroes, nineteen were white. The eight persons executed for rape were all Negroes. On December 31, 1960 there were 210 prisoners awaiting death, of whom 110 were Negroes and one hundred white. . . .

Sensational news stories, television, and radio programs are advertising most effectively murder, guns, knives, and

[35] *San Francisco Chronicle*, March 5, 1955.

[36] Statement of Attorney General J. D. Bove, Jr., April 26, 1960.

[37] *Congressional Record*, July 25, 1958, testimony of Richard McGee.

[38] *National Prisoner Statistics*, No. 23 and No. 26, *Executions*, 1959 and 1960. Federal Bureau of Prisons, Washington, D. C. See also Franklin Williams, "The Death Penalty and the Negro," *The Crisis*, October 1960.

[39] See also *New York Times*, October 8, 1961.

violent crimes daily. Some children, highly suggestible, are incited to murder and other crimes. Those from under-privileged and minority groups are the most likely to be condemned and to be executed.

In 1954, ten "teenage" offenders were executed. They were all Negroes: seven in Georgia, two in New York, and one in Florida. During the previous four years nine "teenagers" were executed. Seven were Negroes, two were white.

In New York, Concepcion Correa, a seventeen-year-old Puerto Rican boy, was sentenced to die at Sing Sing on May 10, 1952—the youngest person ever condemned in New York County.[40] He and two others, age seventeen and twenty-two, were convicted of first degree murder for killing an eighty-five-year-old woman while stealing $90. Death in the electric chair is mandatory since the jury did not recommend mercy. Sentencing of the other defendants was postponed when a witness claimed he had testified falsely. Maintaining his innocence, Correa refused to plead guilty and to accept a short reformatory sentence. He had been in this country one and a half years, his family was poor, his father was in Puerto Rico, and his mother was dead. He could not speak or understand English, and he remained entirely mute during the trial.

Paul Giacamazza, who had just turned seventeen, was put to death in Massachusetts in 1942, the youngest person to be executed in this State.[41] However, in another case involving a seventeen-year-old boy in Massachusetts, a judge took the initiative and accepted a plea of "guilty to second degree murder" on the ground that "no Mas-sachusetts governor would ever allow so youthful an of-fender to be electrocuted."[42]

In 1949 in Germany, General Lucius Clay commuted to life the death sentence of a seventeen-year-old German boy convicted of killing two persons. General Clay said he

[40] *New York Herald Tribune*, Saturday, April 3, 1954.
[41] Details are in the files of the Massachusetts Council for the Abolition of the Death Penalty.
[42] Herbert B. Ehrmann, "The Death Penalty and the Admin-istration of Justice," *The Annals*, November 1952, p. 79.

could not bring himself "to approve the death sentence for a crime, no matter how heinous, committed by a young boy of seventeen and a half."

An editorial in the Washington, D. C. *Daily News*, October 7, 1959, expressed the hope that a death sentence of a fourteen-year-old boy who had been sentenced to die in Canada would be commuted:

> The boy should be punished. We do not dispute that fact. But to take his life at such a tender age would only add tragedy to tragedy. . . . Justice is one thing but legal murder is another. To our way of thinking, hanging a fourteen-year-old boy is but legalized murder.

From Arkansas, on September 10, 1960, came news that a fourteen-year-old boy had killed two playmates and quoted him as saying (in explanation), "because I want to die. If I killed one they would just send me to reform schools again but if I killed them both they'll send me to the chair."[43] . . .

The United States Supreme Court has been reversing a number of convictions because the confessions were obtained under duress. Recently the court ordered the release from prison or the retrial of Emil Rick on the grounds that the confession he made to the killing of a Chicago doctor twenty-five years ago was obtained by physical abuse.[44] How many defendants today are able to pay the costs involved in taking their cases to the United States Supreme Court?

False confessions by innocent people are not infrequent. *Coronet Magazine*, September 1957, states that 205 innocent people made false confessions of guilt in the Lindbergh kidnap-murder twenty-five years ago. They state also that the Los Angeles police were harassed by countless "phony" confessions in the "Black Dahlia" case. In New

[43] American League to Abolish Capital Punishment Bulletin, December 1960. *Capital Punishment*, Staff Research Report No. 46, Ohio Legislative Service Commission, January 1961, p. 49.

[44] *Civil Liberties*, September 1961, No. 191.

Jersey, a fifteen-year-old schoolboy confessed that he had murdered his mother with his boy scout knife because she had interfered in his relations with a girl. He retracted this confession four hours later. The school authorities say that he is a "disturbed personality."[45]

An Associated Press dispatch published at Fort Wayne, Indiana, tells of a signed statement made by a thirty-year-old farm hand in which he admitted three Fort Wayne sex killings in 1944 and 1945, two of which had been already confessed by another man who was under sentence of death. The man awaiting execution was Ralph Lobaugh, whose date of execution had been set but who was reprieved by Governor Henry F. Schricker.[46]

The unnecessarily long duration of most murder trials is due almost solely to the presence of capital punishment.[47] A recent study by the American Bar Foundation, "Delays in the Execution of Death Sentences," by Donald M. McIntyre, shows that the federal court calendars are increasingly clogged with appeals of death sentences.[48] What this study does not describe is the frequent agonies through which the condemned person and his family must pass as he awaits the action of the courts. In Connecticut, for example, it was reported that "At least three men had been so close to the electric chair they could almost touch it. Their heads were shaved, their pants' legs slit, last meals eaten . . . when stays were granted."[49] Prisoners in other states have had similar experiences.

Since 1958, four trials have been unable to settle the fate of Silas Manning, forty-year-old Hopkinsville, Kentucky, Negro, twice condemned to die. A fifth trial has been set for next spring. The fourth jury was hopelessly

---

[45] *Boston Herald,* January 4, 1958.

[46] Fort Wayne, Indiana, August 22 (A.P., The year on the press clipping in our files is not legible).

[47] See *Commonwealth of Pennsylvania* v. *James Carter, Robert Lee Williams, George Lee Rivers,* 152 A.2d 259 (1959).

[48] American Bar Foundation, Research Memorandum Series, No. 24, December 1960.

[49] "Should the State Kill," *Sunday Courant,* Hartford, Conn., February 27, 1955.

deadlocked. It was understood that the jurors could not agree on the man's *punishment,* not his *guilt.*[50]

In Illinois a federal judge said "there must come a time when these cases must end," when he granted an eleventh stay of execution to Vincent Ciucci, who has maintained his innocence of triple murders in 1953. The *Daily News,* September 16, 1961, points out that this betters the record of Caryl Chessman, executed in California after eight reprieves and years of delay.

In California, Barbara Graham went to her death after a series of last-minute reprieves. She cried out, "Why do they torture me?" The grim succession of legal maneuvering she endured, as portrayed in the film, *I Want to Live,* "put the Chinese water torture to shame."[51]

While all praise is due our judicial system for the opportunities it affords condemned persons to have their sentences carefully appraised, the fact remains that capital punishment creates an insoluble dilemma—either we increase the risk of executing the innocent by speeding up the judicial process, or we increase the agonies of the condemned by stretching it out—and this can be removed only by abolition.

The willingness with which state and federal courts hear appeals in capital cases suggests a growing reluctance among the judiciary of this country to permit executions to occur. Perhaps the best evidence of discontent with the inhumanities of the death penalty which I have tried to describe in this article is the almost unanimous opposition of religious groups within the last few years.[52] Typical of

[50] Kentucky *New Era.* Hopkinsville, Ky., November 8, 1961.

[51] *New York Times,* November 19, 1958. See also Tabor Rawson, *I Want to Live!* New York: Signet Books, 1958.

[52] Some of the rapidly growing number of religious groups on record as opposed to capital punishment are: American Baptist Convention; American Evangelical Lutheran Church; Augustana Evangelical Lutheran Church of North America; California-Nevada Conference of Methodists; Central Conference of American Rabbis; Christian Churches (Disciples of Christ) International Convention; Church of the Brethren; Church Federation of Greater Chicago; Congregational Conference of Southern California and the Southwest; Connecticut Valley Presbytery; Connecticut Valley Quarterly Meeting

the views of American clergymen today is the statement of the subcommittee of the Massachusetts Investigating Commission of 1960, consisting of the Reverend Dana McLean Greeley, Rabbi Roland B. Gittelsohn, and the Right Reverend Monsignor Thomas J. Riley:

> The only moral ground on which the State could conceivably possess the right to destroy human life would be if this were indispensable for the protection or preservation of other lives. This places the burden of proof on those who believe that capital punishment exercises a deterrent effect on the potential criminal. Unless they can establish that the death does, in fact, protect other lives at the expense of one, there is no moral justification for the State to "take life."[53]

It should be noted, however, that Monsignor Riley dissented from the majority recommendation that capital punishment should be abolished.

It is not possible to indicate here the number of correctional officials who oppose the death penalty. Austin H. MacCormick, dean of American corrections, had this to say,[54] and it is characteristic of unnumbered wardens, penologists, and criminologists:

---

of Friends (Quakers); Connecticut Universalist Convention; Greater Red Bank Area Council of Churches; Massachusetts Baptist Convention; Massachusetts Council of Churches; New York State Council of Churches; Northern California and Nevada Council of Churches; Protestant Episcopal Church in the United States of America; Protestant Episcopal Church, Diocese of Massachusetts; Southern California Council of Churches; Southern California-Arizona Conference of the Methodist Church; Union of American Hebrew Congregations; United Presbyterian Church in the United States of America—General Assembly; United Synagogue of America; Universalist Church of America.

[53] Massachusetts Legislature. Special Commission Appointed to Investigate the Advisability of Abolishing Capital Punishment. *Report and Recommendations.* Boston: Wright & Potter Printing Co., 1958, p. 34.

[54] Part of a statement prepared for presentation to the Massachusetts Legislative Hearing on February 11, 1937 (in a letter to the author of February 5, 1937).

I do not believe in capital punishment because it is an archaic and barbarous practice which has not only failed to accomplish the desired result but has actually had the opposite effect by making convictions on murder charges slower and more difficult. If capital punishment were more effective in curbing murder, I would probably still be opposed to it on the ground that it cheapens the very commodity which it seeks to protect and that capital punishment is itself nothing more than murder of the most cold-blooded and deliberate type.

The foregoing data concerning persons facing execution are merely samples of the vast amount of information concerning capital punishment which should be analyzed and made available to the public. My own office is bursting with newspaper stories, magazine articles, reports, letters, and important historical information which require collating, cataloguing, and careful study.

I have dealt with only a few phases of a large and complex problem. But even this brief and incomplete account given here shows the urgent need. Information, collected on a day-to-day basis, on all capital offenders, must be available to the authorities, who often are unprepared through their own ignorance of the facts to recommend commutation or clemency. Finally, information dealing with all phases of capital punishment, and especially with the human side of the injustices and inhumanities it involves, must be made more generally available to offset the hit-or-miss approach of the tabloids to this vital issue.

But even the brief and incomplete account given here shows the urgent need of some official central office of information which will place the study of capital punishment as it affects the administration of justice on a systematic basis. There is no such information center. Seeking reliable data concerning the operation of the death penalty in this country, the British Royal Commission, the Canadian Parliamentary Committee, and the various state investigating commissions, as well as governors, attorneys general, judges, counsel for the condemned, correctional officials, and the press have been forced to turn to this volunteer, unofficial office as the chief source of vitally needed information.

In the Department of Justice and in the law schools of the country, research departments on capital punishment are lacking.

Human lives are taken according to statute, while evidence produced through the century as to the necessity of capital penalties for public protection is not known by some prosecutors and lawmakers.

The news that Delaware has restored the death penalty over the veto of Governor Elbert N. Carvel (and has made whip-lashing mandatory for some felonies) comes as this paper is written. Perhaps this step would not have been taken if the true facts about capital punishment were publicized as widely as some sensational statements about capital punishment, usually incorrect. . . .

If a means can be found by our Federal Government to provide the facts desperately needed in the neglected area of capital punishment, the voices of the leaders of America will be heard over the decades in protest against the taking of life for civil crimes. These are voices of presidents, justices of the United States Supreme Court and of other courts, governors, and countless others.

One such voice is that of the late Professor August Vollmer, former chief of police at Berkeley, California, and former president of the International Association of Police Chiefs, who was perhaps this country's most distinguished law-enforcement official. In his address to the California Legislature on April 7, 1931, Chief Vollmer said in part: "As a police executive I am opposed to the death penalty for the very practical reason that it obstructs the effective enforcement of the law and more often protects the criminal than society. . . . If capital punishment has completely broken down; if it is an encouragement to crime rather than a deterrent as I believe this review of the case will demonstrate, then it is certainly time to face the facts and adopt a satisfactory substitute penalty. We can ill afford, with our appalling California murder toll, to sacrifice certainty and swiftness of punishment for spasmodic brutality."

CRIME OF PASSION*

BY JOHN BARTLOW MARTIN**

That winter in Colorado, Alvaro Alcorta, a stocky, swarthy man of twenty-seven not long out of the Army, was courting a girl. Her name was Herlinda, and she was pert and beautiful—later the men in the bars would call her *Borada,* "Green Eyes"—and though only fifteen, she was lovely. She and Alcorta were migrant farm workers from San Antonio, Texas, and she had virtually enticed him to Colorado. He boarded there with her parents. Sometimes when he went to town in the truck to buy groceries, he took Herlinda to a show or a dance, though he himself didn't dance. "She was wanting to get married, but I told her she was too young. She said her dad and mother were too strict, she couldn't do nothin'."

Finished with the Colorado sugar beets, they all went in the truck to West Texas to pick cotton. Alcorta was in love. He asked her mother's permission to marry. She told him to ask Herlinda's father. He told him to ask her mother. Alcorta had erred; by Mexican custom, he should have sent four adults to ask her father formally for her hand. He told Herlinda he was leaving. She said, "I'll take off with you." He demurred, but she pleaded, and he consented.

They arrived at his father's house in San Antonio broke. "I didn't know what the heck I was going to do. I got to marry her; her mother would get the law. My sister got scared. She said, 'You got to marry her.' She gave me a twenty-dollar bill and said go right now and do it." They were married in the San Antonio courthouse by a justice

* Reprinted, with omissions, by permission of Harold Ober Associates Incorporated, from *Saturday Evening Post,* vol. 233 (July 30, 1960), pp. 14 ff. © 1960 by The Curtis Publishing Company.

** Author of *Why Did They Kill?* (1953) and many other books and articles on crime and punishment; appointed as United States Ambassador to the Dominican Republic in 1961.

of the peace, Buck Jones. The date was December 17, 1947.

Eight years later Alcorta was back in the same redstone courthouse, charged with stabbing Herlinda to death because she left him. Testifying, he attempted to explain what had gone wrong. And he accused the prosecutor of framing him. The jury was not impressed. It convicted him and fixed his punishment at death.

Let us observe how Alvaro Alcorta was dealt with by our American system of criminal justice. . . . The criminal law has been said to mirror faithfully any given civilization. Let us study the administration of criminal justice in America. How surely does it procure the conviction of the guilty and the acquittal of the innocent? How justly does it assess culpability? Why does it sometimes break down? Let us inquire into the third degree, double jeopardy, mistaken identification by eyewitnesses, the right of the accused to counsel, the rights of the poor and of men with previous criminal records, the death penalty and the quality of judges, jurors, defense lawyers and public prosecutors. We shall find ourselves dealing often with procedure—the rules of the game. Laymen sometimes dismiss them as "mere technicalities." But the rules are critically important. They actually determine in large measure whether justice is done. And often they go to the heart of great moral issues that have been our civilization's heritage, and burden, since Biblical times—moral issues that all of us have faced in one form or another, since none of us are wholly guilty or wholly innocent.

San Antonio is a sprawling, low-roofed city set down on the hot dry Texas plain—blinding sun on white stucco walls, cross-topped churches, burning blue sky, palm trees along the riverbank, the ancient stone Alamo, dust and the Spanish language everywhere. More than half the population is Latin American. The saying goes, "A Latin American is a 'Meskin' who's paid his poll tax." Some are clerks or stenographers downtown, and a few rise to become successful lawyers, doctors and businessmen. But most are migratory workers or laborers and handy men. A *contratista* hauls them off packed like cattle in a ramshackle canvas-topped truck—men, women, children and their ragged belongings, and up north they live in hovels.

They live in hovels too in San Antonio, on the West Side and the South Side. Nogalitos Street runs southwest from the central city; it is lined with little Mexican groceries and restaurants, open-air bars and fruit markets. This is the highway to Laredo. Men hold cockfights farther out. Dust swirls thick at Nogalitos Circle, and on the Circle stand taverns and dance halls—one is the Los Angeles Night Club, a big, bare, barnlike place. Herlinda lived near here. "She liked to dance with all the men," the bartender recalls. The Mexican slums lie in the deep West Side, around Concho Street, near the ancient market place. In the evening, bands of strolling guitarists in Mexican costume serenade tourists here. The reality is less picturesque. Some of the dives nearby are narcotics distribution centers or else they're gambling joints, and the bars are full of B-girls.

Alvaro Alcorta was born October 25, 1919, farther out on the West Side, at Elvira and Zarzamora streets, the second-youngest of seven children. As a lad he was in no trouble. When he was in sixth grade, his mother died, and he quit school. Every season he went to Michigan with his family to work in the sugar-beet fields. He was drafted immediately after Pearl Harbor, was in the assault landings at Kwajalein, Leyte and Okinawa and was discharged in 1945. He was short, dark-complexioned, husky. He had heavy bushy eyebrows and thick black hair. His features were rather coarse, his forehead high, his brow furrowed. There was a certain babyish softness about his face. He was quiet, fatalistic, moody. He was deeply religious and inclined to be righteous and moralistic, rigid. He wanted to better himself, not to remain a migrant worker, and he wanted to live like an American citizen, not like a Mexican.

He and Herlinda lived in a tiny house alongside a repair garage on Guadalupe Street. He went back to school under the G.I. Bill of Rights. They soon had three children and, needing more money, Alcorta quit school and got a sixty-five-dollar-a-week job at Kelly Field. His employer thought him a good worker. Alcorta moved to a two-room house near Nogalitos Circle, then he bought a lot at 426 Eisenhower Street—called Ike Street, a dirt road straggling out through cactus and mesquite to the countryside, all mud in April, all dust in July—and here Alcorta built Herlinda a house out of scrap from Kelly Field.

Herlinda spoke no English. Her mind was on a good time, his on the children. He was twelve years older than she. Once she called him a *sonso,* a square. She was beautiful, tall, slender, very fair, with green eyes and amber hair. Alcorta once recalled, "I used to take her to the Los Angeles Night Club, but most of the time we'd go to the park or out to the river and drink sodas and things like that— picnics for the kids, nice *fiesta* out there," and he sighed, remembering. "My intentions for them kids, what you want your kids to do is have 'em go to school. First I wanted to build the house of brick or tile, something strong, but then I had the idea of saving a little money for the kids."

One night in 1955 Alcorta took Herlinda to a neighborhood tavern, and she danced with another man. Alcorta took her home, and she jumped out of the car and spent the night with a friend. Soon she went west to pick cotton with her parents, taking the children. A private investigator, Neff Limón, says, "She had a boy friend there." Alcorta brought her home. She had been home only fifteen minutes when she told him she was leaving. He told her, "Well, if you leave me and the kids, it's all right, but never come back, please."

"I never will," she said and left.

Alcorta sued for divorce—perhaps to frighten her into returning. He moved back to his father's house. His sister took care of the children. Now and then one of the children would ask where his mother was. Alcorta would pretend she'd be back someday. "During those six months—why, it was so hard," he testified. "Why was it that my wife left me with the kids and just took off like that?"

On Thanksgiving Day, Alcorta took the children to Herlinda's sister's house. He accused Herlinda of misbehaving in West Texas, and she laughed at him. Soon he heard she was prostituting herself. "The cab drivers would tell me. They didn't know she was my wife." For a time she worked as a B-girl in bars. But she also worked as a waitress at

Gonzales's, a respectable neighborhood café, and its owners say she never drank or fooled around with men there.

It was while she was working at Gonzales's that she met Natividad Castilleja, called Nato by his friends. Nato was nineteen, tall and slender but well-muscled, handsome, brown-skinned, with gleaming white teeth and oily black hair combed into a ducktail. "Girls go for him," a man who knows him says. He was a Pachuco—wore a narrow belt and tight shirt and khaki pants pulled low, stood talking with his thumbs hooked in his hip pockets, bore cabalistic tattoos on his hand. He has been involved in at least one fatal gang affray. He lived near Herlinda's mother's house, where Herlinda was living, near Nogalitos Circle. He drove her home from work several times and on the third time parked his car in a vacant lot about three blocks from her home and had intercourse with her. The same thing occurred other times—"I don't remember how many times," he said.

Alcorta found them out. The wife of Jesse Cervantes, who ran a tavern near Herlinda's house, told him that Herlinda had been there with Castilleja. Alcorta took to following her through the streets. Several times he saw her at the Los Angeles Night Club with Nato Castilleja, he has said, "dancing and kissing and drinking beer." He watched them drive down the dark dusty streets at night in Nato's old green coupé. "I even knew where the lot was where they used to go and park," he has said.

Alcorta persuaded her to take the children, perhaps hoping she would take him back, too, for their sake. But then he complained bitterly that she neglected them. On Mother's Day he went to her mother's house, found her missing and the children lying on a dirty quilt on the floor and, when she came home, knocked her down. A judge put him under a peace bond.

Alcorta had taken to frequenting the dives around Concho Street in the deep West Side slums. Often he would go into Manny's Bar and sit alone for hours, morose, drinking beer, talking to no one, weeping. Still, tormented, he tried "to patch things up." Once he took Herlinda to Manny's Bar; when he went to the rest room, she left with another man. She taunted him about her love affairs, telling him she was a whore. Once he took her to Lopez's ice house, near Nogalitos Circle, and called for two beers. She began insulting him loudly, saying, "When we were living together before I left you, you were not jealous of me like you now are," and, "You are not enough of a man for me." Everyone in the place heard it and waited for him to slap her. But Alcorta merely hid his face in his hands.

A few nights later, on Thursday, June 16, Alcorta has said, he went to Gonzales's Café. Herlinda had just left. He crossed the street. In a parked car by a school he saw Herlinda and a man, and Alcorta was sure they had just had intercourse—they were rearranging their clothes. She saw Alcorta and yelled to the man, and they drove off fast.

Next day Alcorta quit his job at Kelly Field and went to Manny's Bar and drank beer with a B-girl, Dominga Soto. He bought her a cheap necklace, bought another for Herlinda and took Dominga to Gonzales's. Herlinda served them. Alcorta offered her the necklace. She threw it at him. Alcorta said to Herlinda, "Well, how about last night," meaning her affair in the parked car by the school. She said nothing.

On Saturday Alcorta packed a suitcase, put a knife in his pocket and went downtown. He had decided to leave town, to go up North and forget the whole thing. He intended to get the one-o'clock bus, but wanted to say good-by to his children first. He fell to drinking with Dominga, Esperanza Huron and two men. The girls testified that he said they would read about him in the newspapers and that if he found Herlinda with another man he would kill her and go to Mexico. At dark he went alone to Herlinda's neighborhood. He maintained he intended to visit his children, but he went instead to Jesse Cervantes's little tavern, where formerly he had gone with Herlinda. He stayed, drinking, till Cervantes closed, then bought six more bottles of beer and took them outside and slowly drank them. He decided to go see his wife. He walked down the dark, deserted dirt street. A car came by. Herlinda was in it with a man. It stopped.

Herlinda had gone to the Los Angeles Night Club on

Nogalitos Circle at 9 P.M. Nato Castilleja was there with a friend. Nato danced with Herlinda a couple of times, then left with his friend and made the rounds of other bars. At 1 A.M. he saw Herlinda walking alone on Zarzamora Street. He stopped and offered her a ride. She got in. He took his friend home first, then parked in front of Herlinda's house, a little whitewashed shack, rising above the weeds in the vacant lot next door.

Alcorta was coming up behind the car. "I saw them kissing and all that. I could see through the rear window." He took out his knife. He had on thick-soled shoes and she heard them on the gravel. She cried, *"Mira,* Alvaro!" and tried to close the door, but Alcorta held it and jumped on the running board and began stabbing her. "I stab her I don't know how many times, I was so mad." He stabbed her thirty-two times. The car zigzagged down the street. Alcorta hung on, stabbing. The car stopped. Nato Castilleja tried to kick Alcorta off Herlinda. Alcorta turned on Nato. Nato fled. Alcorta got behind the wheel and drove away fast. "The door on my wife's side was still open, and my wife's legs were hanging out the car seat." She was dead.

He drove aimlessly through the countryside, stopped at a bridge over Atascosa Creek and dumped Herlinda's body on the dry creek bed. He drove till the car broke down, then he walked, hitchhiking, wandering through Mexican border towns. He came back to San Antonio on July 9, picked up his last check from Kelly Field, headed out of town and was arrested and turned over to the district attorney.

Roy Barrera, a top assistant D.A., handled the case. He was then twenty-eight. Barrera is a tall broad-shouldered, darkly handsome young man whose face has a strong Indian cast—high cheekbones, straight black hair, dark skin. He is smart, quick, aggressive, fast on his feet, an excellent trial lawyer. He believed in vigorous prosecution. "The whip has got to come down where it properly belongs. A lot of people can't understand a Mexican prosecuting a Mexican. Those people on the West Side, humble and ignorant and poor as they may be, they want justice the same as anybody else." So impressive was Barrera's reputation as a tough prosecutor that it became a point of pride among defense lawyers to beat him. And each victory of Barrera's advanced his own reputation.

Alcorta was guilty and should have been punished. But there are varying degrees of guilt, and it is the task of justice to assess guilt properly, taking into account all circumstances. It is the prosecutor's duty to promote justice, not to get convictions. Observe now how prosecutor Barrera went about his work.

In an interrogation room in the county jail, Barrera and investigator Pete Torres warned Alcorta that he need tell them nothing and that anything he said might be used against him, then asked if he wanted to make a statement. He did—he confessed. Torres asked the questions, Alcorta answered them, and Torres dictated to the stenographer. Occasionally Barrera suggested a question. Alcorta signed the statement, making and initialing several corrections.

In the confession Alcorta said he didn't know if he was sorry he had killed her and that if he had it to do over he might do the same thing. As to motive he said only that he killed her because "she was going out and not taking care of the children," because "I wanted to," and because she "had made me mad." Not a word in the entire statement mentions Nato Castilleja or his wife's infidelities.

Barrera says, "He said nothing to me about his wife's unfaithfulness." But Alcorta himself once said, "I told him about what I saw Thursday night by the school. I told him about seeing her with Castilleja. Every time I told about her, he'd whisper to the stenographer. He didn't put it in." An attorney who entered the case much later, Fred Semaan, says, "He told the district attorney about her and other men, but they said that's got nothing to do with it. The poor ignorant guy, he didn't know it was the only evidence that could've helped him and he let them leave it out. That's like tyin' a man's hands behind his back and just sluggin'."

Pete Torres took a statement from the state's key witness, Nato Castilleja, on July 20. In his statement Nato said not a word about his true relationship with Herlinda—only that he had driven her home from work about three times, always accompanied by another lad. Torres, suspecting Herlinda and Nato had been intimate, consulted Barrera, and Barrera himself questioned Nato. Nato admitted it, saying it had happened about four times in the car on the way home from work. So, even if Barrera had not heretofore known the truth about Herlinda and Nato, he knew it now. But he did not requestion Alcorta. Instead, he ordered Torres to omit the truth from Nato Castilleja's statement, thus suppressing it completely.

Castilleja asked what to do if anyone came to interview him. Barrera replied he could give anyone a statement he wanted to, but he didn't have to, and Barrera would rather he did not. But what, Nato asked, should he say in court if he was asked about having been intimate with Herlinda?

Barrera replied, "Under any and all circumstances, you answer each and every question that is asked of you truthfully; however, don't volunteer any information. You just answer the questions that are asked of you and that's all."

Barrera, accused later of suppressing evidence, said he omitted the truth from Nato's statement for two reasons. First, if Nato should prove a reluctant witness at the trial, Barrera might have to use his statement to drag his testimony out of him; and if it contained the truth about his relationship with Herlinda, it would weaken Nato's position with the jury. Second, Barrera felt that evidence of Herlinda's relationship with Nato was inadmissible because, Barrera maintains, Alcorta had not known of her infidelity before the crime, and it therefore could not have influenced his state of mind.

The trial judge, Joe Frazier Brown, disagrees. "Evidence of prior infidelity is admissible to show aggravation or mitigation—it's a question for the jury."

Now all this was of far more than mere technical importance. For if Alcorta had deliberately plotted his wife's murder for no other reasons than those he gave in his confession, he was almost surely guilty of murder with malice; but if, on the other hand, tormented for months by his wife's infidelity, he had accidentally come upon her in a parked car with a man and, in a fit of uncontrollable rage, had killed, then he might be guilty of no more than murder without malice. It makes a difference. Under Texas law, murder with malice is punishable by death in the electric chair; but murder without malice is punishable by a maximum of five years—and that sentence may even be suspended.

Alcorta had retained as his lawyer E. P. Lipscomb. Lipscomb is an old man, white-haired, weak-voiced, anxious, with mottled skin loose on his hands, rheumy eyes and white eyebrows, glasses far down on his nose, wearing a seedy gray suit and suspenders. A banker's son educated at Harvard, Lipscomb was admitted to the bar in 1912 and during the depression drifted into criminal law. He and his wife were divorced—he doesn't remember when. He married again. He says, "Practicing law is a hard field in which to make much money." Then, rather wistfully, remembering the hopes of youth, he adds, "I studied under Roscoe Pound at Harvard." Other lawyers feel sorry for him.

Before Alcorta's case, Lipscomb says, he had handled four death-penalty cases. But a newspaper says he had handled only two, pleading both defendants guilty. How he got the Alcorta case is uncertain. Alcorta paid Lipscomb $250. (Alcorta's relatives later paid him about $250 more to appeal for clemency.) Lipscomb visited him in jail five or six times. Alcorta has said, "I told him she was running around with other men. I told him everything." Lipscomb denies this. Lipscomb did not investigate her activities, did not interview the bartenders or the B-girls. He had no investigator on the case. He did not investigate or interview Nato Castilleja. Barrera says he told Lipscomb he would agree to a life sentence if Alcorta would plead guilty. Lipscomb denies it.

Barrera says that when he learned Lipscomb was to defend Alcorta, he was disturbed—"Lipscomb was a good lawyer in his day, but I didn't feel he was capable any more of giving this boy a run for his money"—so Barrera asked Judge Brown to appoint additional counsel. The idea occurred to Judge Brown independently and he called Lipscomb in and offered to appoint a lawyer to help him. Lipscomb refused. The case went to trial on October 3, 1955.

Barrera was the lead prosecutor. His superior, Hubert Green Jr., "sat second"—sat at the counsel table, but said little. He was there to get experience. Green had been appointed district attorney by the governor only a few months earlier. Green, a tall, thin, pale intense young man, only twenty-nine, with burning bright eyes and small sharp teeth, had practiced law with his father five years and had been San Antonio campaign manager for the governor. A "crusading conservative" in politics, active in civic affairs, a Baptist deacon, Green, as D.A., raided gambling joints and closed the crib houses near Concho Street. He encouraged vigorous prosecution. Under him, a man got life for possessing five marijuana cigarettes. A former prosecutor recalls, "Before Green, in an ordinary Mexican killing, a man would get five years, maybe ten, and might get a suspended sentence on a plea of guilty. We started trying these cases and trying hell out of 'em. When Green ran for election in his own right, on our political platform we listed fifteen cases where we'd got ninety-nine years, life or death penalties."

When the trial began, only a handful of relatives and hangers-on were present. In the little courtroom, ceiling fans whirred, and now and then the judge interrupted a witness's testimony to wait for a noisy truck outside to pass. The trial did not amount to much. Barrera put in the state's case swiftly and expertly, calling fifteen witnesses—a boy who found the body, the medical examiner, investigators, the girls who swore they had heard Alcorta threaten to kill Herlinda. The key to the state's case was Nato Castilleja. He testified he had met Herlinda at his sister's house six or eight weeks before she died. Had he seen her on other occasions? "Well, I give her—about two times, I give her a ride. . . . From where she was working to her house." Had they been alone? No, he said, always a friend had been with him. Had he ever given her a ride home by himself? No. (Barrera did not ask, and Nato did not volunteer, that he had dropped his friend off first and been alone with Herlinda.) When Alcorta stabbed her, she had been asking him to tell his sister to pick her up in the morning on her way to church. Barrera asked, "Natividad, were you in love with Herlinda?"

"No."

"Was she in love with you?"

"No."

"Had you ever talked about love?"

"No."

"Had you ever had dates with her other than to take her home?"

"No. Well, just when I brought her from there."

"Just when you brought her from work?"

"Yes."

He was a convincing witness. Lipscomb cross-examined him only for a minute or two. Lipscomb asked not a single question about Nato's relationship with Herlinda. Barrera had been careful not to ask Nato directly if he had had sexual relations with Herlinda—and, as instructed, he had not volunteered. Certainly the impression was that they had been no more than casual acquaintances. The full truth had not come out.

Lipscomb's cross-examination of the state's witnesses had been pitifully weak. For the defense he presented only three witnesses—two perfunctory character witnesses and Alcorta himself.

Lipscomb invited Alcorta to tell his story "in your own words," and he started off almost eloquently. "Well, it happens this way. It is just like a man meets a girl and gets married and they live happy, yes, for a while, you know, because I have three childrens; I love them." Barrera, listening, was worried. He recalls, "He made out a pitiful case for himself. I could see my death penalty flying out the window." To stop him, Barrera interposed a technical objection, and the judge sustained him; and Lipscomb, instead of helping Alcorta resume his narrative, which might have led to his discovery of his wife's infidelity, told Alcorta to get to the point. What had happened on the night of the murder? Alcorta described it. He said, not very convincingly, that he had seen Herlinda and Nato kissing in the car and that he thought if he had watched a few minutes longer, "something else" would have happened. By this, he explained later, he meant that they would have had intercourse; he did not make this clear to the jury. He said that he had seen Herlinda previously with Nato and others, but this was not very convincing either.

Barrera cross-examined with great skill. Alcorta tried to deny he had threatened to kill his wife; Barrera made him admit he had been put under a peace bond after hitting her on Mother's Day. In the face of indisputable medical testimony, Alcorta argued at great length that he had not stabbed her thirty-two times—maybe nine times or fifteen, but not thirty-two, it was impossible—and this idiotic quarrel enabled Barrera to show the jurors hideous photographs of the butchered body. Alcorta insisted he had gone to Herlinda's house only to see the children, and Barrera asked, "Do you always visit those kids, Alvaro, that you worry so much about, at one o'clock in the morning?" It was a telling blow, and Barrera used it repeatedly. Once Alcorta flared, "I wanted to tell the whole truth, but, anyway, it doesn't have to be a frame-up here like they are doing it." He insisted he had seen Herlinda and Nato kissing that night. Why hadn't he told Barrera and Torres this when he confessed? "You didn't ask me, and I knew if I tell you, why, you won't put it [in the confession] anyway."

"I see," Barrera said coolly and asked if the B-girls had invented his threats to kill Herlinda. "You did," Alcorta said sullenly. And the doctor and the policeman who counted the wounds—was that, too, part of the frame-up? Sure it was—"thirty-two is too many."

Abruptly Barrera stopped. He had handled him perfectly. He recalls, "I gigged him." Alcorta had done well on direct examination but on cross he lost his temper, cried frame-up, lied about such easily provable facts as the number of wounds; and, no doubt, when he tried to maintain that he had seen Nato kissing her, the jury didn't believe him. Of course, it might have believed him if Nato had told the truth. But Nato didn't. The full truth had been suppressed. The jury, ignorant of vital facts, could scarcely escape the conclusion that this was a cold, planned assassination without mitigation. It fixed Alcorta's punishment at death.

Lipscomb appealed on the ground that the inflammatory pictures should not have been admitted. The Texas Court of Criminal Appeals affirmed the conviction.[1] Alcorta was sentenced to die at Huntsville state penitentiary December 19, 1956. He was taken there, 215 miles northeast of San Antonio, on the vast Texas plain.

Lipscomb appealed for clemency to the State Board of Pardons and Paroles at Austin. The hearing was routine. Lipscomb merely pleaded for mercy, citing Alcorta's excellent military record. The board refused clemency. A new date was set. Alcorta would die January 18. Lipscomb planned further appeals. And the cruel game of last-minute reprieves began. Alcorta once said to the present author, "The chair is in a little chamber with a steel door, the green door. About noon they test the thing. You can hear it. Then it comes out on the radio too. The priest comes in. They shave you the last few minutes. While the guy is in the chair, the rest of us are quiet like. You can hear the generator. Three times. You see them when they bring him out afterwards on a four-wheeled cart. Once I got a stay about an hour before the time, and the guard said, 'We'll burn you yet.' " In all, Alcorta got eleven stays.

And then, in January 1957, a new lawyer entered the case—Fred Semaan, one of San Antonio's leading criminal lawyers. He is a blocky, bald man of forty-seven with big round brown eyes, an intense, nervous man, outwardly combative, soft inside. He was born and raised in San Antonio, the son of a Syrian immigrant who got rich importing Oriental rugs and art objects. His grandfather had established schools and churches in Lebanon; the Turks had burned them.

Semaan says, "It could be that has something to do with my being sympathetic with minority groups and underdogs." Admitted to the bar in 1941, he worked three years as a sheriff's investigator, then went into private practice— "I wanted to try murder cases." He has handled about 300 murder cases and never has lost a client to the electric chair —"if I do, I'll die with him."

Politically liberal, he ran unsuccessfully for the legislature, attacking the manufacturers' association, himself at-

---

[1] [Editor's note: See Alcorta v. Texas, 294 S. W. 2d 112 (1956).]

tacked as the candidate of "the underworld elements." He has said, "I'm mean and nasty and tenacious. I've got a hell of a reputation for being a fighter. I don't go into a courtroom to try to prove what a gentleman I am. I go in to help a defendant. If some judge gets his feelings hurt in the rush, I don't care." Semaan has a highly developed social conscience. "People are vicious. They treat a man like an animal. Prosecutors especially have an idea that when a man's indicted, he's fair game; any way you can get him, get him. He's like a wild animal in a hunt. He's running; and all that pack behind him, with all that ammunition, is waiting to cut him down. You just don't do that to human beings; I don't care what crime he's committed."

After Alcorta was taken off to the death house, the brother of a man Semaan had defended told Semaan that Nato Castilleja had told him he'd perjured himself on Barrera's instructions. Nato, however, refused to talk to Semaan. Semaan tipped off the San Antonio *Light*. It got nowhere. On January 24, 1957, the Rev. Francis Duffy, chaplain at the Huntsville prison, inquired at the *Light* on Alcorta's behalf about Alcorta's children and was referred to Fred Semaan. Semaan sent Father Duffy to Nato Castilleja's house. Father Duffy recalls, "I told Nato if he withheld anything, he'd have it on his soul the rest of his days." Father Duffy, Nato and Nato's brother went to Semaan's office. "And Nato spilled the whole works," Semaan says. "The truth finally came out."

Nato gave Semaan a one-page statement. In it he says that he had had sexual relations with Herlinda "about four or five times." He told investigator Torres so before the trial, but Torres told him he need say nothing about it unless he wanted to. "I didn't tell this in court because I didn't want to say it in front of all those people. I was asked in court during the trial whether or not I had had intercourse with Linda Alcorta and I said that I had not." (Actually, as we have seen, the direct question never was asked him on the witness stand.) And in a second statement Nato said he'd been intimate with Herlinda the night she was killed.

Alcorta was granted another stay. The parole board scheduled a new hearing. Semaan and the private investigator, Limón, found new witnesses—bartenders and bar customers who had known Herlinda, some intimately. Esperanza Huron gave them an affidavit recanting her testimony that Alcorta had threatened to kill Herlinda. The case was gathering momentum. All over the West Side jars appeared on bars, soliciting contributions to the Alvaro Alcorta fund. A song, *El Corrido de Alcorta,* blared from jukeboxes. Petitions for clemency were circulated. And the papers took sides, the *Light* espousing Alcorta's cause; the *News* and *Express,* District Attorney Green's. Green and Semaan were enemies—Green was a Baptist and a crusader; Semaan considered him a sanctimonious witch-hunter. Everybody's nerves got taut.

Semaan recalls, "Green was the governor's fair-haired boy and the *News*'s too. I was considered damn near sacrilegious. My sisters, my mother, my law partners and my closest friends all told me to get out of the Alcorta case. Let somebody else do it, they said."

The parole board hearing at Austin on February 8 was uproarious. Barrera said Semaan had been known to try to influence a witness, a newspaper reported, and Semaan shouted, "I say you are lying if you so accuse me." Semaan accused Green of suborning perjury. Barrera jumped up and said, "If you have any questions about perjury, ask me." Barrera admitted he had known that Herlinda had had intimacies with Castilleja, but denied any impropriety in not bringing it out for the jury. The board refused clemency. Alcorta would die on Tuesday.

Semaan filed a petition in the original trial court for a writ of habeas corpus on the ground that Alcorta had been denied due process of law under the Fifth and Fourteenth Amendments. Judge John F. Onion Jr. held a hearing. Alcorta sat through it clutching a Bible, his face blank, saying nothing. Semaan recalls, "I'd never seen him before. But I wouldn't give a damn who he was, knowing what they'd done to him. I don't condone what he did. If the jury had had all the facts, I wouldn't have raised a finger. But I want them to get him legally. Hell, this is lynch law."

As court convened, Semaan asked Nato if he had talked lately to anybody from the D.A.'s office. No, he said. But he had—Green and Barrera had gone to his house last night. And although now he testified that he had had sexual relations with Herlinda several times, he denied having had them on the night of the murder and denied having told Father Duffy he had, and Semaan was obliged to impeach him with his written statement. The hearing lasted all day. Judge Onion denied the writ. The Texas Court of Criminal Appeals at Austin upheld him. Semaan appealed to the Supreme Court of the United States though only as a formality, expecting it to require him to start over in the lower Federal courts. To his astonishment, the Supreme Court granted certiorari—agreed to hear the case fully now.

On October 23, 1957, Semaan, Barrera and Green argued the case orally before the Supreme Court in Washington. None of them had previously appeared before this awesome tribunal in its marble hall. Semaan wouldn't let his wife attend court, fearing the court might embarrass him.

"It was hard," he recalls. "I was groping. And all for a 'Meskin.' That's what they call 'em. Everybody said, 'Why the hell do that for a damn Meskin?' Everybody's attitude—that was the damnedest thing about the case."

Semaan argued first. When he told the court that the prosecutor had known before the trial of Nato's intimacies with Herlinda and had not divulged it, Justice Frankfurter interposed, "You mean to say that this prosecutor knew that and did not divulge it at the trial?" Prosecutor Barrera recalls, "That's when I saw the handwriting on the wall." Barrera argued next. He had scarcely got started when the justices began to question him sharply. He recalls, "I felt like a duck in a shooting gallery."

Justice Black asked, "Did you know, when you heard those denials, that he was in love with the lady, that he had confessed having relations with her?"

Barrera said, "I certainly did."

Black said, "You knew, of course, that no Southern jury would convict for murder if it knew of those prior relations."

Chief Justice Warren said the prosecutor had depicted her relations with Nato as "innocent and platonic," though he knew it false. Justice Clark told Barrera, "You are not supposed to be a persecutor." And Black, "The object of questioning a witness is to bring truth to the jury and not deception." Frankfurter, pounding the bench, demanded of Barrera whether he considered his conduct of the trial fair, and Justice Harlan asked when he had graduated from law school.

Barrera recalls, "There's a little light that warns you when your time is up. It went on, and Green kept pulling on my coat and whispering to me to sit down. You just don't back down at a time like that. Man"—laughing—"they scratched all over me." And Semaan recalls, "When I heard Frankfurter and Warren and the other justices point their finger at Green and Barrera and say, 'Don't you know it's your duty to prosecute and not persecute,' I had all I could do to keep from getting up and shouting, 'Hooray.' Because that was the first time any judge ever saw it my way." After it was over, Green vomited. Barrera says wryly, "It was an experience."

November 12 the Supreme Court decided the case.[2] It related that Alcorta at his trial had admitted the murder, but had claimed he had killed his wife "in a fit of passion" when he discovered her kissing a man late at night in a parked car. Had the jury believed him, it might have found him guilty of murder without malice, punishable by only five years. And it might have believed him had Nato Castilleja told the truth. Instead Castilleja had testified falsely—and with Barrera's knowledge. Thus the jury had been misled. All this, the court held, had denied Alcorta due process, and it reversed the conviction and ordered a new trial.

The new trial began on December 1, 1958. Green and Semaan had been negotiating. Semaan had offered to plead Alcorta guilty for a five-year sentence; Green had started out by demanding life. When they arrived at a compromise of thirty years, Semaan felt he had to tell Alcorta about it. Alcorta was delighted. Semaan says, "I wish he'd just sat tight and let me fight it. But if I'd had eleven dates set for my own execution, I guess I'd grab anything less than the

[2] [Editor's note: See Alcorta v. Texas, 355 U. S. 28 (1957).]

chair." Alcorta pleaded guilty and was sentenced to thirty years. He will become eligible for parole next year, after serving five years.

The Texas State Bar Association asked the court to reprimand, suspend or disbar Lipscomb, charging he had solicited "numerous" cases, including Alcorta's. (It subsequently dropped the charge that he had solicited Alcorta's.) The court suspended Lipscomb for four months. Semaan feels Lipscomb became "the goat." The bar association took no action against Green or Barrera. Green did not run for re-election, though not, he says, because of the Alcorta case. He is practicing law privately, mostly civil law. After the Supreme Court decision, he was dubbed "Outstanding Texas Prosecutor" by a private agency, the Texas Law Enforcement Foundation, "in recognition and appreciation of his signal and matchless contribution to criminal justice in this state." Barrera went into private practice. Semaan estimates that he himself spent $3000 or $4000 on the Alcorta case, plus several months' time. His only fee was $120, raised by donations on the West Side.

Today Nato Castilleja says, "I'm glad it's all over. I wish I'd never heard of her."

Attorney Lipscomb still feels he was right—the conviction should have been reversed because the inflammatory pictures were introduced.

A newspaper columnist who fought Semaan at the time now says, "Alcorta is a brute and he got off because of an overzealous prosecutor."

Green says, "I will say that I have no feeling of bitterness or grudge against anyone or any court. The court did what it thought right and proper, and I have done what I thought right and proper." Green feels that the court decision comes close to saying that the state has a responsibility for the defense, an idea abhorrent to him, since he feels it would "wipe out" the entire adversary system of pitting one lawyer against another. He thinks telling Nato to volunteer nothing was simply good practice, taught every day in law school.

Barrera took defeat philosophically. He insists the crime was murder with malice. "I still feel I did nothing wrong."

Semaan says, "They damn near got away with it. And if they can do that to a poor Mexican like Alcorta, and someday they decide to get you or me, they can do it. What scares you is, this one came to light—but you wonder how many other poor young punks have been convicted this way, and nobody's looked into it."

The case, like so many others, is not simple; it is gray, not black or white. What Nato Castilleja testified to was not, line by line, outright perjury; yet its total effect was to mislead the jury. What Alcorta did was neither clearly murder without malice nor clearly a cold-blooded assassination. No murders are alike, and not all murderers are equally culpable—if they were, the law would recognize no degree of murder, but would punish all alike. Very often in a trial the question to be decided is not guilt but culpability—taking all circumstances into account, how much punishment should be assessed? It was here that the system broke down in the Alcorta case. "All circumstances," the full truth, would have presented the jury with a crucial question: Whether her conduct was aggravation or mitigation of his offense. The system broke down because the full truth was not given the jury. Why was it not? Because the actions of an overzealous prosecutor and an inadequate defense attorney deprived Alcorta of his rights.

A canon of the Texas State Bar Association's code of ethics says, "It should be the primary duty of a member engaged in public prosecution not to convict, but to see that justice is done."

A law professor has said, "The typical D.A. thinks a string of convictions is the way to re-election. And he's right. The evil is that he is led into using perjurious witnesses to get a victory at any cost."

Barrera was overzealous. Other prosecutors have actually procured outright perjury. Moreover, our adversary system can promote justice only if the opposing attorneys are of roughly equal competence. That Lipscomb was no match for Barrera is amply clear.

Alcorta is working in the cement factory in prison. His only worry is about his children. "They'll be grown up by the time I get out."

He does not know it, but they are living with Herlinda's parents in the little house on Ike Road that Alcorta built for Herlinda long ago.

One evening a while back, the investigator Limón took a visitor down to Troubador Lane near Concho Street; a band of strolling musicians came to his car, and he asked them to play *El Corrido de Alcorta*. They had forgotten it. Limón said, "Can you imagine? Life is cheap here." Finally they remembered.

> *Alvaro Alcorta mató,*
> *Y es necesario un castigo;*
> *Pero hay que ser de razón*
> *Y comprender los motivos.*

> (Alvaro Alcorta killed,
> And a punishment is necessary;
> But one must be reasonable
> And understand the motives.)

THE QUESTION OF IDENTITY*

BY JOHN BARTLOW MARTIN

About 11 A.M. on June 25, 1956, Jim Foster was up on a ladder painting a doctor's house in Gainesville, Georgia, when two police officers told him to come down, that they wanted to talk to him. Foster, a wiry cocksure little house painter of thirty-eight, descended. The officers were Fred Culberson of the Georgia Bureau of Investigation and the local police chief, Hoyt Henry.

Foster later testified, "They said do you know anything about anything that happened in Cleveland," a small town twenty-three miles away. "I said I don't know what you are talking about. They said we're talking about a mattress agitting caught afire. I said I guess I know all about it." The preceding Friday—today was Monday—Foster and another man, Robert Dean, though both were married, had

---

* Reprinted, with omissions, by permission of Harold Ober Associates Incorporated, from the *Saturday Evening Post*, vol. 233 (August 13, 1960), pp. 34 ff. © 1960 by The Curtis Publishing Company.

taken two young women—one married, the other widowed
—out drinking and had spent the night with them in two
tourist cabins at Cleveland. The other couple had set the
bed afire, and all four had left without paying their bills
or paying for the damage. Now they were caught. The
police locked up Foster, picked up Robert Dean and the
two women and notified the sheriff at Cleveland.

But the police had something more important on their
minds. A week earlier, on June 19, a prominent storekeeper on the outskirts of Jefferson, twenty-one miles southeast of Gainesville, Charles Drake, had been shot dead by
a robber. Foster fitted the description of the robber given
by Drake's wife. In addition, the police found in Foster's
pocket a document showing that he had recently been released from Florida State Prison in Raiford.

They asked where he had been the night of the Drake
murder. Riding around with Dean and the girls. Where?
Near Jefferson—that is, near where Drake had been shot.
But hadn't he encountered the roadblock? Yes, and he had
evaded it. Why? Because he'd been drinking and had no
driver's license.

Saying all this, Foster seemed unconcerned. He did not
even know Drake had been killed or, if he had read it in
the papers, had forgotten it. He enjoyed bragging about
the girls. The police put Dean in Foster's cell. Foster later
testified, "We stood there and talked. He said, 'Well, I
guess we are in a mess now, ain't we?' I said, 'I guess we
are.' He said, 'What we going to do about our wives?'
I said, 'Well, I'm not worried about mine.' He said, 'Well,
I'm worried about mine.' Tell you the truth, I'm worried
about mine a little bit." Next day they paid for the damage
at the tourist cabin. The others were released. The whole
thing still seemed a lark.

Agents Culberson and Louis Hightower of the GBI took
Foster to Charley Drake's house. He went willingly, to
oblige them. "Mr. Culberson went in front of me into the
house. He opened the door. We walked in through this
room into another room in to the door, and he said, 'Now
stand right here. You stand right here, now—don't you say
anything. You just stand right here.' I said, 'All right, sir.'

I stood right there. . . . Mrs. Drake . . . came out, and the minute she came out around in view of me, she made a lunge like she was going to grab me. Mr. Hightower, he grabbed her. He said, 'Take it easy, Mrs. Drake; it's nothing to git excited about.' I was still standing there. When she got through with the tears, she came up and said, 'Why did you kill my husband? How could you do it?' I was so scared I didn't know what to do, standing there when she said that. I said, 'Lady, for God's sake, please don't make a mistake.' She backed up and she said, 'Don't you talk; don't you say nothing. You let me look at you.' I said, 'O.K., lady, just please don't make a mistake—for God's sake, don't make a mistake.' "

But she did—and started Foster on the way to the electric chair for a crime he didn't commit.

Our American system of criminal justice probably breaks down more frequently because of a mistaken eyewitness identification than for any other single reason. Let us observe what happened to James Fulton Foster.

He was a hard-bodied, muscular little man with hard brown eyes and a sharp-featured face and pointed chin. He spoke with a flat, hard, upcountry twang. He was a simple, humorous man, but shrewd and cocky. He liked a good time, girls, gambling, drinking. He had seven children—the youngest four, the eldest sixteen.

He was born and raised in the hard red hills near Greenville, South Carolina. Cool mountains rise in the distance, but in the summer the sun burns so hot it hurts. His father was a sharecropper. "Ever since I was big enough to pick up a hoe," Foster says, "I been hoeing, then plowing—then tractors. I'm telling you, I've had it tough all my life." He married at twenty in 1937. For two years he farmed. "I didn't make enough off cotton to pay my fertilizer. And it come a rain and washed my field slap away." He quit farming to work in the textile mills, went up to Baltimore and made seventy-five dollars a week in a defense plant, was drafted, saw combat in Europe and, discharged in 1945, went home to South Carolina and worked summers as a house painter and winters in the textile mill. He drew pay to go to school under the G.I. Bill of Rights.

"I'd get both checks Friday. I'd have a hundred and sixty-five, hundred and seventy-five dollars, and I'd go off maybe that night and get drunk and gamble every penny away—and next morning have to buy groceries on credit." He says he began drinking in the Army. "Army made some good men and some bad. I turned out to be a sot. One drink, and I'm gone."

His wife objected to his drinking and gambling. Finally he left her—hitchhiked to Fort Lauderdale, Florida. It was December 1954. He stayed in a rooming house. One night, he says, he went for a ride with another roomer, and the other man held up a store. Foster was sentenced to Raiford for eighteen months as an accessory to armed robbery. His wife had a lawyer draw up divorce papers, but went no further.

Foster was released May 18, 1956. He went to Gaines-ville, Georgia, got a job painting, hitchhiked home to spend a night with his wife and went back to Gainesville to work. A month later he was picked up for murder.

He spent the month house-painting, living in a rooming house and chasing around. One night after work he bathed, put on his "gal gitters"—bright pink pants—went next door to supper and sat down on the porch of the rooming house to read the paper. A girl, Mary Francis Higdon, telephoned and said, "I thought you was going to come out sometime." Another roomer, Robert Dean, drove him to her house. Mary Francis was twenty years old. She had a child; her husband had died a few months earlier. She lived with her mother and her sister-in-law, Leola Forrester. Leola had two small children; her husband was in military service overseas. Foster and Mary Francis and Leola and their three children got into Mary Francis's jalopy and drove back to Foster's rooming house and invited Robert Dean to join them. Dean, a forty-four-year-old illiterate, married, with grown children, later recalled, "I asked 'em where they was going, and they said they was going to ride around and said crawl in. I said, 'Well, it don't look like there's no room.' They said, 'Yes, there's room—crawl in.'" So, he did. They started off, but the brakes were bad, and they parked the jalopy at the rooming house and started off anew in Dean's car, Foster driving.

They drove around the town square, then went out to a café on Dawsonville highway. Foster bought four cans of beer—the county is dry—and he and Dean drank them in the car. They drove around aimlessly, looked for a bootlegger in the woods, got lost, found him, bought two cans of beer. But there was no opener, so they stopped at a drive-in and borrowed one, and Foster bought some cheese crackers for the children. The little boy was asleep in the front seat. They finished their beer, threw the cans out and drove off. It was late. They came to a roadblock. The girls said the police had been checking drivers' licenses. Foster said, "Good Lord, I ain't got no driver's license," and turned off on a side road and told Robert Dean to drive. Directed by the girls, they found a roundabout way into Gainesville and went home.

Unbeknown to all of them, Charles Drake had been murdered on that evening, June 19. Drake was fifty-seven years old, a prominent citizen of Jefferson. A resident says, "He was a good, honest, Christian man." It is the region's highest compliment. Drake and his wife ran a clean, modern country store on the Gainesville highway. They lived in a white house on a little knoll sloping up from the store. Drake's late father always had carried large amounts of cash because he didn't trust banks and, dying, had given Drake $5400 cash. Drake kept it in his shirt pocket.

About 9:30 P.M. Mrs. Drake left her husband watching television in the living room and went to the bathroom to wash. In a moment, "I heard this terrible scream from my husband." He was in the dining room trying to hold a French door shut. A man with a gun was kicking the door in and coming through. Drake ran to the bedroom and got a gun. The robber shot him dead. Mrs. Drake ran to a phone. The robber snatched it from her hand, threw it to the floor, put his gun in her face and, when she turned, hit her on the head. He searched Drake's body hastily, missed the $5400 and ran away.

Great hue and cry arose. In Sheriff John B. Brooks's

seventeen years in office, this was the first robbery murder. A newspaper reported that the crime was "branded the 'most vicious in the history of Jackson County.'" A Gainesville newspaperman recalls, "They wanted *somebody* bad."

James Foster was unaware of the uproar. On Thursday he and Robert Dean took the two girls and their three children out again, swapping partners—Leola was with Foster because she preferred him. They drove out to the country, parked and danced in the road to music from the car radio. The next night, Friday, they went out again, but this time left the children home. They drove north, drank some beer, went on to a motel at Cleveland and spent the night, according to testimony. At daylight they left, Robert Dean and his girl giggling because the mattress on their bed had caught fire. On Monday, Foster was arrested.

Foster was arraigned on August 17, and attorneys Horace Wood and Floyd Hoard were appointed by the court to defend him. Only six days later the trial began. Indeed, when it began, the police had not yet received the results of laboratory tests on the bullets. Six days is not much time to prepare a criminal defense. Wood and Hoard worked frantically.

The trial was held in Jefferson, and it was a great event. Jefferson is just a little country town, a cotton-mill-and-farming town in the Georgia Piedmont. A tractor on a hilly horizon, rusty tin-roofed shacks and pretty farmhouses, a straw-hatted old man plowing with one horse, blood-red earth beneath pine and oak, vines suffocating everything in a creek bottom and a big black snake slithering across a highway—that is the landscape. In the town square rises a Confederate statue. A block up the hill stands the ancient courthouse, worn stone corridors, wooden stairs, unshaded light bulbs—all together, an unpretentious and even somewhat seedy temple of justice. But for one week while James Fulton Foster was on trial it was the scene of great doings.

Jackson County is one of four counties in the Piedmont Judicial Circuit. A judge still rides the circuit here. He holds court at Jefferson twice a year. His court is called

"Big Co't" and hears all felonies, as distinguished from municipal court, which tries misdemeanors. People come from miles around to attend Big Co't, for entertainment is scarce hereabout.

The crowd that came to see James Foster tried was about the biggest ever. Every inch of standing room was taken. The balcony for Negroes was full. The heat was sweltering, and ceiling fans whirred, and spectators mopped their brows and fanned themselves. Some brought their lunch so as not to risk losing their seats at noontime. Church ladies sold lemonade and sandwiches under the shade trees on the lawn, and merchants displayed their wares on the sidewalks. Old men peddled peanuts in the courtroom and small boys sold cold drinks. At lunch hour an evangelist stood on the courthouse steps, exhorting the Big Co't crowd to repent.

Judge Julian Bennett presided. It was his first trial; he had been appointed only a few days before. Solicitor General Hope D. Stark prosecuted, assisted by H. W. Davis and Jack S. Davidson, who were retained by Mrs. Drake. The state put in its case crisply—testimony from doctors, a neighbor, Agent Culberson and Mrs. Drake, the key witness. She identified Foster from the witness stand, pronouncing the fatal words firmly.

"Is that the man that was in your house?"

"That's the man."

"Is he the man that shot your husband?"

"He is the man that shot my husband."

As a clincher, the state produced J. C. Dameron, who had been in jail with Foster and who testified that Foster had told him he had killed Drake. Incredibly, Wood, cross-examining, did not ask Dameron if he had been promised leniency for his testimony. Indeed, Wood's cross-examination often seemed fumbling and confused. Perhaps he was exhausted by sleepless nights preparing the case.

For the defense, Wood produced thirteen witnesses, including the alibi witnesses and Foster himself. On the stand Foster made an unsworn statement not subject to cross-examination, common practice in Georgia. He clutched a Bible as he presented his alibi in convincing detail. He described Mrs. Drake's identification and his own incarceration, took off his shirt to show the jury he was not muscular enough to grapple with Drake, a big man, then launched a peroration remarkable in the annals of criminal jurisprudence.

"I hope to God you fellows will believe me—I hope you will. I ain't give up yet, I ain't give up. I know a Man that can do greater things than I can do, or anybody else, and I'm still trusting Him. I know I'm going to git out of this thing, just about know it. . . .

"I wish to say this to everybody—that I could have a word of prayer, if it would be pleasing to everybody.

"Dear God, as I put my head in their life, God, and approach Thy throne of grace, I want to thank Thee, God, for standing by me and giving me the courage, God, to go on through this terrible strain. Heavenly Father, we want to thank Thee, God, for our beautiful day outside, the beautiful sunshine. Heavenly Father, bless each and every one that's in this courthouse today. . . . Father, bless my mother and father, wherever they may be. Bless my children, God, that they may grow up to be fine young men and women, future people of this world. Heavenly Father, we would ask Thee now to be with us all through the remainder of this day. If it be Thy will, Father, grant, dear God, that we can all meet in the same place in that home which Thou hast prepared for us. These things we ask in Thy name. Amen. That's all I have to say."

The question for the jury was simple: Whether to believe Foster and his misbehaving alibi witnesses—or the eyewitness identification of a leading citizen. It believed Mrs. Drake. The penalty would be death. Foster, eyes closed and hands clenched, said, "I didn't do it; I didn't do it."

They took Foster to Gainesville jail. "I can't tell you how I felt," he once said. "I went blind for a day and a night—totally blind. For breakfast I couldn't eat nothing. I just laid on the steel bunk."

Gradually hope returned. Even during the trial some of

the spectators had thought Foster innocent. They contributed to a fund to finance an appeal. To some it became a holy cause. Attorney Wood appealed; but the Georgia Supreme Court affirmed the conviction,[1] and the United States Supreme Court refused to review the case. So all had failed. "There was not a thing anybody could do," a man who thought him innocent recalls.

But there was. It was done by the South Carolina Law Enforcement Division, a powerful plain-clothes investigative agency headed by J. Preston Strom. Early in 1957 an ex-convict, now dead, told Strom he'd heard that Foster was innocent. About the same time, Strom, together with the division's Lt. B. S. Moss and Sheriff B. B. Brockman and Jack Fowler, investigating some safecrackings and burglaries near Spartanburg, South Carolina, were told that a former policeman turned thief, from Cairo, Illinois—Charles Paul (Rocky) Rothschild—had killed Drake and had driven a car belonging to William F. Patterson, of Greenville, South Carolina. Agent Culberson of the GBI heard the same thing in Georgia. Patterson, arrested and convicted of a Spartanburg robbery, finally gave Chief Strom a statement: Rocky Rothschild, the ex-cop from Cairo, had borrowed his car on June 19 and returned it to him late that night, telling him that he and A. D. Allen, a bootlegger, had tried to rob a storekeeper and had killed him. Rocky Rothschild was arrested and convicted of a Spartanburg robbery. Confronted with Patterson's statement, Rothschild confessed—A. D. Allen had fingered the Drake job; Rothschild had killed Drake. Rothschild's story fitted Patterson's. It was extremely circumstantial. He re-enacted the crime convincingly, Chief Strom says. On August 14, 1958, a jury found A. D. Allen guilty, and he was sentenced to life imprisonment. Rothschild pleaded guilty and was sentenced to life. And Foster was set free.

The case is very painful to Mrs. Drake. She says, "I thought I was right. Now I just don't know. I certainly don't want to see anyone suffer for anything he didn't do, but I was completely honest. It's a terrible thing to see your

[1] [Editor's note: See Foster v. State, 213 Ga. 601 (1957).]

husband killed before your eyes and almost be killed yourself."

The case is not entirely satisfactory. The gun Rothschild said he used was never found. In his confession Rothschild said he had worn a silk stocking over his face during the robbery; Mrs. Drake at the time had said nothing of this. On October 9, 1959, the Georgia Supreme Court overturned Allen's conviction—held that he had been convicted on the uncorroborated testimony of an accomplice, insufficient under Georgia law. And Rocky Rothschild repudiated his confession, saying he had been framed. His repudiation came during a political upheaval at Jefferson and could have been connected with it. Chief Strom, Agent Culberson and Sheriff Brooks are convinced Rothschild is guilty.

Regardless of all this, however, the central fact remains —James Foster was innocent, but almost went to the chair. Laymen tend to consider eyewitness identification more reliable than "circumstantial" evidence. Lawyers and psychologists know better. And the case proves something else—that a man with a criminal record walks always in danger. It is all very well to say Foster was an ex-convict and wouldn't have got in trouble if he hadn't been misbehaving with somebody else's wife—and to smile at his foolishness. But it is still true he spent two years in jail and nearly went to the chair for a murder he didn't commit. . . .

THE MAKING OF A BOY KILLER*

BY IRA HENRY FREEMAN**

A little after midnight on August 30, 1959, fifteen teenagers from a Puerto Rican gang in the West Seventies

* Reprinted, by permission of the author and the *New York Times,* from "The Making of A Boy Killer," *The New York Times Magazine* (February 18, 1962), pp. 14 ff. Copyright © 1962 by Ira Henry Freeman.
** Author of *Out of the Burning* (1960) and many other articles and stories; winner of the George Polk Award for National Reporting in 1951.

attacked six "gringo" youths sitting in a playground in Forty-fifth Street near Ninth Avenue.

The attack was planned to avenge the beating of a Puerto Rican boy by rival gang members, but all of the victims were "innocent bystanders," not gang boys. Two sixteen-year-old "gringos" were stabbed to death and a third seriously wounded by Salvador Agron, also sixteen, who was called the "Cape Man" because he wore a red-lined nurse's cloak. When arrested, he boasted, "I don't care if I burn; my mother could watch me."

Convicted of first degree murder in one of the most shocking cases of boy-gang violence in New York, Agron was scheduled to die in the electric chair three days ago.[1] However, one week before execution, Governor Rockefeller commuted the sentence to life imprisonment on the plea of Mrs. Eleanor Roosevelt, Correction Commissioner Anna M. Kross, Mayor Felisa Rincon de Gautier of San Juan, P. R., District Attorney Frank S. Hogan, who had prosecuted the case, and others.

The basis of their plea was that although Agron had been labeled "Dracula," a monster who wantonly killed, he actually was a weak, timid boy on the borderline of insanity who had been "grotesquely deprived" of parental affection or community care all his life.

Here is the story of his life—uncovered after a year's investigation by social agencies in New York and Puerto Rico at the instigation of Shad Polier, the boy's principal counsel, who served without fee.

Salvador Agron was born on April 24, 1943, in the small town of Mayagüez, Puerto Rico, the son of Gumersindo Agron and Esmeralda Rodriguez. The mother, orphaned at the age of three, was a "headstrong, pretty, illiterate" child of thirteen when she eloped with Agron, a handsome, thirty-two-year-old street cleaner whom she met at a dance. Four years later, the couple were married. They had two children—a daughter, Aurea, born in 1942, and Sal. The four lived in one slum room.

When Sal was about eighteen months old, Mrs. Agron

[1] [Editor's note: For the appellate decision in the case, see People v. Agron, 10 N. Y. 2d 130 (1961).]

fled with both children from her husband, whom she charged with beating her with a machete, neglecting her for other women and drunkenness. She found shelter in a Roman Catholic asylum for the poor, described as a "nineteenth-century" institution for the destitute of all ages, orphans, the aged, sick and mentally ill.

When they arrived at the place, both children were suffering from malnutrition. Sal could not stomach solid food and was so rachitic that he could not walk until he was two and a half; his sister later developed tuberculosis.

The poorhouse was run by Sisters of Charity with strict discipline and segregation of the sexes. The Agron children were put into the nursery, while their mother, working as an $8-a-week attendant in the wards for the aged, was lodged separately. She was allowed to visit her children on Sundays.

Sal became a problem as soon as he could walk, running after his mother, interfering with her work, upsetting the old people in the ward. Despite scolding by the nuns, Mrs. Agron encouraged this, since Sal was her favorite. Mother and son used to hide in corners to embrace. The boy was always disappearing, usually trying to find his mother, sometimes also his father. When Mrs. Agron, off duty, left for town, Sal clung to her skirts and howled. Several times he was picked up wandering the streets late at night looking for his mother or father.

He never adjusted to life in the ward. He cried and wet his bed every night, when awake as well as when asleep. (No punishment cured him of bedwetting, which persisted until the age of fourteen.) He developed a habit of tumbling out of bed and sleeping on the floor. He never could sit still, pay attention or take orders. When spanked, he threw temper tantrums, and ran away from the asylum several times. Unable to play with other children peaceably in the playground, he attacked them with stones.

Mrs. Agron, immature and uneducated, rebelled against the nuns' discipline. She was disaffected with the Catholic faith, to which she conformed outwardly but which she had left, first for a spiritualist and later for a pentecostal sect. She had also broken Catholic rules by getting a divorce. Divine voices, which she still hears, told her what to do.

In 1948, she left the asylum for San Juan, taking her children. She could not support them. Sal, then five and a half, was turned over to his father, and Aurea was sent to a tuberculosis sanitarium.

Mr. Agron, ill with heart disease, admitted he could not control his son during the one year he was in charge of him. Young as he was, Sal ran the streets day and night, rarely returning home to eat and sometimes not to sleep. He was often found sleeping on the sidewalk or in alleys, apparently lost.

It was during this period that Sal's strange compulsion to collect razor blades was first noted. After his arrest for murder, many old scars were found on his arms and chest where, he confessed, he had cut himself with razors and knives for years, although he did not know why. Sometimes he, too, heard voices that told him "to do bad things."

Sal seemed attached to both parents, and wished they would live together again. But Mr. Agron was living with a succession of "wives" (he had ten, legal and common-law, up to the age of fifty-five), some kind to the boy, others indifferent or neurotic.

In November 1949, Mrs. Agron returned to the almshouse. Both children went to school on the grounds. Aurea was a normal pupil, but her brother was dull. Teachers said his speech remained "babyish," that he spent his time making "weird" drawings, that he could not pay attention in the large, ungraded class, that he fidgeted constantly, caused disturbances, and kept wandering out. Once he fled to the garden and buried himself.

He got the equivalent of only one year's schooling up to the time he left Puerto Rico at the age of ten. He could scarcely read or write. (The only available data on intelligence tests give him a below-average quotient of sixty-eight to eighty-six at age sixteen, although observers think disturbances might have lowered his true score somewhat.)

Mrs. Agron eventually married a man named Luis Vargas and lived with him in a nearby town, but her new husband would not take in the children. They remained in the asylum. As usual, Sal cried and kept running away to town, searching for his parents. The marriage to Vargas ended in divorce a few months later, and Mrs. Agron returned to the institution.

Unhappy there, she began saving to emigrate to New York. In 1953, Carlos Gonzalez, who had been a member of the Mayagüez pentecostal sect and was now a hat worker in New York, sent her the air fare. Mrs. Agron went to New York and married him, taking Aurea with her, but leaving Sal in the asylum until she settled into her new home. The nuns recall that he was the "saddest child in the institution" during his six months of waiting.

Ten-year-old Sal arrived in New York alone at midnight to find nobody at the airport to meet him because of a change in the flight date. He wept for hours until his mother, located by telephone at last, came for him.

The family of four lived in one miserable furnished room in midtown Manhattan, paying the comparatively high rent of $22 a week. Since both parents went out to work, the children were left to take care of themselves all day.

Knowing no English, Sal achieved even less in school in New York than in Puerto Rico. Aurea, who was doing well, had literally to drag her brother into the classroom, from which he escaped at the first opportunity. Sporadically he made futile efforts to learn, and beat his head against the wall in frustration.

Giving up, the teachers set him to chores like cleaning the blackboard. Sal's classmates called him "crazy," which drove him to furious attacks upon them or to tantrums. The only playmates he got along with were much younger children, in whose infantile games he joined happily.

At first, Sal called Mr. Gonzalez "little Daddy," greeting him with a hug and kiss. But Gonzalez rebuffed him: "I am not your father; your father is in Puerto Rico." The foster father, who had been self-supporting since the age of eight and had taught himself to read and write both English and Spanish, was rigidly self-righteous and religious.

He punished Sal's tantrums, disobedience, misbehavior at home and truancy from school by beatings with a strap, and once locked him out of the home all night. The mother, although dominated by her husband, tried to comfort the boy, but Gonzalez objected to any show of affection between them.

Before one year had passed, the foster father lost all patience and asked the Children's Court to send Sal to an institution for disturbed boys. Sal was in Wiltwyck School from 1954 until late in 1956. There he was "helped to some extent," but reluctantly discharged at the age limit of thirteen "with many questions and apprehensions as to his ultimate adjustment. . . ." Psychotherapy for "schizoid traits" was recommended, but was unavailable.

Sal came back to a home more uncongenial than ever. The family now occupied a two-story, seventy-year-old tenement backed against the Brooklyn Navy Yard. In a store on the ground floor, Mr. Gonzalez had set up a "Pentecostal Church of Christ" with himself as minister. The four lived on the second floor in four small rooms. Their income came out of the collection and from Mrs. Gonzalez' earnings as a manufacturing worker.

Sal tried to brighten the apartment with pictures and artificial flowers bought at the five-and-ten-cent store, but Mr. Gonzalez opposed him. Harshly puritanical, he banned smoking, drinking, non-religious pictures, television and radio. He forbade Sal and Aurea to play the guitar, sing or dance. Sal, who never defied his foster father, would slink away, muttering, "You don't have the right to be cheerful in this house."

To keep Sal from eating too much, Gonzalez padlocked the refrigerator.

Although Sal had learned some English at Wiltwyck, he still could not adjust to school and was truant half the time. He drifted away from home and soon could not account for his whereabouts. Not being strong, he was not welcome among street clubs in the neighborhood and was beaten up by boys his own age. He enjoyed playing with little children and running errands for old people. He would have occasional moments of religious fervor and even

preached in his father's church, but these moods were
brief.

After five months, Gonzalez sent Sal to an aunt in
Puerto Rico. The aunt promptly shunted him onto his real
father, Agron. Sal liked his father's current "wife." It was
a profound shock to him when she hanged herself. After
that, he ran with juvenile delinquents in Mayagüez, drinking, gambling, staying away from home more and more.

Agron, disabled by a stroke and arthritis, could not control his son. Sal was committed to a reformatory after
assaulting another boy with a broken bottle.

In the reformatory, Sal openly displayed homosexual
tendencies, which the supervisors tried vainly to correct.
He was growing up tall and good-looking, but weak, slender, "soft and smooth like a girl," with very long arms and
legs, joints that bent backwards and "apparently some
deficiency in the body."

He escaped four times, threw rocks at his supervisor,
and "flooded the dormitory with razor blades." He still
banged his head against the wall in school, heard voices,
saw demons in his room, and told boastful lies about his
gang exploits in New York, speaking of himself in the
third person.

The school director recognized the need for psychiatry,
but it was not available.

While Sal was in New York, he had often begged to be
sent back to Puerto Rico; now that he was in Puerto Rico,
he talked of nothing but returning to New York. His
mother made a special trip to the island to try to win his
release. She failed, but arranged for him to flee to New
York while he was visiting his father on a brief pass.

When Sal returned to Brooklyn in November 1958, he
enrolled in a junior high school, but was truant fifty-three
days out of one hundred. Then he obtained working papers,
quit school, but did not take a job either. Instead, he hung
around the streets and playgrounds of the Navy Yard area,
trying to join the street clubs and again being beaten up.

Because of the hostility of his foster father, Sal spent
little time at home. Sometimes he slept at his sister's home
in Harlem. Aurea had escaped from home by falsifying

her age when she was still under fifteen and marrying a twenty-two-year-old worker in a doll shop.

Sal got along fine with his sister and brother-in-law. The young couple let Sal sleep on the floor of their tiny flat and fed him when they could. Having two babies, they could not spare much.

After his sister and brother-in-law broke up, Sal lived "like an alley cat," sleeping in abandoned buildings, scrounging food where he could, doing odd jobs for store-keepers, occasionally getting a handout from his mother or Aurea. He finally found companions on the midtown West Side in a street club of Puerto Rican youths led by a thirty-year-old homosexual.

This was a "bopping" gang, but Sal was not a leader or a tough member. The Mexican dagger with the seven-inch blade used in the attack of August 30 was borrowed from another boy. It is true that he did all the stabbing (two boys were struck in the back and one in the abdomen), but only while his friends were holding them down. The much-publicized cape was borrowed from another member; apparently Sal had never worn it before.

During Sal's detention for trial, Dr. Carl Towbin, a psychiatrist at Kings County Hospital, found "schizoid reaction" of a "severe paranoid type" with evidence of "psychomotor epilepsy." Sal said he had heard people plotting against him on television for years and that he suffered migraine headaches. He expressed no remorse or fear of death, and fell into fits of pointless laughter.

Nevertheless, defense counsel appointed by the court—not Mr. Polier, who did not enter the case until after the trial—did not plead insanity as a defense. For first degree murder, death in the electric chair is mandatory in New York State for any defendant over the age of fifteen. Legislation is being prepared to raise the minimum age and to permit long prison sentences instead of death as the penalty.

By commuting the sentence to "life imprisonment," the Governor made it possible for Agron, who is now eighteen, to be released on parole in a minimum of twenty-five and a half years. Six codefendants have been sentenced to long terms for manslaughter.

Some observers think Salvador Agron can never be rehabilitated; others disagree. In his sixteen months in the death house at Sing Sing, he has greatly improved his reading and writing of English. The Rev. Drury L. Patchell, Episcopal chaplain, says he has become sincerely religious and repentant, studying the Bible. His social worker received a letter from him recently, saying: "I wish I was free that I may put a cure on every heart I have broken. I was one of the most wicked teen-agers that anyone else could ever have the misfortune of meeting."

In pleading for the boy's life, Polier told the Governor that "state and community agencies fell far short" of meeting their obligations to Salvador Agron.

"The circumstances of his life were a clear summons for the community's aid," he said. "The community had full warning that the stresses, added to inner difficulties, might well be more than he could weather. There never was any doubt that he needed ongoing care to substitute for deficient parental attention . . . but no agency was available to give him the help he needed."

REHABILITATION ON DEATH ROW*

BY RONALD BAILEY**

When Warden Jack Johnson met him, Paul Crump was, Johnson says, "choked up with hatred. He was animalistic and belligerent. Self-preservation was the only law he knew."

The men clashed, head on, in a series of showdowns. The first came late in 1955, only two months after Johnson assumed command of the scandal-ridden, riot-scarred prison. Crump and the twelve other condemned men on Death Row decided to test the new warden. They smashed lights, ripped apart wooden benches, set fire to blankets

*Reprinted, by courtesy of *Life* Magazine, from "Facing Death, A New Life Perhaps Too Late," *Life*, vol. 53 (July 27, 1962), pp. 28–29. Copyright © 1962 by Time, Inc.
**Correspondent, *Life* Chicago News Bureau.

and mattresses. Johnson, a six-foot one-inch, 259-pound mountain of a man, strode angrily down to Death Row and ordered the men out of their cells. When they refused, Johnson tossed six shells of tear gas into the cellblock. As the men staggered out, they found—instead of the usual goon squad armed with clubs—only the warden and two doctors.

This was the first battle in what became known as the nineteen-day "cold war" between Johnson and the inmates of Death Row. The warden locked them up in widely separated cells and stripped them of their privileges. They were allowed no visitors, no reading material and no mail. On the fourteenth day they sent for the warden. Paul Crump was their spokesman.

"Look," he said, "you've won. Get the goon squad down here, beat us up and get this thing over with and give us our privileges back."

"There aren't any goon squads here any more," the warden told him. "All I want is your word that you will make no more trouble in this jail."

The men refused. Five days later Crump sent for the warden again. This time he pledged his word and that of the other condemned men. The warden's will, enforced without brutality, had beaten them.

Paul Crump's surrender marked the beginning of a rehabilitation that has lasted for seven years. It also marked the beginning of a deep friendship between the convicted murderer and his warden.

Before Johnson's arrival the jail had been an abomination. One of the country's largest penal institutions, it was overcrowded and understaffed, a grotesque relic of outmoded days. The guards wore guns and carried arsenals of brass knuckles, blackjacks and miniature baseball bats.

In Death Row, condemned men were locked up for twenty-two hours a day in four-by-eight-foot cells. For two hours daily they exercised, tightly handcuffed and dragging leg irons, in the cellblock corridor. "Maximum security" was stamped across the chests of their khaki uniforms like a brand.

The slum-bred Crump described coming to jail as being "transplanted from one jungle to another. If I hadn't been an animal, I wouldn't have survived."

When he took on the job as warden, Johnson went from tier to tier hearing prisoners' complaints. He saw that archaic treatment bred many of the hatreds of his 2,000 caged inmates and barred any chance for rehabilitation. The tough ex-cop, who had had no prison experience before, found that "a simple word of love was what was lacking in this jail."

Johnson reduced the emphasis on punishment, disarmed the guards, ended the Death Row lockup and tried a few simple words of love. He had success with some of the short-term prisoners, but a more convincing proof of his new philosophy was needed. He had to work with extreme cases, those convicted of murder and awaiting death. Paul Crump and his condemned comrades became the subjects of Warden Johnson's brave experiment.

After the cold war truce, Johnson took personal charge of Death Row. He made daily visits there. He installed two telephones outside the tier and told the inmates: "Anytime you guys want to talk to me, call me up." He started bringing them in groups of three and four for discussions with the new prison sociologist and psychologist. The men aired their gripes—lousy food, not enough books to read, brutal guards—and the warden listened. But for a while Crump did not join the sessions in the warden's office. When Johnson wanted to see Crump, he had to go to his cell.

"Finally, I began to see that the Old Man was serious about this philosophy," recalls Crump. "The things he wanted done started happening. There was a guard who beat up an inmate with a baseball bat. The next day I was sitting in the office next to the warden's and I heard him tell a bunch of guards: 'If I hear of this happening again, I'll break your goddamned leg.' "

A new climate pervaded the jail, a climate in which Crump found his chance to change and grow. He sought out the prison chaplains. Although a convert to Catholicism, Crump was befriended by rabbi, Protestant minister and priest alike. Crump told Father James Jones, the Episcopal chaplain, that he wanted to write, and Father Jones gave him $10 for writing materials.

Crump immediately started work on his autobiographical novel, *Burn, killer, Burn*. But in his writing Crump soon felt the bounds imposed by his ninth-grade education. Hans Mattick, a gifted sociologist who was then assistant warden, offered to give Crump an informal course in analytic reading. Three times Mattick had Crump read *Moby Dick*, each time asking him to write a ten- to fifteen-page essay on the different facets of the book. In his second essay Crump explained the message of the book: "Though evil might seem to triumph, the spirit of man will rise again." His third essay, Mattick says, would have done credit to an English major in college.

In Crump's cell the cheap paperback novels and the few law books, which he had purchased for his own defense by giving up cigarets for six months, gave way to Thomas Wolfe's *Look Homeward, Angel,* Will Durant's *The Story of Philosophy* and books on sociology. Crump read the English metaphysical poets and found a poignant relevance for himself in John Donne's famous line: "No man is an *Iland. . . .*"

"I read and read and read," says Crump, "and some old distortions were swept away. I had thought that anything good that happened to me was all gravy, just accident. I started seeing that things don't happen by accident, but because of the good will of people and their belief in the basic goodness of man."

A fellow inmate, Ed Balchowsky, plucked at the strings of Crump's new-found curiosity about life and the world. Balchowsky, in jail on a narcotics rap, was also a rebel against society—a bohemian, an itinerant artist, writer and composer. He introduced Crump to the poetry of Max Bodenheim and sang songs for him in Russian, Spanish and Italian. Night after night the two men worked late editing the crude, handwritten manuscripts of Crump's book.

Crump needed a typewriter, so Balchowsky wrote a letter to the prison newspaper, *The Grapevine,* asking other inmates not to complain if Crump got one. More than 1,000 letters supporting Crump flooded the paper, and Warden Johnson got Crump a typewriter. On it Crump wrote short stories, articles and poems, which were published in small magazines. He started a second novel—his first will be published this fall—and developed a voluminous correspondence with interested and sympathetic people around the world.

He began to take an interest in the problems of his fellow prisoners. The stories they told him were familiar: slums, broken homes, high school dropouts. By comparing their experiences with his own, Crump understood himself better. "It helped me to see the real me," he says. "The start of rehabilitation was when I saw the real me." Through the irony of living under prolonged death sentence, the old Paul Crump was dying, just as surely as if he had been burned in the electric chair.

Looking back on those days, the warden recalls that Crump was "beginning to realize that he had a conscience, realizing that life was not just taking—that there was such a thing as giving. He actually became a man."

The change was best mirrored in Crump's relationship with the warden. Crump became a frequent visitor to Johnson's office. Until the 9 P.M. lock-up time they would discuss "everything from sex to psychology." For Crump, whose own father had deserted his family when Paul was six, "This was the first time I could talk to someone in a language you would use in talking to your father. He told me that life is not just Paul Crump. He said that I'm just as responsible for the people around me as they are responsible for me."

In February 1958, Johnson abolished Death Row. He distributed the condemned men throughout the jail and gave them each responsibilities. Six, including Crump, were put in charge of separate tiers. Crump's job was "barn boss" of the convalescent tier for the new jail hospital.

As barn boss, Crump became, in the words of a guard,

"mother, father, priest and social worker" for some fifty prisoners. To his tier came epileptics, diabetics, heart patients, old men suffering from the DTs, dope addicts on withdrawal. Johnson also sent Crump problem prisoners and inmates who needed special protection from other prisoners and from themselves—fourteen-year-old kids, former policemen, potential suicides. Crump ministered to his charges at all hours of the night and told the youngsters: "Get smart. Stay out of trouble when you get out of here." His tier became the best in the jail.

Shortly after Death Row was abolished came the decisive point in Paul Crump's rehabilitation. It was a particularly bad time for him. He was between stays of execution and fighting desperately to stave off the electric chair. He fired his lawyer and laboriously wrote his own petition for a writ of habeas corpus. The petition—unprecedented in Illinois because it went directly to the federal court—was turned down.[1] But then Crump received a letter which informed him that the warden had offered to talk to the judge on his behalf.

"The letter knocked the props out from under me," he remembers. "It cracked me up. Until then I was still a little suspicious of the Old Man because he was an ex-cop and because he was white."

Crump, clutching the letter in his hand, fell down on his knees in the warden's office and wept for nearly an hour. "He whimpered like a baby," the warden remembers. "I think it was the first time in his life Paul ever completely let himself go. And for the first time, he really believed in another person."

"I had a father," Crump says. "A white father."

Thereafter the tales of Paul Crump's deeds in the convalescent tier grew legendary. He got in the shower with senile men who were unable to bathe themselves. He set aside a corner of the cellblock so that a seventy-year-old Orthodox Jew wearing his skull cap and prayer shawl could

---

[1] [Editor's note: See 295 F. 2d 699 (1961). The Illinois Supreme Court had earlier granted Crump a new trial; see 5 Ill. 2d 251 (1955).]

worship in privacy. He broke up fights and on several occasions prevented guards from getting hurt. A cousin of one of the guards was born with a heart defect and needed blood. The guard spoke to Crump. Within twenty minutes Crump had signatures of fifty men who promised to donate blood.

One poignant story illustrates how Crump's racial animosity changed to tolerance. An epileptic, in jail for bombing Negro homes, was put in his tier. One day the man had a seizure and Crump grappled with him to keep him from hurting himself. When the man came to, he screamed: "Get away from me, you black nigger!" Crump released his hold and went back to his cell. Ten minutes later the man came to Crump, sat down and cried. "I'm sorry," he said finally. "As long as I live I'll never hurt another person because of his race."

During one late bull session in the warden's office, Johnson was accidently locked in the radio room next door. Crump was alone, and Johnson could not reach him. The possibility that Crump might escape flickered across the minds of both men. "I let him knock three times," says Crump, "then I opened the door." He told the warden: "If you opened the gates now, I wouldn't run. You kept faith with me, and I'm going to keep faith with you."

If Paul Crump has undergone a great change in the past seven years, so has Jack Johnson. As Crump responded like a son, Johnson grew like a father. When he came to the jail, the warden had no strong feelings about capital punishment. Now he vigorously opposes it.

"Paul Crump is completely rehabilitated," he says. "Should society demand Paul's life at this point, it would be capital vengeance, not punishment. If it were humanly possible, I would put Paul back on the street tomorrow. I have no fear of any antisocial behavior on his part. I would stake my life on it. And I would trust him with my life."

Now, as the sovereign State of Illinois prepares again to decide Crump's fate, the warden is a man with a heavy burden. Crump has requested, if he must die, that Johnson push the button that will send 1,900 volts of electricity into his body.

"He trusts me," says the warden. "He wants a friend to do it. It is my duty."[2]

2 [Editor's note: Paul Crump's death sentence was commuted by Governor Otto Kerner on August 1, 1962 to 199 years imprisonment without possibility of parole. In commuting the sentence, Governor Kerner wrote in part, ". . . The embittered, distorted man who commited a vicious murder no longer exists . . . Under these circumstances, it would serve no useful purpose to take this man's life . . . The most significant goal of a system of penology is the rehabilitation of one of its members . . ." See *New York Times* of August 2, 1962.]

BIBLIOGRAPHY*

I. BIBLIOGRAPHIES AND COLLECTIONS

Bedau, Hugo A. "A Survey of the Debate on Capital Punishment in Canada, England, and the United States, 1948–1958." *The Prison Journal* 38 (October 1958), pp. 35–40.

Beman, Lamar T. (ed.) *Selected Articles on Capital Punishment.* New York: The H. W. Wilson Co., 1925. lxviii, 366 pp.

Fanning, Clara E. (ed.) *Selected Articles on Capital Punishment.* Minneapolis: H. W. Wilson Co., 1913. xxiv, 239 pp.

Johnson, Julia E. (ed.) *Capital Punishment.* New York: H. W. Wilson Co., 1939. 262 pp.

MacNamara, Donal E. J. "A Survey of Recent Literature on Capital Punishment." *American Journal of Correction* 24 (March–April 1962), pp. 16–19.

McClellan, Grant S. (ed.) *Capital Punishment.* New York: H. W. Wilson Co., 1961. 180 pp.

McGehee, Edward G. and William H. Hildebrand, (eds.) *The Death Penalty: A Literary and Historical Approach.* Boston: D. C. Heath and Co., 1964. 160 pp.

II. PUBLIC DOCUMENTS

California. Assembly Judiciary Committee. Subcommittee on Capital Punishment. *Report. . . . Pertaining to the Problems of the Death Penalty and Its Administration in California.* Sacramento: State of California, 1957. 55 pp.

California. Senate Judiciary Committee. *Report and Testimony . . . [on a proposed bill] to Abolish the Death Penalty.* Sacramento: State of California, 1960. 176 pp.

Canada. Joint Committee of the Senate and House of Commons on Capital and Corporal Punishment and Lotteries. *Reports.* Ottawa: Edmund Cloutier, 1956. pp. 1–37.

Canada. *Capital Punishment: Material Relating to Its Purpose and Value.* Ottawa: Queen's Printer, 1965. 141 pp.

Ceylon. Commission of Inquiry on Capital Punishment. *Report.* Colombo: Government Press, 1959. 118 pp.

Florida. Special Commission for the Study of Abolition of Death Penalty in Capital Cases. *Report.* Tallahassee: State of Florida, 1965. 45 pp.

Great Britain. Royal Commission on Capital Punishment. *Report, Together With the Minutes of Evidence and Appendix.* London: H.M.S.O., 1866. 671 pp.

Great Britain. Royal Commission on Capital Punishment. *Minutes of Evidence.* London: H.M.S.O., 1949–1951. 678 pp.

Great Britain. Royal Commission on Capital Punishment. *Report.* London: H.M.S.O., 1953. 505 pp.

* For further references, consult the footnotes throughout this volume, as they contain many titles not gathered into this Bibliography.

Great Britain. *Report . . . Together With the Proceedings . . . and the Minutes of Evidence, Taken Before the Select Committee. 1929–1930.* London: H.M.S.O., 1931. 681 pp.

Illinois. Legislative Council. "Bills to Abolish the Death Penalty in Illinois." Research Memorandum 1–549. Springfield: State of Illinois, 1951. 13 pp.

Illinois. Legislative Council. "Capital Punishment for Serious Sex Offenses." Bulletin 2–130. Springfield: State of Illinois, 1954. 10 pp.

Kentucky. Legislative Research Commission. *Capital Punishment.* Frankfort: State of Kentucky, 1965.

Maryland. Legislative Council Committee. *Report . . . on Capital Punishment.* Baltimore: State of Maryland, 1962. 80 pp.

Massachusetts. Special Commission Established for the Purpose of Investigating and Studying the Abolition of the Death Penalty in Capital Cases. *Report and Recommendations* (House Document 2575). Boston: Commonwealth of Massachusetts, 1958. 120 pp.

Michigan. Legislative Research Bureau. "History of Capital Punishment in the State of Michigan." 1957. 4 pp.

New Jersey. Commission to Study Capital Punishment. *Report.* Trenton: State of New Jersey, 1964. 51 pp.

New York. Commission on Capital Punishment. *Report.* Albany: Argus Co., 1888. 100 pp.

New York. Temporary Commission on Revision of the Penal Law and Criminal Code. *Special Report on Capital Punishment.* Albany: State of New York, 1965.

North Carolina. Board of Charities and Public Welfare. *Capital Punishment in North Carolina.* Raleigh: State of North Carolina, 1929. 173 pp.

Ohio. Legislative Service Commission. *Capital Punishment.* Staff Research Report, No. 46. Columbus, Ohio: State of Ohio, 1961. 88 pp.

Pennsylvania. Joint Legislative Committee on Capital Punishment. *Report.* Harrisburg: Commonwealth of Pennsylvania, 1961. 32 pp.

United Nations. Department of Economic and Social Affairs. *Capital Punishment.* New York: United Nations, 1962. 76 pp.

United States. Eighty-sixth Congress, second session. House of Representatives. Committee of the Judiciary. *Hearing. . . . on H.R. 870 to Abolish the Death Penalty.* Washington, D. C.: Government Printing Office, 1960. 181 pp.

United States. Library of Congress. Legislative Reference Service. *Capital Punishment: Pro and Con Arguments.* Washington, D. C., 1966. 71 pp.

Wisconsin. Legislative Reference Library. "Capital Punishment in the States with Special Reference to Wisconsin." Madison: State of Wisconsin, 1962. 12 pp.

III. GENERAL

Abramowitz, Elkan and David Paget. "Executive Clemency in Capital Cases." *New York University Law Review*, 39 (January 1964), pp. 136–192.

Alexander, Myrl. "The Abolition of Capital Punishment." *Proceedings of the American Correctional Association*, 96 (1966), pp. 57–59.

American Bar Association. Section of Criminal Law. "Pros and Cons of Capital Punishment." *Proceedings* (August 24–26, 1959), pp. 5–25.

American Law Institute and American Bar Association. Joint Committee on Continuing Legal Education. *The Problem of Punishing Homicide*. Philadelphia: American Law Institute, 1962. 92 pp.

Bacon, G. Richard (ed.). "Capital Punishment." *Prison Journal* 38 (October 1958), pp. 34–74.

Barrows, Samuel J. "Legislative Tendencies as to Capital Punishment." *The Annals* 29 (May 1907), pp. 618–621.

Beccaria, Cesare. *On Crimes and Punishment* (tr. Henry Paolucci). Indianapolis: Bobbs-Merrill Co., (1764) 1963. 99 pp.

Bedau, Hugo A. "A Social Philosopher Looks at the Death Penalty." *American Journal of Psychiatry*, 123 (May 1967), pp. 1361–1370.

Bedau, Hugo A. "Capital Punishment in Oregon, 1903–64." *Oregon Law Review*, 45 (Fall 1965), pp. 1–39.

Blackie, Donald K. "What Does the Bible Say about Capital Punishment?" *The Church Herald* 18 (April 21, 1961), pp. 5 ff.

Block, Eugene B. *And May God Have Mercy . . . The Case Against Capital Punishment*. San Francisco: Fearon Publishers, 1962. 197 pp. Supplement 1965.

Brown, Edmund G. [Excerpts from a Message to the Legislature Relating to the Abolition of the Death Penalty.] *The Californian* 1 (May 1960), pp. 1–12. Reprinted in McClellan (ed.), *Capital Punishment* (1961), pp. 112–115.

Brown, Edmund G. "A Matter of Conviction." *Fellowship* 26 (July 1, 1960), pp. 14–16.

Brown, Edmund G. *Statement . . . On Capital Punishment* (transmitted to the California Legislature, Thursday, January 31, 1963). Sacramento: State of California, 1963. 8 pp.

Calvert, E. Roy. *Capital Punishment in the Twentieth Century*. 5th rev. ed. New York: G. P. Putnam's Sons, 1936. 236 pp.

Camus, Albert. "Reflections on the Guillotine." *Evergreen Review* 1 (1957) No. 3, pp. 5–55. Reprinted in Camus, *Resistance, Rebellion, and Death* (1961), pp. 173–234.

Clark, Francis H. "The Death Penalty in Illinois." *Proceedings of the Illinois State Bar Association*. (1927), pp. 173–181.

(Also "Status of Legal Executions in Illinois by Counties," pp. 181–184).

Cutler, S. Oley, S.J. "Criminal Punishment—Legal and Moral Considerations." *The Catholic Lawyer* 6 (Spring 1960), pp. 110–125.

Darrow, Clarence. "Is Capital Punishment a Wise Policy?" (1924) In: Arthur Weinberg (ed.), *Attorney for the Damned* (1957), pp. 89–103.

Darrow, Clarence. "Why Capital Punishment?" Chapter 10. In: Darrow, *The Story of My Life* (1932), pp. 359–375.

DiSalle, Michael V. "Special Message on Capital Punishment." *Senate Journal* [State of Ohio], (February 10, 1959), pp. 5–13.

DiSalle, Michael V. with Lawrence V. Blochman. *The Power of Life or Death.* New York: Random House, 1965. 214 pp.

Donnelly, Richard, Joseph Goldstein and Richard Schwartz, (eds.) *Criminal Law.* New York: The Free Press, 1962. 1169 pp.

Drzazga, John. "Capital Punishment." *Law and Order* 9 (December 1961), pp. 88–89.

Duff, Charles. *A New Handbook on Hanging.* Chicago: Henry Regnery Co., 1955; London: Hamilton and Co., 1956. 192 pp.

Edwards, Stephen W. "The Death Penalty." *Journal of the California State Bar* 25 (January–February 1950), pp. 98–101.

Ehrmann, Sara R. "The American League Looks at Capital Punishment." *Proceedings of 86th Annual Congress of the American Correctional Association* (1956), pp. 300–308.

England, L. R. "Capital Punishment and Open-end Questions." *Public Opinion Quarterly* 12 (1948), pp. 412–416.

Eshelman, Byron, with Frank Riley. *Death Row Chaplain.* Englewood Cliffs, New Jersey: Prentice-Hall, 1962. 252 pp.

Ferkiss, Victor C. "Life for a Life?" *Commonweal* 63 (October 7, 1955), pp. 11–12.

Fraser, Albert G. (ed.). "Capital Punishment Issue." *The Prison Journal* 12 (October 1932), No. 4, pp. 1–28.

Gardiner, Gerald. "Criminal Law: Capital Punishment in Britain." *American Bar Association Journal* 45 (March 1959), pp. 259–261.

Geis, Gilbert. "The Death Penalty in Oklahoma." *Proceedings of the Oklahoma Academy of Science* 34 (1953), pp. 191–193.

Ginsberg, William R. "Punishment of Capital Offenders: A Critical Examination of the Connecticut Statute." *Connecticut Bar Journal* 27 (1953), pp. 273–281.

Goetz, Richard J. "Should Ohio Abolish Capital Punishment?" *Cleveland-Marshall Law Review* 10 (May 1961), pp. 365–377.

Gold, Louis H. "A Psychiatric Review of Capital Punishment." *Journal of Forensic Science* 6 (October 1961), pp. 465–478.

Gottlieb, Gerald H. *Capital Punishment*. Santa Barbara, Calif.: Center for the Study of Democratic Institutions, 1967. 16 pp.

Gowers, Ernest Arthur. *A Life for a Life? The Problem of Capital Punishment*. London: Chatto and Windus, 1956. 144 pp.

Grant, Fr. John. "Is the Electric Chair Condemned?" *The Ave Maria* 85 (1957), pp. 8–11, 29.

Grinnell, Frank W. "The Jury and Death Sentences." *Massachusetts Law Quarterly* 31 (October 1946), pp. 60–61.

Hankins, Leonard, as told to Earl Guy. *Nineteen Years Innocent*. New York: Exposition Press, 1956. 110 pp.

Hale, Leslie. *Hanged in Error*. Harmondsworth, England: Penguin Books, 1961. 160 pp.

Harley, Herbert. "Segregation versus Hanging." *Journal of Criminal Law, Criminology and Police Science* 11 (February 1921), pp. 512–527.

Harper, Frank. "California's Death Penalty Fight." *Dissent* 8 (Winter 1961), pp. 99–102.

Harriman, W. Averell. "Mercy Is a Lonely Business." *Saturday Evening Post* 230 (March 22, 1958), pp. 24–25, 82–84.

Hartmann, Raymond. "The Use of Lethal Gas in Nevada Executions." *St. Louis Law Review* 8 (April 1923), pp. 164–168.

Herman, Lawrence. "An Acerbic Look at the Death Penalty in Ohio." *Western Reserve Law Review*, 15 (1964), pp. 512–533.

Hill, Denis, and D. A. Pond. "Reflections on One Hundred Capital Cases Submitted to Electroencephalography." *Journal of Mental Science* 98 (January 1952), pp. 23–43.

Hopkins, J. V. and L. L. "Seven in Death Row." *The Nation* 183 (December 1, 1956), pp. 476–478.

Huey, F. B., Jr. "Murder By Proxy." *Baptist Standard* 72 (April 20, 1960), pp. 18–19.

Huie, William Bradford. "A Tale of Two Lynchings." *Cavalier* 10 (April and May, 1960); Reprinted in Huie, *The Hero of Iwo Jima and Other Stories* (1962), pp. 120–159.

Innerst, J. Stewart. *Is Capital Punishment the Answer?* Richmond, Indiana: Board of Peace and Social Concerns, The Five Years Meeting of Friends, 1959. 6 pp.

Johnston, Norman, Leonard Savitz and Marvin E. Wolfgang (eds.), *The Sociology of Punishment and Correction: A Book of Readings*. New York: John Wiley & Sons, 1962. 416 pp.

Kalven, Jr., Harry and Hans Zeisel. "The American Jury and the Death Penalty." *University of Chicago Law Review*, 33 (1966), pp. 769–781.

Kevorkian, Jack. *Medical Research and the Death Penalty*. New York: Vantage Press, 1960. 75 pp.

Kingsley, Robert. "The Case Against Capital Punishment." *Los Angeles Bar Bulletin* 32 (May 1957), pp. 200–202.

Kinsolving, Lester. "Capital Punishment: A reaction from a

Member of the Clergy." *American Bar Association Journal* 42 (September 1956), pp. 850–852.

Kinsolving, Lester. "Christianity and Capital Punishment." *Pastoral Psychology* 11 (June 1960), pp. 33–42.

Kinsolving, Lester and Jacob Vellenga. "Does Society Have the Moral Right to Take Human Life?" *Together* 6 (May 1962), pp. 34–36.

Kirkpatrick, Clifford. *Capital Punishment.* Philadelphia: Committee on Philanthropic Labor, Philadelphia Yearly Meeting of Friends, 1925. 55 pp.

Koestler, Arthur and C. H. Rolph. *Hanged by the Neck.* Harmondsworth, England: Penguin Books, 1961. 143 pp.

Larrowe, Charles P. "Notches on a Chair." *The Nation* 182 (April 14, 1956), pp. 291–293.

Laski, Harold J. *Political Offenses and the Death Penalty.* 6th Roy Calvert Memorial Lecture. London: E. G. Dunstan and Co., 1940. 11 pp.

Laurence, John. *A History of Capital Punishment* (with a comment on Capital Punishment by Clarence Darrow), 2nd edition. New York: The Citadel Press, (1932) 1960. 230 pp.

Lawes, Lewis E. "Capital Punishment." *Encyclopedia Americana* 5 (1956), pp. 560–564.

Lawes, Lewis E. "Capital Punishment," in Branham, V. C. and S. B. Kutash (eds.), *Encyclopedia of Criminology* (1959), pp. 43–45.

Lazell, J. Arthur. "The Churches and Capital Punishment." *National Council Outlook* 9 (March 1959), pp. 21–22.

Lunden, Walter A. "Time Lapse Between Sentence and Execution: the United States and Canada Compared." *American Bar Association Journal* 48 (November 1962), pp. 1043–1045.

Lunden, Walter A. *The Death Penalty, An Analysis of Capital Punishment and Factors Related to Murder.* Anamosa, Iowa: Iowa State Reformatory Printing Department, 1960. 28 pp.

Mannes, Marya. "The Murder of In Ho Oh," *The Reporter* 18 (June 26, 1958), pp. 21–25.

Martin, John Bartlow. "The Rights of the Accused." *Saturday Evening Post* 233 (August 20, 1960), pp. 34–35, 64 ff.

Martin, John Bartlow. "Why Does Justice Fail?" *Saturday Evening Post* 233 (August 27, 1960), pp. 29, 88 ff.

Mattick, Hans W. *The Unexamined Death.* Chicago: John Howard Association, 1963. 33 pp.

McCafferty, James A. "Major Trends in the Use of Capital Punishment," *Criminal Law Quarterly* 1 (February 1963), pp. 9–22.

McGrath, W. T. *Should Canada Abolish the Gallows and the Lash?* Winnipeg: Stovel-Advocate Press, 1956. 95 pp.

MacNamara, Donal E. J. ["Capital Punishment"] Address to the Legislature of Virginia. *Congressional Record* 106, # 42

(March 7, 1960), pp. A1973–A1974.

Meiners, Robert G. "Justice or Revenge?" *Dickinson Law Review* 60 (June 1956), pp. 342–347.

Meyners, Robert. "Two Chairs at San Quentin." *The Christian Century* 77 (March 16, 1960), p. 316.

Michigan State Bar Association. Committee on Capital Punishment. "Report." *Michigan State Bar Journal* 8 (November 1928), pp. 278*–*305.

Mill, John Stuart. "Remarks on Capital Punishment Within Prisons Bill." *Hansards Parliamentary Debates,* III Series, 191 (April 21, 1868), pp. 1047–1055. Reprinted in: *Westminster Review* 91 (April 1869), pp. 429–436.

Mironenko, Yuri P. "The Re-emergence of Death Penalty in the Soviet Union." *Soviet Affairs Analysis Service* # 28 (1961–1962), pp. 1–5.

Morris, Arval. "Thoughts on Capital Punishment." *Washington Law Review* 35 (Autumn 1960), pp. 335–361.

New York. District Attorney's Association. "Symposium on Capital Punishment." *New York Law Forum* 7 (August 1961), pp. 247–319.

Paine, Donald F. "Capital Punishment." *Tennessee Law Review* 29 (Summer 1962), pp. 534–551.

Partington, Donald H. "The Incidence of the Death Penalty for Rape in Virginia." *Washington & Lee Law Review,* 22 (1965), pp. 43–75.

Patrick, Clarence H. "The Status of Capital Punishment: A World Perspective," *Journal of Criminal Law, Criminology, and Police Science,* 56 (1965), pp. 397–411.

Phelps, Harold A. "Rhode Island's Threat Against Murder." *Journal of Criminal Law, Criminology and Police Science* 18 (February 1928), pp. 552–567.

Phelps, Harold A. "Effectiveness of Life Imprisonment as a Repressive Measure Against Murder in Rhode Island." *Proceedings of the 89th Annual Meeting of the American Statistical Association;* in: *Journal of American Statistical Association* 23 (March 1928), # 161 A, pp. 174–181.

Reichert, William O. "Capital Punishment Reconsidered." *Kentucky Law Review* 47 (Spring 1959), pp. 397–419. Reprinted in *Congressional Record,* March 14, 1962, pp. 3773–3777.

Reik, Theodore. "Freud's Views on Capital Punishment." In: Reik, *The Compulsion to Confess* (1959), pp. 469–474.

Remick, Paul A. "What About Capital Punishment?" *Gospel Messenger* (July 12, 1958), pp. 6–8.

Riley, Thomas J. "The Right of the State to Inflict Capital Punishment." *Catholic Lawyer* 6 (Autumn 1960), pp. 279–285.

Robbins, Jhan and Julia. "Let's Abolish Capital Punishment. Special Interview with California's Governor Edmund G. Brown." *Good Housekeeping* 151 (August 1960), pp. 57, 153–158.

Rubin, Sol. *The Law of Criminal Correction.* St. Paul, Minnesota: West Publishing Co., 1963. 728 pp.

Rush, Benjamin. "Considerations on the Injustice and Impolicy of Punishing Murder by Death." *American Museum* (1792). An earlier version was published in *American Mercury* 4 (July 1788), pp. 78–82; a later version is in Rush's *Essays* (1798), pp. 164–192. Reprinted in D. D. Runes (ed.), *The Selected Writings of Benjamin Rush* (1947), pp. 35–53; and in Negley K. Teeters (ed.), *A Plan for the Punishment of Crime by Benjamin Rush* (1954), pp. 19–24.

Schwartz, Louis B. "Capital Punishment: United States." *Encyclopedia Britannica* 4 (1958), pp. 811–812.

Schwartz, Louis B. (ed.) "Crime and the American Penal System." *The Annals* 339 (January 1962), pp. 1–170.

Scott, George Ryley. *The History of Capital Punishment.* London: Torchstream Books, 1950. 312 pp.

Sellin, Thorsten (ed.). "Murder and the Death Penalty." *The Annals* 284 (November 1952), pp. 1–166, 231–238.

Sellin, Thorsten. *The Death Penalty* (Tentative Draft No. 9, Model Penal Code). Philadelphia: The American Law Institute, 1959. 84 pp.

Shaffer, Helen B. "Death Penalty." *Editorial Research Reports* 2 (1953), pp. 573–588.

Shalloo, J. P. (ed.). "Crime in the United States." *The Annals* 217 (September 1941), pp. 1–163.

Shaw, George Bernard. *The Crime of Imprisonment.* New York: Philosophical Library, 1946. 125 pp. (Reprinted from the Preface to Sidney and Beatrice Webb, *English Prisoners Under Local Government* (1922), pp. vi–lxxvi.)

Sickler, Joseph S. (ed.). *Rex et Regina v. Lutherland* (facsimile of *Blood Will Out* . . . 1691). Woodstown, New Jersey: Seven Stars Press, 1948.

Slovenko, Ralph. "And the Penalty Is (Sometimes) Death." *Antioch Review,* 24 (Fall 1964), pp. 351–364.

Smith, Mapheus. "Spontaneous Change of Attitude Toward Capital Punishment." *School and Society* 47 (March 5, 1938), pp. 318–319.

Smith, Mapheus. "Concordance in Change of Attitude With Reference to War and Capital Punishment." *Journal of Social Psychology* 12 (1940), pp. 379–386.

Smith, Mapheus. "Attitudes Toward War and Capital Punishment as to Size of Community." *School and Society* 58 (September 18, 1943), pp. 220–222.

Society of Friends. Conference on Crime and the Treatment of Offenders. Continuation Committee (eds.). *What Do the Churches Say on Capital Punishment?* 7th ed. Philadelphia: Friends World Committee (1960) 1961. 64 pp.

Soper, Donald. "Donald Soper Speaks Out Against Capital Punishment." *Observer* (June 1, 1958), pp. 11–12.

Springer, Charles E. "Against the Death Penalty." *Nevada State Bar Journal* 25 (October 1960), pp. 210–215.

Star, Jack. "The Bitter Battle Over Capital Punishment." *Look* 27 (May 7, 1963), pp. 23–29.

Start, Raymond R. and Thomas D. McBride. "Abolish the Death Penalty." *Pennsylvania Bar Association Quarterly* 31 (June 1960), pp. 408–414.

Story, Joseph. "Punishment of Death." *Encyclopedia Americana* 4 (1830), pp. 140–145. Reprinted in Hogan (ed.), Joseph Story on Capital Punishment", *California Law Review* 43 (March 1955), pp. 76–84.

Thomas, Trevor. *This Life We Take*. 3rd. rev. ed. Washington D. C.: Friends Committee on Legislation, 1965. 34 pp.

Tuttle, Elizabeth Orman. *The Crusade Against Capital Punishment in Great Britain*. Chicago: Quadrangle Books; London: Stevens and Sons, 1961. 177 pp.

Von Moschzisker, Michael. "Capital Punishment in the Pennsylvania Courts." *Pennsylvania Bar Association Quarterly* 20 (January 1949), pp. 174–188.

Von Moschzisker, Michael. "Capital Punishment." *The Shingle* (Pennsylvania Bar Association), 14 (June 1951), pp. 153–157.

Walker, Gerald. "Young Man, Be an Executioner." *Esquire* 60 (August 1963), pp. 62–63.

Weihofen, Henry. *The Urge to Punish*. New York: Farrar, Straus, and Cudahy, 1956. 213 pp.

Werkheiser, Richard M. and Arthur C. Barnhart. *Capital Punishment*. New York: The National Council of the Episcopal Church, 1961. 32 pp.

Williams, Brad. *Due Process: The Fabulous Story of Criminal Lawyer George T. Davis and His Thirty Year Battle Against Capital Punishment*. New York: William Morrow & Co., 1960. 336 pp.

Williams, Franklin H. "The Death Penalty and the Negro." *The Crisis* 67 (October 1960), pp. 501–512.

Wilson, Victor. "Capital Punishment in the United States." *Congressional Record* 106 (March 4, 1960), pp. A1882–A1883.

Wolf, Edwin D. "Analysis of Jury Sentencing in Capital Cases: New Jersey, 1937–1961." *Rutgers Law Review,* 19 (1964), pp. 56–64.

Wolfgang, Marvin E., (ed.) "Patterns of Violence." *The Annals,* 364 (March 1966), pp. 1–157.

Worley, Francis. "A Bill to Abolish Capital Punishment in Pennsylvania." *Dickinson Law Review* 60 (January 1956), pp. 167–169.

Ziferstein, Isidore. "A Psychiatrist Looks at Capital Punishment." *Frontier* 8 (January 1957), pp. 5–6.

IV. CLASSIC CAPITAL CASES

Ehrmann, Herbert B. *The Untried Case: The Sacco-Vanzetti Case and the Morelli Gang.* (Foreword by Joseph N. Welch, Introduction by Edmund N. Morgan). 2nd ed., New York: Vanguard Press (1933) 1960. 268 pp.

Huie, William Bradford. *The Execution of Private Slovik.* New York: New American Library, 1954. 152 pp.

Kunstler, William M. *Beyond a Reasonable Doubt? The Original Trial of Caryl Chessman.* New York: William Morrow and Company, 1961. 304 pp.

Leopold, Nathan F. *Life Plus 99 Years.* Garden City, New York: Doubleday & Company, 1958. 381 pp.

Machlin, Milton and William Read Woodfield. *Ninth Life.* [Caryl Chessman] New York: G. P. Putnam's Sons, 1961. 321 pp.

Russell, Francis. *Tragedy in Dedham: The Story of the Sacco-Vanzetti Case.* New York: McGraw-Hill Book Co., 1962. 478 pp.

Schneir, Walter and Miriam. *Invitation to an Inquest.* [Rosenberg-Sobell case] Garden City, New York: Doubleday & Company, 1965. 467 pp.

Wexley, John. *The Judgment of Julius and Ethel Rosenberg.* New York: Cameron & Kahn, 1955. 672 pp.

V. UNPUBLISHED SOURCES

American Civil Liberties Union of Georgia. "The Death Penalty in Georgia." Atlanta, Ga., 1965. 47 pp.

American Jewish Committee. Institute of Human Relations. "The Death Penalty for Economic Offenses in the Soviet Union." 1962. 10 pp.

Balogh, Joseph K. *Capital Punishment: A Study of Social Attitudes.* 1961. 303 pp. (typescript).

Carter, Robert M. *Capital Punishment in California: 1938–1953.* Berkeley: University of California, 1953. (thesis).

Feiertag, Erwin L. *Capital Punishment in New Jersey: 1664–1950.* New York: Columbia University, 1951. 100 pp. (thesis).

McCafferty, James A. *Capital Punishment in the United States: 1930 to 1952.* Columbus: Ohio State University, 1954. 328 pp. (thesis).

Prisoners Aid Society. Herbert Cobin (ed.). *Material: Senate Bill No. 299.* 1957.

Society of Friends. New York Yearly Meeting. Prison Committee. Edmund Goerke, Jr. (ed.). *Materials: New Jersey Assembly Bills 33 and 34.* 1958.

INDEX

ANCHOR BOOKS

PSYCHOLOGY